A TEXTBOOK OF PSYCHOLOGY

A TEXTBOOK OF PSYCHOLOGY

Edited by

JOHN RADFORD, B.A., Ph.D., F.B.Ps.S., F.R.A.I., F.R.S.A.
and
ERNEST GOVIER, B.Sc., B.Sc., A.B.Ps.S.

SHELDON PRESS
LONDON

First published in Great Britain in 1980 by
Sheldon Press, Marylebone Road, London NW1 4DU

Printed in Great Britain by
Lowe and Brydone Printers Ltd
Thetford, Norfolk

ISBN 0 85969 321 X (cased)
ISBN 0 85969 170 5 (paper)

Acknowledgements

The authors and publishers wish to acknowledge the assistance of the Division for Staff and Educational Development of the North East London Polytechnic. We especially wish to acknowledge the skill of Gloria Shayler who prepared all the diagrams in this book.

Acknowledgement is due to the following for permission to use figures and tables in this volume.

Fig. 13.3, from 'A Comparative and Analytical Study of Visual Depth Perception' by R. D. Walk and E. J. Gibson published in *Psychological Monograph* Vol. 75 No. 519. Copyright © 1961 by the American Psychological Association. Reprinted by permission. Figs. 13.4 and 13.7, from 'Plasticity in Sensory-Motor Systems' by Richard Held. Copyright © 1965 by Scientific American, Inc. All rights reserved. Fig. 13.5, from *Optics: An Introduction for Opthalmologists* by K. Ogle published by the W. B. Saunders Company, Philadelphia, Pa., 1961. Fig. 13.9, from 'The Role of Frequency in Developing Perceptual Sets' by B. R. Bugelski and D. A. Alampay published in the *Canadian Journal of Psychology*, 15. Fig. 13.10, from 'Pictorial Depth Perception in Sub-cultural Groups in Africa' by W. Hudson published in *Journal of Social Psychology* Vol. 52, 1960, by Human Sciences Press, 72 Fifth Avenue, New York 10011, USA. Fig. 18.1, from *A Study of Thinking* by J. S. Bruner, J. J. Goodnow and G. A. Austin, 1956, published by Wiley, New York. Fig. 26.1, from *Prejudice and Racism* by J. M. Jones © 1972, Addison Wesley Publishing Co, Reading, Massachusetts. Reprinted with permission. Tables A.1, A.4, A.5 and A.10, from Tables 1, 13 and 18 of *The Biometrika Tables for Statisticians, Vol. 1*, edited by E. S. Pearson and H. O. Hartley (3rd edition 1966). Table A.13, from 'A Distribution-free k sample Test against Ordered Alternatives' by A. R. Jonckheere, *Biometrika Vol 41*, pp 133–45, 1954. Tables A.2 and A.3, from Tables III and IV of *Statistical Tables for Biological, Agricultural and Medical Research* by R. A. Fisher and F. Yates (6th edition 1974). Published by Longmand Group Ltd., London (previously published by Oliver and Boyd, Edinburgh), and by permission of the authors and publishers. Tables A.8, A.9, A.12 and A.14 reprinted by permission from the *Journal of the American Statistical Association* as follows: Table A.8, from Table 1 of 'Extended Tables of the Wilcoxin Matched Pair Signed Rank Statistic' by R. L. McCormack, 1965 Vol. 60 pp 864–71; Table A.9, from 'Significance Testing of the Spearman Rank Correlation Coefficient' by J. H. Zarr, 1972 Vol. 67 pp 578–80; Table A.12, from 'Use of Ranks in One-Criterion Variance Analysis' by W. H. Kruskal and W. A. Wallis, 1952 Vol. 47 pp 584–621; Table A.14, from 'Ordered Hypotheses for Multiple Treatment: A Significance Test for Linear Rank' by E. B. Page, 1963 Vol. 58 pp 216–30. Table A.7, from table L of *Nonparametric and Shortcut Statistics* by Merle W. Tate and Richard C. Clelland. Danville, Illinois: The Interstate Printers and Publishers, Inc., 1957. Used by permission. Table A.11, from Table I of *Nonparametric and Shortcut Statistics* by Merle W. Tate and

Richard C. Clelland. Danville, Illinois: The Interstate Printers and Publishers, Inc., 1957. Used by permission. Values at the left of the broken line were derived from Appendix 5A, 5B, 5C and 5D of M. G. Kendall's *Rank Correlation Methods* (4th edition 1970). Reproduced by permission of the publishers, Charles Griffin & Company Ltd. of London and High Wycombe. Other values were obtained by the method described by Kendal, *ibid.*, p 84.

The authors and publisher are grateful to the Literary Executor of the late Sir Ronald A. Fisher, F.R.S., to Dr. Frank Yates, F.R.S. and to Longman Group Ltd., London, for permission to reprint Tables III and IV from their book *Statistical Tables for Biological, Agricultural and Medical Research* (6th edition 1974).

The Authors

JOHN RADFORD, joint editor of this book, is Dean of the Faculty of Human Sciences at the North East London Polytechnic. He took B.A. in English, History and French at Goldsmiths' College, London in 1955, B.A. Hons in Psychology at Birbeck College, London in 1961 and was awarded a Ph.D. in 1965. He was Chief Examiner for GCE 'A' Level Psychology for the Associated Examining Board from 1970–9 and Head of the Department of Psychology at the North East London Polytechnic. He is Chairman of the Association for the Teaching of Psychology; Chairman of the Standing Advisory Committee on Education in Psychology, British Psychological Society; Chairman of the Psychology Board, Council for National Academic Awards; Fellow of the British Psychological Society, and Fellow of the Royal Anthropological Institute.

ERNEST GOVIER, joint editor of this book, is Principal Lecturer in Psychology at the North East London Polytechnic. He obtained B.Sc. in Zoology from London University in 1968 and B.Sc. in Psychology in 1972. He is a member of the British Psychological Society.

CLIVE GABRIEL is Principal Lecturer in Psychology at the North East London Polytechnic. He obtained B.Sc. in Physics and Maths in 1965 and B.Sc. in Psychology in 1970. He is a member of the British Psychological Society.

JEREMY COYLE is Principal Lecturer in Psychology at the North East London Polytechnic. He obtained B.A. Hons in English from Bristol University and B.A. Hons in Psychology from London University.

SIMON GREEN is Lecturer in Psychology at Birkbeck College, London. In 1969 he obtained B.Sc. in Psychology from University College, Cardiff and did graduate research at Birkbeck until 1972 when he joined the North East London Polytechnic as a Lecturer. He is a member of the British Psychological Society, the Brain Research Association, and the British Association for Psychopharmacology.

PHILIP EVANS is Senior Lecturer in Psychology at the North East London Polytechnic. He read Philosophy and Psychology at Emmanuel College, Cambridge in 1969 and obtained Ph.D. from University College, Cardiff in 1972 with research into Behavioural Psychotherapy. He is a member of the British Psychological Society.

HEATHER GOVIER is a teacher. She read Natural Sciences at Newnham College, Cambridge specializing in psychology. She graduated in 1970 and then moved to the Chelsea Centre for Science Education where she obtained a M.Phil. in the Psychology of Education.

BRIAN CLIFFORD is Senior Lecturer in Psychology at the North East London Polytechnic. He obtained D.P.E. from Jordanhill College of Education in 1967. Dip.Ed. from the University of London Institute of Education in 1969, and B.A. Hons from North East London Polytechnic in 1974. He is a member of the British Psychological Society, the British Sociological Association, the British Society for the Philosophy of Science, and the British Society of Sports Psychology.

HARRY FISHER is Principal Lecturer in Psychology at the North East London Polytechnic. He obtained B.Sc. in Psychology in 1971 and is a member of the Mathematical Association and the British Psychological Society.

MARION PITTS is a Senior Lecturer in Psychology at the North East London Polytechnic and a tutor for the Open University. She read Psychology at University College, Cardiff and then obtained a Ph.D.

JUDY GAHAGAN is Senior Lecturer in Psychology at the North East London Polytechnic and a Lecturer at the University of London Institute of Education. She obtained B.A. Hons in Psychology in 1964. She is a member of the British Psychological Society.

DENIS GAHAGAN is Principal Lecturer in Social Psychology at the North East London Polytechnic. He obtained B.A. in Philosophy from the University of Southampton in 1960 and B.A. in Psychology in 1964. He is an associate of the British Psychological Society, an affiliate of the American Psychological Association, a member of the Association for the Teaching of Psychology, and Chairman of the Educational Writers Group of the Society of Authors. In 1979 he became Chief Examiner in 'A' level Psychology for the Associated Examining Board.

CLIVE HOLLIN was awarded an honours degree in Psychology from the North East London Polytechnic in 1975. He was Research Assistant to Dr John Radford from 1975–8.

Contents

Editorial foreword

If either of the editors had known in advance how difficult the production of this book would prove to be, neither would have undertaken it. The preparation of the manuscript took about three years, mainly because of the problems of co-ordinating the efforts of so many people.

The first and, to some extent, the most difficult problem we faced was how we should organize the material. Our plan, which we hope will make sense to the reader, is to group the material in five Sections. We start with a historical-methodological Section and progress through Sections on animal behaviour and information processing to a Section on the psychological development of the individual. We have put the Chapter on Abnormal Psychological States in this Section because it is so closely related to the Personality Chapter. Our last Section deals with social psychology, which, in a sense, uses the widest perspective to investigate human behaviour. This, we thought, would be the best order for anyone reading the book straight through; but it should not hinder anyone reading separate Sections or separate Chapters.

Our next problem was to try to diminish any stylistic variations between the authors to the point where the reader would not be distracted by them, while, at the same time, we had no wish to erase completely each author's individual stamp. This proved an interesting task, in which we have probably failed.

We hope that this book reflects the emphasis on experimentation which characterizes the British psychological tradition.

J. K. R.
E. G.

Preface

It was not so very long ago that I happened to mention to an elderly teacher that I had just taken a degree in psychology. 'How interesting', she said, 'which book did you use?'

The days of using *a* book for a degree have long gone: and there cannot either be one book for 'A' levels (or any other levels, probably). This is an introduction. In preparing it, we have been reminded of the famous Monty Python 'summarize Proust' competition. There is far, far more interesting and useful psychology than can go into one book. (Further reading is suggested wherever it may be useful throughout the book.)

There are also in existence large numbers of introductory text books, many of them (I have certainly not read them all) excellent. What distinguishes this one?

First, it was planned with a specific sort of student in mind: one who is starting the subject for the first time, and is preparing to take a fairly demanding examination after one or two years. The most obvious body of such, and that which we had primarily in mind, are those taking G.C.E. 'A' level. We hope, though, that other students whose work is comparable, for example first-year degree students, will also find the book useful. At the time of writing, there is only one 'A' level examination, but others may follow. As far as we can judge, this book should prove useful for such new examinations.

We hope, too, that there may be comparable courses in other countries than ours for which what we have to say will be of interest.

The book consists of Chapters written by individuals. This is deliberate. Not only is it almost impossible for one person to write on the wide range of material covered: in our view it is better to have separate treatment of each major area. The book is rather like what you would get if you were taught psychology by the authors: there is overlapping, and there may be disagreements. The authors all agree, however, on their common purpose: they share common standards and the same attitude towards psychology and to teaching it. All the authors work, or have worked, together in one large department of psychology. They have, between them, a quite enormous experience of teaching a variety of subjects (from arithmetic to zoology) to a variety of students from five to fifty-five; but in particular, of course, psychology to those taking first courses in it. And here they share a great deal of experience in examining and in course-planning.

This does not mean that this book is the last word. Another set of authors, even from the same department, would give you a somewhat different book. And the introduction that suits one student will not suit another.

To summarize the view of psychology shared by this particular group: they consider that, as a discipline, it is, or should be, objective, empirical, eclectic, and humane. *Objective* means that one tries to distinguish what commands general agreement, because it can be demonstrated by reference to fact or logical reasoning, from what is the outcome only of opinion, tradition, hearsay, or prejudice. It does not mean that psychology can, or should, avoid value judgements: it means being aware of such judgements and of their sources and their implications. *Empirical* means that, whenever we can, we look for evidence. Generally, the preferred way of getting evidence is by experiment, for the reasons given in the first Section. But that is not the only useful way; and, indeed, the experience of each individual student is a valuable bonus for psychology which other disciplines, not concerned with human beings, cannot share. *Eclectic* means that we do not rule out in advance any source of information. There have been many scientists, and psychology has had it share of them, who have felt that their methods or their theories were all that was necessary or even permissible. This seems to us fundamentally unscientific and, in the end, self-defeating. A really eclectic approach also means that, ideally, a psychologist should be familiar with many other conventionally-labelled disciplines such as anthropology or mathematics. These connections can only be suggested here. Finally, *humane* means concerned with, and about, human beings. In the last few years there has been a lot of fuss about so-called 'humanistic' psychology. (This is actually a misnomer: humanistic is a technical word in the history of ideas, referring to the study of antiquity by Renaissance scholars.) Proponents of this approach attack conventional psychology for concentrating on rats in laboratories. This may be a fair charge against some of the stricter Behaviourists, but the British tradition in which this book is, we hope, written—the tradition of Galton, Bartlett, Burt, Broadbent, and many others—has always put human beings, with all their perplexing attributes, at the centre of its concern.

Psychology is sometimes accused of having only a very small body of really well-established facts, in contrast to other sciences. This stems partly, in my opinion, from a misconception about the nature of science. Science does not consist essentially in the collection of facts: rather, it is a particular way of tackling problems—systematically, objectively, etc. The problems constantly change, and, indeed, every problem apparently solved gives rise to a new one. This is true of all sciences, but above all of psychology. Not only is human behaviour continuously changing under different social and physical conditions, we have the peculiarity that psychology itself causes changes, for example, through education. Partly for these reasons, psychology has always been rather prone to fashions. Some new idea, such as the conditioned reflex, or scheduled reinforcement or feedback loops, seems, for a time, to explain all, or a great deal, of behaviour, only to fall out of fashion as its limitations become clear. It is not altogether a bad thing, since the temporary enthusiasm can often give rise to a lot of useful investigations and hard thinking. However, it is partly why, in this book, there is a good deal of emphasis on both methods and history. Indeed, we start with substantial pieces on each. These, we hope, bring out the idea of psychology as a way of going about problems.

A further small book could be written at this point on how to study psychology and how to pass examinations in it. Without attempting this, let us make the general point that very seldom does either reduce solely to learning lists of facts. Some material must be known, but, nearly always there are such questions as: What sort of problem is this? How has it been approached? What has been discovered so far, and what are we to make of it? What should be done next? One of my own favourite devices for stressing this is an imaginary companion who constantly asks you to tell him what you know on each issue. I imagine him (or her) saying, for example: 'Well, you're studying psychology, you're supposed to know about intelligence—is it really inherited, or not?' Or, 'Of course, psychology is just common sense, isn't it?' What answer can you give?

Psychologists have yet to tackle more than a fraction of the questions they might, and this book is necessarily even further selective. But we hope our introduction leaves you wishing to pursue the acquaintanceship.

London 1980   JOHN K. RADFORD

PSYCHOLOGY AS A SCIENCE

This Section describes some of the historical background to psychology and how it was developed, and, in doing so, gives an overview of psychology as a whole. Thus, many of the things said here are picked up and further discussed in later Chapters. It may be useful to compare the two. This Section also includes Chapters on the method *par excellence* of psychology, that of experiment, and the essential accompanying statistical procedures.

Experimentation, in its broadest sense, is really absolutely fundamental to all modern psychology; and experiments cannot be done or understood without at least minimum techniques of design and analysis. The non-mathematical should not be put off: the computation involved is very small. The muddle-headed may find their confusion at first exposed, and then removed. And one of the most gratifying rewards of tackling psychology is the elegant simplicity of a well-designed investigation.

1 The development of psychology as a science

CLIVE GABRIEL

Introduction

One of the major difficulties encountered when starting to study psychology is to find out what it is. It is tempting to take the easy way out by looking up the word 'psychology' in a dictionary and satisfying oneself with some neat definition, such as 'the science of behaviour and experience'. But this way will not provide you with any adequate picture of the subject, because 'psychology' has meant (and does mean) quite different things to people, depending on when they lived, where they worked, and, also, on what sort of person they were. The aim of the first two Chapters of this book is to present an adequate, if necessarily very brief and simplified, view of the nature of psychology, by discussing its development in the last hundred years or so. This Chapter gives an account of the history of the subject until about 1950. The second Chapter will bring the overview up to date.

3

Before scientific psychology

The history of wondering, and pronouncing, on human behaviour and motivation is as old as history itself. That which took place before the 1870s (as well as some since) is now generally thought of as philosophy rather than psychology. One great step which marks the possibility of a clear division between philosophy and psychology was the founding by Wilhelm Wundt (1832–1920) of the first psychological laboratory in Leipzig, Germany, in 1879. Like so many 'firsts', this one is disputed, and it is sometimes claimed that the event first happened in Harvard University in the U.S.A., the founder being William James (1842–1940); but whichever place, date, and person you accept, the 1870s were a uniquely important time for psychology.

The development of the early psychology laboratories was adumbrated particularly by the two-and-a-half preceding centuries of philosophical activity, during which the appeal to the authority of dogma for knowledge was replaced by an appeal to observation. The atmosphere for these brave ways of speculating about human mental acitvity was provided by contemporary discoveries from other areas of science. The most striking of these were Galileo's rejection of the belief that the Earth was at the centre of the universe and Harvey's discovery of the rudiments of the blood circulatory system. The one shattered the picture of man as being something quite exclusive in all creation, and the second reduced his body to something as mundane as a machine. Much later, Darwin removed the last obstacles to regarding man, not as a unique product of God's will, but as a part of a continuous evolution of animal life.

The people who most prominently made clear the implications of this new picture of man for the study of what we now call Psychology were the Frenchmen Descartes (1596–1650) and Compte (1798–1857) and the group of what are often outrageously known as 'English Empiricists', a large proportion of whom were Scottish and one of whom was Irish.

Descartes delineated the distinction between mind and body, supposing' that the body needed no more than the rules of mechanics to understand it, it was, in his view, a machine. He further proposed that the interaction between body and mind took place in the brain (although, for the love of unity, he chose a rather improbable part of that organ).

The main difference between the philosophies of the British Empiricists and Descartes was in the latter's supposition that some ideas are present at birth, whereas the Empiricists believed that the development of mind happened by an accumulation of sensory experiences after birth.

By the mid-nineteenth century there was a strong current of philosophical thought which held that the organization of conscious experience was a fit subject for study; that sensation (stimulation impinging on

4

sense organs) was a vitally important process in the gaining of ideas about the external world; and that the association of ideas or elements of experience was an important explanatory mechanism to show how simple ideas could combine to provide the complexity which is characteristic of (some!) human thinking. The next step seemed, to some thinkers of the time, to be to examine these ideas by experimentation. Thus, psychology, in something akin to its present day meaning, came about.

Schools of psychology

Once psychology had established itself as an empirical study, that is, a study based on systematic observation rather than on reason alone, it developed and separated into different schools of thought, traces of which are still with us today. These schools differed in their subject matter, in what they thought psychology should be about, as well as in their methods of investigation. Each school has handed down some ideas and attitudes which are of value to contemporary psychologists; but some of the schools were much more diffuse in their formulations than others, resulting in their present-day influence being uneven in importance.

The idea of 'schools' is a convenient one which enables contemporary psychologists to look back and make sense of the welter of ideas and experiments which lie behind their own. From the point of view of members of the various schools, the organization of psychology may sometimes have seemed as clear as it can be made to look now but, most often, it must have seemed nothing of the sort: rather, a busy confusion with an occasional transient clear direction. But, as long as we are aware of this, we may usefully use the method to get a bird's-eye view of the past.

Structuralism

Wilhelm Wundt

Although Wundt founded his *Psychologisches Institut* in 1879, he was titled Professor of Philosophy in Leipzig from 1875–1920. His laboratory, with its many students, worked with a great solemnity of purpose on a range of problems, particularly those of physiological psychology, psychophysics, and reaction times, as well as on the analysis of experience, for which he is best remembered. He defined psychology as the science of consciousness and believed that its subject matter should be immediate experience rather than that experience which has been subject to conceptualization. For example, Wundt was not at all satisfied if a person told him that he saw a blue book. For Wundt, this was a far too high level of interpretation of the experience. The level he was trying to elicit was that expressed by 'blueness', 'rectangularity', 'depth', and so

5

on. Two questions immediately occur: why should Wundt want to deal in such a low level of experience and how could he possibly obtain this seemingly unnatural type of information from people?

The chemistry analogy
Wundt wanted to build his new science of psychology along the lines of other sciences, hoping to achieve successes comparable to theirs. He dealt with the elements of experience in a way that was analogous to the way in which chemists discussed the elements of matter. Wundt believed that consciousness consisted of compounds which could be broken down into their constituent elements for our fuller understanding of them. Further, he considered that the elements of experience could be divided into two kinds, the ones 'out there' being 'sensations', and the others, within the person, being 'feelings'. He also used the word 'image' to describe elements of ideas, a concept closely related to sensation, but perhaps less vivid. Wundt systemized feelings and their compounds in various ways at various times, but none of his attempts convinced the scientific world for long. His best-known system of feelings was obtained by carefully examining his own mental processes whilst listening to clicks sounded in various rhythms and speeds and noting his feelings during and at the end of the sets of clicks. Wundt suggested from his procedure that feelings could vary along three independent dimensions: 'excitement–calm', 'pleasure–displeasure', and 'strain–relaxation'. However, these were just the dimensions of simple feelings or elements of conscious experience. Wundt believed that these elements of conscious experience were built into compounds and beyond these into complexes of experience; this idea became known as Structuralism. Yet in Wundt's scheme of things the attributes and characteristics of compounds could not necessarily be discovered by knowing the attributes and characteristics of their elements. This was, in Wundt's view, because the mind performs a 'creative synthesis' of elements when putting them together. This rather unsatisfactory way of linking elements and compounds was defended by Wundt with the chemical analogy: who, without knowing chemistry, would predict on 'seeing' the two gases hydrogen and oxygen that they could be synthesized into water?

Introspection
The method which Wundt and his students used to obtain their information about the elements of consciousness was that of introspection. This simply means that people were asked to examine and report on their own mental processes. Everyone has done this, and some people, you may have noticed, do little else, but Wundt's contribution was to bring order into the process. His idea was that introspection should be made to be replicable and lawful; that is, it should give similar results on different

6

occasions, even when carried out by different people, and, further, differences in results should follow differences in instructions or problems in a systematic way. To become an 'observer', that is, one who introspects using Wundt's terms, involved a great amount of training. To see commonplace objects in the analysed way required by Wundt meant attaining what he called a state of 'strained attention' to the contents of consciousness.

The method of introspection by itself in the end proved inadequate as a way of gaining knowledge about mental processes. There were several reasons for this but the most basic was that, when different laboratories gave different results, there was no way of settling the issue. The most famous example of this happening was in a conflict between Wundt's laboratory and that of Oswald Külpe (1862–1915) in Würzburg.

Külpe, originally a student of Wundt, became professor at Würzburg in 1894 and, within a short time, had established a laboratory, working along similar lines to that at Leipzig. However, whereas Wundt claimed that it was possible to study experimentally only the elements of conscious experience, Külpe saw no reason why higher mental processes should not be studied as well and picked on 'thinking' as a start. Külpe's studies repeatedly showed that problem-solving took place without the appearance in consciousness of images; that is, without the elements of conscious experience to be expected by Wundt's chemical analogy. It was like water resisting all efforts at reduction to hydrogen and oxygen. Wundt responded to this state of affairs by attacking the finer points of Külpe's introspective methods. Thus began a debate which exposed the weakness of the method of introspection when faced with conflict between two sets of researchers. It is a very fundamental weakness, depending ultimately on the impossibility of observing another person's mental processes in the way that any reasonable number of people may observe what goes on inside a retort in a chemical experiment.

Edward Titchener

Titchener (1867–1927) was born in England and became a disciple of Wundt in Leipzig. Later, he exported Wundt's methods and beliefs about the essential subject matter of psychology to the U.S.A.

Titchener was every bit as awesome as Wundt, and he painstakingly, perhaps relentlessly, compiled a list of the distinct conscious elements of sensation which he published in *An Outline of Psychology* in 1896. The majority of the sensations were visual and most of the rest auditory. They came to a total of more than 44 000.

Although Titchener produced various reformulations of Structuralism during his life, he cannot be said to have introduced any new essence into psychology and, with his death, Structuralism also died. The analysis and presentation of the structure of the contents of consciousness no longer seemed to psychologists a useful way to proceed. There were two separate circumstances which made this the case: the inability and lack of promise of Structuralism's method of introspection to provide a cogent, generally agreed account of human mental life and the existence of practicable alternative sorts of psychology.

Functionalism

Whereas it is easy to say what Structuralists believed—that it was essential for psychologists to study the structure of consciousness—it is not such a simple matter to say what Functionalists believed. As you might expect, they generally held that the function of conciousness was an important topic to study, but members of the school worked at a wide variety of topics.

The greatest single influence on functional psychology was Charles Darwin's work on the origin of the species. Functionalists were also influenced to work on a relative diversity of subject matter by rebellion against the dogmatic insistence of the contemporary Structuralists that psychology was essentially concerned with the structure of consciousness. In particular, they were influenced by the brilliant writing and inventive thinking of William James (1842–1910).

In one sense, structural psychology owed most in its underlying attitudes to philosophy, whilst functional psychology owed most to biology; and perhaps for this reason the attitudes underlying functional psychology are still with us, whilst no parallel situation exists with structural psychology.

Charles Darwin
The idea of evolution, that living organisms change and develop over time, is a very ancient one. Darwin's great contribution, in a series of publications from 1858 to 1877, was to provide the world with a carefully worked out account of the mechanisms of evolution. Darwin, however, failed to do the decent thing by stopping the account just before the arrival of man. This last fact, particularly, provided a great shock to very old habits of thinking, causing Victorian theologians to express anger and despair and psychologists to start work on a rich source of ideas.

Darwin's main thesis was that members of a species exhibit variability of characteristics and this means that some of them will be better suited than others to any given set of environmental conditions. By 'characteristic' is meant anything which may be attributed to the organism, for example, height or ferocity. Those members of the species who are best suited to the environment will be the ones who will reproduce most prolifically; indeed, under extreme conditions they will be the only ones to survive to maturity and be able to reproduce at all. These survivors of the struggle to reproduce will tend to transmit to the next generation that advantage, ability, or physical characteristic which enabled them to survive. This advantage will tend not, merely to be transmitted, according to Darwin, but, because of the variability of characteristics, some of the new generation will have the advantage to a greater degree than others. If the environmental pressures remain similar over several generations, the process may be repeated until the advantage is so pronounced that a major change has taken place in the type of animal. Darwin proposed this mechanism of natural selection as one of the ways in which new species emerge.

The thesis caused uproar when first presented because of its implications for the origin of man; and, because of the enormous body of observation presented by Darwin in support of it, it could not easily be dismissed.

If the function of other abilities were to be discussed, why not the function of consciousness? Thus, Darwin raised the issue of the utility of consciousness. The importance of individual differences between members of species was also made clear by Darwin, and this lead was taken up by a group of statisticians and psychometricians who form a tradition of psychology in themselves.

Darwin's ideas also provided an immediate reason for supposing that observing animal behaviour would be of use in understanding human behaviour and, indeed, during nearly all of this century, a great deal of animal experimentation has taken place. This is a very clear case of biology having had greater influence on psychologists than has philosophy. Descartes had held the opposite view to Darwin, that studying animals was a pointless pursuit. His reason for this was his belief that animals were radically different from man in having no soul.

In *The Expression of the Emotions in Man and Animals* (1872), Darwin presented evidence and argued for the notion that emotional expressions are vestiges of actions and movements that, at one time in the evolutionary history of the species, had served some practical function. Again, by considering the use of emotional expression, Darwin focused on a field eagerly taken up by functional psychology and also provided modern psychology with its first look at Man as an emotional being—unless you count Wundt's feelings of tension and relaxation to metronome clicks as emotions. Perhaps Wundt may have.

Finally, Darwin provided psychologists with an early example of the study of infant development. In 1877, he published *Biographical Sketch of an Infant* which comprised details of the development of his own son. Of Darwin's four main contributions to psychology, the importance of a functional approach (asking about the *uses* of mechanisms and characteristics) is the most pervasive. It will appear throughout this

9

discussion of Functionalism and also as a declared or tacit assumption through the whole of this book. The other three main contributions, the importance of animal work, child psychology, and the study of individual differences, will be discussed at various points.

William James

William James' central place in the Functionalist school of psychology was not chosen by himself. The school was, in fact, labelled by Titchener in 1898. At that time, Titchener was attacking non-Structuralist psychology, and, for this purpose, he found it convenient to provide the sort of psychology practised by James and his associates with a name.

James was as different in personality from Wundt and Titchener as can be imagined. He had, in common with Freud, a wonderful literary gift combined with little or no interest in experimentation. James travelled much throughout his life and his attitudes were always very eclectic. He would have been incapable of declaring allegiance to any school or set of ideas; certainly none could have contained his divergence of thought. He was born into a wealthy and talented family and, for several years, threatened to become merely a wealthy dilettante. James looked at several possible careers: painting, chemistry, biology, medicine and nearly became a full-time hypochondriac. He failed to qualify in any of these with the exception of medicine, in the efficacy of which he had little faith. From medicine, via emotional and physical crises, he went on to teach physiology, and a while later he taught a course on the relationship between physiology and psychology.

James remained principally a psychologist for a remarkably long time for him, but towards the end of his life he published in philosophy and in education. We are lucky that he dropped in on us: he brilliantly expressed a much-needed corrective to the all too pervasive Structuralism.

The influences on James included the overriding one of Darwin, often as transmitted by Galton, an important figure whose work will be discussed with the account of psychometry. James spent nearly twelve years writing a major account of psychology, *Principles of Psychology* (1890), which states his position on the whole range of psychological topics in which he was interested. The *Principles* presents a picture of man far more complete than that of the Structuralists. James pointed out that people act and feel and show emotion: they do not just think. Further, he tried to place all of the activities of man in a biological framework. Psychology was regarded at this time by James as the study of peoples' adaptation to the environment.

Consciousness

James believed that, to understand consciousness, one had to

10

understand its function rather than its structure. This function, according to James, was to enable the organism to behave in ways most likely to lead to survival. Otherwise, he reasoned, why would it have been evolutionarily selected at all? James supposed that many repeated actions are first performed by the use of conscious thought but that, by practice, they became properly relegated to unthinking habit, thereby freeing consciousness for the acquisition of new actions and for functionally vital decision-making.

James believed the Structuralists to be mistaken in thinking that conscious experience was made up of analysable elements. He supposed that in their analyses they saw what they expected to see—a common enough occurrence! James saw consciousness as a unity and as something that flows; the 'stream of consciousness' is one of the most striking images he used to describe this view. He argued that the continuity of the stream of consciousness was not interfered with even by sleep: we pick up in the morning from where we left off at night, with no real break in our conscious experience of life.

James' view of consciousness is also one of a system of organic growth. Experience increases by a process of inclusion rather than one of association. As James pointed out we can never perceive the same event twice because on the second occasion the event is perceived by a person with different experience.

Habit

As can be gleaned from James' view of consciousness, unconscious habit also has a crucial part to play in his account of human life. He provided a theory of habit at two levels, physiological and social. His physiological explanation that habits are established by increased plasticity of pathways in the nervous system is plausible but, by now, very outdated. The account of the function of habit in running society also reflects an outlook of 'a place for everything and everything in its place', which is certainly weaker now than in James' day, but still the social function of habit is clear. Whilst 'stream' was the image used for consciousness, 'flywheel' was that for habit. James saw habit as the great stabilizing force in society. It is the device by which the predictability of the behaviour of others can be kept within biologically efficient bounds.

Emotion

Unusually for James, in the area of emotion, he presented a clear, testable formulation. That is, he presented a point of view which suggested empirical ways in which it can be supported or refuted. He argued that if we see a frightening object and run, we feel afraid because we are running (due to the accompanying autonomic and skeletal changes), whereas common sense tells us that we are running because we feel

11

afraid. This problem, concerning the order of the various components of emotion (experience, behaviour, and expression), is one which still concerns psychologists. As usual, common sense is inadequate and fails to deal with the complexities of the problem. James' theory of emotion is contemporary with a similar (although not identical) one presented by the Danish physiologist Lange. The two formulations have tended to be thought of together as the James—Lange theory.

The self

James attempted an analysis of the concept of self, proposing a hierarchy of 'selves' stretching from the 'spiritual me', to the 'bodily me', via a number of levels of 'social me'. The 'spiritual me' has, since James, tended to be left to theologians and mystics and the 'bodily me' to the medical profession. Social psychologists have, however, made much of the various types of 'social me', particularly during the last decade, when accounts of real people have tended to re-enter psychology after a long period, during which only aspects of people were being considered by many (although not all) psychologists.

These topics do not exhaust the huge range covered by James. Before his arrival in psychology the subject was narrower and doctrinaire in its approach; he let fresh air into the subject and enabled a much broader view to be taken of the areas which psychology could encompass.

James' methods

James' contribution to methods by which we may gain knowledge about human life was not as far reaching as his widening of the subject area. James stayed with the Structuralists in regarding introspection as the psychologist's basic tool, he saw it as the exercise of a natural gift. This way of proceeding was, however, not the only one James recognized. Experimentation he accepted as valuable and was happy that others would use it. He himself, however, lacked the inclination and the patience.

James emphasized the desirability of comparative methods, that is, attempting to gain knowledge about the workings of one group by observing its similarities and differences with those of another; for example, human adults against animals or children.

Dewey and Angell

John Dewey (1859–1952) and James Angell (1867–1949) each published a paper which served to codify the achievements thus far of Functionalism as a school and to point out its advantages, not only over the, by then, ailing Structuralism, but also over atomism in general. Atomism is the doctrine that to understand the workings of a system it is best to break it down and understand the parts first.

12

Dewey (1896) continued the Functionalist argument that there was no point in regarding behaviour as an object of study unless it was in the context of understanding the organisms adaptation to the environment. Angell (1906) provided a very thorough exposition of the Functionalist position in which he represented its basic tenets.

The ends of Structuralism and Functionalism

Both schools were transformed: Structuralism into a matter of little more than historical interest; Functionalism into a belief in the importance of a biological substratum to experience and behaviour which was to underlie all future psychology.

Despite the huge difference between Structuralism and Functionalism there were many ways in which they were similar and every one of these similarities encountered a reaction. Both Structuralism and Functionalism stressed the importance of the unconscious part of mental life. The earlier schools agreed that introspection was a valuable method but Behaviourism was to attempt to dismiss it entirely, supposing only observable behaviour to be worthwhile data. Structuralism insisted upon and Functionalism partially tolerated the idea of atomism, that is, the idea of analysing phenomena in trying to understand them; Gestalt psychology was to reject this approach entirely, believing that, by disregarding the holistic aspects of mental life, one was disregarding its essence.

Structuralism and Functionalism were largely concerned with discovering statements concerning the similarities between people, but individual differences were studied by Galton (during the heyday of Structuralism and Functionalism) and later by a line of researchers who were particularly connected with the use of psychology in the selection and testing of people.

Both Structuralism and Functionalism accepted the existence of associations of greater and lesser complexity. They inherited the notion of association from philosophy. Three psychologists in particular, however, instead of accepting the association of ideas, events, and so on, chose to create associations and to study the circumstances under which this could be done. The rest of this Chapter will discuss first these Associationists and then each of the reactions to the ideas shared by Structuralism and Functionalism.

Associationism

The three scientists in this part of the Chapter hardly form a school, but they provide us with a convenient grouping to help understand the early work on the forming of associations.

Hermann Ebbinghaus

Hermann Ebbinghaus (1850–1909) originally trained in philosophy. Amongst other events in his early life he was involved in the Franco-Prussian war of 1870. Despite this, or perhaps because of it, 1876 found Ebbinghaus looking through the second-hand book stalls which then, as now, line the Seine in Paris. There he found a copy of Fechner's *Elemente der Psychophysik*, which event in the psychology of association is akin to the tale of the falling apple in Newtonian physics. Ebbinghaus, with an independence of spirit, engendered, no doubt, by many factors, but including a good private income, decided to ignore the edict of Wundt that higher mental processes were not amenable to psychological investigation and began to investigate learning by adapting Fechner's techniques.

Although the meaning of 'learning' in psychology will be made clear in later Chapters it is important to realize now that 'learning' means those changes in humans or animals which are not attributable to maturation or disease. This definition, like so many others, causes more trouble than it clears up, but it will suffice to make it clear that 'learning' in psychology is not specifically connected with the concept of education or even of training.

By inventing a device called a 'nonsense syllable' Ebbinghaus was able to investigate the formation of associations between items which he supposed could not have been associated previously. Examples of nonsense syllables are ceg, zut, tis.

The result of his several years of utterly dedicated and very isolated endeavour was considerable understanding of learning and forgetting. Ebbinghaus discovered that forgetting, the lack of availability of associations, happens quickly at first and then progressively more slowly, but, most importantly for psychology, he quantified this and his other results.

For a subject for his work Ebbinghaus used himself and it is a tribute to his patience and his thoroughness that, although his work has been elaborated by now to a vast extent, his contribution still provides the firmest of foundations. From Ebbinghaus we learnt that, for verbal material with humans, strength of association depends on repetition and meaning and, further, we learnt about this quantitively.

The other two 'Associationists' we shall discuss concerned themselves mainly with associations in animals.

Ivan Pavlov

Ivan Pavlov (1849–1936) was a dour man who did not like psychologists. He regarded psychological nomenclature as pretentious and useless. His own training was as a physiologist, to which study he stuck, investigating initially the innervation of the heart and digestive system and then brain function.

Pavlov discovered the rules governing the association between external stimuli, such as sights and sounds, and some types of glandular secretion. The experiments for which he is most famed amongst psychology students are those in which he taught dogs to salivate to the sound of a buzzer. Because he demonstrated that untaught dogs fail to do this he can be said to have formed an association between the sound of a buzzer and salivation. This process is now known as classical or Pavlovian conditioning. The description is not reserved only for the special case just mentioned but whenever a learned stimulus (for example, the buzzer) replaces a natural stimulus (for example, food).

Around this basic process, Pavlov worked to provide an enormous amount of information about the variables which, when manipulated, provide greater or lesser, stronger or weaker, learning. Further, Pavlov was a great quantifier. He did not, for example, content himself with the observation that a dog salivated slightly or copiously but, rather, measured the rate and total amount of saliva secreted. The importance of quantification is a topic to which we shall return when summarizing the contribution of the Associationists.

Edward Thorndike

Edward Thorndike (1874–1849) took the principles known to circus trainers for generations and transmitted them into knowledge of great scientific value. Whereas Pavlov had investigated the associations between stimuli and glandular responses, Thorndike investigated the association between situations and voluntary muscular responses. To do this, he invented the 'puzzle box', which is a cage, out of which animals may learn to escape by some manipulation, such as pulling a wire loop. Thorndike motivated the animals to escape by enabling them to thus obtain food or to join their fellows. He used the time taken by an animal to escape as a measure of learning or, if it had previously learned, as a measure of remembering.

Thorndike explained his earlier work in two 'laws'. The first of these is the 'Law of Effect' which holds that the effects on itself of an action by an animal influences the likelihood of the animal repeating the action given the opportunity. This is an informal way of stating the law which, it is hoped, is clear. In Chapter 11 you will find its formal statement, together with an account of the conceptual difficulties to which such a seemingly simple idea can lead. Earlier in his career, Thorndike also supposed that associations were strengthened or weakened in ways independent of the outcome of the situation. This he called the Law of Exercise.

Although Thorndike's early work was with animals, he attempted to apply his learning principles to education, but this is not the part of his work for which he is now best known.

The contribution of the Associationists

At first sight, the contributions of Ebbinghaus, Pavlov, and Thorndike might appear disappointing in that, sometimes, their discoveries seem self-evident. But this is only true of the grossest account of their work. At this very gross level, they simply confirmed that humans and animals tend to associate certain events with certain behaviour. Their work is important, however, because they made, and led others to make, a very fine study of the conditions under which the formations of associations—learning—could be expected. This work was largely continued by a school of psychologists who have become known as Behaviourists: even Ebbinghaus' work was to be put under the heading of verbal behaviour.

The emphasis on quantification in psychology has been mentioned as something for which the Associationists should be given special credit. It is important that one realizes why working with quantities or scales is a matter of importance to psychology or, come to that, to science in general.

If we think we understand a system or part of a system we may check our understanding by predicting how it will behave. The more finely we can check the system the more we can confirm our understanding or realize that we did not understand it as well as we thought. Fineness of checking improves with our fineness of measurement. If, for example, we predict that it will rain over Southend Pier in fifty days time, and it does so, we might or might not have discovered the key to the laws which govern the falling of rain. However, if we predict correctly that it will rain from 19.08 hours to 20.03 hours at that place on that day and at no other time we can be surer that we have understood the laws. To predict an event roughly is a less impressive demonstration of our comprehension of the rules governing it than to predict the event finely. We wish to be as impressive as possible in this way, and fine prediction involves finely quantified prediction.

The type of analysis of associations discussed here is dependent upon the notions of a stimulus, something which effects the organism, and a response, something the organism does because of the stimulus. Thus, the three scientists we have been dealing with needed to break down behaviour somewhat artificially. They adopted an atomistic attitude. The same type of attitude had been taken by Wundt concerning his chosen subject matter of the contents of consciousness. Atomism and a great concern with the problems of learning, characterize an American-based school known as Behaviourism. A total rejection of trying to understand behaviour by breaking it down into small components characterizes a German-based school known as the Gestaltists. We need, now, to discuss these two schools.

Gestalt psychology

The German word 'Gestalt' is translated in several ways such as 'form', 'shape', 'configuration', or 'whole'. The word in psychology represents a school whose main tenet is that the subject matter of psychology should be treated holistically wherever possible. Favourite words of Associationists, 'stimulus' and 'response', were anathema to Gestalt psychologists.

The school's founder was Max Wertheimer (1880–1943) who was joined by Kurt Koffka (1876–1941) and Wolfgang Köhler (1887–1967). It began and flourished mainly in Berlin, but its three leading protaganists emigrated to the U.S.A. during the 1930s because of the threat posed by the Nazis. Thus Gestalt psychology was thoroughly introduced to the English speaking world.

Max Wertheimer

Wertheimer began his constructive campaign against atomism by doing experiments on apparent movement. Using a tachistoscope (a device for presenting visual stimuli for timed periods), Wertheimer illuminated two slits, one vertical the other at an angle, one after the other. He found that the subject's perception depended on the interval between turning off the light behind one slit and turning it on behind the other. If the interval was long (by visual perception experiment standards) say 300 msec (msec stands for millesecond which is one-thousandth of one second) then the subject typically saw one slit go off and the other come on. If the interval was very short, say 30 msec, then the subjects saw first one slit on and then the other, but the fascinating case for Wertheimer was the intermediate interval of about 60 msec. At about this interval subjects reported seeing the slit of light move from one place to the other. This phenomenon, which has often been exploited in illuminated advertising hoardings, Wertheimer dignified with the name 'the phi-phenomenon'.

Wertheimer believed the phi-phenomenon was important to psychology because it provided a perception which defied analysis by Wundtian methods. You will remember that Wundt was not content with reports from his observers that they saw 'a book'; rather, he required an analysis of this percept into, for example, darkness, rectangularity, and so on. Wertheimer showed that his subjects, having observed the phi-phenomenon, could not analyse it into its elements in a Wundtian manner, even though those elements were there. This remained the situation however many times they cared to watch the phenomenon.

Thus, Wundt's atomistic type of analysis failed, nor could an Associationist approach of some other kind explain why two incidents in a particular relationship should look like something else. Wertheimer's

17

solution to the problem was to point out that there was no problem if one accepted a Gestalt approach, that the phenomenon needs to be considered as a whole to provide a sensible unit with which to work. This principle is usually expressed in the phrase, 'the whole is greater than the sum of the parts'. In fact, the phrase has become such a cliché that it is tempting to suppose that it is devoid of meaning; but this is not true, it really does convey very clearly the main principle of Gestalt psychology. Later, Gestalt psychologists were to refer to atomistic, Associationistic psychology as 'bricks and mortar' psychology, the bricks being the atoms or elements and the mortar the associations between them. They believed that the important part of the matter was the wall. Further, in cases like the phi-phenomenon it was important (we are nearing the end of the analogy) to discuss walls because there were no bricks or mortar to be seen.

Wertheimer developed his early work on the phi-phenomenon until, in 1923, he published a set of principles of perceptual organization. In those he expressed the view that perceptual organization is spontaneous whenever an organism looks round its environment. We do not have to learn this organization because it is based on fundamental principles which can in turn be related to the organization of brain function.

The main principles of perceptual organization, according to Wertheimer are proximity, similarity, closure and pragnanz. The first three can be made clear by diagrams:

```
X  X      X  X
X  X      X  X
```

Fig. 1.1

The principle of proximity is illustrated by the fact that we most readily see the eight crosses as two squares made up of four crosses each. The elements of the diagram which are closest to each other are perceived as wholes.

```
□ □ □ □ □ □
○ ○ ○ ○ ○ ○
□ □ □ □ □ □
○ ○ ○ ○ ○ ○
□ □ □ □ □ □
○ ○ ○ ○ ○ ○
```

Fig. 1.2

The principle of similarity explains, according to Wertheimer, why we tend to see six rows rather than six columns in Figure 1.2.

Fig. 1.3

18

Closure, as a principle, is demonstrated by the observation that we tend to perceive Figure 1.3 as three circles rather than two back to back semi-circles with a spare at each end. We tend to complete incomplete figures.

The principle of pragnanz is more difficult to illustrate, as you might have guessed from the fact that it remains in German, *Prägnanz*, which is simply the German for pregnant, or concise. It refers to the belief in a tendency for figures to be perceived as 'good' as possible. A figure attains goodness by being orderly, stable, simple, reduced to its simplest terms. One is not obeying the principle of pragnanz if one saw

Fig. 1.4

as representing a state of affairs which could happily exist indefinitely.

Wertheimer supposed that all perception was organized according to these principles but he believed also that the experience of the perceiver would affect the perception.

Apart from his work on perception Wertheimer also carried out major work on the topic of 'thinking' which is discussed in Chapter 18.

Gestalt psychology and the brain

The Gestalt psychologists imagined brain processes underlying the organization of perception to be quite different from those imagined by the Associationists. Instead of a series of representations of outside events connected by associationist links, the Gestaltists supposed that isomorphism existed between the outside world and its representation in the cerebral cortex (that part of the brain where sensory input is primarily represented—see Chapter 7). 'Isomorphism' means literally 'same form'. The Gestaltists supposed that the brain was a map of the outside world. This means that if, for example, two objects are close to one another in space they will automatically be represented close to one another in the brain. This proximity, according to the Gestaltists would cause an automatic interaction of the representations enabling them to be perceived as parts of a whole, the whole being the result of physiological inevitability, not the result of learning.

To understand more accurately the Gestaltists' notion of interaction by virtue of proximity, it is important to realize that they were influenced by the contemporary topicality of field theories in physics. These theories postulate (and, in the case of physics, clear evidence is available for this) that entities such as electric currents are not limited to their conducting wire but radiate a field all around them, strongly when close to the wire, and rapidly falling off but reaching zero only at infinity.

To use this kind of idea for the cortical representation of the outside world needs more direct physiological evidence, in fact the Gestaltists notions received indirect support from the unlikely quarter of Karl Lashley (1890–1958) a Behaviourist.

Learning and problem-solving

The Gestaltists extended their principles of perception to provide accounts of learning and problem-solving. Learning was the central topic, not only for the Associationists, but also for the Behaviourists who were contemporary with them. Problem-solving was a topic which the Structuralists had considered previously.

During the first world war Köhler was interned on Teneriffe. He took advantage of his confinement by studying the behaviour of apes who were given various problems to solve. The type of problem Köhler used was not totally unlike that used by Thorndike. The animal had to discover a technique in order to obtain food. By using apes, Köhler had rather splendid subjects in that he did not find it necessary to have the animals very hungry as Thorndike often did. To an ape, it appeared, a banana in the distance was a challenge.

Köhler's observations led him to conclude that the solution to problems are 'seen' in the literal rather than the metaphorical sense. Once the elements required for a solution are in reasonable proximity (e.g., a banana and a stick with which to drag it into the cage) then the solution may come, and, once it does, it comes quite suddenly as the Gestalt of elements forms. Thorndike's results with cats, however, needed explaining. Köhler held that they resorted to trial and error because Thorndike hid a vital element for the solution of the problem which is what prevented the sudden appearance of the solution.

Thus, for the Gestaltists, learning and problem-solving involved a holistic reorganization of the perception of the environment which is in strong contrast to the atomistic approach of the other schools. Wertheimer, in a late work, extended Gestalt ideas on learning and problem solving to the case of human beings, but this work is perhaps of rather more pedagogical than psychological interest.

The great criticism of the Gestalt school's account of problem-solving, which does not seem to have been satisfactorily answered, is that their solution to problems often seems to be the same as ignoring them. This is a tempting way to run one's life but an ultimately unrewarding one. To criticize Thorndike for not presenting his animals with part of the solution seems strange when problems are problems just because some part of the solution is obscured.

The Gestaltists did, however, stimulate a great deal of work on the relative contributions of genetic endowment and learning to perception, which is described in Chapter 13.

Behaviourism

Behaviourism was as American in its main development as Gestalt psychology was German. The main tenet of the school, that psychology should be the study of behaviour, however, is attributable to the British psychologist William McDougall (1871–1938).

Whereas Gestalt psychology has, by modern times, shrunk greatly in its width of application, Behaviourism has become an essential ingredient of mainstream psychology. At the time of writing this situation still holds, although, as we shall see in Chapter 2, there is some sign of change—both perhaps a less broad concern with the contributions of Behaviourism and even some renewed interest in Gestalt psychology, together with a number of other types of psychology. By the 1950s the idea that psychology was, to a huge extent, to be the science of behaviour, as distinct from that of consciousness, had become almost universally accepted and, thus, Behaviourism, as a widespread school, ceased to exist. This is parallel to the end of the Functionalist's clear existence as a school, once Functionalism had been widely accepted. Schools, in fact, seem to have been generated by a wish to protest against currently accepted ideas. If and when the ideas of schools become accepted, then the school loses its strong identity.

John Watson

John Watson (1878–1958) was the person who changed psychology from the study of conscious experience to the study of behaviour. That he was able to do this in a very short time speaks for the existence of two factors. The first of these was a readiness, particularly on the part of American and British psychologists, to accept change because of the difficulties into which introspection as a method had led Structuralism. The second factor was the ability of Watson as a polemicist as well as a scientist.

Watson began life as the sort of child most parents prefer not to have, eventually displaying socially delinquent behaviour. After his relatively short working life in academic psychology, during which he made his greatest achievements in the subject, he returned to 'delinquency' in the guise of divorce and re-marriage to a research assistant. For the United States of the 1920s this was delinquency indeed, and he was forced to resign his job at John Hopkins University. He spent the rest of his life making a great deal of money in the advertising industry and producing an occasional book on Behaviourism. As time progressed, Watson became increasingly concerned with the implications of learning theory for education and the organization of society. B. F. Skinner is another Behaviourist who, more recently, has turned his attention to the same kind of concern.

Watson's first published written account of Behaviourism came in an article in *The Psychological Review* of 1913 and in his book *Behaviour* (1914). He was clearly impatient with the in-fighting of the Structuralists particularly over the dispute between Wundt and the Würzburgers over the possibility of imageless thought. Watson felt that, if psychology was to progress, it would have to desert the method of introspection which, he pointed out, was turning psychologists into a 'debating society'. For introspection Watson wished to substitute objective data.

Although Watson did not concern himself greatly with this point, it is worth considering the meaning of the term 'objective' because it is not always clear when a piece of evidence is to be regarded as objective. The problem becomes clear when one considers that all of the knowledge we have of the world is essentially private. We do not, in the last analysis, know if we see an object in the room; we simply know we have a sense-impression, a perception of the object. This knowledge is subjective. Even if the object is clear and plain to see, an armchair, for example, we only know of it subjectively; and if we are the only person who has ever been in the room or ever will go into the room, the statement, 'there is an armchair in the room', is a subjective one. In principle, the situation is not altered if a procession of observers peer into the room and note the existence of the armchair. But the situation is to some extent altered if the observers hold a meeting and agree that there is an armchair in the room. We are tempted, then, to say that the statement, 'there is an armchair in the room' is an objective statement. This idea of objectivity, as an agreement between observers, will have to do as its definition. Karl Popper thus defines objectivity as 'inter-subjectivity'.

One problem with introspection as practised by the Structuralists was that, given a dispute about what was in consciousness, there was no way in which more than one observer could check the situation. A further problem was that, to obtain the 'right' things in consciousness, one had to be trained properly and this reduced to being trained by the right people. This kind of psychological 'establishment' was not destined to appeal to Watson.

Watson, then, in the short term, substituted objective data for introspective data but it is essential to realize that, very soon, the Behaviourists were slipping in introspection, usually under the euphemism of 'verbal report'. But it had become complementary to and an aid to understanding the objective data rather than the main data itself. The new definition and methodology of psychology insisted upon by Watson opened the doors completely to animal psychology. Apart from the Cartesian objection to animals being used in psychology, that they had no souls and were thus fundamentally different to mankind, the Structuralists had ignored animal psychology on the grounds that they possibly had no conscious experience but that, even if they had, they were distinctly inadequate at introspecting.

Like the Structuralists and unlike the Gestaltists, Watson was atomistic in his approach; he believed that, however complex a piece of behaviour appeared to be, it could be analysed into basic stimulus-response (S-R) units which he called 'reflexes'. In Watson's system these were of two types: those called by Pavlov unconditioned responses, for example salivation to the smell of food, which he supposed were instinctive, and those which he supposed were learned. A major task for psychology, according to Watson, was to identify those responses which were instinctive and those which were learned and to discover the laws governing learning (or habit formation as Behaviourists sometimes called learning). However, whilst others took this up, Watson, true to his concern with practicalities in life dealt most of the time with stimuli and responses of a molar common sense size rather than a molecular, analytic size.

Watson's insistence on observing behavioural measures, rather than worrying about conscious states, led to some results of great interest, but also to what now seem to be almost absurdities. His account of learning depended largely on a basis of Pavlovian conditioning and he strongly opposed Thorndike's law of effect. An enormous amount of work has been done in learning theory since Watson's day, so that his own account of learning is now a matter for history rather than contemporary scientific interest.

Similarly, his account of memory is distorted by his determination to see human beings as S-R machines. The brain is simply a complex switch-room or telephone exchange, a passer on, not an originator or storer of messages. To avoid the plausible assumption that memories are stored and recalled in the brain, Watson put forward the implausible assumption that memories are largely after-effects in sensory organs. The lack of more than a 'telephone-exchange' brain in Watson's scheme presented him with particular difficulties in accounting for thinking, which he described as being simply implicit speech movements, a view which has received only circumstantial empirical support and which belongs to times past.

Whereas the difference between the common sense and the Jamesian view of emotion was in the order in which its components were supposed to occur, Watson predictably dismissed the component of emotional experience, restricting himself to the view that emotion consists of profound bodily changes particularly of the visceral and glandular systems. The viscera are the smooth muscled parts of the body such as the stomach and gut which, as you probably know if you have ever sat an examination, seem to be highly involved in emotion. In the case of emotion, Watson's assumptions led to some fascinating demonstrations of conditioned acquisition and loss of emotional responses which were a precursor of important later work, especially in clinical psychology.

Watson as a scientist

At first sight, Watson's simplified way of regarding human beings may seem pointless or just perverse, but it is important to realize that this enabled him to formulate clear predictions which were testable by experimentation. Furthermore, that experimentation was often able to decide between Watson's view and that of others. Whilst it is clearly desirable that we should formulate testable predictions which turn out to be supported by experiment, nothing is less constructive than to formulate ideas which are simply not testable. In this respect Watson was admirable; he was not frightened to stick his neck out.

Edward Tolman

Edward C. Tolman (1886–1961) accepted a Behaviouristic approach to psychology but one which was tempered by his interest in and knowledge of Gestalt psychology. The fact that the Gestalt school placed emphasis on perception and the organizing function of the brain led Tolman to change the S-R model of Watson to an S-O-R model, where 'O' means organism.

Tolman's major contribution was his theory of learning which was expounded in various publications covering 40 years, nearly up to the time of his death. The theory demonstrated his wish to re-introduce the person into psychology insofar as it used the notion of cognition. Cognition means knowing and Tolman suggested that even animals come to know a part of their environment. Further, these pieces of knowing coalesce to form an internalized map of the environment in the animal's brain: shades of Gestalt psychology, indeed. Tolman's theory has received considerable empirical support, although it has some enormous difficulties, particularly in the area of relating knowing to action, which demonstrate that it is far from a completely satisfactory story.

Clark Hull

Clark Hull (1884–1952) was the person who most thoroughly developed the Behaviourist account of learning. His theory went through three major formulations and attempted to predict the behaviour of rats in mazes. It was the last theory which attempted anything so ambitious. Hull's followers, notably K. W. Spence and N. Miller have tended to concentrate on more limited problems within learning theory as the solving of any one of these has proved to be a formidable task.

Hull's theory of learning reflects his interest in mathematics as well as in the physiological research of Pavlov. The theory can be likened to Euclidean geometry. By starting with a set of axioms, Hull hoped by means of deduction to produce predictions concerning behaviour. He then tested the predictions experimentally, thereby supporting, or otherwise, his axioms. In the cases where the predicted behaviour did not occur, attempts were made to modify the axioms to put this right, whilst not at the same time putting wrong deductions which had been confirmed in other experiments. The scheme of continuous guessing and checking was envisaged by Hull early on as a corrective to what he regarded as the half-baked formulations of other schools who did not, in his view, make the effort to follow through their assumptions to their logical conclusion. So that you may recognize it, it should be pointed out that the method of guessing and checking is usually glorified by the title of 'hypothetico-deductive method'. The guesses, the hypotheses, are not, however, usually as random as the word 'guess' may imply, but are guided by previous experience and knowledge which, when codified, is known as theory.

The difficulty which Hull and his co-workers met with in their grand scheme was that it failed to converge to the point where the number of explanatory devices was adequately smaller than the observations to be explained. Hull's lasting contribution to psychology is the provision of a variety of terms which have become part of its language and are most often found nowadays in learning theory and its applications in clinical psychology.

B. F. Skinner

Burrhus Frederic Skinner (born 1904) has also largely concerned himself with learning theory and like Hull has often used animals, although his work has been extended by himself as well as others to account for and to attempt to modify human behaviour, most notably in educational and clinical settings.

Skinner's attitude to research methods in psychology was originally inspired by Pavlov's view that if variables are adequately controlled, then the underlying order in the nature of things will become apparent. This view of research has contributed to Skinner's use and development of a characteristic approach to experiment which may be contrasted with that most often used by Hull and others. Skinner's method is to observe one animal or person rather than a group. Even if he does this several times it is not for the purpose of averaging the results, the typical Hullian procedure, but to check that the results obtained with one organism are not the result of some idiosyncracy of that organism. Accounts of Skinner's work in various settings will be found in Chapter 11.

It is in Skinnerian work that an 'anti-organism', behaviourist, S-R rather than S-O-R, approach still survives as a useful complement to much modern psychology, which is concerned with the analysis and comprehension of the organism. This does not mean that users of Skinnerian techniques as a group have any particular beliefs about the organism. In fact, it is unlikely that many of them do think that con-

25

sciousness is simply a more or less useless by-product of a basically S-R system. However, the simplified S-R scheme of things is found to be useful in various settings and excellent at predicting the behaviour of animals in some situations, which allows us to create further hypotheses about human behaviour. This is more than adequate justification for the approach which has come to be known as the 'experimental analysis of behaviour'.

Psychology of the unconscious mind

The modern consideration of the unconscious mind was developed largely by Sigmund Freud (1856–1939) beginning from about 1895. Thus, we go back to the time before Behaviourism and Gestalt psychology. The reason for leaving discussion of Freudian and related work to this late stage in the Chapter is that it had little debate with the other schools, coming as it did from a different mix of antecedents and developing a different subject matter. Before considering any relationship of the psychology of the unconscious to other schools a word about terminology will be useful.

The system founded and developed by Freud was called by him and is still known as 'psychoanalysis'. Freud had many disciples at various stages of his career, two of whom founded major systems branching from his. That founded by Carl Gustav Jung (1870–1961) is known as 'analytical psychology' and that founded by Alfred Adler (1870–1937) is known as 'individual psychology'. These three systems, together with other related ones, form a school, having in common the belief that much human experience and behaviour springs from motives of which the individual is unconscious. Collectively, the various systems are most often known as 'psychoanalysis', which is all right as long as the context makes clear whether the term is referring to the specifically Freudian system or to the systems as a group.

Sigmund Freud

Freudian psychoanalysis is both an account of human mental life and behaviour and a therapeutic technique. This is a lot and it took someone of Freud's singularity of purpose and confidence about the rightness of his ideas to produce it all. He was, like Wundt, a tireless worker and an autocratic man. He rethought parts of his system as time went on, yet was extremely antagonistic to friends or colleagues who offered criticisms or even suggested modifications to his system.

Freud was a medical graduate who was initially influenced by the French hypnotist Charcot (1825–1893). He used hypnosis with patients when he returned after a year in Paris to Vienna in 1886. However, he found his results only partially satisfactory. A medical colleague in

Vienna, Joseph Breuer (1842–1925) also used hypnosis to deal with a case of hysteria (a psychiatric disorder), but the patient not only seemed to remember emotional experiences to which symptoms were attributed, but found that, after discussing these under hypnosis, the symptoms disappeared (usually temporarily, as it turned out). It was from Breuer's hint that Freud proceeded with working out psychoanalysis, soon dropping the part played by hypnotism.

The ideas of Freud are discussed in later Chapters. Here it will have to suffice to describe his ideas very briefly so that the elements of particular interest and difficulty may be pointed out.

Freud invented a theory of personality based on the notion of 'fixation' at various developmental stages. These developmental stages Freud called 'psychosexual' stages, indicating the importance he wished to allot to sexuality in his system. Indeed the very life force, the prime motivator, in Freud's system is 'libido' which, at least in early versions of his system, is clearly sexual in nature. Freud also put forward an account of the forces which, in their dynamic (i.e., not static) equilibrium, constitute mental life. For this reason psychoanalysis (in general) is sometimes known as 'dynamic' psychology. The prime actors in this dynamic system are the id exerting instinctive, libidinous force, the superego representing cultural, civilized forces and the ego which achieves some balance between the other two.

Freud's system in general has caused a great deal of controversy in psychology, but there are perhaps two points in particular to which people have often reacted strongly. The first of these is Freud's insistence that children enter a phase of sexual activity at about the age of four to five years, after which there follows a decline, the latency period, until puberty. The second point is his belief that much human motivation, especially that from the id, is unconscious. This means that humans may sometimes do things for reasons of which they are unaware and cannot normally become aware.

Psychoanalysis, as a therapeutic technique, includes free association to the elements of the patient's dreams and the interpretation of the patient's statements in terms of symbolic meanings. The process, in its classical form, is extremely lengthy, involving what Freud described as transference of libido to the psychoanalyst. In broad terms, the technique is conceived as a means of obtaining controlled regression back to the psychosexual stage at which the patient is supposed to have been fixated, that is, unable to progress through. Whilst at this stage (in some emotional sense) the analyst attempts to right the previous wrongs so that the desired emotional maturity may be reached by the patient.

Freud came to his conclusions by seeing patients over many years and also by the process of self analysis. Freud's system is often criticized, indeed dismissed as mere fancy, on the grounds that his conclusions were obtained in a way open to the possibility that he simply recorded his own prejudices and views and that, by the undoubted charisma of his personality, he persuaded his colleagues to reach the same conclusions as himself. This criticism is neither of scientific nor pragmatic relevance for the following reasons: if one reduces Freud's beliefs to a set of statements, it is the job of scientists, in the case of dispute, to check these by replication, that is, by observing relevant cases, such as current patients, to see if they reach similar conclusions. To look at the reliability of the origin of the sources is to practise history, a practice only justified when the events are not still there to be observed. However, it is as useful to check Freudian hypotheses as to check Jamesian or Wundtian ones: they are not even entertained in their original form by those who would describe themselves as Freudians. Further, Freudian and neo-Freudian psychology is so vast in its aims that one should never fall into the trap of discussing the standing of Freudian hypotheses; always specify which ones. Several attempts have been made to test empirically Freudian-derived hypotheses in more or less modified forms, and the results, as one might expect, are mixed.

Carl Gustav Jung

Jung's analytical psychology differed from Freud's system, from which it stemmed, in several respects. The most radical of these were his account of the unconscious and the dismissal of libido as the central life-force.

Jung believed, obtaining his evidence in a similar way to Freud, that the unconscious was of two types, the personal and the collective. The personal unconscious is broadly similar to Freud's conceptualization, but the collective unconscious is an inherited unconscious knowledge of the essential experience of all mankind. The mechanisms of transmission of the collective unconscious have always been obscure. According to Jung, the collective unconscious expresses itself in an archetypal way, that is, its products represent concepts which are universal. One purpose of Jungian analysis is to recognize the archetypes behind dreams and fantasies. Jung believed that archetypes also occur in myths and fairy tales and are cross-cultural. Jung's attitudes to the notion of archetypes and their transmission showed a tendency to mysticism which pervades much of his work. The effect this tendency had on Freud, who was a convinced atheist, may be imagined. To go with his attitudes, Jung posited that the essential life force was essentially spiritual in nature, not sexual as it had been in Freud's system.

Jung was concerned with psychological 'types' and introduced into psychology the ideas of introversion and extraversion which were to become important in theories of personality (see Chapter 23). He is perhaps one of the most difficult psychologists to comprehend and it is certainly impossible to do anything like justice to what one is tempted to call his muse in such a short space as this. Like many original thinkers, his work can seem at times utterly profound but at others equally absurd. What is clear is that those parts of Jung's system which overlap in their coverage with that of Freud are probably even more difficult than Freud's to submit to investigate empirically.

Alfred Adler

Adler produced an acccount of human behaviour and mental life which, for scrutiny, needs to be considered in terms of outcome rather than in terms of cogent structure as a system. This is not a criticism; there is no intrinsic merit in producing a grand scheme of things, and Adler certainly provided ideas and theoretical formulations even though these were often modified piecemeal.

Where Freud had libido and Jung a spiritual life force Adler has the extraordinarily down to earth will for power, a striving after superiority. He saw the essential part of human motivation as being conscious although he in no way denied the existence of unconscious motives. His emphasis was not, as with Freud and Jung, on the history of the patient's emotional life, but on its future. Largely as a result of this an Adlerian analysis is far shorter and less likely to become a way of life in itself than a Freudian or Jungian one.

None of these divergencies from the Freudian orthodoxy were destined to endear Adler to Freud, and Adler went his separate way in 1911.

The three systems

We have seen earlier the huge methodological difficulties encountered in trying to investigate psychology as a science of consciousness, but these difficulties become trivial when compared with those arising from trying to create a science of unconsciousness. Because of this, psychoanalysis has always stood apart from the other schools. It was born of medicine rather than biology or philosophy, and its subject matter has prevented it from really joining with and interacting with other schools. Psychoanalysis, being born of medicine, has been centrally concerned with clinical problems and, in its final assessment, whenever that will be, it will be important to consider it not only as a form of therapy but also as a description of human mental life and human behaviour.

Psychometry

From the end of the last century throughout the whole period we have been considering, there have been psychologists who, usually with an eye to immediate application of their studies, have concerned themselves with the problems of mental measurement. They do not form a school in the sense that they actively worked together, hoping to solve the same problems; rather, they have usually been people who were faced with the need to solve a problem and who had the inventiveness to develop the solutions.

Galton, who has been mentioned already in the context of Functionalism, was the forerunner of modern psychometry. He supposed that intelligence was correlated with sensory ability (he had invented the first measure of correlation a little earlier in 1888). Thus, to measure intelligence, he set out to measure sensory ability. Not one to betray lack of enthusiasm for the task in hand, he arranged the collection some six years later of data from over 9000 people. James McKeen Cattell (1860–1944) had by then met Galton in London and published his paper *Mental Tests*, which gives an account of the uses to which such tests may be put as well as providing the term 'mental test'.

The progress of mental testing was threatened for a while by statistical objections to its validity but the situation was saved by the work of Charles Spearman (1863–1945) who worked under Galton in London. Spearman presented a two-factor theory of intelligence which held that any test result depended on tapping the general ability (g) of the subject as well as special ability (s). This theory was immediately challenged and has often been so since, but it remains a usable underpinning for the theory of mental measurement.

Alfred Binet (1857–1911) was a French psychologist who faced the administrative problem in Paris of allocating some children of deficient intelligence to special schools. To solve this problem, he devised a series of graded tests each consisting of a group of different tasks, thus providing a broad tapping of the child's abilities. Unknown to Binet at the time, he had solved, in practical terms, what Spearman had solved theoretically. The result was a success and the Binet scale was translated into English. The need for testing conscripts in the First World War so that they could be successfully allocated to different tasks completed the acceptance of mental testing and since those days it has been a part of all our lives. Recently, however, the very basis and meaning of mental testing has again been called into question. Discussion of the problems will be found in Chapter 17.

Conclusion

This Chapter has not attempted to present every contribution to psychology in the 75 years or so it covers. Some of the grosser omissions will be repaired in the next Chapter. They involve work which makes more sense looked back upon rather than being sliced off at about mid-century.

It is customary to point out that schools in psychology were a developmental phase, akin to that seen in other sciences in their early days. They were weakened in about 1930 when their founders were dead and when there was dissension from within and psychologists realized that no school really did justice to the huge gamut of human experience and behaviour. The extent to which this is so is something we shall have to examine in the next Chapter.

What is clear from our examination of the schools is the conflict between the poetic imagination and the influence of the machine. On the one hand, we have the Gestalt psychologists and the Psychoanalysts, who have a vision of man which is born of the notions of completeness and uniqueness with full recognition of the place of awareness. On the other hand, we have the Associationists and Behaviourists with their vision of man strongly influenced by the development of machines. Both seem useful models. The extent to which they have guided, and even made compatible, recent work is the essential if often tacit subject of the work we now need to examine.

2 Different approaches to the study of psychology

CLIVE GABRIEL

Recent psychology

A number of differences may be seen between recent psychology and the psychology of the schools discussed in the last Chapter. The emphasis on doctrine has lessened and that on empiricism increased: it is rare nowadays to hear the confident prescriptions as to what psychology should be about or the level of analysis, holistic or atomistic, at which it should be conducted. This change has not come about because psychologists have all suddenly become especially tolerant people, but because it is now clear that what we have embarked upon in studying psychology is most probably centuries of endeavour, rather than the few years to clear up the details, optimistically supposed by some of the earlier schoolmen. With the recognition of the complexities of the problem that we have set ourselves has come the acceptance that the routes to the answers cannot be clear and that the plural 'routes' is probably the realistic way of expressing the situation. Individual psychologists, being people, still, however, have their preferences for subject areas, as well as for methods, so that different areas of psychology are still recognizable.

One of the biggest changes that has occurred in psychology during the last thirty years or so has been the growth of 'cognitive' psychology. Social psychology, developmental psychology, and applied psychology have all developed greatly since the era of the schools, and physiological psychology has revealed a great deal about the workings of the 'machine' which correlate with behaviour and conscious experience. It has also made some particularly exciting contributions to the area of motivation. Let us begin the account of recent psychology with the problem of motivation.

Motivation

The problem of understanding why people do anything at all, and if they do something, why that and not something else, is very basic to psychology. The problem may be broken down into the need to understand two components of motivation: driving force, and direction. Following is a sketch of the types of approaches to motivation which have been used to account for its problems.

Instincts

An early theorist who attempted to answer both parts of the question was William McDougall in his *Introduction to Social Psychology* (1908). As the title of his book implies, McDougall was concerned with the area of social psychology, but his aim was to find, for those involved in all types of work concerning societies (sociologists, economists, and so on), a firm psychological basis for their accounts of human behaviour. For McDougall, that firm basis was biological and based on the idea of 'instinct'. McDougall presented a list of twelve human instincts which grew to a list of eighteen by 1932. His idea was that all human motives could be derived from his list of basic instincts. McDougall was not really happy with the use of the word 'instinct' in this context, which is as well because neither was anyone else. He later used the term 'propensity' instead. Instincts, or propensities, in McDougall's sense, were said by him to be analysable into three compotents: a predisposition to notice particularly relevant stimuli in the environment; a tendency to feel an appropriate emotional impulse; and a predisposition to make appropriate movements.

In fact, McDougall's theory was very sophisticated, involving a concept of sentiments which were derived from instincts, the final behaviour not being supposed to be purely instinctual at all, but involving considerable learning. The reasons why the theory fell out of favour after a period of great success were threefold. Firstly, Behaviourism was emphasizing the importance of learning for behaviour. Secondly, the sociologists, economists, etc., for whom McDougall's theory was so obligingly prepared, made it clear that they did not want it: for them, 'society' was a concept they felt they could deal with without considering individual psychology. Thirdly, the concept of 'instinct' came under great suspicion for not explaining anything, but just stating the problem in a new way. For example, saying that one is eating because of an instinct to eat may sound acceptable, but then, why not say that one is roller-skating because of one's roller-skating instinct? This process could be continued indefinitely—renaming everything and explaining nothing.

The 1950s saw the return of the idea of instinct to psychology, but this time with clear circumscription. The term itself is usually replaced by 'species-specific behaviour', one of a set of concepts introduced by animal ethologists such as Lorenz, Tinbergen, and Hinde to describe the genetically-determined behaviours of various species. However, even these genetically-determined behaviours are more or less modified by learning, although some to a very small extent indeed. Species-specific behaviour has been described in sub-human species, but there is no reason to suppose that we do not exhibit it, although the very adaptability of mankind speaks for the likelihood of a great proportion of learning in human behaviour.

Drive theories

Before the problems with McDougall's theories were clear, Freud had put forward his idea of libido as the energizing force behind behaviour. Other later theories, related to Freud's, supposed that the driving force was different in origin, and it was given different names; but the idea was essentially similar. In Freud's system, any particular type of behaviour could be supposed to be a transformation and canalization of libido, and Freud suggested mechanisms such as 'repression', by which these processes could occur. However, his and similar systems fail to say much more than that they suppose people behave because they live. There is no part of these systems which explains the vital point: why the general driving force takes the form of violin playing in one person, for example, and rock-climbing in another.

A different theory of drive came from the learning theorist Clark Hull. Hull's system related hours of deprivation of a basic biological need such as food to variables, such as speed of running to reach food. Hull's system was extremely complex and he took note of many variables in the rat's behaviour other than drive. However, it is important to note two points: that Hull had no way of measuring drive—he inferred it from deprivation; and that he found his data best fitted the assumption that drives are not specific. This last assumption means that, generally, a thirsty and hungry rat will seek food more energetically than a rat which is only hungry. This last idea, that of generalized drive, has much in common with the idea of arousal which was to become important to the theory of motivation.

Arousal theories of motivation

The concept of arousal seemed to have a clear physiological basis in the activity of part of the brain-stem known as the ascending reticular activating system (ARAS). Indeed, for several years from the late 1940s it seemed that there existed a physiologically mediated continuum of general arousal or activation. Sadly, like so much in science, what seemed simple has proved to be complex. Nevertheless, arousal states of various types are still identifiable and the concept of arousal in one form or another has featured widely in motivation theory.

The arousal theory of motivation supposes, and evidence has supported this to some extent, that the organism will work to obtain intermediate levels of arousal, too little arousal leading to no behaviour or aimless behaviour, whilst too much arousal leads to panic or frantic agitation. This picture is adequate insofar as it explains why humans and animals will behave to avoid staring at blank walls for long periods of time on one hand, and do not sit by idly whilst the house is burning down on the other. There are also, however, all of the middle levels of arousal which cover most of life. To explain which response is made by humans at these levels of arousal, cognitive and social theories of motivation are usually called upon. For animals, hierarchies of preferences for different types of behaviour are often supposed to operate. In the human case, these further theories usually involve the notion of hedonism.

Hedonistic theories of motivation

Hedonism is the ethical doctrine that seeking pleasure is the purpose of life. As pleasure is a conscious experience which animals cannot report and maybe cannot have, the notion is modified in their case. This is done by treating as 'pleasurable' those stimuli which the animal will work to obtain.

In his formulation of the 'law of effect', Thorndike supposed that animals repeated actions when they were followed by 'satisfiers' and would avoid repeating them when followed by 'annoyers'. It was soon pointed out that this formulation led to a circular argument. Thorndike supposed food was a satisfier because animals would press levers for it and he supposed they pressed levers for it because it was a satisfier. However there was no way of predicting, other than in this circular way, what would be a satisfier or what would be an annoyer. Meehl (1950) and Premack (1962) have solved this problem by demonstrating that satisfiers and annoyers have a general role by whch they can be identified other than by the circular argument of Thorndike. Premack has presented a system of arranging behaviours in order, which enables one to predict the proportion of time an animal is likely to spend emitting any one behaviour. Further, he has shown that the proportions may be altered by depriving the animals of particular requirements.

Social psychologists have taken up the idea of hedonism in their accounts of motivation. A series of 'exchange theories' have been developed, the exchange referring to rewards and costs. These theories are also open to the criticism of circularity and again, as may be seen in Chapter 26, ways have been found to meet this criticism.

Conclusion on motivation

Because motivation is at the very core of psychology one cannot expect all, or even many, of the problems it presents to be neatly solved. Animal and human studies may still offer perspectives for each other, but it seems that the two areas are perhaps best considered separately, if only because of the greater use of secondary or learned motivation (the cognitive and social sort) in explanations of human behaviour (McV. Hunt 1963). One difficulty with the psychological study of motivation is that the history of the subject has persuaded psychologists to look for answers by studying organisms in one environment, the laboratory. It has been apparent for some while now that the situation in which the behaviour takes place, especially in interaction with the organism's idiosyncrasies, plays a large part in the cause of behaviour exhibited.

Physiological psychology

Physiological psychology is concerned with discovering the physiological mechanisms whose action is concomitant with behaviour, experience and, indeed, all psychological phenomena. The relationship between physiological and psychological events is often complex, cause and effect by no means being always in one direction. Indeed, the relationship is often interactive, the physiological events and the psychological events serving to build up each other's intensities or damp them down. There are people who believe that, ultimately, all psychological events will be explicable in terms of physiological events, and this belief is known as reductionism. Whether or not reductionism is ultimately shown to hold, it is not a view which need concern us now; pragmatically there is more than enough for us to discover in both physiological and psychological language.

The scope of physiological psychology is wide and covers a number of different subject areas. Research has developed rapidly in recent years (on the firm basis laid by medical physiologists) on the mode of action of brain cells (neurones) and, most importantly, their junctions, which are known as synapses. These are important to psychology because of their role in learning and remembering.

At a gross level, physiological structures have been shown to mediate various psychological functions. Details of these systems and their functions will be found in the chapters on physiological psychology. Physiological psychology has also been important in the investigation of sleep cycles (sleep has been found to comprise a cyclical arrangement of different physiological and behavioural states), as well as in the wider investigation of the whole range of consciousness from coma, through sleep and wakefulness, to alert attention.

One of the most dramatic findings in physiological psychology over the past decades has been that by Olds and Milner (1954) and Olds (1956) identifying centres in the brain which, when stimulated, lead animals to behave as though they were strongly rewarded or strongly punished. These findings have been important in helping to understand the physiological mechanisms operating in the motivation of behaviour.

Methods of physiological psychology

Activity of the cerebral cortex, the outermost layer of the brain, is interpreted from records known as electroencephalograms, which term is mercifully usually abbreviated to EEG. This is the method beloved of illustrators of sensational articles about the horrors of mind-reading, thought control, and other Orwellian ideas. Electrodes are affixed to subjects' scalps, and these electrodes are sensitive to the very small electrical effects arising from the activity of the cortex. The signals from them are amplified and a continuous graph of the signals is automatically drawn. Readings from the graph may be correlated with sensory stimulation the subject receives or tasks he is asked to perform.

Measures may also be taken of the activity of the subjects' autonomic nervous system (ANS), which can be crudely defined as the nervous system controlling involuntary responses (Chapter 6 gives more detailed explanation). These measures are usually of heart rate, breathing depth and rate, galvanic skin responses (GSR), as well as readings of muscle tension. The galvanic skin response is a measure of conductivity between two points on the skin. Skin potential is also sometimes read. A further technique used by physiological psychologists is to implant an electrode at a specific point in the brain by means of surgery. The electrode may then be used either to stimulate that area of the brain with small electrical currents or else, by larger currents, to burn away a small area of surrounding tissue. This latter process is known as ablation. Stimulation and ablation are carried out mainly on animals, very rarely on humans, and then only for good clinical reasons.

Physiological psychology and psychology

As you will appreciate from this brief account of the activities of physiological psychologists, their work is not confined to one area of psychology (although it is more applicable to some areas than to others) but covers many areas in a symbiotic relationship with work which is behavioural or introspective.

Social psychology

Like physiological psychology, social psychology offers more than just its subject matter; it can be used as a viewpoint for all psychology.

The start of social psychology is usually taken as dating from the work of McDougall, who has already been mentioned in the context of motivation. His aim was to provide a firm biological basis for others who concerned themselves with the structure and function of society. It is important to note that social psychology is very concerned with the individual although it takes especial note of his relationship with others. Social psychologists do not often talk of 'society' as a concept for study; this is the job of sociologists. Ironically, given McDougall's aspirations for a biological basis for social studies of various types, social psychology is often regarded by psychologists as being as far as one can get from physiological psychology, the two types of study involving very different techniques.

One of the earliest influential theoretical systems in social psychology was that of Kurt Lewin (1890–1947). Lewin was greatly influenced by Gestalt psychology; indeed, he is often regarded as a Gestalt psychologist. Like the other members of the school, he was impressed by and used the field theories then, as now, current in physics. However, he used the idea of a field to represent the person's interactions with various forces in their 'life-space', whereas the other workers had used the idea as the basis of a theory of brain function.

Lewin's idea of a person's life-space comprised a psychological map of their environment, that is, a map representing the physical world as mediated by their perceptions as well as the rest of their psychological world. Lewin's aim was to comprehend behaviour by supposing it to be the resultant of the vectors (lines representing forces in direction as well as magnitude) representing all forces in the life space. This model, therefore, incorporates the influence on behaviour of the environment as it is perceived by the individual. The idea of representing psychological 'forces' by vectors has been influential in social psychology, as a glance at most textbooks on the subject will show.

Content of social psychology
A considerable proportion of social psychology is concerned with the problem of social motivation in humans, that is, motivation which does not relate directly to basic biological needs without some intervening learning process; and in most human society that amounts to just about all behaviour. Attempts have been made to identify such motives, as well as to provide models for the resolution of situations where motives would be expected to oppose each other. Some of these social motives such as the postulated need for achievement (N Ach) are hypothetical constructs (complex ideas supported by evidence which is largely circumstantial), whose measurement is by questionnaire-type tests. These tests need to be subjected to procedures for ascertaining their reliability and validity. That is, we have to discover that the tests are measuring what we believe them to be measuring and are doing so reliably at different times.

Another major topic of investigation in social psychology is the study and measurement of attitudes and attitude change. An attitude is another hypothetical construct which is supposed to have a cognitive, an affective (pertaining to mood), and a behavioural component. The study of the influence of groups on their members' behaviour and beliefs, of non-verbal communication and interpersonal attraction comprise a few of the further topics which make up social psychology and which you will find discussed in later Chapters. The study of how children become socialized, that is, learn the enormous amount of social skills and number of attitudes society requires them to have is sometimes placed under the heading of social and sometimes of developmental psychology. Here it is discussed in Chapter 22.

The methods of social psychology

Social psychologists' data cover the gamut of possibilities: behavioural, introspective, and various other kinds of report, free or structured by questionnaire. The data has most often been collected in laboratories but field work is also common.

For several years now social psychologists have been questioning the validity of their procedures. The problems they have encountered are of two types: those which are difficult to put right but clearly could be, given the will; and those which seem part of the very activity of social psychology. There has been concern about the heavy bias of samples of subjects used in social psychology experiments. Counts done on journal articles report that well over half the subjects used are students. Concern has also been expressed about the effects the experimenter has on the subjects by consciously or unconsciously communicating to them his requirements from the experiment. Another criticism is that social psychology is inadequate in predicting behaviour; that is, it fails to discover general laws governing social behaviour. The fact that students are so often used as subjects is a greater problem in social psychology experiments than in, say, physiological psychology experiments because the variables the social psychologist observes (social skills, for example) may be functions of socioeconomic class, intelligence, and so on. The trouble is that students are already biased in these ways: they are more intelligent than the general population and tend to come more from middle-class families than from working-class families. One is, therefore, developing the social psychology of a small group which may lead to statements which are quite untrue for the rest of the population, who were not represented in the experiments. The problem exists for all types of psychology but has been emphasized by social psychologists, not without reason. In short, the problem is that students are more likely to be atypical of the general population on social psychological variables than they are on some other types of psychological variables. This problem is of very great practical importance. Its remedy may well be extremely costly in effort. It is not, however, a fundamental problem.

Rosenthal (1966) raised the problem of experimenter effects which, again, might occur in most psychology experiments but will be more powerful in an area of study which frequently requires responses involving value, rather than purely behavioural, responses. Various ways have been used to remedy this problem which have in common the use of 'blind procedures'; that is, all those who come into contact with the subject do not know the experimental condition to which the subject is to be allocated. There are, however, other demand characteristics of experiments. It is often the case that subjects hypothesize what is expected of them and, depending on how nice or nasty they are, will tend to give either the results they suppose are desired or the opposite results. Both niceness and nastiness are obstacles to undistorted results, and experiments need to be designed to minimize this effect. There are no general rules for this; the experimenter needs to exercise his wits to the maximum to reduce the problem.

The problem of the relative lack of predictive power in theories in social psychology is more fundamental but not at all hopeless. The underlying model behind much social psychological thinking is that people behave according to an economic calculus. Various actions are seen as having positive or negative utility, and an attempt is made to understand human behaviour as being the result of a reckoning of which choice of action will provide the best pay-off. The predictive power of this kind of theory is limited by the same matter which so lamentably limits that of economic forecasting: the problem is that the effects are so highly interactive. This means that any general statement such as 'people will like those similar to themselves' will be contradicted many times because so many factors will affect it and in real life these are not held constant. The same problem occurs in all science: the extent to which it can be dealt with depends on matters of complexity and measurement. We have to draw the distinction made by Karl Popper whilst discussing physics, between prediction and prophesy. While it is often difficult to *predict* the outcome of a situation in social psychology, it is often possible, using theory, to provide a rationale for the outcome; that is, to show it fits the theory once one knows what the outcome is. Prediction is one of the severest criteria scientists demand before they are satisfied that an explanation of a phenomenon has been provided. However a rationale is a type of explanation, if not one which is ultimately satisfying. We shall have to return to the topic of what constitutes a satisfactory explanation towards the end of this Chapter.

Cognitive psychology

Associationists and Behaviourists had concentrated on a stimulus-response (S-R) model of animals and man. Tolman (1932) had taken the step of modifying this scheme to an S-O-R model, where 'O' standing for 'organism' indicated the view that the brain, indeed the central nervous system in general, was probably more than a busy telephone exchange. Cognitive psychology has attempted to analyse the structure and function of 'O'.

'Cognition' means knowing, and cognitive psychology has studied all of the abilities we use in knowing: perceiving, remembering, thinking, and so on. A very clear indication of how to proceed in cognitive psychology came from D. O. Hebb in *Organization of Behaviour*. Hebb suggested that, in order to understand the flow of information through the nervous system, one need not have a complete knowledge of the finest aspects of brain structure and function. Instead, one could race ahead of physiological knowledge by inventing a conceptual nervous system. Whilst any account of the brain's working must ultimately be subject to the check of physiological credibility, the approach of the conceptual nervous system, building information flow models, has proved extremely constructive.

Early empirical work was begun by Colin Cherry an engineer who concerned himself with what he called the 'cocktail party problem'. This is the problem of discovering how one may listen to the speech of one person whilst surrounded by many others speaking equally loudly in a crowded room. Why, if the person who is talking to one, is saying 'we had an awfully good time yesterday' and someone nearby is saying quite as loudly, 'the cow jumped over the moon', does one not hear some conflation of the two messages such as, 'the cow had an awfully good moon yesterday'? Cherry's method of answering this problem was to give various dichotic listening tasks to subjects. In these, different information was fed into each ear and the subject was asked to report what he had heard or else to 'track' the message from one or other ear; that is, to repeat what he heard as he heard it. The investigation of these and related problems was soon taken up, at first by Donald Broadbent, and then by a number of workers particularly in the U.K. and North America (for details see Chapter 14).

Eventually, models were developed, and these are still being modified, to account for the known facts about perception, selective attention, memory, and other aspects of the information processing system. The development of computers, which has occurred at the same time as the development of cognitive psychology, has provided inspiration for the building of some models and has also provided a useful analogy for higher level models designed to show the organization of other models. One of the best known attempts to show how higher organization may take place is that by Miller, Galanter, and Pribram in their book *Plans and the Organization of Behaviour* (1960).

41

Cognitive psychology, then, is not simply the science of behaviour, nor the science of conscious experience, but the science of information flow through people. Some of this flow may lead to behaviour and some of it may be conscious but neither is necessarily the case.

The methods of cognitive psychology

One method of psychologists in this field is to ask people what they saw, heard, or remembered after some sensory stimulation (and sometimes after a delay, during which they may be asked to perform some task or be subjected to other sensory stimulation). That is, subjects are asked to introspect. Watson's way out of the difficulty, when he had lambasted introspection as a methodological disaster, yet wanted to take notice of what his subjects said, was to say he was not using introspection at all; it was 'verbal response'. This need not be just casuistry; the distinction is in the attitude held by the psychologist. If a subject is asked to look into a tachistoscope (an instrument used for presenting visual stimuli) and say what he sees, the psychologist may get a response such as, 'it says ZRT'. If the psychologist assumes that the statement has meaning which is akin to that with which other subjects (and he himself) would endow the statement were they looking, he is using introspective method. If, however, the psychologist treats the statement as though it were a mere reflex in Watson's terms, something akin to conditioned salivation, then he has obtained a verbal response. It is hard to imagine why anyone would want a verbal response in this sense, unless they could not understand the language of the subject (an unpromising practice), or else were trying hard to defend a silly doctrine. It is clear that what cognitive psychologists ask subjects to do is to introspect.

A fundamental reason for objecting to introspection as far as Behaviourists were concerned was that, in cases of dispute, the problem sometimes proved to be unresolvable, but there are practical differences between the practice of cognitive psychologists and that of Structuralists. Wundt and his disciples were concerned with a type of report from subjects which did not occur spontaneously and which took careful training to obtain. They often succeeded in finding agreement between subjects at different places but hit trouble when they pursued more and more difficult tasks. Apart from straightforward instructions about where to look or listen, the subject in the type of experiment usually done in cognitive psychology is asked simply to report what he or she heard. During the last twenty-five years or so disputes have indeed arisen, caused by conflicting experimental results, but they have not led back to the mysteries of the training of subjects. Instructions given to subjects have often been found to alter results but instructions may be and have been compared and problems resolved.

While the methods of cognitive psychology have frequently included introspection, this has been a matter of convenience, not doctrine, as has been the case in the past. Other methods are indeed used, as may be seen from the Chapters on memory, perception, and thinking. It is typical of the attitudes of post-school psychology that any other methods available will certainly be grabbed very quickly, as long as they help to solve the problems which concern cognitive psychologists.

Cognitive psychology and a model of man
In the last Chapter it was pointed out that some schools of psychology worked with a machine-like model of man, whereas others took a view which had more in common with the products of a poetic imagination. Clearly, the methods and model building activities of cognitive psychologists subscribe to the 'man as a machine' view; but a machine with a difference. It is seen as much more complex than that postulated by the Associationists and Behaviourists. Also, there is in general no claim by psychologists that their account of information processing is sufficient to explain all human behaviour and experience. Some believe this, with the corollary that the 'machine' needs to be complex enough to produce poetry; a sort of computer. Others believe that the production of poetry is not within the province of even the most complicated machine; they suppose that the machine is a mediator. Whilst these conjectures are fascinating, it is not necessary to take one side or the other or even to indulge in them at all to practise cognitive psychology; the important thing is to understand the workings of the machine as accurately as possible.

Developmental psychology

In 1887, Darwin published an account of the diary he kept of the development of his own son. This is normally taken to be the start of modern developmental psychology. The first person to make the study a major part of their life's work was Granville Stanley Hall (1844–1924).

Hall was a remarkable person who investigated everything with superb enthusiasm. The fact that he was not one to do things by halves may be judged from the title of his magnum opus, *Adolescence: its Psychology, and its Relations to Physiology, Anthropology, Sociology, Sex, Crime, Religion, and Education* (1904). Hall was a strong proponent of evolutionary theory, especially that aspect which holds that ontogeny follows phylogeny; that is, that the development of the individual goes through stages representative of the development of the species. Hall left a wide, encyclopaedic basis for future study as well as a look into the future in his late study of geriatrics, until quite recently a lamentably neglected end of developmental psychology.

In general, developmental psychologists have been distinguished from

43

others by the questions they have asked, rather than by their theoretical background, although there is one giant exception to this rule.

The contents and methods of developmental psychology

Developmental psychology rests on the notion that behaviour and experience at any stage of life is related to previous states. The early years, from conception to young adulthood, have received most attention from developmental psychologists and old age has the next share of attention. Middle life does not so often show such sudden changes of behaviour or experience, so that it has been comparatively neglected. This is like historians of ancient times mentioning only the great battles and other crises of society, thus giving an unnaturally exciting account of life to the unwarned reader.

Psychological theories of early life stress two types of unevenness in the flow of development: stages, and critical periods. Development is found to occur in more or less the same order (although at differing times) in all normal children. Thus crawling precedes walking while holding furniture precedes free walking. Further, these stages of locomotion will roughly correlate with development of speech and other achievements. Various workers, foremost amongst whom are Freud and Piaget, have used the concept of stages to delineate periods when particular abilities first appear, or during which characteristic behaviours are produced. Critical periods are periods during development in which it is supposed that a child is ready to take advantage of some particular set of experiences. Some critical periods seem more critical than others. The extent to which various successful adult functions depend on childhood experience is a topic discussed in later Chapters.

Both the concepts of stages and of critical periods imply that development is neither simply a function of learning nor simply of maturation, that is, of the pure consequences of genes making themselves known at the appropriate times. Rather, development is, in general, the result of an interaction between heredity and environment. The meaning of 'interaction' is that any statement concerning the effect of learning on development must be qualified by describing the hereditary attributes of the person concerned, and, similarly, any statement about the effect of heredity on development must be qualified by describing the experiences encountered by the organism. At a common sense, qualitative level, the idea of interaction between heredity and environment is very clear; it is in attempts to quantify it that difficulties arise, indeed, the meaning of quantification in this area is a difficult concept. One way of dealing with this problem of quantification is to give scores to some piece of behaviour, aggressiveness, for example, and attempt to discover how much of the variance amongst scores is explained by heredity and how much by environment. Variance is a statistical term, it is simply a

44

number which represents the dispersion of the scores; the smaller the variance the more the individual scores tend to crowd around their mean. Difficulty then arises in controlling both the learning available to the children as well as their heredity. These points will be taken up at various places in this book, but it is important that you realize now that any statement concerning the various contributions of heredity and environment to any human function is a statement in which there can only be a limited amount of confidence. Knowledge is hard to come by, and bold assertion with little evidence, or a dozen or so shaky steps between the evidence and the assertion, is no substitute for it. The task of obtaining this type of knowledge is, however, far from hopeless— simply arduous.

The main approaches to the development of childhood have been those by Freud, Piaget, and various learning theorists (Bandura, for example); these approaches have differed in both their content and their methods. All three have investigated various aspects of socialization, with Freud predictably concentrating on emotional development and Piaget on intellectual and moral development. Learning theorists have concentrated, to some extent, on mechanisms of imitation, which has led to a theoretical debate as to whether or not imitation may be understood in terms of the basic types of conditioning introduced in the last chapter. Whereas learning theorists have adapted conventional laboratory methods to the study of development, the methods of Freud and Piaget are idiosyncratic and their validity needs to be considered. Freud's discussion of development stems from his psychoanalytic methods which, as has been mentioned in Chapter 1, leave much to be desired. Piaget's methods are semi-structured; that is, in his questioning of children, the aims and basic questions are standardized but, in recognition of the fact that children are not standardized, supplementary questions are sometimes added *ad lib*. These raise the methodological difficulty of distinguishing between asking and teaching.

The developmental psychology of senescence (old age) comprises distinguishing between normal and abnormal senescence and attempting to find successful management regimes for both. This is an area where psychology works with a range of other disciplines: psychiatry, neurology, and social work.

In all developmental work the need for more accurate observation has been felt. Children and the old are ready victims of anecdotal evidence, an awful combination of wishful thinking and sloppy observation, fit only for first wanderings in science. Developmental psychology is one area where theory has come almost too early and psychologists, aware of this, are successfully pushing the clock back, using techniques, such as time-sampling of behaviour, which have become readily available with the widespread use of aids such as video-tape recording.

45

Individual differences

One may consider people as being extraordinarily similar to one another or extraordinarily different from one another. Which view-point you take depends on how you compare them. A huge amount of psychology has arisen from studying the similarities between people; that which studies the differences comes under the heading of individual differences. Traditionally, this field has been divided into the main areas of personality and intelligence, with their attendant problems of measurement.

'Personality' is a term which, whilst easy enough to grasp roughly, is not easy to define, and it is even harder to make the definition operational. The problem is one of knowing where to stop studying the differences. Whilst viewing everyone in the world as being more or less the same is clearly a gross oversimplification, viewing everyone as unique in every respect may be wonderful for the biographer but not for the scientist who usually wishes to see patterns in his subject matter.

Trait and type theories

Although these are commonly distinguished, they may be regarded as fundamentally similar, trait theories allowing more 'types' and being more flexible in the labelling of those they allow.

Trait theories, as typified by that of R. B. Cattell are developed by obtaining, by various means, such as rating and behavioural observation, people's positions on various scales. Most of the scales used by Cattell (he began in 1946 with 171 of them) are bipolar, that is they have adjectives of opposite meanings at either end of the scale: examples are 'sociable-shy', 'wise-foolish'. Left like this, with a person rated on 171 variables, we might as well write a biography, indeed a biography may well be more digestible and give a clearer picture of the person than 171 numbers. Because of this, Cattell has, by various statistical means (cluster analysis and factor analysis), reduced the number of traits by taking advantage of correlations between them. The principles of these techniques are very simple, although in pre-computer days the arithmetic was hideously tedious. The idea of taking advantage of correlations can be readily understood by considering two of Cattell's original 171 traits. It is found that people's scores on the 'confident-submissive' scale is highly correlated with their scores on the 'conceited-modest' scale. This being so, we may reduce these two scales (together with several others) to one scale, say 'dominance-submissiveness'. Thus, several of the 171 originals may be reduced to one 'source' trait. Cattell, in fact, ends up with no more than 16 source traits altogether with which to summarize his 171 original traits. It is worth noting immediately, however, that personality ratings alone have proved to be rather disappointing in the prediction of behaviour. Situational variables, especially when considered in interaction with personality, are far more predictive of behaviour than personality alone.

The best-known, contemporary type theory is that of H. J. Eysenck, who proposes that people may be scored on three continua: neuroticism, extraversion, and psychoticism. Thus, people are typified by these scores. Although developed quite independently, Eysenck's three dimensions may be likened to Cattell's by regarding them as the result of taking advantage still further of correlations which may be found between the source traits.

The origins of individual differences

The origins of individual differences is a topic which has received much attention in the past few years. Special attention has been paid to the particular problem of intelligence, especially because of the suggestion that scores on intelligence tests may be largely genetically determined, a suggestion that has caused social, political, and moral opinions to be expressed on all sides in answer to psychological and statistical problems. This overspilling of inappropriate, often affective reactions into a problem of cognition has slowed progress of our understanding of the issues involved.

As you will probably already have realized, the topic of the origins of individual differences is yet another place in which the heredity-environment issue is of major concern.

Method in psychology

Whilst far from complete, these two chapters have presented a picture of what psychology has been, and is, about. The existence of several tensions in psychology will, it is hoped, have become apparent during the discussion. These tensions often reduce to conflict between intuitive and methodical methods of gaining knowledge about mankind. This raises a basic and very interesting distinction between psychology and other sciences: other sciences study objects and events which are not the objects and events doing the studying. Because each of us has such immediate experience of being human, it is very tempting to indulge our intuition in trying to understand humans; but the pitfalls in this method make it unacceptable. The major problem with proceeding by intuition is that people's intuitions are different, as are our own at different stages of our life. By depending on intuition, we thus consign ourselves to a modern 'Tower of Babel', everyone talking what to them is sense, and all the talk falling on non-comprehending ears. The claim science has to uniqueness is its ability to make statements which are regarded as true according to criteria which are there for all to see. This view of science does not mean that its practice is without assumptions or declared or tacit values, nor does it mean that science is in any way anti-intuitive. Intuition, in fact, has a worthy and recognized place in science as being one means by which hypotheses may be generated; but, once they are generated, we insist that they go through some system of checking, which may, or may not, seem intuitively reasonable, depending on who you are.

Intuition is not, however, the only way in which scientists obtain hypotheses for checking; a more formal way is by the use of a theory. A theory is a general statement which serves two fundamental purposes: to enable us to remember various disparate experimental results and discussions, and to provide us with hypotheses for checking. These are known respectively as the mnemonic and heuristic functions of a theory. An example of a general statement serving as a theory in psychology is: 'the more predictable is reward during the training of an animal to make a response, the fewer trials it will take before the animal stops making the response once reward has ceased'. Because this is a general statement, it is not immediately testable. To test it, we need some initial conditions. For example, group of rats A has been rewarded for every fifth trial in training, group of rats B has been rewarded every nth trial, where the mean of n is five. With the theory and the initial conditions, we may immediately form the hypothesis that group of rats A will stop making the trained response after a fewer number of trials than will group of rats B.

If, on running the appropriate experiment and interpreting the results according to the methods in Chapter 3, we find that our prediction is confirmed, then we may say that our theory is corroborated. Note well, 'corroborated' not 'proved'. 'Proof', in the way the word is commonly used, has no place in science: we have not demonstrated that our theory is true for goldfish, elephants, people, or even mice, just for some rats.

When we have tested a hypothesis, we may assume that our result would hold for all organisms which had an equiprobable chance of being in the sample tested. However, once a theory has been shown to hold for several species, we may use our knowledge of the relations between species to make a reasonable guess at which other species may also come under the domain of the theory. All of the remarks about species may also apply to types of people or any other convenient categorization. Those individuals, species, or groups for which a theory can be corroborated are called the domain of convenience of the theory.

The concept of domain of convenience presents a useful way of regarding theories. They are not edifices which are put up to be lauded or else knocked down with malicious glee. Rather, the process of defining domains of convenience may be fed back to a theory by slightly altering it so as to increase or decrease its domain or simply to define its domain so that other adjacent theories may be successfully joined with it.

Hypothesis-testing is also commonly used to decide between the usefulness of two theories which have predicted different outcomes.

Some theories are cowardly about predicting outcomes and yet are tempting because they seem, intuitively, to be so reasonable. In cynical moments one can feel that the choice facing psychologists is between making a clear precise statement within some theory whose domain is so narrow as to be almost trivial, and making a vague statement within a theory which explains nearly all human behaviour. However poetic you feel, however inspired by a muse (or even all of them) it is wisest to be as precise as possible about what is perhaps not much, than to be grandiose but vague about 'life'. The first is a sometimes arduous, but rewarding, path towards reasonably stable statements; the second is liable to be both unconstructive science and bad art. Examples of grandiose theories which are cowardly in predicting but which nevertheless have sometimes caught the imagination of some psychologists are psychoanalysis, and the psycholinguistic theory of Chomsky. This is not to say that both sets of theories do not have great value in providing hunches from which testable statements may be derived. It is the temptation to treat the hunch as a testable statement, or even a statement which does not need testing, which presents the problem.

A near synonym for 'theory' which is in common use is the word 'model'. 'Model' is often used for 'theory' by writers in psychology under two circumstances: either when they feel that the domain of convenience they are discussing is so small as to make the word 'theory' seem rather pretentious, or when their expression of the theory is in diagrammatic or even physical form (such as the building of a machine which operates like a human or animal in some way). The use of 'model' or 'theory' is a matter of taste and, as often used, there is no logical distinction between the two terms.

Chapters 1 and 2 are meant to have provided you with some historical and conceptual landmarks to enable you not to lose sight of overall subject of psychology whilst studying the contents of the following Chapters. The rest of the book consists of Chapters on statistics for the purpose of hypothesis-testing and very much more detailed accounts of the large range of subject matter which comprises contemporary psychology.

FURTHER READING

Wright, D. S. *et al* (1970) *Introducing Psychology*. Penguin.
Brown, R., and Hernstein, R. J. (1975) *Psychology*. Methuen.

Eysenck, H. J., and Wilson, G. D., eds. (1976) *A Textbook of Human Psychology*. M.T.P. Lancaster.

Lindsay, P. H., and Norman, D. A. (1977) *Human Information Processing*. Academic Press.

3 Experimental design

JEREMY COYLE

A psychologist may employ a variety of methods to study behaviour. He might watch how children play together and note how they converse, how they co-operate or fight with each other, or how they withdraw to play alone. He might give a questionnaire to a representative sample of the voting population to discover their attitudes towards political issues. Alternatively, he could ask detailed questions of one person in order to establish why he chose a particular career. To such methods as these—observation, survey, interview—he can add the method of experiment.

An experiment can be thought of as a method for speeding up the rate at which observations can be made. Consider for a moment the position of an early astronomer. He would look at the various heavenly bodies, note the pattern of movement, make conjectures about how one governed the movement of another, and make predictions about future events based on the theories he had formulated about the mechanics of the universe. Events would confirm or deny the truth of his propositions. Some of his theories might have to wait a hundred years for the crucial testing event to occur.

If his calling had not made a patient man of him, he might long to intervene in the processes he observed. If he could move the sun a little closer to the earth, would that merely allow him to grow peaches in his garden, or would it scorch the moon, or disorientate the pole star, or bring the Trade Winds to the doors of St Pauls? Alas (for him, if not for us), he is powerless to intervene. He cannot manipulate things and see their effect. He cannot, in other words, experiment.

How does the psychologist stand in relation to our astronomer? In some respects, he, too, is restricted to observational techniques, as in the case mentioned above, for example, when he wishes simply to see how children play together. He can, however, manipulate this situation as well. He could introduce a stranger into the group, or change the number of boys or girls in the group and see what happened. This ability to intervene and change things in order to see the resultant effects gives him an enormous advantage over our astronomer, for he need no longer wait for nature to produce the conditions in which he can make his observations. He can construct the conditions himself. Forcing the pace in this way is the function of the experimental method.

Designing an experiment

How does he set about using the experimental method? He might start with a theory that is based on his own, or others', observations, or with a hunch that comes to him almost haphazardly. He might start with what seems to him to be a sound piece of common sense or the received opinion of the community. The source of the idea does not really matter, but the first thing to do with it is express it in a form that allows it to be tested. Let us suppose he has the notion that treating people kindly is a good thing. To test the truth of this proposition, he would need to know, for example, what was meant by 'kindly'. Does it mean justly, mercifully, indulgently, liberally—which, if any, of these? How could 'kindness' be applied? What is meant by 'a good thing'? Would people be more virtuous, more efficient, more contented if treated kindly? How would he measure this effect?

Formulating a hypothesis

In order experimentally to assess the idea, the psychologist has to formulate it in more precise and measurable terms. He will first look for *operational definitions* of 'kindness' and 'good thing'. Perhaps he will represent 'kindness' as rewards, or positive reinforcers, and look for their effect on the efficiency with which people perform certain tasks.

His original idea, of course, has lost its overtones and has been narrowed to the comparatively impoverished statement, 'positive reinforcement will increase efficiency'. This, unfortunately, is the sort of price that must be paid when we employ experimental methods. However, the compensating advantage is that we have a clearly defined, testable proposition which can lead us to reliable conclusions.

Let us consider this kind of statement more formally. When a psychologist states that 'positive reinforcement will increase efficiency', or says that 'noise will impair learning' he is putting forward a *hypothesis* that one thing has an effect on another. Putting this in technical terms, he is suggesting that the manipulation of an *independent variable* will produce a change in a *dependent variable*. In the two examples we have quoted, the independent variables are reinforcement and noise; the dependent variables that are influenced by these are, in the first case, efficiency, and in the second, learning.

Now that we have formulated an experimental hypothesis, a number of decisions need to be made before we are in a position to put it to the test. These include (a) how to represent and manipulate the independent variable, (b) how to represent and measure the dependent variable and (c) what type of experimental design to employ.

Manipulating the independent variable

The first of these is very much under the control of the experimenter. He is free to do virtually as he likes. Consider the second of the hypotheses quoted above ('noise will impair learning') and see what he might do with the independent variable, 'noise'. He might represent it in the form of pop music or of a tape recording of traffic in Piccadilly Circus and compare the efficiency with which people learned with that background noise with their learning in fairly quiet conditions. It is possible, however, that in a psychological laboratory he would use 'white noise' (a mixture of sounds at all frequencies within the audible range, so called by analogy with the visual spectrum where all colours, when blended, produce white). Let us suppose he adopts this course. He might then decide to compare the effects of white noise over a wide range of decibel values. This is quite possible, but it involves techniques that are beyond the scope of this book. We are concerned here with comparisons between just two experimental treatments, e.g., 'noise' versus 'no noise'. (These experimental treatments, incidentally, are also known as *experimental conditions* or as *levels of the independent variable*.) Now our experimenter can finalize things. He decides that he wishes to compare the effect of a fairly loud background noise with that of the normal ambient noise one might be exposed to in a classroom. He accordingly determines that his two conditions shall be of 60 dB and of 85 dB.

Representing and measuring the dependent variable

His next concern is with the dependent variable. What material shall be learned? A passage of poetry? A set of complex instructions? A Chapter from a textbook of psychology? A common recourse in psychology is to use lists of words or of nonsense syllables. These, at least, can easily be marked right or wrong. But there are still several ways in which the experimenter can obtain measures of this dependent variable. They include counting how many items a subject gets right or, alternatively, how many he gets wrong after one presentation of the list; noting the number of times the list of words has to be presented before a subject learns all the words perfectly; or taking the total time a subject requires to master the entire list. A decision must be made between these, and the experimenter may consider which will give his experiment the greater 'realism', as well as which is the most convenient or expedient to use.

53

Choosing a design

The decision about the type of design to employ is an important one. Many things need to be considered, such as the nature of the task the subjects have to do, the number of subjects available or the kinds of irrelevant variables that might intrude on the experiment and confuse or obscure the finding. The choice of design will also, be important in determining the way in which the experimental data are to be analysed.

There are three basic designs available to us. They are:

1. Independent measures designs
2. Repeated measures designs
3. Matched subjects designs

We need to examine each of these in detail.

Independent measures

This design involves taking all the people who are to be the subjects of an experiment and dividing them into two groups. If we return to our experiment on the effect of noise on learning, what would happen there is that one of these groups of people would learn the list of words under the 60 dB condition and the other would learn the list under the 85 dB condition. We would then want to compare the performance of the groups to see if they differed. There are obvious problems here. What would happen if the first (60 dB) group contained all the highly-motivated people or people with a higher average intelligence than the other group? If we looked at the scores and found those for the 85 dB condition to be lower, we could not conclude that this was due to the noise level, for it might equally be attributable to these differences in motivation or intelligence. Clearly, the groups must be as equal as possible. But in what respect? The answer must surely be in respect of all those abilities which could influence their performance on the learning task, for what we are trying to do is isolate the effect which is due to noise and noise alone. But, here, we have perhaps twenty people doing our experimental task, and they will differ with respect to practically any variable that we care to name as having a potential effect on their performance—age, sex, previous experience, educational background—as well as the two variables already referred to. We also know that introverts and extraverts are differentially affected by noise. How, then, can we create two groups that are equal? The best answer is to allocate the subjects at random to our two experimental conditions. This can be done very simply by writing the numbers 1 to 20 on pieces of paper and asking each person to draw a number. Those who select odd numbers form one group, whilst the other group contains those who select even numbers.

Random number tables can also be used to create the groups. This random allocation of subjects to the two experimental conditions ensures that all the potentially interfering variables are divided quite unsystematically between the two groups.

It is important that this sorting process should be *random* as opposed to arbitrary. If, for example, the experimenter merely picked out what he thought was a 'random' group of ten, it is possible that he would alight initially on the people who were looking at him. They might well be the more highly-motivated or co-operative subjects and there could be a difference in the performance of the two groups which was primarily due to these variables. This would either enhance or obscure the differences due to noise and vitiate the experiment, for the experiment would have confused—or, to use the technical term—*confounded* the effect of his independent variable (noise) with that of an irrelevant variable (motivation, or 'co-operativeness'), thereby making his data impossible to interpret.

It is obvious, however, that even if he randomly allocates his subjects to each of the two conditions he will not eliminate these irrelevant variables. They will always be present in his experiment, but if his sample is of reasonable enough size, the effects they create will be dispersed through the two conditions as 'random error'—as it is properly known—or, to use a more familiar term, 'noise'.

'Random error' or 'noise' is something which the experimenter cannot eliminate, he can only aim to minimize it and to prevent its sources from being confounded with the effects of his independent variable.

Let us see how this kind of design looks and when it might be used:

60 dB	85 dB
S_1	S_2
S_3	S_4
S_5	S_6
S_7	S_8
S_9	S_{10}

—where S stands for 'subject' and the numbers are those which each subject drew from the hat.

This design would be used, for example, in the following circumstances:

1. Where there is an adequate supply of subjects for the experiment to allow the randomization procedure to be effective (say, twenty to thirty in all).
2. When the stimulus material used in the experiment has to be the same for each level of the independent variable but cannot be exposed twice to the same subject.
3. When the experiment involves only one subject.

This last circumstance needs commenting on. We will quite often want to do an experiment on a single subject; sometimes we will be obliged to, simply because of the shortage of subjects. Suppose we wish to compare someone's visual and auditory reaction times. The statistical analysis we would have to perform would require that all these measures were independent of one another, that is to say, that the value of one reaction time is not influenced by the value of another. This, in principle, seems rather unlikely where a single subject is involved. There are two ways, however, of looking at this problem. One is to think of the subject as a source of a *population of potential reaction times*, from which an experimenter with a good experimental technique (e.g., using suitable time-intervals between collecting scores, adequately preparing the subject for the task, etc.) can obtain two samples of responses under the headings 'visual' and 'auditory'. If we are satisfied that this has been done, we might reasonably assume that the measures are independent. The second way to view this is to consider whether the reaction times we obtain can be organized in any way other than in two columns, with the headings 'visual' and 'auditory'. For example:

Visual	Auditory
RT_a	RT_q
RT_x	RT_i

Can one say that RT_a influences RT_q any more than it influences RT_x or RT_i? Does RT_x influence RT_i any more than it influences RT_q? Having collected these data, would it make any material difference if, within the columns, the scores were shuffled and written down in a different order? (To put this point in statistical terms, an independent measures design is one that assumes that scores are not paired across the two conditions, and that if we calculated a correlation coefficient for the two sets of scores, it would be as good as zero). The essential point is that these scores do not come in pairs. Scores relate to other scores, perhaps, but in such an unsystematic, even chaotic way that they may as well be treated as independent measures.

Related measures

It is perhaps already clear by implication that this type of design assumes that the scores we obtain are *correlated*. Indeed, some writers use the term 'correlated measures' to describe this sort of design.

Let us see what it looks like.

56

	60 dB	85 dB
S_1	—	—
S_2	—	—
S_3	—	—
S_4	—	—

Here, we have our subjects working in each of our two noise conditions. An advantage of this type of design that can be seen immediately is that, for a given number of subjects, twice as many raw scores are obtained this way as in an independent measures design. It is not difficult to understand why the resulting pairs of scores are considered to be correlated. Suppose the task the subjects performed was one which required arithmetical skills, and we had three subjects of differing ability. They might produce scores that looked like this:

	60 dB	85 dB
S_1	10	8
S_2	6	4
S_3	3	1

By inspecting these scores, we can see not only that the 85 dB condition impairs performance, but also that our subjects have very different arithmetical abilities. S_1 performs best in both conditions, whilst S_3 performs worst. These scores very definitely come in pairs: they *correlate* perfectly. It would also be confusing if we shuffled the scores within each column, for, although that would not change the average score for each condition, it would obscure the identity of the score pairs and thereby cause us to lose the important 'second dimension' of this design.

Had we used an independent measures design in this particular example with, say, twenty subjects, all of different mathematical ability, the differences between our subjects, although divided at random between the two conditions, would still be, as it were, jostling within the columns, and the influence of our independent variable would have to compete against them in order to make its presence felt. In this related measures design, by having the second dimension of organization, we pin down this source of what otherwise would be random error and can thus see more clearly the differences that are due to subjects and those that are due to our main variable (noise).

Some precautions, however, need to be taken with this sort of design. If a subject is tested first under one condition and then under the second condition, he might well carry over the experience he has gained by performing under the first to benefit the second. Alternatively, he might find the tasks he is required to do boring or tiring. If so, he will perform worse in the second condition than in the first. This kind of effect is

57

known as an *order effect*. If we were to compare his performance under the two conditions, we would not know whether the difference we observed was due to the independent variable or to some irrelevant variable, such as practice or fatigue.

Now, as we have said, it is essential in an experiment to isolate the effect of the independent variable alone and not have our observations distorted by the irrelevant variables that tug and fret at these efforts of ours to see just the one effect. In the case of the independent measures design, we endeavoured to neutralize the effect of irrelevant 'subject variables' by randomization. Here, although we have controlled those that are to do with subjects (e.g., intellectual ability), we find ourselves exposed to new ones that are to do with the order in which our subjects are exposed to the two conditions.

The solution to this new problem is known as *counterbalancing*—one subject is measured under Condition I first and Condition II second, another is measured under Condition II first and Condition I second. The 'order effects' such as 'practice' or 'fatigue' will consequently tend to cancel each other out. Of course, we would need to have half the subjects performing under one condition first and half of them performing under the other condition first. Naturally, the order for a particular subject must be randomly determined, and it is evident that, to counterbalance properly, an even number of subjects is required.

It should be emphasized that this, although the best available solution to the problem, is nevertheless not a perfect one. If, for example, a subject benefits more from performing first under Condition A, than under Condition B, the 'carry over' from A to B will be greater than that from B to A. In such a case, the order effect is said to be 'asymmetrical', and the counterbalancing procedure will be unsuccessful. The experimenter, therefore, must judge these effects to be symmetrical before he can confidently employ this technique.

Matched subjects designs

This type of design is really only a special case of a related measures design. It assumes that each subject in one condition is paired off, or 'matched' with another subject in the other condition. Let us take our original problem and suppose that we wish to see whether the ability in mathematical tests is influenced by noise. We might think we should 'pair off' clever subjects with other clever ones and dull ones with dull ones. That way, differences in intellectual ability would be 'damped down'. If we represent 'cleverness' and 'dullness' in the form of scores in an intelligence test, we would have this kind of design:

58

	60 dB	**85 dB**	
S_{1A} (IQ 130) —		— S_{1B} (IQ 130)
S_{2A} (IQ 100) —		— S_{2B} (IQ 100)
S_{3A} (IQ 70) —		— S_{3B} (IQ 70)

We have matched our subjects by IQ score, and we might therefore expect to obtain correlated measures, with the 'clever' subjects producing the highest overall scores and the 'dull' subjects producing the lowest. The effect of noise would be seen 'overlying' this, as it did in our example on page 57.

But is it good enough in this experiment to match subjects only on IQ scores? Perhaps one of our 'dull' subjects is much more highly motivated than the subject we have paired him with. Perhaps one of our 'average' subjects hates mathematics. Perhaps one of our 'clever' subjects is off his form. Our 'matching' could be very unsuccessful. It is quite evident that, in principle, our 'pairs' should be matched on every variable that might influence their performance in this experiment. It would be impossible to list all the variables that might influence their performance; it would, in any case, probably be impossible to measure all these 'irrelevant variables' in such a way as to permit matching. And how many subjects might we need to produce even a dozen pairs of people matched perfectly, or even adequately, for IQ, motivation, attitude towards the experiment, and so forth? It is better, surely, to use an independent measures design, where all these variables are defined as 'noise' and committed to the neutralizing care of our randomization procedure. Better still, perhaps, to allow each subject his idiosyncrasies and let him, in a related measures design, bring them to each of our experimental conditions as (hopefully) a constant.

In practice, these designs are rare. They are mostly used in studies of twins, where the process of matching is more justifiable than in the case of other subjects. Even in these studies, however, the method is open to the sorts of criticism we have made.

Some further considerations

Situational variables

The designs considered above have one common purpose: they aim to reveal the effect of the independent variable in spite of the host of other variables that crowd the experimental scene and set up a confusing clamour. They use different techniques (e.g., randomization and counterbalancing) to deal with some of these irrelevant variables, but there are others that are not so much associated with particular designs as with the ordinary working conditions of a psychological experiment. They are known as *situational variables*. This term is used to refer to such things as the ambient noise in which an experiment is conducted: people conversing nearby, perhaps; the clatter of typewriters or the ringing of a telephone in an adjacent office; or traffic in the street outside. But in the experimental room itself there are others—differences between say, two tachistoscopes which are used to present stimuli, or, more important, differences in the way in which the experimenter deals with his subjects.

This last problem can be a very acute one. There is a considerable literature, much of it attributable to Rosenthal, on 'experimenter effects', which demonstrates that effects which appear to be due to the independent variable are sometimes due to the experimenter's unwitting influence over his subjects' performance. Let us suppose that he expects his subjects to perform better under one condition. Whenever a subject does so, the experimenter might display almost imperceptible signs that reinforce the subject. He might hold his breath in anticipation, change his facial expression or shift his posture. Neither the experimenter nor the subject may be aware that these cues are being given and responded to, but they can have a marked, systematic effect on performance that is confounded with the effect of the independent variable and so makes the experimental findings impossible to interpret.

What can be done with such variables? We can endeavour to rid ourselves of them by conducting experiments in sound-proof rooms and using sophisticated computer-controlled apparatus. But this is a costly, tedious, and, possibly, unnecessary thing to attempt. What we normally do is try to avoid the grosser distracting influences on subjects by conducting experiments in places where a subject can concentrate reasonably on the task in hand, by using our apparatus sensibly and skilfully and by reducing the possibility of 'experimenter effects'. The latter can be accomplished, for example, by using standardized instructions and by keeping what might be called the 'social relationship' between experimenter and subject strictly controlled and minimal.

By these methods, the effect of many situational variables will be rendered unimportant. Some of them (e.g., variations in background noise) will tend to cancel each other out over the time-span of the experiment rather than obviously help or hinder the subjects' performance in any particular condition. There will, of course, be some occasions when an experimenter will want to examine very subtle behavioural effects which need elaborate (and costly) protection from the influence of situational variables if they are to be detected at all. In these cases, the experimenter has no choice but to take the necessary precautions. Such occasions will be comparatively rare, for there is a wide range of psychological phenomena robust enough to be studied experimentally without the fear that they will be 'drowned' by the effect of situational variables. It is also sensible to ask ourselves whether the search for very subtle differences is always worth the investment of time, energy and money. Is the difference we are looking for going to be of any consequence? William James once remarked that 'a difference that makes no difference is not a difference'. Any experimental psychologist might usefully ponder this.

Perhaps at this point we might draw together the main points that we have covered so far in this Chapter so that they might be made to stand out more clearly.

First, an experiment involves the manipulation of an *independent variable*. It is the effect of that, and that alone, on a *dependent variable* that we wish to isolate. Other variables will tend to obscure this effect. Some of these are *subject variables*, (e.g., motivational differences) and some are *situational variables* (e.g., background noise). We endeavour, by various means, to ensure that none of these works systematically to favour one of our experimental conditions and so become *confounded* with the effect of the independent variable.

In the case of an *independent measures design* we control irrelevant variables by randomly allocating subjects to each of our conditions. When a *related measures design* is employed, counterbalancing will eliminate *order-effects* provided that they are symmetrical. *Matched subject designs* have limited utility because of the difficulties inherent in the matching process.

Control groups

We often use the word 'control' to refer to the process of managing the effects of irrelevant variables. This word is used in another, more restricted, sense in the phrases 'control group' or 'control condition'. A control group is used to give the experimenter a baseline against which he can compare the performance of another group. Let us suppose that he wants to see whether rewarding children with sweets will improve their performance in a weekly spelling test. He would take a group of children and divide them at random into two sub-groups. One sub-group would merely take the spelling test each week, with no special reward being given for success; the other might be promised, say, a bag of sweets if they spelt all the words correctly each week. Perhaps at the end of one term, the marks would be compared. The children who received no reward would be described as the 'control group'; those who were rewarded would be described as the 'experimental group'. The 'control condition' is the 'no reward' condition, the other is the 'experimental condition'.

This method of experimenting (in which either independent or related measures designs may be employed) assumes that the two groups differ only in respect of the variable we are interested in (in this case reward), and that otherwise they are equal both in composition and the way in which they are treated.

61

Correlational studies

The designs we have looked at already seem implicitly to have the purpose of looking at differences between two conditions. An experimenter, however, might well be interested in whether scores in two conditions or on two variables 'go together', or *correlate*. Does a child's performance in mathematics resemble his performance in English? Is his performance on a choice-reaction time task related to his intelligence? Such investigations are perfectly possible to conduct. There are two things to be noted about them, however. First, there is the interpretation of our findings. If we do discover that one variable 'goes with' another, we cannot conclude that they are causally related. In human beings, for example, height and weight tend to be correlated, but obviously height does not cause weight, nor vice versa. Nowadays, most of us are aware of the correlation between smoking and lung cancer, and equally aware that some people dispute whether the relationship is causal. It has been suggested, for example, that both smoking and cancer are the result of a possible genetic predisposition, which, therefore, must be regarded as the common causal factor. The distinction between correlation and causality is very clear when one considers what are known as 'spurious correlations', such as that which has been found between the increase in alcoholism and the increase in the salaries of Methodist ministers.

Generalizing from experimental findings

Over-generalization from experimental findings, is, unfortunately, all too common. It must always be borne in mind that, if a difference is found between two experimental conditions, the difference is specific to the conditions that have been used. If, for example, a psychologist is interested in the effect of delay on recall, he might ask one group of subjects to recall a list of words after a delay of ten seconds after presentation of the list, and another group of subjects to recall them after a delay of thirty seconds. He finds that his subjects remember fewer words after a thirty-second delay than after one of only ten seconds. On the basis of this finding, he cannot conclude that all possible delay periods produce similar effects. Perhaps performance after a sixty-second delay would not be materially worse than after a delay of thirty seconds. Equally, he cannot draw conclusions about the effect of twenty-second delay. It might well be the case that recall after twenty seconds is as good as after ten seconds or just as bad as after thirty seconds. To state the matter more formally, neither extrapolation nor interpolation is easily justified; each experiment gives us only a fragment of the total picture.

Another sort of generalization is sometimes discussed. It is pointed out that many psychological experiments are conducted on under-graduate students of psychology. Surely, it is argued, these subjects are an unrepresentative group; what is true for them may not be true for the general population.

Such an argument often mistakes the nature of psychological experiments. They are not surveys. If a profile of the population at large is required, a survey, not an experiment, is required. An experiment is primarily concerned with the effects of independent variables and usually treats the varying characteristics of the subjects who participate in it as random error, about which nothing can be said except that the smaller it is, the better. It follows, therefore, that using a fairly homogeneous group of subjects is an advantage rather than a liability for random error, in the form of individual differences, is thereby reduced.

It is with his independent variables, not with his subjects, that an experimental psychologist models the world and it is by his success in this that he must be judged. If his model does not reflect the 'real world', his conclusions will, to use Gerard Manley Hopkins' phrase, 'fable and miss'. However cleverly he controls extraneous variables, however pure his randomization procedures or elegant his counterbalancing techniques, his success ultimately depends on the importance of the independent variables that he manipulates and the way in which he represents them. Although it is often difficult to represent or manipulate many important psychological variables one must remember that methods other than experimentation exist. One must also be prepared to accept that knowledge accumulates in a slow, piecemeal fashion, in spite of the ingenuity with which it is sought.

4 Statistics

JEREMY COYLE

The statistics used by psychologists are of two main kinds: those that describe data, and those that are analytical tools, capable of showing whether what we have observed is unusual enough to be taken seriously. The first of these are *descriptive*, the second *inferential* statistics.

Descriptive statistics belong to the tradition of 'statists' sums' which Mark Twain criticized in his much-quoted remark, 'there are lies, damned lies and statistics'. But descriptive statistics can only describe. They tell us what is the average national wage, what a horse's track record is, or how many families own freezers. The inferences we draw from them are our own. Mark Twain's criticism, therefore, applies not to statistics themselves, but to the familiar inclination of politicians to go mendaciously beyond the facts.

Describing data

The descriptive statistics we are concerned with here are of two kinds: measures of central tendency and measures of dispersion. Let us suppose we wish to state how much money we normally carry on our person. We might say that, on average, it is five pounds. This piece of information is useful enough, but it would be desirable to know, in addition, whether the sum we carried varied much about this average. Do we always carry, say, between four and six pounds, or is this average based on very variable sums between a few pence and twenty pounds? Our friends who wanted to rely on us for the occasional loan of a couple of pounds would, in fact, be less interested in the average sum we carried (i.e., the measure of central tendency) than in knowing how much variability there was about this central value. For them, the measure of *dispersion* could be the critical one. Similarly, a teacher dealing with a class whose average IQ was 100, with all the members of that class varying between IQ 95 and IQ 105, would find it easier to 'pitch' his lessons at the right level than if he were confronted with a class of the same average IQ but with children in it whose IQs ranged from 70 to 130.

Let us now consider the various measures of central tendency and dispersion that we might use.

Measures of central tendency

All measures of central tendency are 'averages'. There are three of them: *the mean*, the *median*, and the *mode*.

The mean is the arithmetical average, the median is the 'middle' value, and the mode is the value that occurs most frequently.

Here are fifteen values:

$$3, 4, 5, 5, 5, 5, 6, 6, 8, 8, 10, 10, 10, 32, 33$$

To find the mean of these numbers, we add them all together and divide by fifteen. This gives us $150 \div 15 = 10$.

To find the median, we must first be sure that the scores are arranged in ascending or descending order and we then choose the middle one. In this case, it is the eighth one, which is 6.

For the mode, we find which value occurs most frequently. In this case, the most common value is 5.

These measures of central tendency, applied to the same set of members, yield three different values. Which one is the most apt? Which is the 'best' one to use? The answer depends partly on the nature of one's data, partly on what features of the data need to be brought out, and partly on the way in which measures of dispersion can be used to indicate how apt or representative our measure of central tendency happens to be. We will deal with this last point first.

Measures of dispersion

Measures of dispersion are also known as measures of 'spread', 'scatter' or 'variability'. They are used in such a way as to complement the measures of central tendency that we employ.

This time, we shall start with the mode. Its associated measure of dispersion is the *variation ratio*, which simply tells us what proportion of our observations are not 'modal'. Considering the numbers we had previously:

$$3, 4, 5, 5, 5, 5, 6, 6, 8, 8, 10, 10, 10, 32, 33$$

we saw that four of them were 'modal'. Eleven of them are not. The variation ratio for these data is found by determining what eleven is, as a proportion of fifteen. To do this, we divide eleven by fifteen:

$$11 \div 15 = .733$$

and state that .733 of our observations are *not* modal. By implication, of course, .266 *are* modal. (If you are not happy with proportions, you can transform them to percentages by multiplying them by 100, and saying, in this instance, that 73.3 per cent of the values we had are not accounted for by the mode.) We now have a measure that tells us how representative, or otherwise, the mode is. In this case, it does not seem to be very representative at all.

The median is complemented by measures of range. The *range* itself is simple to calculate. It is the difference between the highest and the lowest score. For the above data, the range is $33-3 = 30$ units.

The two measures together, therefore, tell us that the middle value is 6 and the range of values is 30. This indicates to us (as is, indeed, the case) that the values are mostly fairly low (in fact, half of them are below 6) and that there is a wide spread of values. This seems a fairly satisfactory description of the numbers we have. Suppose, however, that the last score were 100, instead of 33. 100 would look rather unusually high in relation to the others and the range of values now would be 97 (although the median would still be 6). Because of the sensitivity of the range to extreme, possibly freakish, scores, it is more common to eliminate the highest and lowest scores—to 'top and tail' the set—in order to avoid such misleading extreme scores. One way of doing this is to ignore the top 25 per cent and the bottom 25 per cent of scores and quote the range of the middle 50 per cent. This measure is known as the *interquartile range* (IQR).

Let us see what this does for our set of scores:

3,   4,   5,   5,   5,   5,   6,   6,   8,   8,   10,   10,   10,   32,   100

| 25% | 25% | 25% | 25% |

The interquartile range is found by subtracting the score that cuts off the top 25 per cent of all the values from the score that cuts off the bottom 25 per cent. Thus:

$$IQR = 10 - 5 = 5$$

We now say that the median is 6, and the middle 50 per cent of scores lie within a range of five about that central point. This seems a more satisfactory way to describe our set of values than by quoting the full range, for the 'freak' score of 100 is not permitted to distract our attention from where the bulk of the scores lie.

It is more common, however, to use the *semi-interquartile range* (SIQR)

66

than the IQR. This is simply half the IQR and in this case it would be $5 \div 2 = 2.5$. (This value is to be understood as 'plus or minus 2.5'; that is, 2.5 units either side of the median.)

The last measure of dispersion complements the mean. It is the *standard deviation*. Although it is a less intuitively obvious measure than those we have seen so far, it is a very 'powerful' descriptive statistic which can cross the border, as it were, into the territory of inferential methods. It merits detailed treatment.

The standard deviation gives us an idea of how much, on average, the individual scores in our set differ from the mean of the set. To make things very simple, we will take only five scores and consider how we can obtain the standard deviation:

$$1, 2, 3, 4, 5.$$

Firstly, the mean of these numbers is $\dfrac{1+2+3+4+5}{5} = 3$

The difference from the mean of each score is:

$$(1-3); \quad (2-3); \quad (3-3); \quad (4-3); \quad (5-3)$$
$$\text{i.e.,} \quad -2; \qquad -1; \qquad 0; \qquad +1; \qquad +2$$

Now in order to *average* these differences, we must add them up and divide by the total number of differences. The problem is obvious. These values sum to zero; zero divided by five is zero. Our efforts to aggregate the differences will always come to nought unless we do something about their signs. The first thought is that we might ignore them:

$$2+1+0+1+2 = 6; \quad 6 \div 5 = 1.2$$

We now state that the average distance of all values from the mean is 1.2 units—and 'plus or minus' is understood. What we have just done is calculated what is known as the *mean deviation* (i.e., the average deviation from the mean). This is satisfactory enough for many purposes but there are some problems. The first can be seen if we look at the formula we use to calculate it.

$$MD = \frac{\Sigma (|X = \overline{X}|)}{N} \tag{1}$$

where: $X =$ a given score
$\overline{X} =$ the mean of the scores
$N =$ the total number of scores
$\Sigma =$ the conventional summation sign (the Greek capital letter 'S') which simply instructs us to add up all the $X - \overline{X}$ differences that we have found

Note the two vertical lines that embrace $X - \overline{X}$. This is a modulus sign which tells us to treat all differences as positive—which is what we did.

67

A mathematician looking at this formula, however, might be less satisfied with it than we are, for the modulus sign effectively puts a block on algebraical manipulation. He would suggest, perhaps, that we remove the modulus sign, and get rid of the troublesome positive and negative values by *squaring* the differences. We would, of course, have to square the other side of the formula appropriately to preserve the equation; so we would have:

$$\text{Mean } squared \text{ deviation} = \frac{\Sigma(X - \overline{X})^2}{N} \qquad (2)$$

Treating our five numbers this way we obtain the following:

$$\frac{(-2)^2 + (-1)^2 + 0^2 + (+1)^2 + (+2)^2}{5} = \frac{10}{5} = 2$$

and we present our finding that the set of scores has a mean of 3 and a 'spread' (i.e., dispersion) of two squared units.

At this stage, we would surely protest to our mathematician that his desire to manipulate formulae had led him to commit a nonsense. What can 'two squared units of dispersion' possibly mean? His first rejoinder might be that we could easily take the square root of our calculated value and so return to the original units of measurement. Thus:

$$\sqrt{2} = 1.414*$$

We might be inclined to accept this reply as merely a hollow little triumph of legerdemain and still resent the sacrifice of our common sense measure, the mean deviation. Have we watched it having its parts squared and then square-rooted for no better reason than to please a mathematician?

The answer, as you will suspect, is no. Let us first consider what our mathematician has done and then see why it makes such good sense.

When he took the sum of squared deviations (Formula 2) he was in fact calculating the *variance* of the scores. The variance, therefore, is the *mean (or average) squared deviation from the mean*. The symbol for variance is s^2 and the formula therefore would normally be written thus:

$$s^2 = \frac{\Sigma(X - \overline{X})^2}{N} \qquad (3)$$

The standard deviation (S) is simply the *square root of the variance*. Its formula would therefore be:

$$s = \sqrt{\frac{\Sigma(X - \overline{X})^2}{N}} \qquad (4)$$

* Those who are not very comfortable with mathematics might wonder why this answer is different from the original mean deviation. The reason is that our mathematician did not square the mean deviation itself. He squared the individual deviations and then averaged them. Squaring the mean deviation itself would have meant averaging the individual deviations first and then squaring them.

Both of these formulae can be manipulated algebraically to produce:

$$s^2 = \frac{\Sigma(X^2) - \frac{(\Sigma X)^2}{N}}{N} \qquad (5)$$

and

$$s = \sqrt{\frac{\Sigma(X^2) - \frac{(\Sigma X)^2}{N}}{N}} \qquad (6)$$

These formulae are mathematically identical to formulae (3) and (4) and more convenient when using a calculating machine.

Now to consider why these measures of dispersion are superior to the mean deviation. Firstly, note that the fundamental index is variance. (The standard deviation, by taking the square root of the variance, merely restores the original unit of measurement). Variance is about squared deviations. This need not surprise us, for often squared units are the only apt units with which to describe the physical world. A glance at any textbook of physics will reveal formulae using all kinds of squared units to describe physical relationships. Acceleration, for example, is distance divided by time *squared*.

But why should this concern an index of dispersion? Solomon Diamond (*Information and Error*, 1963, N.Y. Basic Books) tells the story of 'the scatter-brained boy' who was surrounded by birds roosting on a heath. He shouted and clapped his hands to startle the birds into flight. In a few seconds they settled down and he noted how he had scattered them. He decided to repeat the experience, and shouted and clapped again equally loudly. Again the birds rose, dispersed and settled. He considered the sum of the distances of all the birds from their original roosting places. It seemed greater than after the first alarm, but not twice as great. Given that both alarms had been equally effective surely there should be twice as much scatter, or dispersion? Diamond points out that if the boy measured the *squared distances* of the birds from him and added them up, the second *sum of squares* would be twice the size of the first. The boy, in effect, was standing at the centre of a circle, measuring the distances of the birds around him. Those distances can be thought of as radii of the circle. To double the area of a circle, one doubles the square of its radius, for the area of a circle is given by πr^2. Diamond notes that 'the dispersion of scores of any kind is, in principle, not different from the scattering of birds on the heath'.

By using the variance (and the standard deviation), we thus capture an essential quality of dispersion that the mean deviation, for all its intuitive appeal, misses.

Choosing a descriptive statistic

We have now seen three measures of central tendency and their associated measures of dispersion. It is necessary to consider the circumstances in which they can be used appropriately. Let us suppose we stood at the entrance to the British Museum and noted the nationality of seventy visitors who entered during one half-hour period. Our observations were as follows:

British	American	European	Japanese	Arab
12	20	15	13	10

It seems evident that the most appropriate summary statistics to use here are the *mode* and the *variation ratio*. These will tell us that American is the most common nationality and that .714 (or 71.4 per cent) of the visitors are of other nationalities. We could not use the median, for who is 'the middle-ranking person'? How can one get a mean if that involves adding up all our observations and dividing by N? Such a procedure would be meaningless.

It is clear from this example that we are not at liberty to use just any of these statistics whenever we wish. One of the crucial things that governs their appropriate use is the level of measurement we have achieved.

Levels of measurement
Psychologists ordinarily use three levels of measurement: nominal, ordinal, and the interval scales. Ratio scales are less common.

THE NOMINAL SCALE

The nominal scale, the crudest of the three, involves classification, or sorting things into mutually exclusive categories. An ornithologist, for example, might record each observation he makes during the day and do so by species. Someone less familiar with all the different species of bird might sort the same observations into different, cruder categories (e.g., gulls/waders as opposed to kittiwakes; herring gulls/redshanks; bartailed godwits). Both these people, in statistical terms, are employing nominal scales although, clearly, the expert ornithologist has the more sensitive method of classification, that is, the more sensitive nominal scale.

It is useful to think of the nominal scale as being essentially about naming things. When someone says 'my name is Oliver Twist' he is, to put this statistically, establishing a category and entering the number of observations that belong in that category, i.e.,

Category: Oliver Twist
No. of observations: 1

70

It can sometimes be slightly confusing when numbers are used nominally—that is, as classifiers, identifiers, as mere labels. The usual example given of this type of usage is that of numbers on footballers' shirts, which serve only to identify a player. Their numerical value is quite immaterial. The most skilful or expensive players, for example, are not necessarily given the highest numbers. In such cases, one must remember that the numbers in themselves are meaningless. They do not imply rank, nor can they be added, subtracted, multiplied, or divided in any informative way, for they are being used categorically, for purposes of discrimination only.

THE ORDINAL SCALE

This represents a higher level of measurement than the nominal scale. It involves ranking. With this scale, we can say which is first, second, third, and so on in a sequence; which is biggest, smallest; highest, lowest; most beautiful, or ugliest. It involves comparison of one thing with another, or others. What it does not involve is the comparison of things with some objective yardstick. In the racing pages of newspapers you will find the previous record of horses presented as a list of finishing positions only, that is, as how they ran against other horses in particular races. We are not given their times for the course, which could be one possible objective yardstick.

When we use an ordinal scale to identify which is first, second, or third we must remember, therefore, that we do not imply that the difference between first and second is the same as the difference between the second and third. If we ranked Cinderella and her sisters according to their beauty, the difference between the first and second would be much greater than the difference between the second and third. The ordinal scale involves ranks and ranks only.

THE INTERVAL AND THE RATIO SCALE

Interval scale measurement has the great advantage over ordinal scale measurement that there are defined differences along the scale. We can say that the interval between one and two is exactly the same as the interval between fifty-five and fifty-six. Scores that people obtain in tests are typical interval scale measures. There is no true zero point, however, for a score of zero, say, in a geography test does not mean that the person who obtains it knows nothing at all about geography. Such things as height, weight and volume, however, involve ratio scales which do have true zero points.

There is one important point to note about these levels of measurement. Consider any interval scale measurement: say an I.Q. of 100. As well as telling us what fixed unit of measurement is involved, this statement implicitly conveys the information that 100 *is less than*, say, 120 and that *is different from* any other number. In other words, interval scales contain the characteristics of both ordinal and nominal scales. The ordinal scale, of course, includes the features of the nominal scale. Thus, higher levels of measurement implicitly have all the qualities of the levels of measurement which are below them.

We can return now to the question of how to choose an appropriate descriptive statistic, and present the answer in a simple, tabular form:

Table 4.1

Level of measurement		Index of central tendency	Index of dispersion
(lower)	*Nominal*	The mode	The variation ratio
	Ordinal	The median	The semi-inter-quartile range
(higher)	*Interval*	The mean	The standard deviation

Note that any measure which can be used at a lower level of measurement can also be used at higher levels of measurement. The mode and the median, for example, could be used at the interval scale level, but the mean cannot be used at either of the lower levels of measurement. Traffic, so to speak, is one-way only—in the direction indicated by the arrow. This is because the characteristics of lower levels of measurement are present in the higher levels. For example, the mode can, as it were, attach itself to the 'nominal' features of an interval scale but the mean, depending as it does on arithmetical operations, cannot cope with scales that are too imprecise to make such operations permissible.

Frequency distributions

Whenever we have a set of values, or scores, and a count of how many times each occurs, we have a frequency distribution. The following data, showing the frequency of scores that occur within particular class-intervals, are from an aptitude test given to fifty-three apprentices:

Score:	30–35	36–40	41–45	46–50	51–55	56–60	61–65	66–70	71–75	76–80
Frequency:	2	1	5	8	11	10	9	4	2	1

We can represent these data graphically by plotting *frequency against value* and could produce either a frequency polygon or a histogram. Both of these graphs do essentially the same job. They show in a simple pictorial fashion how our scores are distributed, and we could use either

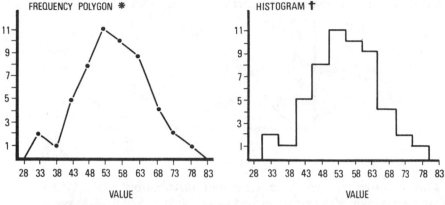

Fig. 4.1

method of representation. There are two subtle differences, however, between the two graphs which are worth noting in order to establish some concepts which will be of importance to us. Firstly, by joining up the points plotted on the frequency polygon, we imply that scores exist between those which we have plotted. We could read off the implied, theoretical frequency, say, of the value 43.5. If this statement sounds sensible enough to you, reflect for one moment that you are thereby implicitly acknowledging something which statisticians are perfectly comfortable with—namely *theoretical frequencies* (which could, of course, be fractional).

Now consider the histogram, and imagine it were constructed by filling in a square on graph paper for each frequency. (i.e., column one would consist of two squares, column two of one square, and so on). What obviously follows is that the *sum of the frequencies* will be given by the total *area under the histogram.*

The idea of a normal distribution

One very important theoretical frequency distribution, in which the area under the delineating curve is constantly used, is the normal probability

---

* The frequency polygon is conventionally constructed by joining the mid-points of class intervals with a straight line. Two extra points, for when the frequency is 0, are added at each end of the distribution in order to 'close' the Figure.

† The histogram is constructed by erecting rectangular columns the width of the class interval; the height is equal to the frequency.

Note that in these graphs the class intervals are marked off in what are known as 'real limits' as opposed to the 'apparent limits' shown in the data above. It is more precise to do this. The implication is that theoretically possible scores can be accommodated, e.g., 35.4 would be included in the first class interval, whilst 35.7 would be included in the second.

curve. It is bell-shaped and symmetrical—and looks like this:

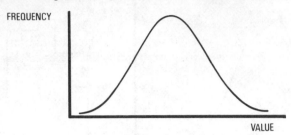

FREQUENCY

VALUE

Fig. 4.2

This is often known as a Gaussian distribution, after Gauss, the mathematician who first described its properties. We need to consider it in some detail.

The first thing we might note about it is that it seems to correspond with our intuitive understanding of the distribution of many variables. We have mentioned height already. If we write 'midgets' on the left hand side of the 'value' axis and 'giants' on the right hand side, we can see immediately that most of us feature somewhere between these extremes. A box of apples would have a similar distribution, with some apples being distinctly under-sized, others being very large, but most of them being of 'middling' size. Indeed, it is the case that the normal distribution represents how a great number of variables are usually distributed. One can almost think of it, instead, as the 'usual distribution'. Because of its importance, we must understand some of its properties. One way to do this is consider another distribution, known as the binomial distribution, which resembles it quite closely.

The binomial distribution

Let us suppose that a couple wish to have four children. They wonder how many boys or girls they might end up with.
The possibilities are:

No. of boys: 4 3 2 1 0
No. of girls: 0 1 2 3 4

How probable is any of these outcomes? If we assume that the sex of a child is randomly determined, it is obvious that the couple is less likely to have four boys or four girls, than a family of mixed sexes. The way we determine these probabilities is by listing the various possible combinations. An all-boy family is quite simple (statistically speaking). It can have only the following *sequence* of births:

B, B, B, B.

74

An all-girl family is accomplished with the same statistical ease:

G, G, G, G.

But how about one boy and three girls? The combinations are more complex. The children could be born in several different orders, namely:

B G G G
G B G G
G G B G
G G G B

The same would apply for one girl and three boys:

G B B B
B G B B
B B G B
B B B G

Two boys and two girls? You can list the six possible sequences for yourself. This process, however, yields the following:

Table 4.2

Sequence of boys and girls	No. of possible arrangements
Four boys and no girls	1
Three boys and one girl	4
Two boys and two girls	6
One boy and three girls	4
Four girls and no boys	1
Total	16

We can state the probabilities. There is a one in sixteen chance of having four boys and no girls, a four in sixteen chance of having three boys and one girl, and so on. The following Table shows these chances as percentages and as proportions.*

Table 4.3

	No. of possible arrangements	Percentage	Proportion
4 boys and no girls	1	6.25	.0625
3 boys and 1 girl	4	25.0	.25
2 boys and 2 girls	6	37.5	.375
1 boy and 3 girls	4	25.0	.25
4 girls and no boys	1	6.25	.0625
Total	16	100.00	1.0000

* For the non-mathematical, percentages are based on 100, whilst proportions are based on 1. Proportions are fairly commonly used in statistics, which is why they have been introduced here.

We can make a histogram for this distribution:

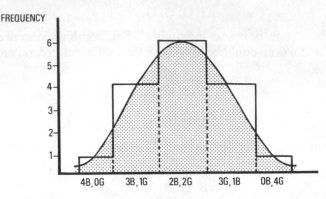

FREQUENCY

6 -
5 -
4 -
3 -
2 -
1 -

4B, 0G   3B, 1G   2B, 2G   3G, 1B   0B, 4G

Fig. 4.3

and, looking at the *area under the histogram*, we can obtain the *probability* of any of the combinations of children. Column 2, for example, contains four out of the sixteen possibilities; it is one quarter, or 25 per cent of the total *area*. Now probabilities are usually expressed as *proportions*, so we would say that the probability of having three boys and one girl is .25.

Imagine, if you can, a couple who wished to have twenty-four children. We could make similar lists of possible combinations and draw a histogram of them. The histogram would have many more steps to it. But it would, of course, always be 'stepped', no matter how many frequencies were plotted, for this distribution involves a *discrete* variable, that is, one that can assume only particular values—in this case, 'boy' or 'girl'. This particular distribution is known as the binomial distribution for it is derived from theoretical outcomes of the combination of two kinds of event. However, it does begin to resemble the normal probability curve which we have superimposed on the histogram above. If we imagine that we had been dealing with a *continuous* variable, such as height, which can assume any value, including fractional ones, the 'steps' would disappear, and we should have a smooth curve whose shape is essentially the same as the binomial distribution. Thus we can think of the normal distribution as a theoretical or idealized representation of certain very common frequency distributions for which N (the total number of scores or observations) is very large.

Note, however, that even when N is quite small, as in the above example, the 'fit' of the line to the histogram is quite good and the *area* it encloses, when you consider the pieces of the histogram that have been clipped off compared with additional areas the curve includes, is practically the same.

Some characteristics of the normal distribution

This distribution, as we have said, is of great importance in statistics. This is not only because it aptly describes how a great number of variables in the physical sciences, in biology, botany, and psychology are distributed; it also has certain mathematical properties which can be used to great advantage.

One such property relates to the descriptive statistics we considered earlier. Firstly, note that the peak of the curve marks the most frequent value, the middle value, and the arithmetical average of all the values in the distribution; in other words, the mode, median, and mean coincide at the axis of symmetry. The next, and very important, fact about this curve concerns the standard deviation, which measures dispersion or the 'spread' of scores. It can be shown mathematically (although to do so would be beyond the scope of this Chapter), that within one standard deviation either side of the mean, 68.26 per cent of all scores will be found, within two standard deviations either side of the mean, 95.44 per cent of all scores will be found and within three standard deviations either side of the mean, 99.74 per cent of all scores will be found. Let us consider an example. It is a fact that IQ scores are pretty well normally distributed. We will graph them as if they were. Thus:

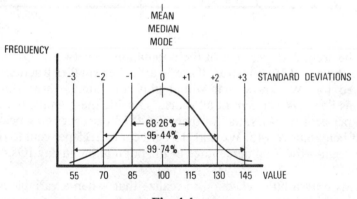

Fig. 4.4

Average IQ, as we know, is 100. Furthermore, the standard deviation of test scores works out at 15 or 16 IQ points. Here, we have taken it to be 15, and marked off the values of *plus* one, two, and three standard deviations (115, 130 and 145) and *minus* one, two and three standard deviations (85, 70, and 55) from the central point, or mean, of 100. (Remember that the standard deviation is to do with distance from the mean. The mean itself is obviously no distance at all from the mean, so it must have a standard deviation of zero).

We can now state the following:

1. 68.26 per cent of the population have IQs between 85 and 115 (i.e., within −1 and +1 standard deviation from the mean.
2. 95.44 per cent of the population have IQs between 70 and 130.
3. 99.74 per cent of the population have IQs between 55 and 145.

Note that these statements are based on areas under the curve that are delimited by the different units of standard deviation.

Let us take the matter a little further. If we have a person whose IQ is 100, we know that 50 per cent of the population will have IQs as great or greater. We also know that if we find a person with an IQ of 130, 2.28 per cent of the population will have IQs as great or greater. We can see how this is done by taking another look at the normal curve.

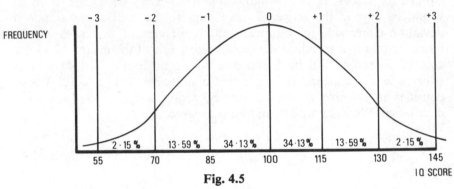

Fig. 4.5

As can be seen, 2.15 per cent of the population lie between IQ 130 and IQ 145. Beyond 145, however, there is a further smaller fraction to be accounted for. We know that within plus and minus three standard deviations lie 99.74 per cent of all scores. Outside these limits, therefore, lie 0.26 per cent of cases; half of them (i.e. 0.13 per cent being below 55 and half being above 145. We add .13 per cent to 2.15 per cent to obtain 2.28 per cent—the total percentage of the population having IQs of 130 and above.

It needs only a little reflection to realize that, when a variable is normally distributed, the mean and the standard deviation do more than merely describe it. For we know immediately how rare or common particular values of the variables are. We know, in other words, about their *probability* and this is why we pointed out earlier that the standard deviation goes beyond description into the realm of inference.

Inferential statistics

Inferential statistics are concerned with the probabilities associated with particular values of a statistic. They enable us to say, for example, whether a difference we observe between two measures of central tendency is a 'real' difference or not. The process by which we come to such decisions, however, is slightly unusual to those approaching statistics for the first time. What we must first do is establish some concepts that are basic to this process; but whilst we do so, it may help if one constantly bears in mind the origins of inferential statistics. These are to be found in the law courts of nineteenth century France, to which mathematicians were summoned to give evidence on the fairness or otherwise of the various games of chance played in casinos. How often would a fair roulette wheel favour the house? How often could a croupier draw the card he needed from a pack before he could be judged a crook? The critical thing to be resolved was the part played by chance. For, once the probabilities of particular events occurring purely under the influence of chance were known, comparisons could be made with what actually occurred, and the necessary conclusions could be drawn. The mathematicians provided the courts with theoretical distributions of outcomes when chance alone was assumed to be responsible for them.

(It is worth emphasizing at this point that the statistician's function is to calculate theoretical probabilities of one sort and another and to provide the instruments (i.e., the statistical testing procedures) that permit us to compare various features of our data with these theoretical distributions. The psychologist is responsible for collecting data, applying a suitable statistical test and drawing appropriate conclusions. This Chapter is concerned only with these processes).

Hypothesis testing

When we conduct an experiment, we look to see if an independent variable has an effect on a dependent variable. We might wish to see, for example, whether by varying the rate of presentation of stimuli, there is an associated change in the number of stimuli recalled. Accordingly, we prepare a list of twenty words and, in one case, present it at the rate of one word per second and, in the other, at the rate of two words per second. Recall is measured under each condition of presentation for each subject and our results look like this:

Table 4.4

	Condition I	Condition II
Rate of presentation:	1 per sec.	2 per sec.
Mean no. of words recalled:	8	6

and we ask ourselves is this a 'real' difference or not.

Whenever we do such an experiment, we should be aware that there are no less than three hypotheses which must be made quite explicit before we can either make full sense of what we are doing or perform any statistical analysis on our data.

The first thing is our *research hypothesis*. This is the 'larger scale' general hypothesis that 'rate of presentation of stimuli influences recall of those stimuli'.

The second is our *experimental hypothesis*. This is specific to what we propose to do. Here, it might state that 'words presented at the rate of one per second will show a different level of recall from words presented at the rate of two per second'. (This is the *operational statement* of our research hypothesis and it is important to recognize that evidence that confirms the experimental hypothesis does not automatically confirm the research hypothesis.

The third is what is known as the *null hypothesis*. This lies at the very centre of statistical hypothesis testing.

The null hypothesis
The null hypothesis denies that any 'real' differences exist and holds that any observed differences are attributable solely to chance fluctuations in score levels. It plays devil's advocate to the experimenter and challenges him to prove that the differences he has obtained are due to the independent variable and could not reasonably be thought to be the product of chance variability.

Let us see how the experimenter contends with this. He has two samples of scores, whose means are 8 and 6. His experimental hypothesis states that they differ. More precisely, his experimental hypothesis states that *the populations from which these samples are drawn have different means*. Countering this, the null hypothesis states that *these samples are drawn from the same population*.

At issue is whether all possible scores in Condition 1 are qualitatively different from all possible scores in Condition 2. If we suppose that recall measures are normally distributed we can represent this conflict graphically:

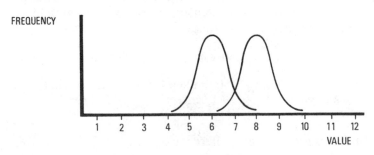

Fig. 4.6

This is the experimental hypothesis: the two means, 8 and 6, belong to two quite different distributions.

The null hypothesis, however, claims that these two values belong to the same distribution. Thus:

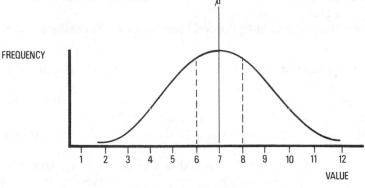

Fig. 4.7

How do we decide between these competing claims?

Firstly, imagine that Figure 4.7 represents a plot of an indefinitely large number of scores, each of which is printed on a slip of paper and placed on a box. We then pick out fifty of them at random and calculate the mean of that sample. It turns out to be, let us say, 6.5. We replace the slips, shake the box to randomize the contents and draw another sample of fifty. Its mean is 7.4. The difference between the two, therefore is 0.9, which we record. We take another two samples similarly and compare their means; and so on until we amass a large number of such 'difference' scores. It is fairly obvious that big differences would be less common than small ones, and that, after doing this, we would be able to make some such statement as 'smaller differences of, say, up to 0.5, are common; but differences of, say, 2.5 or greater are extremely rare'.*

This is one way of approaching the problem of how we can decide between the experimental and the null hypothesis. The null hypothesis, remember, is claiming that any difference that is found is purely a product of chance. We now know, however, as a result of all our random pairings, that there is something quite lawful about the distribution of these chance differences. Small ones are common, but some

* This statement would be based on our knowledge of the *distribution* of difference scores. The standard deviation of this distribution is known as the *standard error* of the difference. If you look at the formulae for related and independent *t*-tests in the next Chapter you will see that their denominators have a form which closely resembles the formula for the standard deviation. In the case of the related *t*-test, the difference scores (in the numerator) are divided by the *standard error of the differences* to produce *t*, whereas in the independent *t* test the difference between means (in the numerator) is divided by the *standard error of the means* to produce *t*.

differences are so large that, by chance alone, they occur very rarely indeed. They are, in other words, very improbable if chance alone is responsible, and, as a consequence, the null hypothesis seems difficult to believe. Would it not be more sensible to believe instead the experimental hypothesis which claims that the difference is due to the effect of the independent variable?

Let us review the process of hypothesis testing as we have described it so far.

1. The null hypothesis states that chance alone is responsible for the effects we see in an experiment.
2. The experimental hypothesis (commonly known as the alternative hypothesis because it stands in opposition to the null hypothesis) states that what we see is attributable to the effect of the independent variable.
3. If the null hypothesis stands only a slim chance of being true, we prefer to believe its alternative, i.e., the experimental hypothesis.

Rejecting the null hypothesis

The last point, 3, above needs elaborating. Very simply, there is a fairly firm convention in psychology (and in most other sciences) that we refuse to believe the null hypothesis if it has only one, or less than one, chance in twenty of being true. This is usually expressed in percentage or proportional terms, i.e., 'a five per cent (or less) chance of being true'; or (more commonly) 'a probability of being true equal to or less than .05'. The short way of writing the latter is $p \leqslant .05$.

Thus, when we find a difference between two sets of scores that is so large that it could occur by chance alone only one in twenty times or less we reject the null hypothesis and accept the experimental hypothesis. In other words, we say that we are not prepared to believe the difference is a chance one; we prefer to believe it is a product of change in the independent variable; that it is, in fact, a *significant* difference.

The concept of significance

At this point, it is worth attempting to describe what 'significant' means. In statistics, something is significant if it is unlikely to be the product of chance alone. The probability of its being the product of chance alone, must, by convention, be .05 or less.

How do we know when a difference is significant? How do we know when $p \leqslant .05$? In general this provides no problem. We carry out a statistical test on our data and then consult Tables which show what the probability is that our result could occur by chance alone. It would be quite beyond the scope of this Chapter to deal with the origin and genesis of significance tables, but if you turn back to page 75, you will see how one such table of probabilities can be constructed. Suffice it to say that a variety of tables exists to inform us of the probability of the null hypothesis being true under a variety of different circumstances. Statisticians create them; psychologists use them. Unless you are prepared to spend some considerable time on statistical theory, you would be better off concentrating your efforts on the task of becoming a competent *user* of statistical tests: You do not, in other words, have to understand the inside of a car engine in order to become a competent driver.

Type I and Type II errors
It may be clear already that, even if we declare that we have found a significant difference between two sets of scores, we have not eliminated the possibility that we are wrong in believing that the difference is attributable to the effect of our independent variable. The null hypothesis could still be true—in fact, we have stated that it has a one in twenty chance (or less) of being true. Overall, our conclusions will be more often right than wrong but there will certainly be occasions when we reject the null hypothesis when it is true. This is known as a *Type I error*, and it is obvious that the probability of committing this type of error is equivalent to the significance level that we choose. When we set our significance level at p = .05, we are settling for being wrong 5 per cent of the time. Sometimes, we will want to be especially careful before we are prepared to say that a difference is significant. We would not wish to market a drug, for example, whose efficacy was not assured. In these cases, we might set our significance level more stringently at .01 or .001, for the more stringent the significance level*, the less the risk of a Type I error.

But there is a price to be paid for defending ourselves so well against the chance of being wrong. We might fail to detect a difference that is really there. This is known as a *Type II error*.

The position is therefore as follows:

1. If our significance level is not stringent enough, we will commit a relatively large number of Type I errors, that is, we will be reporting that differences really exist when, in fact, they do not.
2. If our significance level is too stringent, we will commit a relatively large number of Type II errors; that is, we shall fail to report differences which actually are present.
3. Any scientist would rather err on the side of caution and risk a Type II error rather than a Type I error.
4. A decision must therefore be made about significance levels which,

* All pre-set significance levels are known as 'criteria of significance'. A criterion is denoted by the Greek letter α. Hence one reads in statistical texts such formal statements as 'Let $\alpha = .05$'.

83

while restricting the number of Type I errors, does not entail an unacceptable number of Type II errors.

5. The .05 level of significance is commonly judged to strike roughly the right balance between the risks of these two complementary types of error.

One- and two-tailed tests

Experimental hypotheses can be one-tailed or two-tailed. If you, the experimenter, have reason to predict that the values in one sample will be greater than those in the other, your hypothesis will be *one-tailed* and will have some such form as, 'the mean of Sample A will be higher than the mean of Sample B'. If, however, your experimental hypothesis has the form, 'the means of Samples A and B will differ and you are implicitly adding 'but I am not sure which sample will have the higher mean', your experimental hypothesis is said to be *two-tailed.*

The word 'tail' here refers to some theoretical distribution of a statistic. Suppose that the distribution concerned is the normal distribution. It has a central 'hump' and two 'tails' that trail off indefinitely. Now, we already know that if we want to reject the null hypothesis, we must have some value that is so unusual that we judge it unlikely to have been produced by chance alone. In the case of the normal distribution, where are these 'unusual' values to be found? Clearly the answer is that they are to be found in the 'tails', for the more common values cluster round the mean to produce the central 'hump'.

FREQUENCY

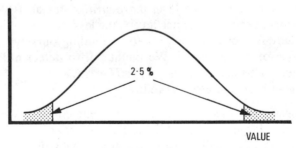

Fig. 4.8

We also know that only values that can occur by chance 5 per cent, or less, of the time are extreme enough to be deemed 'significant', that is, extreme enough to allow us to reject the null hypothesis. The shaded areas of the distribution show where the most extreme 5 per cent of scores are to be found—2.5 per cent of them in one 'tail' and 2.5 per cent in the other.

A two-tailed experimental hypothesis is in effect saying 'the effect of the independent variable will be to produce a value which is extreme, but

84

which could be located at either end of the distribution'. A one-tailed hypothesis is quite different. In effect, it says that 'the effect of the independent variable will be to produce an extreme value which is located at the end of the distribution that the experimenter specifies'. And if we now shade in the area occupied by the most extreme 5 per cent of values in only one end of the distribution, we have the following:

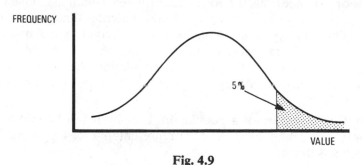

Fig. 4.9

Whichever kind of hypothesis is involved, the *region of rejection* (as it is known) of the null hypothesis covers *5 per cent of the total distribution*. However, in the case of a one-tailed hypothesis, a less extreme value is needed to achieve significance. This is a benefit which comes from having a more specific hypothesis.

It is important to note that when you formulate a one-tailed hypothesis, the *region of acceptance* of the null hypothesis includes the other 'tail' of the distribution. What happens if, having predicted that values in Sample A will be larger than values in Sample B, the opposite turns out to be the case, and the size of the difference is so great that it would have proved significant if we had had the opposite hypothesis? The answer is that you have already defined such an event as one which does not permit the rejection of the null hypothesis. You have made your bed and must lie in it. The logic of hypothesis testing cannot be turned into caprice.

Types of statistical test

The tests we are primarily concerned with in this book are predominantly two-sample tests, although some multi-sample tests are included for those who might have the occasional need or desire to go beyond the limitations imposed by two-sample techniques. The specific function of each test is briefly described in the introduction to the tests presented in the following Chapter. Here, we are concerned with some more general points which will help us to choose an appropriate test for our data.

85

Parametric and non-parametric tests

Although it is not difficult to distinguish between these two types of test, it seems worthwhile to define some basic concepts and terminology in order to acquire a clearer understanding of this distinction.

First, *a population*: this word is used in statistics to stand for all of anything. Although 'all the people in the United Kingdom' defines a population; so does 'all the foxes on Bromley common', or 'all the chimney pots in Ipswich', or 'all Mr Jones' reaction times to a visual stimulus'. The concept of a population can be broad or narrow, concrete or abstract. It can lack all utility; it can even be absurd. When a statistician, however, talks about a population, he is very often talking about a theoretical population of numbers or scores or some such.

A sample is a portion of a population. Usually it will be selected in such a way (e.g., randomly) as to be representative of the population from which it is drawn.

A parameter is a value referring to some characteristic of a population. Usually, such values will be denoted by Greek letters. For example, the mean of a population is denoted by μ (the Greek letter 'm', pronounced mu) whilst its standard deviation is denoted by σ (the Greek letter 's', pronounced sigma).

A statistic is a value referring to some characteristic of a sample. Usually, such values will be denoted by letters from the Roman alphabet. For example, the mean of a sample is usually denoted by $\overline{X}$ ('X bar') whilst its standard deviation is denoted by 's'.

Assumptions of a parametric test

As you might expect from the foregoing, parametric tests involve parameters. They, in fact, estimate population parameters and capitalize on the known properties of the normal curve. One such test is the *t*-test. There are two versions of it: one for independent samples and one for related samples. The following comments apply primarily to the independent *t*-test.

The theoretical distribution of *t*, from which significance tables are constructed, and against which we check the value of our test statistic, is derived on the assumption that the population distributions are normal and have equal variances.

Strictly speaking, if we are to use a t-test, our data should come from populations with these characteristics. However, it has been repeatedly demonstrated that even if these assumptions of normality and homogeneity of variance are violated it makes little difference. The t-test is therefore said to be robust in that it will tolerate quite marked departures from these assumptions.

To be more practical about these matters:

1. The normality assumption is not very important. If you can reasonably imagine that if you collected an indefinite number of scores, the majority would form a roughly central 'hump' in the middle of the distribution with the higher and lower scores tailing off at each end, that will be good enough.

2. Check the ranges of scores in each sample. If they are roughly the same, you can assume that their parent populations have similar variances. If they are markedly different, carry out an F test (see page 117 which will tell you whether they differ significantly. Be particularly cautious about assuming homogeneity of variance if your sample sizes are unequal; for in such cases, your test could much more easily be invalid.

3. Remember that the independent t-test assumes that the data in both samples come from normally distributed populations with equal variances; you should check both samples for similarity with respect to these parameters. And this test is the one that can have unequal sample sizes. In the case of the related t-test you are not concerned with the parent populations of the two samples, but with a single set of difference scores. These should be from a (roughly) normally distributed population. No assumption about variances is involved. Furthermore, difference scores, even if derived from population distributions of quite different shapes, tend to be normally distributed. You can, therefore, afford to be much less diffident about using the related t-test than about using the t-test for independent samples.

It might be worth coming back to this part of the Chapter when you have seen more of the tests we are talking about (see next chapter). In turn, we will revert to our treatment of the different types of test available to us.

Within the broad division into parametric and non-parametric tests, there are further subdivisions. There are tests of difference, and measures of correlation. There are also, if we go beyond the limits of two-sample methods, tests of trend.

Tests of difference
These are probably the most commonly used tests in psychological experiments. They may be tests of differences in central tendency, or differences in dispersion. We can, for example, test whether the *means* of two samples differ significantly (a t-test will do this for us) or whether two *variances* differ significantly. In order to choose an appropriate difference test, we must make the following decisions:

1. What sort of difference are we looking for?
2. What level of measurement have we for the dependent variable?

3. Are we dealing with an independent or related measured design?

That much will allow us to select a test; but, in addition, we must decide whether the test we use is to be one or two-tailed. At the end of Chapter 5, we will present a 'decision-map' (not unlike that on page 72 which covers descriptive measures) but we must first deal with other types of inferential techniques before it can be made complete.

Measures of correlation

Two variables are said to be correlated when the values on one of the variables allow us to predict the values on the other. Let us suppose I have a motor car that does exactly thirty miles to the gallon. If I tell you that I have ten gallons of petrol in my tank, you can instantly predict that I can travel three hundred miles. One variable, which we shall call Y, is the amount of petrol; the other, which we shall call X, is the number of miles I can travel. We can plot this relationship:

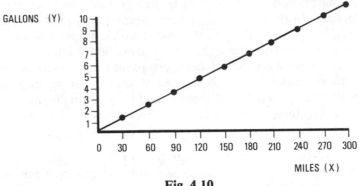

Fig. 4.10

These two variables are *perfectly correlated*, that is to say, an accurate prediction is possible from one variable to the other. If, for example, I tell you that I have travelled 180 miles, you know that I have used exactly six gallons of petrol. X and Y are also *directly correlated*, which is to say that as mileage increases, consumption increases. The 'direction of movement' so to speak, on each variable, is the same.

Suppose, however, that I start with a tank full of petrol (ten gallons) and measure how much petrol I have left after thirty, sixty, ninety miles, and so on. As mileage increases, the quantity of petrol remaining in the tank decreases (see Figure 4.11).

The variables are still perfectly correlated, but the relationship is an *inverse* one, for 'the movement' on each variable is in *opposite directions*. A direct relationship as in Figure 4.10 yields a *positive correlation coefficient*: an inverse relationship, as in Figure 4.11 yields a *negative correlation coefficient*.

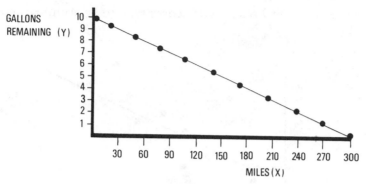

Fig. 4.11

The values of a correlation coefficient can range from − 1 through zero to +1. Perfect correlation gives a coefficient of unity (positive or negative); where no prediction is possible, the coefficient will be zero; but most of the time we have to deal with coefficients that are somewhere between these extremes.

If we plot the values of two variables that are imperfectly related, we get, instead of a straight line, a scattergram which will show a rough 'straight-line' relationship. When two variables do not correlate at all (i.e., when the coefficient is zero) no straight line relationship can be seen at all. Thus:

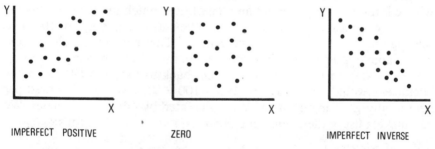

Fig. 4.12

Suppose we wish to see whether children who do well in an English examination also do well in a French examination. We obtain the scores of ten children on each of these two variables, as follows:

English X: 12 23 13 15 11 18 17 14 16 15
French Y: 11 17 18 15 12 21 16 13 17 12

Clearly, by knowing the scores on one variable, we cannot predict (perfectly) their corresponding values on the other variable. But a roughly direct relationship seems to exist: good scores in English tend to

89

go with good scores in French; bad scores tend to go with bad scores. Let us plot them:

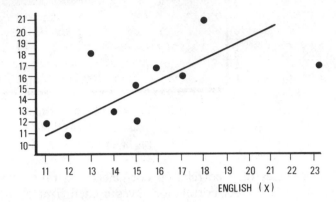

Fig. 4.13

This approximates to the sort of direct relationship shown in Figure 4.12. In fact, for these data the correlation coefficient works out at + 0.58 (which is significant). What does this tell us? Firstly, the positive sign tells us that the relationship is direct. Higher scores in English are associated with higher scores in French, and so on. Secondly, the value of 0.58 for the coefficient tells us that it is a less than perfect relationship. As a result, predicting French scores from the basis of the English scores will be imprecise. We can get an idea of how much imprecision there is by simply squaring the correlation coefficient, multiplying by 100, and reading the resulting value as a percentage. That percentage tells us how much 'guessing error' for Y scores is eliminated by knowing X scores. This is perhaps a little complicated. Go back to Figure 4.10. There, the coefficient would be $= + 1$. $1^2 = 1$; $1 \times 100 = 100$ (%). One hundred per cent of any guessing error for Y is eliminated by knowing X values. We can make a list of these *'guessing-error' elimination values* thus:

Value of correlation
coefficient (whether
+ve or −ve):　0　.1　.2　.3　.4　.5　.6　.7　.8　.9　1.0

'Guessing error'
eliminated:　　0% 1% 4% 9% 16% 25% 36% 49% 64% 81% 100%

As you see, until the coefficient is quite high, only a comparative small proportion of 'guessing error' is eliminated.

This concept is not to be confused with the *significance* of a correlation coefficient. That tells us whether such a coefficient could occur by chance only very infrequently. Imagine any four scores on each of two variables, X and Y. The X values are shuffled and set down; the Y values are shuffled and set down alongside the X values. What chance is there that the high scores will be 'paired off' on each variable, likewise the medium score and the low ones? Obviously, with only a few scores on each variable, the chances are quite good. If, however, we had a hundred scores on each variable the likelihood of obtaining consistent pairings is remote. The significance of a correlation coefficient is to do with this—namely the scope that chance alone has to produce systematically paired scores.

The implication of this is that when the number of scores on each variable is small, the correlation coefficient needs to be high before it can be regarded as significant, but as N increases, a smaller coefficient will be significant (see Table A.10, which clearly illustrates this point).

It is important to remember that the correlation coefficient presented in this book identify only the *linear* (i.e., straight-line) relationship between two variables. You can think of them as statistical techniques for drawing the best-fitting straight line through a scattergram. If our scattergram was as follows:

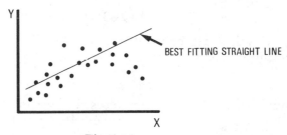

Fig. 4.14

The best-fitting straight line does not fit very well because the relationship between the two variables is curvilinear. There are techniques for dealing with non-linear relationships but in this book we are restricted to identifying only the linear component.

Finally, note that, when a correlation coefficient is tested for significance, the null hypothesis usually states that the population coefficient is zero*, a one-tailed alternative hypothesis specifies the sign of the coefficient (i.e., the direction of the relationship), and a two-tailed alternative hypothesis does not.

Trend tests
The word 'trend', as used in statistics, has a more restricted meaning than it has in ordinary usage. It is used to describe a progressive increase, or decrease in values across three or more levels of an

* Other null hypotheses can be formulated, but this is the most usual one. It is beyond the scope of this Chapter to treat such variants of H_0.

independent variable. A trend test can therefore be thought of as an extension of a one-tailed test where more than two samples are involved. Like any other one-tailed test, trend tests require that the directional hypothesis is formed in advance of data collection. If, for example, you predict that scores will increase across three levels of an independent variable and it turns out that they actually decrease, you cannot switch your hypothesis to match the effect, for your data have fallen into what you had defined as the rejection of acceptance of the null hypothesis (see also the section on one- and two-tailed tests).

Degrees of freedom
You will find that statistical tests involve degrees of freedom. To use statistical tables, you often have to use the appropriate number of degrees of freedom in order to find the required critical value of a statistic. The concept is a difficult one to grasp in all its complexity, but it can be stated, in general, that the number of degrees of freedom associated with a statistical calculation reflects the number of observations or scores that are free to vary within certain restrictions. If we have a simple sum:

$$1+2+3=6.$$

How many values can be freely altered within the restriction that their total must be 6? The answer is any two of them, e.g.:

$$10+12+X=6.$$

We have changed the first two values, but the third, x, is now determined. It is not free to vary. It must be -16. This calculation, therefore, has two degrees of freedom associated with it.

There is only one degree of freedom associated with the choice of which leg you put into your trousers first. If you put your left leg in first, you are no longer free to vary which leg goes in second. The restriction within which you are operating here is, of course, that human beings, and trousers, have only two legs.

Now consider a more complicated example. Imagine we intend to shoe a horse. Theoretically, we could start on any hoof we liked—front, back, left or right. We could then choose any of the three remaining hooves; after that either of the remaining hooves; but the fourth hoof would be prescribed by our first three (free) choices. We can represent our choices in this way:

	Left	Right
Fore		
Hind		

Fig. 4.15

92

(You can place a tick in any three boxes you wish, but when you have done so, you have no choice about which box to put your fourth tick into).

So, as novice blacksmiths, we have three degrees of freedom associated with the order in which we shoe our horse's hooves. Before we embark on this venture, however, we decide to consult an experienced blacksmith. He tells us that we should not shoe a hind leg first, for there is a danger of being kicked if we do so. We must therefore start with a foreleg. Are we free to choose either of these? The blacksmith would tell us that we are not. Horses prefer to be approached from the side on which they are usually led—their left hand side—otherwise they can become nervous, and, again, we would be in danger of being kicked. In the interests of safety, therefore, we sacrifice one of our degrees of freedom by deciding to shoe the front left hoof first.

A blacksmith would now tell us that we should shoe the left hind hoof next, for it is easier to move the tools down the flank of the horse than to the other side of it. In the interests of convenience, therefore, we sacrifice another degree of freedom and shoe that hoof next.

Two hooves remain to be shod. We appear to have one degree of freedom, for we seem free to choose the right front *or* the right hind leg. The blacksmith would not give himself this freedom, however. To be on the safe side, he would start at the front. For him, therefore, the order of shoeing is wholly prescribed. By imposing the restrictions we have described he sacrifices *all* the degrees of freedom that appeared to us to exist.

Perhaps these things will give you the idea of degrees of freedom. Unfortunately to take the concept further we would have to enter the realms of theoretical statistics and that is well beyond our brief. From the practical point of view, however, it can be said that it is generally advisable to ensure that you have as many degrees of freedom as possible, for that increases your chances of detecting significant effects. Although—odd as it may seem—it is possible to have too many degrees of freedom, the problem almost rarely in psychological experiments because of their small scale.

We come finally to the 'decision map' we discussed earlier in this Chapter and which is to be found on page 132. As you will see, the things that determine which is an appropriate test to use are:

1. the type of effect you are looking for (i.e. difference, correlation, trend)
2. the number of experimental treatments (samples)
3. whether your design involves independent or related measures
4. the level of measurement (i.e. nominal, ordinal or interval)

Other considerations, such as whether you can assume normality and homogeneity of variance, will also determine the choice of test, but these organizing principles are fundamental and need to be well 'over-learned'.

FURTHER READING

Harshbarger, T. R., *Introductory Statistics—A Decision Map.* Collier Macmillan 1971.

Hoel, P. G., *Elementary Statistics.* Wiley 1971.

Runyon, R. P., and Haber, A., *Fundamentals of Behavioural Statistics.* Addison-Wesley 1967.

5   Statistical procedures

JEREMY COYLE

Introduction

This Chapter is primarily concerned with tests of significance. The descriptive measures it contains are the mean and the standard deviation (here presented for more complex data than were used for illustrative purposes in the preceding Chapter. But as these are arguably the descriptive measures most useful to psychologists Chapter 4 should be consulted for further information about them).

The function and assumptions of each test are given in a brief introduction and the procedure for calculating each statistic is given step by step, with an accompanying worked example. With the exceptions of the mean, the standard deviation and χ^2, the data that are analysed are basically the same for all two-sample and multi-sample treatments. The reason for adopting this rather unorthodox way of doing things is to permit the user of this book to see for him- or herself how different designs affect the way in which data are analysed and how tests differ in power.

The power of a statistical test

The 'power' of a test can be seen as its ability to detect the effect of the independent variable on the dependent variable. To put this another way, it is the probability of avoiding a Type II error. The power of a test is influenced by a number of things. One of them, obviously, is α, our criterion of significance; another is the size of sample (larger samples being better than smaller ones); yet another is the variance of the parent populations. We can, however, look at this in a simple way and say that the more the experimenter can, as it were, 'tell' the analysis, the more effectively it can operate on the data. For example, when you can 'tell' the analysis that the parent populations from which your data are drawn are normally distributed and have equal variances your data can be treated in a more sophisticated and effective fashion than if such information were not available. Similarly, if you 'tell' the test that two samples are related, you are giving it the information that the values in each sample tend to come in pairs; they are organized other than in just two columns, they are also organized by 'rows'. Again, if you 'tell' the analysis that the units of measurement are precisely defined (as inches or seconds, etc.,) it has more to go on than if it merely assumes that the sample measures represent rank order only.

In general, therefore, what we might call an 'interval scale analysis' is more powerful than an 'ordinal scale analysis', which, in turn, is more powerful than a 'nominal scale analysis'. And, as we saw in the case of descriptive statistics, whilst statistics appropriate to lower levels of measurement may be used for data at a higher level of measurement, the reverse is not the case. In spite of this possibility, however, it must always be advisable to use the most powerful analysis, and the potential 'upward mobility' of statistics appropriate to lower levels of measurement should not be encouraged.

Note for the non-mathematical
It is perhaps worth reminding those who dislike mathematics that statistical formulae, although capable of algebraical manipulation, can be seen simply as a set of coded instructions which tell you how to calculate a statistic. You 'read the code' in the sequence specified in the old school-room mnemonic BOMDAS, standing for 'Brackets, Of, Multiplication, Division, Addition, and Subtraction'. First, work out what is in brackets; then do any multiplications, then divide, and so on. Here is an example:

$$x = \frac{a(b+c)^2}{n} + n - 15$$

where: a = 1
b = 2
c = 3
n = 5

Start inside the *brackets*: b+c = 2+3 = 5; still associated with the bracket is the instruction to square, so: $5^2 = 25$
Now *multiply*: a(25) = 1×25 = 25
Now *divide*: $\frac{25}{n}$ = 25÷5 = 5

96

Now *add*: $5+n=5+5=10$
Now *subtract*: $10-15=-5$
And do not worry about having negative values as your answer. They are common enough. Remember, however, that

positive×positive=positive
positive×negative=negative
negative×negative=positive

Note that Σ ('sigma', the Greek capital letter S) is an instruction to add things up. It is a summation sign. Also, X stands for any given score, and it may have a subscript such as X_A, X_B, etc. These subscripts tell you which set of scores you are dealing with. Suppose we have two conditions under which we have collected test scores:

Table 5.1

Condition A	Condition B
1	5
2	6
3	7
$\Sigma(X_A)=(1+2+3)=6$	$\Sigma(X_B)=(5+6+7)=18.$

The mean from grouped data

The mean is an appropriate index of central tendency when data are measured at the interval scale level. Here we will calculate it for data which are grouped in class intervals.*

Table 5.2 shows the IQ scores of a random sample of 150 twelve-year-old schoolchildren.

Table 5.2

IQ:	61–70	71–80	81–90	91–100
No. of children	5	13	21	44

IQ:	101–110	111–120	121–130	131–140
No. of children	39	20	7	1

Formula:
$$\overline{X}=\frac{\Sigma(fg)}{N}$$

where: f=the number of scores within a given class interval
g=the mid-point of a given class interval
N=the total number of scores

* The mean from *ungrouped* data is presented on page 65.

97

Calculation
Step 1: Subtract the real† lower limit of each class interval from its real upper limit and divide the result by two. (e.g., for the first class interval):
$$70.5 - 60.5 = 10; \quad 10 \div 2 = 5$$
Step 2: Add this value to the real lower limit of each class interval and re-cast the table thus:

Table 5.3

IQ:	65.5	75.5	85.5	95.5	105.5	115.5	125.5	135.5
No. of children:	5	13	21	44	39	30	7	1

Step 3: Find the product of the mid-points of the class intervals and the frequencies; add these up and divide by N to obtain $\overline{X}$.

$$\overline{X} = \frac{(65.5 \times 5) + (75.5 \times 13) \ldots + (135.5 \times 1)}{N}$$

$$\overline{X} = \frac{14745}{150} = 98.30$$

The mean IQ score of these children is 98.30

The standard deviation

The standard deviation is an appropriate measure of dispersion when data are measured at the interval scale level. We will calculate it for the following random sample of ten IQ scores:
$$108, 92, 85, 121, 113, 76, 95, 103, 104, 94$$

Formula

$$s = \sqrt{\frac{\Sigma(X^2) - \frac{(\Sigma X)^2}{N}}{N-1}}$$

where: X = any given score
N = the total number of scores.

Calculation
Step 1: Square all the scores and add these squares. This gives $\Sigma(X)^2$.
$$(108^2 + 92^2 \ldots + 94^2) = 99825$$
Step 2: Add up all the scores and square them. This gives $(\Sigma X)^2$
$$(108 + 92 \ldots + 94)^2 = 991^2 = 982081$$
Step 3: Divide $(\Sigma X)^2$ by the total number of scores and subtract the resulting value from $\Sigma(X^2)$.
$$982081 \div 10 = 98208.1; \quad 99825 - 98208.1 = 1616.9$$

† See page 73 for an explanation of 'real' and 'apparent' limits.

Step 4: Divide the outcome of Step 3 by $N-1$
$$1616 \div 9 = 179.655$$
Step 5: Find the square root of the outcome of Step 4. This gives s.
$$s = \sqrt{179.655} = 13.40$$

The standard deviation of these scores is 13.40. If we assume IQ scores to be normally distributed, we can infer from this that 68.2 per cent of all scores lie within 13.4 IQ points either side of the mean. Here, the mean is 99.1, so between 85.7 and 112.5, 68.2 per cent of scores are to be found.

Note
1. Refer to pages 67 to 69 for more details on this statistic.
2. Notice that, in the above formula, the denominator is $N-1$. In general this is the more common formula, for it gives an estimate of the standard deviation of the *population*. The dispersion in a *sample* is found by dividing by N (see page 68). The reason for this is that the standard deviation of a population is always likely to be larger than the standard deviation of a sample and we compensate for this by reducing the denominator by 1. This boosts the final value of s (see Diamond op. cit. for an explanation of this).
3. The percentage of scores in a population that fall within plus and minus one, two or three standard deviations from the mean is as follows:

Table 5.4

Type of distribution	Number of standard deviations from the population mean		
	± 1	± 2	± 3
Normal	68.2%	95.4%	99.7%
Symmetrical but unimodal	at least 57%	at least 89%	at least 95%
Any	—	at least 75%	at least 89%

The standard deviation from grouped data

This is a method of calculating the standard deviation when data are grouped in class intervals of equal size.

Formula

$$s = \sqrt{\frac{i^2}{N-1}\left\{\Sigma(fw^2) - \frac{(\Sigma fw)^2}{N}\right\}}$$

where: i = the real class interval size
f = the number of scores within a given class interval

99

w = the weight given to a class interval
N = the total number of scores

Calculation
This rather fearsome formula can easily be broken down into a step by step calculation. Thus:

Step 1: Estimate which class interval includes the mean of all the scores and give it a weight of zero. Give the class intervals *above* it positive weights, in ascending order, and the class intervals *below* it negative weights, in ascending order.

Step 2: Square all the weights.

Step 3: Multiply each frequency by the weight given in Step 1 and add up these values (remembering to take their signs into account). This gives Σfw.

Step 4: Multiply each frequency by the squared weight in Step 1 and add up these values. This gives $\Sigma(fw^2)$.

Step 5: Add up all the frequencies to obtain N.

Step 6: Square Σfw, found in Step 3; divide this by N and subtract the resulting value from $\Sigma(fw^2)$, found in Step 4.

Step 7: Find the real* length of the class intervals by subtracting the real lower limit of any one of them from the real upper limit. This gives i.

Step 8: Square i and divide by $N-1$.

Step 9: Multiply the results of Step 6 by the result of Step 8 and find the square root. This gives the standard deviation.

To illustrate this method of obtaining a value for the standard deviation, we will use the same data as we used for the mean from grouped data.

Table 5.5

IQ:	61–70	71–80	81–90	91–100	101–110	111–120	121–130	131–140
Frequency (f):	5	13	21	44	39	20	7	1

Step 1: (w)	-3	-2	-1	0	$+1$	$+2$	$+3$	$+4$
Step 2: (w^2)	9	4	1	0	1	4	9	16

Step 3: $\Sigma fw = (5 \times -3) + (13 \times -2) \ldots + (1 \times 4) = 42$

Step 4: $\Sigma(fw^2) = (5 \times 9) + (13 \times 4) \ldots + (1 \times 16) = 316$

Step 5: $N = 5 + 13 + 21 + 44 + 39 + 20 + 7 + 1 = 150$

Step 6: $(\Sigma fw)^2 = 42^2 = 1764; \dfrac{1764}{150} = 11.76; \quad 316 - 11.76 = 304.24$

*See page 73 for an explanation of 'real' and 'apparent' limits.

Step 7: Taking the first class interval (61 − 70); its real lower limit is 60.5, and its real upper limit is 70.5.
Thus i = 70.5 − 60.5 = 10.

Step 8: $\dfrac{i^2}{N-1} = \dfrac{10^2}{149} = 0.671$

Step 9: s = 304.24 × 0.671 = 204.15; $\sqrt{204.15} = 14.29$

The standard deviation is 14.29.

Some general notes on the χ^2 test

χ^2 is used to test data which are in the form of frequencies. Especially, it tells us whether the frequencies which we have differ significantly from the frequencies that we would be expected to have if the null hypothesis were true.

The case of one sample
Suppose we toss a coin 100 times and obtain a result of 54 heads and 46 tails. Are the frequencies we observe significantly different from those which we would expect on the basis of chance alone (i.e., 50 heads and 50 tails)? The χ^2 test will deal with this kind of question. Similarly, by observing the frequencies with which winners come from each of the six traps in a greyhound stadium we can check whether there is a significant discrepancy between what actually happens and our theoretical expectation that there will be an equal number of winners from each trap. In these two instances, we are talking about *a single set of frequencies*. There are two frequency counts involved in the first, and six in the second. Thus:

Heads	Tails		Trap No:	1 2 3 4 5 6

and

and the expected frequency for each 'box' can be obtained by adding up all the observed frequencies and dividing by the number of 'boxes', or categories. The χ^2 test, used this way, is known as a one-sample test because there is only a single dimension to the arrangement of categories; and this, the most common way of generating expected frequencies, gives us a *rectangular distribution* of expected frequencies.

The 2 × 2 case and the (r × k) case
χ^2 can also be calculated for a 2 × 2 contingency table. Suppose that 100 children are given the choice of studying either statistics or geography.

We can cast the choices of both the boys and the girls into a 2×2 contingency table:

	Statistics	Geography
Boys	40	20
Girls	20	20

How do we now discover whether our observed frequencies differ from the frequencies expected under the null hypothesis? The important thing to note is the nature of expected frequencies. In the previous one-sample case, it made good sense to derive the expected frequencies by dividing the sum of frequencies by the number of categories. But, as far as the statistical test is concerned, what in fact we did there was allocate *equal proportions* of the total frequency count to each of the 'cells' or categories.

The same applies here, and the question that we are asking is whether the *proportion* of boys who choose each of the subjects is the same as the *proportion* of girls. The null hypothesis, of course, would state that the proportions are the same. How do we derive expected frequencies which have this proportional similarity? We take the *marginal totals* that are common to a particular cell, multiply them together and divide by N. Thus:

	Statistics	Geography	Marginal totals
Boys	40 (A)	20 (B)	60
Girls	20 (C)	20 (D)	40
Marginal totals:	60	40	**Grand Total (N)=100**

Note that we have labelled the cells A, B, C and D for simplicity's sake. The expected frequencies would now be as follows:

$$A = 60 \times 60 \div 100 = 36$$
$$B = 60 \times 40 \div 100 = 24$$
$$C = 40 \times 40 \div 100 = 24$$
$$D = 40 \times 40 \div 100 = 16$$

	Statistics	Geography
Boys	36 (A)	24 (B)
Girls	24 (C)	16 (D)

This allows for the different number of boys and girls making up our 100 people (sixty boys and forty girls). And, by using these expected frequencies, we are setting up a null hypothesis which states that the proportional split of boys and girls between the two subjects is the same (i.e., 36 is to 24 as 24 is to 16; the proportions are .66 and .33 for both boys and girls). The method for calculating expected frequencies in the $(r \times k)$ case (i.e., where the contingency table is larger than (2×2)) is exactly the same.

There is, however, a general rule about expected frequencies that must be made clear:

Expected frequencies in at least 80 per cent of all cells in the contingency table must be 5, or more. In no case may an expected frequency be less than 1.

In the 2×2 case, no expected frequency can be less than 5. If this condition is not met, the Fisher Exact Probability test must be used instead (see Siegel, S., *Non Parametric Statistics*, McGraw Hill 1956.)

If this condition is not met in the $(r \times k)$ case, adjacent cells may be collapsed together if it is sensible to do this.

Finally, whenever there is only one degree of freedom, Yates's Correction should be applied. This is known as a *correction for continuity* and involves subtracting 0.5 from the absolute value of each difference between an observed and an expected frequency. What this does is correct for the effect of forcing our observations into discrete categories. When, for example, we count the number of people who vote for and against a proposal, the division we observe is not truly a hard and fast one. Some who vote 'yes' will be only marginally in favour, whilst others will have no hesitation about doing so. Yates's correction allows for this mathematically and has the effect of reducing the final value of χ^2, thereby compensating for the effect of an over-simplication of the 'true' state of affairs.

The χ^2 test (rectangular distribution)

This test tells us whether the frequencies we observe in a single set of categories differ significantly from those expected under the null hypothesis which states that all the frequencies should be the same. All observations are assumed to be independent.

Formula:

$$\chi^2 = \frac{\Sigma (O - E)^2}{E} \qquad\qquad df = c - 1$$

where O = an observed frequency
$\quad\quad E$ = an expected frequency
$\quad\quad c$ = the number of categories

Suppose that we have counted the numbers of winners coming from each trap in a greyhound stadium during the course of a week's racing and we wish to test whether all the traps produce an equal number of winners. Our data are:

Table 5.6

Trap No:	1	2	3	4	5	6
No. of winners:	11	6	7	5	3	4

Calculation

Step 1: Add up all the frequencies and divide by the number of categories. This gives E, the expected frequency for each cell:
$$11+6+7+5+3+4=36; \quad 36 \div 6 = 6$$

Step 2: Take E from each observed frequency, square the resulting value and add up the squares. This gives $\Sigma(O-E)^2$
$$(11-6)^2+(6-6)^2 \ldots +(4-6)^2 = 40$$

Step 3: Divide the result of Step 2 by E to obtain χ^2.
$$\chi^2 \text{ is } 40 \div 6 = 6.66.$$

Step 4: Consult Table A.2 with $c-1$ degrees of freedom to find the critical value of χ^2 for p$=.05$.
Table A.2 gives $\chi^2 = 11.07$ for 5 degrees of freedom.

Our calculated value is less than this and is therefore not significant. We cannot therefore reject H_o.

This means that although our observed frequencies may look different from the theoretically expected frequencies, the discrepancy is simply not large enough to be considered significant. (A practical implication of this, in this instance, is that perhaps we need more data in order to test the hypothesis adequately.)

The χ^2 test (2×2) case

This test tells us whether the proportional split of frequencies between different categories differs significantly from that which would be expected under the null hypothesis. All observations are assumed to be independent.

Formula*

$$\chi^2 = \frac{N\left\{|AD-BC|-\dfrac{N}{2}\right\}^2}{(A+B)(C+D)(A+C)(B+D)} \qquad df=1$$

* Note that this formula incorporates Yates's Correction (in the $\dfrac{N}{2}$ expression in the numerator).

where: A, B, C, and D = cell frequencies in a 2×2 contingency table which has been labelled in this way:

$$\begin{array}{c|c} A & B \\ \hline C & D \end{array}$$

N = the sum of all four frequencies.

Suppose that of fifty people in a room, twenty-eight were men, and twenty-two were women. Eighteen of the men and eight of the women were smokers. Is there a significant difference between these men and women with respect to smoking? We can draw up these data into a 2×2 contingency table:

	Smokers	Non-smokers	
Men	18 (A)	10 (B)	(28)
Women	8 (C)	14 (D)	(22)
	(26)	(24)	N = 50

Calculation

Step 1: Always check the expected frequencies first to ensure that the test will be valid. In any contingency table the best way to do this is to take the two *smallest* marginal totals common to a particular cell, multiply them together and divide by N. If this value is 5 or more, all is well. Here, the smallest marginal totals are 22 and 24:

$(22 \times 24) \div 50 = 10.56$ —We may proceed.

Step 2: Multiply together the frequencies in cells A and D; do the same for cells B and C, and take the smaller value from the larger. (The two vertical lines in the formula are a *modulus* sign which tells us to treat the difference between these two values as *positive*. Hence always take the smaller from the larger.)
AD = $(18 \times 14) = 252$; BC = $(10 \times 8) = 80$; $252 - 80 = 172$

Step 3: Divide N by 2, subtract this from the value found in Step 2, square the result and multiply it by N. This gives the numerator of the formula.
$N \div 2 = 25$; $172 - 25 = 147$; $147^2 = 21609$;
$(21609 \times 50) = 1080450$

Step 4: Multiply together all four marginal totals and divide this into the value found in Step 3 to obtain χ^2.
$28 \times 22 \times 26 \times 24 = 384384$; $\chi^2 = 1080450 \div 384384 = 2.81$

105

Step 5: Consult Table A.2 with 1 degree of freedom to find the critical value of χ^2 for p = .05.
Table A.2 gives $\chi^2 = 3.84$ for one degree of freedom. Our calculated value is less than this and is therefore not significant. The proportional split of men and women into smokers and non-smokers is not significantly different.

The χ^2 test (r × k) case

This test tells us whether the proportional split of sets of frequencies across several categories differs significantly from that which would be expected under the null hypothesis. All observations are assumed to be independent.

Formula

$$\chi^2 = \sum \frac{(O - E)^2}{E} \qquad\qquad df = (r-1)(k-1)$$

where   O = an observed frequency
E = an expected frequency
r and k = the number of rows and the number of columns in the contingency table.

Suppose that 100 people from different social classes were asked how they kept their trousers up and we classified their replies as follows:

	Belt	Braces	Belt and braces	
Aristos	8	14	1	(23)
Bourgeois	17	12	10	(39)
Proles	14	4	20	(38)
	(39)	(30)	(31)	N = 100

Is there a significant association between social class and preferred method of trouser-suspension?

Calculation
Step 1: Find the expected frequencies for each cell by multiplying together the marginal totals common to it and dividing by N, the sum of all the frequencies. (Check that at least 80 per cent of the cells have expected frequencies of 5 or more and that no cell has an expected frequency of less than 1).
The expected frequency for the top left-hand cell, for example,

106

is: $(23 \times 39) \div 100 = 8.97$ and the complete set of expected frequencies is as follows:

	Belt	Braces	Belt and braces
Aristos	8.97	6.90	7.13
Bourgeois	15.21	11.70	12.09
Proles	14.82	11.40	11.78

Step 2: Find the difference between each observed and expected frequency, square it and divide by that expected frequency. Add up all the resulting values to obtain χ^2.

$$(8 - 8.97)^2 = 0.9409; \quad 0.9409 \div 8.97 = 0.1048$$
$$(17 - 15.21)^2 = 3.2041; \quad 3.2041 \div 15.21 = 0.2106$$
$$(14 - 14.82)^2 = 0.6724; \quad 0.6724 \div 14.82 = 0.0453$$
$$(14 - 6.90)^2 = 50.4100; \quad 50.4100 \div 6.90 = 7.3057$$
$$(12 - 11.70)^2 = 0.0900; \quad 0.0900 \div 11.70 = 0.0076$$
$$(4 - 11.40)^2 = 54.7600; \quad 54.7600 \div 11.40 = 4.8035$$
$$(1 - 7.13)^2 = 37.5769; \quad 37.5769 \div 7.13 = 5.2702$$
$$(10 - 12.09)^2 = 4.3681; \quad 4.3681 \div 12.09 = 0.3612$$
$$(20 - 11.78)^2 = 67.5684; \quad 67.5684 \div 11.78 = 5.7358$$
$$\chi^2 = 23.8447$$

Step 3: Consult Table A.2 with $(r-1)(k-1)$ degrees of freedom to find the critical value of χ^2 for $p = .05$.

Table A.2 gives $\chi^2 = 9.49$ with 4 degrees of freedom. Our calculated value exceeds this and is therefore significant. (In fact the table value for $p = .01$ is 13.28, which is also exceeded. We may say therefore that this is significant beyond the .01 level.)

Interpreting such a finding can be quite difficult. By inspecting the tables of observed and expected frequencies, however, we can see that some large discrepancies make up the bulk of the overall effect. Remember, however, that this is strictly an 'overall' analysis. In many cases it is not so easy to see where the bulk of the effect comes from.

Model data for all subsequent analyses

The data below will be used in all subsequent analyses with the object of showing how tests differ in their power to reject the null hypothesis and how the analysis you use depends on the question you ask, on the design of your experiment and on the assumptions you make.

75	65	56	57
77	57	48	52
58	42	49	34
41	38	21	18
47	27	19	25
39	24	36	28
51	39	53	37
46	41	55	41
45	24	35	43
74	73	54	45

In each worked example that follows, these figures will be assumed to have come from hypothetical experiments which are described. If you compare the outcome of the various analyses, you will begin to appreciate what they each accomplish.

The Sign test

This test applies to two related samples when measurement is at the nominal scale level. It identifies the *kind* of difference that exists between pairs of observations (e.g., positive or negative) and determines whether there are more differences of one kind (or the other) than would be expected under the null hypothesis.

Dealing with our model data

Suppose that the data above are the results of an experiment on the Muller-Lyer illusion. Let us assume that ten subjects each produced scores under two conditions. Condition I used 'fins' and 'barbs' at an angle of 45° to the 'shaft'; Condition II employed an angle of 60°. The subjects used apparatus made up of a sleeve and an insert. To eliminate the bias resulting from either pushing in or pulling out the insert, the subjects used both methods of setting the apparatus under each condition. The order in which they did so was counterbalanced, and the scores are error expressed in millimetres. The experimenter hypothesizes that the values in Condition II will be higher (a one-tailed hypothesis).

Thus, our raw data would actually look like this:

Table 5.7

	Condition I (45°)		Condition II (60°)	
	Push	Pull	Push	Pull
S_1	75	65	56	57
S_2	77	57	48	52
etc.				

We now combine 'push' and 'pull' scores to produce a single combined score for each subject under each condition. Thus:

Table 5.8

	Condition I (45°)	Condition II (60°)	Sign
S_1	140	113	−
S_2	134	100	−
S_3	100	83	−
S_4	79	39	−
S_5	74	44	−
S_6	63	64	+
S_7	90	90	0
S_8	87	96	+
S_9	69	78	+
S_{10}	147	99	−

Calculation

Step 1: Mark the direction of difference between each pair of scores with a positive or negative sign, giving zero where no difference exists. (See column headed 'sign' above). If you have a two-tailed hypothesis, go now to Step 3).

Step 2: If you have a one-tailed hypothesis, check that the majority of signs are in the predicted direction otherwise you must at this stage accept the null hypothesis. (In this case the majority of signs are in the predicted direction).

Step 3: Count the number of times the less frequent sign occurs and call this value x.
Here $x = 3$.

Step 4: Count the number of pairs of scores that show a difference *other than zero* and call this value n.
Here n = 9.

Step 5: Consult Table A.6 with these values of x and n to obtain p. If p is less than .05, reject the null hypothesis. Here, for $x = 3$, n = 9, p = 0.254 (one-tailed), so we must accept H_o and conclude that there is no significant difference between the conditions.

Note

1. The Sign test deals only with the direction of these differences. Because it is a nominal scale analysis, it is insensitive to the *size* of the differences. As far as the Sign test is concerned, we might as well have written 'H' (for 'higher score') and (L' for 'lower score') and had data like this:

Table 5.9

	Condition I (45°)	Condition II (60°)
S_1	H	L
S_2	H	L
etc.		

In other words, if ever you have data like these (say ticks and crosses, 'yes' and 'no' responses) or any such simple dichotomies in a related measures design, the Sign test is the test to use.

2. If you have more than twenty-five pairs of scores, use the following formulae:

$$z = \frac{n - (2x + 1)}{\sqrt{n}}$$

To find z, get twice x and add 1; subtract this from n, the number of pairs of scores; divide the result by the square root of n and consult Table A.1 for the significance of z. Do not forget what is said in Step 2 above, however.

The Wilcoxon Rank Sum test

This test tells us whether the average of the ranks in one sample differs from the average of the ranks in another. It applies when we have two independent samples. The null hypothesis states that the two sets of ranks are, on average, the same.

Dealing with our model data

Let us suppose that the data on page 108 are the results of an experiment conducted on twenty children to see if their performance in arithmetical tests was worse in the afternoon than in the morning (i.e., a one-tailed alternative hypothesis is involved). Each child drew from a hat a ticket with a number on it between one and twenty. Those who chose odd numbers were tested in the mornings, those who chose the even numbers were tested in the afternoons. Each child was tested twice to help get a more representative index of his ability than a 'one-off' test would provide, and the two scores were combined to produce the following:

Table 5.10

Condition I (am)		Condition II (pm)	
140	(2)	113	(4)
134	(3)	100	(5.5)
100	(5.5)	83	(12)
79	(13)	39	(20)
74	(15)	44	(19)
63	(18)	64	(17)
90	(9.5)	90	(9.5)
87	(11)	96	(8)
69	(16)	78	(14)
147	(1)	99	(7)
Sum of ranks:	94		116

Calculation

Step 1: Rank all the scores from highest to lowest regardless of which sample they are in. When ties occur, give average ranks. Add up the ranks in each sample. The smaller of these two values is T.
(Ranks are shown in brackets in Table 5.10, together with the two sums of ranks). T=94.

Step 2: If you have a two-tailed hypothesis, go now to Step 3. If you have a one-tailed hypothesis, check that the difference between the two rank sums is in the predicted direction, otherwise you must at this stage accept the null hypothesis.
(Here the higher rank sum is where it should be—the worse scores are in the pm condition).

Step 3: Consult Table A.7 using n_1, the number of scores in the smaller sample and n_2, the number of scores in the larger sample to obtain the critical value of T for p=.05. Our sample sizes here are equal: both n_1 and $n_2=10$. Table A.7 gives T=82 for p=.05 (one-tailed). Our calculated value of 94 exceeds this and is therefore not significant. The two sets of ranks do not differ significantly.

Note

1. Giving tied scores an average rank makes the test slightly more conservative, that is, it tends more towards a Type II error, or, if you prefer, leads us to err on the side of caution. Even if ties are numerous and extensive their effect is so small as to make it rarely worth the labour to correct for them.

2. Compare the outcome of this analysis with that which results from the Wilcoxon Signed Rank test and with the *t* tests.

3. When n_2 exceeds 20, use the following formula:

$$z = \frac{2T - n_1(N+1)}{\sqrt{\frac{n_1 n_2 (N+1)}{3}}}$$

To obtain z, add one to the total number of scores (N), multiply this by n_1 and subtract the result from twice T. This gives the numerator of the formula. Multiply together the number of scores in each sample; multiply that by N+1; divide by 3. Take the square root of all this and divide into the numerator. Consult Table A.1 for the significance of z. Do not forget what is said in Step 2, however.

The Wilcoxon Signed Ranks Test

This test applies to two related samples when the differences between score-pairs can be meaningfully ranked. The null hypothesis states that the ranked differences, when their signs are taken into account, will sum to zero. If we reject the null hypothesis, we can conclude that the values in the two samples differ significantly.

Dealing with our model data

Suppose that the experimental design and hypothesis were the same as for the Sign test (see p. 109). We would have the same data, but on this occasion we can see how this test makes use not only of the *direction* of the differences but also of their *magnitude*. Thus:

Table 5.11

	Condition I (45°)	Condition II (60°)	d	Rank
S_1	140	113	−27	
S_2	134	100	−34	
S_3	100	83	−17	
S_4	79	39	−40	
S_5	74	44	−30	
S_6	63	64	+1	1
S_7	90	90	0	
S_8	87	96	+9	2.5
S_9	69	78	+9	2.5
S_{10}	147	99	−48	

Step 1: Find the difference between each pair of scores and note its direction with a positive or negative sign (see column headed 'd' above).

Step 2: Ignoring the signs for the time being, rank the differences giving the smallest difference Rank 1. Disregard any zero differences.

Step 3: Find the smaller sum of ranks which have the same sign. This gives T. If you have a one-tailed hypothesis and this value comes from differences whose sign does not conform to the direction of your hypothesis you must at this stage accept the null hypothesis. (Here, things are as we predicted, so we may continue).
$T = 1 + 2.5 + 2.5 = 6$.

Step 4: Consult Table A.8 using n, the number of pairs of scores showing a non-zero difference, to obtain the critical value of T for $p = .05$. From Table A.8 for $n = 9$, $T = 8$ for $p = .05$ (one-tailed). Our calculated value is less than this and is therefore significant. We can conclude that the values in the two conditions differ significantly.

Note

1. When difference scores are the same, they should be given an average

112

rank. (see Siegel, S., *Non Parametric Statistics* McGraw-Hill 1956, for tie-correction technique, if you wish).

2. Compare the outcome of this analysis with that from the Sign test and the Wilcoxon Rank Sum test. This test is more sensitive than the Sign test, which failed to find a significant difference, because it takes the *magnitude* as well as the *direction* of differences into account. The Sign Test is sensitive only to the latter. The difference between this test and the Wilcoxon Rank Sum test is to do with *Design*. Here we have 'told' the test that the scores are *paired*; in other words, that they *correlate* (see p. 88). The Rank Sum test did not 'know' this. As far as it was concerned, subject differences were mere 'noise' (see p. 55) and had no such orderliness about them.

3. When there are more than twenty-five pairs of scores, use this formula:

$$z = \frac{n(n+1) - 4T}{\sqrt{\dfrac{2n(n+1)(2n+1)}{3}}}$$

To obtain z, add 1 to n and multiply this by n. Subtract from this $4 \times T$. This gives the numerator. Find twice n and add 1; multiply this by $n(n+1)$ and double the resulting value. Divide all this by 3, find the square root and divide this into the numerator to obtain z. Consult Table A.1 for the significance of z. Do not forget, however, what is said in Step 3.

The independent *t*-test

This tests whether the means of two independent samples differ significantly against the null hypothesis that the means are the same. As it is a *parametric* test, it requires interval scale measurement and depends for its validity on the assumption that the data are drawn from populations which are normal and which have equal variances. However, the test is robust enough to tolerate quite distinct violations of these assumptions.

Formula:

$$t = \frac{\overline{X}_A - \overline{X}_B}{\sqrt{\dfrac{\left\{\Sigma(X_A^2) - \dfrac{(\Sigma X_A)^2}{n_A}\right\} + \left\{\Sigma(X_B^2) - \dfrac{(\Sigma X_B)^2}{n_B}\right\}}{N-2}} \times \dfrac{N}{n_A n_B}} \qquad df = N - 2$$

where $\overline{X}_A$ = the mean of Sample A
$\overline{X}_B$ = the mean of Sample B
n_A and n_B = the number of scores in Samples A and B
N = the total number of scores

113

Dealing with our model data

We can assume exactly the same design and a similar, one-tailed hypothesis as was described for the Wilcoxon Rank Sum test (see p. 110) but here we would make the assumption that the parent populations from which our samples are drawn are normally distributed and have equal variances. Thus:

Table 5.12

Condition A (am)	Condition B (pm)
140	113
134	100
100	83
79	39
74	44
63	64
90	90
87	96
69	78
147	99
$\Sigma X_A = 983$	$\Sigma X_B = 806$

Calculation

Step 1: Add up the scores in each sample and divide by the number of scores in each sample to find the two means, $\overline{X}_A$ and $\overline{X}_B$. Their difference gives the numerator of the formula. (If you have a one-tailed hypothesis, check that this difference is in the predicted direction, otherwise the null hypothesis must be accepted at this stage.)

$\Sigma X_A = 983;\quad \overline{X}_A = 983 \div 10 = 98.3;$
$\Sigma X_B = 806;\quad \overline{X}_B = 806 \div 10 = 80.6$
$$98.3 - 80.6 = 17.7$$

(The difference is in the predicted direction).

Step 2: Square all the scores in sample A and add up these squares. This gives $\Sigma(X_A^2)$. Do the same for sample B to obtain $\Sigma(X_B^2)$.

$\Sigma(X_A^2) = 140^2 + 134^2 + 100^2 \ldots + 147^2 = 105281$
$\Sigma(X_B^2) = 113^2 + 100^2 + 83^2 \ldots + 99^2 = 70412$

Step 3: Square ΣX_A and divide by the number of scores in Sample A. Repeat this for the corresponding B values.

$$\frac{(\Sigma X_A)^2}{n_A} = \frac{983^2}{10} = 96628.9$$

$$\frac{(\Sigma X_B)^2}{n_B} = \frac{806^2}{10} = 64963.6$$

Step 4: Find $\Sigma(X_A^2) - \dfrac{(\Sigma X_A)^2}{n_A}$ and $\Sigma(X_B^2) - \dfrac{(\Sigma X_B)^2}{n_B}$

$105281 - 96628.9 = 8652.1;\quad 70412 - 64963.6 = 5448.4$

Step 5: Add together the two values found in Step 4 and divide the result by $N-2$.

$$8652.1 + 5448.4 = 14100.5; \quad 14100.5 \div 18 = 783.361$$

Step 6: Multiply n_A by n_B and divide this into N.

$$10 \times 10 = 100; \quad 20 \div 100 = 0.2$$

Step 7: Multiply the outcome of Step 5 by the outcome of Step 6 and find the square root of that value.

$$783.361 \times 0.2 = 156.672; \quad \sqrt{156.672} = 12.516$$

Step 8: Divide the numerator found in Step 1 by the outcome of Step 6 in order to obtain t.

$$t = 17.7 \div 12.516 = 1.414$$

Step 9: Consult Table A.3 with $N-2$ degree of freedom to obtain the critical value of t for p=.05.

From Table A.3 with 18 degrees of freedom, $t = 1.734$ for p=.05 (one-tailed). The calculated value of t is less than this and is therefore not significant. The means of the two conditions do not differ significantly.

Note

1. Compare the outcome of this analysis with the results of the Sign test, the Wilcoxon Rank Sum test, the Wilcoxon Signed Ranks Test and the related t test.
2. t may have a negative sign. This merely reflects which mean is the larger and does not affect the way you use the significance table.

The related t test

This tests whether the means of two related samples differ significantly, against the null hypothesis that they are the same. As it is a parametric test, it requires interval scale measurement and depends for its validity on the assumption that the differences between related scores are normally distributed. However, the test is robust enough to tolerate distinct violations of this assumption.

Formula:

$$t = \frac{\Sigma d}{\sqrt{\dfrac{n\Sigma(d^2) - (\Sigma d)^2}{n-1}}} \qquad df = n-1$$

where d = the difference between a pair of scores
n = the number of pairs of scores

Dealing with our model data

We can assume exactly the same design and a similar, one-tailed hypothesis as was described for the Sign test (see page 109), but here we

115

would make the assumption that our data were measured at the interval scale level and that the differences between score pairs were normally distributed. Thus:

Table 5.13

Condition I (45°)	Condition II (60°)	d
140	113	−27
134	100	−34
100	83	−17
79	39	−40
74	44	−30
63	64	+1
90	90	0
87	96	+9
69	78	+9
147	99	−48
		$\Sigma d = -177$

Calculation

Step 1: Find the differences between each pair of scores and add them together, taking their signs into account. This gives Σd. (If you have a one-tailed hypothesis, check that the sign of Σd is in line with it, otherwise the null hypothesis must be accepted at this stage).

See column headed 'd' above. (Σd is negative, which reflects the fact that scores in Condition II are generally lower, which is as predicted).

Step 2: Square all the differences and add up these squares. This gives $\Sigma(d)^2$, which must be multiplied by n.
$$\Sigma(d^2) = (-27)^2 + (-34)^2 + (-17)^2 \ldots + (-48)^2 = 7141;$$
$$7141 \times 10 = 71410$$

Step 3: Square Σd to obtain $(\Sigma d)^2$; subtract this from the outcome of Step 2.
$$(\Sigma d)^2 = (-177)^2 = 31329; \quad 71410 - 31329 = 40081.$$

Step 4: Divide the outcome of Step 3 by $n-1$ and find the square root of the resulting value.
$$40081 \div 9 = 4453.444; \quad \sqrt{4453.444} = 66.734$$

Step 5: Divide Σd (found in Step 1) by the outcome of Step 4 in order to obtain t.
$$t = -77 \div 66.734 = -2.652$$

Step 6: Consult Table A.3 with $n-1$ degrees of freedom to obtain the critical value of t for $p = .05$.

From Table A.3 with 9 degrees of freedom, $t = 1.833$ for $p = .05$ (one-tailed). The calculated value of t exceeds this and is therefore significant. The means of the two conditions differ significantly.

116

Note

1. The sign of *t* may sometimes be negative, as in this case. This merely reflects the nature of the difference scores, and does not affect the way you use the significance table.
2. Compare the outcome of this test with the results of the Sign test, the Wilcoxon Rank Sum test and the independent *t*-test. The outcome of this test is in fact that $p < .025$. This measures its power against its non-parametric counterparts, the Sign test and the Wilcoxon Signed Ranks test. It also demonstrates how, in a related measures design, more information is, as it were, given to the analysis. Its parametric counterpart, the independent *t* test, found no significant difference between the two conditions because it lacked this extra information.

The F test

This is the only test presented in this book which is concerned with differences in dispersion as opposed to differences in central tendency. It tests whether the variances of two samples differ significantly. It is a parametric test requiring interval scale measurement and it assumes that the data are from normally distributed populations. It is, however, robust and will tolerate distinct violations of this assumption. The null hypothesis would state that the variances are the same.

Formula

$$F = \frac{\sigma_A^2}{\sigma_B^2} \qquad \text{df } (n_A - 1) \text{ and } (n_B - 1)$$

where σ_A^2 and σ_B^2 = the variances of the two samples under comparison

n_A and n_B = the number of scores in Samples A and B

Dealing with our model data

Suppose we took the scores in the first two columns of our model data on page 108 and asked if their variances differed significantly. Thus:

Table 5.14

Sample A	Sample B
75	65
77	57
58	42
41	38
47	27
39	24
51	39
46	41
45	24
74	73

117

Step 1: Calculate the variances of both samples using the method described on page 98 but omitting Step 5.
$$\sigma_A^2 = 218.455; \quad \sigma_B^2 = 289.333$$

Step 2: In the case of a one-tailed hypothesis, divide the variance you predict to be larger by the variance you predict to be smaller to obtain F. In the case of a two-tailed hypothesis, divide the larger by the smaller variance to obtain F.

Here, we had no directional hypothesis therefore,
$$F = \frac{289.333}{218.455} = 1.324$$

Step 3: Consult Table A.4 with $(n_A - 1)$ and $(n_B - 1)$ degrees of freedom to obtain the critical value of F for $p = .05*$.

From Table A.4 with 9 and 9 degrees of freedom, $F = 4.03$ for $p = .05$ (two-tailed). Our calculated value is less than this and therefore the difference is not significant. The two variances do not differ significantly.

Note. The fact that the difference between two variances is not significant is no proof at all that they are the same. The null hypothesis exists solely to be disproved in a probabilistic fashion and is by its very nature incapable of proof. This test, therefore, must not be used to give positive support to the assumption of homogeneity of variance.

Spearman's Rank-Order Correlation Coefficient

This is a non-parametric correlation coefficient which applies when measures on both variables are ranked. It gives an estimate of Pearson's product-moment correlation coefficient, which is its parametric counterpart. The null hypothesis against which the coefficient is (most commonly) tested is that the population coefficient is zero.

Formula
$$r_s = 1 - \frac{6\Sigma(d^2)}{n(n^2 - 1)}$$

where d = the difference between a pair of ranks
n = the number of pairs of ranks

Dealing with our model data

We will treat the combined scores of the first two and the second two columns, and suppose that they represent the scores on a test that we had devised to measure people's motivation. We pilot the test on ten people to whom it is administered twice—the second occasion being six months after the first—because we wish to see whether their scores are consistent. If they are, we can conclude that our new test is *reliable,*

---

* In the case of a one-tailed test, the levels of significance shown in Table A.4 should be halved. Thus the 5% significance level should read 2.5%, and the 1% as 0.5%.

118

which is to say that it tends to produce similar results on each occasion that it is used. Thus:

Table 5.15

Initial Score		Score after 6 months		d	d²
140	(2)	113	(1)	1	1
134	(3)	100	(2)	1	1
100	(4)	83	(6)	2	4
79	(7)	39	(10)	3	9
74	(8)	44	(9)	1	1
63	(10)	64	(8)	2	4
90	(5)	90	(5)	0	0
87	(6)	96	(4)	2	4
69	(9)	78	(7)	2	4
147	(1)	99	(3)	2	4

$$\Sigma(d^2) = 32$$

Calculation

Step 1: Rank the scores separately on each variable. (You may do so from highest to lowest or vice versa as long as you treat each variable in the same way).
(Ranks are shown in brackets above, the highest scores on each variable having been given Rank 1).

Step 2: Find the differences between all pairs of ranks, disregarding their signs; square them, and add them up. This gives $\Sigma(d^2)$ which must be multiplied by 6.
(See column headed d above, and column headed d² above).
$$\Sigma(d^2) = 32; \quad 32 \times 6 = 192.$$

Step 3: Square n, the number of pairs of scores; subtract 1 and multiply the resulting value by n. $n^2 = 100; (100-1) \times 10 = 990$.

Step 4: Divide the outcome of Step 3 by the outcome of Step 4 and subtract the resulting value from 1 to obtain r_s.
$$192 \div 990 = 0.194; \quad r_s = 1 - 0.194 = 0.836$$

Step 5: Consult Table A.9 using n, the number of pairs of scores, to find the critical value of r_s for p = .05.
From Table A.9 for n = 10, r_s = .564 for p = .05 (one-tailed). Our calculated value exceeds this and is therefore significant. There is a significant positive correlation between the two sets of scores.

Note

1. r_s is significant beyond the .05 level—beyond even the .005 level.
2. We used a one-tailed test because our *implied* alternative hypothesis was that the scores would be positively related.
3. The fact that these scores correlate gives some account of why the

119

'difference' tests for related (i.e., correlated) samples detected significant differences between these two sets of values whilst the tests that assumed independence did not. (See the Wilcoxon Signed Rank test and related t-test, and the Wilcoxon Rank Sum test and independent t test. See also Pearson's Product-Moment Correlation Coefficient for these data.)

Pearson's Product-Moment Correlation Coefficient

This is a parametric correlation coefficient. It reflects the linear (i.e., 'straight line') relationship between two variables. It requires interval scale measurement and its significance can be tested if both variables are normally distributed and have equal variances. The null hypothesis against which the coefficient is (most commonly) tested is that the population coefficient is zero.

Formula

$$r = \frac{\Sigma N \Sigma (XY) - (\Sigma X)(\Sigma Y)}{\sqrt{[N \Sigma (X^2) - (\Sigma X)^2]\ [N \Sigma (Y^2) - (\Sigma Y)^2]}} \qquad df = N - 2$$

where X and Y = scores on the X and Y variables
N = the number of pairs of scores

Dealing with our model data
We can adopt the same data as for Spearman's r_s (see page 119) and also suppose that the same test of motivation is being assessed. On this occasion, however, we are making the assumption that the scores come from normally distributed populations with equal variances. (Incidentally, when the product-moment correlation coefficient is used for this purpose, it is known as a 'reliability coefficient').
Thus:

Table 5.16

Initial score (X)	X^2	Score after 6 months (Y)	Y^2
140	19600	113	12769
134	17956	100	10000
100	10000	83	6889
79	6241	39	1521
74	5476	44	1936
63	3969	64	4096
90	8100	90	8100
87	7569	96	9216
69	4761	78	6084
147	21609	99	9801
$\Sigma X = 983$	$\Sigma (X^2) = 105281$	$\Sigma Y = 806$	$\Sigma (Y^2) = 70412$

120

Calculation

Step 1: Multiply together each pair of scores and add up these products. This gives $\Sigma(XY)$, which is then multiplied by N.
$$\Sigma(XY)=(140\times113)+(134\times100)\ldots+(147\times99)=84276;$$
$$N\Sigma(XY)=10\times84276=842760$$

Step 2: Add up the scores on each variable to obtain ΣX and ΣY and multiply together these two totals. This gives $(\Sigma X)(\Sigma Y)$.
(See above for these two totals. $(\Sigma X)(\Sigma Y)=983\times806=792298$

Step 3: Subtract the outcome of Step 2 from the outcome of Step 1. This gives the numerator of the formula. (If you have a one-tailed hypothesis, check that the sign of this value is in line with the prediction. If not, the null hypothesis must be accepted at this stage).
$$842760-792298=50462$$
(We have predicted a positive relationship. The above value is positive, so we may continue).

Step 4: Square each value of X and add up these squares. This gives $\Sigma(X^2)$, which must be multiplied by N. Repeat this for the Y scores, too.
(See columns headed X^2 and Y^2 above).
$$N\Sigma(X^2)=10\times105281=1052810$$
$$N\Sigma(Y^2)=10\times70412=704120$$

Step 5: Square ΣX and subtract that from $N\Sigma(X^2)$; square ΣY and subtract that from $N\Sigma(Y^2)$.
$$(\Sigma X)^2=983^2=966289;\quad 1052810-966289=86521$$
$$(\Sigma Y)^2=806^2=649636;\quad 704120\ -649636=54484$$

Step 6: Multiply together the two values found in Step 5 and find the square root of their product. This gives the denominator of the formula.
$$86521\times54484=4714010184;\quad \sqrt{4714010184}=68658.48$$

Step 7: Divide the numerator found in Step 3 by the denominator found in Step 6 to obtain r.
$$r=50462\div68658.648=0.735$$

Step 8: Consult Table A.10 with $N-2$ degrees of freedom to find the critical value of r for $p=.05$.
From Table A.10 with 8 degrees of freedom, $r=.632$ for $p=.05$ (one-tailed). Our calculated value exceeds this and is therefore significant. There is a significant positive correlation between the two sets of scores.

Note. The value for this coefficient is less than that for Spearman's r_s. To understand why this has occurred, look at the third and the eighth pair of scores. The Spearman coefficient sees the discrepancy between the *ranks* of these score pairs as 2 in each case; the Pearson coefficient is

121

more sensitive and takes into consideration the fact that the 'real' discrepancies are not the same. In one case, the discrepancy is 27 and in the other 9. The Spearman coefficient, by taking into account only the rank position of each score, exaggerates the amount of agreement.

The Cochran test

This test applies when data in three or more related samples are measured at the nominal scale level. It can be thought of as the extension of the Sign test in that it deals with dichotomous measures and tests the null hypothesis that the two sides of the dichotomy are similarly represented in each sample. Here, however, the dichotomy is expressed as '1' or '0', rather than as '+' or '−' as is conventional in the case of the Sign test.

Formula

$$Q = \frac{(k-1)\{k\Sigma(T^2) - (\Sigma T)^2\}}{k\Sigma L - \Sigma(L^2)}$$
$$df = k - 1$$

where T = the total for a given condition
  L = the total for a given 'row'
  k = the number of conditions

Dealing with our model data

Let us assume that all these scores were split at the median (44.5) to produce scores which were classified as 'high' or 'low', or 'pass' and 'fail'. Suppose ten candidates had each taken a four-paper examination: 'pass' is indicated by 1, 'fail' by 0. We now have a nominal scale and there are more than two related samples. The appropriate analysis is Cochran's Q, if we wish to find whether the papers are not of equal difficulty.

Table 5.17

	Paper I	Paper II	Paper III	Paper IV	L	L^2
S_1	1	1	1	1	4	16
S_2	1	1	1	1	4	16
S_3	1	0	1	0	2	4
S_4	0	0	0	0	0	0
S_5	1	0	0	0	1	1
S_6	0	0	0	0	0	0
S_7	1	0	1	0	2	4
S_8	1	0	1	0	2	4
S_9	1	0	0	0	1	1
S_{10}	1	1	1	1	4	16
T:	8	3	6	3		

Calculation

Step 1: Add up all the 'ones' in each condition and find the sum of these

totals. This gives ΣT, which is then squared.
(The column totals are shown above).
$$T = 8+3+6+3 = 20; \quad (\Sigma T)^2 = 400.$$
Step 2: Square each column total and sum these squares. This gives $\Sigma(T^2)$.
$$\Sigma(T^2) = 8^2 + 3^2 + 6^2 + 3^2 = 118.$$
Step 3: Multiply $\Sigma(T^2)$ by k, the number of conditions, and from this subtract the outcome of Step 1.
$$118 \times 4 = 472; \quad 472 - 400 = 72.$$
Step 4: Multiply the outcome of Step 3 by $k-1$. This gives the numerator of the formula.
$$72 \times (4-1) = 216$$
Step 5: Add up all the 'ones' in each row and find the sum of these totals. This gives ΣL; which is then multiplied by k.
(The row totals are shown above).
$$\Sigma L = (4+4+2 \ldots +4) = 20; \quad 20 \times 4 = 80.$$
Step 6: Square each row total and sum these squares. This gives $\Sigma(L^2)$ (see column headed L^2 above)
$$\Sigma(L^2) = (16+16+4 \ldots +16) = 62.$$
Step 7: Subtract the outcome of Step 6 from the outcome of Step 5. This gives the denominator of the formula.
$$80 - 62 = 18.$$
Step 8: Divide the outcome of Step 4 by the outcome of Step 7 to obtain Q.
$$Q = 216 \div 18 = 12.00$$
Step 9: Because Q approximates closely to χ^2, consult Table A.2 with $k-1$ degrees of freedom to obtain the critical value of χ^2 for $p = .05$. From Table A.2 for 3 degrees of freedom, $\chi^2 = 7.82$ for $p = .05$.

Our calculated value exceeds this and is therefore significant. The performances on each paper differ significantly.

Note
This is an 'overall' analysis. It provides us with a general conclusion that subjects' performances on these papers are not the same. It does not, however, tell us which particular paper (or papers) differ from which other (or others).

The Kruskal Wallis test

This test applies to three or more samples of independent measures when data are at the ordinal scale level of measurement. It tests whether the sets of ranks differ significantly, against the null hypothesis that they are the same. This can be thought of as the extension of the Wilcoxon Rank Sum test to deal with cases involving more than two samples.

Formula:

$$H = \frac{12\Sigma\left(\dfrac{R^2}{n}\right)}{N(N+1)} - 3(N+1) \qquad\qquad df=(k-1)$$

where R = the sum of ranks in a given condition
       n = the number of scores in a given condition
       k = the number of conditions
       N = the total number of scores

Dealing with our model data

Suppose that these scores were obtained by 40 children who had been allocated at random to do four tests (A, B, C, D) which were supposed to be graded in order of difficulty from A (easiest) to D (most difficult). When the tests were completed we simply ranked the performances of all the children (the highest score being given Rank 1) to produce the following:

Table 5.18

Test:	A	B	C	D
	2	5	9	7.5
	1	7.5	16	13
	6	22	15	32
	24	28	38	40
	17	34	39	35
	26.5	36.5	30	33
	14	26.5	12	29
	18	24	10	24
	19.5	36.5	31	21
	3	4	11	19.5
R:	131	224	211	254

Calculation

Step 1: Rank all the measures from 1 to N, regardless of sample, giving tied scores an average rank. Then add up the ranks in each sample. This gives the values of R.

(Scores are already ranked above, and the sample totals (R) are shown).

Step 2: Square each value of R and divide by the number of measures it is based on. Add up the resulting values and multiply this by 12. This gives the denominator of the formula:

$$12\Sigma\left(\frac{R^2}{n}\right) = 12\left\{\frac{131^2}{10} + \frac{224^2}{10} + \frac{211^2}{10} + \frac{254^2}{10}\right\}$$
$$= 12 \times 17637.4 = 211648.8$$

Step 3: Add 1 to the total number of scores and multiply this by N. This gives the denominator of the formula which must be divided into the numerator found in Step 2.

$$N+1=41; \quad 41 \times 40 = 1640; \quad 211648.8 \div 1640 = 129.054$$

Step 4: Multiply $N+1$ by 3 and subtract this from the outcome of Step 3 to obtain H.

$$41 \times 3 = 123; \quad H = 129.054 - 123 = 6.054$$

Step 5: If the number of scores in the largest sample does not exceed 5, consult Table A.12 for the critical value of H for $p=.05$. Otherwise, treat H as if it were χ^2 and consult Table A.2 with $k-1$ degrees of freedom.

From Table A.2 with 3 degrees of freedom $\chi^2 = 7.82$ for $p=.05$. Our calculated value is less than this and is therefore not significant. The four tests do not differ significantly in difficulty.

Note
1. This is an 'overall' analysis which simply tells us whether the difference between the average ranks of each condition are big enough to be considered significant. It does not tell us which particular condition, or conditions, differ from which other, or others. Compare the outcome of this analysis with the Two-Way Analysis of Variance by Ranks and with Jonckheere's Trend test.
2. See Note 1 on the Wilcoxon Rank Sum test.

Friedman's Two-way Analysis of Variance by Ranks

This test applies to three or more samples of related measures when data are at the ordinal scale level of measurement. It tests whether the average ranks for each sample differ significantly, against the null hypothesis which states that they are the same. This can be thought of as an extension of the Wilcoxon Signed Ranks test to deal with cases involving more than two samples.

Formula:

$$X_r^2 = n(k-1)\frac{12\Sigma(R-\overline{R})^2}{n^2k(k^2-1)} \qquad df=(k-1)$$

where R=the rank total for a given sample
$\overline{R}$=the mean of the rank totals
which always equals $\dfrac{n(k+1)}{2}$
k=the number of samples
n=the number of scores in each sample

Dealing with our model data

Suppose that the same four tests were being used as in the case of the Kruskal Wallis test, but instead of forty subjects, only ten subjects were involved and they each did all four tests. The order in which they took the tests was randomized. We then ranked the scores of *each subject in turn* giving the highest scores Rank 1, to produce the following:

Table 5.19

Test:	A	B	C	D
S_1	1	2	4	3
S_2	1	2	4	3
S_3	1	3	2	4
S_4	1	2	3	4
S_5	1	2	4	3
S_6	1	4	2	3
S_7	2	3	1	4
S_8	2	3.5	1	3.5
S_9	1	3	3	2
S_{10}	1	2	3	4
R:	12	27.5	27	33.5

Calculation

Step 1: Rank the scores of each subject in turn, giving tied scores an average rank, then add up the ranks in each condition. This gives the values of R.

(Scores are already ranked above and the sample totals (R) are shown).

Step 2: Multiply (k+1) by n and divide this by 2 to obtain $\overline{R}$.
$$(4+1)10=50; \quad \overline{R}=50\div2=25$$

Step 3: Find the difference between $\overline{R}$ and each value of R; square these differences, add them up and multiply this by 12. This gives the numerator of the formula.
$$12\Sigma(R-\overline{R})^2=12\{(12-25)^2+(27.5-25)^2+$$
$$(27-25)^2+(33.5-25)^2\}=12\times251.5=3018$$

Step 4: Square n and multiply this by k; square k and subtract 1; multiply these two values together. This gives the denominator of the formula.
$$n^2k=10^2\times4=400; \quad (k^2-1)=4^2-1=15; \quad 400\times15=6000.$$

Step 5: Divide the outcome of Step 3 by the outcome of Step 4.
$$3018\div6000=0.503$$

Step 6: Multiply n by (k−1) and then multiply the outcome of Step 5 by this value to obtain χ_r^2.
$$10(4-1)=30; \quad \chi_r^2=30\times0.503=15.09$$

126

Step 7: Treating χ_r^2 as χ^2, consult Table A.2 with $k-1$ degrees of freedom for the critical value of χ^2 for p = .05.
From Table A.2 with 3 degrees of freedom, $\chi^2 = 7.82$ for p = .05. Our calculated value exceeds this and is therefore significant. The tests differ significantly in difficulty.

Note
1. This is an 'overall' analysis. It tells us whether the differences between conditions are large enough to be considered significant, but it does not tell us which particular condition, or conditions, differs significantly from which other, or others.
2. When $k = 3$ and n is less than 9 *or* when $k-4$ and n is less than 5, X_r^2 does not approximate too closely to χ^2 and Table A.2 should not be used. In these cases, take the value that is found in Step 5, treat it as W, and use Table A.11 instead. See also the note on p. 95.
3. Compare the outcome of this test with that of the Kruskal Wallis test, which found no differences between the conditions. The reason for this is that, here, we 'told' an analysis that the scores were related, row by row. We found a similar effect working in the two-sample tests, where the Wilcoxon Signed Rank test revealed a difference that the Wilcoxon Rank Sum test failed to detect. (See the note appended to those two tests).
4. Compare the outcome of this test also with that of Page's test for trend.

Jonckheere's Trend test

This test applies to three or more related samples when data are at the ordinal scale level of measurement. It tells us whether scores show a progressive increase or decrease across the samples. It involves what can be thought of as an extended one-tailed hypothesis and, because of that, you must predict *in advance* the direction of the trend, otherwise the test is not valid.

Formula
When sample sizes are equal, no formula is involved. All that is required is a counting process which is described below. See the note below for dealing with unequal sample sizes.

Dealing with our model data
We shall assume exactly the same design as was described for the Kruskal Wallis test, but here we shall suppose that the experimenter was not hypothesizing merely an overall *difference* between the tests but had formulated the rather more specific hypothesis that scores would get

127

progressively lower over the four tests. In this case, Jonckheere's test would be appropriate.

Table 5.20

Test:	A	B	C	D
	2	5	9	7.5
	1	7.5	16	13
	6	22	15	32
	24	28	38	40
	17	34	39	35
	26.5	36.5	30	33
	14	26.5	12	29
	18	24	10	24
	19.5	36.5	31	21
	3	4	11	19.5

(Your data may be in the form of ranks, as above, or remain as interval scale measures as our model data were. It is not necessary actually to rank them, for the counting process in effect does that for you. It is concerned only with whether one value is higher or lower than another).

Calculation

The counting procedure is determined by our hypothesis. Consider the sample on the extreme left. Our hypothesis in effect states that samples to the *right* of it will on average have lower scores in them. What we do, therefore, is tally the number of scores that are in line with our hypothesis.

This process involves comparing each individual score with every score in the other samples. We start with the first score in Test A and count how many scores in Test B are lower than that. The answer is that *ten* of them are. We then tally the number of scores in Test C that are lower than this first score in Test A. Again the answer is *ten*. Moving to Test D and making the same comparison, the answer is *ten*. So far the count is thirty.

We next consider the second score in Test A, and repeat the counting process. The third score is treated likewise and we continue until all the scores in Test A have been compared in this way with all the scores in the other tests. We then move to Test B, start with the first score there and go through the entire process again. Thence to Test C which is treated in the same way.

The sum of all the counts is P, and we consult Table A.13 with the appropriate values of k (the number of samples) and n (the number of scores per sample), to find whether it is significant.

For these data, the counts are as follows:

128

Table 5.21

											Total
Test A values	2	1	6	24	17	26.5	14	18	19.5	3	
No. of lower ranks in Test B.	10	10	8	5	7	4	7	7	7	10	75
No. of lower ranks in Test C.	10	10	10	4	4	4	6	4	4	10	66
No. of lower ranks in Test D.	10	10	10	5	8	5	8	8	7	10	81
Test B values	5	7.5	22	28	34	36.5	26.5	24	36.5	4	
No. of lower ranks in Test C.	10	10	4	4	2	2	4	4	2	10	52
No. of lower ranks in Test D.	10	9	6	5	2	1	5	5	1	10	54
Test C values	9	16	15	38	39	30	12	10	31	11	
No. of lower ranks in Test D.	9	8	8	1	1	4	9	9	4	9	62

Grand total, $P = 390$

From Table A.13 for $k = 4$ and $n = 10$ the critical value of P is 138 for $p = .05$. Our calculated value exceeds this and is therefore significant. There is a significant tendency to get progressively lower scores across the four tests.

Note
When sample sizes are unequal, the following formula must be used.

$$z = \frac{2P - \Sigma(n_i n_j) - 1}{\sqrt{\frac{1}{18}\{N^2(2N+3) - 3\Sigma(n^2) - 2\Sigma(n^3)\}}}$$

where n = the number of scores in a given sample
n_i and n_j = the number of scores in any two samples under comparison*
N = the total number of scores

Page's trend test

This test applies to three or more related samples when data are at the ordinal scale level of measurement. It tells us whether scores show a progressive increase or decrease across the samples. It involves what can be thought of as an extended one-tailed hypothesis and, because of that,

* For example, if three samples were involved containing 5, 6 and 7 scores, $(n_i n_j) = (5 \times 6) + (5 \times 7) + (6 \times 7)$.

you must predict *in advance* the direction of the trend, otherwise the test is not valid.

Formula

$$L = \Sigma(wR)$$

where R = the rank total for a given sample or condition
w = weights assigned to the conditions according to the hypothesized direction of the trend.

Dealing with our model data

We shall assume exactly the same design as was described for the Friedman Two-Way Analysis of Variance by Ranks, but here we shall suppose that the experimenter was hypothesizing not merely an overall *difference* between the tests, but had formulated a more specific hypothesis that scores would get *progressively lower* over the four tests. In this case, Page's test would be appropriate.

Table 5.22

Test	A	B	C	D
S_1	1	2	4	3
S_2	1	2	4	3
S_3	1	3	2	4
S_4	1	2	3	4
S_5	1	2	4	3
S_6	1	4	2	3
S_7	2	3	1	3
S_8	2	3.5	1	3.5
S_9	1	3.5	3.5	2
S_{10}	1	2	3	4
R:	12	27.5	27	33.5
weight (w):	1	2	3	4

Calculation

Step 1: Rank the scores of each subject in turn, giving tied scores an average rank, then add up the ranks in each condition. This gives the values of R.

(Scores are already ranked above and the sample totals (R) are shown).

Step 2: Assign a weight of one to the sample which is expected to contain the highest ranks, a weight of two to the sample expected to contain the next highest ranks, and so on until all samples have been weighted.

(Weights are shown above. Note that the highest ranks were expected for Test A, which has a weight of one. Do not confuse *ranks* and *numerical values*. Although 1 is the *highest* rank, *numerically* it is the lowest number).

130

Step 3: Multiply each rank total by its assigned weight and add up all these values. This gives L.

$$L = (12 \times 1) + (27.5 \times 2) + (27 \times 3) + (33.5 \times 4) = 279$$

Step 4: Consult Table A.14 using the number of conditions (k) and the number of subjects (n) to find the critical value of L for $p = .05$. From Table A.14 for $k = 4$, and $n = 10$, $L = 266$ for $p = .05$. Our calculated value of L exceeds this and is therefore significant. There is a significant tendency for scores to get progressively lower across the four tests.

Statistical tests—decision map

| | Tests of difference | | | | Tests of trend 3+ samples | | Measures of correlation |
| | 2 samples | | 3+ samples | | | | |
	Independent	Related	Independent	Related	Independent	Related	
NOMINAL	χ^2 (2 × 2) case	The sign test	χ^2 (r × k) case	Cochran's Q			
ORDINAL	Wilcoxon's rank sum test	Wilcoxon's* signed ranks test	The Kruskal Wallis test	Friedman's test	Jonckheere's test	Page's test	Spearman's r_s†
INTERVAL	Independent t-test	Related t-test					Pearson's product-moment correlation coefficient (r)

* The requirement of this test is that the differences between the pairs of measures must be able to be meaningfully ranked. This means that the raw data must be virtually at the interval scale level.

† r_s is an index of agreement between *two* sets of ranks. If you have more than two sets of ranks and want to obtain an index of agreement between them, Kendall's Coefficient of Concordance (W) can be calculated. W can adopt any value between zero and one, but cannot be negative, as r_s can be. To calculate W, use the first five steps of the calculation for Friedman's χ_F^2. The value obtained at the end of the fifth step is W. χ_F^2 in fact is equal to $Wn(k-1)$.

PSYCHOLOGY AS A NATURAL SCIENCE

This is, perhaps, not an ideal title for the Section, since human beings are at all times part of nature. But, conventionally, 'natural science' refers to non-human species. Here we group the study of the behaviour of such species, and also investigations of the physiological basis of behaviour. Both these can be, and are, studies in their own right. But they have also various applications to human beings.

In the case of physiology, it may be suggested that, in principle, every sort of behaviour must have a physiological substrate. In only some cases has it been possible to demonstrate that this is so. Much more is known, for example, about the physiological conditions of emotion than about those for intelligence. Even if all physiological conditions were known, however, it would be a reductionist fallacy to suppose that we would then have a complete explanation of behaviour.

Animals, apart from their intrinsic interest, may provide a more convenient population for some experiments than humans. The white rat in particular has often been used as a sort of test-tube in which it was hoped to study some basic mechanism of learning. Or it may be—especially with the ethological studies—that the other species offers a sort of model of the human, useful for suggesting hypotheses that can then be tested.

6 Physiological Studies I

SIMON GREEN

Physiological psychology is concerned with the relations between the observable behaviour of organisms and their physiological make-up. Psychology itself uses observable behaviour as its subject matter, and there is no reason why every psychologist should concern himself with physiology; in fact, many psychologists specifically reject any 'physiologizing' as the thin edge of the wedge of reductionism. Reductionism, briefly, is the attempt to explain phenomena by reducing them to their component parts; thus, in physics, the explanation of the behaviour of gases in terms of our knowledge of sub-atomic particles. But some are worried that the application of reductionism to psychology is leading to physiological explanations of behavioural phenomena which are somehow preferable to or more valid than psychological ones.

As physiological psychology is not yet sufficiently advanced to offer complete explanations of perception, memory, emotion, motivation, etc., in terms of brain mechanisms or hormonal levels, the argument is in one sense irrelevant, or, at least, anticipatory. A more constructive approach would be to accept that observable behaviour is the product of, or mediated by, the physiology of the organism; it has physiological correlates, which may be studied and which represent an alternative level of explanation to the psychologist's observations and measurements. A complete description and explanation of behaviour would, therefore, involve both psychological and physiological investigations.

135

The physiological psychologist is interested mainly in the nervous system. Although respiratory, circulatory, hormonal systems, etc., are also involved, the overall integration of stimuli and responses found in complex behaviour is achieved via the nervous system; and the specific structure to have attracted and held the imagination of physiological psychologists, neuro-psychologists, brain scientists, and philosophers generally, is the brain. Thus, most of this and the next chapter will be concerned with brain structure and function; but remember, the adjective is 'physiological', and a complete description of the physiological correlates of behaviour would have to go beyond the brain. It is this complete description that physiological psychology aims at.

Basic units and methods of study

The body is composed of millions of cells, organized into tissues and then into organs. Each cell is specialized for some function—hormone secretion, oxygen transport, filtration of waste matter, etc. All have many functions in common—they respire, metabolize, absorb nutrients, etc. We may therefore concentrate on what makes one cell different from another, rather than their common possession of basic structures such as nucleus and cytoplasm.

The unit of nervous system organization is the neuron. The unique feature of this cell is that it is specialized for electrical conduction along its length, by virtue of its electrically-excitable outer membrane. An impulse begins with stimulation of a dendrite, the fibre that carries activity towards the cell body; from the cell body, the impulse passes along the elongate axonal fibre, or axon, towards the next neuron.

Impulses are always carried from dendrite to cell body and outward along the axon. Each impulse, or action potential as the wave of electrical disturbance is called, is identical to every other impulse; i.e., if the original stimulus to the dendrite is sufficiently intense, an action potential is triggered on an all-or-none basis. The cell either fires or it does not fire. If the stimulation is prolonged, action potentials (or 'spikes') are repeatedly triggered, with a short delay in between to allow the neuronal membrane to recover.

Spiking frequency along the neuron may be of the order of hundreds per second. Variations in spiking patterns constitute 'information' for the brain—all our sensory, perceptual, meditative, experiences consist of spike discharges along neurons. That we can translate such simple patterns of electrical activity into our conscious experience is the problem of brain research.

The axon of one neuron connects with the dendrite of the next one in the pathway. The connection is not physical, as there is a minute gap between the two membranes, but chemical. The gap is termed the synapse. An action potential reaching the end of the axon (the pre-synaptic terminal) causes the release of a few molecules of chemical into the gap (the synaptic cleft). These molecules diffuse across the cleft and combine with receptor sites on the dendritic surface (the post-synaptic membrane). The combination causes a slight imbalance in the membrane's electrical properties.

If sufficient frequency of spikes reach the pre-synaptic terminal, enough chemical will be released to so disturb the post-synaptic membrane that an action potential is set off in the dendrite. Thus, information would have been transferred from one neuron to the next.

The chemicals are called synaptic transmitters, and some, such as noradrenaline, dopamine, and acetylcholine, we will be meeting later.

For now, I would emphasize that the transmission of information through the nervous system is electrical and chemical; electrical along the neuron, chemical at the synapse.

These properties immediately give us methods of looking into the brain's functioning. We may record gross electrical activity (the EEG, or electroencephalogram), which may correspond to general arousal state; we may record electrical responses to single stimuli (the visual or auditory evoked potential); we may record from single cells (particularly valuable for studying the visual system—see p. 148. On the other hand, we may use electrodes to stimulate activity artificially, thus, it is hoped, mimicking the brain's normal functioning.

On the chemical side, we can inject drugs known to have specific actions on synaptic transmitters, or we can measure levels of transmitters and try to correlate variations with variations in behaviour. Later, I talk at more length on the recent advances in brain chemistry, one of the more dramatic developments in brain research.

These rather more subtle techniques are now used in conjunction with the traditional approaches to manipulating the brain. These involve removing tissue via lesions, or ablations (which often involve removal of whole structures, and consequently are becoming relatively less common). Techniques used include intense electric current via electrodes implanted in the brain, direct knife-cuts in specific structures, or, more recently, use of rapid freezing or radio-active pellets. The trend, generally, has been towards more controlled and smaller lesioning techniques, in parallel with our increasing awareness of the brain's complexity.

Many of the methods mentioned above will crop up again during the next two Chapters. This will, it is hoped, show how useful they have been, and are still, to physiological psychology.

A note on terminology

Some terms will be met repeatedly. A few of the more important ones are listed below:

Fibres: axons or dendrites

Nerve: collection of axons and/or dendrites running to and from similar target areas, and bound together in a protective outer covering. Nerves may contain of the order of millions of fibres. In the central nervous system, the protective sheath is unnecessary, and such a collection is then termed a tract or pathway.

Ganglion: collection of cell bodies within a protective outer coat. The central nervous system parallel is a nucleus, a set of cell bodies in close proximity with no outer coat.

Afferent: conducting to a structure, often the brain, and therefore sometimes analagous to sensory.

Efferent: conducting from a structure. If referred to the brain, analagous to motor (i.e., leading to the effector organ of the S-O-R pathway).

Functional neuroanatomy

Experimental psychology assumes that responses are associated with stimuli, however complex that association may be (for instance, in human social interaction it is often impossible to specify the stimuli that produce a given verbal response). The simple, but useful, S-R (stimulus-response) model of behaviour, is best exemplified by the knee-jerk reflex in man, where a stimulus (tap, or hammer-blow, on the knee) evokes a response (knee-jerk) directly, with no intervening variables. It is also seen clearly in the behaviour of simple organisms: the earthworm contracts (response) to vibration (stimulus); the sea-hare withdraws its gills (response) to a jet of water (stimulus); the flatworm Planaria planorbius curls up (response) when given a mild electric shock (stimulus). It is also, incidentally, seen in phototropic plants, which grow (response) towards light (stimulus).

Simple organisms have been studied in physiological psychology because, although their nervous systems are rudimentary, they can exhibit comparatively complex behaviour, e.g., elementary forms of learning. When the S-R model is applied to this behaviour, the physiological correlates involved in the stimulus input and response output are to be sought in a finite nervous system, composed of a limited number of neurons.

138

When we look at the nervous system of primates, including man, we see the products of evolution; although pathways for stimulus input (sensory processes) and response output (motor processes) can still be identified, much of the nervous system cannot be classified as either sensory or motor. Instead of an S-R model, we need an S-O-R one, where O represents the organism generally; more specifically, at a psychological level O would represent intervening variables contributing to the response such as motivation, introversion-extraversion, emotional state, past experience etc., and at a physiological level millions of neurons in the central nervous system (CNS).

Besides this vast increase in the non S-R aspect of brain function, the stimulus and response pathways themselves have become many times more complex. From the simple sensory receptors of earthworm and sea-hare we move to the highly differentiated and specialized senses of the vertebrate, exemplified in the mammalian visual and auditory capabilities.

The significance of sensory evolution
The significance of this sensory evolution for brain structure and organization is two-fold. Firstly, the animal that has vision, that can perceive objects in three dimensions and in colour, needs more 'brain', or neural material, than the animal who has either no visual sense or a simple one, e.g., no three dimensional (depth) perception. (This point is elaborated later.) Secondly, these more specialized and valuable sensory processes became concentrated in that part of the body entering a new and possibly hostile environment first, i.e., the front, or anterior, end. The increase in neural material associated with these senses would then also, logically, be found at the anterior end of the nervous system, and this increase formed the basis of the evolutionary development of a brain at the head of a spinal cord, the basic organizational plan of the vertebrate nervous system. The gradual process by which a 'brain' evolved at the anterior end of the nervous system is termed 'encephalization'; the extremes would be represented by the nerve net of the flatworm, with no identifiable subdivisions beyond individual neurons, and the human nervous system, with its subdivisions both structural and functional. It is to these latter that we now turn.

The organization of the nervous system
The human nervous system is composed of approximately ten billion neurons. It has been idly calculated that if each neuron was represented by one hot dog (sausage plus surrounding bun), then the brain could be represented by the Colosseum in Rome packed with hot dogs, multiplied six-fold—a sobering thought.

Fortunately the organization of the nervous system lends itself to a

139

reasonably simple breakdown into its major components; these are presented below (Fig. 6.1):

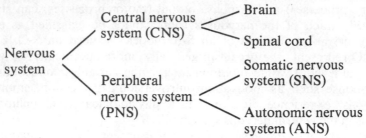

Fig. 6.1   Major components of the nervous system.

The peripheral nervous system (PNS)
The stimuli processed by the brain have to reach it. Messages from brain to effector (response) structures such as muscles and glands must have pathways to travel along. The PNS may therefore be seen as connecting the brain with sensory receptors on the one hand and effector structures on the other.

The division of the PNS into somatic (SNS) and autonomic (ANS) components is based upon environmental considerations. The SNS involves receptors dealing with external stimuli, and motor pathways controlling skeletal striped muscle, whose activation leads to movement (response) in or on that external environment. The ANS is a purely motor system, with efferent pathways controlling the smooth muscle of the gut and vascular system, glands such as sweat, salivary, and adrenal medulla, and the muscles of the heart. The effects of ANS activity are reflected in changes in the internal environment of the body, and are especially important in the study of emotional arousal.

The sensory side of the structures innervated by the ANS consists of the visceral afferent system of fibres, connecting receptors in internal organs with the CNS. Thus, we have two matched S-R networks for the external environment and the internal environment respectively.

The afferents and efferents of each network enter and leave the spinal cord via the spinal nerves. These are arranged in thirty-one pairs, one for each vertebra of the spinal column, and emerge between the vertebrae. The exact organization and distribution of the two systems is covered in any of the general references at the end of Chapter 7; for the present, we will consider each in a little more functional detail.

SOMATIC NERVOUS SYSTEM (SNS)

All movement involves the SNS as it involves skeletal muscle activity. The stimulus may be visual, auditory, smell, taste, pressure on the skin, heat, or cold, etc. A sensory receptor is stimulated, impulses pass along

140

the sensory afferent fibre into the CNS, where the motor response is integrated. Often, of course, movement is voluntary rather than reflexive, the stimulus being internal ('I shall climb the Eiger'); however, reflexive behaviour to sudden stimuli is common, and even complex responses like walking rely on continual sensory feedback from eyes and receptors in muscles and joints.

Some responses, such as the knee-jerk reflex, do not need the brain, only the spinal cord. We are aware if our knee is tapped; so information is passing into the spinal cord via the spinal nerve and then ascending to the brain. However, the reflex is still present in paraplegics (i.e., where the spinal cord has been severed), although the sensation is not; the ascending pathway has been cut, so the patient is unaware of the stimulus; but the S-R pathway is intact, so the motor response occurs. Simple reflexes have simple S-R pathways contained within the spinal cord; they do not need the brain to organize them. Complex behaviour utilizes the same sensory and motor pathways as do simple reflexes, but the brain mediates, integrates and organizes in between stimulus and response. We move from S-R to S-O-R.

AUTONOMIC NERVOUS SYSTEM (ANS)

The subjectively-felt correlates of 'fear' involve heart pounding, palms of the hands clammy with sweat, skin prickly, hair on end (piloerection), stomach churning, etc. These are responses controlled by the ANS.

The internal organs—intestines, blood vessels, heart, glands—for the most part function without our conscious awareness; activity is regulated, by the ANS, in accord with the homeostatic demands of the body (see p. 154), and independently of higher cognitive processes. We do not say 'heart-rate speed up, adrenal medulla release adrenaline' when we indulge in exercise or are subjected to emotion or stress; they occur automatically in response to situational demands.

The ANS has two sub-divisions, the sympathetic and the parasympathetic nervous systems. Internal structures are innervated by both sub-divisions, and, as a rather gross generalization, respond in opposite ways to each. Thus, sympathetic activity increases heart-rate, sweating, and blood-pressure, while decreasing intestinal motility; parasympathetic activity decreases heart-rate, sweating and blood-pressure, and increases motility of the digestive tract. Sympathetic dominance characterizes high-arousal situations, parasympathetic dominance characterizes low-arousal, non-stressful situations. Usually the two are in balance, but psychologists may manipulate stimuli to produce dominance of one or the other—usually sympathetic arousal.

The highest level of control of the ANS is at the levels of brainstem and hypothalamus. Nuclei within the brainstem control heart-rate, blood-pressure, and respiration (and therefore destruction of these via a bullet through the back of the mouth is much more effective than the classic self-destruction via gun to side of temple—this latter destroys the frontal lobes of the hemisphere and the visual pathways, but need not necessarily result in death), while centres within the hypothalamus produce an overall dominance of one sub-division or the other. Thus, electrical stimulation of the hypothalamus in the *ergotrophic* area results in a state of sympathetic arousal, while stimulation of the *trophotrophic* zone of the hypothalamus leads to parasympathetic dominance. Destruction of either will completely disrupt the body's autonomic balance.

Stimulation and lesions of the higher brain structures of the telence-phalon may also affect autonomic regulation. However, these effects are probably mediated by pathways to the hypothalamus; modulation of hypothalamic activity by higher centres is a feature of the brain's organization, and one to which we return when considering homeo-stasis and motivation.

Central nervous system (CNS)
The brain itself may be divided into literally hundreds of nuclei, tracts, cortical areas, etc. Many of these are, as yet, of purely neuroanatomical interest, in the sense that their psychological relevance has not been determined. A more functional approach would pick out those structures and areas most commonly encountered within physiological psy-chology; these are outlined below (Fig. 6.2).

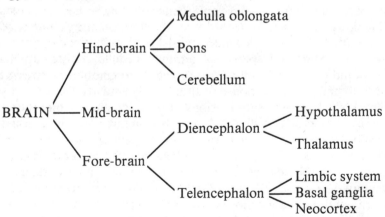

Fig. 6.2 Areas of the brain of importance to physiological psychology.

The fore-brain contains the most recently evolved structures, in which reside the complex behavioural functions typical of advanced mammals, such as memory, emotion, problem-solving, etc. Language, that most distinctively human capability, is mediated by areas of the neocortex. This structure is found in a rudimentary form in reptiles and birds, and

142

increases in amount relative to total brain weight as one ascends the phylogenetic scale. The position of man at the head of the scale correlates with his possession of the most highly developed neocortex; whale and elephant have larger brains, but man has a larger proportion of neocortex (for further discussion of this area, see Chapter 7).

Memory, emotion and cognition, are not essential for life. Amoeba cannot be said to possess any of these in abundance, and yet lives perfectly adequately, moving, respiring, ingesting, reproducing, etc. From the reverse angle, higher primates, including man, may possess complex cognitive abilities, but still need to respire, maintain blood-pressure and body-temperature etc. Thus there is an obvious distinction between 'essential' functions, and 'non-essential' functions which do, however, define what we mean by 'higher', or 'complex', animal behaviour.

This distinction is also represented neuroanatomically. Essential functions tend to be concentrated in hind- and mid-brain, and in the diencephalon of the fore-brain. Non-essential functions are found in the fore brain. What this implies is that damage to the fore-brain tends to be less harmful than damage to hind-brain structures. In a condition known as 'anencephaly', the fore-brain in its entirety fails to develop in the fetus, and yet the newly-born baby will survive for some hours.

This is not to imply that the structures controlling 'essential' functions are independent of those controlling 'higher' ones; each of the ten billion neurons in the brain has in the order of a thousand synaptic connections each with other neurons, and this degree of inter-connectivity means that no one part of the brain is entirely separate from any other. One aspect of brain function, to be emphasized further in the part of this chapter on Homeostasis, is that of 'higher' structures—those appearing later in evolution—controlling or 'modulating' more primitive areas. An example of this is the observation that it is much easier to elicit a rage response in cats who have no neocortex. Normally, it appears, the neocortex has an inhibitory influence over feline emotional response, although not actually necessary for the response itself to occur.

We will meet most of the fore-brain structures listed in Figure 6.2 later, so their functional significance will not be described at present.

As implied above, the hind-brain contains structures essential for behaviour to occur. Nuclei are found in medulla, pons and also the mid-brain, controlling respiration, blood-pressure, heart-rate, and other primarily autonomic functions. Major parts of the medulla, pons, and mid-brain are given over to fibres and tracts ascending and descending between spinal cord and brain, and, in fact, cross-sections through these three structures do resemble those through the spinal cord; so much so, that the three have been classified together as the 'brain-stem', effectively a continuation of the spinal cord within the brain (see Fig. 6.3).

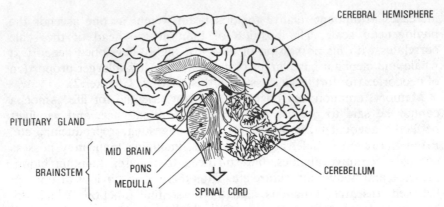

Fig. 6.3 Midline section through the brain.

However, the brain-stem does contain one structure of immense functional importance for behaviour, and that is the 'reticular formation' (RF). This reticulum, or net, of vastly interlaced and interwoven neurons occupies the core of the brain-stem, and conveys impulses via ascending pathways to fore-brain areas; these ascending influences from the RF are a major contribution to the maintenance of 'arousal' or 'activation' in the brain, and will be further discussed in the next part of the chapter.

The cerebellum stands dorsal to the brain stem. It is a large organ (approximately 10 per cent of brain weight), of distinctive structure (see Fig. 6.3). The major part of its functions relate to the integration and patterning of motor responses, involving a subtle interplay of those ascending and descending pathways controlling limb movement and position in space. This integration is carried out in co-operation with other brain structures, particularly neocortical areas and the reticular formation; it is especially sophisticated in animals, such as cats, which exhibit supreme control in locomotory behaviour.

This part of the chapter has provided an overview of the brain's organization, and a more detailed, but still brief, description of hind-brain structures and their function. We now move on to more specialized topics, which will involve a closer examination of fore-brain areas.

Sensory processes

We have considered some of the behavioural processes involving central nervous system structures. Any consideration of behaviour must take as given the passage of information into the CNS; emotion, hunger, thirst all assume normal functioning of visual, olfactory, gustatory systems, etc. In mapping the psychologist's S-O-R model on to the nervous system, our emphasis on the 'O' must not disguise the reliance of all behaviour on stimulus input, on sensory processes.

The world we behave in, the subjective reality of our own experience, the stimuli which can be shown to be relevant to the rat, are all defined by the properties of the appropriate nervous systems. We cannot be aware of or respond to any stimulus that is not accessible to our nervous system; each of our senses has a range of sensitivities beyond which stimuli exist (e.g., ultrasonic sounds), but of which we are unaware as they do not induce electrical change in sensory afferent fibres.

Classification

Our sensory systems may be classified in various ways. All possess sensory receptors, specialized to convert various forms of stimulus energy into electrical activity in a sensory neuron; they are transducers, converting mechanical, thermal, chemical, air-pressure, or light stimuli into a common form that the nervous system can handle.

The receptors may deal with external stimuli (exteroceptors, such as those for vision, hearing, taste, smell, heat and cold, and touch), or with internal stimuli (interoceptors, such as those for internal sensations of pressure and pain, and those in limb joints and tendons). They may be activated by mechanical deformation (mechanoreceptors, such as auditory and pain receptors) or by chemical interaction (chemo-receptors, e.g., taste and smell). There are, therefore, several ways of approaching their study, and we shall use one of the more common ones.

This involves a division of the sensory systems into those dealing with complex environmental stimuli, such as sight, hearing, taste, and smell, and those, rather less specialized, dealing more with our own body; these latter include the proprioceptive, or skin, senses of pressure, warmth, cold, and pain, and the kinaesthetic sensory systems, dealing with body and limb movement and position in space. Proprioception and kinaesthesis together comprise the somatosensory system.

Here, I shall briefly summarize some features of somatosensation. This will be followed by a similar review of hearing, taste, and smell; and, finally, I shall consider the visual system in detail.

Somatosenses

PROPRIOCEPTORS

Our skin is sensitive to touch or pressure, temperature, and painful stimuli. Precisely which receptors relate to which stimuli has not yet been fully determined. Do heat and cold affect two different receptors? How is pain produced by intense stimulation of almost any sensory modality?

Several types of receptor have been identified in the skin. Free nerve endings—basically unspecialized axonal processes—are most common and these are thought to mediate sensations of pain, warmth, and cold.

145

A few types of more specialized receptors also exist, such as Pacinian corpuscles and Krause end bulbs. These more complex structures respond to the mechanical deformation induced by touch or pressure on the skin.

One of the difficulties in the study of the cutaneous senses is that areas of the skin exist with only free nerve endings, but from which the whole range of sensation may be elicited. This phenomenon may relate to an alternative division of proprioception into epicritic and protopathic sensation. *Epicritic sensations* include specific touch and pressure on the skin, and are thought to involve the more complex receptors. *Protopathic sensation* consists of diffuse touch and pressure and pain, and involves free nerve endings. This division is also related to the somatosensory pathways into the CNS; the sensory fibre passes from the cutaneous receptor to the spinal cord, within which there are specific pathways carrying somatosensation up to the brain. Epicritic and protopathic pathways appear to follow slightly different routes within the somatosensory system.

Like the rest of the sensory systems, except perhaps olfaction, the somatosensory pathways, after ascending the spinal cord, synapse within the thalamus. Then their route lies from the thalamus to the somatosensory cortex of the post-central gyrus in the parietal lobe. Here, the highest level of analysis of cutaneous stimuli occurs, and where damage or electrical stimulation has predictable consequences for proprioception.

KINAESTHESIS

Movement is a sophisticated process. We take our fairly automatic regulation of body position and movement for granted; however, a momentary consideration of how any movement depends on our knowing where the limb is to begin with, and where it is at any particular time during the action (otherwise how do we know when to stop?). A constant interplay of motor response and sensory feedback underlies even the scratching of a nose, especially if it is not yours.

The sensory receptors involved in movement concentrate, quite logically, in muscles and joints. Stretch receptors in skeletal muscle and in tendons respond to changes in muscle length; receptors within the joints report amounts and direction of limb movement.

Muscles and joints, like most of the internal organs, also contain free nerve endings and various corpuscular receptors. These mediate the sensations of pain and pressure, heat and cold, from the structures they serve.

Before leaving kinaesthesis, mention must be made of the vestibular system. This involves a receptor complex situated within the inner ear, and concerned specifically with the position of the head in space. Our

146

eyes and ears are paired structures whose horizontal alignment is essential to our normal perceptual orientation in space; their positioning depends upon the head and, therefore, the vestibular system. The physiology of the actual receptor complex is too involved to be adequately summarized.

Hearing

The ear is fundamentally a mechanoreceptor, responding to rapid variations in air pressure; these variations must be of the order of fifteen to 20 000 per second to be effective in generating a receptor potential. The receptor is hugely complicated, possessing three units of varying sophistication: the external ear canal leading to the tympanic membrane (or ear drum); the middle ear, with its three small bones (or ossicles) connecting the tympanic membrane at one end to the membrane covering the entrance to the inner ear at the other; and the inner ear, containing the cochlear apparatus (Fig. 6.4).

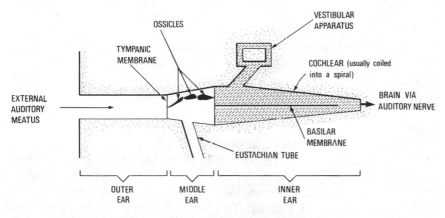

Fig. 6.4 Diagrammatic representation of the human ear.

Sounds vibrate the tympanic membrane. The vibration is transmitted via the ossicles to the inner ear. The cochlear is fluid-filled, and contains several stretched membranes which are differentially vibrated by pressure waves in the fluid generated by the original sound. Hair-cell receptors are stimulated by movement of the basilar and tectorial membranes, and generate potentials in the afferent fibres of the auditory nerve.

Although apparently unnecessarily involved, the system is highly efficient; very good hearers can detect the random movement of air molecules under ideal conditions. In other organisms, the range of sensitivity is very different, reflecting alternate life-styles; the cat can detect up to around 70 000 vibrations per second (frequency is measured

147

in cycles per second, or hertz. 70 000 vibrations per second is therefore 70 000 Hz, or, as 70 kilohertz, 70 kHz), and the bat up to 100 kHz.

The auditory pathway, after several relays, eventually runs via the thalamus to the auditory cortex in the temporal lobe. Here, the processing of sound sensation into auditory perception of speech, music, etc., occurs. As a point of general interest, especially for dichotic listening studies in the psychology of attention, the auditory pathways are predominantly crossed; the left ear projects predominantly to the right hemisphere, and the right ear to the left hemisphere.

As with the vestibular system, to which it is anatomically closely related, further detail on the neurophysiology and psychophysics of the auditory system may be obtained from the references quoted later.

Taste

Taste (gustation) and smell (olfaction) are chemical senses. To be effective, molecules of a given stimulus must be dissolved in solution and interact directly with a receptor molecule; conformational changes then generate the receptor potential in the afferent neuron.

There are few basic tastes—bitter, sweet, salt and sour. They are mediated by around 10 000 taste buds, mostly on the tongue but also on palate and pharynx. These receptors group around the papillae, small protuberances on the tongue; our sensations of taste then reflect patterns of activation of the four different types of taste bud.

Smell

Effective olfactory stimuli must dissolve in the mucous lining at the top of the nasal cavity, where the olfactory receptors are situated. It seems probable that a molecular interaction must occur between stimulus molecule and receptor molecule, to generate the receptor potential that leads to sensory neuron activity. The details, however, are less clear than for gustation. It is known that a few hundred molecules can be an adequate stimulus, even in man, who is not renowned for his olfactory prowess. We are much better smellers than tasters.

Vision

Man is very much a visual animal. Although not at the top—we would have trouble spotting a mole from 500 feet up in the air—it is the sense we rely on most, and this is reflected in the complex anatomical and neurophysiological bases of visual sensation and perception.

Before launching into the visual system, a note on sensation and perception is called for. There is no easy distinction between the two, as they relate to level of processing of stimulation. Sensation is more related to the immediate experience of the stimulus, perception to later products of cortical analysis. Do we perceive touch or cold, or are they pure

148

sensations? Do we sense a flash of light, and perceive a sofa? The argument is insoluble, but the visual system, with its multiple processing levels, may lend light to it.

Photic energy is focused by the cornea and lens onto the retina at the back of the eye. The retina is a layered structure (Fig. 6.5), with the visual receptors connecting to bipolar cells, and bipolar cells to ganglion cells. The axons of ganglion cells form the optic nerve.

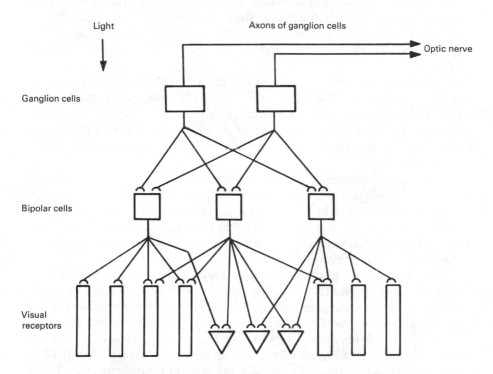

Fig. 6.5   Cell layers of mammalian retina. (Note convergence of many receptors onto few ganglion cells, and overlap of connections.)

Visual receptor cells are of two sorts, rods and cones. In either case, light striking a receptor initiates a chemical change within the cell, which in some, as yet unknown, way produces an electrical potential. The difference between the receptors hinges on the chemicals they contain. Rods contain rhodopsin, a visual pigment which breaks down on exposure to light into retinene and opsin; cones contain iodopsin, which is broken down to retinene and photopsin. The visual pigments in both cases are re-synthesized under appropriate conditions.

The functional difference between rods and cones is that rods are specialized for vision in dim light, and cones for high acuity and colour

149

vision which require relatively more intense light. In normal daylight vision, rods are inactivated, bleached by the bright light such that their rhodopsin is in a permanently broken down state. If you pass from daylight into gloom, the phase of adjustment everyone experiences reflects the re-synthesis of rhodopsin in the rods, necessary before they can function.

In the eye, there are around 125 million rods and only six million cones. The cones are concentrated in the fovea, that area of the retina which is the centre of the visual field (the region we see most clearly when we view an object). As we move peripherally across the retina, fewer cones are encountered, and the periphery is exclusively composed of rods.

There are 131 million receptors in the retina, but only around one million optic nerve fibres. Thus, there has to be massive integration and channeling of information from receptors to nerve fibres. In the fovea, the ratio is round 1:1, accounting for the high acuity of cone vision, but elsewhere in the retina one optic nerve fibre is connected to many receptors.

This retinal processing of visual input is beyond the scope of this Chapter. I will just emphasize that the layers of bipolar and ganglion cells, connected and interconnected horizontally and vertically by the amacrine cells, are designed to enable electrical activity in the optic nerve fibres functionally to represent activation of the visual receptors, despite the great convergence from receptors to nerve.

The visual pathways from retina to visual cortex in the occipital lobe (Fig. 6.6) are straightforward. The optic nerve passes through the optic chiasma and synapses on cells in the lateral geniculate nucleus (LGN) of the thalamus. These LGN cells then project to visual cortical cells in Area 17 of the occipital. Surrounding this primary receiving area are secondary and tertiary visual processing regions in Areas 18 and 19 of the occipital lobe; when we consider the perception of form, we will see how visual stimuli appear to be serially processed through each of the cortical areas in turn, with a progressive increase in complexity.

As Figure 6.6 shows, our visual pathway is partially crossed, in that half the fibres from one eye decussate at the optic chiasma over to the other side of the brain, and project finally to the contralateral visual cortex. Notice that it is the fibres from that half of the retina nearest the nose (the nasal hemiretina) that decussate, while the other half project from the temporal hemiretina to the ipsilateral ('same-side') visual cortex. As the visual fields of our eyes have substantial overlap (close each eye rapidly in succession and see how similar the view is), it is clear that some cells in the cortex will receive information about the same point in the visual field from both eyes; the integration of the input from the two eyes is an important factor in our binocular depth perception.

150

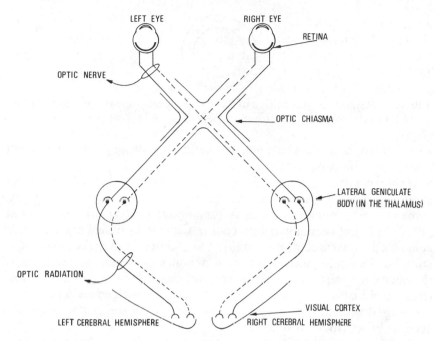

Fig. 6.6   Optic nerve and optic radiation from retina to visual cortex.

Receptive fields and form perception

The technique used in analysing the neurophysiological basis of visual perception revolves around the 'receptive fields' of various cells. Receptive field refers to an area of the retina, stimulation of which by tiny points of light elicits a response in a given fibre or cell. By plotting and comparing the receptive fields of ganglion cells, LGN cells, and neurones in the various cortical processing areas, a picture has been built up of how feature detection—the perception of form—occurs in the visual system.

In 1953, Kuffler identified what has since been established as the most basic type of receptive field in the mammalian visual system. He recorded from retinal ganglion cells (and would have obtained similar results from optic nerve fibres, as these are the axons of ganglion cells), and showed that their receptive fields consisted of concentric rings; a central circular area and a surround, each containing many receptors. A maximal 'on' response was obtained from the ganglion cell when a light stimulus exactly filled the centre area of its receptive field; response ceased if the stimulus moved to the surround area. The cell could, therefore, be classified as a centre-on, surround-off responder (Fig. 6.7).

The opposite arrangement of these concentric receptive fields has also been found—centre-off, surround-on—and in both cases a light

151

Fig. 6.7   Retinal receptive fields of cat ganglion cell—centre-on, surround-off
type.

stimulus covering the whole field evokes no response; positive and negative stimulation cancels out.

Until recently, it had been thought that mammalian retinal processing,
shown by ganglion cell receptive fields, was elementary compared to
some non-mammalian systems. A remarkable analysis by Lettvin *et al.*
(1959–1961) of retinal ganglion cells in the frog identified five classes of
cells, each responding maximally to a different and complex light
stimulus; examples include cells responding to a general dimming of
illumination, cells responding to well-defined boundaries between
objects, and cells responding to moving, curved, dark edges. These latter
are best stimulated by a small spot, moving jerkily across the retina, and
seem to be specific 'bug detectors'.

Such visual processing seems analogous to what the mammalian
cortex does, rather than the mammalian retina, and in primates this
certainly seems the case even now. However, Levick (1967) and Cleland
and Levick (1974) claim to have discovered equally sophisticated
processing in the retinal ganglion cells of rabbit and rat; and it may be
that all visual systems incorporate a substantial amount of peripheral
processing.

To return to our basic mammalian concentric receptive fields, Hubel
and Wiesel (1959), in a series of classic investigations, determined that
the receptive fields of visual cortical cells in the cat were elongate; the
most effective stimuli were lines or edges, often of specific orientations. It
appeared that 'simple' cells of the primary receiving area responded best
to a line of specific orientation on a specific part of the retina; 'complex'
cells of the secondary visual cortex responded to lines of a specific
orientation anywhere on the retina; and 'hypercomplex' cells of the
tertiary region responded similarly, but only to lines of a specific length.
This latter region also contains cells which seem to respond to specific
angles between lines and to specific movements.

How do the spots of light to which retinal ganglion cells respond
become the lines to which cortical cells are best adapted? The answer
involves a continuation of the convergence of information from visual
receptors to optic nerve mentioned earlier.

Ganglion cells project to LGN cells, which also passes concentric
receptive fields. A group of LGN cells, however, projects to a single

simple cortical nerve; the LGN cells represent receptive fields on the retina which lie in a straight line. Given some degree of overlap, we can see (Fig. 6.8) how a *bar* of light on the retina most effectively stimulates the field centres, while avoiding the antagonistic surrounds. For this group of LGN cells—and also the single cortical cell which receives their input—the best stimulus is of line shape, and of a specific orientation to match the line of receptive field centres on the retina.

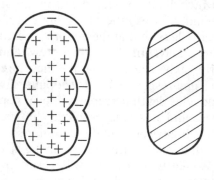

Fig. 6.8   Overlapping retinal fields produce receptive field of visual cortical cell. Most effective light stimulus = line-shape.

If a complex cell receives its input from a number of simple cells, all of which respond to lines of specific orientation on different parts of the retina, it will respond to such a line anywhere on the retina. Finally, the input of many complex cells can explain the more sophisticated functions of the hypercomplex visual cortical neurons.

It appears that lines, edges, angles, and orientations are the basis of mammalian form perception, although their integration into subjective visual perception is still very much a mystery. Perception also involves depth, colour, and movement, which we will not discuss here; and there are still major areas in vision research about which we know little. We have emphasized serial processing through the visual pathways, but it is clear that parallel processing may occur, with hypercomplex cells receiving inputs directly from both LGN and simple cells. Cortical cells also project downwards (efferent pathways) to superior colliculus and the opposite hemisphere via the corpus callosum. The superior colliculus is of major importance in the control of eye movements, receiving input directly from the optic nerve and projecting back to eye muscles.

Combine these findings with known and predicted species differences and it is clear that vision research is, as they say, ongoing. But the classic studies of Kuffler, Lettvin, and Hubel and Weisel still serve as a more than adequate basis for future investigations.

Early experience and the visual system

Over the last seven or eight years, a series of studies, beginning in 1970 with Blakemore and Cooper in England and Hirsch and Spinelli (1971) in the USA, have shown that early visual experience may greatly influence the properties of the mature visual system. It is clear that in the normal cat visual cortex cells are 'orientation-selective'—they respond maximally to lines of specific orientation on the retina. This orientation selectivity can be modified or abolished by early experience.

Blakemore and Mitchell (1973) reared cats in the dark. Exposure to a vertically striped cylinder for as little as one hour at about four weeks of age modified cortical cells such that the majority were selectively responsive to vertical lines only. In 1973 Pettigrew and Freeman found evidence that early experience without lines prevents orientation selectivity or even line-responsivity developing. Even more general features such as binocular depth perception appear dependent upon early binocular experience, and it seems probable that visual perception in mammals is very much environmentally determined. This, of course, is highly adaptive, in that one's early environment is usually one's later environment, and so early moulding will result in a visual system maximally geared to environmental contingencies.

Homeostasis

Homeostasis is the physiologists' term for the way the body regulates its 'internal environment'. This latter concept was introduced by Claude Bernard in the middle of the 19th century, and represents the totality of bodily activities contributing to the overall physiological state of the organism. It therefore includes blood-pressure, temperature, concentration of salts, ions, and metabolites both inside and outside cells, levels of blood oxygen and carbon-dioxide, etc.; it involves the activity of digestive, cardiovascular, respiratory, and hormonal systems, to name but a few. Homeostasis, meaning 'uniform state', was coined by Cannon in the 1920s to represent the maintenance by the organism of a relatively constant internal environment.

The relevance of this physiological concept to psychology is in terms of what makes animals behave at all, i.e., motivation. Any form of behaviour depends upon the production of energy from food; constant behaviour needs a constant supply of energy, which would rapidly deplete the body's reserves. However, the level of the body's food reserves, e.g., carbohydrates and fat, is homeostatically controlled, such that a departure from the 'maintained' level leads to the sensation of hunger and the search for food. Thus, food-seeking behaviour is motivated, or directed, by homeostatic mechanisms.

This simple model may be applied to other areas of behaviour, such as

154

drinking by thirsty rats or lying in the shade on a hot day; responses designed to maintain homeostasis, and induced by a change in the internal environment. In the influential theory of learning put forward by Hull in the 1940s, these homeostatically-based drives play a major role: not only does a change in body fluid balances lead to a thirst drive and consequent water-seeking behaviour, but the alleviation of the internal water-shortage functions acts, quite naturally, as a powerful reward for the animal. In Hullian terms, behaviour leading to drinking reduces the original drive; animals find drive-reduction rewarding, and all learning is based on drive-reduction. It is not the present purpose to describe Hull's attempt to explain all animal learning—even human complex problem solving—in terms of satisfying homeostatic drives; suffice it to say that, although now seen to be massively over-ambitious, it has left, at the very least, an awareness that much of animal behaviour is devoted to maintaining homeostasis, and that the most effective learning occurs when a hungry or thirsty animal is rewarded with food or water.

Before considering the homestatic drives of hunger and thirst in more detail, the overall regulation of homeostasis will be discussed.

The internal environment is the province, in the main, of the autonomic nervous system and the endocrine system. The ANS has already been briefly described and the endocrine system is about to be discussed, but mention must be made at this stage of the hypothalamus in connection with both.

The hypothalamus lies at the base of the brain in the diencephalon. In weight, it represents about 0.3 per cent of the brain (4 g) only, and yet may be divided into twenty-two anatomically identifiable nuclei; even functionally, between six and ten major groupings are accepted. So, despite its small size, the hypothalamus has the complex organization necessary for a structure that has immediate control over both autonomic and endocrine systems.

This control may be demonstrated in various ways. As previously mentioned, autonomic functioning depends upon the integrity of trophotropic and ergotropic regions of the hypothalamus. Hormonal and autonomic responses to stress and emotion, be they vasodilation, increased blood-pressure, release of adrenaline and ACTH (see p. 183), piloerection, sweating, etc., rely on an intact hypothalamus; removal of the hypothalamus destroys the integration, patterning, or appropriateness, of such responses. Thus, an integrated and directed rage response may be elicted from a cat with no fore-brain structures except the hypothalamus; remove this, and the response becomes fragmented and undirected.

To simplify, the hypothalamus, although it may be overridden or modulated by higher centres, is capable of maintaining control over those 'essential' functions necesary for homeostatic regulation. It is the highest representative of what might be called 'primitive' brain structures, as opposed to the more advanced areas of the fore-brain mediating 'higher' functions.

To perform its functions, the hypothalamus has two main efferent pathways. One is via nerve tracts descending through the brainstem to autonomic control centres in the pons, medulla, and spinal cord. The other is via the infundibulum, or pituitary stalk, and from there to the pituitary gland (see Fig. 6.9). It is to this latter structure we now turn.

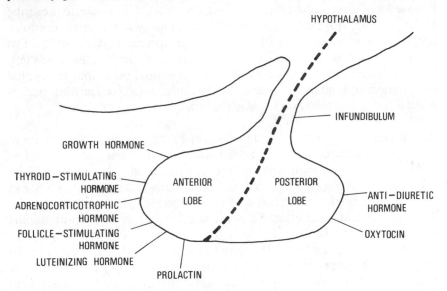

Fig. 6.9   The pituitary gland and its hormones.

The pituitary gland

The pituitary is the most important component of the endocrine system of ductless glands. The importance of the system generally is encapsulated in a listing of other components; for instance, the adrenal cortex, the thyroid gland, and the gonads. All these structures secrete chemicals, known as hormones, into the circulation system; each hormone, be it thyroxin, progesterone, growth hormone, or oxytocin, has a target organ upon which it has a profound and sustained effect.

It should be noted that the chemical neurotransmitters of the nervous system are occasionally referred to as neuro-hormones, or neuro-humors. However, their relatively brief period of action and the close proximity of secretory and target zones make similarities with hormones purely technical; they do not come within the scope of endocrinology.

The pituitary gland is the master gland of the body. It releases a number of hormones, a few of which act directly on target structures,

156

but most of which are involved in the control of other glands. Thus, release of thyroxin from the thyroid gland, cortisol or corticosterone from the adrenal cortex, and oestrogens or androgens from the gonads, all depend upon prior stimulation by pituitary hormones. Damage to the pituitary gland produces atrophy of thyroid, adrenal cortex, gonads, liver, and kidneys, all of which may be reversed by injection of pituitary gland extract.

I hope it is now clear that the body's metabolism is dependent upon endocrine function in general, and upon the pituitary gland in particular. But there is, as implied earlier, a yet higher level of endocrine regulation residing in the hypothalamus. How is this exercised?

Figure 6.9 shows diagrammatically the pituitary gland and its hormones, and the close anatomical correspondence of pituitary and hypothalamus. Via the infundibulum, blood vessels and neuronal processes interconnect them, and provide the basis for hypothalamic regulation of pituitary function.

The posterior lobe of the pituitary—the neurohypophysis—releases, as shown, anti-diuretic hormone (or vasopressin) and oxytocin. It is now thought that these hormones are manufactured in hypothalamic cells and transported intracellularly to the neurohypophysis, where they are stored prior to release. So they are, in a sense, hypothalamic rather than pituitary hormones.

The anterior lobe—the adenohypophysis—does not have direct neural connections with the hypothalamus. Instead, they are linked via a system of blood vessels which transport 'releasing factors' manufactured in the hypothalamus down to target cells within the adenohypophysis. Each hormone released by the anterior pituitary into the circulation has a specific hypothalamic releasing factor; the terminology is logical and clumsy, producing, for instance, growth-hormone releasing factor and thyroid-stimulating hormone releasing factor (TSH RF)!

So the pituitary gland, or hypophysis, is directly under the control of the hypothalamus via their neural or vascular interconnections, and this regulation of endocrine function, when combined with hypothalamic control of the autonomic nervous system, gives this tiny brain structure its pre-eminence in homeostatic circles.

Maintenance of a constant internal environment usually proceeds automatically. We do not consciously order a speeding-up of heart-rate, or a slowing-down of thyroxin release, but rely on homeostatic mechanisms with their own built-in stability. We have already talked of the balance between sympathetic and parasympathetic branches of the ANS which matches activity of circulatory and digestive systems to demand; with the endocrine system, stability is most commonly produced via 'negative feedback' systems. We deal with this concept in detail when discussing stress and emotion, but, in simple terms, it represents the regulation of glandular activity by the hormones that activity produces, i.e., release of ACTH from the pituitary is regulated by the level of ACTH and corticosteroids in the bloodstream. The higher the circulating levels, the lower the pituitary release, and vice-versa; thus the endocrine system tends to a stable and constant pattern of activity.

The internal environment needs a regular supply of raw materials from the external world. Oxygen-intake is involuntary and continuous, but eating and drinking are voluntary and spaced; the sensations of hunger and thirst arise automatically from a state of homeostatic imbalance, but the consummatory responses involve complex behaviour. So we now move from the general area of homeostasis to a consideration of how hunger and thirst, the two major homeostatic drives, are regulated.

Hunger

An adequate diet includes fats, carbohydrates, proteins, mineral salts, and vitamins. In the 1940s, Richter demonstrated, in a series of 'cafeteria' experiments, that rats and human infants can, to some extent, self-select a balanced diet. It was already known that mature animals, in general, regulate their body weight within extremely fine limits; to maintain an adequate calorie intake, rats will automatically eat more of a less rich food.

Given these basic phenomena, what are the questions to be answered, and how has physiological psychology tackled them? The whole thrust of research has been directed at caloric intake, meal size, and body weight; it has, thus, been concerned with fats and carbohydrates, rather than proteins and mineral salts etc. One major reason for this is the relatively simple relation that seems to exist between energy consumption, energy (caloric) input, and body weight, and the remainder of this part of the Chapter deals with this relation.

As stated earlier, 'tissue-need' leads to behaviour which reduces the need; when satisfied, behaviour ceases. Hunger leads to food-seeking and eating, followed by cessation of eating. One obvious problem that has occupied researchers up to the present day is that animals stop eating before the food has been sufficiently ingested, absorbed, and metabolized to satisfy any central tissue-need; a logical extension of this observation was the arbitrary division of theoretical explanations into 'central' and 'peripheral', according to whether the emphasis was on central (sugar or fat in the bloodstream or in cells) or on peripheral (presence of food in mouth, oesophagus, or stomach) factors.

The early peripheralist position was adopted by Cannon in the 1930s, who related hunger pangs directly to stomach contractions, recording the latter with swallowed balloons. However, simple observation of precise food regulation in patients or rats with stomachs either removed or denervated (so that nerve impulses could not reach the brain) raised insurmountable objections. Subsequent experiments on rats used the legendary 'oesophageal fistula', in which the oesophagus is cut and both cut ends brought to the surface; thus food may be passed in through the mouth and out via the oesophagus, eliminating stomach (gastric) factors, or directly into the stomach via the lower cut end of the oesophagus, eliminating mouth (oral) factors.

The results of these studies are somewhat confused but, generally, support the proposition that short-term regulation of food input, i.e., meal size and duration, could be roughly achieved via either oral or gastric factors; either is sufficient, but neither is necessary. Work over the last few years has further clarified this proposition and, in addition, has investigated the function of the small intestine in signalling satiety to the brain. As a result, the present position *viz-a-viz* short-term regulation of food intake may be taken as relying on the presence of food in the stomach and small intestine, with oral factors being of less importance, though still necessary for the full expression of satiety, e.g., patients feeding via a chronic gastric fistula (because of oesophageal blockage) can regulate their input adequately, but also report a desire to taste and chew their food, and will, in fact, do so before placing it in their stomachs.

The role of the hypothalamus
The study of peripheral factors in hunger and satiety was overtaken in the 1940s by the discovery of brain centres apparently involved in the regulation of body weight. Hetherington and Ranson (1940, 1942) showed that lesions in the hypothalamus could produce an 'obesity' syn-drome—the rat would eat voraciously (hyperphagia) until grotesquely fat. The most effective lesions appeared to be in the ventro-medial nucleus of the hypothalamus (VMH); as damage prevented the normal cessation of feeding, the function of the VMH seemed to involve the inhibition of feeding in response to satiety; and it became known as the 'satiety centre'.

In 1951, Anand and Brobeck suggested that the VMH satiety centre was backed up against a 'feeding centre' located in the lateral hypothalamus. Damage to this area produces a prolonged failure to eat (aphagia), eventually, if allowed, resulting in death. Thus, the normal function of the LH appeared to be to stimulate feeding in response to deprivation signals from the internal tissues.

Over the last twenty years, the study of hunger has been substantially in two directions. The first is towards an understanding of the precise brain mechanisms involved in hunger and satiety, and the second is towards an analysis of the physiological and psychological factors in

159

experimental and natural obesity. The two directions obviously overlap to some extent, and both involve more general questions concerning hunger, e.g., what is the relevant signal to which the feeding centre responds?

The understanding of the brain mechanisms involved in hunger and satiety has followed a path along which all physiological psychology has gone or will go; the simple models of twenty years ago are being replaced by more complex ideas of how the brain works, and these ideas are based on the exponential growth in empirical data. Thus we now know that VMH obesity is probably not due to damage involving specific hypothalamic centres, but to an interruption of nerve fibres passing through the hypothalamus; obesity may be produced by cutting these fibres well posterior to the hypothalamus. Further, the LH aphagia may be mimicked by damage to a bundle of fibres ascending from the substantia nigra in the brainstem to the corpus striatum in the fore-brain; intriguingly, the same effect is obtained in pigeons by severing the trigeminal nerve, which brings sensory input from the oral regions.

So, specific brain lesions may prevent or encourage feeding, but the concept of specific 'centres' controlling an aspect of behaviour is being replaced by an awareness that control is more diffuse, and that 'pathways' may be a more useful concept than 'centres'. This point is more fully discussed in the next Chapter.

The importance of the body weight set-point

The obese animal, either the experimentally obese rat, or the naturally obese man, is in some ways a contradictory subject. Despite a voracious appetite and massive body weight, he is more finicky, more sensitive to the sensory aspects of food—if a meal is adulterated with quinine, the obese animal will cease eating while his normal hungry counterpart carries on; conversely, sweetened foods lead to increased intake in obese, but not normal, subjects. There is also a reduction in motivation—VMH animals will not work so hard for food rewards, as in a Skinner box.

So, obesity does not seem to be due to a 'love' of food *per se*. What does appear to have happened is that the body weight is, in fact, regulated, but at a higher level than normal; the simple observation is that VMH animals eat massively immediately following the operation, but eventually settle down at a much higher body weight and regulate their food intake to maintain this weight as precisely as they maintained their pre-operation weight. That the body weight set-point is crucial to understanding obesity was demonstrated by Keesey and Powley in 1975. They showed that VMH lesions in a rat made obese before the operation, by a particular feeding schedule, resulted in post-operational *aphagia* until the rat hit his set-point, which was still well-above his fellows. Conversely, a food-deprived rat given an LH lesion becomes

160

hyperphagic post-lesion, until he hits his new set-point, well below that of his normal colleaues.

These experiments demonstrate that post-operational feeding behaviour is aimed purely at, and controlled by, the alteration in body weight set-point. In VMH animals, it is shifted up, in LH animals down.

Feeding, in normal rats and people and in obese rats and people, is regulated so as to maintain body weight. What signal, representing some index of body weight, triggers central mechanisms to instigate or inhibit feeding? The question is still unresolved. Favourite at present, as it has been for the last twenty years, is some aspect of glucose metabolism—either circulating glucose in the bloodstream, or perhaps the rate of glucose utilization by cells. Glucoreceptors (cells responsive to glucose) have been identified, both centrally and peripherally in the walls of blood vessels.

The demonstration, by Powley and Opsahl (1974), that VMH obesity could be reversed by cutting the vagal nerve just before it reaches the pancreas, along with the production of obesity in normal animals by injections of the pancreatic hormone insulin, also supports an interpretation of central mechanisms responding to some aspect of glucose metabolism. This interplay of brain mechanisms and the body's metabolic state emphasizes the arbitrariness of central/peripheral divisions—the brain and the body, not to be too philosophical about it, need each other.

Although the rat and man have been considered together so far, naturally-occurring obesity in man obviously may involve substantially more complex mechanisms than those considered so far. Personality and social factors may interact to produce an obesity or aphagia (anorexia nervosa) which does not have the simple physiological explanation outlined above. That, however, is not to deny that some obese individuals may be fighting to maintain a physiologically-based higher set-point, and are therefore in an almost permanent state of hunger; although a full description is beyond the scope of this book, it should be mentioned that the body weight set-point seems to depend upon the number of fat, or adipose, cells, and this number is determined genetically in the main, although dietary experience in the first months may influence it.

Conclusions
To summarize briefly, caloric input is regulated to maintain a relatively constant body weight in the face of varying energy output. Short-term regulation, involving cessation of eating at any given meal, seems to depend mainly upon the presence of food in stomach and small-intestine. Longer-term regulation probably depends upon glucose metabolism in the body, involving pancreatic production of insulin and glucose levels in the bloodstream. Both short- and long-term regulation depend upon

161

brain mechanisms, including the hypothalamus and extra-hypothalamic areas, and damage to these areas may produce aphagia or obesity.

Thirst

Hunger has been presented in some detail as a representative homeostatic drive state with both physiological and psychological correlates. Thirst will not be dealt with at length, not because it is of any less importance, but because an adequate description of the mechanisms involved would lead us into the physiological intricacies of intracellular and extracellular fluid balances. The ratio of behaviourally to physiologically relevant data is massively in favour of the latter, concentrating on the posterior pituitary hormone ADH and the renin-angiotensin systems of the kidney. Central mechanisms, as might be expected, involve the hypothalamus, within which cells sensitive to osmotic pressure (osmoreceptors) appear to control drinking behaviour. Interestingly, lesions to the lateral hypothalamus, besides producing aphagia, also produce adipsia—a prolonged failure to drink; the LH syndrome therefore describes an animal whose ingestive behaviour is almost entirely lacking.

Thirst will be mentioned again in connection with the chemical coding of behaviour by the brain. For the moment, we will consider, briefly, some non-homeostatic instances of motivated animal behaviour.

Non-homeostatic motivation

Rats will explore a novel maze. They will learn to press a bar, purely to make a light come on. Harlow's work with monkeys shows that they find the sight of other monkeys more rewarding than a view of an empty room. They will solve small wire puzzles out of an apparent unconditional 'interest'. The young, and in some cases, the old, of more advanced animals 'play', a term referring to a seemingly aimless indulgence in physical activity.

All these examples represent perfectly understandable (with a little anthropomorphizing) facets of behaviour, but do not relate in any simple manner to eating when hungry or drinking when thirsty. If one wishes to apply a similar homeostatic model, one needs to specify what the animal is being deprived of, to what drive it leads, and how the consummatory response satisfies the drive.

The attempt has been made, and gives rise to various suggested drives—curiosity, exploratory, manipulative. Unfortunately, this area is bedevilled by circularity of the sort that explains observed behaviour in terms only of the observed behaviour; thus, animals explore because they have an exploratory drive (elicited by exploration deprivation?), and we know they have an exploratory drive because they explore.

More constructive recent approaches have emphasized species-relevance in relation to some of the non-homeostatic drives. It is always adaptive for animals to explore a novel environment thoroughly; exploration is a complex stimulus-dependent response enabling the animal to function more effectively in its environment because it knows its environment. Recently, Blanchard (1977) has shown that a rat given an opportunity to explore a maze from which there is no exit, will freeze when confronted by a cat in the maze—he knows there is no escape and figures that safety lies in immobility and possible anonymity; in contrast, a rat to whom the maze is novel will run when the cat appears—he does not yet know there is no exit and, in the circumstances, running is a better bet than freezing. Exploration, therefore, has specific relevance to adaptive behaviour.

Similarly, it makes much more sense to see 'play' as contributing to sensory-motor development, rather than a consumatory response elicited by a need-for-play drive produced by play-deprivation. The context is broadened to see the animal in three dimensions, interacting with a complex environment in ways which cannot realistically be modelled on hunger and thirst.

This is not to say that the physiological correlates of such behaviours cannot be studied. Exploration, in particular, has been a popular research area, and we can now say that the attentional and adaptive responses to novelty involve neocortex and the hippocampus and amygdala of the limbic system. Novelty is also one of the most effective activators of the anterior pituitary adrenal cortex system in the periphery.

It is probable that, apart from exploration, non-homeostatic behaviour generally involves higher brain structures than the hypothalamus, but it should be remembered that virtually all overt behaviour necessitates pituitary and autonomic activation and, therefore, an intact hypothalamus.

Even where behaviour, such as eating and drinking, seems predominantly based on the hypothalamus, it may still be subject to modulation by higher centres. Thus, feeding and aphagia may be induced, though usually not so dramatically, by a variety of limbic lesions and stimulation, while a circuit of structures has been described by Fisher and Coury (1962) as participating in the control of drinking. This pattern of hierarchical control in the brain is one we meet continually within physiological psychology; the concept of pure localization of any one function in any one structure cannot adequately cope with the variety of interconnections in the brain, and at best we can only associate function with structure flexibly.

Electrical self-stimulation of the brain (ESB)

Self-stimulation was discovered by Olds and Milner in 1954. They noticed that an animal stimulated through an electrode near the septum (part of the limbic system) would return persistently to the area of the cage where it had been stimulated. Building upon this accidental finding, they demonstrated that ESB can function as a powerful reinforcer and that, if an animal is allowed to control stimulus presentation himself, i.e., by pressing a bar, he will voluntarily self-stimulate to exhaustion, at rates of over 1000 bar-presses per hour.

Over the last twenty years, a huge amount of data has accumulated on self-stimulation. It can be obtained in rats, cats, monkeys, pigeons, and, in some rare studies, man. Not all electrode sites will support ESB; some are neutral, some positive, and some negative in that animals will press a bar to terminate stimulation in that area. The reward sites can be mapped out, and appear to follow the path of a major fibre tract ascending from the brain-stem to the fore-brain, the median fore-brain bundle (MFB); this tract courses through the lateral part of the hypothalamus, from which powerful ESB had been reported early on. There is also some evidence that rewarding ESB relies on the activation of neurones in which the synaptic transmitter is either dopamine or noradrenaline; if the brain is depleted of these catecholamines, ESB tends to fade out. Incidentally, this is one area where the early neuroanatomical mapping does match with the later neurochemical work, as dopamine and noradrenergic neurones contribute a major part of the MFB fibres.

The negative sites seem not so clear cut. In the early 1960s, Stein proposed, on the basis of ESB studies, a 'punishment' system backed up against the 'reward' system; but, however neat in theory, in practice a 'punishment' pathway analogous to the MFB 'reward' pathway has been difficult to identify. Neurochemically, also, the situation is unclear, with an early emphasis on acetylcholine as the relevant transmitter being replaced by one on serotonin.

Behaviourally, ESB is the most dramatic phenomenon found in physiological psychology. A male rat with an electrode in, say, the lateral hypothalamus, will self-stimulate in preference to eating if hungry, or to drinking when thirsty, or to access to a sexually-receptive female. It is, to him, the most potent reinforcer.

However, the relevance of ESB to the study of motivation is difficult to define. It is certainly not a homeostatically-based drive, and, indeed, seems to be largely independent of the physiological state of the organism. Until recently, it was thought to differ fundamentally from naturally-rewarded behaviour in that it extinguishes almost instantaneously—one or two presses only when no current is delivered, then responding ceases. This contrasts with food-reinforced behaviour, which

164

tends to persist for some time in the absence of the reward, allowing an extinction curve to be constructed.

However, if food-rewards are delivered in a comparable manner to ESB i.e., immediately upon response rather than with a delay to allow the animal to locate and eat the pellet of food, very high rates of responding can be elicited and extinction is almost immediate. Observed differences between ESB responding and food-reinforced responding appear to depend upon the time parameters involved in each case, rather than upon fundamental differences in their nature.

The non-specific nature and widespread distribution of these reward centres in the brain led to the early suggestion that they represented the neural substrate of 'pleasure', and that any behaviour defined as pleasurable, e.g., eating when hungry, would involve activation of the reward pathway. ESB was a short-cut to pleasure, eliminating the need for natural drives and reinforcers. The fact that many sites in the limbic system of the fore-brain support self-stimulation strengthens the view that, during evolution, higher brain centres have developed a generalized sensitivity to reward, somewhat independent of the highly specific reward sites associated with the hypothalamus and homeostatic drive states.

There is, still, much debate on the subject of ESB, and its full significance for models of brain function has not yet been ascertained. Its relevance, though, is generally accepted. For instance, the concept of reward pathways has a major explanatory role in the human schizophrenic syndrome, with some people defining the major symptom of the illness as a failure to react normally to reinforcers. Given this, one may search for a breakdown in the reward pathway which may be either structural or neurochemical; the favourite at the moment is for an over-activity in the dopamine component of the reward system.

7   Physiological Studies II

SIMON GREEN

Cerebral hemispheres

The terminology used in relation to fore-brain structures, especially by psychologists, may lead to confusion. Briefly, therefore, I will run through some of the more important terms you need to know.

The cerebral hemispheres are the structures of the telencephalon (see Fig. 7.1). Together, neocortex, basal ganglia, and limbic system

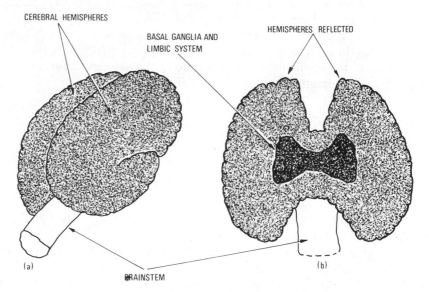

Fig. 7.1   Cerebral hemispheres. (a) Position of paired hemispheres relative to brainstem. (b) Hemispheres reflected to show rough position of basal ganglia and limbic system.

represent about 80 per cent of the human brain by weight (total brain weight is around 1400 g, although wide individual and sex differences are found) and it is this vast proportional increase in the fore-brain which gives man his uniqueness in the animal world.

The brain is bilaterally symmetrical; that is, it is in two halves. Each structure, with one or two exceptions, is therefore represented twice, once in each half, or, where the telencephalon is concerned, hemisphere (see Fig. 7.1). Thus, there are two hippocampi, two amygdalae, two hypothalami, etc. At lower levels, this bilateral representation does not seem to be important; findings on hypothalamic function are consistent whichever side is considered, although most lesion or stimulation techniques are more effective if performed bilaterally.

However, there is increasing evidence that the function of hemisphere structures does vary depending upon their lateral (right or left) position; thus a division into a right and a left cerebral hemisphere appears to make sense functionally as well as anatomically.

Most interest in laterality effects has focused on the neocortex, the outermost layer of the hemispheres and the highest point so far of brain evolution. When discussing cortical function, or referring to cerebral cortex, most workers mean neocortex; the distinction is not of great moment, as long as the reader understands, but it should be remembered that other structures, such as the hippocampus, are also cortical structures—in their case, the cortex (purely a descriptive term) is primitive archicortex, in contrast to the neocortex, which appeared in evolution as recently as birds and reptiles.

Each cerebral hemisphere may be split into several lobes; each of these lobes, therefore, includes both neocortical and sub-neocortical structures, e.g., the temporal lobe includes neocortical zones involved in processing sound, and sub-neocortical structures such as the hippocampus and amygdala. The distinctions may be subtle and often unimportant, but should be borne in mind when considering possible behavioural functions of hemispheres or lobes.

The findings from surgery
Some of the most interesting and useful findings on brain function in man have derived from surgical intervention in cases of chronic epilepsy. Epilepsy is a result of a massive uncontrolled electric discharge in the brain, sometimes produced by physical irritation (e.g., scar tissue after a brain operation) but sometimes of unknown origin. One form of epilepsy involves a focus in one specific area; the discharge begins here, and, as the brain consists of highly conductive material, may spread rapidly to other areas, eventually incorporating the whole encephalon. The symptoms include loss of consciousness during the attack and an amnesia for the seizure and the period leading up to it.

In the 1930s, an operation was devised, not to prevent the epileptic attack, but at least to prevent its spread from one side of the brain to the other in cases where the focus was unilateral (one-sided). This involved cutting the corpus callosum.

The corpus callosum connects the two hemispheres. It is a broad band of fibres connecting cortical areas on one side of the brain with cortical areas on the other. Although other bridges exist—particularly the anterior commissure—the corpus callosum is the means by which most impulses traverse the hemispheres. To accomplish its function, the callosum has in the order of 200 million fibres within it, as compared to the three million in the anterior commisure. If it is cut, effective communication between the hemispheres ceases.

But is this communication important? The severing of the corpus callosum to alleviate severe epilepsy was performed partly because it did not appear to have any after-effects on normal behaviour. However in the late 1940s and early 1950s, Sperry and his group looked at some of these patients again, using the rather sophisticated testing techniques of the experimental psychologist. They were able to show that the split-brain patient (i.e., with corpus callosum transected; also referred to as a brain bisection) does have severe behavioural problems which, however, he can adapt to in everyday life.

To give, for the present, one example: you may remember from the anatomy of the visual system that stimuli hitting the right side of each eye transmit to the visual cortex in the right hemisphere, while stimuli hitting the left side of each eye pass to the visual cortex of the left hemisphere (see last Chapter). If the eyes are fixated straight ahead, this phenomenon means that objects on the subject's extreme right (i.e., in his right visual field) will be seen by his left hemisphere, and, conversely, objects in his left visual field will be seen by his right hemisphere. Think about that for a moment—it is a popular and important experimental technique.

Now, as will be detailed later, we know that in about 90 per cent of people the centres for perceiving and producing language are in the left hemisphere only; reading and talking are left hemisphere functions. So when Sperry projected words to the split-brain patients' right hemisphere, the subject reported no awareness of them; when they were projected to the left hemisphere, they were read out as normal. Objects held in the right hand (which is controlled by the left hemisphere) could be correctly described and named; objects held in the left hand could not.

It appeared that reading and naming, as left hemisphere functions, are unavailable to the right hemisphere when the corpus callosum is cut. Normally, the right hemisphere has access to these functions via the interhemispheric fibres—thus we can read and recognize objects in our left visual field. The split-brain patient cannot, but in everyday life he can move external stimuli into his *right* visual field simply by moving his eyes and/or head, thus compensating for the deficit.

Referring back to our diagram of the visual system (Fig. 7.1), you can see that if the optic chiasma is cut longitudinally along with the corpus callosum, the input to the left eye goes to the left hemisphere, and to the right eye to the right hemisphere—no crossed fibres remain. Sperry has performed this operation on monkeys, and shown that, when separated, the two hemispheres can function completely independently. So, if one eye is covered, the other eye-hemisphere system can be taught that, for instance, green means reward. Now cover the other eye, and you may teach the unexposed eye-hemisphere system that blue means reward; and in each case, learning is equally fast, with no apparent interference effects from the previous learning.

What response the monkey actually produces depends purely on which eye is exposed: if both are open, one response will tend to dominate, although it may vary from day to day.

Sperry concludes that, in the split-brain monkey, each hemisphere is completely independent, and may function as a whole brain in its own right. Generally, one hemisphere will be a slightly less efficient learner than the two hemispheres working together, but not dramatically so.

Of course, in man, language has become our major means and mediator of communication and learning, and we will see in a moment how this has apparently altered the functional equivalence of the hemispheres found in the monkey. But we shall return to epilepsy for a moment.

A case history
The knowledge that severing the callosum functionally disconnects the two hemispheres, plus the inevitable improvement in neuroanatomical knowledge and techniques, meant that surgical intervention in chronic epilepsy became less dramatic during the 1950s. A major finding was that epileptic focii often centred on the hippocampus, a limbic system structure buried deep in the temporal lobe of the cerebral hemispheres. So a procedure was developed whereby the hippocampus was lesioned, which also meant that some of the overlying temporal neocortex was removed. Usually, epileptic focii are unilateral, and a hippocampectomy was often efficacious in alleviating symptoms. Indeed, the same technique, although more precise and sophisticated, is still in use today. However, in 1957, Scoville and Milner reported on a patient operated on four years previously for severe chronic epilepsy which had extended over ten years. This patient, known then and subsequently as H.M., was given a bilateral medial temporal lobectomy, which included hippocampal tissue; postoperatively he exhibited relief from his

symptoms, no obvious personality change, and a massive memory impairment which has lasted up to the present day.

The impairment consists of an uneven retrograde amnesia for events in the two years leading up to the operation, and failure to remember most events occuring post-operatively i.e., a persistent anterograde amnesia. This latter syndrome is obviously dramatic and completely disruptive. Neighbours and doctors he has met day after day for literally years are treated as strangers. Information given during routine psychological examination can be retained for some minutes if practice is allowed; once a second task is attempted, original learning is lost. There is apparently no transfer of information from short-term to long-term permanent storage.

Sperry's work on split-brain patients and the case history of H.M. have been emphasized here because they relate directly to the functioning of the human brain. The aim of physiological psychology is to be a scientific and controlled discipline, aimed at the brain-behaviour relation. For various moral and methodological reasons, virtually all our data comes from (non-human) animals, but the goal is still to understand the human brain. As the cognitive functions of animals are somewhat limited, the analysis of language and complex problem-solving must use data from human studies. Logically, to study the physiological correlates of functions which we feel make us qualitatively different from other animals, we cannot use animals.

In the area of memory and problem-solving, we can, of course, find points of contact. Animals learn sometimes quite complex tasks, and such data may point us in useful directions. However, the confirming evidence for our hypotheses about human brain function must come from studies on patients suffering from brain damage through various causes or who have had brain operations. The latter tend to inflict more controlled and systematic tissue damage and can be used to relate structure to function more accurately. Split-brain patients and H.M. are prime examples of this and of the value to physiological psychology of the unforeseen and usually unfortunate behavioural consequences of brain surgery.

Cortical function

One of the central debates within this broad area has concerned the possible localization of behavioural functions to one specific cortical region. This debate does not involve those areas of cortex given over to pure sensory or pure motor functions; when discussing the visual cortex (Ch. 6) we are talking about an area concerned only with the primary reception and analysis of visual stimuli, i.e., a pure sensory area. The other sensory pathways mentioned in Chapter 6 also have cortical

170

receiving areas, and these are shown in Figure 7.2; note that the more complex sensory systems, vision and hearing, involve relatively much larger amounts of cortex than the non-specific somatosensory pathways.

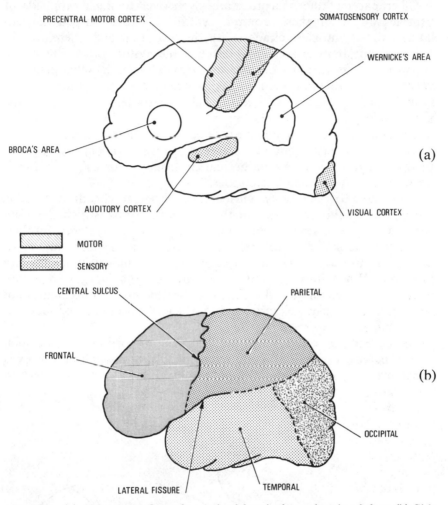

Fig. 7.2 (a) Side view of man's cerebral hemisphere showing lobes. (b) Side view of cerebral hemisphere showing sensory and motor cortex.

Localization
Localization of a high order is found in regard to the sensory areas; electrical stimulation in the visual cortex will produce the subjective sensation of light, in the auditory cortex of sound, and in the somatosensory area, of touch or pressure. Note that the neurophysiological equivalent of the experience of light is an electrical impulse

171

traversing the visual pathway and registering at the cortex, and that this may be mimicked by an appropriate electrical stimulus applied to the visual cortex by an implanted electrode.

Other parts of the neocortex are given over to the motor side of behaviour. The highest control centres for the striped musculature—those muscles attached to the skeleton and therefore involved in any body movement—reside in the motor cortex. Figure 7.2 shows how this region—the precentral gyrus—lies in relation to the general somatosensory area in the postcentral gyrus. Note that the motor area is in the frontal lobe, while the somatosensory is in the parietal lobe.

Stimulation within the motor cortex elicits muscle activity. A stimulus of the correct intensity and in the appropriate spot will cause a finger to twitch or a leg to jerk. Again, normal electrophysiological control may be mimicked via implanted electrodes.

The whole of the body musculature, from forehead to toes, is represented in this neocortex of the precentral gyrus, which therefore supplies the motor components to our sensory-motor systems. Further, we can now look at the neocortex of our cerebral hemisphere, and mark off those regions in which pure sensory and motor functions are localized. When this is done, we can see that large areas are unaccounted for, and it is these areas of 'association' cortex that are of major interest to psychologists, and to which the discussion on localization of function is directed.

As one ascends the phylogenetic scale the proportion of association cortex increases (Fig. 7.3). In lower mammals, almost all neocortex is given over to sensory-motor functions, and later cortical evolution

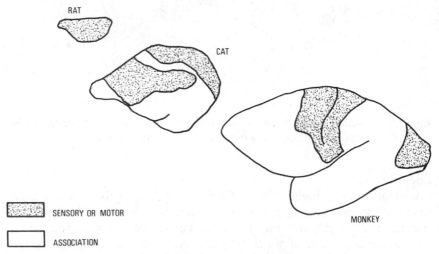

Fig. 7.3   Cortical areas in three mammals.

involves mainly association areas—our sensory and motor systems are not significantly better, generally speaking, than those which may be found elsewhere in the animal kingdom, so the increase in neocortex found in man will be mostly association cortex.

Psychologists divide behaviour into various components; perception, learning and memory, attention, emotion, language, problem-solving, etc. It is probable that some, if not all, of these will involve the association areas of the neocortex, while all will involve some part of the cerebral hemispheres. The problem is to try to locate them rather more specifically, if possible, than these general statements do.

The localization of language processing

Language is the key to our position as top animal. Complex social interaction, cultural evolution, cognitive processes, all depend on our language ability. Do we know how a language is organized in the brain?

As a general principle, we may approach the problem of a specifically human attribute by assuming that it will involve recently evolved brain structures; it is less likely to depend on older parts of the brain. This contrasts with, say, emotion, which is found in non-human animals and which, as we shall see later, is mediated by limbic and diencephalic structures.

So, if we were to begin from scratch, the neocortex would be the target for the search; but as it happens, the clues to the neuroanatomical substrates of language were identified back in the nineteenth century, by Wernicke and Broca. By observation of brain-damaged subjects and some judicious guess-work, two cortical areas were isolated which seemed to be crucially involved in linguistic processes.

Wernicke's area lies mostly in the parietal lobe, but spreads ventrally into the temporal lobe. Broca's area lies in the frontal lobe of the cerebral hemispheres (Fig. 7.2). Damage to either of these regions produces language disturbances, or aphasias; the exact nature varying between the two sites; an inability to comprehend the spoken work (a receptive aphasia) is associated with damage to Wernicke's area, and an inability to produce meaningful speech (a production aphasia) with damage to Broca's area. This would fit in neatly with the close anatomical proximity of Wernicke's area to the cerebral sensory regions, and the close proximity of Broca's area to the precentral gyrus motor regions.

Language involves sensory and motor processes, as well as central mediating mechanisms. To read you need to see, and to speak you need to move your mouth. It is therefore naive to expect a complete localization of language to any one brain structure or region. The effects of a simple sensory deficit such as deafness on language development and performance are well known, and it is clear that a complete specification of the neurophysiological basis of language must involve a whole com-

173

pendium of brain structures. What one may say is that, given normal sensory and motor pathways, certain areas of the neocortex appear to be more concerned in linguistic processing than others, such that aphasias can be predicted if brain damage involves these areas.

A similar analysis can be applied to any sort of complex behaviour. Without input and output, behaviour cannot occur regardless of how intact the so-called central mechanisms may be. So the problem of localization of function becomes a debate on what one means by localization; it does appear to be a useful concept, as long as it is not used to justify simplistic notions of how the brain works.

Language and cerebral dominance

It was mentioned earlier that the language centres described above are found only in the left hemisphere of the majority of people; between 85 and 90 per cent of the population are right-handed, as measured on a variety of manual tasks, and it is in this group that language is lateralized to the left hemisphere. In ambidextrous and left-handed people the situation is somewhat different, as will be described.

The pathways descending from the prefrontal gyrus motor cortex of either hemisphere are so organized that the muscles of the right side of the body are controlled by the left side of the brain, i.e., the pathways cross (incidentally, the crossing of the fibres from one side to the other in the brainstem produces the characteristic bulge from which the pons gets it name).

So, the right-hand is controlled by the left hemisphere, and vice-versa. As language in right-handers also appears to be a left-hemisphere function, one can see how the concept of a dominant hemisphere arose. In most of the population, damage to the left hemisphere may severely restrict the use of our favoured side and impair those intellectual capabilities dependent on language, i.e., the majority of them. Damage to the right hemisphere may affect our left arm and hand, but will generally leave our language abilities unimpaired, i.e., the effects would be much less drastic.

The concept of a dominant hemisphere left open the question of what purpose the non-dominant right hemisphere might be fulfilling. We have language lateralized to the left; is anything lateralized to the right?

The function of the right hemisphere

The investigation of hemisphere differences has now become possibly the biggest research area within psychology. The current view is that dominance is an outmoded concept; the two hemispheres mediate different functions, and each, in its own specialized way, is essential to normal cognitive processing.

Sperry's split-brain work offered early clues. While his patients could not report seeing a word presented in their left visual field (and therefore processed by their right hemisphere), they could select with their left hand, blindfolded, an object matching the word. Apparently, the right hemisphere can carry out some elementary verbal processing.

Evidence also began to accumulate, demonstrating that the right hemisphere is actually superior at some tasks, specifically, those not requiring verbal mediation. Thus it can learn mazes and recognize shapes and faces better than the left hemisphere. Corsi, working in Milner's laboratory with patients operated on for chronic epilepsy, showed that the anterograde amnesia associated with unilateral hippocampal damage varied in character with side of lesion. Left hippocampal damage produced difficulties in performing verbal tasks (such as learning lists of words and retaining them over a period), while right-sided damage produced difficulties in performing tasks of a visuo-spatial nature (such as learning a finger-maze). In the case of H.M., with bilateral hippocampal involvement, both types of task were impaired.

This sort of work led to the present position where the right hemisphere is thought to be specialized in cognitive processing of a non-verbal, visual-spatial, mode. The left is specialized for cognitive processing involving verbal mediation. As most complex tasks have both visuo-spatial and linguistic aspects, the two hemispheres usually complement each other, and it is only in unusual, laboratory-designed, situations that their different modes of operation can be dislocated. However, this has not prevented theorizing on the grand scale.

Ornstein, in 1974, suggested that society itself may reflect a hemisphere 'dominance'. Associating the left hemisphere with verbal, analytical, sequential processing typical of mathematics and scientific thought in general, he feels that the technological paradise and spiritual vacuum this has created could be reconciled by an emphasis on the attributes of the right hemisphere. These he characterizes as the products of a holistic, parallel, synthetic mode of processing, typical of the creative and divergent arts disciplines and also representative of eastern, rather than western, thought.

Whether or not experimental data eventually supports such a neat division of labour, this type of theorizing illustrates both the purpose and the problems of investigating the functioning of the human brain. Findings have immediate relevance, and the media are all too ready to popularize ideas prematurely; to do this effectively, the simplicity of a given notion must be exaggerated for the layman's consumption, often ignoring the provisos and reservations of the original investigators. What should be remembered is that, despite years of work, we are still being surprised daily at how unimaginably complicated the brain is.

175

Handedness and gender effects

Between 10 and 15 per cent of the population are left-handed. Do they therefore have a dominant right-hemisphere, controlling both the favoured hand and linguistic processes?

The answer seems to be sometimes yes, sometimes no, and sometimes in between. Findings on brain-damaged people suggested that left-handers have a lesser degree of lateralization of language, such that damage to either side may produce aphasia, but that prospects for recovery were quite good—as if the undamaged hemisphere can take over.

More recent work on normal subjects, using tachistoscopic presentation of material to either hemisphere, complicates the picture. Although no clear-cut conclusions can yet be drawn, it seems likely that familial left-handers (those with a family history of sinistrality) may have language more strongly lateralized to the right-hemisphere; non-familial left-handers may have language on the left or right side, and left-handers in general may be less strongly lateralized. I must emphasize, though, that this is very much an evolving area, and the only definite statements one can make is that left-handers less frequently have language lateralized to the left-hemisphere than right-handers.

The developmental basis of hemisphere functional asymmetries is now coming under scrutiny. A complicated genetic model for the inheritance of left-handedness has been proposed (Annett, 1975), and anatomical asymmetries associated with the language areas of the left-hemisphere have been found in both adults and the newborn. It thus appears that at least handedness and language asymmetries may be predominately inherited, although both can be affected by early experience. Certainly, the brain is very plastic soon after birth, and early damage can be compensated for by switching the destined functions of the damaged area to another part. There are cases of massive injury to the newborn's left hemisphere not preventing the development of normal speech in the child. Left-handedness has also been subjected to a gradually lessening cultural bias over the years; but the interaction of this bias with a physiologically-based bias can only be guessed at.

As further evidence of physiologically-based hemisphere asymmetries is the suggestion, now widely accepted, that males and females differ in respect to certain hemisphere-specific functions. Thus, females are superior at the characteristic linguistic processes of the left hemisphere, and males dominate in the visuo-spatial, map-reading type tasks of the right hemisphere. (To some of us, mostly men, it also seems natural to associate males with the divergent creative nature supposedly associated with right hemisphere dominance; however, there may be an element of subjective prejudice in this.) But, unfortunately, this sex-based differentiation is another example of a popularized finding that, if one

176

goes back to the original research, is not securely based. The literature abounds with conflicting and inconclusive results; and statements beginning 'males are better at ...' should be treated with constructive scepticism.

Summary

We have considered some of the functions of the cerebral cortex, but the picture is still very incomplete. We may mark off areas associated with language, and areas, such as the hippocampus, associated with memory. However, even when the pure sensory and motor regions are also struck off, there are still large areas of association neocortex unaccounted for. Work is in progress, especially on the frontal lobe, which contains the highest proportion of association neocortex; it has been suggested that it is involved in a behavioural inhibition—the mechanisms whereby animals stop doing things, such as entering a box, in which they have previously been shocked. In the 1930s, the frontal lobectomy was devised, an operation to disconnect the frontal lobes from the rest of the brain in cases of chronic mental illness. The fact that you could do this at all is another fine example of higher, but non-essential, brain structures, although the inconclusive therapeutic results and the associated personality changes make it a fine example of unjustified psychosurgical intervention. Until the involvement of given areas in complex psychological phenomena, such as personality, social adjustment, aggression, etc., has been established there is absolutely no theoretical justification for any sort of surgical procedure for behaviour disorders, leaving aside the associated massive moral problems.

We have looked at cortical function in some detail, as it is here that the man/non-human animal differences must lie. The rat, cat, and monkey do not have inherited asymmetries of cerebral function, although paw preferences may be established through practice. They do not have language, and it is this that probably determines the presence or absence of inbuilt hemispheric asymmetries; one view is that the development of language in the left hemisphere has, in the course of evolution, forced other psychological processes to become lateralized in the right hemisphere. But one may then ask why language should have evolved unilaterally in the first place; and so the questions keep coming. But at least we are beginning to realize how difficult the questions are, and are coming up with what may prove to be the beginnings of answers.

Brain chemistry and behaviour

Impulse conduction in the nervous system involves both electrical and chemical mediation; electrical along the neuron, and chemical across the

177

synapse. This gives us two general approaches to the stimulating and recording of brain activity, the one using electric current and EEG machines, the other using drugs and biochemical assay.

Chemical transmission across the synapse was first demonstrated by Loewi in 1921, and was rapidly and comprehensively investigated in the years that followed. However, only synapses in the peripheral nervous system were accessible, and all we know of synaptic structure and function has come from them. The central nervous system (CNS) was a closed book; indeed, as late as the 1940s the view that transmission within the CNS was completely electrical was quite acceptable.

Even today, no CNS synapse has been described in as much detail as those, for instance, in autonomic ganglia; the technical problems have still not been fully solved. However, a mountain of circumstantial evidence has persuaded us that CNS synapses do exist, and probably function in a similar fashion to peripheral cues.

There are major differences in detail. In the periphery, only acetylcholine and noradrenaline are considered as neurotransmitters; in the brain there are four major candidates, and several aspiring ones. It is generally accepted that acetylcholine, noradrenaline, dopamine, and serotonin function as central neurotransmitters, while there is quite good evidence for other substances such as gamma-aminobutyric acid and glutamate. So, when we try to relate the behavioural effects of drugs to synaptic transmitters within the brain, we have quite a choice.

Psychopharmacology

The study of drug effects on behaviour is called psychopharmacology. Over the last twenty-five years it has shown the most rapid growth of any area in physiological psychology, the major stimulus being the proven use of drug therapy for psychiatric disorders. The clinical use of drugs in psychiatry—or clinical psychopharmacology—has been around for many years, but really took off in the early 1950s. The discovery of chlorpromazine in 1952 revolutionized the treatment of schizophrenia, eliminating the need for surgical intervention (the frontal lobotomy) or insulin coma therapy; and nowadays we possess a battery of drugs, useful in a variety of psychotic and neurotic disorders.

That is not to say that we can cure these disorders, or even that we can help every patient. There has been a great leap forward, but still we do not know the precise brain malfunctions presumed to underly abnormal behaviour. This is especially the case with a broad category such as the schizophrenias, which can appear as various subtypes, each with its own genetic and environmental background. Even 100 per cent effective drug therapy would be only a partial answer—behavioural abnormalities involve a spectrum of interacting factors, the end result of which

178

may be a malfunctioning brain, but whose cure involves sorting out the predisposing variables.

Chlorpromazine was originally synthesized for its central anaesthetic properties; its antischizophrenic potency was discovered more or less accidentally, and this process has been characteristic of clinical psychopharmacology. In the 1950s, little was known of brain chemistry, although drug effects on behaviour were presumably mediated by it. So, clinical psychopharmacology became a very pragmatic discipline—drugs were used which worked, regardless of their chemical nature or origin. As one drug was shown to be effective, its chemical relatives would be synthesized and tried out, bringing some sort of system to pharmacological research. Then, as more was found out of brain chemistry, drugs could be classified according to their actions on transmitter substances; and if the best anti-depressants all stimulated noradrenaline release, we could relate depression to a breakdown in normal noradrenaline function. From this hypothesis, we could then predict that more effective noradrenaline releasers would be more effective anti-depressants; this prediction could be tested, and the hypothesis supported or rejected. So, over the years, clinical psychopharmacology has acquired a more rigorous scientific approach.

Experimental psychopharmacology
One can approach the behaviour/brain chemistry problem from another angle. Once the major transmitters have been identified, we can produce drugs which have specific actions upon them, but which do not necessarily have any clinical potency. Thus we now have a range of noradrenergic stimulators (or agonists) and blockers (antagonists), of dopamine agonists and antagonists, and of cholinergic agonists and antagonists. We can study the effects of these drugs on animals, and attempt to relate specific neurotransmitters with specific aspects of behaviour such as learning, motivation, sleep, attention, arousal, etc.

This more systematic experimental psychopharmacology received a massive stimulus with the discovery in the mid-1960s that transmitters in the brain were found in clearly defined pathways. It has been known since the 1930s that a single neuron releases the same transmitter at all of its axonal endings; it now appears that the cell bodies of neurons using the same transmitter cluster together, and send out long axonal processes that travel together through the brain until their various destinations.

So we can identify two dopamine pathways, each with a cluster of cell bodies in the mid-brain, with bundles of axons passing forwards and terminating either in the basal ganglia or in the limbic system. Electrical stimulation of the cell bodies will cause dopamine to be released at the

179

axon terminals, while lesioning the mid-brain cell body clusters will effectively eliminate all brain dopamine.

Similarly, noradrenergic, cholinergic, and serotonergic pathways have been localized, all conforming to the general pattern of having cell bodies towards the posterior end of the brain with axons travelling towards the anterior end.

Thus, the terminology has altered. Instead of the behavioural functions of a neurotransmitter, we look for the behavioural functions of a neurotransmitter pathway. The brain, instead of being a conglomeration of linked, but anatomically distinct, structures, each of which may be studied independently, is now conceptualized as a set of transmitter pathways, each of which interacts with the others but may also be studied individually. The advantage of the neurochemical approach to brain function is that the units are much larger; instead of the hundreds of anatomically defined nuclei, each of which may have a behavioural correlate, we have four major transmitters, and perhaps eight or nine transmitter pathways. If the analysis of behaviour, i.e., psychology, produces a similar number of basic concepts, the possibility arises of correlating the one with the other.

To give the flavour of this sort of theorizing, one could choose Tim Crow's hypothesis of a dorsal noradrenergic pathway mediating 're-inforcement', and a central dopaminergic pathway mediating 'drive'. Or the partially contradictory view of Larry Stein that 'pleasure', 'reward', or 'reinforcement', are completely under the control of brain nor-adrenaline. We know from the work of Michel Jouvet that serotonin and noradrenaline are involved in the control of sleep, while David Warburton has suggested that stimulus discrimination and attention are a function of cholinergic pathways ascending to the cortex.

The favourite psychological concept studied has been 'reinforce-ment', sometimes masquerading as 'reward' or 'pleasure'. Electrical self-stimulation of the brain, as described earlier, has been used to map out 'reward' pathways; with the improvement in pharmacological techniques and increased interest in brain neurochemistry, the chemical bases of the reward pathways rapidly became popular subjects for study. Currently, the data favour a major role for dopamine as the central substrate for reward, i.e., all rewarding situations would involve an increase in neurotransmission in dopamine pathways. However, the whole field of behavioural neurochemistry is in a state of flux; in brain research generally, it has been estimated that at the current rate of data collection 99 per cent of all we will know at the end of the next half-century will have been discovered in that half-century. So we cannot pretend to be completely confident of our hypotheses at present.

Schizophrenia

Clinical psychopharmacology has produced masses of data on drug effects in people. Many of the drugs have now been characterized in terms of their main chemical actions on the brain. This information can be combined with our knowledge of brain pathways and behaviour from experimental psychopharmacology, to produce models of the possible chemical breakdown in some psychiatric disorders.

The best example of this type of combination comes from drug therapy in schizophrenia. Chlorpromazine, mentioned earlier, has been used as an effective anti-schizophrenic agent for the last twenty-five years; but its discovery was fortuitous, and only over the last ten years has its chemical nature been related to its behavioural effects and to neurotransmission in the brain. Chlorpromazine has a range of pharmacological actions, affecting several transmitters. However its main mode of action, probably responsible for its therapeutic value, is as a dopamine blocking agent. This would reduce dopamine transmission in the brain, and implies that schizophrenia involves (besides genetic, cultural, and social aspects) overactivity in dopamine pathways.

From our animal work, we strongly suspect that dopamine is involved in mediating 'reward', and that abnormalities in dopamine transmission would result in abnormalities in response to 'rewarding' or 'pleasurable' stimuli; and certainly schizophrenics may show bizarre or absent responses to stimuli most people find rewarding. We also know that a major dopamine pathway goes to the limbic system, which, as will be described, is involved in the control of emotion; therefore dopamine overactivity should produce changes in emotionality, and inappropriate emotional responsiveness is a feature of schizophrenia.

There are many problems with this sort of theorizing. Schizophrenia has many sub-types and many symptoms which must involve many brain areas and pathways; it might be unjustifiably naive of us to use animal behaviour as a comparative model. Dopamine systems in animals seem also to be involved in the control of homeostatic drives and memory, while pure dopamine blocking agents may have no therapeutic effect at all in human schizophrenia. The picture is not entirely straightforward. However, the dopamine hypothesis at least gives us something to aim at, even if it is finally discarded (at least in its present form).

There are similar models for other disorders based on the therapeutic value of drugs. Most anti-depressant agents increase levels of dopamine, noradrenaline, and serotonin in the brain, and it is currently felt that an imbalance between serotonin and noradrenaline pathways may be at the root of depressive disorders.

Any models of brain function must be built against the background of the exponential increase in experimental data, in what we know about

181

the brain. I have mentioned four major candidates as neurotransmitters. The recent discovery of enkephalin, thought to be involved in pain perception and possibly functioning as a synaptic transmitter, is just another in a list of around ten other candidates. It is certain that we are still only scratching the surface in our search for the behavioural correlates of brain function, but it is equally certain that an approach combining our knowledge of both neuroanatomy and neurochemistry is at least heading in the right direction.

Emotion

The study of the physiological correlates of emotion has produced two almost incompatible bodies of evidence, one from humans and one from non-human animals.

That the two fields must differ is obvious if we consider the nature of emotion. Although overt responses may be involved, constituting emotional behaviour, a large component of what we call 'emotion' lies in the subjective experience of the state. We can often identify emotions in other people, especially if high arousal is involved as in rage, aggression, love, etc. However, there are many fine distinctions and subtleties in emotional states which can only be identified by asking the subject to report on them himself.

So, the study of emotions in man has usually involved subjective self-report, and an attempt to tie this in with an artificial or natural change in his physiological state. This type of approach, which is discussed fully below, became popular in the 1930s and has consistently emphasized the more extreme emotional states such as fear and anger; this latter point also applies to animal studies. As we cannot, as yet, obtain subjective self-reports from cats, rats, and monkeys, we have to use emotional states whose overt expression is obvious and unambiguous. Thus, the most convincing body of data from animal studies involves the control of aggression in the cat, and it is arguable that the term 'emotion' in this context is inappropriate. Rather, we should study these responses and their physiological correlates, leaving 'emotion' as specifically human attribute whose analysis goes beyond observed behaviour.

Unfortunately, work with people has not yet reflected the diversity and richness of human emotions, at least on the physiological side; when considering animals or man, we usually concentrate on anger or fear. There is, therefore, no semantic reason to distinguish the two bodies of evidence, but there are major methodological ones.

The study of aggression in animals has concentrated on brain mechanisms, and has led to models of 'emotion' whose building-blocks are brain structures. The standard technique, traditionally, has been to lesion an area of the brain and observe the effects on rage and aggression.

However, in man, the tradition has been, until recently, to emphasize the roles of the peripheral autonomic and endocrine systems in emotion, with only lip-service being paid to possible central mechanisms. The reasons for this necessitate a brief description of another branch of psychology.

Psychophysiology

The physiological correlates of behaviour in the intact human may be studied insofar as they may be measured. We cannot intervene in brain function via lesions or stimulation, but we can measure and record physiological variables which may reflect aspects of brain function. The psychophysiologist can try to correlate variations in blood-pressure, heart-rate, hormonal levels in the bloodstream, activity of the salivary or sweat-glands, or the electrical activity of the brain (either evoked potentials or the electroencephalogram, see Chapter 14), with various aspects of behaviour. Does heart-rate fall during sustained attention? Do levels of ACTH vary during simple problem solving? Does the EEG vary with state of vigilance? Do schizophrenics have abnormal patterns of autonomic activity such as raised blood-pressure or increased sweating?

Generally, the dependent variable is a measure of autonomic, endocrine, or brain electrical activity, and the independent variable some aspect of behaviour. This stands in direct contrast to most of physiological psychology, where the dependent variable is usually some aspect of behaviour and the independent variable a direct manipulation of the brain.

There are areas of overlap between the two disciplines, and these are, happily, increasing. We have techniques for psychophysiological recording in animals, and much psychophysiological work involves brain-damaged patients. But it cannot be denied that communication between the two approaches has been minimal, and the study of emotion is a good example of this.

Emotion in man has been the province of the psychophysiologist. This began with one of the earliest models of the way in which physiological changes might influence emotional state, put forward by James and Lange simultaneously in 1878, and involving the autonomic nervous system. Their suggestion was that the emotion experienced depended absolutely on the pattern of peripheral changes elicited by a stimulus. These somatic (skeletal muscle activity) and autonomic (changes in heart-rate, blood pressure, etc.) changes were perceived by the brain, and elicited the subjective experience of the given emotion.

So, presented with a slavering, rabid mongoose, we run—a conditioned response to the stimulus. This running involves a pattern of peripheral muscle activation and general autonomic arousal; this pattern registers in the brain as fear. We are afraid because we are running, and do not run because we are afraid, i.e., emotional expression precedes emotional experience.

This superficially bizarre theory has functioned as an Aunt Sally for many years. In the 1930s, Cannon put forward several major objections and an alternative. His objections centred on such problems as whether peripheral changes occurred fast enough, whether there was sufficient variety in peripheral patterning to account for the variety of emotional states, and why paraplegics can still feel emotional when they have restricted feedback from their peripheral systems. His alternative was a central theory of emotion; the thalamus was responsible for emotional experience, and the hypothalamus for emotional expression. This theory (the Cannon-Bard model of emotion) has some merit in emphasizing the role of the hypothalamus in emotional expression (as we shall see when we look at the animal experiments), but had little basis for its view of thalamic function.

The James-Lange/Cannon-Bard dispute anticipated the subsequent schism in emotion research; peripheral theorists studied people, central theorists worked with animals. There were some attempts to combine the two, most notably in the work of J. W. Papez. In 1937, on the basis of observations he had made on the brains of people dying of rabies (in which substantial emotional changes occur), he proposed a central model of emotion.

Both emotional expression and experience were to be mediated by various interconnected structures that formed the bulk of what we now call the limbic system. His model, built on by MacLean in 1949, has been the source of most ideas concerning the brain and emotion in man, but relies heavily on evidence from animal studies, as we shall see later.

Adrenaline and noradrenaline

The study of emotions in people has concentrated on the peripheral measures first emphasized by James, most notably the release of adrenaline and noradrenaline from the medulla of the adrenal gland. These hormones are liberated into the bloodstream upon stimulation by the autonomic fibres innervating the adrenal gland. Their action is basically to mimic sympathetic arousal (you may recall that noradrenaline is the transmitter at the synapses of the sympathetic branch of the ANS; thus noradrenaline from the adrenal gland prolongs the action of noradrenaline released at sympathetic terminals).

Although both adrenaline and noradrenaline are released from the adrenal gland, and their physiological effects are similar—increase in heart-rate, blood-pressure, metabolic rate, generally preparing the body for activity of some sort—they are not always found in the same proportions. Usually much more adrenaline is produced, but even within this generalization the relative amounts of each appears to vary with the situation. It is this variation which psychophysiologists have attempted to relate to different emotional states.

One of the earliest and still most interesting of these attempts was by Albert Ax in 1953. He induced 'emotion' by manipulating the environment, and recorded blood levels of adrenaline and noradrenaline. An incompetent technician, hopefully making the subject angry, produced an increased output of noradrenaline. Smoke rising from the apparatus to which the subject was attached—probably producing fear—increased adrenaline levels. Ax therefore associated anger with noradrenaline release, and fear with adrenaline.

Using slightly different terminology, Funkenstein in 1956 concluded that a relative preponderance of noradrenaline release in response to various situations typified 'anger-outward' people, while a preponderance of adrenaline typified 'anger-inward' people; the relations between these concepts and the 'anger' and 'fear' of Ax are fairly clear.

More recently, Marianne Frankenhauser has performed a number of studies on the links between the environment and the adrenal medulla. By broadening the range of experimental manipulations beyond fear and anger, she has shown that adrenaline and noradrenaline are released in response to many stressors, and cannot be tied down to just certain emotion-laden situations. Adrenaline release is much more copious and responsive to situational demands; these latter include physical stressors such as prolonged running, and psychological stressors such as performing complex arithmetical problems.

There are individual differences in the adrenaline response; generally, better performance, even at psychological tasks, is associated with a large response which returns to baseline fairly rapidly. There are also sex differences—females tend to have a less pronounced adrenaline response to stressors, which may be associated with their greater resistance to stress generally.

This type of approach has greatly broadened the scope of the field. The idea that by choosing two hormones and two emotional states one could pin down one with another, can now be seen to be rather naive. Adrenaline and noradrenaline have profound effects on the arousal state of the body, an arousal state that is fundamental to all behaviour. A more realistic picture of their role will, therefore, only come about by studying as many behavioural situations as possible, and trying to specify what is common to those affecting the release of adrenaline and noradrenaline.

Ax and Frankenhauser use hormone release as their dependent variable. An alternative approach has been to give hormones and observe behaviour—to use adrenaline as an independent variable, with behaviour as the dependent one.

185

Maranon, in 1924, gave adrenaline to subjects, and asked for self-reports. As adrenaline mimics sympathetic arousal, he hoped that if, as James and Lange felt, peripheral changes led to emotional experience, then induced peripheral arousal would lead to some degree of felt emotion. However, although some of his subjects reported feeling 'as-if' emotions, i.e., not the real thing, the results did not support the prediction. Peripheral change *per se* did not seem to be enough.

In 1962, Stanley Schachter followed up Maranon's work in one of the classic experiments of psychology. As an additional feature, he modified his subjects' cognitive environment as well as their arousal state, and obtained evidence that both are necessary for emotional experience.

Subjects were given either adrenaline, disguised as 'suproxin', or an inert placebo. They were either informed of the drug's effects (increase in heart-rate, face flushing, etc.) or left ignorant, and stooges were used to induce either 'euphoria' or anger. In the former case the stooges pranced around maniacally, and in the latter became obviously irate when all subjects were asked to fill in a long and highly personal questionnaire.

The final stage of the experiment was to get subjects to produce a self-report on their emotional state, and results generally supported the predictions. Subjects given the inert placebo or informed of the expected effects of suproxin tended not to report a high degree of emotion; subjects given suproxin without information as to its effects reported feeling emotional, with the reported emotion matching whichever stooge they were paired with.

Schachter concluded that induced peripheral arousal is not in itself sufficient to generate subjective feelings of emotion. However, when the arousal is unexpected, subjects will account for it in terms of a cognitive appraisal of the environment. They are aware of heart pounding and free flushing; why should this be? Well, that other person is obviously irate (or euphoric), so perhaps I should be too.

So emotion, on this view, is based on central and peripheral factors. Peripheral change does not play such a major role as in the James and Lange approach, but still predisposes towards emotional experience. As further support for the importance of peripheral feedback, Hohmann, also in 1962, reported that subjects with spinal cord damage (which would reduce feedback from the peripheral nervous system, which passes up to the brain via the spinal cord) did suffer a loss of subjectively-felt emotion—in direct contradiction to Cannon's earlier supposition that paraplegics suffer no emotional deficit.

Central mechanisms in emotion
The psychophysiological approach to emotions in humans has suggested some of the peripheral mechanisms which may be involved. To determine the central mechanisms mediating emotion, we have to turn to

186

animal work and physiological psychology. The study of emotion in animals has concerned itself almost exclusively with aggression. The behavioural manifestations are clear and easy to interpret, and it is found in a wide range of species, including man.

In the 1920s, Hess had begun a series of studies demonstrating, amongst other things, that rage could be elicited in cats by hypothalamic stimulation. Around the same period Bard had shown that the whole of the cerebral hemispheres could be removed without destroying the rage response; tail-pinch would still produce integrated aggression. Only if the hypothalamus was removed did the response fragment, so that one might see hissing without pilo-erection, or unsheathed claws without the arched back.

It therefore appeared that the hypothalamus was essential for the full expression of aggression, and this was generalized to all emotional behaviour in the Cannon-Bard theory mentioned earlier. There was a measure of dissent: Masserman felt that the aggression elicited by hypothalamic stimulation was a 'sham' rage, as in his studies the cat could be stroked and might even be purring while simultaneously exhibiting all the signs of rage!

These early findings were to some extent co-ordinated by Papez's limbic theory of emotion. The structures in the limbic circuit included the hypothalamus, hippocampus, septum, amygdala, and cingulate gyrus, and although at the time experimental data were pretty thin on the ground, it does now seem that limbic areas are important in the control of aggression. Kluver and Bucy, in 1937, had produced a syndrome of hypersexuality, hyperorality (putting objects into the mouth), and placidity in monkeys by removing the temporal lobe. Of all the structures contained in the temporal lobe, it is now clear that the placidity, a taming effect, is due to amygdala damage. Specific amygdala lesions may produce all the components of the Kluver-Bucy syndrome.

The obverse is found with septal lesions; the 'septal' animal is well-known to be hyperemotional, aggressive, and often impossible to handle. So it appeared that the septum and amygdala had opposing effects on aggression, probably mediated by their connections to the hypothalamus. (Remember that the hypothalamus is essential for the integrated response to occur at all, while the septum and amygdala are not.) As with hunger and thirst, the picture is again one of higher brain structures having their effects on more primitive behaviours via their modulation of the hypothalamus.

However, the situation is more complicated than this. There are species differences—septal aggression is very difficult to obtain in monkeys. Small lesions of the amygdala may produce placidity or rage, depending on their precise location. We now know (Moyer, 1968) that aggression may be of various types—predatory, fear-provoked,

187

territorial, irritable, maternal, hierarchical—and presumably each may have its own central mechanism.

So the analysis of aggression must become more detailed, although, perhaps, further removed from our global concept, emotion; and the way has been pioneered by John Flynn and his associates over the last ten years or so.

They have analysed the aggressive responses of cats to rats. Surprisingly, the majority of cats do not spontaneously attack rats, but will do if given appropriate brain stimulation. Flynn has shown that attack always takes one of two forms; either a 'quiet biting', predatory assault, or an 'affective', hissing, claws out, back-arched attack that may be related to Moyer's 'irritable' aggression. Each form has its separable central substrate, although, as would be expected, they are closely related. Thus, quiet biting attack can be elicited from medial areas of the hypothalamus, while affective attack seems to rely on the lateral hypothalamus. Both forms are also obtainable from limbic stimulation, and Flynn's group has mapped out the connections between hypothalamus and amygdala, septal and hippocampal areas, through which this limbic control may be exerted.

More interestingly, and in the long term perhaps more importantly, they have shown the subtle dependence of the aggressive response on sensory feedback. The normal emphasis in the study of emotion is on initial sensory input and subsequent central and motor processes. In the cat, the complete sequence of aggressive behaviour leading to killing and eating of the prey depends upon a continual supply of feedback from already initiated responses. This was demonstrated in one dramatic experiment. Stimuli in and around the mouth region of the cat are sensed via the trigeminal nerve, which supplies sensory fibres to upper and lower jaws. If the trigeminal nerve is severed, no sensory input from oral regions is possible. Such a cat will approach the rat, upon appropriate brain stimulation, using a combination of visual and olfactory cues. He will open his mouth and place it around the rat's neck. However there will be no biting, as biting is dependent, in its turn, upon the 'feel' of the rat's fur on the upper surface of the jaw. The consumatory response is not the inevitable end of a one-way, all-or-none, sequence of aggressive behaviour; each component in the sequence itself reflects a direct and often simple stimulus-response connection. Although the patterning of the behaviour is undoubtedly central, it depends upon sensory feedback for the sequence to be maintained.

This elegant analysis of aggression in the cat is far removed from the study of emotion in man. It is the best example of how the improvement in techniques and the accumulation of experimental data combine to provide a more realistic model of how behaviour is controlled by the brain; but to try to relate it to the psychophysiology of human emotions

188

is not easy, that is to say, impossible. Is there any reason, therefore, why we should not eliminate the infra-human animal studies from our consideration of emotion?

Psychosurgery

Surgical intervention in psychopathological conditions has had a controversial history, beginning with the first pre-frontal lobotomy by Moniz in 1935. This technique, as modified and technically improved by Freeman and Watts, became a popular treatment, typically for chronic, deteriorated schizophrenics. Between the 1930s and 1955, it is estimated that something in the order of 45 000 operations were performed.

The idea was either to remove or to separate the frontal lobe of the hemispheres from the rest of the brain. It was based on some observations on monkeys that removal of frontal cortex appeared to make the animal placid and 'happy'.

The dubious therapeutic effects and occurrence of undesirable side-effects such as blunted affect and impaired intellect, meant that the operation faded out as a major means of treatment when drug therapy became established in the 1950s. However, there has been a recent resurgence of interest in psychosurgery, particularly as related to aggression.

It is, nowadays, recognized that schizophrenia is a broad and heterogeneous classification, and that the multitude of types and symptoms will not share a common central mechanism. No one brain operation could be universally therapeutic. But a component of some schizophrenias is uncontrollable aggression, directed at self or others; aggression is also found in autistic children (usually self-mutilatory), in various other psychiatric groups, and is commonly held to characterize certain psychopathic criminals.

From infra-human animals we have data implicating certain brain structures in the control of aggression, particularly the link between amygdala lesions and placidity. Ignoring the problems of types of aggression, subtleties and complexities of the central substrate, social, cultural, and developmental factors, etc., one might conclude that amygdalectomy would be useful in treating human inappropriate aggression. And this is what is done in some parts of the world. Aside from the dubious morality of lesioning the brains of eleven-year-old children, I hope that enough has been presented of the experimental study of aggression to show that human psychosurgery has an insecure theoretical basis. One can appreciate the pressure to find 'cures' to psychiatric disorders, and in many ways a single brain operation would be ideal. But, given the failure to localize even simple behaviours such as predatory aggression to single brain structures, the chances of localizing those cognitive and personality systems involved in, for instance, schizophrenia are at present zero. We do not know enough about the brain to justify psychosurgery on theoretical grounds.

Conclusions

We have considered the study of emotion from several viewpoints, but must remember that there are many more. The development of emotional behaviour, the recognition of emotions in others, social and cultural factors in emotional expression.

Against this rich tapestry the advances made within physiological psychology and psychophysiology seem rather paltry. Certainly the most promising lines—Frankenhauser's work on adrenaline and stress; Flynn's analysis of aggression in the cat—do not seem to be leading towards the concept of emotion as used by William James. The awareness that cognitive factors are involved, demonstrated by Schachter, was timely, but has not been developed to any great extent. We always come up against the subjective experience that characterizes emotion, and that seems pretty well immune to our battery of physiological methods.

However, we are being forced to re-define our use of behavioural and physiological concepts. In all areas of physiological psychology, the responses studied have turned out to be more complicated than first thought, and the brain has turned out to be more sophisticated than we ever dreamt. We may have lost much of the early attractive simplicity ('emotion is . . .') but we have gained a sense of realism sufficient to state that, while we cannot define emotional expression or experience in physiological terms, we do have more productive ways of studying them; we are asking the sort of questions which might just be answerable.

FURTHER READING

Carlson, N. R. (1977) *Physiology of Behavior*. New York, Allyn & Bacon.

Schwartz, M. (1978) *Physiological Psychology*. New Jersey, Prentice-Hall.

Thompson, R. F. (1975) *Introduction to Physiological Psychology*. New York, Harper and Row.

8 Ethological Studies I

PHILIP EVANS

What is ethology?

What is an ethologist? The derivation of the term *ethology* is Greek, but the meanings that it has had over the centuries are various. Sometimes it has been used to describe a study of ethics and·moral science; nowadays, we use it to describe that branch of science which seeks to examine the behaviour of animals in their natural environment. It is important to make a distinction immediately between ethology, as we have just defined it, and that branch of psychology that we usually refer to as *comparative psychology.*

Comparative psychology also deals with the behaviour of animals, but the comparative psychologist has traditionally been interested in manipulation and scientific control of behaviour under stringent laboratory conditions. At the same time, to be aware of this distinction between comparative psychology and ethology does not mean to say that the ethologist does not engage in any form of experimentation. What it does mean is that he will use experimentation where necessary to examine the conditions under which naturally occurring behaviour takes place. He might also use experiments to illuminate the processes underlying naturally occurring behaviour.

In this Chapter and the following one, we intend to look at some of the types of behaviour which have been investigated by ethologists. Then in Chapters 10 and 11, we shall look more closely at the work of the comparative psychologists in the field of animal behaviour. But before we begin it is worthwhile to make one more distinction between ethology and comparative psychology. Ethologists have, in the main, stressed that the purpose of their work is to elucidate the function of an animal's behaviour. Now it is an obvious truism to say that function depends very strongly on what species of animal one is looking at. The question which is often asked by the ethologist is: how can I find out how this particular bit of behaviour (e.g., zig-zag dancing in the male stickleback) fits into the organism's general life; in other words, what function does this behaviour have for this species? The comparative psychologist, on the other hand, more often uses animals with the quite explicit intention of finding general laws about behaviour. The species that he is actually experimenting with is of little importance, except convenience—rats may be good for studying simple principles of learning; cats may be good for studying sleeping, insofar as they do sleep rather a lot. This second distinction we have made is not, however, cut and dried. Ethologists do generalize some of their findings in order to try to shed light on problems of human society—that is not, however, the purpose they have in mind when they commence their work. Similarly, comparative psychologists, especially recently, have become more enlightened about the limitations of generalizing from one species to another. The distinctions we have made, therefore, should be seen more as matters of emphasis, and one hopes ultimately for a synthesis to take place.

Why do psychologists concern themselves with animal behaviour?
When students begin psychology courses, they are often surprised by the number of studies, experiments and reports which devote themselves to infra-human species. The student's expectation is often that psychology is the business of understanding his fellow men, albeit in a more systematic and, he hopes, scientific manner than is the case when mere common sense is the guide. And so, we imagine a student with such an expectation on his way to his first lecture about principles of learning. The word 'learning' conjures up the very class-room or lecture theatre that he is enthusiastically entering. He sits down and the lecture begins. Immediately, his expectations seem to be discountenanced. He hears not of teachers and pupils, books and learning, but of dogs salivating, and white rats eating. Indeed, you will read something of that in a subsequent Chapter. The question is why do animals get such wide coverage? The nineteenth century might help us to answer that question. Psychology, insofar as it claims to be a natural science, finds its roots in the exciting revolution that overtook biology in the middle and end of the last century.

The revolution of which I speak is of course the Darwinian revolution. It is hard nowadays to recapture the excitement and the air of progressive blasphemy which greeted the publication of such books as *Origin of Species* and *Descent of Man*. However, it is very clear what ideas were swept away by those books, and what sorts of roads were opened up for future investigation. Before Darwin, orthodoxy had taught that man's behaviour was not and could not be the subject of scientific investigation. Man's behaviour was, in principle, unpredictable because he chose to behave in certain ways. The philosophical position, which was rigidly held to, was that of free will. Scientific laws could apply to objects, other animals (not blessed with free will), and even the human body (hence the already existent science of medicine) but not to man's behaviour. Man's behaviour was held ultimately to reflect man's soul, and that was free to choose. Psychology, insofar as it existed before Darwin, was a branch of philosophy, and could comfortably be studied in the same way, that is to say, without leaving one's arm-chair.

Yet the very essence of Darwin's ideas was that man could not be singled out as separate from the rest of the animal kingdom. With the erosion of belief in man's special status, and with the spreading of the belief, even in the popular mind, that man was descended from the apes, there was no longer any obstacle to including man's behaviour in the broader field of animal behaviour. Psychology, conceived of as a natural science, had permission to begin.

The term 'instinct'

If man's behaviour was not the result of free will, it seemed to follow that it was in some sense compelled or determined. Nineteenth century investigators had already noted fixed patterns of behaviour in various species of animals, and the word 'instinct' was used to explain why animals seemed blindly to engage in certain activities. Early psychologists, eager to make their discipline respectably biological, took up the concept. Psychologists, such as William James and McDougall, underpinned much of human behaviour with a plethora of separate instincts. We laugh because we have a 'laughing instinct', we weep under the influence of a 'weeping instinct', and so on. Nowadays, when we see that something can explain everything, we quite rightly suspect that it really explains nothing. So it was with the term instinct—it became overworked. When, a little later, psychologists began to discover the phenomenon of 'conditioning', the chaining of stimuli and responses by association (see Chapter 10), this seemed a much better way of broadly explaining man's extremely variegated behaviour. The adage was born that we are all 'products of our conditioning'. Innate factors in man's behaviour were banished from the main-stream of psychology, and only now are they making a powerful resurgence.

And yet, interest in innate patterns of behaviour did not die completely. There were scientists who continued to look at instinctive behaviour in animals generally, and though they tended not to make *homo sapiens* the object of their enquiry, they did, nevertheless, occasionally raise speculative questions about the viability of the 'infinitely conditionable' man of the experimental psychologist. These men, of course, were the ethologists. Notable amongst them have been two important figures: Niko Tinbergen and Konrad Lorenz. These two men laid the foundations of present-day ethology. Apart from amassing a large scientific literature of their findings, they also wrote extremely

193

interesting popular accounts of certain parts of their work, e.g., *King Solomon's Ring* by Lorenz.

Fixed action patterns

Although it is natural to introduce the subject-matter of the ethologists by a mention of the term instinct, that particular word no longer occupies pride of place in many people's vocabulary. It seems immediately to beg too many questions about innateness. Rather, it is better to say that ethologists have found it easy to concentrate on apparently functionally important behaviour patterns which, nevertheless, can be easily identified and reidentified by different independent observers. It may, or may not, be appropriate to call such behaviours instinctive. Such rigid stereotyped behaviours have been called by Lorenz *fixed action patterns*. A multitude of examples could be given to illustrate the nature of fixed action patterns, but limitations of space enable us only to mention a few.

One of the classic examples which can be cited is the behaviour of the grey-lag goose. This bird builds its nest on the ground, and one of the constant problems that it faces is the tendency of an egg to roll out of the nest. The greylag goose then has to retrieve it. What interests us is just how it achieves the retrieval. The bird leans its head forward, puts its beak on the far side of the egg and gets the egg back into the nest using a scooping movement. The whole behaviour pattern is extremely stereotyped and admits of no variation. The bird could conceivably use its feet or its wing; the point is that it never does.

Another example which illustrates the amazing constancy of fixed action patterns comes from a study of courtship movements in the golden-eye drake. Observers recorded a particular part of the ritual known as the 'simple head throw'. Studying one particular invividual, this movement was found to have an average time of 1.29 seconds. However the variation from this average time could at most be measured only in hundredths of a second.

There is no doubt that there is a strong innate component in most fixed action patterns, and this is clearly seen when experimenters try to interfere with the naturally-occurring situations. For example, Lorenz and Tinbergen, having outlined the egg retrieval behaviour of the grey-lag goose which we mentioned above, proceeded to present the bird with an egg of gigantic proportions. The bird nevertheless attempted to retrieve this egg using the same rigid method (see Fig. 8.1).

Ethologists have tended to see fixed action patterns as the nearest thing to purely inherited behaviour. Often, it can be clearly shown that learning is not necessary in any way to the exhibition of such behaviours. Nor are such behaviours usually capable of serious modification, even when the circumstances may be altered either naturally or artificially. However, it is necessary to sound a note of caution here. It is, of course, possible to conceive of behaviour, even complex behaviour, being wired in to the nervous systems of species, which predispose the animal to perform fixed action patterns. But innateness should not be assumed in this way until the most rigorous investigations are done (Manning, 1973).

Fig. 8.1 Egg retrieval in the greylag goose. (After Lorenz and Tinbergen, 1938.)

Certainly, rigidity of behaviour and stereotyped sequences of movement lead one to suspect the importance of innate factors; so also does the finding of a high degree of intra-specific similarity. However, such factors cannot in any way serve as criteria, since we see equally rigid and stereotyped movements in neurotic patients and experimental animals subjected to conflict. We would not want to say that these behaviour patterns were innate—quite the contrary. We have a good idea of the kinds of learning experience likely to produce them. The same argument applies to intra-specific similarity; we know that cultures can be so powerful in their influence as to lead to a very high degree of such intra-specific similarity in man.

However, even when innateness appears to be a very probable important factor, one should be careful.

Manning (1973) gives several examples of environmental factors which are vital for the development of fixed action patterns, but which are not obvious. As an illustration, let us consider the bladder-emptying reflex in the rat. A reflex is just about the simplest fixed action pattern we can conceive of. Infant rats, in a particular experiment not concerned with the bladder reflex at all, were removed from their mother by Caesarian section. After the first day all the infant rats were dead. It was discovered that they had died from rupturing of the bladder. What was subsequently discovered was that the reflex of bladder emptying has to be triggered from the environment, in this case the actions of the mother in giving a slight kick to the offspring at birth. Once triggered, its action is autonomous and needs no further prompting. Other examples could be given of reflexes and fixed action patterns being at least partly determined by environmental factors. Perhaps, therefore, we ought to speak of inherited predispositions rather than inherited behaviour. In some cases, the interaction of heredity and environment in the genesis of behaviour patterns is much more complicated. In a moment we shall discuss one example in full. First we should mention the powerful experimental technique of the *isolation* experiment. Given that the simple observation of stereotyped behaviour and rigidity cannot be sufficient to assume a high degree of innateness, an obvious technique is to take young animals at birth (neonates) and isolate them from their normal environment. If the behaviour in question still appears, this is good *prima facie* evidence for innateness. Notice I have not said firm evidence, since the reader should bear in mind that there is an equally important prenatal environment in the womb, which the simple isolation experiment does not control for. Let us now look at the use of isolation and other techniques in just one example, chosen because it illustrates a complex testing out of innate and environmental factors.

Bird song: inherited and learned components

Marler and Tamura (1964) and Konishi (1965) have given us a good account of the development of characteristic bird song in the American white-crowned sparrow. This species is very widely dispersed along the Pacific coast of the United States and birds from different areas are known to have distinct 'dialects', superimposed on the standard bird song of the species as a whole. If birds are reared in total isolation they do show as adults the characteristic song, even though they have in no way been exposed to the song of the adult during their development. Thus, clearly, the song itself is innately wired into the bird in some sense. The dialect, however, is not to be found in such experimental isolates and, therefore, involves learning experiences. Marler and Tamura found that the specific learning of the dialect takes place relatively early, indeed before the bird has ever sung a note. If birds are taken into isolation after three months, a recognizable accent is still present when the bird in isolation eventually begins to sing. Even more interesting, and something which we shall have more to say about later, the exposure to the dialect seems to be required during a critical period. Isolates who are exposed to adult dialect song after four months are not affected by it, and the future song is the crude standard version.

Konishi continued the work of Marler and Tamura. By means of deafening the fledgeling birds (by surgical removal of the cochlea) he was able to show that birds need to hear their own song in order to produce even the inherited standard song. The mutilated birds were capable of producing only disconnected notes. Konishi also showed that deafening birds at any time before the birds had sung resulted in the same complete deficit. Only when the bird had actually produced a song, was it possible to deafen the bird and still leave the song unaffected.

How do we interpret these results to form a final picture of the interaction between inherited and environmental components? First, it

196

appears, as we have said before, that what is inherited is not the song itself but the predisposition. We can call this a *template* of the song which is innately wired into the bird's nervous system. What the bird has to do is to use this template as a guide and ultimately match its own singing to it. We might say that the bird is *learning* to sing by copying a model; the model, however, happens to be internal and innate. Where, now, does the question of dialect fit in? It would appear that experiences in the environment, during a critical period, can modify the innately laid-down template, so that when the bird finally comes to using its template, that template has environmentally added accretions, i.e., dialect.

We have outlined the story of the white-crowned sparrow at length because it serves as a good example to establish how necessary it is in ethological investigations to be prepared for complex interactions between heredity and environment in the development of even those behaviours which the layman is likely to see as examples of good old instinct!

The role of external stimuli

So far, we have concentrated on the development of the fixed action patterns so often studied by the ethologist. We have done this in order to show the limitations of the old concept of instinct, and the improvement that is reaped by talking instead of innate and environmental components of behaviour. We now move on to look at the immediate environmental factors which determine the occurrence of fixed action patterns, regardless of how they have developed.

Sign-stimuli

One of the most widely-investigated species, with respect to the work of Tinbergen, has been the three-spined stickleback, a very common fresh-water fish. The fish does, in fact, spend much of the winter in estuaries, or even in the sea, but in the spring it migrates to the rivers and streams. The male stickleback finds a suitable place for building a nest on the river-bed, and sets about finding a female to court and mate with. What is interesting to us is the different patterns of behaviour which are elicited by intruding male and female strangers. Male intruders are automatically attacked, females are courted. How does the stickleback know the difference? There are two distinctions which might be important: the male has a bright red underbelly whereas the female has not; secondly the abdomen of the female is swollen with the eggs she is carrying. What feature is important? Tinbergen first showed that it was indeed visual stimuli to which the fish responded. By putting a mirror in front of the male fish, he was able to demonstrate that the fish would attack its own reflection. Having established this, he went on to build a number of 'model' sticklebacks, in which he varied the features that might be important in eliciting behaviour of attack. He showed that the shape of the fish was unimportant; only the red underbelly seemed to be the relevant feature (see Fig. 8.2). The ethologists have called such highly selective stimuli in the control of behaviour *sign-stimuli*.

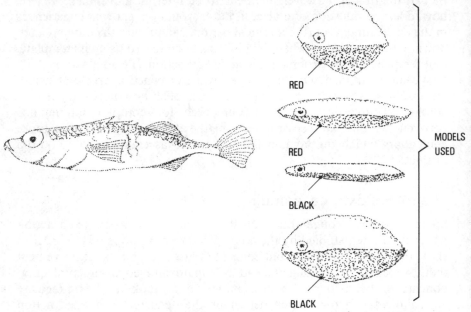

Fig. 8.2 Models used to test for aggressive responses in the stickleback. (After Tinbergen.)

Let us consider one more example of sign-stimuli in operation. The chicks of the herring-gull obtain food quite reliably by pecking at the tip of the parent's bill. Regurgitated food is then given to the chick. The parent's bill is yellow with a red spot on the lower part. Once again Tinbergen was able to construct model bills in order to investigate just what were the important sign-stimuli in eliciting the vital pecking response of the chicks.

The features of the bill which were found to be important were (a) redness of the bill, and (b) the contrast of a spot against background.

The innate releasing mechanism controversy
We have now paid attention to specifiable behaviour sequences, and the specifiable situations which give rise to such sequences. For example, we have discussed the aggressive responses of the stickleback when faced with a male intruder. We discovered that the sign-stimulus of crucial importance is the red under-belly. It follows that there must be, somewhere within the organism's nervous system, mechanisms which mediate

198

between the stimulus and the response. It is in this area that a good deal of controversy has been aroused.

In the 1930s, Lorenz coined the term *innate releasing mechanism* (IRM) as an explanatory device. Unfortunately, this term has proven to be more of a hindrance than a help. For a start, we have seen already how cautious one has to be in applying the word 'innate' in any circumstances; its application can all too easily be questioned. Secondly, is it always true to say that the important property of the stimulus is that it releases the behaviour under study? We can conceive of many other functions for such a stimulus, such as an arousing or orientating function, or in some cases, indeed, an inhibiting one. Thirdly, the use of the singular term 'mechanism' implies just one single and, presumably, as far as the nervous system is concerned, central mechanism responsible for the behaviour. Once again, this is disputable. All in all the choice of the term IRM seems most unfortunate.

Let us look at some particular instances where the term IRM can be seen to go astray. In a well-known experiment by Lorenz and Tinbergen, the alarm response of young turkeys, confronted with a model hawk passing overhead was studied. The model was intriguing because, depending on which way one looked at it, it could be perceived as a goose or a hawk (see Fig. 8.3). When the model was drawn across in direction A, so as to resemble a hawk, the young turkeys exhibited a great deal of alarm. However, when the model was drawn across in direction B, so as to resemble a goose, there was little reaction in the turkey pen. It is tempting to see the alarm response being associated

Fig. 8.3 Hawk-goose silhouette. (After Tinbergen.)

with an innate releasing mechanism, triggered by certain environmental stimuli, which have achieved importance for very obvious reasons during the course of evolution. However, more recently, criticisms have been made of the original experiments, suggesting amongst other things that the young turkeys had had prior experience of geese flying over their pen. The fleeing response might, therefore, have been habituated to geese, but remained intact to hawk-shapes. The controversy over the innateness of this particular stimulus-response relationship continues, but it is clear that the term IRM cannot sensibly be used in 'explaining' such behaviour. Another critic of the early experiments was Schneirla, who argued that the actual resemblance to a hawk or a goose might be of little importance, and that what was important was the more primitive response of most organisms to an unexpected and sudden change in illumination, induced, in this case, more unexpectedly and more suddenly when the model comes in 'blunt end first', rather than tapering end first. Schneirla argues therefore that a simple triangular model would work just as efficiently. We shall leave that particular argument in the air, so to speak, but note that the original experiment did not control for this more parsimonious explanation.

Let us now move on to the second objection to the term innate releasing mechanism. This, if you remember, centred on the term 'releasing'. Let us look at an example of behaviour where the term 'releasing' is clearly inappropriate. Young turkey chicks emit certain specific vocalizations which serve as discrete stimuli for the adult birds. But their function is not to elicit a response; it is, in this case, to inhibit one. Specifically, the sound of the young turkeys serves to prevent the adults from attacking and killing them.

Think back now to the egg-retrieving behaviour of the greylag goose that we mentioned earlier in this Chapter. We mentioned that the egg did serve as a stimulus to elicit or release the retrieval, but retrieval is a complicated business, and it can be shown that the egg also serves to orientate the animal's response. Our examples, then, show us that stimuli do a lot more than just release behaviour; they can *inhibit*, as in the first case, or *orientate*, as in the second.

Our final objection to the term innate releasing mechanism was over the use of the singular form 'mechanism'. A single mechanism might indeed seem appropriate if we were talking always of just one single sign-stimulus controlling one single fixed pattern of behaviour. However, that is not always the case. While it is true that a herring-gull chick will peck most at a model which best resembles the parent's beak, we saw that pecking is recorded in other conditions, too, when the model is not maximally approximate to the real bill. This shows that the IRM, so-called, is only a kind of short-hand in the explanation of behaviour, and what we really require is a thorough knowledge of how the animal *processes* information (sorts out relevant from irrelevant detail) at all stages from the peripheral (the eye, the ear, the nose, etc.) right through to the central stage (i.e., the brain). First, let us look at an instance of fixed action pattern which depends solely on a peripheral mechanism. The example we choose comes from the mating behaviour of the silk-

200

moth. The male moth reliably flies towards the female moth—not surprisingly really. However, when we look at what triggers this response we find that it is a certain odour given off by the female. Where do we find the mechanism which accounts for the selectivity of this response sequence? The answer is that we find it at the most peripheral level possible, i.e., the sense-organs of smell. Tiny *chemoreceptors* in the male send impulses through the central nervous system only when a particular odour is detected.

If we refer back to the pecking behaviour of the herring-gull chicks, we see that the stimulus which elicited the behaviour was not at all simple. It had at least two components. The contrast of the spot on the beak was the one component; the over-all colour, red, was the other. Clearly more central analysis of the stimulus is required in this example.

So, our conclusion must be that the term 'innate releasing mechanism' is at best, and only in certain cases, a crudely descriptive one. True explanation can only come about by a thorough examination of the way in which a particular organism *filters* the relevant from the irrelevant aspects of the totality of environmental stimulation which impinges upon it.

Imprinting

To end this Chapter let us look at a phenomenon midway between what is usually called innate and what is usually called learned.

A lecturer friend of mine once illustrated his lectures on animal behaviour with *Tom and Jerry* cartoons. You may be aware that in one of these cartoons some fowl-like chick decides that Tom, the cat, is its mother, and follows its adopted mother everywhere across the celluloid.

The point of the anecdote is to introduce the topic of *imprinting*. Imprinting is a subject which has been closely studied by ethologists. It is of interest because, on the surface at least, it seems to be neither an innate nor a learned phenomenon. It would appear to involve both innate and learned components and is of interest insofar as we have already stressed the need to keep both components in mind when dealing with the analysis of naturalistic behaviour.

Despite what we have said above, however, imprinting is by most standards a learning phenomenon. Nevertheless it is a learning experience which takes place at a predetermined and highly sensitive period in the development of the young animal. Let us look at an illustration.

It was back in the last century that systematic observation first demonstrated that young chicks (two or three days old) had a tendency to follow any moving object. They would, in psychologists parlance, *attach* themselves to one so-called mother figure. Incidentally, and as one might expect, this kind of attachment is most often seen in those

201

species of birds which have the capacity to wander away from the nest very soon after hatching. The kinds of object on which such a chick can become imprinted seem to be almost unlimited, varying enormously in size, shape, and colour. Experimenters have imprinted young birds on something as small as a matchbox or as large as an observational hide. Auditory stimuli can also play a part in the attachment process. Indeed, it has proved possible in some species to imprint the animal on a simple sound source. This, though, is rare.

Imprinting as learning

One of the most noticeable facets of learned behaviour is that it improves with practice. Also, insofar as learned behaviour tends to be synonymous with environmentally-determined behaviour, it relies crucially on the ability of the organism to discriminate external stimuli. Both these factors can be shown to influence the acquisition of the *following responses*, which form the behavioural evidence for attachment.

Moreover, another well-known principle of learning theory (see Chapter 10) is that a response which an animal learns to make in the presence of a stimulus will be elicited to a greater or lesser degree by any stimulus perceived as similar to the original stimulus. This is the principle of stimulus generalization. It can be shown that imprinted responses obey this particular law of learning. Imprinting, then, seems to occur in such a way as to obey most of the laws which apply to learned behaviour. So what makes it different? Where is its innate quality?

The critical period

It seems that the unique feature of imprinting is that it must be innately laid down when the behaviour is first learned. This is the nature of the 'critical period'. In the case of the chicks' following response this critical period is typically between two and three days old. If one measures the accuracy with which a chick will discriminate and seek out a would-be attachment stimulus, then such a measure will 'peak' at the critical period (see Fig. 8.4 on page 203).

On grosser measures, the chick may indeed show sensitivity to potential attachment stimuli at earlier or later periods, but when it comes to accuracy of learning the critical period is as narrow as depicted above. Scientists have speculated that the critical period develops as it does for the following reasons: before the onset of the critical period one may suppose that the perceptual and discriminatory potential of the chick leads to less accurate following behaviour; after the critical period fear becomes more fully developed and any new stimuli are likely to elicit avoidance behaviour. On this argument the critical period is the ideal compromise: it is the optimal point where discrimination is at its highest relative to fear.

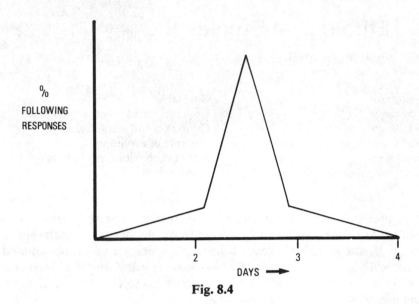

Fig. 8.4

The reader who wishes to delve further into the topic of imprinting can do no better than to refer to the comprehensive account given by Sluckin (1964).

9   Ethological Studies II

PHILIP EVANS

Territoriality	**Courtship**
Dominance	Courtship rituals and appeasement
Social organization	Courtship and identification
Rivalry and aggression	**The role of evolution**
Threat displays	Animal behaviour and human
Displacement activities	behaviour

In the previous Chapter, we looked at the general nature of ethological investigation, the problems arising from a study of naturalistic behaviour, and examined some of the terms which are often encountered in the writings of ethologists. We also saw how the use of at least one term, *innate releasing mechanism*, has itself led to the shaping of argument and controversy in the field.

In this Chapter, we want to concentrate more on specific types of behaviour which have been most systematically studied by the ethologists. Fixed action patterns in response to well-defined situations, which we have already mentioned, are most in evidence when we deal with certain broad topics within the field of animal behaviour. In particular, we can observe them frequently when we encounter an animal in relation to its *territory*, to *rivals* of its own species, and to its *mate*. The topics are not exhaustive, nor are they without a certain degree of overlap.

Territoriality

The importance of the concept of territory is immediately evident when we consider the number of species which indulge in the setting up and defending of territory. The vast majority of birds are territorial. Many mammals also exhibit territorial behaviour, as do fish. Though less common amongst the invertebrate species, territoriality is occasionally present. In social animals, including man, the term territory used as a synonym for a well-defined and defended area of a single member of the species may not appear appropriate.

However, if we extend the term somewhat to a consideration of space, we do see a need for a less strictly defined notion of territory. In the so-called 'social animals', territoriality tends to give way to the idea of dominance, with certain individuals occupying a higher rung on a status ladder. In the wild, conflict in such cases can hardly be said to result from territory consideration *per se*. But in over-crowded situations, where a low status animal is restricted in its ability to avoid confrontation with its higher status colleagues, one does see aggressive results similar to those involving border conflicts between truly territorial animals.

The fact that territoriality has developed in such a wide range of species suggests that the pressures of natural selection have favoured those species which do exhibit it. This does not mean, however, that there is a simple evolutionary solution to the problem. Many ethologists have tackled this particular question (Lack, 1966; Wynne-Edwards, 1962): an obviously possible function of territoriality would come from relating it to the supply of important resources such as food, but such a simple explanation cannot be the whole truth. Territories can vary enormously in terms of size, for example. Certain species such as the herring-gull have territories of limited extent within a colony and certainly do not obtain their food from the territory. Birds of prey, on the other hand, have very large territories (about one square mile) from which they obtain all their food. Apart from food supply, then, there must be other advantages accruing from the holding of territory. Such advantages could be freedom from disturbance by members of the same species, especially during mating periods. We shall leave further discussion of natural selection as a determinant of animal behaviour to a later section of this Chapter and move on to a discussion of the types of territorial behaviour exhibited in different species. The general rule about territoriality is that although its exact nature differs enormously from one species to another, it is usually clearly relevant to the particular ecology of that species.

We begin with a consideration of those cases where the territory holder is for the most part a solitary animal, even though one could say that the group of territories constitutes a society of sorts. This is certainly the formula which applies in a number of bird species, amongst which the willow warbler is a good example. The male takes on a fairly large territory which will supply him with food; eventually he will share that territory with a mate and rear his young there. Although other territories are close by, such that all the ground in a vicinity is occupied, we can still say that each territory belongs to a solitary bird. The robin is also a highly territorial species in this sense, and will not lightly tolerate the presence of a rival of its own species. The other cardinal example of solitary territory holding is seen in that group of mammals known as the carnivores. Anyone who has kept a domestic cat will probably have observed its behaviour as it paces even one's own living room, rubbing up against furniture and indeed people in what appears to be an affectionate manner: the truth of the matter is rather different. Powerful scent glands are to be found on the cat's face which leave an olfactory message pertaining to its recent presence. Outdoors, various scents, and in particular urine traces, mark out the boundaries of his territory.

Here then are two examples of territories occupied by solitary animals. However there are important differences even here: your own cat's territory is not his exclusive domain for a whole twenty-four hour period. The cat has to come to terms with the equally valid needs of all the other cats in the neighbourhood, and there is simply not enough space for all to have exclusive territory. The solution to the problem is as one might expect. The cats operate a time-sharing system. While the smell of urine is fresh, this acts as a signal to other cats which says 'keep clear'; as the smell gets stale the force of the signal is diminished and a neighbouring cat can claim that part of the territory as its own for another limited period. It will be seen that the system is very efficient; though a number of cats may be sharing the same geographical area the olfactory messages ensure that unwanted encounters are kept to a minimum.

Dominance

It might seem from what we have said so far that in any species each animal has the same kind of territory. This, however, is a gross over-simplification of the reality. Quite simply, it is often the case that there are not the resources to allow such an egalitarian notion: in other words animals have to compete for territory. This brings us naturally to a consideration of *dominance hierarchies*. Such hierarchies have long been known to ethological investigators since the initial observations came from a study of hens the term 'peck order' is often used synonymously with 'dominance hierarchy'.

A good illustration of the interaction of territory and dominance is to be seen in species such as the grouse. Here, territories are held for the exclusive purpose of attracting the female during the mating season. All the male grouse in a large vicinity converge on a central area which is called the 'lek': the prime territories within the lek are to be found in the very centre and here the lucky males present a formidable display which attracts the majority of females. The territories on the periphery are correspondingly 'poverty traps' as far as mating is concerned. The dominance hierarchy in this example is usually based on the simple criterion of age: older males often keep the same central territory from season to season, whilst younger birds adopt peripheral positions and wait to replace their elders.

Note that in this example territories only assume importance for a brief period, and for a particular reason, i.e., mating. So it is with many other species. The advantages of solitary territorial existence are, often, much out-weighed by the advantages of some form of social organization. Thus a number of birds which are territorial in the breeding season form flocks at other times; they move together and contribute to the common good by making alarm calls and responding to one another.

206

Territoriality, then, can be transitory. Often, under high density conditions, it is actually replaced by a simple dominance hierarchy for
purposes such as mating. For example white rhinoceroses are normally
highly territorial: however it has been noted that in certain cases a
dominant adult male may allow a subsidiary male to live on his territory
and the lot of this lesser male is not to suffer attack but rather to be completely ignored. Of course, there are many species where group living is
the rule, and, here, the concept of territory gives way completely to the
concept of 'peck order'.

Social organization

In order to complete the transition from discussion of solitary
territoriality to complete group living let us take three types of animals:
the red deer, the wolf, and the primates.

In the case of the red deer the two sexes form separate herds and
group-living is the rule during the summer, when the animals feed
together. In autumn, however, the male herds disintegrate and with their
antlers fully grown the males become very aggressive and put on
elaborate displays for the benefit of the oestrus females. However the
mating season is quite short and the females soon return to their herd;
likewise the males shed their antlers and regroup into their own herd.

Wolves have even more reason to live in groups, since they require to
hunt in packs which means that a stable social organization is highly
desirable. Some males are more dominant than others, but the group
itself is at no time disrupted.

Of all animals, the primates are renowned for their highly developed
social organization. The concept of territory becomes meaningless with
respect to any individual animal. However, troops of monkeys can be
said to have a territory. The troop may be as small as a single family in
the case of the gibbon, for example. As a family they are territorial and
make loud hooting noises if they detect other gibbons in the
neighbourhood. Like the cat, however, the one group of gibbons does
not, strictly speaking, own the territory. Auditory signals—like the
olfactory signals of the cat—serve to minimize potentially threatening
encounters. Other species of primate live in much larger groups than the
gibbon. The gelada baboons live in colonies of up to 400; as one might
expect there are sub-groups within such a large colony.

Within any grouping, there is usually a high degree of stability which
is based on the usual dominance hierarchy. High rank will lead to preference when it comes to obtaining food and mates. Unlike hierarchies in
other animals however, primate groups are usually noted for their lack
of aggressive encounters; threat postures by dominant males are not
needed as much as one might expect, since subservience of the less
dominant animals makes them redundant. Although it would be unwise

to make too many generalizations, it seems to be the case that density of grouping is the important determinant of the amount of aggression to be observed within the group. Monkeys in zoos, where space can be at a premium, do show more intra-group strife: the simplest explanation of this is that the less dominant animals find it physically impossible to get out of the way!

Rivalry and aggression

The above sub-heading immediately leads one to reiterate what was said at the very beginning of this Chapter: that the topics which we are covering overlap considerably. It is impossible, in other words, to talk about territoriality without talking also about how an animal deals with rival intruders on its territory. Here, however, we want to examine the exact nature of aggressive activities which characterize the behaviour of different species, and then to speculate about the evolutionary pressures which determine aggression. One of the hoary old chestnuts constantly grasped, dropped, and grasped again by generations of behavioural scientists is the question of whether aggression is innate or not. Those who believe that aggression is a drive which builds up to inevitable expression have their examples ready to hand. Siamese fighting fish, it appears, will learn to make a response such as swimming through a ring in order to display aggression (Thompson, 1963), and cock fighting would never have become the sport it once was if it were not for the highly aggressive nature of the fowl used. Opponents of the 'inevitable aggression' hypothesis would argue for the view that aggression is not automatic, but is always attendant upon frustration (Miller, 1941). We shall see in the latter part of this part of the Chapter that no generalized and all-embracing view is tenable, and that the aggression or lack of aggression of any particular species should be seen in the light of its own evolution.

But first let us look in a more descriptive way at what happens when animals come into conflict.

Threat displays

We have seen how animals organize themselves in territories, but we have said nothing about what exactly happens when this territory is intruded upon by a rival. Usually the answer is simple—the intruder retreats under the threat of attack by the resident. However, the boundaries of territories are not as fixed as one might suppose. Manning (1973) compares a territory to an elastic disc, the centre of which is well defined as territory since any persistent intrusion will inevitably provoke an extremely aggressive response. As one moves out from the centre the response of the resident gradually becomes less pronounced, until a point is reached where the animal threatens only half-heartedly. In other words there is not a fixed boundary on one side of which we see full-blown defence of territory, and on the other side of which we see no response at all. It is at these peripheral 'no-man's-lands' that threat displays are most in evidence. Threat displays are, essentially, therefore, a compromise when the tendencies to attack and to escape are about equal. Ethologists have made a special study of the idiosyncratic postures adopted by various species during peripheral boundary disputes.

Male cichlid fish face each other motionless with their gill covers fully raised, whilst in many birds and mammals the hair or feathers become erect. This common denominator suggests that the display itself is a more physical corollary to the autonomic activity associated with being in a conflict-ridden situation. Most boundary disputes do not go as far as actual physical aggression. Both animals involved keep up a mutual threatening until one of them retires. This is, of course, an over-simplified picture, and it would be wrong to conclude that for a given species there is a single identifiable threat display. We have said that the conflict—and, thus, the posture—results from the two tendencies of attack and retreat being equal, but they may be equal in different ways: both may be equal and low; both may be equal and high. It is likely that different threat postures are appropriate in the two cases. A nice illustration of the different postures associated with the interaction of increasing aggressiveness and increasing fear in the cat can be seen in Figure 9.1.

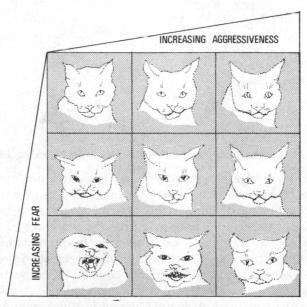

Fig. 9.1 Changes in the facial expressions of the cat with their suggested motivational basis. (After Manning, 1973.)

209

Similarly different results may follow the encounter. If both tendencies are high then the end of the threat situation is likely to be either attack or retreat, but, if both are low, other types of behaviour such as feeding or preening gestures may occur. Ethologists have called such interfering activities *displacement activities*.

Displacement

As a term in ethology, displacement derives from early models of behaviour which assumed the existence of separate instincts (see Chapter 8 each having their own so-called 'reaction energy'. The best known model was that of Lorenz (1950): an energy model, it is probably best described as psycho-hydraulic. Energy specific to an instinct builds up in hypothetical reservoirs and is discharged in the presence of the right sign-stimuli and the amount of accumulated energy. The idea is given a rough representation in Figure 9.2, where the tap represents the source of energy for the instinct, the reservoir stores it, and finally the energy is released into the trough (representing behaviour) by the force of the energy in the reservoir and also the pull exerted by the weight of external sign-stimuli.

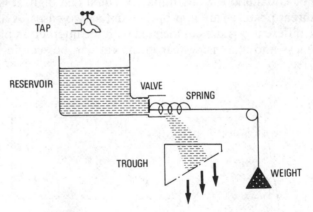

Fig. 9.2 Lorenz's psycho-hydraulic model. (After Lorenz, 1950.)

This model has been sharply and widely criticized, not least because the working of such a model is very far removed from what we know about the functioning of the nervous system. However, a behavioural model does not necessarily have to mirror the workings of the actual nervous system, so long as it represents a good approximation to real behaviour. Does it do this in relation to displacement? Lorenz would argue that, when two instincts come into conflict, as in the example we have mentioned, it is almost as if a suitable response is momentarily blocked but the supposed instinctual energy is still accumulating. The supposition is that energy forces a non-obvious instead of an obvious response. The logic is that the energy has to be released in some way, and the thwarting of the usual response associated with the instinct leads to displacement.

Let us examine how credible is the model. First it is known that not all behaviours can serve as displacement activity. Displacement responses tend to be general foraging movements or elements of nest building behaviour: these behaviours in turn have a high probability of occurring anyway, since the external stimuli associated with them are quite often present. Also, if it were just a case of energy being thwarted in one respect and finding an outlet in another, there should be no reason why the displacement activity should not be clearly and competently carried out. But we find that displacement activity is often incomplete and bizarre in its approximation to the normal form. This is not predictable from Lorenz' model. A better explanation may lie in seeing much displacement activity as a way of reducing anxiety attendant upon the conflict. A bird, for example, during a long boundary dispute, may relieve its anxiety by executing a response immediately available in terms of the stimuli around it, such as pecking the ground. Finally, we may mention one specific experiment. Raber (1948) found that turkey cocks showed displacement activity of a feeding or drinking variety during fights. However the pattern of displacement depended critically on whether food or water was available. This shows that displacement activity is under the control of the external environment, rather than being a result of hypothetical internal energy.

Courtship

Courtship is a convenient term to describe those relatively fixed patterns of behaviour which occur as a preliminary to mating. It is fitting that this section follows on from a consideration of aggression, because we shall see that there is reason to believe that courtship and conflict behaviour are related. Certain species of spider illustrate the fact in a most alarming fashion. Here, the male must treat his mate with the utmost caution if he wants to avoid ending up as her dinner.

Courtship rituals and appeasement

Because of territoriality mentioned earlier, many vertebrate males have strong conflicting motivations when faced with a potential mate; the female's behaviour must, therefore, serve to differentiate her as clearly as possible from that of an intruder. For this reason, many parallels can be seen between sexually motivated postures and *appeasement postures* (i.e., the typical postures adopted by a subservient animal when it gets in the way of a con-specific higher up in the peck order). In fact any behaviour which implies subservience is quite likely to be adopted as

211

part of courtship ritual. Thus, if we look at the great crested grebe we find that the courtship ritual involves an appeasement-type gesture which closely resembles the food-begging behaviour of the chicks. It seems then that the purpose of much courtship ritual is to bring about a reduction of aggressiveness necessary for mating to take place. Sometimes, it is the male who takes the initiative in de-escalating what could otherwise be an aggressive encounter by making movements resembling escape behaviour: we see such a pattern in the male chaffinch.

What we are saying, then, is that the courtship situation almost always involves a conflict between impulses towards sex, attack, and escape. We have already seen that, in the case of conflicting tendencies, displacement activities are almost invariably in evidence. Ethologists have been able to note many instances where such displacement activities have become ritualized and integrated into patterns of courtship behaviour. Tinbergen (1952) has termed these *derived activities*.

In certain cases, the derivation involves little change from the original unritualized behaviour. To return to the great crested grebe, one element in its courtship ritual involves presentation of nest building material; the derivation here is uncomplicated and clearly seen. In other species, however, the origin of derived activities has to be gleaned by looking at gradual changes which can be traced across related species. Morris (1959) has used this particular approach in investigating the courtship ritual of different species of grass finch. In the case of the spice finch, the male courts the female by using an extremely ritualized bow. From an examination of the less ritualized 'bows' of related species of finch, it seems that this particular ritual derives from the common displacement activity of beak-wiping.

It is quite often the case, then, that ritualized behaviour seems to evolve out of displacement activity. Presumably the behaviour begins under the motivation of conflict and later achieves an independence within general sexual motivation.

Courtship and identification

We may suspect that courtship rituals serve more than just one function: they certainly do seem to reduce conflict elements potentially present prior to mating. We may imagine, however, that another function may be important. An animal has to be able to identify an opposite sex member of his own species. Hybridization is almost always a 'bad thing' for a species; and yet we can often succeed in mating hybrids with the greatest of ease once we have introduced a male to a female. So, why does hybrid mating tend not to take place in the natural environment? The answer lies in the fact that species have developed clear courtship signals which lead an animal to its correct conspecific. In a number of lower species, for example, during the mating season the males get together and deliver *assembly calls* which serve to attract the females of their particular species. If we take two species of frog as our example, we can examine the function of these assembly calls in greater detail.

In certain areas, two quite related species of frog may share the same pond. In order to avoid hybridization it is clear that the assembly calls will have to be distinctly different so that discrimination leading to correct intra-specific mating can take place. This is, indeed, what we find. Interestingly, in other areas the two species are not found together, and one species will have a pond to itself. Ethologists have found that, in this case, assembly calls are quite similar. The rule, then, seems to be: related species inhabiting the same area will have different mating calls. Where there are exceptions there is usually a good reason; for example, two species of cricket living in exactly the same area have been found to have identical 'songs'. However, if we look more closely, we find that these two species have two different and non-overlapping mating seasons, so therefore there is no need for song differentiation.

A parallel to this line of argument can be seen in a comparison of alarm calls and mating calls in different species of birds. Analysis of the 'sound pictures' reveals a similarity of alarm call across different species, whereas mating calls are distinctly different.

The harmonious adaptations which we have just been considering seem to provide a suitable point to return to a discussion of the role of evolution in determining animal behaviour; a discussion we postponed until we had dealt descriptively with the topics of the Chapter.

The role of evolution

Let us begin by classifying somewhat the nature of evolutionary selection. Many authors have described aspects of animal behaviour within a species in terms of the evolutionary function which it might have for the benefit and survival of the species as a whole. The implications of altruism and co-operation are not hard to glean. However, such notions are a far cry from the ruthless, competitive self-interest entailed by a strict Darwinian view of natural selection and epitomized in Tennyson's ringing phrase 'Nature red in tooth and claw'. It is individuals, not groups which fight for survival. Indeed, as Dawkins (1976) is at pains to show, it is not even individuals, but genes which are in competition. The individual is merely the transitory bodily machine which acts as a vehicle for the destiny of genes from generation to generation. We therefore have to look twice at those instances of apparently co-operative behaviours whose functions seem to be for the good of the whole species. For example, Lorenz has drawn our attention to the fact that animals engaged in fights over territory or mates seldom go so far as to harm each other seriously; he all too quickly goes on to give reasons why this should be for the good of the species. However, if we want to be orthodox Darwinians, then we must account for such apparent 'gentlemanliness' of conduct by showing how such behaviour satisfies the selfish goals of the individual combatant. Let us look at a specific example in the field of territoriality.

Tinbergen, doing further research with the much researched male stickleback, allowed two males each to build a nest at the opposite ends of an aquarium. The nests formed the basis of each stickleback's territory; Tinbergen then trapped each of the males in a large glass test tube. As we have seen, the sign-stimulus for attack in the stickleback is visual, therefore the glass tubes which separated the two fish would not interfere with any elicited behaviour. Tinbergen moved the glass tubes towards each other and observed the predictable results. The sticklebacks tried to attack each other. He then moved the test tubes into the territory around the nest of one of the protagonists: its rival immediately stopped its attempts to fight and made desperate efforts to escape and retreat. We may predict what happened next when both the test tubes were moved up the tank to the headquarters of the other fish. The erstwhile aggressive holder of its territory immediately went onto the defensive and tried to flee, whilst its opposite number back in home waters resumed the attack.

Without wanting in any way to ascribe consciousness to the humble stickleback, it seems that he follows a certain rule: 'if resident, attack: if intruder, retreat'. It is only incidental that, by following this rule, the good of all sticklebacks is ensured; more to the point it is to the benefit of each stickleback in terms of his own survival to adopt this common strategy. Any mutant who fails to behave in this way will not survive to propagate his aberrant genes: imagine a stickleback who adopted the strategy—'if resident flee, if intruder, attack'. He would not succeed in winning those 50 per cent of encounters which would normally be his by virtue of being resident, and he will only win a proportion of those encounters where his own attack meets inevitably with counter-attack. Moreover, in all probability, he will suffer serious injury and not even survive to fight another day. Even suppose that enough sticklebacks reversed the rule so that this analysis would not hold: what would happen then? If every resident automatically retreats, then, soon, it will pay for everyone to be an intruder, and the concept of residency will become non-existent. Thus, we see that the first rule adopted works for the benefit of the individual, and only seems to be to the benefit of the species, because it is the one solution which offers an evolutionarily stable system. The notion of an evolutionarily stable system is of paramount importance in this line of argument.

We have devoted some time to the role of evolution in territoriality. Natural selection must be the pillar of post-Darwinian biology; and yet it is frequently misunderstood. The reader who wishes to explore further the role of natural selection in relation to animal behaviour is strongly advised to consult the highly readable book *The Selfish Gene* by Richard Dawkins.

Animal behaviour and human behaviour

As we said in the first Chapter on animal behaviour, the aim of the ethologists has not been primarily to shed light on human behaviour, still less on human problems. Animal behaviour is a field in its own right. Nevertheless, it would be untrue to say that the work of ethologists has had no effect on scientists and observers of human behaviour. To be more precise, ethology has had two different kinds of influence on the psychology of human behaviour. First, as a method of study, it has given valuable ammunition to those psychologists who have criticized the artificiality of experimentation as the major research methodology for the behavioural sciences. Indeed, such critics have coined the term 'human ethology' to denote an equally valid, and, for certain purposes a superior methodology based on naturalistic observation. The impact of this school of thought has been greatest in the area of developmental psychology: non-interventionist observation of children in natural situations (see Ch. 19).

The second influence of ethology on the study of human behaviour is best seen against the background of the recent history of psychology (see Ch. 1). Ever since J. B. Watson began the Behaviourist revolution in psychology, it is true to say that the discipline has had a bias towards the 'infinite plasticity' of human behaviour. As little as possible is assumed to be innately determined. Recently, however, 'innateness' has become a more fashionable term again, and, in certain key areas such as intelligence, personality, and racial and sex differences, this swing of the pendulum has led to vociferous controversy. Less controversial, but more closely connected with the material we have considered, behavioural scientists have been more willing to consider the existence of critical periods in human development—the work of Bowlby and others in the field of infant 'attachment' behaviour provides a good example (see Ch. 21).

Ethology, then, should not be seen as totally apart from the main stream of what we call psychology.

10   The laboratory analysis of animal behaviour

PHILIP EVANS

Introduction

Earlier Chapters have described studies of animal behaviour which have often had no more than their own intrinsic interest as a guiding light. However, psychologists have also spent a good deal of this century performing laboratory experiments using animals with the express intention of formulating an analysis of how behaviour in general is shaped, organized and maintained. The role of evolution in adaptively shaping the behaviour of a particular species over the lifetimes of many individual members of that species was pertinent to the earlier Chapters. The aim of the following Chapters will be to see whether it is possible to formulate general rules which govern the adaptation of an individual organism's behaviour to meet the pressures of its own unique environment. Adaptation, in this context, is synonymous with the term learning.

The search for general laws governing the learning process gains its momentum from the basic observation that simple and complex organisms alike seem to be capable of at least rudimentary learning, whilst in the most complex of all organisms—namely man—psychologists have tended to see most behaviour as learned. Roughly speaking, if we compare the balance of innately 'wired in' behaviour and learned behaviour, the balance shifts in favour of learning as we ascend from the lower to the higher animals. There are, however, other considerations. For example, we can, other things being equal, predict that an animal with a short lifespan, which reaches maturity very quickly, will not benefit from being genetically programmed to be a good learner; rather, it would be more helpful if it were endowed with a wide range of suitable innate responses ready for use very soon after birth. In an evolutionary context, then, we should see the capacity for learning itself as a piece of genetic programming, which like anything else, will be tested, for a given species, by the pressures of natural selection. If the idea of being innately programmed to learn seems somewhat paradoxical, the reader has only to think about the latest chess-playing computer programs. Here, the human creator is no longer content to supply his program with the ability to respond to specific moves, nor even to more general situations, but can build in a 'plasticity' which allows the program to alter itself as a result of its 'learning encounters' with its opponents.

But, given that at least rudimentary learning is seen across all species of animals, is it possible to give a general account of its general operation, regardless of the particular species concerned? It might be helpful to draw an analogy with someone wanting to investigate the workings of a particular part of a car; let us say the carburettor. He could take a particular model of car and study its carburettor and he would soon understand its function and method of operation. He might then move on to another model and discover that although the carburettor he finds is of a different make, and indeed might look superficially very different, its method of operation and function are essentially the same. After some more experience with different types of carburettors it would be true to say that he knew something about the principles of carburation in cars. It is in this analogous sense that we want to see whether we can know about the principles of learning in organisms.

So, where do we begin? Pursuing our analogy a little further, our future carburation expert will hardly have begun with a study of the latest 'twin carb' system on the newest high performance model. Likewise, despite the interest it might have, we do not begin our investigation with man himself. As long as we are cautious about premature generalization of our findings we would do well to begin with simpler 'model' species. For very good reasons, psychologists have chosen to carry out a lot of their laboratory experimentation using the white rat. This versatile animal is noted for its learning ability; it is also comparatively easily housed in an animal laboratory; lastly, it is very easily bred! However, many other animals have been used by experimenters, notably cats, dogs and pigeons. For historical reasons that will become apparent, the first experiment which we will consider utilized dogs.

An experiment by Pavlov
Ivan Petrovich Pavlov (1849–1936) was a celebrated Russian physiologist whose major interest, around the turn of the century, was the study of reflexes. In particular, he studied the salivation reflex in dogs. No one, least of all Pavlov himself, would have thought that his research would provide a foundation for the psychology of learning.

217

After all, the reflex can be thought of as the purest example of innately 'wired-in' behaviour—a relatively simple response elicited by a relatively specific stimulus. However, during his work Pavlov became rather annoyed that the answers to his completely physiological questions were being hampered by the fact that, as the dogs became accustomed to the experimental situation, they would start to salivate and secrete stomach acids as soon as he himself walked into the room. These experimental nuisances he termed 'psychic secretions'. Pavlov, in studying them, soon came to see them as important in their own right.

The first question he asked himself was whether it was just the sight or smell of food that caused the salivation, or whether any stimulus, paired often enough with food, would have the same effect. To answer the question, he isolated just one seemingly neutral stimulus which on its own could not elicit salivation: he chose in fact a tone given by a tuning fork. He followed the tone, half a second later, by an insertion of food powder into the dog's mouths. He repeated this pairing several times whilst recording the amount of salivation at every stage in the experiment. At the beginning salivation occurred only after a food delivery; but as the experiment proceeded, salivation commenced earlier and earlier until finally the secretion came before the food: that is to say, salivation was now elicited by a totally new stimulus—the previously neutral tone. This procedure he termed 'Conditioning'. Since it is no longer the only recognized conditioning procedure we shall refer to it as 'Classical conditioning'.

Classical conditioning

If a procedure is to have a wide degree of generality it has to be capable of being expressed in terms of nameable elements. What are those elements in classical conditioning? First, there is the unlearned reflex which one takes as a starting point. In the case of Pavlov's experiment we had a stimulus (food) and a response (salivation). Because, assuming the dog to be hungry, the relationship between these elements is automatic, or, to put it another way, unconditional, the food is known as the unconditioned stimulus (US) and the salivation is known as the unconditioned response (UR). The tone, or in more general terms the neutral element, is known as the conditioned stimulus (CS) and the novel response of salivation to the tone rather than the food is known as the conditioned response (CR). The whole procedure of Pavlov's experiment expressed in this general nomenclature is given diagrammatically in Figure 10.1. Various departures from that procedure are possible which will still result in conditioning, but the optimal interval between CS and US is 0.5 sec. Backward conditioning, where the whole order is changed and the CS follows the US, is a rare phenomenon, if, indeed, it occurs at all and is certainly beyond the scope of these Chapters.

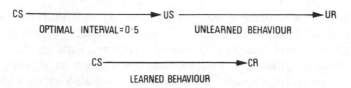

Fig. 10.1 Diagrammatic representation of the standard classical conditioning procedure.

Since the original experiments many more reflexes and many more species have been investigated, with the result that classical conditioning has become established as a precise learning phenomenon, capable of replication from one species to another. Where the same procedure gives the same results from one species to another with such reliability, one is perhaps justified in inferring a fundamental learning process shared by all organisms. Pavlov himself went further and believed that all learned behaviour, however complex, was, in principle, reducible to chains of conditioned reflexes. That belief is now, to say the least, debatable. However, we can outline one type of classical conditioning experiment which may give the reader some idea of the scope of the phenomenon in explaining behaviour.

The conditioning of emotional responses
When a person is anxious or afraid, certain bodily changes occur which can be measured using special instruments. One of these changes is in the electrical resistance of the skin. Because of the activity of tiny sweat glands, the skin becomes wetter and thus offers less electrical resistance. You may have noticed that when you become really anxious, the palms of your hands will feel noticeably clammy; you do not, however, have to be that anxious in order that a sensitive device should measure a change in skin resistance. Indeed, the sensitivity of the response itself has led to its dubious use as a lie-detector in certain parts of the USA. But to return to the laboratory, if we can initiate a change in resistance (a so-called galvanic skin response: GSR) by a specific noxious stimulus, let us say a harmless but mildly painful electric shock, we have a ready-made unconditioned stimulus-response connection. Applying the Pavlovian procedure, it should be possible to pair an established neutral stimulus (CS) with the shock (US) and end up by eliciting a GSR (CR) to the CS alone. This indeed has proved eminently possible using human subjects. What, then, is the explanatory potential of this instance of classical conditioning?

The answer to this question comes from a consideration of the nature of the CS. In the laboratory, we might use a relatively meaningless stimulus such as a tone. However, conditioning also takes place outside the laboratory with an endless supply of possible CSs and noxious USs.

219

Moreover, it takes place over a lifetime. If we say that the 'mental' correlate of our GSR is an emotion (let us say, anxiety) we are in a position to glimpse how conditioning theory may shed light on the acquisition of those bizarre and anxious behaviours seen in severe human neuroses. Moreover, classical conditioning could also explain the way each of us emotionally colours his own perception of the world. In a more general sense, a town, a house, a piece of furniture will have their own 'affective' meaning for us through particular emotional experiences.

We shall postpone further clinical speculations until we have said a lot more about the nature of conditioning. Like the early researchers, we can best approach that task by asking ourselves a series of relevant questions, the answers to which will supply us with a variety of subtopics.

Is conditioning permanent?

In order to investigate this question, let us return to Pavlov's laboratory and follow up those same dogs who have now learned to salivate to the sound of the CS tone. What happens, you may ask, if the experimenter carries on evoking the conditioned salivation response simply by presenting the tone (now on its own unaccompanied by food)? The answer is simple. The dog will eventually cease to salivate. This is a gradual process and is technically known as *extinction*. The first explanation that may come to mind is that the connection set up by the conditioning experience has to be 'reinforced' by the occasional re-presentation of the US (food), otherwise the connection simply breaks up and decays. Now, although the first part of that statement appears to be true (i.e., it seems the connection has to be occasionally reinforced), the second part is untrue, and this can be demonstrated by the following procedure. Let us 'extinguish' the conditioned response in just the way we have described, and let us continue this procedure to the point where the dog no longer shows any salivation in the presence of the CS. If we now interrupt the trial either with a rest period, or, more briefly, by making a loud noise to distract the animal we shall find that the next presentation of the CS will produce the salivation response which we thought we had extinguished. Following a rest period this is known as *spontaneous recovery*. Pavlov discovered this effect and integrated it into his general theory. Basically, what he says is that the original conditioning is a form of active learning but so, also, is extinction. Far from the animal being passive in the extinction process, what it is learning to do is to inhibit the conditioned response. This view gains credibility if we look at Figure 10.2.

In Figure 10.2, we have deliberately omitted the parameters on the vertical axis, since they could be either a measure of the original conditioning or extinction. The point is that both follow the same pattern over time: acquisition and extinction curves have the same appearance.

TIME

Fig. 10.2

An unexpected stimulus, therefore, interrupts the inhibitory process, and the CR resurfaces, as it were. Hence Pavlov attributed the phenomenon to 'disinhibition'. Does this mean that conditioning, even if it goes underground, is really permanent? It would be foolhardy to take such a dogmatic view. Certainly, if we go on presenting unaccompanied CSs to the dog, it will, in time, reach a point called *zero extinction*, when no salivation can be elicited even after a rest or a distraction. And yet, even then, such a zero extinguished dog will be quicker to relearn the response than a completely naïve animal. So, it is not to be concluded that any link between the CS and the CR has decayed completely. Moreover, in the case of emotional conditioning, mentioned earlier, where anxiety or fear responses enter the picture, extinction is very difficult to achieve. This has led some theorists (notably Hans Eysenck) to view certain traumatic conditioning as relatively irreversible. Conditioned anxiety can, as it were, be 'incubated'. The question, 'is conditioning permanent?' is therefore not a very fruitful one to ask; just as, in the related field of memory, it is often a sterile question to ask whether we ever completely forget anything, in the sense of its having decayed in storage.

What adaptive features does classical conditioning have?
If we had to learn a new response in every new situation, the flexibility of behaviour, conferred by learning, would soon be out-weighed, insofar as we would be spending all of our time in new learning and never, therefore, profiting from previous learning. It would make sense if some kind of transferability were built into the learning process. We know, of course, from our own experience that learned skills do transfer: an ordinary driving licence does not give me permission to drive a heavy articulated lorry; however, it is reasonable to suppose that I would be

221

quicker at learning to drive the lorry than someone who had had no driving experience whatsoever. In other words some of my skills can be transferred from one situation to another. Now, learning complex skills is far removed from the simple conditioned responses which we have been considering; and yet such conditioning also has transferability built into it, and this is seen in the phenomenon of *stimulus generalization*. Suppose we specify that the CS tone used in a Pavlovian-type experiment had a frequency of 500 Hz. After the CR has been fully established let us now see what happens if we test the dog with a different frequency CS tone, let us say 100 Hz above or below the training tone. We shall find that there is still a diminished but significant CR to the new stimulus. If we were to plot the magnitude of the CR to stimuli above and below the training stimulus we would get *gradients of generalization* of the type seen in Figure 10.3.

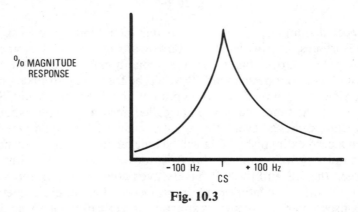

Fig. 10.3

Perhaps we should like to say that stimuli similar to the training stimulus have some natural capacity to evoke the CR. However, it might occur to the reader just how subjective the term 'similar' is. For instance, if we confine ourselves simply to a discussion of tone frequencies, where a physical dimension of similarity seems to be ready-made for us, we nevertheless encounter difficulty. Suppose our training stimulus was the note of middle C. Would a CR be greater in magnitude for the nearest F# above middle C, or the more distant C octave above middle C? The answer (it even appears in rats) is that the more distant frequency is judged more similar and gives the greater response. Apart from the enchanting idea that we can talk of musical rats with a sense of octave, such a finding has other implications. These are most easily appreciated in an experiment by Razran using classical conditioning of human subjects.

He conditioned GSR, in the same way as we have mentioned already using mild electric shock as the US. However, rather than a tone as the

CS, Razran used a visual stimulus consisting of the word 'sea'. When his subjects reliably gave a GSR to the presentation of the word, Razran tested their reaction to two words, both of which could be seen in some sense as similar. The first word was 'see' (defined as physically similar since it is acoustically identical); the second word was 'wave' (in no way physically similar but semantically related). Razran's findings indicated that most response was obtained for the semantically similar word 'wave'. Semantic generalization can therefore be more important than physical generalization. The main problem then is the nature of 'similarity'; when this encompasses semantic similarity, we can envisage the generalization of the conditioned anxiety responses mentioned earlier to a wide variety of objects and situations, which make up totally idiosyncratic clusters of associated meaning for any individual. Perhaps this offers us some further insight into the acquisition of bizarre and neurotic anxieties in clinical patients; their diffuse anxiety may be genetically generalized anxiety responses.

What about unwanted generalization?

It is not always in the interests of an organism to show generalization of its learning. It could well be that a new stimulus, though perceived as similar to an old one, requires a very different response. Reverting to our driving skills example, imagine that you are well practised in the various habits associated with the driving of a manual gearbox car. Let us also suppose that you have the ingrained common, but perhaps not desirable habit of revving the engine at traffic lights. Further suppose that you now drive an automatic car. Unless you consciously prevent generalization of the habit, the consequence of revving up could turn out to be a little unfortunate.

So there has to be a check on generalization. Organisms must have a compensating capacity for learning discriminations, and this is just what we find even in the case of simple classical conditioning.

In a typical Pavlovian-type experiment, dogs were trained to salivate to the CS of a circle. At first, the animals showed typical generalization of the salivation response to circular-type figures, notably an ellipse. However by presenting food powder (US) only in the presence of the circle and not in the presence of the ellipse, the generalization process was halted; the animals had learned a discrimination. Now comes the interesting question. The animal salivates to a full circle and not to a full ellipse, but what happens if we gradually start to introduce more and more ambiguous figures, ending up with a stimulus exactly half-way between a circle and an ellipse? The answer is that not only does the animal's discrimination break down, so does the animal! Emotional responses take over and the animal whimpers and howls as it is taken into the laboratory. Procedures of this kind have been deemed 'experi-

mental neuroses', in the belief that they can shed light on the rudimentary mechanisms that may underlie more complex human conflicts.

Can any neutral stimulus become a CS?

We might as well first raise the fundamental question of whether there
can ever be such a thing as a truly neutral stimulus. To any organism, a
perceived change in its environment (which is what a stimulus really
amounts to) is important. Indeed, any novel stimulus evokes what is
called an orientating response (OR). If we measure that response as we
continue to present the stimulus over and over again, we find the
response wanes to zero. The process is much akin to extinction, but
because the OR to the stimulus did not require prior learning, the term
habituation is used.

Now, the usual method of establishing the 'neutrality' of a potential
CS, prior to conditioning, is to test it out by presenting it on its own
before associating it with the US. If it in no way evokes part of the UR,
then it is assumed neutral. If this procedure were not followed and the
potential CS had already got some association with the UR, it would be
very easy to think that one had established conditioning. However, such
conditioning would be only apparent not real, and the term *pseudo-
conditioning* has been coined for it.

Matters would be very simple if any stimulus (established as neutral in
the sense given above) could be classically conditioned. But matters are
not that simple. Imagine, for a moment, that you are in a restaurant and
along comes the cheese-board with what appears to be a beautiful piece
of Stilton. You take a slice and find it is decidedly 'off'. You immediately
are overcome with a feeling of nausea. Next day you simply see a piece of
Stilton in a shop window; the sight of the cheese causes you to feel somewhat nauseous again. From a commonsense point of view this scenario
might not appear unusual, but from what we have postulated about
classical conditioning principles it is decidedly odd. If we consider that
the taste of the bad cheese is a US to which there is a natural response
(UR) of nausea, then the sight of the cheese has become a CS. The
classical conditioning paradigm would be given further support if you
showed typical generalization of your nauseous response to the sight of
other types of cheese. But now the oddities are apparent. In the typical
conditioning trials, learning takes place gradually and roughly in accord
with the curve shown above in Figure 10.2, and yet in our example it
seems that the conditioned response of nausea has acquired great
strength after what amounts to a single trial. That is not the only oddity
either. If classical conditioning is solely concerned with pairing one
stimulus with another, what about the check table-cloth at the
restaurant, the cheese knife, the biscuit which accompanied the cheese?
Why do they not evoke nausea?

224

It appears that some stimuli are more naturally connected with some responses and that conditioning may be subject to 'biological constraints'. Seligman (1972) has put forward a theory to explain how this might operate. Basically, what he says is that organisms come prepared to learn certain associations, e.g., a bad taste and subsequent nausea; and unprepared to learn others, e.g., the sound of a bell and the delivery of food. Lastly they come contra-prepared to learn certain associations, i.e., conditioning is very difficult, if not impossible; a good example is teaching an association between an electric shock and a taste.

Thus, according to Seligman's theory all possible learning situations lie on a continuum of preparedness which determines how easily or otherwise they may be learned.

Instrumental conditioning

Whilst the Russian researcher, Pavlov, was busy with his experimental dogs, an American psychologist, Thorndike, had been carrying out experiments with cats. Thorndike devised puzzle boxes: boxes from which the animal could escape if it could discover a certain trick, namely unhooking a catch. Thorndike noticed that the animals acquired the correct response in a gradual fashion and likened the process to trial-and-error learning whereby the correct response was gradually 'stamped in' as a result of being 'rewarded' by escaping. This he called the Law of Effect. Later on psychologists extended research to the laboratory white rat (an excellent learner) and to puzzles which enabled better observation and measurement of such learning—a simple T-maze, for example (see Fig. 10.4).

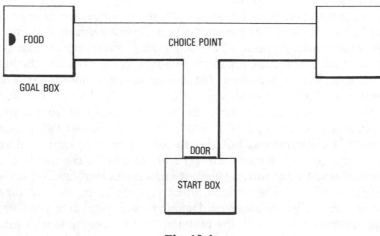

Fig. 10.4

225

Such apparatus enables the researcher to take more than one measurement of learning. He can look at the rate at which errors are eliminated and also look at the so-called 'latency' of the response—in other words the time involved in initiating a correct run of the maze. As research became even more systematic, psychologists such as Clark Hull began to investigate the effects of motivational factors in such learning. *Drive* was objectively defined in terms of the hours of food deprivation; *incentive* was defined in terms of the amount of food offered as a reward at the end of the maze. Hull and his colleagues hoped to build up a mighty edifice of behaviour theory in which the occurrence of any response was, in principle, predictable from a mathematical equation in which a finite number of motivational and learning variables, such as drive and habit strength, interacted to give a final probability value for the particular response. Hull's school of research came to dominate the academic psychology taught throughout the middle period of this century; and yet, the promise of a complete behaviour theory was not fulfilled, despite the efforts of tens of thousands of hungry and hard-working white rats. Psychologists nowadays, quite rightly, shun the idea of such an enterprise coming to fruition, at least for a long time to come.

Despite the failure of the Hullian school, they and other animal experimenters have given us much information about how organisms in general do 'learn by reward'. Thorndike's 'stamping in' procedure is now generally talked about and investigated under the heading *instrumental conditioning*. The barest skeleton of the procedure is to follow a particular response with a 'reward', with the result that that particular response will increase in probability in that situation. Let us now try to put some flesh on the skeleton.

The concept of reinforcement
We have been content so far to talk about responses being learned by 'reward', but that is an oversimplification. In instrumental conditioning, we are really talking about a general learning ability, observable across species, which enables the organism to adapt its behaviour in the light of its environmental consequences for that organism. Consequences which are important for an animal, such as acquiring food when it is hungry, are quite easily spoken of as rewards. However, escaping from a noxious environment (such as one of Thorndike's puzzle boxes) can be just as important a consequence, but the use of the term reward to describe such escape is not so apt. In general, psychologists use the term *reinforcement* to refer to the effect of consequent outcome on response probability. All outcomes which affect probability in the instrumental paradigm are called reinforcers. Defining exactly what a reinforcer is except something that alters the probability of the response with which it is associated is a difficult and, as yet, unsolved question which we will

consider in the next Chapter. For now, let us look in more detail at the different kinds of outcome which affect responding in instrumental conditioning.

Basically, two things are important to an organism: the presence of certain stimuli and the absence of certain others. At the risk of being mentalistic, we can call the former 'pleasurable' and the latter 'painful'. It follows that there will be four conditions which an organism will consider important and which will therefore lead to behavioural consequences. These four conditions are summarized in Table 10.1:

Table 10.1

	Presentation	Removal
Pleasant stimuli	Positive reinforcement	Omission
Noxious stimuli	Punishment	Escape

It can be seen that the loose term 'reward' only applies properly to the positive reinforcement situation. The escape situation is similar in the sense that the associated response will become more probable, hence the term 'negative reinforcement' is sometimes substituted for escape. The other two situations have the opposite effect on response probability; a response followed by punishment, other things being equal, will lead to a lowered probability of that response. Omission of a positive reinforcer will have the same effect as punishment, hence the term 'negative punishment' is sometimes substituted for omission.

What is learned in instrumental conditioning?

Thorndike and the early researchers mostly agreed that the nature of instrumental conditioning was the building up of habits or stimulus-response connections. Now, in an obvious sense this is indisputable. In all experiments, we come to see a functional probabilistic relationship build up between a stimulus and a response. However the early researchers wanted to go further than this. They belonged to the Behaviourist school (see Ch. 1) and, therefore, sought to dismiss the importance of that which was not directly observable: cognition and consciousness. Insofar as they were dealing with animals, it became an anathema to admit that anything of that kind went on inside the animal's head! Thus a direct mechanical link between stimulus and response was held, on faith, to be the actual nature of what was learned. It was as if the stimulus and response were wired up together by the blind operation of reinforcement. However, even in the early days there were 'cognitive' theorists such as Tolman who disputed the over-simplified Behaviourist view and indeed quickly caused modifications to simple Behaviourism as a result of their experiments.

Tolman showed that rats, once they had learned to run a maze, could, if circumstances demanded it, swim through it. He also showed that rats in a cross-maze (see Fig. 10.5) learned where to go rather than what to do, as demonstrated by their ability to proceed to the food regardless of their entry point to the maze. In essence, Tolman showed an animal's flexibility in its mode of response. He believed that the nature of learning was to perfect what he called 'maps in the head'. Rather than learning consisting of simple stimulus-response connections, Tolman believed that learning was about what stimulus goes with what other stimulus (S-S, i.e., stimulus-stimulus connections rather than S-R connections). The organism selects a response on the basis of this 'information'.

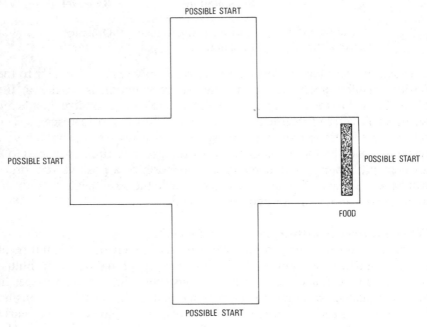

Fig. 10.5

The debate between S-S and S-R theorists has now become largely historical. At a physiological level the attendant questions will not be answered for a considerable time and speculation is not profitable. At a behavioural level, everyone has agreed that, regardless of the physiological nature of learning, it is useful and possible to explore the systematic way in which events in an organism's environment and its responses develop into a functional relationship. Responses become measurably contingent upon events. The field of instrumental conditioning is no longer about speculative S-R connections; it is about observable S-R contingencies.

228

Is reinforcement a necessary condition of learning?

This question is closely allied to the previous one and is also largely historical. It can be seen that if Tolman is right about learning being essentially about the acquisition of information, one can draw a distinction between learning and performance. Reinforcement may not be necessary for learning; it may simply be the important variable which determines whether the animal translates covert learning into overt behaviour. Tolman and Honzig (1930) carried out an experiment to try and demonstrate this. The experiment was to compare three groups of rats in a maze learning task. One group was given reinforcement (food) after each trial; the second group (control) was never given reinforcement; the third group was not given reinforcement till the eleventh trial. Tolman was able to show that the last group resembled the control group until trial eleven, showing little evidence, therefore, of learning. After trial eleven they very quickly caught up with the first group. The results are presented graphically in Figure 10.6.

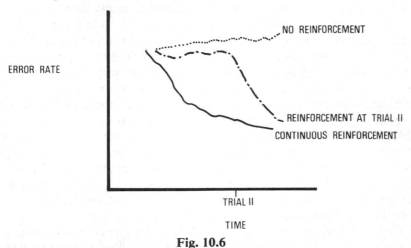

Fig. 10.6

The experiment appeared to confirm Tolman's suspicion that 'latent' learning had taken place in the absence of reinforcement; when reinforcement was later introduced this 'latent' learning made itself apparent in the ease with which the Group three animals caught up with the Group one animals. However, it is hopeless to try and prove anything with regard to this question. Tolman's results could be countered by saying that there was some implicit reinforcement present in the earlier trials, e.g., being returned to the familiar, home cage from the alien, goal box. The trouble is that no one has been able to give a strict definition of reinforcement that covers all instances (see Ch. 11). We have, therefore, to make do with an operational definition, defining a reinforcer in terms of its effect on the probability of a preceding response. This, however, is

229

essentially circular, and its circularity is particularly noticeable when we raise a question, such as 'is reinforcement necessary for learning?', where we need to have an outside criterion of what constitutes a reinforcer. Unless and until the concept becomes more refined any final answer to this question has to be shelved.

Is consciousness necessary for instrumental learning?

This might seem a rather strange question to be raising, given that Behaviourists have not had much time for the concept of consciousness. However, it is a question worth asking because so many people enter and leave this area of psychology with either an enthusiastic or a disparaging notion that it all boils down to what everyone knew already: the power of the stick and the carrot. Such a view needs so much qualification that it is in the end misleading. Nowadays, not many psychologists deny the importance of consciousness or awareness as something that often mediates between stimulus and response. We also know from our own experience that crude attempts to apply stick or carrot to human subjects very often give quite contrary results to those we would expect. A parent hitting a child for bad behaviour might not only fail to curb that behaviour but instead increase its likelihood. A political party holding out some obvious carrot to the electorate might be so mistrusted as to lose votes as a result. These examples demonstrate that, far from consciousness being necessary for instrumental conditioning, it may complicate it to the point of contrary findings. At best, the question of consciousness is somewhat irrelevant. This area of psychology, insofar as it has importance for human behaviour is at its strongest when reinforcement works gradually and blindly at shaping habitual patterns of behaviour which are not very often the focus of conscious control: a person's gait, his habitual mode of speaking, the attitudes he has come to hold (but has never consciously decided to hold).

Keehn (1969) showed quite dramatically the power of reinforcement to shape human behaviour without awareness. Subjects were invited to play a fruit machine type of game and, unbeknown to them, rewards were made contingent upon their rate of blinking. As a result of this clandestine reinforcement the subjects increased their rate of blinking. Goodenough conducted a similar experiment. He brought subjects into a room and held a conversation with them. Unbeknown to them, Goodenough had set out to increase their usage of plural nouns, and to achieve this he gave verbal reinforcement in the form of an 'M-hm' whenever they used a plural noun. As predicted, there was a gradual increase in the use of plural nouns. Both experiments confirm that our behaviour is influenced by reinforcement, whether we want it to be or not. In the next Chapter when we look at schedules of reinforcement we shall see that the principles of instrumental conditioning are powerful and pervasive enough to be able to predict the response rate of a person playing a one-armed bandit machine as easily as predicting the behaviour of a rat pressing a bar for food pellets. No doubt, the person playing the machine would report all sorts of conscious 'reasons' for his behaviour: expectation that the jackpot will occur in the next three goes; disappointment that it does not. Such conscious reports are largely irrelevant since the graph of his behaviour will still match that of a rat whose reward contingencies are identical.

Classical and instrumental conditioning compared

We have described, quite rightly, two rather different conditioning *procedures*. What we could however ask is whether these two different procedures reflect two fundamentally different learning *processes*, or whether, at root, there is just one process called conditioning. A quick look at the conditioning phenomena that we have mentioned suggests that the differences may only be superficial. After all, both classical and instrumental responses undergo the same extinction process when either the US or reinforcer respectively is omitted. Moreover, the extinction curves in both instances follow the same pattern. The same similarity between the two kinds of conditioning procedure is seen when we examine the phenomenon of generalization. A rat which has learned (instrumentally) to press a bar for food when a tone sounds will show generalization of its behaviour in the event of similar tones being sounded.

Despite these similarities, a number of psychologists have put forward strong reasons for isolating two separate kinds of conditioning underlying the procedures. Perhaps most importantly, they have drawn a distinction between the type of response which is conditioned in each case. Classical conditioning deals with essentially involuntary emotional or glandular responses which are mediated by the autonomic nervous system; instrumental conditioning deals with essentially voluntary responses, which may be described as deliberate skeletal movements. This major division has been upheld by many notable Behaviourists including, in particular, B. F. Skinner. However, very recently it has been dealt a severe blow by a series of experiments conducted by Neal Miller. By ingenious techniques, Miller managed to train rats to alter their 'involuntary' autonomic functioning in order to obtain reward. Even before these well-controlled experiments, it had been shown that human subjects could also control supposed involuntary responses, such as heart-rate and blood-pressure, if they were provided with so-called bio-feedback. What Miller showed in his experiments was that this was not due to mediation by essentially voluntary responses, such as indulging in exciting fantasy, or making certain muscular movements. Miller's rats were totally paralysed and received reward in the form of direct stimulation of 'pleasure' centres in the brain (see Ch. 6). The only interpretation was that the rats were directly controlling autonomic responses.

However, Miller's experiments cannot be said to show positive evidence in favour of a one-process view of conditioning, since it leaves open the possibility that the two kinds of procedure might still be more appropriate for different kinds of response, even if, in principle, involuntary responses can be instrumentally conditioned.

And so, yet another debate continues.

11 Reinforcement

PHILIP EVANS

In this Chapter we take up in more detail the concept of reinforcement and address ourselves to a variety of questions concerning its nature and its effects. We shall also elaborate on the special considerations that attend the shaping and maintenance of behaviour by punishing consequences.

Schedules of reinforcement

We have scarcely yet mentioned one of the key figures in the development of and, indeed, in the current exposition of behavioural psychology, namely B. F. Skinner (b.1904). And yet, it is to him and his colleagues that we owe most concerning our knowledge about the operation of reinforcement, particularly reinforcement *contingencies*. What do we mean by contingencies? Till now, our brief perusal of the field of instrumental conditioning has tended to assume a situation in which simple responses are stamped in by the operation of continuous reinforcement after each correct response. Skinner's work takes us beyond this simple outline in two respects.

Skinner's work

First, he has been concerned with how more complicated responses can be shaped by reinforcing, at first, only gross approximations to the eventually desired response. In this way, quite extraordinary behaviour was engineered, the best known Skinnerian feat being the ping-pong playing pigeons. Secondly he has been interested in how conditioned behaviour can be maintained, not just by continuous reinforcement, but by *partial* (or *intermittent*) reinforcement. Such work is of great interest, since the behaviour of men and women in the real world is not usually followed by its due reward on every occasion. In other words, intermittent reinforcement of responding is nearer the real-life situation.

Before we outline some of Skinner's major findings, it is necessary to give a brief description of his typical laboratory method and apparatus.

Skinner was the inventor of what has naturally enough become known as the 'Skinner-box'. This is essentially a chamber (see Fig. 11.1), in which a small animal (usually a pigeon or white rat) is exposed to a highly-controlled environment. Reinforcement can be given automatically by a special mechanism linked to a bar, which the animal presses, or a key, which is pecked. Skinner conceives of the organism continuously 'operating' on its environment. The behaviour can be studied in terms of small units called 'operant' responses. For this reason, Skinner uses the term *operant conditioning* instead of instrumental. The two terms are, however, identical in meaning.

Fig. 11.1   A pigeon in a Skinner-box.

To return to the Skinner-box; obviously a naive rat cannot go straight up to a bar, press it, and receive a food reward. The behaviour is shaped: at first, the rat will find out where the food-cup is located and a few carefully delivered pellets will keep the animal predominantly on the correct side of the box; later, the experimenter will demand more of the rat so that it must now at least be in contact with the bar; thus the final bar-pressing behaviour is shaped. Once a rat is fully trained in emitting the correct operant response, the Skinner-box comes into its own as a method of studying behaviour. One can introduce *discriminative stimuli* such as a green or red light which signals to the animal that reinforcement will or will not follow a bar press. Importantly, one does not have to follow a response with reinforcement on every occasion, and we now come on to a consideration of partial reinforcement.

234

One of the most important findings with regard to partial reinforcement of any kind is that the extinction process (see Chapter 10) is lengthened. Let us examine what that, in fact, means. When a response is reinforced on every occasion (continuous reinforcement) the sequel in the extinction process of withdrawing reinforcement is a speedy diminution of responding. If however the organism's responding has been maintained by partial reinforcement, the extinction process is lengthened and, in some exceptional cases, can be avoided altogether. This is known as the partial reinforcement effect (PRE). Psychologists have put forward a number of theories to try to explain PRE, all of which possibly contain an element of truth. One common sense theory is that the animal has to learn to discriminate clearly between the acquisition/maintainance situation and the extinction situation before it can change its behaviour (remember from Chapter 10 that extinction itself is a form of active learning not to respond). Now, in the instance of partial reinforcement the discrimination is not so easy since the organism has already learned not to expect reinforcement on each and every occasion; hence, the extinction process will take that much longer. Yet another theory bases PRE on inferred emotional responses which may be considered to be akin to conditioned frustration. These frustration responses can normally be thought of as motivating the inhibition of responding. However, in the partial reinforcement situation, such responses have been associated with the occasional presence of reinforcement; hence, the organism will tolerate much more frustration without a deterioration in performance. Although frustration responses are not directly observable, there is supportive evidence for this view in the common finding that the usual extinction process does lead to signs of emotionality in all organisms.

Specific types of schedule

Let us now be more exact about partial reinforcement. One can omit to reinforce an organism in many different ways. One could decide to reinforce every fifth, every tenth, or every fifteenth response; equally, one could, when the animal is responding properly, gradually make the reinforcement contingent upon the passage of time rather than the number of responses emitted; in other words the animal may be given a reward every minute, two minutes and so on. Ferster and Skinner (1957) discuss such schedules in great detail, but for our purposes we shall simply outline the two major types of schedule: they are *ratio* and *interval*, and they approximate to the examples given above. A ratio schedule requires the animal to make a fixed number of responses per reward; an interval schedule dictates that an animal will get a reward after a fixed time interval of responding regardless of how many responses it may make. Note the qualifying adjective 'fixed'—the schedules are known as fixed ratio (FR) and fixed interval (FI). However, it is equally possible to vary the ratio and vary the interval. Instead of reinforcement following every fifth response, for example, one could simply determine that on average the reinforcement will follow five responses. This is known as a variable ratio schedule (VR). Likewise, the reward which comes every five minutes on average would be an example of a variable interval schedule (VI).

These four major types of schedule give rise to typical patterns of responding which we can illustrate by the use of cumulative graphs (see Fig. 11.2) where we record the number of responses on the vertical axis and the time intervals involved on the horizontal axis—a diagonal slash indicates an instance of reinforcement.

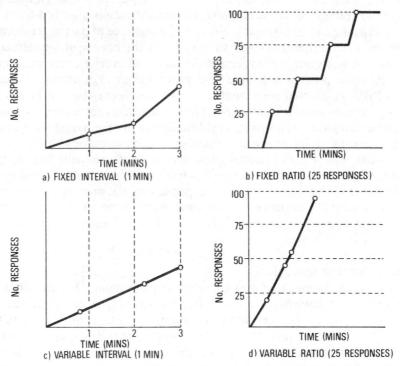

Fig. 11.2 Cumulative records of different schedules (circles denote reinforcement).

Note that in the case of the fixed schedules there is a falling off of responding immediately after a reinforcement. This is followed by an increase in responding as the time for reinforcement (FI) or the number of responses needed (FR) is approached. This gives rise to a 'scalloping' effect on the graph. Apart from obtaining for rats pressing bars or pigeons pecking keys, such patterns of responding could be seen in equivalent human activities. If you were to wait at a bus-stop, where the bus was expected in ten minutes, one could think of it as a (relatively!) fixed interval situation; whatever responses one makes the time of reinforcement (arrival of bus) is preordained. However human beings are not immune from making superstitious responses such as looking intently down the road as if to will the bus to appear. If you used a fellow would-be traveller as your subject of investigation and made a record of his superstitious peeps, his response rate would map very neatly on to a typical FI record. Another example: 'a watched pot never boils'—and yet we do watch them from time to time and our peeping responses would once again represent typical FI performance.

Turning our attention back to Figure 11.2, let us now consider the variable schedules. Here we can see that the scallops have been removed. The consequence of making any schedule variable rather than fixed is to make responding steadier and smoother. As a human example of VR, we can take the activity of playing a one-armed bandit. Here reinforcement is dependent on bar-pressing rather than time, but the number of bar-presses required for a reinforcement is variable. The kind of behaviour elicited in the gambler is obviously just what the machine's owner wants. The VR schedule is to be found lurking behind most gambling situations and explains the compulsive nature of the respond-ing which it engenders: the fact that the investment of the responder is not usually equalled by his pay-off offers only a cognitive awareness which in some cases may be of little value in limiting his compulsive responding.

What is the nature of reinforcement?

This question was raised and quickly dropped in the preceding Chapter. However, we did pose the difficulty of circularity which is attendant on defining a reinforcer simply as something which increases or decreases the probability of the response which it follows. Such a working defini-tion does not help us to identify those reinforcers which are not apparent to begin with; it will often become a matter of faith, rather than fact, to say that an increasingly probable response is being reinforced. We need, therefore, some additional criterion as a definition, and theorists have been eager to suggest suitable candidates. We present here a few attempted solutions.

The drive-reduction hypothesis
This is associated with the psychologist Clark Hull and offers a very plausible first attempt. According to Hull the concept of reinforcement begins with the concept of biological need: an organism has many such survival needs such as food, water, air, avoidance of tissue damage from

noxious stimuli. When any of these needs are thwarted, Hull supposed that a state of drive came into being, which energized the organism into random activity. By trial and error, certain responses would be made which satisfied the need and thus reduced the drive. Reinforcers are thus, in a primary sense, drive-reducers. The fact that animals will work for 'reinforcers' which do not apparently reduce drive was not damning to Hull's hypothesis, since his general theory allowed for so-called 'secondary reinforcers' which could be learned through association with primary reinforcement. Thus Bugelski (1938) showed how rats would continue to press a bar in a Skinner box simply to obtain a noise of a click from the apparatus, even though the original food-pellet reward had been withdrawn. He argued that, in the past, by its consistent pairing with the food, the click had acquired secondary reinforcing characteristics. Now the question of whether this is the explanation of Bugelski's results or not is beyond the scope of this text; what is important is that even the sometimes dubious concept of secondary reinforcement is not enough to rescue Hull's drive-reduction hypothesis from more serious criticism. It certainly is the case, for example, that animals will, in some instances, work for what can only be described as drive increase. Among the more bizarre experiments in the psychological literature is one by Sheffield *et al* (1951) who used a sexual reinforcer as the goal in maze learning; male rats were allowed to copulate with a female in the goal box. Well, not quite. In fact, Sheffield took the male rats out of the goal box before they had the chance to ejaculate. By no stretch of the imagination could this experience be described as drive-reducing, and yet, apparently, the rats continued to treat the goal box as a reinforcement. Other experiments have shown that animals which have all their survival needs satisfied do not, as one might predict from Hull's theory, sink into a state of blissful inactivity; rather they continue to explore their environment, even seeking out novel and complex places and objects rather than simple ones, and making bar presses to turn on lights and buzzers. One could, of course, postulate a 'curiosity drive' but this is a very dangerous kind of *post hoc* invention which could lead to an endless multiplication of drive sources. Also, in this case, it does not help since the behaviour that the drive supposedly motivates does not result in the satiation that one might expect from drive-produced responses.

The drive-reduction hypothesis, then, does not allow us to say anything definite about the nature of reinforcement. Nor do closely related hypotheses such as Miller's 'stimulus intensity' view. This states that all stimuli (internal hunger pangs, external noise) are potentially aversive when they reach excessively high intensities. Reinforcement is the business of reducing stimulus intensity. It can be seen that the flaws of Hull's drive-reduction view are also shared by this theory. If we are to speak in terms of level of stimulation, it appears that an organism seeks to achieve a balance, avoiding excessive under-stimulation just as much as avoiding excessive over-stimulation. This, of course, might be the nature of reinforcement—to achieve such a balance—however, it is not very helpful since it is still impossible to say just how under- or over-stimulated it is at any one time.

Response theories of reinforcement

Certain psychologists have attempted to define reinforcement in terms of the kind of responses made in a reinforcing situation rather than the stimuli delivered by the environment. Thus, it might be said that in an ordinary Skinner-box task where a rat presses a bar for a sugar-pellet reward, it is not the food itself which is reinforcing; rather, it is the opportunity thereby provided to make the pleasurable response of eating. Sheffield has put such a theory forward based on the idea of *consummatory responses*.

Consummatory responses typically include eating, drinking, and sexual activity. Note that Sheffield's own experiment quoted above is readily explained by the consummatory response theory. Ironically, then, Sheffield's theory is most effectively compromised by an experiment carried out by the drive-reduction theorists. Miller and Kessen used food reward for rats in the usual way, except that they by-passed the consummatory response of eating by passing a fistula into the animals' stomachs. The food thus satisfied the underlying drive produced by hunger, but did not satisfy a consummatory response.

An interesting and more recent theory of reinforcement, based on responding rather than stimuli, is associated with the psychologist David Premack. It is a theory which claims to be useful rather than universal. It offers us some insight into the shifting nature of what is and is not reinforcing. You may have noticed that I have tired of adding 'assuming the animal is hungry' when talking about food as a reinforcer. What happens when animals are not desperately hungry as a result of planned deprivation? It is here that Premack's theory comes into its own. Let us illustrate this by looking at what might be called Premack's paradigm experiment. In the usual scheme of things, a rat may be trained to turn an activity wheel in order to achieve access to food. Now, let us imagine the rat fully satiated. Anyone who has kept pet rodents knows that they spend a good deal of their time running activity wheels without the arranged contingency of a food reward. Premack, therefore, reversed the normal experiment and made the opportunity for wheel turning contingent on the satiated animal's eating. If the satiated animal ate some presumably unwanted food, the wheel-brake would be freed allowing the animal access to it.

We can put Premack's theory in more general terms, as follows.

Observation of an animal's activity in a free situation will reveal a number of typical behaviours. Because the animal freely engages in them all, we can assume that they are all to some extent, and at different times, reinforcing. At certain times, Premack says, one response is *pre-potent*, that is to say that it is more probable than others. Thus, in the case of a hungry animal, eating response is going to be pre-potent over a wheel-running response. However, in the case of a well-fed rat the opposite becomes true. Premack simply states that if all the responses of the animal are put in the form of a hierarchy from the most pre-potent to the least, then a more pre-potent response can always serve to reinforce a less pre-potent one. Thus, there is nothing paradoxical about a rat learning to eat in order to run; it is just that the early psychologists had been too eager to study reinforcement using a limited range of obvious necessities such as food and drink.

Premack's theory is both interesting and challenging. It does not, however, shed any final light on the question about the nature of reinforcement, nor does it explain instances of reinforcement where no response appears to be made. For example, the fistula feeding experiment described above as evidence against the consummatory response theory of reinforcement could also be quoted here against Premack's theory and that is because it, too, is a response theory. In the next part of this Chapter we shall see the ultimate in passive reception of reinforcement with no response involved when we look at electrical brain stimulation.

Hedonistic theories of reinforcement

Thorndike, in his pioneering days, referred to reinforcing events as 'satisfiers' and 'annoyers'. These terms were starkly mentalistic in the same way as terms such as 'pleasure' and 'pain'. Hence, psychologists have been unwilling, until recently, to admit them, since they do not help us explain behaviour in any way. The notion that reinforcing events have to do with pleasure and pain has always, however, had a common sense appeal and such theories as are based on this notion are called 'Hedonistic' theories—from the Greek word for 'pleasure'.

In 1954, James Olds and Peter Milner, two physiologists, were conducting experiments on rats with electrodes implanted in their brains. With great serendipity, they noted a curious observation: when the rats were stimulated by turning on the electrodes they tended to return to that part of the cage where the stimulation had occurred. The researchers decided to investigate further. Using electrode implantations in the mid-brain, they went about making stimulation (a very mild current of about 1/10000 ampere) contingent on bar-pressing. Although the stimulation only lasted for about half a second, Olds reported that rats would press a bar thousands of times an hour for up to twelve hours

240

or more for such brain stimulation. Obviously, such stimulation was extremely reinforcing and it was not long before there was speculation that these 'pleasure-centre' sites represented a neurological basis for all instances of reinforcement. Additional sites were also discovered which seemed to act as 'pain' centres, where stimulation led animals to learn an avoidance response.

Obviously, we are nowhere near being able to trace every instance of reinforcement to the operation of these centres, so the hedonistic theory is not as yet of great explanatory value. However, it does enable us to pin such mentalistic notions as pleasure and pain to observable nervous system functioning. In this way, there is at least a glimpse of what might turn out to be a final answer to the question what is the nature of reinforcement.

Behaviour and aversive events

Many of the rules governing the acquisition and maintenance of behaviour using rewarding consequences of the positive reinforcement variety have parallels when behaviour is shaped by aversive consequences. Thus, if an animal learns that it can escape a shock by pressing a lever, or jumping over a hurdle we would find that that response will increase in frequency just like a positively reinforced response. For this reason *escape learning* is also referred to as negatively reinforced behaviour, and it appears to satisfy all the obvious canons of instrumental conditioning.

It is far more debatable to say that *punishment* procedures are so alike, since no particular response is being shaped. All that punishment appears to do is suppress a target response, and suppression and unlearning are not the same thing, as any parent should be able to testify. Child psychologists do not usually recommend using punishment as a standard way of shaping and controlling a child's behaviour. This is not only because child psychologists are kind people. There is a good deal of evidence to suggest that punishment techniques are, firstly, not particularly effective and, secondly, often have unwelcome consequences as side-effects. Let us examine some of these disadvantages of punishment procedures.

The disadvantages of punishment
In a laboratory we have almost complete control of an animal subject, so it is not surprising that a rat which receives a punishment for going down one alley rather than another will cease that particular response quite soon after the delivery of a few mildly painful electric shocks. Even in the laboratory we are not always likely to get such clear-cut results

241

and a little later we shall discuss some of the paradoxical effects that can result from such procedures. In normal life, the amount of control we have over people is very properly limited and that applies to a parent and a child. Let us suppose that a father punishes a child for aggression against other children, obviously in the hope that punishment will reduce the frequency of future aggressive encounters. This consequence, on its own, is, however, just one of many. Let us consider some other consequences:

1. The child learns to be selective about his aggressive encounters avoiding only those which are likely to come to the attention of his parents.

2. The child learns to avoid the presence of the aversive source of stimulation, i.e., the father, thus keeping punishment encounters to a minimum.

3. The child learns by example that his father can control him by what psychologists call 'power-assertive' techniques. Thus, as long as he also learns the first lesson that we outlined he should convince himself that, apart from the dangers of being caught, his own power-assertive ways of dealing with other children are just the thing.

None of the three outcomes above is desirable, nor were they intended. There is good evidence, however, to believe that they are very common outcomes. Albert Bandura (1969), a psychologist who has made a study of imitative learning, quotes the well-established statistic that parents who use 'power-assertive' techniques of discipline tend to have distinctly more aggressive children on average.

There is another distinct disadvantage of punishment as a means of control. This derives directly from its vagueness in terms of goals. Punishment, at most, can only indicate what is undesirable or unwanted behaviour, it cannot indicate what is desirable or wanted. If a parent resorts to punishment as a way of bringing up a child, only offering criticisms, slaps, and shouting sessions, then it will not be surprising that the child will have little idea of what is expected of him. Add to this the established finding that power-assertive parents are also inconsistent in their demands of their children, and we have a very sorry picture and a very confused child.

There is yet another factor which needs to be mentioned, and that is that punishment, whether it be applied to a laboratory white rat or human kind, has attendant emotional consequences. Some years ago, Neal Miller carried out an experiment in which electric shock was given to a rat in a cage containing another rat. The shocked rat immediately attacked the other rat. Across species, aggression is a very common response to punishing consequences.

242

Avoidance

We have so far looked at two procedures involving aversive events: escape and punishment. There is a third procedure which has been extensively researched by those involved in the laboratory analysis of behaviour. It is called avoidance. Suppose we introduce in the normal escape procedure an additional stimulus which reliably predicts the arrival of the shock—for example it might be that a red light comes on a few seconds before the shock. We shall find that it is not long before the animal starts to make its response before the arrival of the actual shock. Rather than simply escaping the shock, it can now successfully avoid it altogether. This procedure is known as *signalled avoidance.*

One of the most characteristic findings about avoidance learning is that responses which animals learn in this fashion are very difficult and sometimes impossible to extinguish. Why should this be?

We know that what maintains responding in a situation is reinforcement. Could it be that there is a kind of intrinsic reinforcement in these situations? Two psychologists, Neal Miller and Hobart Mowrer, thought that there was. They have both developed what have become known as two-factor theories of avoidance. Avoidance, they say, involves both a classical conditioning component, and an instrumental component. First of all, we consider the automatic or unconditioned response to receiving an electric shock. We should expect to see a great variety of peripheral physical responses involving the autonomic nervous system: changes in heart-rate, respiration, galvanic skin response. These may be said to represent some more central state which we may conveniently call 'fear'. The argument of two factor theorists is that fear is a response which becomes classically conditioned to the bell by virtue of its close associaton with the shock. Fear, however, is also an aversive state to experience; psychologists who still object to words like 'experience' would probably say the conditioned responses give rise to internal feedback stimuli which are aversive. Hence, in the same way that hunger pangs are supposed in Hullian learning theory to drive the animal into responding, so these latter-day Hullians suppose that stimuli associated with fear drive the animal into activity. Also, in strict analogy with hunger pangs, whatever reduces the intensity of these fear-stimuli is reinforcing.

This last sentence gives us the instrumental component of the two-factor approach to avoidance. The organism performs some response such as pressing a bar or jumping a hurdle in order to reduce what may be thought of as a conditioned fear drive. Now, let us make some additional assumption that fear is conditioned in an extra strong fashion to a previously neutral stimulus (indeed, Eysenck has suggested that traumatic conditioning of this kind is subject to something called 'incubation'—a kind of self-strengthening process which can lead to almost irreversible conditioning). We now have some sort of answer

243

to the peculiar paradox that avoidance learning is difficult to extinguish, even when the obvious negative reinforcer—the shock—is not experienced. The answer is that fear acts as an internal negative reinforcer.

A critique of the two-factor theory

So much for the theory. We can recognize its neatness. We can recognize the importance of having an explanation for the phenomenon, since avoidance responses and their typical and irrational persistence seem, in microcosm, to resemble the mysterious phobias, obsessions, and persistent rituals of some neurotic patients. An understanding of general mechanics would, therefore, be quite valuable. However, is the two-factor theory more than just neat and plausible? Is it, in fact, useful? At the moment the answer must be no, for the simple reason that it does not do what is demanded of a good theory: it does not take us any nearer to explaining anything.

All the crucial, so-called explanatory, links are pushed inside the organism—fear-responses, fear-derived aversive stimuli—which makes them unobservable; it thus becomes a simple matter of faith as to whether they are there or not. Another weakness of the two-factor theory of avoidance comes from studies of *unsignalled avoidance*. A psychologist called Sidman developed a method of training animals in avoidance without any obvious warning stimulus. Rats, for example, could be put in a Skinner-box situation, where electric shocks were delivered at fixed intervals. The animals were, however, capable of reducing the frequency of these shocks by pressing the bar. Thus, a bar-press effectively turned the timer back to zero, and as long as the rats kept up with regular bar-presses they could successfully avoid shocks. Sidman, and many others since, have found that rats are quite capable of learning this kind of unsignalled avoidance. Where, then, is the warning stimulus which elicits the mediating fear of the two-factor theorist? The stimulus would have to be internal: some kind of neural trace associated with the passage of a calculated amount of time. Once again, we are given a theory which depends on the *post hoc* invention of key unobservable stimuli. Of course, such inventions may eventually turn out to be realities but, for the moment, they only detract from further explanatory potential. Also, the invocation of mediating fear in this kind of unsignalled procedure does not seem to fit what is observable, i.e., the animal's behaviour. Rats in this kind of situation do not seem to be frightened or anxious and it therefore seems unlikely that fear motivates responding. It is often claimed that much human social behaviour is maintained as avoidance responding rather than in a directly positive way—behaving in company in a way which avoids disapproval, not really wanting to be the odd man out, etc.— here again, we do not expect such behaviour to occur necessarily against a background of fear and anxiety even if the goals are avoidance goals.

Learned helplessness
We have spent some time on this topic of avoidance, not only because it has always been one of lively debate in the literature of behavioural analysis, but because it serves as a good example of how modern Behaviourism (see Rachlin, 1976) diverges from classical Behaviourism. The early theorists were 'connectionists'; they believed, in other words, that learning was about the building up of a connection between stimulus and response. However, more and more, recent experiments have shown that even simple organisms can show sophisticated learning when crude contiguity of stimuli and responses has been much surpassed. In the example, above, of unsignalled avoidance we have no close contiguity of overt stimuli and responses, rather the organism seems capable of learning a correlation between frequency of shock and frequency of responding—in this case a negative correlation. The move towards treating learning in terms of correlations rather than connections is most strikingly illustrated by looking at a particular phenomenon associated with the field of avoidance. The phenomenon is known as *learned helplessness*.

In 1967, two researchers, Maier and Seligman, reported an interesting, and unexpected, finding. They had been trying to improve avoidance learning of the signalled variety already described. Following a two-factor position, they predicted that animals already exposed to the contiguity of bell and shock would learn to avoid faster since they had already come to fear the bell and associate it with impending danger. To test this, they put dogs into restraint harnesses and exposed them to unavoidable but signalled shock. After this experience the animals were put into a box—called a shuttle-box—in which the shock could be avoided by a 'shuttling' response, i.e., jumping a hurdle and moving to the opposite end of the box. Surprisingly the experimental animals were worse not better than control animals which had not had the prior exposure to shock. It seemed that the animals which had been unable to avoid first time, had developed a lasting incapacity for successful avoidance. The simplest explanation of the result was that the animals had learned a competing response (lie still and wait for the shock to go away), which interfered with the development of a new, and very different, active response. However, a variety of subsequent experiments showed that this was not so. They had learned something far more 'cognitive' than a passive response. They had learnt that there was a zero correlation between their responding and events in the environment: they had learnt that they were helpless—a state of affairs which had drastic effects on their motivation and ability to respond to future contingencies.

Now in the old connectionist scheme of things there was nothing in the first part of Maier and Seligman's experiment to learn (at least not in the instrumental sense) since the animal could do nothing. Instrumentally speaking, the situation was neutral. If however learning is about correlations, the situation is different. A correlation can be anything between perfect negative correlation (-1) and perfect positive correlation ($+1$) and there is reason to believe that any correlation can be learned, including a zero correlation as in this instance. Responding and external events are independent—*that* is what is learned; the consequences of this are disastrous. Seligman and his co-researchers have replicated their findings across many species, and recently Hiroto and Seligman have shown such effects in human subjects on a great variety of learning tasks. Moreover, the phenomenon of helplessness seems to serve as a very good model for what happens in clinically depressed patients.

This quick look at learned helplessness completes our survey of that branch of psychology known as the laboratory analysis of behaviour. The reader who wishes to study further in this area is recommended to read one of the many texts available, such as Rachlin (1976).

SECTION 3

INFORMATION PROCESSING

Different aspects of what we are labelling information processing, for long periods, constituted virtually the whole of experimental psychology. Sensation and perception were the main preoccupation of Wundt and his immediate followers, 'thinking' that of Külpe, memory that of Ebbinghaus, while the Gestaltists concerned themselves with perception and problem-solving, and the Behaviourists with learning. Added to this was the vast cognitive development system of Piaget and much of the work of the classical British psychologists, such as Bartlett. Further, there was the newer 'cognitive psychology' exemplified in the work of George Miller, Ulric Neisser, and others—to say nothing of language; and this group of studies seems to overshadow the others. Sheer amount of published work, however, does not necessarily mean greater theoretical importance.

It does make for a formidable task for the student. We present our account in a slightly unusual way but in a way that we hope will make things clear. The usual Chapter on Learning is lacking, partly because the emphasis of research has shifted, and partly because it is not easy to make a sharp distinction between learning and memory, or, in some aspects, perception. Other 'learning' material is dealt with in Section 2. Language comes mainly in Sections 4 and 5, and Piaget in Section 4.

12 Basic perceptual processes

HEATHER GOVIER

An organism has access to information from its environment by way of sensitive tissues, which range from the simple photoreceptors in single-celled animals to sense organs as complex as the human eye. The basic physiology of such organs is discussed elsewhere; this Chapter will be concerned with the cognitive processes involved in perception, that is to say, the way in which stimuli are interpreted by the organism.

Not all impinging stimulation is perceived. In experimental terms, perception always involves discrimination. We test whether or not an organism has perceived something by its ability to discriminate between the presence and absence of the stimulus or between two different stimuli. In the case of human beings, the discriminating response is usually a verbal one—the subject tells us whether he has seen or heard the stimulus. For animals, the response must be non-verbal—we know that a pigeon can discriminate between a red light and a green one by training it to peck at a key when a red light shows, but not to respond to a green light.

Two of the principal factors which affect the organisms perception of a stimulus, are its past experience and its sensory thresholds. Many experiments have been performed which show that various experiences in an organism's development can contribute to later perception of the environment. This is true for experimental animals as well as man and will be fully discussed in Chapter 13.

Thresholds

The absolute threshold

Stimuli with intensities below a certain minimum value will not evoke any sensory experience. This minimum value is known as the absolute threshold and occurs for all sensory systems. However, the absolute threshold occurs at different stimulus intensities with different subjects and on different occasions with the same subject. It is not a constant value and must be measured afresh for each subject and on each occasion. One way of determining the absolute threshold, for example, of the visual system, is to seat the subject in a totally dark room, directing him to fix his gaze in a certain direction. The subject is then presented with a series of light flashes of varying intensities and must report whenever he sees a signal. When the data from such an experiment is analysed, it is found that there is no one intensity value *below* which the stimulus is never detected and *above* which it is always seen. Instead, there is a gradual gradient from intensities which the subject always reports seeing, through those which are sometimes detected and sometimes not, down to the lower intensities which are almost never perceived. An explanation of why this should be uses the concept of 'neural noise'. At any one moment in time, some of the neurones in any sensitive system will be firing spontaneously. For example, in the visual system, recordings made in cats have shown residual neural activity in the retina and optic nerve, even when there is no light stimulation to the eye. When neural impulses are received by the brain, it must make a decision as to whether those impulses represent external stimuli or whether they are mere 'noise' or background activity. This decision process complicates the ascertainment of the absolute threshold because, with a given low intensity stimulus, the brain may sometimes 'decide' that a stimulus was present and on other occasions 'decide' that it was not. The intensity of stimulus which evokes a positive decision varies, depending on many factors in the internal and external environment of the subject.

If a graph is plotted of stimulus intensity against percentage of 'seen' responses, the following type of curve is obtained (see Fig. 12.1). This curve is called a psychophysical function because it expresses a relationship between a psychological variable (the perception of the stimulus) and a physical variable (its intensity). The sloping part of the curve shows a region of stimulus intensities where detection occurs part of the time. In order to give a definite value to the absolute threshold, psychologists have agreed to define it as the intensity of stimulus which is perceived 50 per cent of the time (marked 'A' in Fig. 12.1).

Difference thresholds
As well as being interested in the *minimum* intensity of stimulation which can be perceived, psychologists are also concerned with the *differences* in intensities between two stimuli required for them to be perceived as dissimilar. The minimum amount of intensity difference necessary before the subject can tell two stimuli apart is known as the difference threshold. As with the absolute threshold, the intervention of

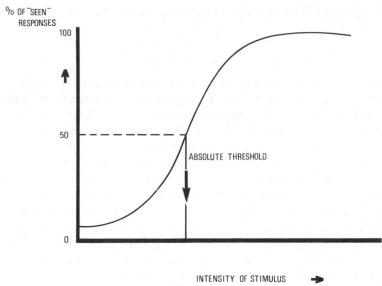

% OF "SEEN" RESPONSES

100

50

ABSOLUTE THRESHOLD

0

INTENSITY OF STIMULUS ➡

Fig. 12.1

'noise' and a decision process means that there is no one absolute value of the difference threshold. Again, it is defined as the magnitude of intensity difference between two stimuli, required for them to be perceived as different 50 per cent of the time. This value is alternatively known as the 'just noticeable difference' or j.n.d., a term invented by Gustav Fechner (1801–1887) who was the first psychologist to study sensory thresholds empirically.

The difference threshold, like the absolute threshold, varies for different subjects and also for the same subject depending on his motivation, physical condition, etc. However, the difference threshold also varies with the absolute stimulus intensity. This variation, unlike the personal and interpersonal ones, can be predicted according to a given law. This law is called Weber's law after Ernst Weber (1795–1878), who first discovered the relationship in 1846. He states that the smallest difference in intensity which can be detected is directly proportional to the original stimulus intensity. For example, the sound of someone dropping a pencil can be heard quite clearly when the room is quiet, but would not be noticed if a party were in progress. In numerical terms, if a subject is judging weights and is given a 100 g weight to start with he will be able to detect a difference between that and weights of 102 g with 50 per cent success. His j.n.d. will be 2 g. If he starts with a 200 g weight the j.n.d. will be 4 g. With a 400 g weight it will be 8 g and so on. The ratio of j.n.d. to background level is always constant.

$$\frac{2}{100} = \frac{4}{200} = \frac{8}{400} \text{ etc.} = 0.02$$

251

The mathematical formula which expresses Webers Law is

$$\frac{\Delta I}{I} = K$$

if ΔI is the increase in stimulus intensity required for a j.n.d. and I is the original intensity of stimulation. The quantity K is known as Weber's constant and differs widely between various sense modalities. For the change in pitch of a tone, $K = \frac{1}{333}$; in other words, we can detect a very small change in pitch. For the change in concentration in a saline solution, $K = \frac{1}{5}$; we are not very sensitive to change in saltiness. This is broadly true, although there is of course the complication of different units being used to measure intensities in different modalities.

Webers Law holds fairly well over a wide range of background intensity but it does break down at the extremes, particularly at very low levels of stimulation. This is probably because at such levels the 'noise' in the system (i.e., the spontaneous residual firing of neurones in the absence of stimulus) becomes a significant factor.

Signal detection theory
In the last 20 years it has become apparent that the methods of determining a subject's threshold developed by the early psychologists presented the experimenter with some problems. For example, the experiments designed to find a subject's perceptual threshold used low energy stimuli, this means that on some proportion of trials the subject would be unsure about whether or not a stimulus had been presented. This of course provided fertile ground for the subject's guessing habits to affect the results. Furthermore the experimenter had no guarantee that his subject was not dissembling.

In order to deal with these problems experimenters introduced trials when no stimulus was presented. Originally when this was done the experimenters tried to use the data collected from these 'catch trials' to account for the subject's guesses. However, if we deliberately set out to study the effect of the subject's guessing behaviour and to separate out this effect from his true perceptual sensitivity, then we may use the methods derived from so called Signal Detection Theory. This is a mathematical model of stimulus detection, developed by communication engineers, from which it is possible to derive two supposedly independent measures of the subject's behaviour. First, his ability to perceive stimuli (d') correctly and secondly, his willingness to make a positive decision that a stimulus was presented (β). This latter measure, β, is the subject's criterion of caution, that is to say, the subject may decide to operate with a lax criterion in which case he will make more correct detections but he will also make more *false positive* errors, i.e., he will more often report the presence of a stimulus when no stimulus was in fact

252

presented. Or he can operate with a stricter criterion, making fewer correct detections and fewer false positive errors. His criterion will be affected by many factors, his general motivation, his guessing habits, his expectations on each trial that a stimulus will be presented, his appraisal of what sort of accuracy is expected of him during the experiment etc.

It is of course apparent that the subject's responses may be categorized as follows, correct detection, missed stimuli, false alarms and correct negatives, but we are only interested in the proportion of hits (correct detection) to the total number of stimulus presentations and the proportion of false alarms to those trials on which no stimulus was presented. If we run a subject nine times through our experiment, with the same signal strength while varying the proportion of trials on which a stimulus is really presented from say 10% of the trials to 90%, we should be able to study the effect of his altered expectations upon his criterion level, β. If we then plot the hit rate to false alarm rate for each presentation rate we will have a curve known as a Receiver Operating Characteristic Curve which is an indication both of the subject's changing β and his sensitivity d'.

A detailed discussion of the mathematics upon which calculation of d' and β are based is beyond the scope of this treatment, but one or two points should be mentioned. First, it is assumed that the subject has no threshold below which he will not detect the stimulus. Second, the model assumes that the subject's spontaneous neural activity fluctuates in a manner which is characteristic of the normal distribution and that when stimuli are presented the subject's neural activity is still characterized by the normal distribution but with a raised mean.

The first of the above assumptions seems odd as a 'trigger' or threshold is often built in to machines to make them more efficient, and the second assumption seems far too simple a description of the workings of the perceptual apparatus. It therefore seems likely that signal detection theory will be modified in the future to take account of these points. The reader who wishes to pursue the theory in greater detail may consult the treatment by J. P. Egan.

The general effects of stimulation

Stimuli above threshold level acting upon an organism may produce a response. The effects of stimulation fall broadly into two categories: the general effects, and the specific effects relating to object perception. We shall first discuss the general effects.

Sensory restriction

A number of experiments, started over twenty years ago, have indicated that efficient behaviour degenerates in human subjects who are deprived of all types of stimulation. In these experiments, college students have been paid to stay in isolation in sound-proofed cubicles, wearing goggles, and with their limbs tied up to prevent any tactile stimulation. Alternatively, they have been required to lie in baths of water at blood temperature, blindfolded, and using breathing apparatus. After a period of time under these conditions (which can vary from a few hours to a few days), subjects report great mental strain. They are unable to think clearly and logically, their minds wander, and they reach a state in which they are unsure whether they are awake or asleep. Some subjects have reported visual and auditory hallucinations. These effects may even continue for up to two days after the end of the stimulus deprivation. The interpretation of these results is complicated by the large variations in the experiences of individual subjects and also the discrepancies among the results obtained by different investigators. However, it is broadly true to say that subjects under such conditions of restricted sensory input function at less than their normal level of efficiency. This type of degeneration in efficiency is apparent in certain monotonous tasks such as radar scanning where the subject (or operative) is required to watch out for infrequent signals. Performance on this type of vigilance task can be improved by, among other things, the introduction of general stimulation such as background music for a visual task, or pictures to look at for an auditory task. In these cases the subject is not undergoing total *sensory deprivation* but his sensory input is so monotonous and unstructured that he could be said to be *perceptually deprived*. In experiments on perceptual deprivation subjects are for example, required to wear diffusing goggles instead of blindfolds and, strangely, these subjects seem to show at least as much mental disturbance, if not more, than subjects in sensory deprivation experiments. It would appear that it is the lack of change in stimulation rather than the absolute reduction which leads to behaviour breakdown. Our brain seems to require a constantly changing sensory input for maximum efficiency.

This is not only true of the brain but also applies to the individual sensory systems. The ears, or the auditory centres of the brain, are very responsive to change in auditory stimulation but soon ignore persistent monotonous signals. For example, the ticking of a clock is easily ignored but if the clock for some reason stopped, the cessation of the ticking would be noticed. The eye reacts quickly to a moving stimulus but can be very unattentive to familiar objects which are still. This attention to changing stimuli has obvious survival value in a world where predator and prey are usually moving features.

Stabilized retinal images
As our sense organs normally respond largely to changes in the environment, it is interesting to see what happens when they are presented with

an entirely stable perceptual field. This approach to the study of vision was first developed by R. W. Ditchburn in 1952.

When we survey a scene we make continuous eye and head movements which change the fix of our gaze. It is possible to prevent some of these movements by clamping the head and instructing the subject to fixate steadily on a small target. However, even under these conditions, the eye is constantly making small oscillating movements of which the subject is unaware and which he is unable to control. This tremor results in a constantly changing pattern of retinal stimulation even when the subject stares fixedly at one thing. It is impossible to stop these movements safely, but various devices have been produced which cause the image to move along with the eye. One such device is a tiny slide projector which is mounted on a contact lens. When the subject wears the lens the projector moves with the eye, causing the projection of the slide on a screen to move also. Wearing such a device, the subject is at first able to see the image projected onto the screen very clearly. However, within a few seconds the image begins to fade and. may disappear entirely. More often, though, parts of the image disappear, and it has been noted that the disappearances are usually of an entire unit or block of the image rather than just random patches. For example, if a subject views a target like this in a stabilized vision

Fig. 12.2

he is likely to see any of the following fragments of the image:

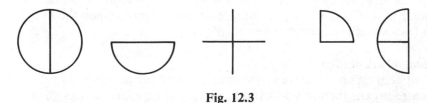

Fig. 12.3

Frequently, the subject reports that as some parts of the image fade from view other parts come back so that he sees a changing pattern.

It is not clearly understood exactly what causes this phenomenon to occur. Some kind of neural inhibition or neural fatigue may be involved. This does not seem to occur at the retina, and the fact that meaningful elements of the stimulus disappear and reappear suggest that it may

255

occur at quite a high level of neural processing, for example, the lateral geniculate body (see Chapter 6).

Sensory adaptation
Another of the general effects of stimulation is the way in which the sense organs are able to adapt to stimuli impinging upon them. If a stimulus persists, we become less sensitive to it, and, conversely, in the absence of stimulation, sensitivity increases. On first walking into a room, we can clearly smell both pleasant smells such as flowers or perfume, and unpleasant ones such as stale smoke. However, after we have been sitting in the room for some time we become less aware of the smell, even though there may be just as much smoke or even more than there was at first. Bath water may seem very hot when we have just stepped into it but it soon becomes comfortable as our senses adapt, even though the water temperature may remain the same. This phenomenon is perhaps most marked for the visual system. On first walking into bright sunlight it seems to hurt our eyes, but, as we adapt to the glare, we are able to see quite clearly. On returning to a dimly lit room, it is often impossible to see anything until our eyes have become adapted or accustomed to the lower light intensity.

One mechanism by which such adaption occurs in the visual system is the contraction of the muscles in the iris which change the size of the pupil. However, this does not account for much of the adaptation. The main peripheral mechanism involved in dark adaptation seems to be biochemical changes which take place in the pigment cells (the rods and cones) in the retina. Exposure to bright light bleaches the photo-chemicals in the cells of the retina, making these cells less sensitive to light stimulation. When the bright light is removed these photochemicals regenerate, enabling the eye to respond to lower intensities of light. These changes in sensitivity are very dramatic. The eye at its most sensitive state, after a long period in total darkness, will respond to a stimulus $\frac{1}{100\,000}$ as intense as that required when the eye is at its least sensitive, after exposure to bright light.

Perceptual adaptation
Not all adaptation in sensory systems occurs at the peripheral level (in the sense organs themselves). Another series of experiments has shown that humans are capable of adapting to quite drastic changes in stimulation. Various psychologists, the first of whom was George Stratton (1897), have devised a variety of optical devices for distorting the visual world. The simplest of these are inverting lenses: pairs of spectacles which project an upside down image of the world to the wearer. When subjects first put on such spectacles they find it very difficult to do anything, and the world appears very bizarre. However, after some time

256

things begin to look more normal, and after wearing the lenses for some days subjects find themselves able to move around quite well. They have adapted to their distorted world. Moreover, subjects report confusion over their perceptions. They may be unable to say whether things still look upside down to them, although they do realize that there is something strange about what they see. On removal of the lenses after they have been worn for several days, subjects report confusion and bewilderment which may last for several hours before their perceptual world returns to normal.

This type of adaptation is different from sensory adaptation, which is largely a physiological process, taking place mainly within the sense organ. Perceptual adaptation, on the other hand, must occur at a more central level of processing (i.e., in the brain itself rather than in the eye) and seems to involve an aspect of 'learning'. Interestingly enough, other animals do not seem able to adapt to this type of distortion of the visual field. Hens wearing distorting prisms show no improvement in their disturbed behaviour, even after three months. Monkeys show some sign of slight adaptation but nothing like as much as humans. Clearly, some quite complex processing must be involved in this type of adaptation. For a fuller discussion see Chapter 13.

The perception of objects

In the real world we are not much concerned with the general effects of stimulation such as those discussed above. Most of us never experience stabilized retinal images and few of us walk about wearing defusing goggles. We are concerned, however, with the perception of specific meaningful objects. Although our sense of taste and smell are stimulated by an elaborate pattern of chemicals, we do not perceive this pattern. We are aware, however, that we are having kippers for tea today! When listening to an orchestral concert only the trained ear is aware of individual notes or instruments; most of us hear only the music. This is even more true when we listen to speech; we are concerned with the meaning, not with the series of tones. Despite these examples, most of the work on object perception has been concerned with seen objects and, thus, much of the following discussion will be concerned with the human visual system.

Gestalt psychology

Any sensory experience is a product of a series of often quite discrete stimuli impinging on the organism. These individual stimuli are rarely perceived as such. The perception is of a pattern, not of its component parts. A television picture is composed of thousands of points of light but we are never aware of this. We see only the image shown on the screen. This type of phenomenon was the basis of a school of psychology known as Gestalt psychology. This grew up in Germany and Austria towards the end of the nineteenth century and the name Gestalt comes from a German word which means form or pattern. It was led by Max Wertheimer (1880–1943), Kurt Koffka (1886–1941) and Wolfgang Köhler (1887–1967). Proponents of the Gestalt school hold that components of a perceptual field are synthesized by the mind into a pattern or a Gestalt, i.e., that the whole perception is more than the sum of the individual parts and that the extra significance has been added inside the organism. There are four basic principles of Gestalt psychology: 'figure and ground'; 'segregation and differentiation'; 'closure'; and 'good Gestalt', or 'Prägnanz'.

The figure/ground principle relates to the problem of how the visual system is able to distinguish an object from its background. If all stimuli are simply arrays of coloured dots, how do we make out where one object ends and the next begins, i.e., how do we distinguish the figure from its background. This is not simply a matter of picking out identifiable objects, because figure-ground structuring in perception still occurs in the absense of these. Black and white patterns and certain wall-paper designs are perceived as figures upon grounds and in some cases figure and ground spontaneously reverse. A classic example is shown in Figure 12.4. This picture can be seen either as a white vase upon a dark background or two silhouetted faces looking at each other.

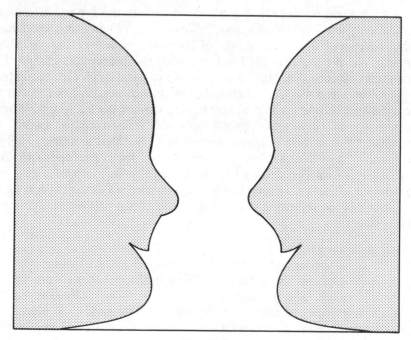

Fig. 12.4

258

It is interesting to note that the ability to distinguish figure from ground is not learned. Studies of subjects who, blind from birth, have had their sight restored later in life show that they are able to distinguish figure from ground immediately, while other features of perception must be learned (see Ch. 13).

The second principle of Gestalt psychology, that of segregation and differentation, is closely related to the first. The principles may be illustrated with dot patterns.

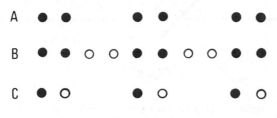

Fig. 12.5

In diagram A, the dots are seen, not as a row of single dots, but as a series of pairs of dots. This is because of the segregation of the pairs. In B, the dots are seen as pairs because of the differentation between filled and unfilled dots. In C, it is apparent that the spacial nearness is more important than similarity in determining how the pairs appear.

The Gestalt principle of closure is exemplified by the following diagram:

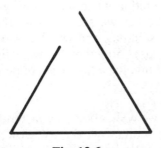

Fig. 12.6

We perceive this as a triangle with a piece of one side missing. It has been found that subjects shown such shapes in a tachistoscope for brief intervals of time report seeing the completed shape and are unaware of the break in the outline. They mentally 'close' the shape. The same happens when such shapes are used as stimuli in memory tasks. The subject, when asked to reproduce what he saw will frequently draw a complete figure.

All these principles combine together to give the principle of 'good

259

form' or 'Prägnanz'. The brain organizes a perception in such a way that the stimulus appears orderly, or a good figure. Take the following illustration:

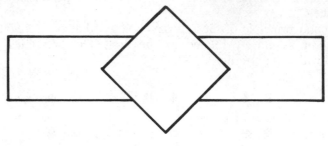

Fig. 12.7

This figure is perceived as a square superimposed upon a rectangle. The rectangle is completed mentally according to the principle of closure. The square is the figure and the rectangle the ground. We do not see a ten-sided figure with two right-angled patterns inside it, as this would not be such a neat interpretation or good Gestalt.

Object constancy
Not only are we able to distinguish a figure from its background, but we are also able to recognize a known object in a variety of different orientations. This ability is known as object constancy. The pattern of stimulation falling on the retina when we see our grandmother may vary wildly, depending on whether we see her from the front, back or side, whether she is sitting or standing and whether she is partly obscured by some object between us; nonetheless we still recognize her as Grandmother. This must involve a high level of perceptual processing.

Location constancy
As our eyes move, or as we walk about, a constantly changing pattern of stimulation falls on our retina. We do not, however, see the world as constantly moving about. We know that the table is stable even though its image is moving. The ability to perceive objects as enduring and stationary is partly dependent upon the organs of balance in the middle ear.

Size constancy
Objects may be viewed at different distances. When they are so viewed, the image of the object falling on the retina will differ in size. The retinal image of a book held ten inches away is twice the size of that when the book is held twenty inches away, yet the book does not appear smaller

when it is further from us. We tend to see it as more or less invariant in size, whatever our distance from it. This does break down somewhat at unusually great distances, a village viewed from a hilltop seems to be made up of dolls' houses and the people in it look like ants. This is an indication that size constancy may result from learning. We know by experience that objects in our immediate environment do not change their size when we move away from them and this affects our perception. When unusually large distances are involved we have less experience on which to draw and thus the constancy mechanism tends to be less effective.

Colour and brightness constancy

Familiar objects appear to remain the same colour, despite variation in lighting conditions. Even coloured lights do not obscure our perception of the constancy on an object's colour, provided that there are sufficient contrasts and shadows. We perceive our writing paper as white, despite the fact that it may be covered by grey shadows or reflecting yellow light from a coloured street lamp. Colour constancy depends entirely on our having some knowledge of the perceived object and/or seeing it against a background of information about the intensity of illumination and the colour of surrounding objects. When these cues are removed colour constancy disappears entirely and we see the colour of objects as true to the wavelength of the light reflected from them. For example, when a familiar object, such as a tomato, is viewed through a tube which obscures the outline and all background, its colour is no longer seen as invariant as the illumination of it changes.

Perception of depth

One of the problems in this field is how we manage to perceive a three-dimensional world when the image on the retina is necessarily a two-dimensional one. We believe that this is facilitated by recourse to certain 'cues'—aspects of the perception which gives us information about distance and depth. These fall into two classes: binocular and monocular cues.

Binocular cues to depth

The image on the retina of the eye is two-dimensional, but the normal human observer has two eyes and thus two retinal images. These images are not identical. Because the eyes are separated in our head, the left eye receives an image which is slightly different from that received by the right eye. (This was first realized by Euclid in the third century B.C.) If these two images are combined, a stereoscopic effect results. This effect can be clearly reproduced in a three-dimensional viewer or stereoscope.

This device is similar to a pair of binoculars but instead of lenses each eye tube holds a two dimensional picture. By simultaneous presentation of two slightly differing pictures, one to each eye, a dramatic three-dimensional picture can be seen.

In normal vision, the slight difference between the two retinal images is termed retinal disparity and is easily demonstrable. Hold a pencil up in front of you at arms length and closing one eye align the pencil with some distant object such as the window frame. Now open the closed eye and close the other. The pencil will appear to jump to one side as the second eye views it from a different angle. The image from one eye usually dominates the overall perception and in a right handed person the right eye is most commonly dominant. Eye-dominance can be determined in a similar way to the above. This time the pencil and window frame should be aligned with both eyes open. If you then close each eye in turn, the pencil will probably appear to shift more with one eye than with the other. If the greatest jump occurs when the right eye is closed then you are right eye dominant and vice versa.

Another depth cue which is dependent on the use of both eyes is convergence of the eyes. The nearer an object is, the more the eyes must turn inwards in order to focus on that object. Thus information from the orbital muscles which turn the eyes could be available as a further cue to depth.

Monocular cues to depth

It is clear that people who have lost an eye are nevertheless capable of judging depth as are two-eyed observers with one eye covered, and so there must therefore be some alternative monocular cues available. The two binocular cues result from processes and structures which are inherent in the organism and are thus assumed to be independent of learning or experience. Such cues are called *primary cues* to depth perception, and there is one monocular primary cue which depends upon the accommodation of the eye. In order to focus objects at different distances from the eye, the lens must change its shape. These changes are brought about by the activity of the lens muscles. It is possible that information could be available from these muscles in much the same way as information from the orbital muscles. Of course, we are conscious of neither of these muscular changes as they are autonomic responses, but this does not preclude the possibility that the information may be being used at a subconscious level. However, this process only works over short distances. Anything further away than twenty-five feet is at optical infinity, in other words no further changes in lens shape occur after the object is further away than twenty-five feet. Therefore, there must be other cues available.

These final cues are called *secondary cues* and are assumed to be

262

acquired through experience. They are not dependent on biological processes but are features of the visual field itself, and may be used by artists to create an illusion of depth in a flat picture. These cues are as follows:

1. *Overlap or superimposition.* If one object overlaps and appears to cut off the view of another then we presume the first object to be nearer.

Fig. 12.8

2. *Relative size.* In an array of similar objects smaller ones appear to be further away. This is especially true if the object is one which is known to have a constant size, e.g., a teacup.

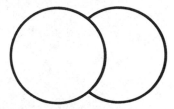

Fig. 12.9

3. *Height in the horizontal plane.* Objects which are placed higher up in a picture appear to be further away.

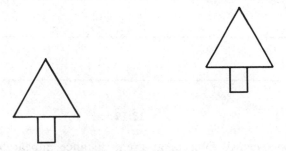

Fig. 12.10

4. *Texture gradient.* The grain or texture appears to become finer as distance becomes greater.

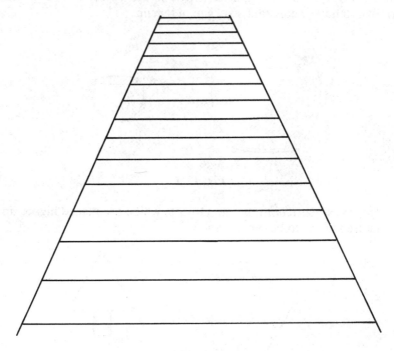

Fig. 12.11

5. *Linear perspective.* Parallel lines such as railway track appear to converge as they recede into the distance.

Fig. 12.12

6. *Aerial perspective.* Objects at great distance appear to be slightly different in colour, e.g., the bluish tint of distant mountains.

264

7. *Relative brightness*. Brighter objects appear to be nearer if all other things are equal.
8. *Shadowing*. Three-dimensional objects present variations in light and shade. This can be used by an artist to create three-dimensional illusion.
9. *Motion parallax*. When the observer is moving, e.g., as a traveller in a train, the apparent movement of distant objects is slower than that of objects close by. Telegraph poles by the side of the track appear to flash by, while similar poles on a distant hillside move quite slowly.

Although the sensation of depth or distance produced by each one of these cues in isolation is not very strong, they can combine together to create a very compelling impression of depth.

To summarize, the cues to depth perception are as follows:

1. *Primary cues*
   Retinal disparity
   Convergence
   Accommodation
2. *Secondary cues*
   Overlap
   Relative size
   Height in the horizontal plane
   Texture gradient
   Linear perspective
   Aerial perspective
   Relative brightness
   Shadowing
   Motion parallax

Visual illusions

In the foregoing discussion of perception, various references have been made to situations in which our eyes seems to play tricks on us leading us to perceive something very different from reality. Such phenomena may be grouped together under the heading of visual illusions, and their study can tell us much about perceptual analysis.

Illusions of movement
Our perception of the movement of an object depends on changes in its position on the retinal image. However, as we move our heads around we produce a constantly-changing retinal image, and yet we do not perceive the world spinning around us. Despite the movement across the retina of their image, objects in the room appear to be stationary. Kinaesthetic feedback from the muscles and organs of balance is

265

integrated with the changing retinal picture at a high level to inhibit the perception of movement. The disruption of this process results in dizziness when the world does appear to reel around. In the absence of this kinaesthetic feedback then, changes in position of objects in the retinal image are perceived as movement. It is thus possible to create the sensation of movement without any movement actually occurring. This creation of apparent motion is the principle by which moving films work. It was brought to the interest of psychologists by Max Wertheimer (1880–1943) in 1912 and is commonly known as the *phi phenomenon*. A subject in a darkened room is seated in front of a line or sometimes a ring of lights. If these lights are flashed on and off in sequence, the subject perceives the illusion of a single light moving in a line or circle. This effect is sometimes used to create the illusion of movement in neon street signs.

The stroboscopic motion of cinema films is essentially similar to the phi phenomenon. The illusion of motion is created by presenting stationary stimuli one after the other.

When the eye perceives real relative motion the brain always tends to assume that the small objects are moving while large objects are stationary. If a subject is shown a stationary spot of light within a moving frame he will report that the spot is moving. This phenomenon is called *induced movement* and an everyday example of it is the apparent racing of the moon through the clouds in a windy sky. Similar illusions can be experienced when travelling by any kind of vehicle. In a train, it is often difficult to judge whether one's own carriage is moving or that of an adjacent train. Pilots and astronauts are so well aware of such confusions that they tend to trust their instrument panels rather than their eyes.

A third type of movement illusion is termed the *autokinetic effect*. If a small point of light is presented in a totally dark room, an observer will frequently report that the light is moving, although, in fact, it is not. This effect seems to be connected with eye movements, as, when such movements are minimized, the autokinetic effect is reduced. A theoretical explanation lies in the inability of the brain to 'decide' whether it is the movement of the eye itself or of the stimulus dot of light which is producing changes in the position of the retinal image. The brain has not enough data on which to base a decision and may come to the 'wrong' conclusion. This theory is supported by the fact that the introduction of any other features into the visual field will reduce and frequently abolish the autokinetic effect. It may be that a similar explanation could apply in the case of all the movement illusions discussed here. In each case the brain has not enough information on which to make an accurate decision and is, consequently, often mistaken. A similar theory will be put forward with regard to the geometric illusions described below.

Geometric illusions

The two most famous visual illusions are the Muller Lyer and the Ponzo illusions.

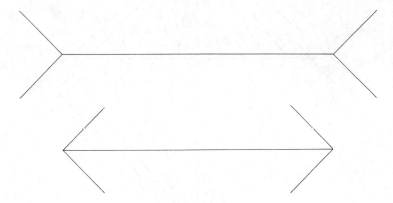

Fig. 12.13

The Muller Lyer illusion (Fig. 12.13) is created by pairs of fins attached to the ends of straight lines of identical length. The line with the outgoing fins always appears longer. Not only is this true for most human observers but the illusion is also experienced by animals. We can ascertain this by training an animal to produce a response to the shorter of two lines. If such a trained animal is presented with the Muller Lyer lines, it will respond to the one with the ingoing fins.

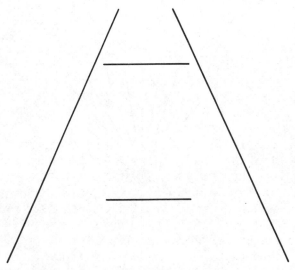

Fig. 12.14

267

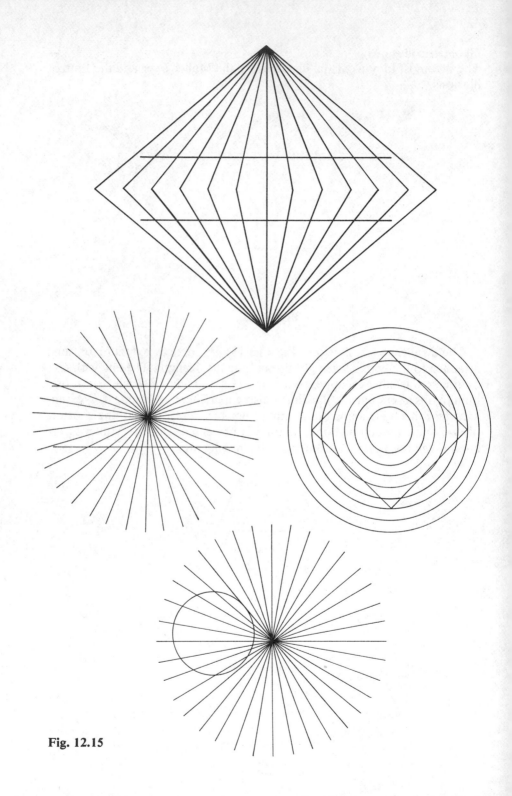

Fig. 12.15

In the Ponzo illusion (Fig. 12.14) two lines of identical length are placed between a pair of converging line segments. Here the top line appears longer.

Other illusions involve the distortion of lines by superimposing them upon certain backgrounds. In the drawings in Figure 12.15, straight lines appear to be curved and arches distorted.

A third type of illusion involves a change in the apparent size of an object in changed surroundings:

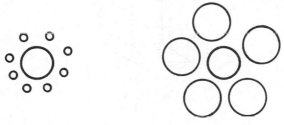

Fig. 12.16

The two centre circles are the same size but the one on the left appears to be larger. Similarly with the horizontal-vertical illusion below, the vertical line appears longer, although in fact, the two lines are of equal length (Fig. 12.17).

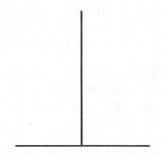

Fig. 12.17

Towards an explanation

Although these illusions and many others have been known for a long time, their explanations are still controversial. One strongly-favoured theory relates illusions to the perception of visual constancies. The perceptual system is not a passive recipient of all stimulation. Given

269

a specific input the brain attempts to apply meaning and searches for an hypothesis which is most consistent with all aspects of the stimulus. Sometimes this hypothesis changes from one moment to the next as in figure-ground illusions such as the one illustrated in Figure 12.4. Another well-known instance of this is the illusion of the Necker cube.

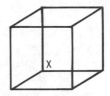

Fig. 12.18

The above drawing is seen to represent a transparent cube the depth properties of which appear to change spontaneously. The corner x sometimes appears at the front of the Figure and sometimes at the back.

The problem here seems to be lack of adequate information on which to base our hypothesis about what we are seeing. If the cube were a real three-dimensional object set against a background of other objects we would be able to ascertain its true orientation easily by means of the multitude of depth cues available to us. This illusion appears even more marked when the cube is a luminous three-dimensional framework suspended in a dark room. Here, as in the two-dimensional drawing, all cues which might help us to formulate a hypothesis about its orientation have been removed.

The same process may be involved in the perception of the Muller Lyer, Ponzo, and other geometrical illusions. We use available cues to enable us to formulate an hypothesis about our perception but, these cues being misleading or inadequate, we are brought to the wrong conclusions.

In the case of these geometrical illusions however it is not so easy to determine why a mistake is being made. Clearly, there is no spontaneous reversal as with the Necker cube and thus a firm but mistaken hypothesis must have been made as to what comprises the stimulus. Several explanatory theories have been put forward. For example it has been suggested with regard to the Muller Lyer illusion that the fins serve to draw the eyes past or within the lines. This at best, is a rather vague description and can clearly be shown to be untrue. If the image of the arrows is stabilized on the retina (see p. 255), the illusion is still apparent, although, clearly, no eye movement is possible.

Gregory's contribution

A more convincing approach is made by R. L. Gregory who, in his book *Eye and Brain*, relates the perception of illusions to the various constancy scaling devices discussed earlier in this Chapter (p. 260), in particular size constancy. A book, or our hand appears to be the same size whether it is viewed from a distance of ten inches or twenty inches despite the fact that its retinal image will be only half the size in the second instance that it was in the first. By the reverse of this scaling process, a given size of retinal image will be interpreted differently, depending on the estimated distance of the stimulus producing that image. If we believe the object to be further away, we will hypothesize that it must be larger for a given retinal image size. Both the Muller Lyer and the Ponzo diagrams contain features which could be analysed as depth cues. In the Ponzo illusion, the outer pair of lines could be considered to be cues to linear perspective (see p. 264). If this were the case, then combination of that and the third monocular depth cue, i.e., height in the horizontal plane (see p. 263) should combine to give a strong illusion of depth. In this three-dimensional percept the upper of the two inner lines is seen as further away and, as it produces the same size of retinal image as the lower one, the system will hypothesize that it must be larger.

A similar explanation can be put forward for the case of the Muller Lyer illusion. Here, the line with the ingoing fins provides linear perspective cues which suggest that it might be the corner of an object which is pointing towards us such as the corner of a building.

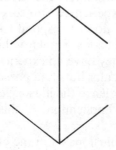 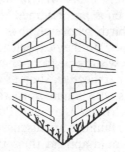

Fig. 12.19

The line with the outgoing fins looks more like the internal corner of a room, where the corner is pointing away from us (see Fig. 12.20).

The cues of linear perspective lead us to hypothesize that the vertical line is nearer to us in Figure 12.19 than in Figure 12.20. Consequently, the equal-sized retinal images of the vertical lines are interpreted as representing different-sized objects, the more distant one appearing larger.

271

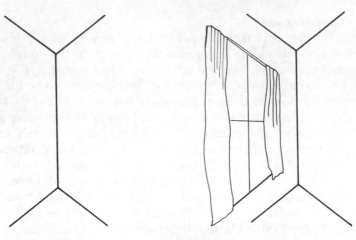

Fig. 12.20

In support of this hypothesis is the fact that when the illusion Figures are removed from their flat paper background and presented as luminous models suspended in a dark room, their three-dimensional interpretation is very striking. Gregory argues that it is only their superimposition on a flat paper background with its consequent conflicting cues (e.g., no texture gradient) that prevents us from seeing the Figures as three-dimensional objects.

Another piece of supporting evidence is the fact that the illusions only occur in organisms whose previous experience has taught them the basic depth cues. As was mentioned earlier in the Chapter, the secondary depth cues are assumed to be learned from experience. Subjects blind from birth whose sight is restored in later life do not respond to such cues, nor do they experience the usual visual illusions. Similarly, human beings who come from an environment where they have no experience of linear perspective, such as Zulus who live in circular huts and possess no objects with square corners, usually fail to experience the illusory effects of the Muller Lyer and Ponzo diagrams. (The implications of this, and further findings are discussed in Chapter 13.)

It would appear, then, that the geometrical illusions as in the case of the Necker cube and reversible figure-ground drawings result from errors being made in the formation of an hypothesis about what is seen. These errors, yet again, result from incorrect interpretation of inadequate constancy cues.

However, Gregory's interpretation has been criticized and one most compelling illustration of where the theory falls short concerns a variation on the Muller Lyer illusion (Fig. 12.13).

In Figure 12.21 the two lines appear to be different lengths, as do the Muller Lyer lines. However, in this variation there are clearly no linear

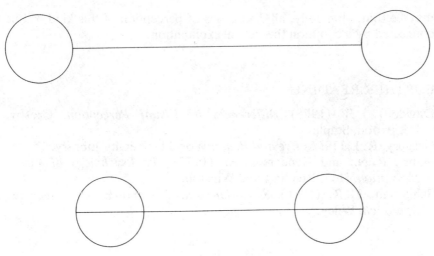

Fig. 12.21

perspective cues and it is very difficult to see how any 'misinterpretation of cues' hypothesis could account for the illusion.

We are left with an enigma.

Figural after-effects
In the case of the visual illusions discussed so far the observer experiences the illusion when he first sees the stimulus involved. A further category of illusion is the figural after-effect, where the illusion is only experienced after viewing the stimulus for some time. If certain figures are viewed for a prolonged period with the eyes held as still as possible, distortions in vision may arise. For example, James Gibson noted in 1933 that if a curved line is viewed in this way and the gaze is then immediately transferred to a straight line, this line appears for a few seconds to be curved in the opposite direction.

Another famous after-effect is the waterfall illusion which was first recorded by a psychologist in 1834. He stared at a waterfall for several seconds and noticed that when he subsequently looked at the adjacent bank it appeared to be moving in the opposite direction. A similar illusion is created by watching a parade for a long period: stationary objects viewed subsequently appear to move against the line of march. This effect can be produced experimentally by showing a subject a rotating spiral for several minutes and then instructing him to transfer his gaze to a stationary target. Subjects report that this appears to spin in the opposite direction to the spiral.

The explanation for these illusions probably lies in some inhibitory response within the nerves of the visual system. Inhibition theories have also been put forward as explanations of the geometric illusions, and it may be that, ultimately, all distortions of perception of this kind will be connected by a common theoretical explanation.

FURTHER READING

Davidoff, J. B. (1975) *Differences in Visual Perception.* Crosby, Lockwood, Staples.

Gregory, R. L. (1966) *Eye and Brain.* World University Library.

Haber, R. N., and Henderson, M. (1973) *The Psychology of Visual Perception.* Holt, Reinhart and Winston.

Schiffman, H. R. (1976) *Sensation and Perception: An Integrated Approach.* Wiley.

13 The development of perceptual processes

HEATHER AND ERNEST GOVIER

One of the most long-standing controversies in the history of psychology has been concerned with the relative influences of innate factors and the environment on the development of perceptual processes. There have long been two opposing schools of thought: that of the Empiricists; and that of the Nativists.

The Empirical position is that all knowledge comes through experience. This point of view was expressed in its most extreme form by John Locke (1632–1704), who held that the mind at birth is a *tabula rasa*, a complete blank, requiring experience to fill it with meaning and understanding. Thus, the newly born can derive no meaningful perception from his environment, such perception being built up as his experiences multiply. A less extreme expression of the empirical view is attributable to Hermann Von Helmholtz (1821–1894), who accepted that something was brought to perception by the physiological features of the organism. He held that it is by complex interaction between this physiological structure and the environment that the resulting perception is developed.

The Nativists, on the other hand, believed that most fundamental perceptual processes are innate and independent of experience. Such a view was taken by many of the Gestalt psychologists and notably by Ewald Hering (1834–1918). For them, the infant comes into the world with a mind fully able to grasp all essential features of its perceptual field.

A third, and more recent, position finds some sort of middle ground between these two extreme philosophies and was expounded by Donald Hebb. He argued that studies of the structure of cell assemblies in the brain suggest an innate basis for visual perception (c.f. the Nativists) but that these cell assemblies are built upon and influenced by the experiences of the organism, to form the perceptual processes of the adult (c.f. the Empiricists).

Evidence on which to assess these divergent theories comes in modern psychology from a variety of different fields of study. Clearly, the examination of the physiological features of perceptual systems in both developing and adult organisms can shed some light on the issue. However, this aspect is fully discussed in Chapter 6 and will not be considered here. The study of visual illusions too is covered in Chapter 12. This Chapter will be concerned with four basic sources of insight:

1. Studies of neonates both human and animal.
2. Studies of the adaptations made by subjects to distortions in their perceptual world.
3. Studies of the influence of various cognitive dispositions on perception.
4. Studies of the effects of cultural differences on perception.

Examination of these four types of research as set forward below represents a contemporary reassessment of the development of perceptual processes.

Studies of neonates

One way to assess the relative importance of nature and nurture in determining what we perceive is to compare the perceptual world of the adult with that of the newly born (or neonate). Any differences between the two must be due either to the influence of the environment or to maturational processes. Various controls enable us to disentangle these two influences, as we shall see below. Both human and animal neonates have been used in these studies, the most important of which have been carried out by five noted psychologists, Fantz, Gibson, Walk, Held and Hein.

The work of Robert L. Fantz

Research by Robert L. Fantz and his colleagues has been concerned with the ability of the infant to perceive form, i.e., shape, pattern size and solidity. The early work used newly hatched chicks as experimental subjects. Immediately after hatching, chicks begin to peck at small objects in their environment in order to find food. In these experiments the chicks were offered a variety of items to peck at and their pecking preferences were noted. All stimuli were encased in perspex to exclude

276

the possibility of smell, touch, or taste influencing the choices. As the chicks were hatched in darkness and had no experience of real food, any discrimination must have been made exclusively on the basis of innate perceptual abilities.

The results of this experiment were quite conclusive. Chicks consistently preferred a sphere to a pyramid and a circle to a triangle, indicating an ability to perceive shape. That they could also perceive size was shown by selection of circles of $\frac{1}{8}$ inch diameter more frequently than circles of any other size, and, when tested for perception of three dimensionality, the chicks selected a sphere in preference to a flat disc. Clearly, the chick has innate ability to perceive the shape, size and solidity of possible food objects. Moreover, the preference for spheres of this particular size is highly adaptive, as this is approximately the size and shape of the food grains which constitute the chicks' diet.

From studying chicks, Fantz turned to the study of human infants. But here he was presented with a major problem. Human babies are not self-sufficient organisms with the mobility and range of responses of chicks. They have, in fact, very little way of showing preferences between stimuli. Fantz however was able to use the only one available. He studied the eye movements of the young babies when presented with a choice of visual test objects. If the baby is seen to look consistently at one object more than another he must be able to perceive some difference between the two stimuli. This experiment is thus essentially similar to the one conducted with chicks and concerns itself with the question of whether the innate abilities seen in the chick persist higher up the evolutionary scale. Human infants are, clearly, less developed than newly hatched chickens with regard to motor abilities, so perhaps this is also true of their perceptual processes.

Fantz tested a group of human infants at weekly intervals from the age of one week until they were fifteen weeks old. The stimuli used were four pairs of designs of varying complexity. One of these pairs consisted of two identical triangles, which were included to control for the possibility of differential response to some factor other than form. In the other three pairings, the infant was able to choose between the alternative figures shown in Figure 13.1.

Both in the case of the identical triangles and the cross and circle, the infants spent an equal amount of time looking at each figure in the pair. Moreover, with each of these pairs the infants quickly 'lost interest' and either looked elsewhere or went to sleep. The more complex figures illicited far more interest, and, in both cases, the infants showed a preference by looking at one stimulus more than the other. Generally the checkerboard was favoured in preference to the square, and the bulls eye in preference to the stripes. Curiously, in younger babies (under two months) this preference lay in the other direction, i.e., the stripes were

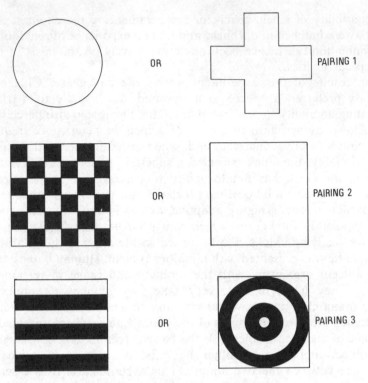

Fig. 13.1

fixated more than the bull's eye. The reason for this is unexplained. The important point, however, is that a preference is shown in the case of both complex pairs, indicating that the infant is able to discriminate between the two stimuli. This is true for all the ages tested. Human infants, then, are able to perceive form from the age of one week. Ethical considerations clearly exclude the possibility of keeping human infants in the dark, and it is thus conceivable that this level of perceptual skill is the result of influences occurring in the first week. However, similar findings have since been made for infants below the age of one week, strongly indicating that some degree of form perception is innate in humans.

In the case of the experiment with the chicks, it was suggested that their preferences were biologically adaptive in that they opted to peck at grain-like stimuli. An equivalent stimulus to the human infant is, perhaps, an adult face, as this will always accompany any attention to his needs. Accordingly, Fantz investigated infants' preferences among stimuli which approximated by varying degrees to an image of a human face.

In this experiment the stimuli were three flat objects the size and shape of an adult head. On one of these a stylized face was painted, on the second the same features were included but in a jumbled order, and on the third an area equal to that of the features was included at one end of the 'face'. All 'features' were black on a pink background.

Fig. 13.2

The three stimuli, paired in all possible combinations were shown to infants ranging from four days to six months old. In all cases the realistic face was preferred to the jumbled face and the third figure stimulated hardly any interest at all. In this study, although the degree of preference for the real over jumbled face was not large, it was consistent. However, in later studies Fantz failed to replicate this finding or found the effect only at certain ages. A cautious conclusion, then, would be that while preferential attention is given to those figures with a complexity similar to that of a drawing of a face the exact configuration of the features does not seem to matter much to the infants. Thus, the innate predisposition seems to be less specific than in the case of the chick, which responded to spherical objects of a particular size. The human infant is simply programmed towards complex visual patterns but not specifically to faces.

Results using three-dimensional stimuli, however, were more clear cut. Infants over the age of two months consistently preferred to look at a three dimensional dummy of a head rather than at a white board of the same size and shape. Under the age of two months the flat object was preferred, perhaps because it was brighter than the solid model. These results suggest that, as the baby develops, changes occur either in his ability to perceive three-dimensionality or in the attention holding value of solidity.

In the next phase of his research, Fantz concerned himself with ascertaining the visual acuity of human infants. A similar procedure was used, but this time a plain grey stimulus was paired with a series of striped patterns which varied in the width of the stripes. Results here showed that newborn infants placed at a distance of nine inches from the stimuli fixated longer on $\frac{3}{8}$ inch stripes than on grey. This suggests quite a remarkable acuity on the part of these infants. Even from birth, their perception of form has considerable detail. However, acuity does improve with age, which may be due either to maturation or to learning. With human subjects it is difficult to disentangle these influences, and therefore, it is necessary to refer back to animal studies.

The work of Eleanor J. Gibson and Richard Walk

Whereas Fantz studied the perception of *form* in developing animals, Gibson and Walk have investigated *depth* perception. Their work centres around a piece of apparatus which has become known as the 'visual cliff'. In the centre of this structure is a narrow plank on which the subject is placed. On either side of the plank there is a step down to a level floor area. To the right of the plank this step is very small, just a few inches, whereas to the left there is an apparent sharp drop of three or four feet. For the safety of the subject, a plate of glass covers this drop so that he cannot fall over. The experimental subject is able to choose between the two sides of the apparatus. A reluctance to move to the left (onto the glass over the cliff), as opposed to the right, would indicate that the subject is able to perceive the greater depth of the left hand cliff.

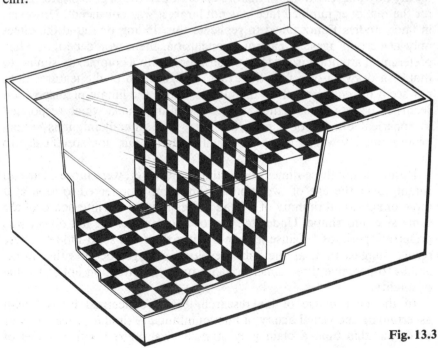

Fig. 13.3

When human infants were used as experimental subjects they consistently refused to cross the glass on the deep side to reach their mothers but happily crawled across to them when they stood on the shallow side. This would seem to indicate that human infants are able to perceive depth and are aware of the dangers involved in a cliff. However, there are several difficulties in interpretation of these results. The sample of children tested was rather small and there were some individuals who did, in fact, move onto the deep side either by backing onto it or by resting one foot on it for support. The experimenters interpreted these events as accidental, arguing that it was the infant's poor motor control which would have led to his falling over the cliff but for the glass floor. Secondly, all the infants involved must be able to crawl to perform the experimental task and so we are not able to discover anything about depth perceptual abilities in very young babies. With a child of six months or more, environmental and maturational influences have been long at work and we are unable to draw any conclusions about whether the ability to perceive depth is innate.

However, the same apparatus has been used with a variety of animals and the results here are clearer and more easily interpreted. Chicks less than twenty-four hours old are able to perceive the visual cliff and never hop down on the deep side. The same is true of goat kids and lambs tested as soon as they can stand. Moreover, if placed on the glass over the 'deep' side these animals show marked fear despite repeated tactual experience of the solidity of the glass.

Rats, on the other hand, are less inclined to accept the evidence of their eyes over other senses. If they are able to feel the glass with their whiskers, rats will step down onto either side of the cliff but if the glass is lowered out of reach the cliff is avoided.

Kittens are not mobile until four weeks of age but, tested at this time, they are able to avoid the visual cliff. Similar findings were made for a variety of other animals, an exception being aquatic turtles which showed less avoidance of the deep side. Clearly visual depth is less biologically important to aquatic turtles and thus we are unable to say whether their depth discrimination is poorer than other animals or if they simply pay less attention to perceived visual depth, having no fear of a fall.

Gibson and Walk next investigated which of two visual cues was most important in determining depth perception. The two cues investigated were pattern density and motion parallax. In all the visual cliff experiments described so far the floor level was marked by a sheet of patterned material which was pasted directly under the glass on the shallow side and laid upon the floor some feet below the glass on the deep side. Thus the retinal images of the pattern elements and the spacings between them were smaller when viewing the deep side, giving greater pattern density than on the shallow side. This cue can be removed by using an enlarged pattern on the low side of the cliff such that the retinal image size of pattern elements on both sides is the same.

The second visual depth cue which could be used in assessing the visual cliff is motion parallax. When a subject moves its body or head, the apparent motion of the pattern elements is slower for the more distant elements than for the nearer ones. This is similar to the effect seen from a railway carriage, where nearby objects seem to flash by while distant ones move much more slowly. In the case of the visual cliff this can be removed by pasting patterns directly below the glass on both sides of the cliff with the 'deep' side pattern elements reduced in size to maintain pattern density differences.

In the first condition, with pattern density equalized, chicks and rats still prefer the 'shallow' side. Clearly, both species can discriminate depth using motion parallax alone. In the second condition, with motion parallax cues removed, day-old chicks showed no preference while rats preferred the side with the larger pattern, i.e., the 'nearer' surface. However, the rats used in this experiment were somewhat older than the chicks and it is possible that they had learned to respond to pattern density. This suggestion is supported by experiments with dark-reared rats which, like the chicks, stepped down equally on both sides when motion parallax cues were removed but not when they were present. It would appear then that motion parallax is the innate cue for depth perception while responses to pattern density are learned later.

Experiments involving dark-rearing
Before we can declare that an animal has innate ability, we must be certain that there are no opportunities for learning between birth and testing. In the experiment described above the rats appeared to show an innate response to pattern density. However, when rats which had been kept in the dark from birth were tested there was no such response.

Rearing animals from birth in darkness would seem to provide an answer to the problems encountered with those species in which the infant at birth is very limited in his range of responses. Kittens, as has already been pointed out, are not mobile until four weeks old and therefore cannot be tested on the visual cliff or any similar task before this age. During these four weeks the normally-reared kitten receives much visual stimulation, giving opportunities for perceptual learning to occur. Thus, their avoidance of the 'deep' side of the visual cliff may be seen as a result of learning rather than innate factors. This suggestion is supported by the fact that dark-reared kittens will step or rather fall down equally on either side of the visual cliff apparatus. Apparently, in kittens, the ability to perceive depth is not innate as it is in rats and chicks.

By rearing animals in the dark, we remove all possible opportunities for visual learning. Thus, we should also be able to draw some conclusions about the relative influences of learning and maturation using this technique.

Fantz found that monkeys reared in the dark showed no improvement in performance on perceptually guided tasks with increasing age, unlike normally-reared monkeys. Deprived of opportunities for learning, the animals make no progress. This would seem to suggest that improvements with age in the normally-reared animals are due to learning rather than maturation. However, the dark-reared animals do not simply fail to improve, they, in fact, show distinct deterioration as they get older. Older animals take longer to learn perceptual skills after removal from the darkness than do younger ones. This poorer performance of the older animals was originally thought to indicate that there is a critical age for the development of visual perception. Deprived of stimulation during this period the animal later learns perceptual skills only after extensive experience and training. Again maturational influences seem to be compounded with learning.

There is, however, an alternative explanation for the poorer performance of the older, deprived animals which confounds the issue still further. Perhaps rearing animals in the dark actually leads to a physical deterioration in the perceptual system. Such an explanation is supported by evidence from a variety of sources. Chicks which have been reared in the dark from hatching to ten weeks of age are unable to recognize and peck at grains, although normal chicks are able to do this immediately on hatching. Clearly, there has been loss of ability in the dark-reared group. Development of cataracts on the eyes of some of the groups suggests that physical deterioration of the eyes may be involved. Such deterioration has been clearly seen in the dark-reared monkeys and cats, where post mortem examinations of the eyes have found retinal damage. This seems also to be true in rats, but only after extensive periods of light deprivation. Rats reared in the dark for thirty days perform as well as light-reared rats on the visual cliff apparatus, indicating an innate ability to perceive depth, as has already been discussed. However, rats reared in darkness until ten months of age no longer discriminate depth when first brought into the light.

Physical retinal damage is reduced if animals are reared, not in total darkness, but in diffuse light. In such experiments, the animals are fitted with diffusing goggles which allow a homogenous field of light to impinge upon the retina, but there is no patterned stimulation. Although physical damage to the retina is not found in animals so reared, their performance on perceptual tasks is still poorer than that of normally-reared controls. However, they rapidly learn visual skills when exposed to a lighted environment. Perhaps this does provide evidence that maturation cannot occur without the opportunities for perceptual learning. On the whole, however, the procedure of dark-rearing has not proved as useful a tool as was hoped, since the results are open to a variety of different interpretations.

Similarly, the few cases of humans who have had their sight given to them after being blind from birth have provided less insight into the processes of perceptual learning than might be imagined. There are only some sixty documented cases and very few of these have been carefully studied. In recent years, a typical case would involve a man or woman having an operation for removal of cataracts or, very recently, a corneal graft in patients having opacity of the cornea. Generally, such people are at first unable to name or distinguish between simple objects and even with prolonged training sometimes never achieve useful vision. Perhaps the most interesting finding to emerge from these cases is the frequent occurrence of severe emotional disturbance following the patients experience of vision, to such an extent that they sometimes reject their new faculty, keep their eyes firmly shut during daylight hours and refuse to use artificial light at night. Not all patients react so severely and one or two (generally the more intelligent and better educated) are able to use their vision quite well very soon after the operation. But, overall, such cases throw little light on the nature/nurture problem.

The work of Richard Held and Alan Hein
We have seen that dark-reared kittens seem effectively blind with regard to the visual cliff on first exposure. Held and Hein have further investigated the perceptual abilities of neonate kittens. Their hypothesis is that, in the case of those animals in which perceptual abilities are not innate, such as kittens, the acquisition of these skills depends not only on exposure to visual stimulation but also on motor activities. They argue that it is only by moving about in a visually rich environment that normal sensory-motor coordination can develop. Passive exposure to such an environment is not adequate to produce normal behaviour. They tested this hypothesis using a piece of apparatus which has become known as the kitten carousel (see Fig. 13.4).

Two kittens are placed in the apparatus together. One kitten is housed in a basket, from which only the head protrudes. There is room inside the basket for limb movement but the kitten's legs cannot touch the floor of the apparatus. The second kitten is allowed to move about freely within the confines of a drum. It is attached to a harness connected to the basket containing the first kitten in such a way that its movements are transmitted and thus both kittens receive the same visual stimulation whilst inside the drum. The walls of the drum and centre post are covered with a repeated, striped pattern.

In the classic experiment, the pairs of kittens were reared in darkness until strong enough to be able to move the basket containing a kitten

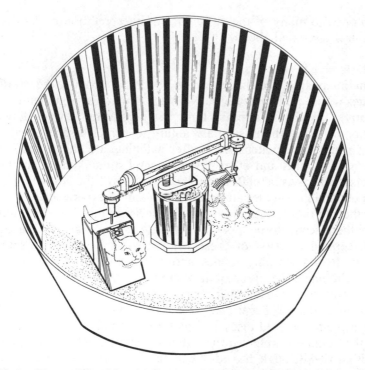

Fig. 13.4 (From 'Plasticity in Sensory-Motor Systems' by Richard Held. Copyright © 1965 by Scientific American, Inc. All rights reserved.)

(eight to twelve weeks of age). They were then placed in the carousel, with the same kitten in the basket on each occasion, for three hours each day, spending the rest of the time in darkness. After thirty hours in the apparatus the active kitten showed normal sensory motor coordination. It avoided the deep side of the visual cliff, blinked when an object approached its eyes, etc. The passive kitten however showed no such responses although it soon learned to do so after being allowed to run about in a lighted environment.

Kittens, then, must learn sensory-motor skills of this nature. They are not innate. Moreover, in order to require such skills it is necessary for the animals to move around under the power of their own muscles in a lit environment where they can see the results of their movements. However, we must draw a distinction between perception, on the one hand, and sensory-motor coordination, on the other. The experiments of Held and Hein do not prove that the passive kitten cannot perceive the increased depth on the one side of the visual cliff or the objects moved towards their eyes. It may simply be that the kitten has not learned the correct response for such situations. This is a confounding factor in the case of most of the experiments with developing animals. This experiment

285

is also open to many of the difficulties of interpretation of dark-rearing procedures discussed above.

Conclusions

Several interesting conclusions can be drawn from these studies of neonates which contribute to the Nativiste-Empiricist argument.

Firstly, it would appear that in organisms lower down the evolutionary scale there is innate ability to perceive salient features of the environment. Chickens, soon after hatching, are able to discriminate between food items and other environmental stimuli, and both chickens and rats avoid a visual cliff. Such findings support the Nativist view that perceptual abilities are innate and independent of experience.

Further up the evolutionary scale however, in humans, apes and even kittens there seems to be less that is innate. There is greater plasticity in the perceptual systems of these organisms, giving greater scope for maturation and learning to act upon what innate predispositions do exist. In humans, the paramount of these predispositions is attention to form or pattern above all other aspects of a stimulus. This is shown most clearly in a further experiment by Fantz, wherein neonates selected between plain coloured discs and patterns such as bulls eyes and faces. Even the youngest preferred the patterned stimuli. Such an emphasis on form is carried through into adult perception, where it is principally form which underlies all object and person perception. The removal of other features such as depth, colour, usual size, and movement does nothing to impair our recognition, as the success of black and white photography proves. For humans, then, the position taken by Donald Hebb seems to be the most accurate. There is some innate basis for visual perception, but it is only by complex interaction between this and the maturation and environment of the individual, that the adult perceptual capabilities are developed. Such a system underlies the greater adaptability of higher organisms.

Adaptation to perceptual distortion

Johann Kepler (1571–1630) was the first person to argue that the image of an object falling on the retina is inverted by the lens of the eye. His theoretical analysis was subsequently confirmed by Scheiner (1575–1650), who cut away the opaque outer layers at the back of the eyeball, making the image on the retina visible. From this time on, philosophers and natural historians speculated on how this inverted image comes to be perceived as upright. Perhaps Lotze (1852) made the most sensible contribution to this argument when he pointed out that the orientation of the image on the retina is irrelevant as every other geometrical property of the image is distorted on the retina, which, after

286

all, is a most peculiar shape on which to project an image. One of the implications of this view, especially in the light of empiristic arguments, is that, given the opportunity for perceptual-motor experience, the perceiver could perceptually and behaviourally adapt, even were the image to be artificially reinverted. Further, it would be intriguing to find out what would happen to a subject's perception if he were exposed to grossly transformed visual input for long periods. Would he adapt to his new visual world by altering his motor responses to it, or would he adapt by sorting out his new perceptual problem so that the world once again looked 'normal'? In any event, if he adapts at all to this new world this has implications for our understanding of the role of experience in the development of perception.

Stratton's experiments with inverting lenses

With the background outlined above, George Stratton (1896) devised an experiment which has become one of the most widely cited investigations in the history of psychology, which is rather odd because, as we shall see, his results are controversial even to this day. His apparatus was a tube containing a lens system which produced an inverted image which was then re-inverted by the lens of the eye to produce an upright image on the retina. This apparatus was worn over his right eye, the left being blindfolded. Stratton used himself as the subject because he found it difficult to persuade others to wear his apparatus for days or weeks.

The main part of his investigation lasted for eight days, during which he wore the lens system for a total of eighty-seven hours. While he was not wearing the apparatus, both his eyes were blindfolded. During the time that he wore the apparatus, Stratton just went about his usual routine; he did not engage in any controlled perceptual motor tasks.

Stratton reported that, at first, he experienced a great deal of visuo-motor disruption, so much so, that at times he shut his eyes to avoid considering the visual data with which he was presented. As the first day wore on, he became better able to accept the scenes around him as they were presented. But he was still aware that the part of his environment not in his immediate vision was in a different orientation. By the fourth day, Stratton reported that he was starting to imagine the unseen parts of his environment as also being inverted and by the eighth day everything appeared harmonious by which he seems to mean that he had begun to feel himself to be upside-down and to feel normal in this state.

The feeling one sifts from Stratton's reports is that his visual sense of up and down was not affected by his experiences, even though he had learned to adapt his behaviour. This feeling is supported by Stratton's report of his experiences as the apparatus was removed. He immediately recognized the visual orientation as the pre-experimental one, but, even so, he found it surprisingly bewildering, though definitely not upside-down. This absence of an up-down after-effect is strong evidence that perceptual adaptation did not take place to the inversion effect of his apparatus. However, he did experience an after-effect which caused the scene before his eyes to swing and sweep as he moved his eyes thus indicating that location constancy had been disrupted by adaptation to a different set of rules.

More experiments with inverting lenses

In 1930 P. H. Ewert tried to repeat Stratton's experiment but, as is so often the case with an attempted replication, Ewert began by altering the apparatus; he used a binocular optical system. His subjects wore the inverting goggles for between 175 and 195 hours. Ewert's aim was to determine finally whether, during such an experiment, there was any perceptual adaptation, rather than just an improvement in the subject's ability to cope with his transformed vision. To this end, he devised two tests which he administered on each day of the experiment. In the first test, the subject was presented with coloured blocks placed in a line extending from his observation point. The subject was asked to name the colours of the nearest and farthest blocks. The results were quite clear; up and down and right and left judgments were always inverted with no evidence of up/down adaptation even after the 14th day of the experiment. Ewert also tested for motor adaptation and found considerable improvements, for example, in touch localization.

A further series of experiments by Frederick Snyder and Nicholas Pronko (1952) and J. Peterson and J. K. Peterson (1938) which focused mainly on the question of motor adaptation contributed the findings that these newly learned visuo-motor adaptations are extremely resistant to forgetting, to the extent that, two years after their experiment, performance wearing inverting goggles was not significantly poorer than at the end of the thirty-day experimental period.

The final set of experiments that we shall discuss in the context of inverting lenses were performed by Ivo Kohler (1964). For all three experiments Kohler used an optical device which utilized a mirror; its effect was to invert the image on its vertical axis without reversing left and right. He carried out three experiments, but we shall be concerned only with the third, which lasted for ten days. Kohler concluded on the basis of this third experiment that upright vision could be achieved if the subject was encouraged to move about and touch objects in his environment. The familiarity of objects was also found to be important: the more familiar the object, the greater the probability that it would be seen upright. Kohler also reported that, on removal of the inverting apparatus, subjects sometimes saw objects as upside down, but this happened only for the first few minutes.

Thus, Ewert's findings appear to be contradicted by those of Kohler.

Perhaps we may explain their differences in terms of the different experimental apparatus and procedures. Kohler's apparatus only inverted the image, it did not reverse left and right; Ewert's apparatus not only inverted the image but also reversed right and left, as well as producing depth inversion. Although Ewert's experiments lasted for up to 195 hours his subjects were not encouraged to practise a wide variety of perceptual motor tasks; in fact, most of their time was spent being assessed in the laboratory. This is in contrast with the experience of Kohler's subjects, who were encouraged to move around and pick up objects. Lastly, we must note that in the experiments discussed here a total of nine subjects were used—a very small number when we consider the problem of individual differences which must limit extrapolation.

The prism experiments

In 1928 experiments along the lines of Stratton's transformed stimulation studies were begun by James J. Gibson. This researcher used prisms set in goggles as well as other devices, but for the moment we shall confine ourselves to a discussion of the effects of wearing prisms. One of the effects produced by a prism is to distort vertical lines by making them appear curved. A prism with its base to the left will make a straight vertical line appear curved with its centre pulled to the left (Fig. 13.5).

Furthermore, this curvature of lines is only part of a more comprehensive property of prisms by which variations in the angle, curvature, and distance of observed objects may be produced. This comes about because the angle at which a light ray is caused to deviate varies as the angle that it makes with the front face of the prism changes, such that rays entering at an oblique angle are made to deviate more than rays entering at right angles. Thus, if the eyes move behind the prism or the head and goggles move while the eyes remain fixed on an object, very complex 'variable' distortions will arise. Prisms also produce colour fringes which appear along the borders of light-coloured objects. This is because light rays of shorter wavelengths are bent more than long ones. Finally, prisms produce colour displacement effects, whereby adjacent areas of different colours are separated leaving a dark area between the colours.

Gibson's subjects were the first to discover adaptation to line curvature and colour fringes produced by prisms. The subjects adapted to these constant distortions in the relatively short duration of Gibson's experiment, but adaptation to the more complex variable distortions produced by prisms was not noted until Kohler (1951) reported such adaptations in his subjects. The so-called variable distortions take the form of concertina effects, such that, wearing prisms with bases pointing to the right, a subject who turns his head to the left but his eyes to the right sees an image which contracts horizontally. If he turns his head to the right and his eyes to the left the image expands horizontally. Kohlers subjects suffered severe after-effects when they removed their goggles at the end of the experimental periods, which resulted in contraction or expansion of the image depending on the position of the head and eyes. These after-effects disappeared after two or three days.

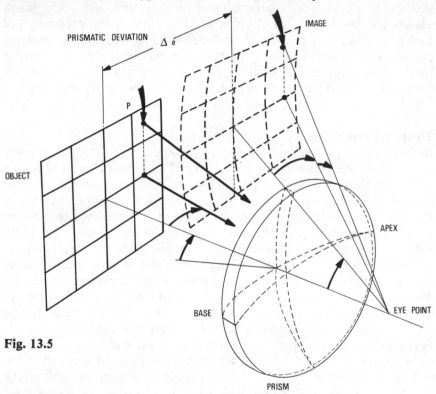

Fig. 13.5

The colour stereo effect

Several devices apart from the prism arrangement described above were used in Kohler's series of experiments, but we shall discuss only one further type of prism device here. Kohler found that if his subjects wore goggles with the base of each prism pointing outwards (away from the nose) this produced a variety of distortions; the most interesting from our point of view is known as the colour stereo effect. The two prisms refract colours at different angles according to their wavelengths, but in opposite directions. As the bases face outward the blue end of the spectrum is bent outward more than other colours. This means that the eyes must converge more to focus blue images than red images, making blue appear closer than red, with other colours appearing to lie between them.

290

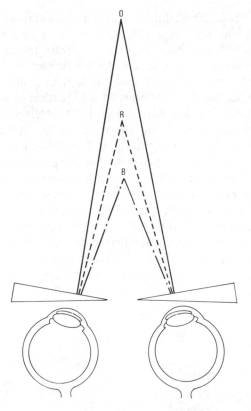

Fig. 13.6

One of Kohler's subjects, wearing these goggles, described an incident in which he saw a woman wearing a red blouse walking along a street. She appeared to have no upper body with the red blouse following a few feet behind her moving its empty sleeves in time with the movements of the arms!

Now, the most important finding about the colour stereo effect is that even after wearing the prisms for fifty-two days Kohler's subjects did not report the slightest adaptation to this distortion. So far, this finding remains without any completely satisfactory explanation.

The role of active movement in adaptation

In 1965, Richard Held published a review of several experiments which he and his co-workers carried out in order to clarify the role of 'reafference' in the organization of the perceptual-motor system. Reafference is the term used to describe the neural activity which follows movement initiated by an organism and which provides the organism with information about the results of this self-produced movement (sometimes called 'feedback').

In the first experiment, the subject was seated at an apparatus in which he could see a simple lattice under a glass screen. Actually, what the subject saw was an image reflected by an angled mirror. His task was to put his hand into the apparatus and mark the apparent location of the four intersections of the lattice. As will be seen from the schematic representation of the apparatus below, the subject could not see his hand while he carried out his task. He marked the location of each intersection ten times, withdrawing his hand after each attempt. After this, the marking sheet was removed and the mirror was replaced by a prism which displaced the images to the right. The subject then spent several minutes looking through the prism at his hand as he moved it in the apparatus. None of the movement involved deliberately trying to touch a target. Next, the original conditions were restored and the subject was again required to mark each lattice intersection ten times. The results showed that the subjects had begun to adapt to the effects of the prisms, the second set of marks being further to the left than the original set. Furthermore, it is apparent from this study that recognition of error is not necessary for adaptation to occur (the subject did not attempt to reach for a target while moving his hand under the prism).

Fig. 13.7

Held then set out to see whether it was just movement that was necessary for adaptation or movement controlled by the subject. He repeated the procedure outlined above, except that, during the time the subject was looking through the prism, he had his arm strapped to a

292

board which was pivoted at the elbow. Subjects looked through the prism under three conditions:

1. No movement of the arm.
2. Passive movement: he kept his arm limp and it was moved from side to side by the experimenter.
3. Active movement, in which he moved his arm from side to side himself.

The results showed that approximately half an hour of active movement, i.e., Condition 3 was all that was required to produce complete compensation for the displacement caused by the prism, whereas passive movement, Condition 2, produced no adaptation. Thus, Held concluded that as the same visual feedback was available to the subjects in the active and passive condition the differences in adaptation must have been due to the element of self-initiation of movement in Condition 3. For a comparison with Held's work using animals see the kitten carousel experiment in the first part of this Chapter. Held went on to argue that it is important that movement is self-produced because an organism will only be able to gain information about the movement of objects relative to its own anatomy if it has information about its commands to its own muscles.

The studies of adaptation to distorted visual input reviewed here lead us to conclude that the visual apparatus is, in adults, extremely flexible and able to adjust to severe interference and changing conditions. It is difficult to see why we should have developed this facility if learning plays no part in the normal development of perceptual processes.

The effects of cognitive disposition on perception

Here, we shall consider the proposition that our perception is dependent, not only upon the structure of the environment and objects in it, but also upon certain dispositions within the perceiver and, further, that these dispositions are a function of the past experiences of the perceiver. More specifically, we shall deal with the effects of expectation, value, and motivation on perception. Actually, the term motivation is somewhat of a bugbear in psychology because it has been used in connection with so many different psychological states: for example, some emotional states are said to be motivating; attitudes may motivate; beliefs may motivate; primary sensations such as hunger, thirst, pleasure and pain are motivators. Here, we shall focus on the apparently motivating aspects of emotionally coloured words to produce the so-called 'perceptual defence' effect. But first we shall look at the interaction between expectation and perception.

Expectation and perception

It is well known that if someone is predisposed or 'set' to perceive certain features of his environment he will more readily perceive them. An early experiment performed by Jerome S. Bruner and A. Leigh Minturn in 1955 demonstrated this effect quite simply. They presented twenty-four subjects with strings either of letters or of numbers, followed by an ambiguous test figure which was a broken B, in which the curved part of the figure was separated from the vertical line by a distance of one millimetre. Before presentation the subjects were told which class of stimuli to expect (letters or numbers). Each stimulus was initially presented for the very brief exposure time of thirty milliseconds and then successively with twenty millisecond increases until the subject reported perceiving the letter or number three times in succession. The subjects were required to draw exactly what they saw as accurately as they could. Bruner and Minturn found that when a subject had been presented with a string of letters he developed a 'letter' set and drew and presumably saw a closed B when he was actually presented with the ambiguous test figure. When the test figure was preceded by numbers it was drawn as the number 13. Bruner and Minturn conclude by observing that when the conditions of stimulation are such that some ambiguity is present then resolution is brought about on the basis of the context in which the stimulus is set.

A series of experiments which appear to illustrate the same sort of process in a rather different way, has a long pedigree going back to a piece of work by Leeper in 1935.

Leeper found that, if he presented a subject with a figure which portrayed a young woman (B), followed by an ambiguous figure (A),

A   B   C

Fig. 13.8

then the subject reported that (A) was a picture of a young woman. The parallel effect was produced by prior presentation of (C) in which case (A) was seen as an old woman.

This powerful predisposing effect is probably not simply due to expectation, because, if you present a subject with a sequence of C-B-C-B-C-B-C-B stimuli, he expects C (the old woman); but if you now present A he usually sees B (the young woman). So it seems that we must add a recency memory effect to the organizing principles which determine perception.

Recently, Bugelski and Alampay (1961) have shown that a 'set effect' can be induced without verbal instructions. They presented half their subjects with several pictures of animals after which they presented all subjects with an ambiguous 'rat-man' figure for identification. The pre-trained subjects generally saw a rat, while subjects, who had not been given the pretraining usually saw the man.

Fig. 13.9 From 'The Role of Frequency in Developing Perceptual Sets' by B. R. Bugelski and D. A. Alampay published in the *Canadian Journal of Psychology*, 15.

This brief look at set and perception indicates clearly that we may sometimes see what we expect to see. However, the experiments cited here have been concerned only with ambiguous stimulus arrays, and these findings may not apply to any significant extent in the perception of unambiguous stimuli. Moreover, expectation is not always the dominant organizing factor in set effects.

Value and its effects on perception
Perceptual overestimation (accentuation) of the size of objects due to their value has been noted in many experiments. The results of the overwhelming majority of these studies confirm the following general conclusion: we tend to perceive valued objects as larger than they really are but

only if the value of the objects has been associated with their size, e.g., increasing coin size is related to increasing value of those coins (with some exceptions, this is true for the specie of many countries of the Western world). It was formerly thought that the size of any objects of 'importance' to a perceiver would be over estimated, e.g., the size of a swastika as perceived by a survivor of a concentration camp, but this is not so. A typical early experiment was designed by Jerome Bruner and Goodman and reported in 1947. In this experiment thirty ten-year-old children were used as subjects, ten poor children, ten rich children and ten children drawn at random from the population of Boston (a control group). Each child sat in front of a screen, on which was a spot of light. A knob under the screen controlled the size of the spot. All the subjects first had to estimate (by manipulating the size of the spot of light) the size of a penny, nickel, dime, quarter, and a half dollar in that order and then in reverse order. Two judgments were made in each run, one starting with the spot of light at its smallest setting and the other at its largest. In the first condition all the judgments were made from memory.

In the next condition, the subjects had to repeat the process but this time with the coins held in the palm of the hand normal to the line of vision. Control subjects had to judge the size of grey cardboard discs which were the same size as the coins used. The results of these trials were expressed as percentage deviations of the size of the spot of light from the true size of the coins being judged.

The main finding of this experiment was that all children significantly overestimated that the size of the coins by an amount which increased with the value of the coin, not its true size. Thus, even though a dime (10 cents) is smaller than a penny (1 cent) its percentage overestimation was greater. The one exception to this was the half dollar which Bruner and Goodman suggest may be too valuable for a ten-year-old child to be able to form any real feeling of its worth. These findings, then, seem to substantiate the hypothesis that attitudes may have an organizing effect on perception. Further evidence for this notion was provided by the finding that poor children showed more overestimation than rich children, the difference increasing with value. The argument here would be that poor children have a different attitude to the coins from rich children, in that they value them more. However, when children made their judgements from memory, poor children showed less overestimation than when coins were present, whereas rich children showed no consistent difference in this respect. This is contrary to the obvious prediction from the hypothesis because the presence of the coins should have reduced any error in judgment due to memory. This remains an unexplained finding.

Those studies which have produced findings which are apparently contradictory to those of Bruner and Goodman have one thing in common: the 'value' of the stimuli used has nothing to do with their size. For example, concentration camp survivors do not reliably overestimate the size of discs bearing a swastika. Clearly, whether a swastika is large or small or on an object that is large or small is of no relevance to its importance. Thus, size is not associated with the importance of swastikas in any special way.

Perceptual defence and sensitization
Much of the interest among psychologists investigating the effects of motivation on perception, has been focused on the phenomena known as perceptual defence, perceptual sensitization, and subception. Leo Postman, Jerome Bruner, and Elliot McGuinnies utilized the concepts of perceptual defence and sensitization in 1946 when they put forward the hypothesis that personal value systems were determinants of perception. This led to a series of experiments which indicated that subjects had lowered visual recognition thresholds for words which had highly valued or pleasant associations and higher thresholds for words which had unpleasant or taboo associations. In their main experiment Postman, Bruner and McGuinnies used twenty-five subjects, all of whom had completed Allport-Vernon personal value questionnaires. Each subject was then shown thirty-six words, one at a time, in a tachistoscope. The words represented the six scales of the personal value profiles (theoretical, economic, aesthetic, social, political, and religious) thus the theoretical value scale words were: *theory, analysis, logical, science, research*, and *verify* while the social value scale words were: *sociable, kindly, loving, devoted, helpful*, and *friendly*. Now, if a subject has a low social and high theoretical value profile, his thresholds for words like *logical* and *analysis* should be lowered because of 'perceptual sensitization' and raised for *sociable* and *loving* because of 'perceptual defence'. The results of the experiment seemed to confirm the existence of the mechanisms of sensitization and defence, and, further, early experiments, notably by Elliot McGuinnies, concentrated on replicating the perceptual defence effect. Again this was done by tachistoscopic presentation of words, but, this time, half of the words were chosen as emotionally neutral, e.g., apple, broom, glass and the other half as emotionally arousing taboo words, e.g., whore, penis, belly (our sense of what is a taboo word has obviously changed since 1949)! The subjects' recognition thresholds were determined by exposing the words at 0.01 seconds then at 0.02 seconds, etc., until it was correctly reported. McGuinnies found that his subjects displayed significantly higher recognition thresholds for the emotionally-toned words than they did for the neutral words. This, of course, was interpreted by him as clear evidence for perceptual defence; however there are alternative interpretations.

297

Howes and Soloman (1950) made two main points:

1. The difference in threshold between neutral and emotional words is due to the greater familiarity with the written form of neutral words because they occur with much higher frequency in generally available literature than 'taboo' words.
2. It is not that subjects fail to recognize the emotional words as quickly as neutral words; it is merely that they feel loath to report their perceptions until they are absolutely sure about what they have seen.

This perceptual defence versus response bias controversy has continued more or less to the present day, with perhaps the best attempt to settle it being an elegantly designed experiment by Worthington (1969), in which he utilized brightness scaling at the threshold of awareness. Worthington used 160 subjects, who were required to judge which of two faint spots of light presented successively on a screen was brighter. In fact they were objectively identical. Embedded in each spot of light was a very faint subliminal word. Nine different words were used which had previously been rated for emotionality by an independent group of judges. Worthington found that when one of the spots of light had a word rated high on emotionality embedded in it, it was rated as dimmer than a spot of light with an emotionally neutral word embedded in it even though the subjects were completely unaware of the verbal stimuli.

This experiment very neatly provides us with firm evidence that the perceptual defence effect is not due to a reluctance on the part of the subject either to say out loud or even admit that he is aware of any taboo words. In fact, in the Worthington experiment, the subjects had no idea that any words were being presented to them at all. If this experiment is successfully replicated we will probably be justified in regarding the perceptual defence effect as a manifestation of a sensory regulation mechanism. However, we must now introduce a note of caution in our interpretation of the 'perceptual defence' effect. It seems most odd that we should have evolved a mechanism which would allow our unconscious minds to censor emotionally arousing stimuli, especially as this effect only seems to occur with stimuli which are very faint either because they have been presented very fast or at a very low intensity. Indeed, one would have imagined that the selection pressures on our evolutionary ancestors would have been in the direction of making us as sharply aware as possible of faint but threatening stimuli. As perceptual defence seems to be a fact of life, how are we to deal with the evolutionary arguments outlined above?

A possible explanation might rest on the evolution of consciousness itself. This new development would require the parallel development of a mechanism which would control the input into consciousness, which is a limited capacity system. Once a mechanism which controls entry into consciousness is arrived at, it becomes easy to see that the organization of the system which may produce the most efficient selection under most conditions, may, under the special conditions of a perceptual defence experiment, result in what appears to be an anomaly. In any event, there would seem to be absolutely no necessity to imagine that the 'perceptual defence' effect results from an attempt by our unconscious psyche to protect us from rude words.

The subception effect

Further evidence for pre-conscious analysis of stimuli was provided by Richard Lazarus and Robert McCleary (1951), who coined the term 'subception' to label a process by which some kind of correct discrimination is made when the subject is unable to make a correct conscious discrimination. These two workers paired certain nonsense syllables with electric shock in order to condition their subjects into producing galvanic skin responses on presentation of these nonsense syllables. They then tachistoscopically presented ten nonsense syllables to their subjects (five previously shocked and five non-shocked) at each of five different exposure durations, the slowest allowing 100 per cent accuracy in syllable recognition and the fastest allowing accuracy to be achieved only by chance.

Lazarus and McCleary found that their subjects reacted with significant GSRs to nonsense syllables which had been previously associated with shock even when these nonsense syllables were presented so quickly that the subjects could not correctly identify them. This subception effect has been used to investigate the mechanisms of selective attention but, instead of using fast stimulus presentation to prevent conscious awareness, the selective attention studies employ higher energy supraliminal stimuli with awareness directed, by the use of shadowing, towards an alternative source of stimulation (see Ch. 14).

Cultural influences on perception

If learning plays a role in the development of perception, it may be true that different cultural backgrounds will produce people whose perception of their environment reflects these differences. But it is not really satisfactory to conclude that culture affects perception; it ought to be possible to show how. Here, we shall review the notions that attitudes may be implicated in certain perceptual phenomena and that familiarity with the methods, materials and conventions of the pictorial art of a particular culture is necessary in order that it may convey the appropriate information.

Attitudes and the perception of race

One of the most controversial investigations in this field of enquiry was carried out by Thomas Pettigrew, Gordon Allport, and Eric Barnett in 1958. They, rather ingeniously, used binocular resolution to investigate how members of the five main ethnic groups in South Africa perceived one another. These researchers used 122 subjects drawn from the Afrikaner, English, Coloured, Indian and African populations of Durban. Each subject was presented with pairs of head and shoulder photographs of members of four ethnic groups, African, Coloured, Indian, and European in all combinations plus intra-group pairs. These pairs of photographs were presented stereoscopically for an exposure duration of about two seconds. Immediately after exposure, each subject was required to name the race he thought he had seen. The responses fell into several different categories. When both eyes were presented with photographs of members of the same race the subject could be either right or wrong in his judgment. When he was presented with photographs of members of two different ethnic groups the subject could report both correctly, suppress one and report the other, or report that he had seen what Pettigrew called a 'manifest fusion'. An example of a manifest fusion would be when a subject reported 'coloured' when in fact he had been presented with a European-African pair. The researchers reported that they were convinced that their subjects were not consciously guessing but were in fact reporting what they 'saw'.

The results of this study were rather startling. The main finding was the Afrikaners (Dutch-descended whites) tended to be comparatively accurate when they were judging European one-race pairs but frequently judged as African all other one-race pairs. Furthermore, when judging European-African pairs the Afrikaners tended to suppress one of the images and report either European or African more often than the other groups of subjects. When they were presented with the Coloured-Indian pairs, Afrikaners again produced more European and African judgments than the other groups of subjects.

Pettigrew, Allport, and Barnett interpreted these findings as being consistent with previous research which has shown that judgments made by highly emotionally-involved subjects tend to be extreme, i.e., that people with strong beliefs tend to see issues in 'black and white' (in this case both literally and metaphorically). The argument here seems to be that questions of race are of paramount importance in the life of Afrikaners and this tends to polarize their judgments in racial issues and, furthermore, this mechanism can influence perception.

Some points to bear in mind, however, are that this study uses highly artificial stimulus arrays, briefly presented, and that, even if the subject reports his perceptions rather than his guesses this does not mean that his real-life perceptions are in any way similar. Secondly, this study has

300

now been replicated but we are left with the central issue. Do Afrikaners really 'see' exactly what the other races see but differ from them in their willingness to attach labels to these perceptions, or are they actually less likely to 'see' a fusion. At the moment we cannot be certain.

Visual illusions

The above experiment is rather out of the main stream of investigation into the effects of culture on perception. The principal thrust of work in this area has been concerned with visual illusions and constancies. This work originated with W. H. R. Rivers who worked with the natives of the Torres Straits as long ago as 1901. He concluded on the basis of his findings that the reactions of his subjects to the visual illusions with which he presented them were largely determined by their own particular environment. A later, and much more extensive, investigation was carried out by Marshall Segall, Donald T. Campbell, and M. J. Herskovits who published their results in 1963. This study took six years to complete during which 1878 subjects were studied from locations in Africa, the Philippines, South Africa and America. These researchers found that non-European subjects were less susceptible to the Muller-Lyer illusions but that some groups of non-Europeans were susceptible to the two horizontal-vertical illusions in the study. (For information on these illusions see Chapter 12.)

Segall, Campbell, and Herskovits hypothesized that the greater susceptibility of the Europeans to the Muller-Lyer illusions was due to the relatively widespread occurrence of rectangularity in their environment which results in a bias to interpret angles drawn on a two-dimensional surface as representative of rectangular, three-dimensional objects. The relatively less 'carpentered', non-European environment would not encourage the development of such a perceptual bias; hence the Muller-Lyer illusion tends to 'fail' with individuals developing in these conditions.

Now, this explanation must be treated with caution for the following reasons. First, the mechanisms underlying the perception of geometrical, visual illusions are still under debate. Thus it is by no means certain that the experience of rectangularity is especially important. Secondly the variable of race was not controlled in this study, i.e., there may be other cognitive or biological differences between the Europeans and non-Europeans which account for the experimental findings. Some evidence for this comes from a study by A. C. Munday-Castle and G. K. Nelson (1962) who studied an illiterate community of white forest workers in South Africa. In spite of the 'rectangularity' of their environment they were unable to give appropriate three-dimensional responses to two-dimensional symbols on a standard test. Neither were their responses to the Muller-Lyer illusion significantly different from a sample of non-

Europeans; but they were very significantly different from those of ordinary white adults.

Similarly, the finding of Segall *et al.* that some groups of non-Europeans were more susceptable to the horizontal-vertical illusion cannot be attributed simply to the openness of the terrain on which these groups lived because G. Jahoda (1966), working with Ghanaian subjects, found no support for the hypothesis that groups living in open country would be more susceptible to the horizontal-vertical illusion than groups living in dense tropical forest. Moreover, Gregor and McPherson (1965) found no significant differences between two groups of Australian aborigines on the Muller-Lyer and horizontal-vertical illusions, in spite of the fact that one group lived a relatively urbanized life in a 'carpentered' environment while the other group lived primitively in the open.

So we have evidence that there do appear to be differences between ethnic groups in how they respond to some illusions. However, we also have some evidence that these differences do not seem to be caused by the different physical environments of the groups (Jahoda, 1966; Gregor and McPherson, 1965), but that perhaps familiarity with the test materials, drawings and pictorial representation in general, may be an important factor (Munday-Castle and Nelson, 1962).

The perception of line drawings
Further evidence highlighting the importance of this last factor comes from an intriguing study reported in 1966 by A. C. Munday-Castle. He set out to investigate how Ghanaian children responded to depth cues in pictorial material. He used 122 children aged between five and ten years, who were shown the pictures in Figure 13.10 and asked a series of questions about them.

From the children's answers it became clear that they frequently misinterpreted details in the pictures, but their mistakes were not haphazard. They frequently correctly recognized the class to which the object belonged but seemed to guess which member of that class was represented, using their own experience as a guide, e.g., the deer was called a goat, sheep, cow, dog, ass, horse, or camel. More interestingly, it was clear that, with the more abstract representations, the children did not even get the class right, their mistakes being often the result of failing to respond to cues of three-dimensionality; e.g., in Card 3, the road was often mistaken for an object such as a mill or tree which the children said would prevent the man and the deer seeing each other. Similarly, the horizon line was almost always described as a ruler, stick or piece of string.

The second problem highlighted by this study was that of cultural effects on responses, by which I mean the rather striking finding that

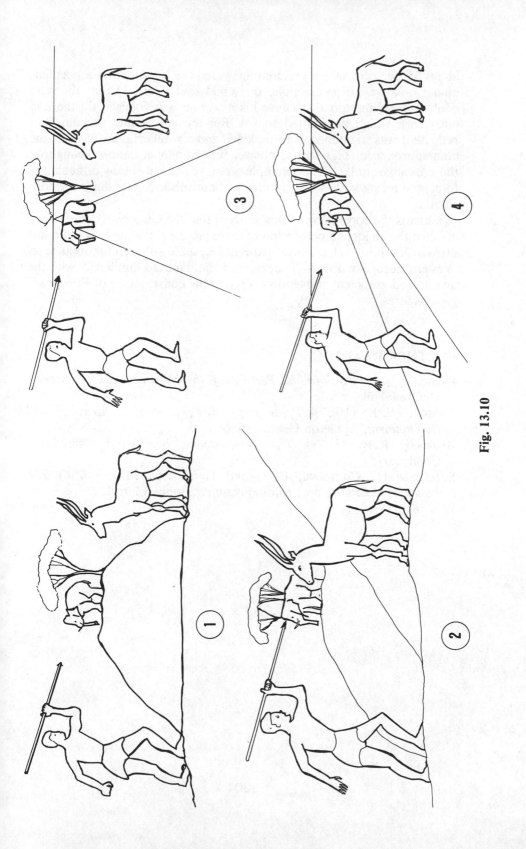

Fig. 13.10

about 35 per cent of the children answered the questions in a peculiar, imaginative way. For example, one child said (Card 1) that the man could not see the 'goat' because his attention was focused on the lion (elephant), which he wanted to kill. But the goat could see the man because it was frightened of being killed and it would run away when the man approached. This sort of answer was equally common throughout the age-range studied. This example serves to show just how difficult it is to communicate with other cultures without misunderstandings on both sides.

Perhaps the conclusion of this study is that the Ghanaian culture only affected the children's perception of these pictures inasmuch as it did not provide for informal pictorial experience, such as is commonplace in Western European homes. They consequently lacked familiarity with the artistic and graphical conventions used in the construction of European-type pictures.

FURTHER READING

Dixon, H. (1971) *Subliminal Perception, the Nature of a Controversy.* McGraw-Hill.

Gibson, E. J. (1967) *Principles of Perceptual Learning and Development.* Appleton-Century-Crofts.

Rosinski, R. R. (1977) *The Development of Visual Perception.* Goodyear.

Segall, M. H., Campbell, D. T. and Herskovits, M. J. (1966) *The Influence of Culture on Visual Perception.* Bobbs-Merrill.

14   Attention
ERNEST GOVIER

The concept of attention

Origins
Edward B. Titchener, writing in 1908, credited the formulation of the concept of attention to the German introspectionist Wilhelm Wundt. Titchener felt that Wundt's discovery of attention (which he dated at about 1860) was one of the few outstanding achievements of psychology up to that time, but that even this had itself brought to light a host of more ticklish problems.

In 1890 William James published his textbook, *The Principles of Psychology*, which contained a section describing many of the phenomena associated with the concept of attention. He raised the issue of the number of ideas or things to which we may attend simultaneously, deciding that we could only carry out two tasks simultaneously if one of them is 'habitual' and does not require attention. James also proposed that attention affects perception, thought, memory, and reaction time. As regards perception, James noted that, if two stimuli are presented simultaneously and attention has been directed to one of them, then this stimulus will appear to have been presented first. He also pointed out that paying more attention to a stimulus seems to increase the clarity of our perception of that stimulus. Finally, James linked attention to memory by asserting that we do not remember things to which we have paid little attention.

This work was systematized and more precisely documented by Titchener in his book, *The Psychology of Feeling and Attention*, published in 1903. Research into attention carried on until about 1920 when it almost vanished from the psychological literature. This was mainly due to the way in which experiments on attention were conducted: they were mostly carried out using introspection as the only source of data and were thus not objectively verifiable. This lack of objectivity was rightly attacked by the rising school of Behaviourists, and research into attention fell into disrepute.

The return of attention

It became respectable to be able to attend to things once again in about 1958. The rejuvenation of work on attention has been attributed by Neville Moray to three factors. Firstly, 'operational' definitions of processes hitherto defined in terms of private experience were developed. This allowed for objectivity in research into attention. Secondly, the Second World War, catalyst of so much innovation, provided the conditions of urgency necessary to overcome prejudice against experimentation on attentional phenomena. The rapid increase in the sophistication of communication systems provided human beings with situations in which they were presented with a great deal of information from multiple sources. This, of course, required answers to problems such as: how should the information be presented? how fast can a human operator switch his attention from one dial to another? Lastly, Moray highlighted the importance of the development of the tape-recorder, which has tremendously improved research into auditory attention.

Cherry's contribution

So, the stage was set for the general acceptance of attention research. The first important landmark in the 1950s was the development by Colin Cherry of dichotic listening experiments in which the subjects had to 'shadow' or repeat aloud the verbal message that was presented to him through one ear while a different message was played to him through the other ear. Cherry published the results of his investigation in 1953 as did E. C. Poulton, who had simultaneously developed the same technique. Poulton's findings differed from those of Cherry, but, for reasons which will be explained later, it was Cherry's work that was accepted and it provided the inspiration for a plethora of experimentation which is still very lively over twenty years later. But, in spite of the brilliance of Colin Cherry's early contribution, perhaps the most influential figure in the renaissance of attention was Donald Broadbent. His book, *Perception and Communication*, published in 1958, provided the theoretical structure from which all of the recent work on attention has sprung either as a continuation or as a reaction. One of the central problems dealt with by Broadbent was the mechanism which allowed human beings to attend to some stimuli and ignore others. This quality of selectivity in attention will be the main theme of the next part of this Chapter.

Selective attention

The problems
Let us first look at the particular puzzle which originally inspired Colin Cherry and which he described as 'the cocktail party problem'. Imagine that you are at a noisy party surrounded by people enjoying their animated conversations; you are trying to listen to just one conversation and, by and large, you are succeeding. Now Cherry was interested in how we achieve this complex feat of perception. What factors affect our ability to select one conversation from the babble which surrounds us? This ability requires extremely complex analysing mechanisms, so complex in fact that no electronic device can as yet mimic our performance. The second question which Cherry posed for himself was, how much of the rejected conversations can we remember?

Cherry's experiments
As mentioned earlier, Cherry used what have become known as dichotic listening tests. They fall into two groups. Firstly, he presented two different messages to the subject through both ears. In the second group of experiments Cherry presented one spoken message to the subjects right ear and a different spoken message to his left ear.

The results of the first set of experiments tell us something about the subject's ability to separate the two messages which are presented to him as a 'babel'. Many tests were carried out using pairs of messages which varied in similarity, but the results consistently showed that the messages could be separated even when they were taken from adjacent paragraphs in the same book. However, the subjects reported great difficulty in separating the messages and often they would listen to the same section of the tape recording up to twenty times. It was possible to construct messages which could not be separated. If the messages consisted of strings of clichés then, even though they are spoken with continuity and natural emotional content, the subjects could not separate them.

The dichotic tasks
The second set of tests proved to be in many ways the most fruitful. Two different prose messages were recorded, both by the same speaker. One of the messages was presented to the subject's right ear and the other to the left ear. The messages were presented via headphones. The subject's task was to repeat one of the messages as he heard it. This is now referred to as shadowing. The point of requiring a subject to shadow one

of the messages is to make sure that his attention is directed towards it. This provides an experimental equivalent of the cocktail party situation where someone is listening to one conversation and ignoring others. Cherry was now able to determine exactly how much of the unattended (non-shadowed) message the subject could report. He found that they could always correctly identify it as speech, but they could not identify any words or phrases or even definitely identify the message as being English. A change of voice from male to female could be detected and a 400 cps pure tone was always reported. Reversed speech was thought to be normal by most subjects but was thought to have 'something queer about it' by others. This all seems quite straightforward really, the conclusion of course is that only the physical properties of the unattended message are 'heard' by the listener and the semantic content is completely lost.

Perhaps at this point we should try to explain why the work of E. C. Poulton failed to be as influential as Cherry's. Poulton found that subjects could not shadow a message accurately in a dichotic listening task. In fact, although his subjects were apparently unaware of it, they were, according to Poulton, 'speaking drivel'. For a long time nobody could reconcile the performance of Cherry's subjects with Poulton's but Neville Moray has recently pointed out that Poulton's subjects whispered their responses. It therefore seems possible that they could not hear their own voices clearly, and this imperfect auditory feedback interfered with normal speech production.

The first theories

The filter theory

The earliest comprehensive theory of attention was proposed by Donald Broadbent in 1958. The essential feature of Broadbent's theory was that we are unable to analyse all the information which falls on our sensors. He therefore proposed that somewhere in our brain is a mechanism or 'filter' which limits the amount of information which has to be analysed to a very high (semantic, in the case of spoken words) level. He therefore identifies the higher levels of analysis as being where the bottleneck occurs (see Fig. 14.1).

Broadbent based this model on a great deal of research but a set of experiments now referred to as the 'split span' experiments are regarded as having been critical to Broadbent's thinking. In a typical split span experiment a subject was presented with three pairs of digits each pair being presented simultaneously, one digit to each ear, at the rate of one pair every half-second. After presentation, the subjects were asked to recall the digits, which they did by recalling the three digits presented to one ear followed by as many as they could recall from the other ear.

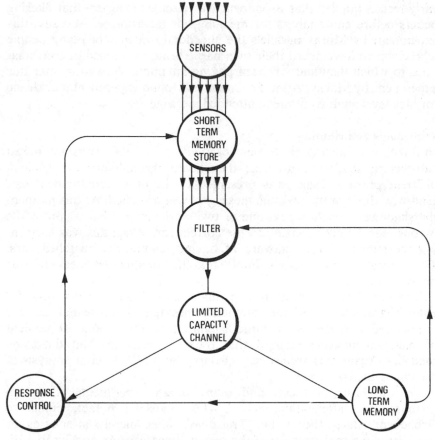

Fig. 14.1   Broadbent's filter theory. (After Broadbent, 1958.)

From these results and those of Cherry, Broadbent concluded that, when we select a message for high level analysis, we do so on the basis of its physical properties, (in the case of the split-span experiments this would be the location of the input, i.e., the relevant ear). Furthermore, information which is not selected is only retained for a very short period in a short term store, where it decays rapidly. If a message is allowed through the filter, it enters the limited capacity channel where high level analysis takes place with the aid of the long term memory store. The results of this analysis may then produce a response.

A new development
In 1959, experimental evidence was published which conflicted with Broadbent's conclusions. In that year, Moray found that if you presented the subject's own name in the unattended message of a dichotic listening task he would hear about one third of the presentations. These

early results implied that Broadbent was wrong to suggest that filtering occurs before any analysis for meaning has taken place. Actually, this experiment by Moray parallels the anecdotal evidence of many people who claim to have heard their own name being mentioned in conversations to which they had not been paying attention. Very soon after this experiment by Moray, Anne Treisman also found experimental evidence for high level analysis of the unattended message.

Treisman's contribution
In a dichotic listening experiment carried out in 1960, Treisman asked subjects to shadow a message they heard through one ear while a different prose message was presented to the other (unattended) ear. Half-way through the task the messages were switched. At this moment the shadowers would repeat one or two words from what was now the 'wrong' ear, before reverting to the correct ear. While this was happening the subjects were unaware of having temporarily switched ears. These results very strongly imply that the unattended message was analysed for meaning.

Treisman has shown, in an experiment carried out in 1964, that if a French translation of the attended message is presented as the unattended message in a dichotic listening task, then about 50 per cent of bilingual subjects realized that the two messages had the same meaning. Again, this argues very strongly for a high level of analysis of the unattended message.

On the basis of these, and many other, experiments, Treisman proposed her 'attenuation model'. This model is, in fact, similar to Broadbent's filter theory but Treisman's filter merely attenuates or weakens the signal strength of the rejected message. As applied to a dichotic listening task, both the attenuated rejected message and the attended message go deeper into the perceptual system for further analysis. Here, we find a major difference with Broadbent because Treisman is allowing for all inputs to be analysed at a high level. However, at this higher semantic level a second stage of selection takes place in which so called 'dictionary units' or word analysers are triggered if their signal strength is high enough. The triggering of a dictionary unit is perceived. Thus, as the thresholds of dictionary units are all different and variable, so biologically relevant and emotionally important words will fire their low-threshold dictionary units even when the signal strength of such a word has been attenuated.

Thus Treisman's model allows a subject to hear his own name and a few other very special words even when they have been presented in the non-attended ear. The main problem with this model is that the first stage of filtering really appears to be redundant. If the thresholds in Stage II are variable, why not allow Occams razor to cut off Stage I, and

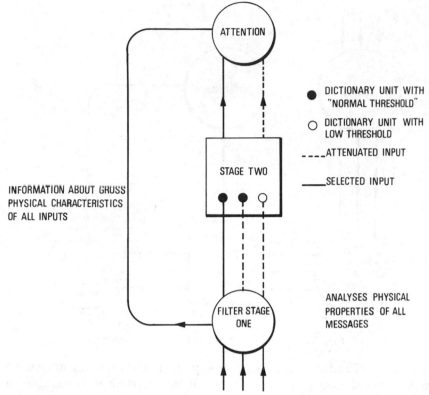

Fig. 14.2   Treisman's attenuation model.

have the filter do its work after a high level of analysis of the input. Treisman admits that all inputs are analysed to a high level, so, obviously, the bottleneck appears to be a function of consciousness not analysis.

Single filter, late selection

This brings us to the final theory of selective attention that we shall discuss. This theory was developed in 1963 by Anthony and Diana Deutsch. Its main feature is that it allows for filtering or selection only after all inputs have been analysed to a high level, i.e., after each word (if the message is prose) has been recognized by the memory system. From Figure 14.3, we can see that a message is analysed for its physical qualities and, on the basis of this, each word 'activates' its representation in the memory store. Simultaneously, the items most pertinent to the ongoing activity also excite their representations in the memory store. Those items which are excited by both mechanisms are allowed to pass into attention.

In summary, we may say that there are two major theories which

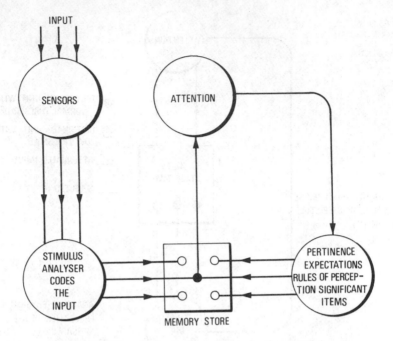

INPUT

SENSORS

ATTENTION

STIMULUS
ANALYSER
CODES
THE
INPUT

PERTINENCE
EXPECTATIONS
RULES OF PERCEP-
TION SIGNIFICANT
ITEMS

MEMORY STORE

Fig. 14.3 A single filter, late selection model.

have been offered in recent years as explanations of the phenomena so far discovered in the field of selective attention. Both theories allow a high level of analysis of the information processed by the sensors, although one theory (Triesman's) carries the implication that when two messages are physically different, i.e., presented dichotically or spoken in different voices, then the unattended message will be attenuated, and it will not be analysed quite as efficiently as the attended message.

The GSR studies

In 1969, Moray briefly mentioned in a publication that he had found that subjects would produce galvanic skin responses (minute increases in the electrical conductivity of their skin) to words which had been coupled with electric shock and then embedded in the unattended message of a dichotic listening task. The procedure he used was as follows: a subject was presented with a neutral word such as 'country' followed by an electric shock to his hand. After about fifteen trials Moray found that his subjects produced strong GSRs just to the presentation of the word country. He then presented 'country' to his twelve well-conditioned subjects, first in the unattended message and then in the attended message (AM). Three of his twelve subjects produced marked GSRs to the target word when it was presented in the unattended message (UM) even though they did not hear it. As Moray indicated, this experiment was carried out using very primitive equipment but if it could be replicated using more sophisticated machinery then this would constitute strong evidence that information could be analysed to a semantic level without the awareness of the subject.

In 1972, R. S. Corteen and B. Wood replicated Moray's findings and, further, found that synonyms of the target word would also produce GSRs when they were embedded in the UM. In 1975 Von Wright and his colleagues also replicated Moray's findings, so that by this time the effect has come to be regarded as very robust.

Sustained attention

We are all familiar with the problems involved in maintaining our alertness while engaged in a boring task. This phenomenon is common throughout our lives but, apart from in motorway driving, it rarely endangers our wellbeing. There are however, specialized professions such as those in aviation and radar defence, in which errors made by people who are unable to maintain alertness for long periods while engaged in tedious tasks, may endanger many hundreds or thousands of lives. The tendency to make more errors the longer one is engaged on a monotonous vigilance task is referred to as 'performance decrement', and it is an intriguing fact that subjects tend to be quite unaware of it.

A brief review of the methodology

One of the first researchers to study vigilance performance in a systematic way was Norman Mackworth. Working in the late 1940s Mackworth used three typs of experimental techniques. First, he used the radar test, in which subjects sat watching a radar screen for the occurrence of signals which were presented usually against a background of visual 'noise' (random, non-signal, visual events). Secondly, he used an auditory listening task, subjects sat listening to 1000 cps tones presented about every 18 seconds for a duration of about two seconds. The signals were tones of 2.5 seconds' duration. Finally, he used the clock test. The Mackworth clock has one pointer which moves in jumps at regular intervals. Every so often, the pointer makes a double jump; this is called the signal, and the regular single jumps are called events. The clock test can also be set up so that the pointer moves round with a smooth continuous movement, punctuated by 'signals', during which the pointer speeds up or slows to produce irregularities in the continuous movement. In these and experiments carried out by other workers the responses which were measured included the subject's ability to report signals verbally or mechanically by pressing a button when he saw a signal. The experimenters measured and recorded the latency of each response and, finally, they recorded the cortical evoked response which the subject produced to the presentation of a signal. The experimenters used these responses to consider the subject's overall level of detection and/or his decrement in performance over time.

Some early results

Experiments like the ones described above usually lasted for between half an hour and two hours. The factors in the tasks were varied systematically by Mackworth and others, so that lists could be compiled of all the factors which affected the subject's performance. This information, it was thought, could be used to construct a theory which would explain all the phenomena associated with sustained attention. For example, all the aspects of the signal were investigated, its intensity, rate of presentation, regularity, duration, and its spatial probability. The results were more or less as one would expect. Increasing signal intensity, duration and frequency brought about better vigilance performance, as did presenting signals at regular intervals near the centre of a display. Similarly, motivational factors were investigated and some surprising results were obtained; for example, Mackworth found that giving the subject information about his performance (knowledge of results) reduced his performance decrement; but so, too, did giving him false feedback. Mackworth also found that if a telephone was placed in the experimental room and allowed to ring every so often, this also reduced the subject performance decrement. The presence of other people in the room where the experiment is taking place has also been found to reduce decrement, especially if these extra people have a high status with respect to the subject, e.g., if the subject is a private in the army but the extra observers are officers.

There are a few other miscellaneous findings which are worth mentioning at this point. Some stimulant drugs such as amphetamine reduce performance decrement if administered in moderate dosages. Subjects who score high on the introversion scale of the Eysenck Personality Inventory strangely show no performance decrement at all while engaging in long vigilance tasks; however, normals and extreme extroverts both show the decrement.

An early theory

In 1950, Mackworth formulated his Pavlovian-Inhibition theory of vigilance decrement. He tried to fit the elements of the typical vigilance experiment into the mould of a Pavlovian explanation. He designated the signal as the conditioned stimulus and the response of key pressing became the conditioned response; knowledge of results was the reward, with the observation period (usually up to two hours) being the extinction period because during this time knowledge of results was withheld from the subject. Thus, the performance decrement according to this theory is due to the build-up of inhibition.

There are several very damaging criticisms of this view of vigilance decrement. First, complete response decrement is never achieved in the typical vigilance task, unlike Pavlovian response extinction, which can be achieved very quickly. Second, it could be argued that self-instruction would reinforce the subject and should, if it were acting like a real Pavlovian reinforcer, prevent any decrement. Thirdly, it is very difficult to see exactly what the unconditioned stimulus could be which would produce an unconditioned response of key-pressing. But lastly, and most damaging, the greater the frequency of signal presentation, the lower is the performance decrement in a typical experiment. This is quite contrary to a Pavlovian interpretation in which an increase in the number of unreinforced presentations of the CS results in more rapid extinction.

A clutch of other attempts to explain performance decrement appeared in the 1950s and early 1960s, but they were all either too vague and therefore completely non-predictive or obviously wrong. However, out of this maelstrom of ideas, there gradually emerged a conviction, which was to grow progressively stronger, that the 'arousal level' of the observer was a very important factor in his ability to perform well in vigilance tasks.

Arousal as an explanatory concept

The term 'arousal' has been applied to so many diverse psychological conditions that its use is often most confusing. To describe somebody as 'highly aroused' may imply that his behaviour is characterized by an unusually increased vigour; or it may mean that he is in a state of intense motivation or drive. Finally, it may indicate that the person is sharply alert and sensitive to stimuli in his environment. It is this last definitiion that has brought the term into the arena of vigilance studies. However, to describe someone whose vigilance performance is poor, as being under-aroused, when the word itself is defined in terms of low levels of alertness, is circular. In order to avoid this circularity many theorists have identified the 'arousal level' of the individual with the level of activity of one or more neural centres, which may be cortical, subcortical or in the autonomic nervous system. In this part of the Chapter we shall evaluate four physiological indices which have been thought to provide reliable measures of arousal.

EEG and vigilance performance

We shall first investigate the argument that the degree of alertness of a subject in a vigilance experiment is determined by the degree of activity of his cortex, and that, if we measure the electrical activity of the cortex, then this should show a close correspondence with performance in vigilance tasks. To this end, electroencephalograms (EEG) have been taken from subjects performing vigilance tasks. EEGs are taken by attaching two or more electrodes to a subject's scalp in order to pick up the tiny electrical currents which are generated by his brain. This electrical activity is then amplified and fed into a device which converts it into a visible trace on a paper readout. Now we must proceed with caution. Often these EEGs have been taken via electrodes attached to only two points on the scalp by researchers whose skill at recording and interpreting EEGs was, until quite recently, only rudimentary. The most frequently investigated cortical activity has been the alpha rhythm which is recorded at 8–12 cycles/sec. The experiment which best illustrates the problem involved in this type of research was carried out by Carl Stroh in 1970. He noted the vigilance performance of his subjects during a one hour visual task, during which their alpha activity was also recorded. Stroh's aim was to see if there was a relationship between the level of a subject's alpha activity just before presentation of a stimulus and the likelihood of his detecting it (small fluctuations in alpha occur spontaneously). Stroh used twenty-four subjects and found that they fell into three groups:

1. Those subjects for whom the level of alpha activity immediately preceding a missed signal was lower than their level of alpha preceding a detected signal.

2. Those subjects for whom the reverse was true.

3. A group for whom there was no difference in alpha activity before signals detected and missed.

Stroh then looked for other ways in which these groups differed, and he found that those in the first group were generally younger and more neurotic (as measured by personality inventories). One interpretation of these data is that a decrease in alpha (as it is replaced by other more complex patterns) indicates an increase in cortical arousal and vice versa. Thus the first group (younger and more neurotic) show an increase in arousal before missed signals and a decrease before detected signals; the second group demonstrated the reverse relationship, but the subjects were older and less neurotic. If we plot the following graph perhaps these data make some sense (see Fig. 14.4).

Now, a spontaneous increase in arousal will improve the performance of the older less neurotic groups, whereas a decrease will improve that of the younger more neurotic group.

This study indicates very clearly that individual differences between subjects should be carefully considered.

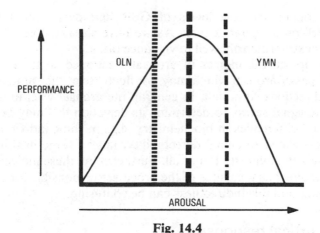

Fig. 14.4

Three more indices of arousal

Both the galvanic skin resistance (GSR) and the pulse rate of subjects
engaged in vigilance tasks have been recorded. Typically the traces were
scanned for changes in GSR recordings in the ten-second period preceding the presentation of a stimulus. However, the studies up to the early
1970s show conflicting results: some workers report that GSR activity
before detected signals was greater than that before missed signals, while
others report no such finding. It is possible that this contradiction would
be shown to be more apparent than real if individual differences between
subjects were taken into account. The same conclusion also seems
appropriate for the studies of pulse rate, which are likewise contradictory. Neither pulse rate nor GSR are reliable predictors of signal
detection, possibly because these two measures do not react quickly
enough to arousal changes or are not sensitive enough. They merely
seem to indicate the general state of the subject and they are very
indirect measures of cortical arousal. Recently, Daniel Kahneman
(1973) has argued very strongly that pupil diameter is the most sensitive
measure of cortical arousal, high arousal being mirrored by an increase
in pupil diameter. However, this has not so far been studied in vigilance
tasks.

To complicate matters even more, some theorists have argued that
we may become aroused in two or more different ways. Hans Eysenck
has argued, for instance, that individuals with labile autonomic nervous
systems can become highly aroused in a manner characterized by
neurotic behaviour, and also that the system controlling cortical arousal
is separate from this. He argues that people with high cortical arousal
levels are characterized by typical introvert behaviour. Thus, a neurotic
extravert would show high levels of GSR and pulse rate but would
perform badly in a vigilance experiment, whereas a non-neurotic

317

introvert would have low levels of GSR and pulse rate but would perform well on a vigilance task. As we have already noted, introverts do perform extraordinarily well in vigilance tasks.

To sum up: all the indices of arousal mentioned so far may reflect different types of arousal which may not fluctuate at the same time or in the same direction. Although, in general, the arousal level immediately preceding a signal seems to determine its detection this may be masked by individual differences in biochemistry, e.g., in some individuals EEG alpha is not related to signal detectability; indeed some healthy people do not have any alpha rhythm at all. Furthermore, these indices seem to be far too indirect as measures of the processes responsible for the detection of signals and this indirectness can be confusing.

Evoked cortical responses

Evoked cortical responses emanate from the cortex near to the top and front of the head and are not specific to any one sensory modality. If we confine our discussion to visual stimuli, then a typical investigation of evoked cortical responses will involve the presentation of a signal to a subject and then measuring and recording the tiny electrical changes that occur in his cortex as a result of his analysis of that stimulus.

Haider's research

Haider, Spong, and Lindsley carried out an important investigation into evoked cortical potentials in 1964. These researchers presented light flashes to the subjects at three-second intervals. Ten per cent of these flashes were dimmer than the others and were designated as signals to which the subjects had to respond by pressing a key. Haider and his colleagues found that the latency of the evoked responses to all the stimuli gradually increased as the experiment progressed and that missed signals tended to be associated with evoked potentials of smaller size and greater latency than were the correctly detected signals.

The complexity of the ECR

A later experiment by Wilkinson, Morlock, and Williams in 1966 has shown that the evoked cortical response is in fact quite complex and can be divided into four components as shown in Figure 14.5.

They found that the amplitude of N_2 was significantly greater preceding missed signals than that preceding detected signals. They also found that missed signals were also associated with a greater latency of the first negative deflection component (N_1).

Conclusions

The evidence thus suggests that detection of signals in a vigilance task is related to changes in electrical activity recordable from the scalp. These

318

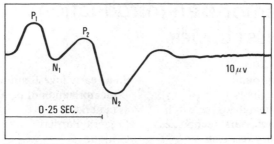

P₁ P₂ POSITIVE DEFLECTION COMPONENTS
N₁ N₂ NEGATIVE DEFLECTION COMPONENTS

Fig. 14.5 Components of an evoked cortical response. (After Wilkinson.)

electrical records reflect the activity of the cortex and appear to be related to changes in attentiveness. It is also interesting to note that the EEG records which indicate a change in EEG activity to the presentation of a signal where that signal is 'missed' provides evidence that our brain processes information of which we may not become aware. This evidence is in line with evidence from other fields, notably subliminal perception and selective attention, all of which encourage the view that much more of the information falling on our receptors is processed at a higher level than we are ever aware of.

Finally, perhaps we should be aware of the difficulties inherent in EEG research. As one scientist working in this area has already pointed out, recording the brain's electrical activity by placing electrodes on the scalp in the hope that we shall be able to devine the mysteries of highly complex cognitive processes, is like standing outside the open window of a factory and trying to guess the details of the processes going on inside from the noises coming through the window.

FURTHER READING
Broadbent, D. E. (1958) *Perception and Communication*. Pergamon.
Davies, D. R., and Tune, G. S. (1970) *Human Vigilance Performance*. Staples Press.
Mackworth, J. F. (1969) *Vigilance and Habituation*. Penguin.
Moray, N. (1969) *Listening and Attention*. Penguin.
Moray, N. (1969) *Attention*. Hutchinson.
Norman, D. A. (1969) *Memory and Attention*. Wiley.
Stroh, C. M. (1971) *Vigilance—The Problem of Sustained Attention*. Oxford-Pergamon.

15 Memory: an introduction

ERNEST GOVIER

Historical background

Most of us take our ability to remember things completely for granted. In fact, this particular facility is an essential component in such diverse activities as understanding sentences and recognizing one's dog, and more than one dedicated psychologist has despaired of ever unravelling its mechanisms. It has become conventional to attribute the origin of this field of inquiry to Aristotle, a man obviously not given to taking things for granted. Aristotle's essay entitled *Memory* is as far as is known the earliest surviving formal attempt to analyse the process of memory. In his essay, he makes the fundamental, if simple, point that one thing reminds us of another. Aristotle felt that there were three kinds of relationship between items in memory, contiguity, similarity, and contrast. The British Empiricists and Associationist philosophers adopted these three principles as their 'laws of association'. Thus, through them, Aristotle's influence on memory research persists to the present day.

Hermann Ebbinghaus

A scientist named Ebbinghaus was the first person successfully to carry out experiments on human memory (one of the higher mental processes previously considered intractable to experimentation). Ebbinghaus, working alone over a period of about five years, with no academic setting in which to work and no supervision or proper laboratory, carried out many superbly controlled experiments. He used himself as the subject of these experiments and he subjected himself to the most rigorous discipline.

It seems likely that in about 1876 Ebbinghaus purchased a copy of Fechner's *Elemente der Psychophysik*. This book appears to have made a very profound impression on him, because he seems to have decided to use Fechner's systematic, mathematical approach to the study of psychophysics, as a model for his own study of the higher mental processes.

In deciding which of the higher mental processes to study, it is quite probable that Ebbinghaus was influenced by the British Associationists to focus on memory. As well as their so-called 'Laws of Association', they had been emphasizing the role played by frequency of association in memory. Ebbinghaus had a series of brilliant ideas. He decided to study the formation of association instead of, as was usual up to then, attempting to study already formed associations. Next, he assumed that the difficulty of learning material was a reflection of the difficulty of forming associations with and among the material. Thus, he reasoned that if he counted the number of times that the material had to be recited before it was learned to the criterion of one error-free reproduction, then he would have a measure of association-formation in the memorization of that material. Finally, Ebbinghaus' most inspired notion was his adoption of nonsense syllables as his experimental material. He argued that words were of no use because of their existing associations, but that syllables formed of two consonants with a vowel between as in '*teg*' or '*mab*' were uniformly unfamiliar and without existing associations. Actually, it must be remembered that Ebbinghaus worked in the German language which has 11 vowels and diphthongs, 11 consonants suited for ending words and 19 suited for beginning words, with ch and sch used as consonants. Ebbinghaus put all possible combinations of consonants and vowels on separate cards which gave him a supply of about 2300 syllables, from which he drew at random those to be learned.

Later, it became apparent that most 'nonsense' syllables really did suggest some meaning to most people in that they could, if so directed, concoct associations to the syllables. Indeed, a psychologist named Glaze, working in 1928, attempted to assess the 'association value' of each nonsense syllable. Each of fifteen students was shown individual syllables and allowed three seconds to say whether the syllable brought anything to mind. Two thousand syllables were tested and only one hundred did not suggest any meaning to any of the students. Moreover, Glaze found these syllables far more difficult to learn than the others. These syllables included such odd combinations as KYH and XIW.

However, as if to forestall this kind of criticism Ebbinghaus undertook as one of his earliest experiments a comparison of speed of memorization of nonsense syllable lists with memorization speed of meaningful material for which Ebbinghaus chose stanzas of Byron's *Don Juan*. Each stanza of this poem is composed of eighty syllables which required about nine readings to learn. A list of eighty nonsense syllables, however, required nearly eighty repetitions. He concluded that nonsense syllables really were qualitatively different to meaningful words from the point of view of memorization, that this difference was due to their lack of existing association, and that this made them about nine times as hard to learn as meaningful words.

The scope of Ebbinghaus' research

Ebbinghaus designed a number of experiments to investigate the effect of various conditions on memorization. For example, he varied the amount of material to be learned and found that the longer the syllable list, the greater the number of repetitions was required for an errorless reproduction. Moreover, it became obvious that the average learning time per syllable was considerably increased as the number of syllables to be learned was increased. Ebbinghaus went on to investigate the influence of the passage of time between learning and recall, overlearning, the formation of intra-list associations, both near and remote, and the effect of repeated learning of the same list over long periods. The importance of his work, which cannot be stressed too much, lies in his meticulous control of the conditions of the experiments and his careful, systematic collection of quantitative data. Indeed, the data from his experiments on the passage of time and its effect on memory which he summarized graphically as a 'forgetting curve' have become famous for their accuracy and have been replicated many times by modern psychologists. Essentially, Ebbinghaus found that material is forgotten very rapidly in the first few hours after learning but that the rate of forgetting becomes slower and slower.

Ebbinghaus published his findings in *Über das Gedächtnis* (On Memory) in 1885. This book has been acknowledged as the manifestation of a truly original mind. It marked the origin of a new field of study and represents the most thorough, creative, and resourceful investigation by a single researcher in the history of experimental psychology.

Some early experimental techniques used in memory research

The anticipation method

Ebbinghaus' idea of measuring the difficulty of memorization of a given list by counting the number of times the list had to be presented before the subject could recite it perfectly is often called the anticipation method. Using this method, the experimenter may know precisely the rate at which the subject is learning. The procedure is simple. The subject is presented with the list once, and then he attempts to recall each item before it is presented again. This is repeated until the subject correctly anticipates all the items in the list. A piece of equipment called a memory drum is usually used with this method; this is just a cylinder around which the material to be learned is wrapped. The cylinder rotates and exposes the material item by item through a window. The memory drum can be set to rotate at a constant speed thus precisely controlling the rate of presentation of the items. Using this method, the experimenter can measure the total time or number of trials that the subject takes to reach the criterion. Alternatively he may count the number of times that the subject needs to be prompted before the criterion is reached. The experimenter may also keep a record of the performance of the subject for each of the items in the list.

The relearning method
A second measure of memory is the relearning or saving method. Here, the subject learns something, e.g., a list of nonsense syllables, some prose or a perceptual motor task to a criterion. Then he is allowed to forget and after an interval he is required to relearn the task to the same criterion as before. The argument here is that if the subject has remembered anything from the first learning period then he will relearn the task quicker. The saving may be expressed as the difference between the time taken to learn the list the first time and the time taken to relearn it. If this difference is divided by the original learning time, we arrive at the percentage saving. Instead of time, the calculation may be based on number of errors or trials; it is interesting to note if these different computations result in the same percentage saving.

The recognition method
This method typically involves the subject being presented with a set of stimuli followed by an interval; then the original stimuli are re-presented to the subject, together with a varying number of similar stimuli. The subject has to choose which of this second larger set of stimuli were in the first presentation. The scoring of this method presents some problems. Consider a subject who is presented with a set of fifteen pictures to memorize. After an interval he is presented with thirty pictures and has to choose which of these he has seen before. He could, purely by guessing, be right on 50 per cent of the trials. Thus, the experimenter has to estimate the significance of a deviation from 50 per cent. Alternatively, the experimenter could reduce the probability of the subject producing artificially good results by guesswork with the use of multiple-choice tests. This just means that each correct stimulus is presented with several 'incorrect' stimuli and the subject has to choose the

correct stimulus from each group. If the group is composed of one correct stimulus and five incorrect stimuli then the subject has only a one in six chance of being right by guessing.

The reconstruction method
Next, we have a method by which the subject's memory for order may be tested. The stimuli are first presented to the subject in a certain order. This arrangement is then completely altered, and the subject is required to reconstruct the original order of the stimuli. Using this method, the experimenter may investigate memory for non-verbal material, such as shape and colours. Of course, the question of how far a subject will covertly verbalize about stimulus material is fraught with danger for the unwary experimenter. Great care must be taken when controlling for verbalization; the stimulus material must be difficult to name, and the subject must be deterred from trying to name it. Perhaps the best method of investigating the role of verbalization in memory for shapes and colours, etc. is to use stimuli varying in the ease with which they can be named as determined by a panel of judges which rates each stimulus prior to the experimental trials. The scoring of the reconstruction method, whatever the type of stimulus used, may be calculated by the correspondence between the efforts of the subject and the original order of the stimuli, or the number of trials necessary for the subject to reach a criterion.

Paired-associates
In using the methods so far described, material can either be presented and learned in serial order (like a list) or it can be presented as paired associates; that is to say pairs of items, usually words, are presented to the subject, who has to remember the assocation, so that when one of the words is presented again he has to respond with the other member of the pair. Care must be taken to randomize the order of the pairs between each presentation in order to reduce the risk that inter-pair associates will be formed. This sort of arrangement is most useful when the experimenter is investigating isolated associates between pairs of items. It is a flexible experimental tool, inasmuch as the experimenter may use as many trials as he wishes and he may score items remembered, percentage saving, items forgotten or trials to a criterion.

Some early findings

Here, we will look briefly at the results of some of the early investigations in the area of memory. A convenient point at which to begin is with the work of C. W. Luh in 1922, who, using nonsense syllables as his material, measured retention by several different methods.

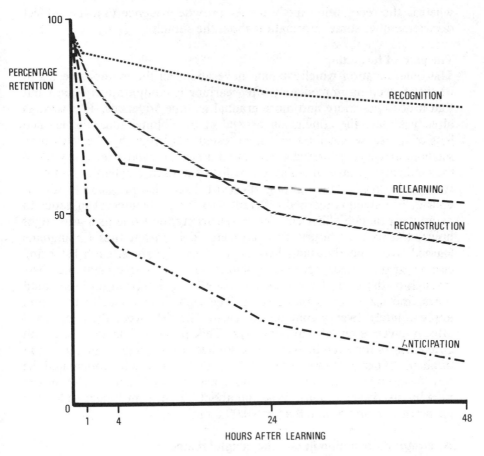

Fig. 15.1 Retention of nonsense syllables. (Adapted from Luh.)

These four different methods of measuring memory will appear to show different rates of forgetting. In fact, all the methods differ in the number of cues with which the subject is provided to jog his memory. In other words, the subject is provided with 'retrieval cues'. The notion that retrieval is very important in memory has gained ground over the past ten years. We shall return to the problems involved in studying retrieval later. Each of the four methods puts different loads on the memory of the subject. The most demanding task is to ask a subject to reproduce the stimulus he was asked to learn (anticipation method). The least demanding task is where the subject is merely asked if he has seen the stimulus before (recognition method). The importance of the different methods may be highlighted by pointing out that, as a result of using the anticipation or recall method, an experimenter may conclude that a subject does not remember anything of the to-be-remembered stimulus, whereas the recognition method may provide evidence that the subject does remember some information about the stimulus.

The path of forgetting

The generalization which we can make about all the methods seems to be that forgetting immediately after learning is comparatively quick but that it becomes more and more gradual as time advances. This was, as already stated, the conclusion arrived at by Ebbinghaus, who learned lists of nonsense syllables and then tested forgetting, by the relearning method, at varying intervals. He found a saving, even after thirty days, thus indicating that something of the list of nonsense syllables had been retained in spite of such a long interval between learning and recall. Of course, Ebbinghaus learned different lists for each interval in order to avoid the practice effect entailed in relearning the same lists after eight hours, twenty-four hours, two days etc. This meant that Ebbinghaus learned over one thousand lists of nonsense syllables, each list being composed of thirteen nonsense syllables. He would read eight such lists through at the rate of about one syllable every $\frac{2}{5}$ second until he could repeat the list twice without error. The eight lists typically took him approximately twenty minutes to learn. The lists were then relearned after a given interval, say six days. This process was repeated with different lists for each interval to be studied. Ebbinghaus found a saving of about 20 per cent even after 30 days. Ebbinghaus also anticipated the now fashionable study of the psychological effects of diurnal rhythms in man by discovering that it took him about 12 per cent longer to learn a list between 6 and 8 p.m. than at 10.00 a.m.

Association-formation in non-meaningful material

Let us now take a closer look at association-formation in non-meaningful material. If a subject is required to learn a list of nonsense syllables so that he can recite them in their correct order, it could be argued that all he has to do is learn the direct association between each nonsense syllable and the next one in the list. But, if this is so, how can we account for partial list learning, in which the subject has omitted some syllables and remembered others in the wrong order? Perhaps associations form not only between adjacent syllables, but also between each item and all the others in the list but with the items which are farthest apart having only weak association. Ebbinghaus devised an experiment to test association formation in his lists which was run as follows. He used the relearning method with a slight modification. He drew up lists of nonsense syllables, each list comprising sixteen syllables, and called them the original lists. He then systematically rearranged each list in one of several ways, either by missing out alternate syllables, or by missing out syllables in successive pairs, or by reversing the order

326

of the lists. If the syllables in the original list are designated by the letters
A to P, then the rearranged lists are as shown in Table 15.1.

Table 15.1

Original	Missing alternate syllables	Missing successive pairs
A	A	A
B	C	D
C	E	G
D	G	J
E	I	M
F	K	P
G	M	B
H	O	E
I	B	H
J	D	K
K	F	N
L	H	C
M	J	F
N	L	I
O	N	L
P	P	O

The same process could be continued for lists missing triads, reversed
lists, and scrambled lists. Now, Ebbinghaus would on one day learn six
original lists which would take him about twenty minutes and on the
next would time himself to learn the six that had been rearranged. This
two-day exercise was repeated seventeen times for each type of
rearrangement. He found that the saving diminishes as more syllables
are missed and that there was only a tiny saving on the scrambled lists.
In fact, Ebbinghaus was a very good subject for studying the formation
of association because he was familiar with the nonsense syllables which
he used, and so any measure of his ability to learn the order of a list was
less contaminated by the effort of learning the syllables themselves. His
overall conclusions were that associations are formed not only directly,
one item to the next, but also remote associations between non-adjacent
items are formed, both forward and backward; the backward associates
being weaker and the remote weaker than the direct.

The above painstakingly executed experiment represents quite a
thorough investigation into the first of Aristotle's three types of association, namely contiguity. The other two, similarity and contrast, do not
lend themselves so easily to investigations which use nonsense syllables
as experimental stimuli.

Overlearning

Material is deemed to have been underlearned when it has not been learned to the criterion of one perfect repetition and overlearned when the subject is required to carry on with the learning trial after the criterion point of one correct repetition has been attained. It has been found many times in the past that retention is approximately proportional to the amount of original learning, although, as with many generalizations that are made in this field of study, this result usually holds only when the subject is well practised in this type of experimentation. In an experiment carried out in 1929, W. C. F. Kreuger studied the effect of different degrees of overlearning on rates of forgetting of lists of monosyllabic nouns. He used two measures of retention: firstly, a recall score, and secondly, a saving score. Both measures of retention showed that, the greater the original overlearning, the slower was the rate of forgetting, but the effect was far more marked for the saving measure than the recall measure. In fact, Ebbinghaus had demonstrated this point very clearly by showing that relearning of nonsense syllable lists required fewer trials each day even though the lists were learned to the same level of performance, i.e., one perfect recitation.

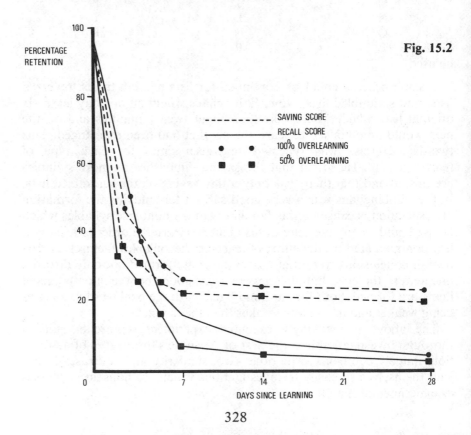

Fig. 15.2

328

Now this, on the face of it, is very odd. Why should it be true that reaching the same standard of performance each day leads to slower forgetting? It is a bit like saying that repeated refilling of a leaking bucket slows the leak; this seems absurd and merely demonstrates how inadequate are such simple analogies. Essentially, the only difference between overlearning and repeated relearning is that in overlearning the learning trials are all massed together, whereas, in repeated relearning, trials are spaced out, so that it is not surprising that both methods should lead to similar results, i.e., that the more times we learn something the better we will retain it. However, the theoretical implications of the result are surprisingly complex.

The retardation of forgetting by overlearning may be due to the laying down of redundant memory traces (the internal representations of the memorized material) in the form of associations between the memorized material and the existing items in memory. The retardation of forgetting by relearning may be caused by the subject putting more 'effort' in relearning forgotten items, perhaps by spending more time in trying to memorize them at the expense of the more easily memorized items. The prediction here, of course, is that relearning is more efficient than overlearning and that if two sets of material are learned, one to the criterion of 50 per cent overlearning, the other to the same number of trials but after some forgetting has been allowed, then forgetting will be slower after the completion of all the learning trials in the relearning condition.

Critique
The main criticism of Ebbinghaus' findings (his methods can hardly be faulted because he was so careful and precise), is that all they tell us about are Ebbinghaus' memory, which may not be typical of the population in general. This criticism has been met, as many studies, using different types and numbers of subjects, all produce essentially the same results as Ebbinghaus. Another important criticism of Ebbinghaus' work is that it does not reflect the everyday working of a human mind in two respects: firstly, people do not generally spend hours learning lists in a very controlled and deliberate manner; secondly, the very choice of nonsense syllables as material to be remembered is odd, in that people rarely have to deal with meaningless material. The first criticism is, of course, valid and applies to almost all laboratory investigations of psychological phenomena. The second argument, that meaningfulness is an important factor in the formation of associations, has provided the impetus for a great deal of recent research into the organization of memory which will be discussed in Chapter 16. Firstly, we will look at some early studies into memory for meaningful material.

Some early investigations into memorization of meaningful material

Frederic Bartlett

So far, our discussion has focused solely on memorization of nonsense syllables, but that is not to say that early work was not also carried out using other types of verbal material, some of which was meaningful, for example, word lists or poetry. However, even these experiments could be criticized as being artificial and not reflecting real-life learning. A famous psychologist Sir Frederic C. Bartlett experimented on memory in a more realistic way and published his results in the noted work, *Remembering*, in 1932. Bartlett examined the way in which a person's memory for stories could be affected by his own attitudes, beliefs, motivation, and general cognitive style. Typically, subjects were presented with a short story and, after various intervals, they were required to reproduce it. Bartlett found his subjects very often appeared to modify the story in such a way as to make it more consistent with their own frames of reference. The most frequently quoted example of this aspect of Bartlett's work is one of his stories which tells of two Indians who are canoeing on a river when they meet a war party and are invited to join it. One of the Indians joins the raiding party but is wounded in the ensuing fight. He is brought back home and dies at dawn the following morning. The story also includes a reference to ghosts, which can either be viewed as central to the whole story or as figments of the imagination of the dying Indian. The English subjects of this experiment seemed to interpret the story in such a way as to make the ghosts unimportant and they were generally omitted from the later reproductions. This and other very common alterations made to the story during recall led Bartlett to formulate several generalizations: some subjects indulged in a lot of elaboration and invention especially after long delays before recall; there was much rationalization so that details were made to fit in with a subjects' pre-formed interests and tendencies. Two other common results were noted: if one subject was asked to recall the story frequently then the form and items of remembered detail very quickly became stereotyped and did not change much with repeated recall; however, in the case of infrequent reproduction, omission of detail, simplification of events and structure, and transformation of items into more familiar detail went on so long as unaided recall was possible. Finally, the most common finding was that accuracy of recall in a literal sense was rare.

Critique

Here lies the great contribution which Bartlett made to the investigation of memory; he emphasized the idea that remembering is not just the reactivation of memories which have been stored and which have remained unchanged during storage. Instead, Bartlett describes the act of remembering as being a process of construction based on the individuals' attitude to the mass of constantly changing, organized past experiences and to some outstanding detail. This mass of organized past experiences Bartlett terms a 'schema'. One consequence of this view of remembering is that it is really exact only very infrequently and then only in cases of rudimentary rote learning. The role of the individual's attitude here is, according to Bartlett, directly a function of consciousness. He seems to be saying that without consciousness we would not have an attitude to our past experiences.

Bartlett took the germ of his idea of schemata from Sir Henry Head who had been working on problems associated with the neurophysiology of movement and body posture. Head had decided, on the basis of observations of patients with certain cortical lesions, that the explanation of how we order skilled movements must involve having a model of our body posture against which we measure all changes. Head termed this ever-changing mental model a schema. Bartlett was attracted to this idea of a central organizing, changing schema and adopted it as an important concept in his theory of remembering. He anticipated criticism of his theory on the lines that it said very little apart from postulating loose collections of memory traces called schemata with a few vivid ones called images. Bartlett defended his position by pointing out that his theory emphasized the active nature of memory; it also highlighted the similarities between remembering and imagining which Bartlett saw as different expressions of the same activity; his theory encompassed a view of forgetting which was very different from that of trace theories; and, finally, he ascribed a very special function to consciousness.

Some recent insights
A number of interesting questions are posed here. Do subjects make these consistently similar errors in Bartlett's experiments because they actually forget elements of the stories, or do they remember these elements but consider them to be so trivial and insignificant that they are not reproduced? There is evidence that a person's memory is profoundly influenced by his own interpretation of the material, even when the correct version is presented many times. In a fascinating experiment, Kay, in 1955, read his subjects two short passages and then asked them to write down as much as they could remember of the passages. After they had completed this task, Kay then re-read the passages to the subjects. The following week the subjects were again required to reproduce the original passages; the correct versions were then read to them yet again. This continued for a total of seven weeks. It was found that sub-

331

jects recalled with uncanny accuracy the material which they had produced in the previous week in spite of having had the correct version read to them after they had produced their own incorrect rendering. It seems that a subject's first interpretation of the material was very dominant and resistant to change. Confirmation of this finding has come from similar experiments, as has the discovery that the subjects were quite aware that they were remembering what they had recalled earlier and that they felt somewhat upset that they were unable to remember as much as they had expected to from the presentation of the correct version.

One of the mechanisms which seem to be involved in the production of these distortions of memory involves the subjects' expectations. A classic experiment which indicated this and also demonstrated the now well-established fact that eye-witness accounts can be extremely inaccurate was carried out as follows. A 'stooge' walked into a room while a lecture was taking place. He briefly interrupted the lecture by asking the lecturer if he could look at a book on the bookshelves. The stooge waited, reading the book for a while, then he left the room taking the book with him. The students did not, of course, know that the stooge was acting and they paid little attention to him. The following week, the students were asked to give an account of the episode and to answer questions about it, including details of the man's appearance and conduct. In general, the students' answers were remarkably inaccurate and, in particular, when asked about the book which the stooge had taken from the shelves, most students reported that he had replaced the book before leaving. As it was strictly forbidden for anyone to remove books from the room, it could be argued that the expectation that the stooge would replace the book on the shelves was very high. One interpretation of this experiment could be that the students were really only providing the answers that they thought were most likely to be correct and later experiments have shown that this may be true in many cases. This problem has been investigated by asking subjects to rate how much confidence they have in their answers, i.e., certain, moderately sure, unsure, etc. When this procedure was carried out, evidence is usually found that some subjects are giving answers which they know are unreliable, presumably because they are just projections based on expectations, while other subjects give incorrect answers which they really do believe are actual memories. This constitutes the best evidence that expectation is an important factor in the shaping of memory.

So, at present, the evidence appears to indicate that we interpret meaningful material in terms of existing knowledge, attitudes, beliefs, and expectations and that this interpretation is accurately remembered and is very resistant to change.

Imagery

Over the last ten years, psychologists have increasingly turned their attention to the investigation of that class of private mental experiences called images. There are very many problems with this type of research. The central difficulty is that a subject's imagery is not available for public inspection; this means that the experimenter is trying to study something of which he cannot have any direct knowledge (except in his own case). Because they cannot measure their subjects' imagery directly, psychologists have tried to find ways of evaluating it by noting its effects on other cognitive abilities. In particular, this discussion will be concerned with the way in which mental imagery may effect memory.

The nature of imagery

Perhaps we should first try to be a little clearer about what we mean by imagery. Images may be characterized as more or less shadowy refabrications of ordinary perceptions. There are several types of imagery: visual, auditory, gustatory, etc. Indeed, a person may experience images in one or several of his ordinary sense modalities. The most commonly-discussed variety is visual imagery, which is also the form of imagery most often studied in relationship with memorization.

Mental imagery has been considered important in memorization since the time of the Greeks, who perfected methods of using imagery as an aid to memory (by developing mnemonics, of which more later). It was not until Francis Galton's investigation in 1880 that it was recognized that not only do people differ in the vividness of their visual imagery, but that some people claim to experience none at all. Galton investigated this problem by simply sending one hundred subjects a questionnaire which directed them to remember details of their breakfast on the morning of the test. Galton's questionnaire instructed the subjects to assess their own memory-images in a way which enabled him to collect information about the clarity of their imagery, and the modality in which it predominantly manifested itself.

Following on from Galton's work, there have been several recent attempts to devise standardized questionnaires which have been designed to make the process of collecting this kind of information more systematic; but the use of more systematic procedures does not overcome the problems inherent in the private nature of imagery. Does each subject interpret the questions in the same way? Do they answer truthfully? In fact, attempts to relate a person's imagery profile, as defined by a questionnaire, with his performance on a variety of tasks have been notoriously unsuccessful. However, in their personal interaction with subjects, researchers have noticed certain characteristics which seem to typify good visual imagers. First, good imagers do not show the hesitation and uncertainty that typifies the response patterns of poor imagers to questions such as: Is your image a picture? Is it in colour? Good imagers tend to react to this sort of question positively and without equivocation. Secondly, good imagers tend to use, or claim they use, certain strategies: when asked to transform their colour images, say of a house, into black and white, most achieve this by imaging the scene as a photograph or on a television screen; poor imagers do not report using this kind of artifice. One quite consistent difference is that good imagers report that their images are, or can be, located in front of their eyes; a small percentage of subjects even claim to be able to 'project' their images onto a wall and even to expand or contract them at will. Finally, poor imagers commonly describe their images as 'pressures' rather than as pictures. Actually, most people are neither good nor poor imagers, but possess an intermediate level of imagery vividness. However, all of the above conclusions are hotly disputed as being without scientific foundation: perhaps the most surprising aspect of the whole issue is the intensity of emotion which may be engendered by a discussion of individual differences.

The relationship between imagery and memory

What is the evidence that people who say they can conjure up mental pictures are better at remembering things than those who say they cannot? One method of investigating this problem is to give groups of good and bad imagers who have been differentiated on the basis of a questionnaire, some task which seems to be related to imagery, in order to see if they perform differently. For example, it has been claimed that good imagers, as identified by a questionnaire, are better able to remember lists of paired-associate words than poor imagers. The procedure here has been explained in a preceding section: either trials to a criterion or number of correct items may be counted.

A rather different approach was initiated by Alan Paivio in the latter half of the 1960s. He presented subjects with word lists composed of either so-called 'concrete' or 'abstract' words. A concrete word in this context is a word which refers to an object, e.g., car, which should more readily evoke an image than an 'abstract' word, e.g., fear, which does not directly refer to an object or class of objects. Paivio's hypothesis was that his subjects should find it easier to remember concrete words than abstract words, because concrete words more readily evoke images which themselves may aid recall. Using a paired-associate technique, Paivio did, indeed, find that concrete words were remembered better than abstract words.

Of course, abstract words may evoke images indirectly, e.g., the word courage may suggest an image of a soldier, and it seems obvious that excellent imagers will find it just as easy to form images to abstract

334

words as to concrete words; but subjects whose imagery is mediocre may well find it easier to evoke images to concrete words than abstract words.

Imagability of words as rated by panels of judges is closely related to rated concreteness, but there are discrepancies: some abstract words are rated high on imagability, e.g., anger; but these words usually have obvious powerful emotional associations. Similarly, some words are rated low on imagability but high on concreteness, the words refer to objects which are rarely encountered and thus there is little opportunity to form images to them, an example would be 'emporium'.

Mnemonics

Thus there seems to be quite a lot of evidence that imagery aids recall of verbal material; it now remains to define a process which would account for this. Obviously vivid pictorial imagery cannot be necessary for recall because some people claim to be unable to form mental pictures and yet they may have perfectly ordinary memories.

For a possible explanation we must return to the early Associationists, who held that part of the meaning of a word lay in the image which the word evokes. The word comes to evoke an image through its repeated occurrence contiguous with the object which it symbolizes. In time, the word comes to evoke an image, just as the object produces its percept. Thus, it could be argued that if the 'recallability' of a word in part depends upon the richness of its association network, then words with images as associations obviously have a greater probability of being recalled than words which do not; assuming that both types of words have verbal associations.

Evidence for this view comes from a study of mnemonics. There are several types of mnemonics but the function of all of them is to provide a means by which new material can be very quickly integrated into an existing memory structure. The user of the mnemonic simply has to form a conscious association between the to-be-remembered material (we shall stick to words) and an item which already firmly exists in his memory. A very simple visual mnemonic would involve the subject in imagining a familiar house during presentation of, say, a word list; he would try to image each word written on the wall of a room in this house. In fact, the more bizarre and eccentric the image association, the greater is the probability that it will be effective: the word could thus be magnified in large letters of a brilliant colour on an unusual part of the room. In order to recall the word list, our mnemonist simply takes an imaginary stroll through the house looking into each room to 'see' which words are there. If the process of association-formation has been successful he will be able to recall the words which have been

335

associated with each room.* An extreme example of a person using visual mnemonics to aid memory is reported in a fascinating book by A. R. Luria called *The Mind of a Mnemonist*, in which he describes a man who could perform amazing feats of memory by using visual mnemonics, which he apparently did quite automatically.

One of the easiest mnemonics useful for remembering short word lists requires that the mnemonist first writes down the numbers 1 to 10 and then writes beside each number the first word that comes to mind which rhymes with that number, for example, 1—gun, 2—shoe, 3—tree, 4—door, and so on. Suppose that the to-be-remembered word list consists of ten words, the first two being chair and lion; the mnemonist has to imagine an association between, for example, gun and the first to-be-remembered word which here is 'chair', then shoe and the second word 'lion', and so on. Again, the more bizarre the association, the better. However, one fact tends to militate against the idea that association between visual images necessarily constitutes the mechanism which brings about improvement in memory using this mnemonic system and that is that people who report poor imagery also show very great improvement in memory when using the system.

Thus, it seems that the use of visual imagery may improve recall of word lists by aiding association-formation; but it also appears that merely instructing subjects with poor imagery to try to form what presumably must be purely verbal associations also improves recall of word lists. So, the explanation is not clear and is certainly not simple.

Eidetic imagery
It has been thought for many years that some people are able to remember what they see in exactly the same form as they see it: that is to say, they remember their visual perceptions more or less in the form of photographs. Actually, real eidetic imagery is very rare indeed; and even when there is quite a lot of evidence that a person possesses it, this is not a guarantee that he can use it to retain his visual memories over long periods. It seems to be more common in young children under the age of eleven; but, even then, only about one in ten show any evidence of it and a large proportion of these children have pictorial memory images which are unstable, so that parts of the picture fade and disappear apparently at random. The classical way in which experiments have been carried out on eidetic imagery was as follows: the subject was seated facing a plain white screen; a complex picture of, for example, a landscape was placed in front of the screen and the subject was allowed about half a minute to look at the picture. When the picture had been removed the subject was asked to look at the plain white screen and describe the

* This technique is sometimes called the method of loci, from the Latin word for a place.

picture. Eidetic imagers could report accurately how many branches a particular tree had or even how many leaves on a branch. In one famous study conducted by George Allport in 1922 some children were able correctly to report the word *Gartenwirtschaft*, letter by letter, forwards or backwards, even though they had never seen it before.

Finally, we must distinguish between eidetic images and after-images. If you stare hard at a small patch of colour on a white background for about thirty seconds and then remove the patch of colour and stare at the white screen, negative after-images will appear which is the colour complement of the original stimulus, i.e., if the original patch was red, the after-image will be green. Positive after-images may be produced by staring at very bright stimuli for very brief periods, for example, by glancing at a bright electric light bulb and then closing your eyes. Positive after-images are transient and are quickly replaced by negative after-images. The main features which distinguish after-images from eidetic images are that after-images move with the eyes, whereas eidetic images may be scanned, they fade rapidly compared to eidetic images which are usually under some degree of volitional control and may be recalled weeks or even years later. Finally, after-images may be eliminated by presenting another stimulus immediately after the first.

Our conclusion must be then, that imagery appears to play one or perhaps more roles in memory, but these functions have, so far, proved elusive.

Perceptual motor learning

Introduction
So far, this Chapter has dealt mainly with memory for verbal material of one kind or another. Now we shall examine the learning of perceptual motor skills. Throughout this discussion it will become apparent that psychologists use the word skill in a much broader sense than the general public. Psychologists use the term 'perceptual skill' to cover all cases in which sensory input is integrated with muscular responses to obtain a goal. Thus, the term would include walking, knitting, typing, and playing football. Psychologists often broaden the area still further to include what are generally thought of as purely mental skills, for example, verbal behaviour and problem-solving.

Up until the early 1940s, most of the research on perceptual-motor skill was dominated by the S-R theory of learning in which skill-learning is viewed as the acquisition of stimulus-response chains. Several ideas began to weaken the hold of this view on psychologists: firstly, as we have seen, neurophysiologists like Sir Henry Head had been emphasizing the complexity of even apparently simple skills like sitting in an upright posture; secondly, Tolman (1932) put forward the idea that behaviour was not necessarily driven by states of deprivation, but by goals which the organism would strive to attain; and, lastly, Lashley (1951) highlighted the shortcoming of the S-R approach to the acquisition of skills in many examples of serially-ordered behaviour.

One of the central concepts in the new approach to skill-learning is the concept of feedback, which originated in control engineering. In a system which uses feedback, information about the output of the system is 'fed back' into the system to help control it. A thermostat in an oven is an example of such a device.

As we saw earlier, Head's idea, that we carry around with us a schema of our muscular system, against which we may measure our movements and which itself is sensitive to any movements we may execute, embodied elements of the more modern concept of feedback and foreshadowed the modern view of man as a very flexible information processer. Actually, man behaves very differently from machines in several important aspects: he is far more flexible than any machine and appears to be capable of learning an unlimited number of skilled behaviour patterns; moreover, man's performance is affected by emotion, motivation, and stress.

The stages of skill-learning
It would seem from our own experience of learning complex perceptual motor tasks that there are several distinct stages that we go through while mastering the skill. First, the beginner will try to 'understand' the task and what will be required to perform it. This is not as easy as it may at first appear. The most difficult thing for a learner is often the conscious appraisal of information about his own limbs; how many of us know, for example, what idiosyncratic mannerisms we perform while speaking? One of the most helpful strategies at this phase of skill learning is to show the learner video recordings of his efforts. This provides him with first class feedback of his actions. The extent to which instruction can be useful in the learning of a new task will, of course, vary with task complexity; but most skilled behaviour is complex enough for instructors to point out cues, events, and responses which are more important than the others. In the very complex skills of flying an aircraft, the learning time before the first solo flight has consistently been reduced from ten hours' flying to about three-and-a-half hours, by the instructor conducting detailed discussions of each manoeuvre and the exact sequence of responses to be made, interspersed with very brief flights. Similarly, anyone who has been coached to a reasonably high standard at a sport, will probably have been surprised at the time spent by good coaches in just discussing the execution of a movement, even to the extent of describing a mental attitude to be adopted.

Next, an intermediate or associative stage is entered, in which the

338

chains or patterns of individual responses are practised and co-ordinated. This period obviously depends on many factors, the complexity of the skill being learned, the accuracy with which it must be mastered, and so on; but in learning morse-code, most errors are eliminated after about ten hours of practice.

One of the questions which relates to this phase is, should the practice trials be massed together or should there be rest periods between sessions of practice trials? Well, as with verbal learning distributed learning trials seem to be best, especially if the skill requires extensive motor activity. Another, more complicated, question is the proper sequence of practice of the individual components of a skill. A very early experiment designed to shed light on this sort of problem was performed by Koch in 1923. His subjects practised typing finger exercises on two separate typewriters simultaneously. Koch found that subjects who began by practising with each hand separately before attempting to use both hands simultaneously made faster progress and then maintained their lead over subjects who began by using both hands simultaneously. This is not true, however, for piano-playing. The discrepancy may be more apparent than real if the following principle holds: where the skill is composed of components which are relatively independent of each other, such as the typing of different passages with separate hands, then it is best to practice each component separately; but where successful execution of the skill depends on the integration of the components, then this obviously must be practised.

During the first stage of skill-learning, the execution of the skill becomes progressively automatic, less under cognitive or conscious control, and less subject to interference from other activities.

An experiment carried out by Bahrick, Noble, and Fitts in 1954 highlighted this. Two groups of subjects had to respond to lights. One group had to respond to lights which appeared in a regular pattern, and the other group had to respond to lights which appeared at random intervals. Both groups also had to do some mental arithmetic, as well as the primary task. After some practice, the group for whom learning was possible on the primary task (the group with the patterned lights) obtained higher scores on the arithmetic task than did the other group. These results add weight to the view that practice of a skill renders it more autonomous and resistent to interference. This experiment also indicates that as a skill is practised, it requires less and less of the brain's processing capacity-learning than for other tasks. The resemblance between well-developed skills and reflexes has been pointed out many times, and brilliant sportsmen often report that they experience a feeling of detachment from the execution of their skills at the times when these skills are at their height.

Plans

In 1960 G. A. Miller, E. Galanter, and K. H. Pribram published a book which proved to be very influential in guiding ideas and thought in the study of skill acquisition. The book was called *Plans and the Structure of Behaviour*. In it, the authors develop the notion that when one learns a skill one begins usually with a verbal description or idea (plan) of the skills involved which through trial and error becomes a well-co-ordinated perceptual-motor skill. In fact, most skilled behaviour, like driving a car, involves the co-ordination of a hierarchy of behavioural units, each unit being guided by its own plan. For example, the first stage of learning to type is to learn the positions of the keys on the keyboard. After some practice the learner acquires a smooth, faster 'letter habit', i.e., see letter-first key-press key-check. The next step is to build up speed for familiar letter sequences, such as -ing, and, the or -ion. Thus 'word habits', build up and become faster. The last stage, or plan, to be reached is the point at which the typist reads the material several words ahead of those actually being typed.

So far, the discussion has centred on communicable plans or strategies which the learner or teacher could verbalize; but there are skills which are extremely difficult to describe, for example walking a tightrope. Thus a plan does not necessarily have to be a verbal description; it just has to be an idea or goal in the mind of the learner or his teacher (as in the case of an animal being taught a trick).

Miller, Galanter, and Pribram also emphasized the 'automatic' nature of well-developed skills, using as an example the extreme difficulty that a good typist will have in typing 'hte' instead of 'the'. They point out that skilled behaviour in humans has many similarities with instinctive behaviour in animals, even going so far as to argue that the starting gun acts as a 'releaser' for a trained athlete, the occurrence of false starts indicating that the athlete's behaviour is not completely under volitional control. However, they do point out that a human being's releasers are generally complex and that he can usually control the conditions under which the releaser is presented, whereas, in animals, the releaser is usually simple and its occurrence is not under the animal's control.

Miller *et al.* develop their thesis that a plan is first processed digitally and then, as it becomes translated into skilled movements, its execution appears to be controlled by the kind of processing seen in analogue computers. An analogue computer is one in which the magnitudes involved in its computations are represented by physical quantities in proportion to those magnitudes. The physical qualities may be lengths, voltages, time lapses, angles, etc. Thus, if you use a slide rule you are computing using an analogue device. On the other hand a digital computer represents the magnitudes involved in its computations by different states of the machine, e.g., by a dial which can be in any one of many positions or by a switch which may be open or closed. Thus, it follows that the relationship between the input to a digital device and the process which represents that input inside the machine is not simple. All of us have used digital procedures when we have multiplied by writing the computations on paper—here, the symbols do not have a simple physical relationship with the magnitudes which they represent.

Now, what has all this got to do with plans and their execution? Well, the idea is that when a plan is formed its representation must involve an abstract kind of process which does not bear a simple physical relationship with the magnitude of the movements which constitute the plan. However, the execution of the plan at its lowest levels seem to be controlled by an analogue process. The better a skill is learned and the more 'automatic' is its execution, the more it looks like the original plan which controlled its execution and which used symbols (words), is replaced by a control process which directly enables the operator to make responses whose magnitude is proportional to the magnitude of the input. Thus, a learner driver starts with plans which are expressed verbally, symbolically (digitally) and gradually learns to translate the plans into continuous proportional movements which appear to be controlled by analogue processes.

This interesting view of the acquisition of perceptual motor skills was, when it was first postulated in 1960, greeted with enthusiasm but it has not, so far, led to the significant advances in our ability to improve perceptual motor learning that it promised. Neither does it seem to have advanced our understanding of the neurological basis of skill acquisition. The guess that 'the cerebellum is a critical component in a digital-to-analogue converter on the output of the neural system for processing information' may well be 'shrewd' but it does not, so far, appear to have provided the theoretical background for any concrete advances in our ability to manipulate skilled behaviour. This is, perhaps, a more forceful criticism than the more frequent comment that the approach adopted by Miller, Galanter, and Pribram was too mechanistic.

Attempts to improve skill-acquisition

A mass of research has gone into this area over the last thirty years, the Second World War providing a catalyst for finding quick, efficient methods of teaching people to shoot accurately or fly aircraft, etc. The research may be divided roughly into that which has concentrated on providing the learner with information about the sort of errors he is making and that which centres on methods of preventing the learner from making many errors while he is learning.

There are many different ways in which a learner may gain information about his performance, but in most ordinary tasks such knowledge is present for the learner to see, hear, or feel. Artificial feedback may be

341

added by an experimenter; for example, a buzzer which sounds while a gun is on target. Generally, it has been found that such concurrent artificial feedback may help if it is used intermittently but, surprisingly, its continuous use seems to impede learning. When experimental groups are provided with continuous concurrent feedback the performance is better than a control group. However, when the feedback is removed their performance is worse than the control group. Providing the learner with information about his performance after he has completed the task (terminal feedback) seems to be effective in aiding the acquisition of simple perceptual motor skills, but if the feedback is delayed too long, i.e., after intervening responses, then its effects may be deleterious.

Attempts to improve skill acquisition by preventing the learning of errors have met with varying amounts of success. We are all familar with the use of floats and inflatable rings for use by people learning to swim: such devices provide partial guidance. More complete guidance is given, for example, by a harness which may be used to control a golfer's swing, the learner merely supplying the force. Yet another kind of guidance designed to prevent the occurrence of errors is termed forced response guidance. Here, the limb or body of the learner is moved by the trainer; an instance of this would be dual control devices; although these are usually employed for safety rather than guidance.

The main finding from such work is that the learner should be allowed to make some errors, possibly so that he may get to know what making a mistake 'feels' like.

FURTHER READING

Bartlett, F. C. (1932) *Remembering*. Cambridge University Press.
Dixon, T. R., and Horton, D. L., eds. (1968) *Verbal Learning and General Behaviour Theory*. Prentice-Hall. (Chapters by Deese, Mandler, and Asch.)
Ebbinghaus, H. (1913) *Memory*, tr. H. A. Ruger, and C. H. Bussenius. Teachers College, Columbia University Press.
Luria, A. R. (1975) *The Mind of a Mnemonist*. Penguin.
Miller, G. A., Galanter, E., and Pribam, K. H. (1960) *Plans and the Structure of Behaviour*. Holt, Rinehart and Winston.
Richardson, A. (1969) *Mental Imagery*. Routledge and Kegan Paul.

16 Recent developments in memory
BRIAN CLIFFORD

The distinction between STS and LTS

Introduction
Psychologists are fond of creating dichotomies in their attempt to furnish explanations of real life events. One such dichotomy is that human memory must be conceptualized as having two distinct parts, a short-term storage (STS) and a long-term storage (LTS) system.

Memory is one of man's essential survival systems: without a memory we would not exist for more than a few hours. In everyday life many different types of demands are placed upon us. Broadly speaking, we use our memories in the 'short-term' when we receive a telephone number from the operator, or when we try to remember directions which have just been given to us. We also use our memories in the 'short-term' when we try to remember how much the cashier demanded, how much we gave her, and whether the change we received was correct. These two senses of 'short-term' memory (as a passive storage system and as a working or processing 'space') differ somewhat, but in both cases STS is regarded as an essential requirement for efficient transaction with our environment. We use long-term memory when we are sitting our 'A' levels, when we try to understand what the teacher is really saying, or again when we dial, almost unconsciously, our familiar home telephone number. Now, these two memory systems are obviously not unrelated because that which is now classifiable as an old memory was, at one time, new input and, as such, employed short term storage. But, while not unconnected, many psychologists feel that they can be separated, and ought to be so, in order to understand better the total system we call memory. It is this question—to separate or not—that has troubled psychology acutely since the 1960s but more generally from the beginning of the science of behaviour.

William James (1890) was one of the first psychologists to make the distinction between primary memory as one type of memory that endures for a very brief period of time, and secondary memory, 'the knowledge of a former state of mind after it has already once dropped from consciousness' Meumann (1913) made the same type of distinction. Now, while these historically very old views were based on introspective evidence, more recently the same distinction between STS and LTS has been suggested by laboratory studies and by investigation of patients in a clinical setting. More specifically, the evidence for such a separation comes from physiological studies, from amnesic patients, and from a number of experimental manipulations based on testing retention over different periods of time.

Physiological studies
The physiological basis of an STS–LTS dichotomy has been most strongly argued by Donald Hebb (1949). Hebb distinguished between reverberating activity (the active trace) and structural change (the structural trace). These two traces are equated with short term and long term storage respectively. Incoming stimulation sets up reverberatory activity in the receptor and effector cells which are involved in the sensation. With repeated stimulation and reverberation, a structural change occurs, possibly of a neuro-anatomical or neuro-chemical nature. During the early part of this process, interference or disruption can be caused by further incoming information. That is, the active trace is very 'fragile'; the structural trace is not. This theory has important affinity with consolidation theory ('give me a minute to let it sink in'), which suggests that perseveration (continuation in time) of neural activity is necessary for the consolidation of the trace. Interference is more likely the shorter the length of time perseveration has gone on.

There is some experimental support for the Hebbian theory. Duncan (1949) applied electric shock to the brains of rats at various times after they had learned a maze and observed its effect on retention of this new learning. If perseveration is necessary for learning, but is interfered with, deficits in retention ought to be observed. This is what Duncan found: the shorter the delay between learning and shocking, the poorer the retention of the learned behaviour. If the administration of shock was sufficiently delayed, no impairment of learning occurred.

Clinical evidence
Studies of amnesic patients give strong support for the belief that

memory has at least two components. Patients suffering from Wernicke-Korsakov's syndrome, an alcohol related illness, exhibit gross long-term storage defects but little impairment of short-term storage. For example, they cannot remember what day, month, or year it is but they can repeat back perfectly a series of digits or letters which they have just been given. This normal STS capacity but impaired LTS has also been well-documented in amnesic patients other than alcoholics.

The converse has also been shown. Patients have been examined who have intact, good LTS in the sense of memory for everyday events but grossly impaired ability to immediately repeat back even two digits.

Thus, the evidence of good memories for long past experiences but poor memories for what has just gone, together with the converse, is strong evidence for the belief that we must distinguish between at least two types of memory.

Laboratory evidence

The third line of evidence for the distinction between STS and LTS comes from the psychology laboratory proper, and especially free recall studies. In free recall, the subject is presented with a list of items which he then must try to recall—but in any order he chooses. When this technique is employed, one of the most reproducible effects in psychology occurs (at least after the first one or two trials). This 'hardy' effect is the serial position curve (SPC). The SPC is characterized by good recall of the first few items presented by the experimenter (the primacy effect) and good recall of the last few items presented (the recency effect). The middle items are usually poorly recalled.

The relevance of the SPC is that the two end peaks (primacy and recency) are held to represent output from LTS and STS respectively. Now, if it could be shown that one peak could be altered while the other remained intact, this would be very good evidence for a distinction between two separate and separable memory systems. This can be achieved. It has been found that the nature of the words presented for recall does not affect recency but does affect primacy. For example, word frequency has no effect on recency, but common words (high frequency of usage) are better retained in LTS than are low frequency words. The imagibility of words has been found to have little effect on recency but large effects on primacy. Again, lists containing either acoustically similar words (e.g., fail, sail, hail) or semantically similar words (e.g., huge, great, large) have little effect on recency but a large effect on primacy. Repetition of a word has no effect on recency but does affect primacy. Delaying recall after presentation of a list has no effect on primacy but does massively depress recency.

These above findings are taken to be powerful experimental evidence for an STS-LTS dichotomy. From everyday life, from physiology, from amnesic patients, and from the experimental psychologist's laboratory much the same story emerges: it seems necessary to distinguish between two distinct memory systems—STS and LTS. The next question to ask is in what ways do they differ.

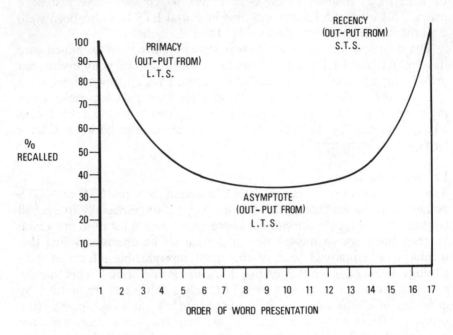

Fig. 16.1 Hypothetical serial position curve (SPC) showing primacy and recency peaks and their source.

The characteristics of STS and LTS

The characteristics of the two main memory stores have been shown to differ along a number of dimensions. These dimensions are:

1. *Entry of information*: how the to-be-remembered items get into the different memory systems.
2. *Maintenance of information*: how a person can go about fixating material to retain it best.
3. *Format of information*: the form of the material held in memory.
4. *Capacity*: the amount that can be held in the various systems.
5. *Information loss*: the reasons why we forget.
6. *Trace duration*: how long we can remember information for.
7. *Retrieval*: how we recall information when we need it.

These different characteristics are shown in Table 16.1

Table 16.1 Characteristics of the short-term store (STS) and the long-term store (LTS).

Features of memory	Levels of memory	
	STS	LTS
1. Entry of information	Requires attention	Rehearsal Semantic processing
2. Coding	Phonemic Articulatory Visual Possible semantic	Semantic Phonemic Visual
3. Storage format	Phonemic Articulatory Visual Images	Lexicons Grammars Knowledge of the world Propositions
4. Capacity	Small (2.5–7 items)	No known limit
5. Maintenance of memories	Continued attention Rehearsal	Repetition Organization
6. Memory duration	Up to 30 seconds (if not rehearsed)	Minutes to years
7. Forgetting	Displacement Possibly decay Possibly interference	Loss of accessibility Possibly interference Possibly repression Possibly systematic distortion of the memory trace
8. Retrieval	Automatic	Search and decision processes

Qualifications

ENTRY OF INFORMATION

Now, while the entries in Table 16.1 have a fair degree of 'truth value' some qualifications are required. While it is generally true that attention is required to enter items into STS, it is not always the case. From the selective attention literature, a study by Donald McKay in 1973 is interesting. He showed that, if one group of subjects was presented with an ambiguous sentence on the attended channel, such as 'the boys were

347

throwing stones at the bank' and on the unattended channel they were presented with the word 'river', their recall of the presented message differed from a group given the same ambiguous message, but the word 'savings' on the unattended channel. Both groups were unaware of the unattended channel word. Thus, although no attention had been allocated to these words, nonetheless they had entered STS and had served to disambiguate a potentially ambiguous sentence.

FORMAT OF INFORMATION

Another area where evidence is not as clear cut as Table 16.1 would suggest is in the format of information. One of the thorniest problems in current memory research is the form of storage of information in STS. Is it acoustic, articulatory, visual, or semantic? The earliest studies suggesting that STS was acoustic were by Richard Conrad in 1962 and 1964, who presented a series of letters which subjects had to remember for later recall. Where errors occurred, they were similar to the correct letter's sound, e.g., 't' was wrongly recalled as 'b' 'p' or 'd'. This acoustic confusion suggested that items are coded or processed on an acoustic basis. From this initial experiment many researchers then went on to argue that *the* coding of items in STS was acoustic. However, at most all that could legitimately be deduced was that acoustic coding was *one* possibility. Because letters were used, it would seem reasonable to argue that semantic (meaning) coding would not (i) be very easy or (ii) be very beneficial, and therefore would not be used. If one used semantic material, and semantic coding was known to be beneficial, or necessary, then the story may be rather different. This was shown to be the case by Harvey Shulman who, in 1970, demonstrated that semantic coding did occur in STS, if it was possible, due to the material, and if it was beneficial or necessary, due to the task demands.

Shulman visually presented lists of ten words and then tested for recognition memory by means of a visually presented probe word which could either be a homonym of a presented word (ball − bawl, pray − prey, board − bored), a synonym of a presented word (talk − speak, leap − jump, angry − mad) or identical to a presented word (board − board, speak − speak, pray − pray). The subjects had to say whether the probe word had been present in the list of ten words. The error rates were very similar for both the homonym and the synonym probes, thus strongly suggesting that semantic coding was going on in STS because to make an error on 'talk' and 'speak' requires that the similarity of meaning has been rendered available. That is, the two words were being matched at a semantic level. Thus experimental evidence now strongly suggests that semantic coding occurs in STS, while logic, and everyday observation of communication, would also support this contention.

CAPACITY

The last qualification to Table 16.1 which we will discuss here (but there are others) is that of capacity. It would generally be conceded that STS capacity is small. But the real question is how small is small? The number of items which a person can repeat back word and order perfect is said to represent his memory span. This memory span is, in turn, held to reflect the limited capacity of the STS. Typically, a person can only repeat back five to nine items, depending on whether the items are digits, letters, or words. However, if input words are in the form of a connected sentence then, at least for oldish children and young adults, the memory span expands to twenty words. George Miller has pointed out that it is not the number of items as such that defines the limitation but the number of 'chunks' or meaningful units. A digit, letter, word, or sentence can be seen as one chunk, but the actual number of items within a chunk can and does differ. This is an extremely interesting aspect of memory which we will pick up again under organization.

Whilst most psychologists working in the area of memory have accepted the possibility of a dichotomy, qualifications like those above have led some to argue that a unitary memory system may be a better way of conceptualizing the known facts (e.g., Craik and Lockhart, 1972). However before we look at this view we will retain the distinction between STS and LTS for its heuristic usefulness in a discussion of how we forget.

Theories of forgetting

Psychologists have been much exercised in elucidating the process of memory failure. All memories do not fade at the same rate, or in the same way, but we do seem to forget over both long and short periods of time. Why should this be? There are a number of possible explanations or theories, such as the passive decay theory, systematic distortion of the memory trace, interference theory, displacement theory, motivated forgetting and retrieval failure. Over and above these psychological accounts of memory failure, physical trauma, drug abuse, and senility are other causes. Only the psychological accounts will be discussed here.

Passive decay theory

This theory suggests that memories fade over time, unless maintained by rehearsal or repetition. Now, while time itself cannot be an explanation it is argued that, as time goes on, so metabolic processes occur which degrade the memory trace which was set up during the initial learning and remembering. Weathering in physical geography would be an appropriate analogy for this theory.

Systematic distortion of the memory trace

The early proponents of this theory of memory failure argued that memories were not so much lost as distorted. They also held that errors of distortion increased over time. Wulf (1922) found that when subjects were asked to reproduce a line drawing which they had been presented with some time earlier, their drawing showed certain characteristic distortions compared with the original. If the presented shape looked like some familiar object the recalled shapes looked even more like the familiar object. Secondly, it was found that the reproduced figures became more symmetrical, and, thirdly, any irregularity in the original stimulus became accentuated in the reproduced figure. It was also found that the longer the time between seeing and reproducing the figure, the greater was the distortion. After the initial flush of success for the Gestalt psychologists (see Ch. 2), who could explain this in terms of 'goodness', problems began to appear in 1945. Hebb and Foord demonstrated that distortions were no greater after long delays, provided you tested different subjects at the different time intervals, and not the same subjects repeatedly. There is now a fair amount of evidence that large distortions are due to repeated reproductions by the same subject. Over and above the time factor, it has also become clear that systematic distortion does not occur only during storage but also at input and at retrieval.

Irrespective of where the distortion comes, and whether it increases over time, distortions do occur in both visual and verbal memory and thus testify to the active striving of humans for coherence, and this coherence stems from the person's pre-existing schemata (see Ch. 15 where we discussed Bartlett's research with verbal material).

Motivated forgetting

A complete account of remembering and forgetting cannot ignore what the person is trying to do—both when he remembers and when he forgets. Repression, a Freudian term (see Ch. 23), suggests that some memories become inaccessible because of the way they relate to our personal feelings. Memories can be 'forgotten' because they are unacceptably associated with guilt and anxiety. Clinical evidence testifies to the reality of motivated forgetting. The amnesic syndrome, often brought about because of physical trauma or pathology, can also be produced by great emotional shock. In these cases forgetting is highly selective and focused. The memories forgotten are those referring to self—name, family, home address, personal biography. However it is somewhat doubtful whether motivated forgetting ever occurs in normal, everyday life, or whether it has ever really been shown in the laboratory. Paul Kline (1972) argues persuasively for its reality in the laboratory, and reviews evidence which shows that if you inform some subjects that they have failed a test which they have just taken, then their recall of these test items is much poorer than subjects given no such feedback. The line of reasoning is that if you provide 'failure' feedback the subject becomes anxious and hence represses the emotional stimuli and this leads to poor recall. The problem, as Michael Eysenck (1975) indicates, is that exactly the same failure to recall occurs if you give 'success' feedback! Thus, an arousal hypothesis may be a better explanation of every day forgetting of this type than Freudian repression.

Interference theory of forgetting
This account of forgetting does not use time as an explanation, but rather stresses that it is what we do between initial memorization and eventual recalling that is crucial. Within this interference account of memory failure there is interference caused by prior learning on later learning (pro-active interference, or PI) and the interference caused by later learning on earlier learning (retro-active interference, or RI). A very basic concept in interference theory is similarity: the more that two things (people, words, situations) resemble each other the greater the potential for interference. Thus, basically put, interference theory explains forgetting by the fact that we constantly learn or do new things which have a greater or lesser degree of similarity to things we have learned or done, or will learn to do, and, thus, we are likely to confuse this old and new learning. From this emerges a real problem for interference theory: do we ever actually forget anything, or do we merely 'hide' it by new or old memories? That is, does new learning cause unlearning of old knowledge, or does it merely compete with it? Although most old, and still a few new, introductory texts on memory devote a large number of pages to interference theories of forgetting it is now being realised that the theory is very paradigm-specific, by which I mean that it seems to hold only for very circumscribed laboratory situations. Thus interference theory, once regarded as 'one of the most successful and established theories in psychology' (Kintsch, 1970), is on the wane. Leo Postman himself, the great exponent of the theory, says that the concepts of PI and RI have 'failed to generate a model of the forgetting process which can be shown to have general validity'.

Retrieval failure
The basis for this theory of forgetting is the belief that memories are seldom lost, they merely become inaccessible. Academic psychology makes the distinction between accessibility and availability (Tulving and Pearlstone, 1966). That is, just because we cannot recall a desired piece of information it does not mean that we do not know it. Quite often, in fact, we know that we know it. This is the famous 'tip of the tongue' phenomenon. Accessibility to stored information is governed by retrieval

cues, or retrieval routes. These retrieval cues can either be encoded along with the to-be-recalled material or they can be provided later as prods or pointers which govern where we will search in memory. Endel Tulving and Donald Thomson have developed this theory most thoroughly; from a cue-dependent forgetting theory, to an encoding specificity hypothesis, to, eventually, an encoding specificity principle. While the encoding specificity principle lacks falsifiability, and is, therefore, of little value, the 'hypothesis' form is useful and informative. Tulving has produced a great deal of evidence for his hypothesis, but perhaps the clearest evidence for it comes from a fairly old study by Abernethy (1940) who presented material to be learned to two groups of subjects. One group both learned and recalled in the same room while the other group learned and recalled in different rooms. The recall of the former group was much higher, suggesting that the closer we can reinstate the environment of learning at the time of recall the better will that recall be. Note how your memories of a holiday come flooding back if you once return there.

Displacement

The last theory of forgetting we will look at is that of displacement. If memories are finite storage banks (see above) then it would seem somewhat obvious that there is a possibility that if you enter yet another piece of information you will 'push out' a previously stored memory. While this theory has been applied to long term storage the evidence is purely anecdotal: the absent-minded professor, or the professor who refused to learn his student's names because for every name learned he lost the Latin name of a flower. The application of displacement theory to STS seems much sounder because here we know that STS is a limited capacity system, unlike LTS, which may be unlimited in capacity, the only limitation being one of retrieval.

All these theories of forgetting have some validity but no one theory explains all forgetting. Further, no one theory fully explains forgetting from either STS or LTS, but some are better than others. It is to these we now turn.

Forgetting from STS

Decay theory, interference theory, and displacement theory have been the chief contenders as explanations of STS forgetting. Two chief techniques can be cited as sources of resolution, the Brown-Peterson technique and the serial probe recall technique of Waugh and Norman. The Brown-Peterson technique involves presenting subjects with a number of trials, each trial comprising the presentation of three items, then asking the subjects to perform a task which prevents rehearsal of these three to-be-remembered items and finally asking for recall of the three items. The important manipulation is the length of time the subjects perform the interpolated rehearsal-prevention task. Brown argued that in the absence of rehearsal, memorized items should decay over time. This was shown. Forgetting of the three items was complete after as little as eighteen to thirty seconds. While this was good evidence for the decay theory (coupled with rehearsal—see below) there remained one possibility in terms of interference theory: if it could be shown that there was little forgetting on the first trial, but progressively more on the second, third, and fourth trials, then pro-active interference could be occurring. Geoffrey Keppel and Benton Underwood (1962) argued that they showed precisely this. In their study using the Brown–Peterson technique no forgetting was shown on the first trial. However, Alan Baddeley and Donald Scott (1971) collected evidence from a number of their own studies and indicated that, providing certain precautions in terms of design were taken, forgetting did occur on the first trial. Thus, it seems that decay rather than interference was the better explanation of STS forgetting.

More recently, there has been a general acceptance that, in fact, displacement may be an even better explanation. The reference experiment is the serial probe technique of Nancy Waugh and Donald Norman (1965), who presented their subjects with series of digits at different speeds, and, when the list presentation was over, re-presented one of those digits and asked the subjects to recall the digit which followed that re-presented item in the original list. The different rates of presentation determined the time in STS and, thus, would indicate the relevance of decay theory, while the probe recall determined the number of items which intervened between a to-be-recalled item and its actual recall, thus allowing investigation of displacement theory. In general, displacement was supported: the greater the number of intervening items, the poorer the recall of the probed digit. There is, however, some evidence for decay theory because slower rates of presentation did produce slightly poorer recall.

The general conclusion which follows from the above is that interference theory has little to recommend it, decay theory has some validity, but that the best explanation of why memory for new information is so elusive resides in a displacement account.

What about these frustrating situations when we cannot remember that which we know we know. This is the problem of LTS forgetting, to which we now turn our attention.

Forgetting from LTS

Several of the theoretical explanations of STS forgetting reappear in accounts of LTS failure. These are trace decay and interference, and to those are added retrieval failure, systematic distortion of the memory trace, and motivated forgetting.

While systematic distortion of the memory trace and motivated forgetting will not be discussed here for the reasons outlined above, it must be borne in mind that, undoubtedly, some forgetting from LTS is due to those factors.

The choice between decay, interference, and retrieval failure is nicely made in an experiment by Endel Tulving (1968), who presented a list of words and then asked the subjects to recall all they could remember. He then took away their answer sheets, and without re-presenting the list, asked them to recall again. This was repeated a third time. The important finding was that the same words were not recalled on each of the three trials. One would have difficulty explaining these results in terms of interference because one would have to argue that that which had been unlearned on Trial 1 was present on Trial 2 or 3. Decay theory would be an unsatisfactory explanation of why items not recalled on either Trial 1 or Trial 2 could be recalled on Trial 3, because more time would have elapsed between presentation and the third recall than presentation and either the first or second recall. The above results are easily explained by assuming that different retrieval cues or schemes are employed on different recall trials. Thus the possibility exists that perhaps much less is forgotten than we believe, and what is fallible is the selection or the provision of the appropriate cues. As with the STS explanation the story is much more complex than this, but for our purposes the generally accepted position is that in normal everyday life we fail to recall that which we know we know because we are unable to set up correct or appropriate retrieval cues.

Special issues

Rehearsal

If there are in fact two memory systems, an STS and an LTS, then we must ask how information gets from one to the other. The traditional answer has been 'rehearsal'. However, the term rehearsal has recently come under attack either as not being necessary or as being too global a concept. Richard Atkinson and Richard Shiffrin (1968) suggest that rehearsal has two functions: maintaining items in STS, and transferring these items to LTS. There are also two associated assumptions which go with this dual function: that time in STS and the number of repetitions are vital for transfer of information to LTS. The longer the stay in STS, or the greater the number of rehearsals, the better the chance of remembering at a later date.

Recent research, however, suggests that neither time in STS nor number of rehearsals predict storage in long-term memory. Fergus

Craik and Michael Watkins (1973) asked subjects to remember only certain critical words (defined as words beginning with a certain letter) in lists which were presented either rapidly or slowly. The placing of critical words relative to non-critical words determined the amount of time an item spent in STS, and potentially the number of rehearsals given to an item. Retention over the long term was unrelated to either duration in STS or number of implicit or explicit rehearsals. This led Craik and Watkins to differentiate between maintenance rehearsal and elaborative rehearsal. The former is sufficient to retain items in the short term, but the latter is necessary for retention over a long term. Maintenance rehearsal can be conceptualized as repetition of the item in its presented form, elaborative rehearsal involves the elaboration of the input item, this often involving a semantic recoding or an associative linking of the words with pre-existing knowledge.

It is possible that if elaborative processing is adequately employed, storage can be achieved without any 'rehearsal' (in the sense of repetition) whatever. That this is possible is indicated by studies on incidental learning where subjects are not led to expect a recall test and therefore are not predisposed to rehearse. James Jenkins (1974) has performed many experiments where separate groups are asked either to 'estimate the number of letters in the words which I will present to you', or 'give a rhyming word to each of the words I will present to you', or thirdly, 'give me an association to each of the words I will present you with'. These are the cover tasks which hide the fact that memory is actually being studied, but they also involve processing the words in different ways. It is found that 'associate' processing produces very good recall. Thus, in the absence of rehearsal, as it was originally conceived, long-term retention can be good.

Thus it is not the amount of rehearsal but rather the type of rehearsal or processing which is crucial. The more meaningful the processing of information the better the eventual retention. What could this 'more meaningful processing' entail? This question, which we shall now address, has raised very serious doubts about the dichotomous nature of memory and has suggested that a 'levels of processing' account may be a better conception of the human memory system.

A 'levels of processing' approach to memory

Together with the criticisms of the 'boxology' approach which we made in terms of capacity, storage format, and attention, the theoretical shift from structure to function or process has driven the conclusion that, rather than looking at memory as a series of holding stages, it may be better to see memory as the by-product of what we actively do with information as it comes to us. Depending upon what we do, the type of memory we have will differ. If we simply wish to retain information momentarily in order to deal efficiently with our environment—such as dialling a person's telephone number—then we will merely process these numbers in a maintenance way, or in what Fergus Craik and Robert Lockhart (1972) called a Type 1 way (we may simply repeat them over and over again). We have no need to store it permanently, therefore we do not expend much 'cognitive effort' on it, and, as a result, the memory we have is not at all durable. If however, for what ever reason, we wish to make sure that we learn something which we will not forget then we expend a greater amount of cognitive effort on the material. This 'cognitive effort' is best characterized as an attempt to relate new information to old, previously learned, information. This view of memory has been most forcibly argued by Frank Restle (1974) who conceptualized memory in terms of a 'degree of organization' principle. The better we can organize new material, i.e., relate it to existing knowledge, the better it will be retained.

This is altogether a more realistic way of viewing memory because it does not treat memory as a system separate and separable from our thinking, perception and knowledge systems. This is especially the case where the material we are trying to remember is new in the sense that words are not. When we are asked to 'remember' a list of words we are not really learning them, because they are in memory already: we are simply being asked to remember that a specific word has been presented. When we read stories or hear sentences, however, they have not been previously stored and could not have been because they are infinite in number. Thus the explanations of memory for digits, letters, and words may not suffice as explanations of memory for novel, complex material. It is precisely in this latter case that a levels of processing or a degree of organization approach is most exciting in its potential. Thus, memory does comprise several levels, but they are not different memory stores with information being transferred unidirectionally from one to the other. When we are asked to remember, we encode into existing cognitive structure, the depth of processing being determined by what we are attempting to do.

Organization

We have argued above that good memory depends upon the subject actively organizing the to-be-remembered material. John Meyer (1973) has stated that to remember is to have organized. Now, while this is not necessarily the whole story, there is a large grain of truth in it. The evidence that people actually do strive to organize material for later recall, and that this organization has beneficial effects, became obvious as a result of what appeared to be a very trivial change in research methodology. The change was from a stress on serial recall to a stress on free recall. In serial recall, the subject must correctly recall the items

356

and recall them in the same order as they were presented, while, in free recall, correct item recall is demanded, but the subject can recall the items in any order he chooses. This simple change unlocked the door on a whole unexplored area of human memory. By allowing free recall of the items, psychologists could begin to see just how subjects were going about memory tasks.

As we mentioned above, psychologists are fond of postulating dichotomies to explain their data, and the explanation of the efficacy of organization is no exception, being polarized into storage and retrieval accounts. The first account states that organization has its beneficial effect at storage because it serves to reduce the amount of material to be remembered by hierarchically grouping the material, or chunking it. For example, the words cat, dog, parrot, and tortoise could all be grouped under the heading 'pets'. The opposing view is that organization has its effect at retrieval due to the fact that organized items have greater uniqueness and hence an increased number of retrieval routes or 'tags' associated with them. However, the assumption we will work on is that organization has a beneficial effect because it aids both storage and retrieval. It is likely that whenever a subject detects the possibility of an organizational scheme he processes the input words into this scheme and retains both the retrieval (organizational) scheme and the individual items. You will remember from our section on 'rehearsal' that, providing an item is processed adequately (deeply), no rehearsal in the sense of repetition is necessary. Fitting the word into an overall organizational scheme may be sufficient processing to ensure recall. At retrieval the subject probably evokes his organizational scheme and then decides if internally-generated words are sufficiently familiar to be output as a response.

It has become clear from a vast amount of research that subjects can organize material either because the material has intrinsic organizational properties (e.g., all the list words refer to either cars, animals and colours), or subjects organize material in terms of some personal idiosyncratic principle. The first type of organisation can be referred to as experimenter-imposed organization (EO). The second type of organization is referred to as subject-based organization (SO). The most researched type of EO is categorical organization. Categorical organization refers to the fact that the input words can be grouped into a greater or lesser number of semantic categories, as, in our example above, cars, animals, and colours. Here the work of Bousfield is seminal, and his technique is still employed today, with various gradations of refinement. He began by sampling a number of semantic categories for exemplars (e.g., category; *animal*: exemplars; *horse*, *lion*, etc.) and then randomly mixing these exemplars into a sixty-item list and presenting them to subjects for memorization. This procedure ensured that all the animal exemplars did not come one after the other in the input list. The important question was whether this random input would be output in a principled, non-random, way. If recall did exhibit category-clustering of exemplars, then good evidence would exist that subjects actively processed and organized the list for later recall. Principled free recall was exhibited, and has been exhibited by numerous other researchers.

Further evidence for categorical organization comes from the study by Pollio and Foote (1971) who studied temporal aspects of recall. These researchers showed that items within categories were output rapidly, but long delays occurred between categories (e.g., lion-tiger-panther——pansy-rose-violet). Segal (1969) supported categorical organization by showing that if category labels ('*animals*') were presented randomly among lists of exemplars (tiger, desk, *animal*, pansy, lion) the category label preceded the category exemplars at output. Lastly a 'some or none' effect has been shown by Cohen (1966) where, with categorizable lists, either several exemplars from a category are output, or none at all.

LIMITATIONS

So predictable has this categorical organization effect become that more recent research has taken for granted that it will happen and has begun to look for other characteristics of organization, such as its limits and mechanisms. Current research seems to suggest that, while categorical organization does exist, it is limited both in the number of categories that can be efficiently handled (about six) and in the number of words in each category. These inherent limitations have been shown most clearly by Endel Tulving and Z. Pearlstone (1966), who varied both the number of categories and the number of exemplars per category by presenting lists of twelve, twenty-four, and forty-eight words containing categories of one, two, or four exemplars, in each. Half the subjects were simply asked to recall the words, while the other half of the subjects were given category names (cues) at recall and were asked to recall the presented exemplars. The cued recall subjects recalled more words (exemplars) than the non-cued subjects, but this was due to recalling from more categories, not from recalling more exemplars from any one category. That is, the cued and non-cued subjects did not differ in the number of exemplars recalled from any one category. This shows clearly that there seems to be a limit to the number of words recallable from each category. The second limitation of organization (the number of categories that can be handled) was shown by providing the category labels to the non-cued subjects after they had indicated that they could remember no more words. If more words were then recalled, this would be good evidence for a limitation in terms of the number of categories that could be remembered. Such additional word recall was exhibited. (Note also that this is an example of the availability-accessibility distinction talked of above.)

While category-clustering served the function of showing that subjects can utilize organizational schemes inherent in the material it fails to show just how 'active' the subject really is in memory experiments. A more powerful demonstration of organization would be achieved if the material to be recalled did not have any (obvious) organizational schemes such as categories contained within it, but principled recall was still observed. This is precisely what SO achieves. This paradigm also avoids the inherent danger of EO in that the latter builds on the assumption that, because the list has intrinsic organizational properties, these properties should be used and therefore be the criterion by which one deduces organization on the part of the subject. The problem with this is that if the experimenter's assumption does not match the subject's actual organizational method then the subject will be assumed not to have shown organization, whereas in fact all that can be said is that the subject did not use the experimenter's organizational scheme. Subject-generated organization has been demonstrated in a number of ways such as looking for repeated output-grouping despite different input orders over a number of lists, but especially by what is called part-list or transfer learning. Tulving (1966) argued that subjective organization involves schemes for memorizing the whole list, i.e., subjects are not merely concerned to organize one or two items into a memorable unit, but rather they are concerned to maximize recall by generating an overall organizational scheme which includes all the to-be-remembered items. If this is the case, then if items a, b, c, d, e and f form a list and then the subject is later asked to learn a list comprising a, b, c, d, e, f, g, h, i, and j, the possibility exists that the organizational schemes for the first and second lists may conflict, resulting in the odd finding that learning part of a list inhibits the learning of the whole list compared with subjects who have no chance to learn the first part of the list. Tulving (1966) showed this counter-intuitive finding. He used two groups, with one group (Group 1) learning eighteen words which would later be incorporated into a thirty-six word list, while the other group (Group 2) also learned eighteen words but these words were not to be incorporated into the later thirty-six word list. The interesting question was whether Group 1 or Group 2 would learn the thirty-six words faster. From trial two onwards the subjects who had initially learned eighteen irrelevant words learned the thirty-six word list faster! Tulving interpreted these results as indicating that Group 1 had initially developed an over-all organizational scheme for the eighteen words, which, when these eighteen words were incorporated into a thirty-six word list, was inappropriate, while Group 2 simply evolved a new organizational scheme for new material. This part-whole transfer effect has also been shown to work in reverse (whole-part).

THE PROCESS OF ORGANIZATION

Research has thus gone beyond simply demonstrating the fact of organization. We now know quite a bit about the process. For example, it seems that organization has its effect both at storage and retrieval (e.g., Mandler, 1972); that the efficiency of organization is limited both by the amount of information we can contain within an organized unit and the number of such organizational units we can effectively utilize; and, lastly, it has become obvious that the number of ways a person can organize any set of information is very large.

But perhaps the most exciting work in the last few years is that concerned with the question of how students organize connected discourse or texts for retention. This literature is very complex but rather clear principles are emerging. These principles basically follow that found in word-list research and are based on heirarchical grouping of content. In any text, the ideas expressed are of differential importance. If one has ever tried to write a precis, this point will be conceded. It seems that, in remembering connected discourse, the relative importance of the idea units clearly predict recall, i.e., the more important or central the idea, the more likely it is to be recalled. It seems that texts can be represented as hierarchical in nature, that is, within the logical structure underpinning the actual text, conceptual units can be isolated, and be shown to interlink in hierarchical form, such that from the central or core idea other ideas lead off in an ever spreading network. The function of a central idea is clearly shown by John Bransford and Marcia Johnson (1973) who presented a difficult-to-comprehend passage to one group of subjects and also gave them the title ('Washing Clothes') before they read the passage. Another group of subjects were given the passage, and then the title after they had read it, while the last group received only the passage and no title at any time. The argument advanced was that the title is the central idea. Recall of words in the passage was then requested and the 'title plus passage' Group was found to far surpass both the 'passage plus title' and 'passage only' Groups. The finding that the 'passage plus title' did not differ significantly from the 'passage only' strongly suggests that either the organizational scheme must be present at input, or, at least, that it must be capable of generation during the ongoing input. Giving a retrieval or organizational plan (title) after encoding has gone on does not aid memory.

Throughout this discussion of organization we have been concerned to stress organizational schemes in terms of hierarchies which have the properties of low storage requirement and high inference components.

From our argument that memory is a by-product of integrating incoming information with existing knowledge, a fairly clear prediction would then be that our existing knowledge has this hierarchical structure. To see whether, in fact, it does is the focus of the final part of this Chapter.

Semantic memory

That part of long-term memory which is concerned with our stored knowledge of facts, laws, and principles is referred to as semantic memory. This should be distinguished from our long-term memories of personal events and episodes which have happened to us in our lives. This latter memory has been referred to as episodic memory. While these two memories are undoubtedly intimately connected they can be conceptually distinguished, and here we shall deal only with semantic memory.

All the knowledge that underlies human cognitive ability is stored in semantic memory. From this premise certain things follow:

1. Semantic memory will be involved in problem-solving and logical deduction, in question answering and fact retrieval, and in the development and utilization of language.
2. The amount of information stored in memory is staggering.
3. Semantic memory organization must therefore be organized, not haphazard.

It was precisely with these assumptions in mind that one of the earliest and best evolved theories of semantic memory was developed. In 1969 Allan Collins and Ross Quillian published their 'cognitive economy model' of human semantic memory, which was developed from a computer simulation model of language processing.

Collins and Quillian argued that knowledge was stored in the form of a hierarchical network of concept nodes, each concept being linked with a number of other nodes in a superset-subset relationship. Their most often quoted hierarchy (see Fig. 16.2) should help render the basic structure of their model clear.

As can be seen, properties are stored non-redundantly, i.e., that which is true of animals, birds and canaries is stored only at the animal node, and is therefore applied to canary by implication, due to the latter's membership in that animal hierarchy. Thus, Collins and Quillian's model is characterized by a low storage requirement but a high inference component. Now, it is all very well generating a computer program which will handle language, but the important question to ask is whether it in any way represents human memory. To test whether, in fact, the simulation model adequately modelled the human system Collins and Quillian used a true-false reaction time (RT) technique whereby subjects were presented with a sentence such as 'a canary is a bird' and the time taken

361

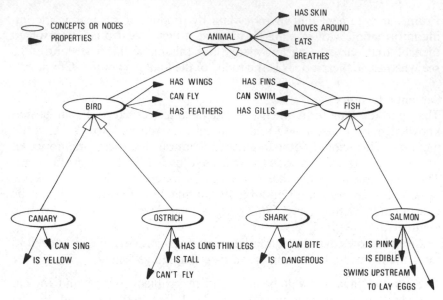

Fig. 16.2 A hypothetical memory structure for animal, bird and canary. (After Collins and Quillian, 1972.)

by the subject to answer true (yes) or false (no) was measured. On the bases of their model Collins and Quillian predicted that it would take times would be additive. Thirdly, they postulated that the average time where one step depended on the completion of another (prior) step the times would be additive. Thirdly they postulated that the average time for any step would be independent of which particular level of the hierarchy was involved. In order to verify or falsify these predictions Collins and Quillian need both property (P) and superset (S) sentences. These two basic types of sentence could each have three levels. For example, 'a canary is yellow' would be called a P_0 sentence (being a property sentence with no links involved); 'a canary has feathers' is a P_1 sentence (see Fig. 16.2) and 'a canary can breathe' is a P_2 sentence because it involved properties but also involves traversing two links to arrive at 'breathes' from 'canary'. Sentences such as 'a canary is a canary', 'a canary is a bird' and 'a canary is an animal' are referred to as superset sentences 0, 1 and 2 respectively (S_0, S_1, S_2).

They found that the time to move from a node to its superset node was in the order of seventy-five milliseconds and that the time taken to move from a node to its property was 225 milliseconds. Now, while these times are somewhat task-dependent a fair amount of supporting evidence exists, at least for the qualitive aspects of the model. The linearity of the effect seems to testify strongly to the reality of the hierarchical structure of semantic memory.

362

CRITIQUE
However, since its inception, and progressively since about 1972, Collins and Quillian's (1969) cognitive economy model of semantic memory has had certain criticisms levelled against it. For example, the model has never adequately handled the problem of false instances such as 'a canary is a fire engine'. The reaction time to such sentences were not predicted or predictable, and despite having looked at five possible explanations Collins and Quillian (1972) had to conclude that no satisfactory or adequate answer was at hand. Obviously an adequate account of human functioning will have to explain both positive and negative instances of knowledge verification.

Over and above this major failing, other problems have arisen, such as the possibility that people do store information repeatedly, and that, because of this, some information is more available than others because of the individual's past learning. A second attack is based on the belief that Collins and Quillian's data (RTs) may be an artifact of category size. For example, there are more animals than mammals and thus verification of an instance of animal should take longer than verification of an instance of mammal. That is, the greater the number of instances the slower RT will be. A third possible explanation of the Collins and Quillian findings could be in terms of imagery (Jorgansen and Kintsch, 1973). They suggest that the higher up the hierarchy ones goes, the less concrete or imagible is the instance or concept. It is very difficult to image an animal—without imaging a specific animal. It is however, easy to image a canary. The last attack on Collins and Quillian which we shall discuss is the argument that the RT data of the cognitive economy model could just as easily be explained by similarity, or what is called 'feature overlap'. Concepts which are more distant in a conceptual hierarchy have fewer features in common (e.g., mammal and collie) than concepts which are close together (e.g., dog and collie). It has been proposed that subjects prime a positive response when two concepts are similar and would thus predict the Collins and Quillian RT findings, without having to postulate that knowledge is stored hierarchically. In fact similarity ratings of concepts are better predictors of judgement times than distances in a conceptual hierarchy.

These various attacks on Collins and Quillian's interpretation of their RT data have led to a suggestion that knowledge is not, in fact, stored hierarchically, but, rather, in some other format. The nature of this alternative organization is not at all clearly specified, and, in fact, when it is given 'flesh' there seems little to differentiate it from the Collins and Quillian model (though this is far from being a consensual statement).

The concept of semantic memory is a very new field of enquiry and errors in theory and methodology are therefore to be expected. The polarization of theories should not serve to frustrate the student of

363

memory but rather should serve to indicate the fruitfulness of the field and its importance. The over-riding concern is that logical models should not carry the day simply because of elegance, power and parsimony: the overall need is for a psychological model of man's knowledge structure and the way he develops and utilizes such a structure. Semantic memory research has a very long way to go, but it has made its first faltering steps, and we must now be concerned with its growth to maturity.

FURTHER READING

Baddeley, A. D. (1972) 'Human Memory'. In P. C. Dodwell, ed., *New Horizons in Psychology 2*. Penguin.

Baddeley, A. D. (1976) *The Psychology of Memory*. Harper and Row.

Gregg, V. (1975) *Human Memory*. Methuen.

Herriot, P. (1974) *Attributes of Memory*. Methuen.

Wright, D., Taylor, A., Davies, D., Slukin, W., Lee, S., and Reason, J. (1970) *Introducing Psychology: An Experimental Approach*. Penguin.

17 Intelligence
JOHN RADFORD with Clive Hollin

The measurement of intelligence

One of the most basic problems faced by psychologists is that, so it seems, no two people are exactly alike. Even identical twins (see below) are not identical in every respect; and each has his own thoughts and feelings which are his alone, however similar they may often be to those of the twin. This problem is not shared by many other sciences, or at least is less serious. Physicists, for example, seek to understand the forces underlying all matter. Dynamics is concerned with general laws of movement, not primarily with particular moving objects. Even biologists deal mainly with classes and sub-classes rather than with individual members of a species.

Some psychologists, however (for example, Gordon Allport, 1897–1967), wish to argue that it is precisely uniqueness that we must study; it is precisely individuality that makes us human. Partly for this reason, some psychologists (for example, H. J. Eysenck (b. 1916) maintain that the central concern of psychology is the study of individual differences.

The differences between people have fascinated scholars, scientists, and writers for centuries. From at least the time of Hippocrates (c. 460 B.C.) there have been attempts to devise some kind of orderly classification. But systematic attempts to measure the differences, to establish their distribution, range, and limits, have been made only in the last two hundred years. For various reasons, the greatest amount of effort, at least until quite recently, has gone into the study of intellectual abilities; and in particular, into the investigation of what has come to be labelled intelligence.

Definitions of intelligence

Psychologists are sometimes criticized for trying to study intelligence when they cannot agree on what it is. This criticism is due to a misunderstanding of the purpose of scientific definitions. These are perhaps best thought of as labels or direction-signs. They are useful if they are generally understood and agreed upon. The sign 'exit' is useful, without having to define precisely the nature of exits or say whether the doors are hinged, sliding, or revolving. The sign 'way out' would do just as well. (Signs can be misleading. There is the story of the showman who, in order to hurry the crowd along, labelled the way out 'This way to the egress'.)

It is only fair to admit that psychologists themselves have, especially in the early years, contributed to the confusion, partly by their disagreements, and partly by apparently thinking that definitions are not so much merely convenient labels as declarations of territorial rights. It will be useful to try to see what psychologists have intended to convey in using the term 'intelligence'.

As Burt (1955) points out, the concept of intelligence came into vogue largely due to an upsurge of interest in the writings of Herbert Spencer (1820–1903) and Francis Galton (1822–1911) who were among the first to use the term more-or-less in its modern sense. For different reasons, they both believed in the existence of a general ability superordinate to and distinct from special abilities; an ability which underlay intellectual achievements of all kinds. This notion received support from the hierarchical view of the nervous system expounded by the leading neurologists of the period John Hughlings Jackson (1834–1911) and Charles Sherrington (1857–1952). Cyril Burt himself accepted the theory of a general cognitive capacity probably dependent upon the number, complexity of connections, and organization of the nerve cells in the cerebral cortex. The concept of 'intelligence' gradually became widely accepted, and attempts to define it proliferated. There have been perhaps three main sorts of definition: *intuitive* definitions have relied on experience and judgement; *logical* definitions try to tease out the implications of the way the word is actually used; and the *empirical* approach which generally starts from accepted usage and from what has been scientifically established so far, derives hypotheses from this, seeks evidence to test the hypotheses, and tries to construct a theoretical model to accommodate the results. Here are some examples:

Intuitive: 'The ability to carry on abstract thinking' (Terman); 'The capacity to acquire capacity' (Woodrow); 'The power of good responses from the point of view of truth or fact' (Thorndike).

Vernon (1960) has classified definitions of this type as biological, psychological, or operational. Freeman (1962) divides them into those

366

emphasizing (a) power of adapting to the environment; (b) capacity for learning; (c) capacity for abstract thinking.

Definitions of this type may be useful starting points, but cannot really be accepted as conclusive.

Logical: Probably the most important analysis is that of Gilbert Ryle (*The Concept of Mind*, 1949). He argued that 'intelligence' is not to be considered as an entity inside the organism, causing it to act in a certain way; nor is it an attribute such as 'tall' or 'British'; rather it is a dispositional concept describing certain sorts of behaviour. However there is no list of behaviours which can be always so described. Rather, any sort of activity can, in principle, be carried on intelligently or unintelligently—playing cards, washing dishes, or resolving mathematical equations. To say that someone is intelligent means that he characteristically acts in intelligent ways in the things that he does. And what that means is that, for example, he acts in ways logically related to the end he wants to achieve; that he is ready to deal with new circumstances if they arise; that he is able to innovate.

Miles (1957) has described intelligence as not only a 'disposition word' but also as 'polymorphous' and 'open'. Polymorphous means that, as with a word like 'games' or 'farming', two examples may have no individual characteristics in common. Open means that the list of possible characteristics of intelligent behaviour is endless.

Empirical: This approach originates with the work of Francis Galton (1822–1911) and was continued by a line of British psychologists, Karl Pearson (1857–1936), Charles Spearman (1863–1945), and Cyril Burt (1883–1971), who were closely associated with University College, London. These men favoured the concept of one general quality of 'intelligence', common to a wide range of activities, though they had somewhat different ideas about the nature of this quality. The idea became famous with Spearman's 'two-factor' theory (1927). He concluded that a number of psychological capacities existed, each involving both a general intellectual factor and another factor specific to that capacity. The first he labelled 'g' or general intelligence; and he considered that it consisted essentially in the ability to see relationships.

A parallel line of thought developed in the United States, where stress was laid rather on the analysis of intellectual abilities into a number of separate factors. Thurston (1938) felt that the evidence justified the naming of seven 'primary mental abilities'. Guilford (1967) has developed this further and defined no fewer than 120 factors which constitute 'intelligence'.

To an extent, this difference depends less on basic theoretical issues than on preferences for what are considered the most economical and practical ways of interpreting the results of factor analyses (see below).

367

Reliability and validity

Given that it is possible to identify, from whatever standpoint, some important intellectual ability or capacity, it is clearly useful to be able to measure it. From the start, the measurement of psychological characteristics—often referred to as psychometrics—has had both a theoretical and a practical purpose. Galton's purpose was to identify those qualities that made for great achievement in individuals and in the race, and then find means of increasing them. Binet and Burt both had very practical educational problems to solve, while the need to classify large numbers of army recruits when the United States entered the First World War in 1915, led to the production of the very influential group tests named the Army alpha and Army beta.

To be of use, any measuring instrument must be *reliable* and *valid*. *Reliability* is often interpreted as consistency; but, as Cronbach (1960) points out, the term often covers two rather different aspects. He distinguishes between the *internal consistency* of a test, the extent to which the different parts or items agree with each other; and *stability*, the degree to which the test produces consistent results when used for successive groups of subjects.

The best-known way of establishing internal consistency is the split-half method. The items of the test are divided into two groups; they are all scored for each of a set of subjects, and the two sets of scores are correlated. An improvement on this is provided by the Kuder-Richardson method, which gives, not just the correlation coefficient for one arbitrary division of the items, but the average coefficient that would result from splitting the items in every possible way. To establish stability, the test-retest method is generally used. The test is given to the same group of subjects on two occasions, with an interval between in which it is hoped that the subjects will have forgotten their first responses but will not have altered substantially in their performance.

It should be clear that reliability is a relative, not an absolute, matter. It depends upon assumptions (such as the stability of subjects) and upon decisions about the selection of groups of subjects and conditions of administration.

Validity refers to the question of whether we know what a test is measuring. It is sometimes said that a test is valid if it measures what it is supposed to measure. This is slightly misleading since, because of the theoretical uncertainties surrounding psychological concepts such as intelligence, we do not always know what a test ought to be measuring. Some cases of invalidity are relatively obvious: for example, if a test involved a lot of writing, we might be measuring handwriting skill rather than intelligence. There are several ways of improving validity, or perhaps better several varieties of validity. These are summarized in a report of the American Psychological Association (1954). The most relevant to intelligence are concurrent validity and predictive validity.

Concurrent validity and *predictive validity* refer to the comparison of scores on the test with scores obtained from some other source. This could be another test; or performance on a task or series of tasks; or judgements of trained observers. The difference between concurrent and predictive validity is that in the first case the two sets of scores are taken at or about the same time; in the second, they are separated by an interval, possibly of several years. It will be seen that both have an element of circularity: for example, if a test is validated on children against the judgements of their teachers, those judgements are almost certain to be affected by what the teachers know of their children's performance on similar tests.

Construct validity hopes to avoid this. The idea is that a test should be derived from some theory which has testable consequences. This is rather obviously desirable, but also obviously difficult, due to the lack of any generally accepted theory. In principle, construct validity, if established, would ensure that the test measured 'real' intelligence or what not. It is, at best, an unsolved conceptual puzzle whether such a term as 'real intelligence' has any meaning. However, the nearest approach to it is certainly provided by factor analysis, which we discuss later.

For completeness we should mention *face validity*, which means, approximately, whether a test looks valid. This makes good sense for tests of, say, history knowledge, for clearly the questions should be about items on the syllabus. But for psychological tests it is much less appropriate.

Standardization
Standardization is a concept analogous to calibration. It is the process of ensuring that the measuring instrument accurately corresponds to the appropriate criteria. Thermometers, for example, can be checked against standards of heat such as the boiling point of water. It was realized by Galton that there are no such objective absolutes for psychological qualities. New tests of intelligence can only be checked against other measures of 'intelligence', which may be tests, or achievements, or the judgements of other people, and so on.

In standardizing a test we are seeking to establish a scale of measurement. Such scales can be more or less informative and the advance in the development of a test consists in moving from a nominal scale (i.e., classifying) to an ordinal scale (i.e., ranking), to an interval scale (in which items are an equal distance apart). There are also ratio scales which start from an absolute zero, but very few psychological measures are of this kind. Intelligence tests are normally of the interval type.

The process of standardizing involves the administration of numbers

369

of possible test items to large groups of people, who represent the 'standard' population. Some items will prove to be valid and reliable and will be retained; others will not and will be rejected. The process is much more complex than this suggests, for judgements must be made about the actual construction of items, their balance in the test as a whole, avoidance of response bias, etc. The last of these, to give one example, can be readily demonstrated. Ask a group of subjects to imagine they are answering a questionnaire, no matter on what, in which the answer to each if item is yes or no. Then ask them to write down their replies to the first three items. On the first item, there will almost invariably be a large majority of yeses.

It must also be noted that no population chosen for standardizing a test can possibly be fully representative of the human race as a whole. The most that normally can be looked for as practical is that it is representative of one race in one country; and even this is a very long and expensive task. This must be remembered when the test is used, as tests often are, to assess individuals from other groups. This is not useless, but does involve a further set of judgements and assumptions.

The result of the standardization process is a set of norms for the completed test which takes the form of a distribution of scores given by the standard population. It is generally assumed that psychological variables, and intelligence in particular, will tend to be normally distributed. The concept of a normal distribution is derived from statistical probability theory and was initially developed by Gauss (1809).

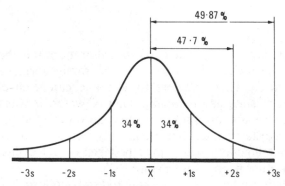

Fig. 17.1 The normal distribution. $\overline{X}$ indicates that the mean, or arithmetic average. s indicates a standard deviation. This is a measure of the spread of the data, such that 68% fall within one standard deviation above and one below the mean. These two figures can be used to summarize results. Thus, if the heights of men were measured, they might be summarized (in inches) as $M = 67 \pm 3$. This would mean that the arithmetic average was 5′ 7″; 68% of men were between 5′ 4″ and 5′ 10″; 95.4% between 5′ 1″ and 6′ 1″; and so on. (After Radford and Kirby.)

The assumption relating 'normality' to psychology was first made by Galton, who argued that, as intellectual abilities must have a physical basis, they should follow the normal distribution as other physical traits (such as height) had been shown to do by Quetelet (1835).

In reality, it is found that natural phenomena tend to fit the normal (or Gaussian) curve which is a mathematical abstraction. An example of such an approximation is given in Figure 17.2.

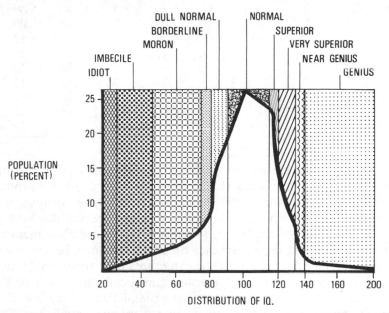

Fig. 17.2 Interpretation of intelligence quotients on the Stanford-Binet. (After Merrill.)

One particular difficulty with psychological phenomena is that they cannot be observed directly, like height, but must be inferred from behaviour. The investigator has to decide what is to count as intelligent in order to measure it; and one criterion for the choice is that the items will yield a normal distribution. There is, however, a logical reason why psychological variables must be normally distributed.

Another important aspect of the normal distribution is that it underlies factor analysis, one assumption of which is that the data do in fact conform to this pattern.

The use of factor analysis in research on intelligence

What is factor analysis?

Factor analysis derives from the concept of correlation (see Ch. 4), the extent to which two variables go together. In studying the structure of human abilities it is usual to administer a number of tests to a large subject population and obtain a score for each test. All these scores can then be intercorrelated, yielding a *correlation matrix*. An example is shown in Table 17.1.

Table 17.1 Correlation matrix for nine aptitude tests (from Guilford, 1967)

Tests	2	3	4	5	6	7	8	9
1	.38	.55	.06	−.04	.05	.07	.05	.09
2		.36	.40	.28	.40	.11	.15	.13
3			.10	.01	.18	.13	.12	.10
4				.32	.60	.04	.06	.13
5					.35	.08	.13	.11
6						.01	.06	.07
8							.45	.32
								.32

The three outlined clusters of correlations, because of their sizeable correlation coefficients, indicate that these are groups of tests with something in common not shared by the other tests. Factor analysis is a mathematical technique which enables us to make specific this kind of interpretation. The final result of a factor analysis is usually a measure of how much variation in performance on all the tests may be accounted for by one common factor, and of the extent to which additional factors are necessary. It is possible to 'extract' statistically the effect of the factor common to all the variables (the general factor) and still find correlation patterns suggestive of further common influences. The process is repeated until all the remaining correlations are statistically non-significant.

Thus if we factor analyse the correlation of Table 17.1, we first compute the correlation of each test with a few factors. Such correlation between test scores and factors are known as factor loadings; if a test correlates 0.02 on Factor I., 0.16 on Factor II., and 0.83 on Factor III., it is said to be most heavily loaded on Factor III. The correlation matrix of Table 17.1 yields the factor matrix of Table 17.2.

The outline factor loadings show tests which are most highly correlated with each of the factors. The clusters are the same as those in Table 17.1, but, due to the analysis, have a greater accuracy. Test 2, since it is loaded equally on Factors II and III, cannot be a 'factor pure' test.

The factors which have been identified must now be interpreted. This is done by inspecting the contents of the tests which are most heavily weighted on each factor. They may be named with a plausible name (such as 'general intelligence') or with one made up for the purpose, or just numbered. Thus, whilst the factor analysis itself is a mathematical

Table 17.2 Factor matrix for nine aptitude tests and three factors. (From Guilford, 1967.)

Tests	Factors I	II	III
1	.75	−.01	.08
2	.44	.48	.16
3	.72	.07	.15
4	.08	.76	.08
5	−.01	.49	−.01
6	.16	.73	.02
7	−.03	.04	.64
8	.02	.05	.66
9	−.01	.10	.47

process, the determining and naming of the factors is a strictly psychological undertaking.

Criticisms and comments

Whilst factor analysis is an important and very useful mathematical tool which may be gainfully employed by psychologists, it has definite limitations, among which are these:

1. As already indicated, the statistically-produced factors do not emerge conveniently labelled 'general intelligence' or 'spatial ability', etc. The interpretation of a statistical factor as a psychological dimension requires careful justification.

2. The method itself can only, like a computer, give answers to the questions it is set about the data presented to it. The method gives no indication as to what material should be analysed at the start. It cannot give us information about abilities for which there is no valid test.

3. The final result of the analysis is not a description of the composition of intelligence, or any other psychological quality. It simply provides a number of mathematically equivalent answers. To fasten upon any of these and form a theory from it involves further assumptions, either mathematical or psychological.

4. There exist alternative methods of factor analysis which yield slightly differing results. There is also some debate about the precision with which the factors are determined. The issues are complex and, as yet, unsettled. As a result of the differing analyses the theoretical interpretations of the test results differ.

Spearman and general intelligence, 'g'
Charles Spearman (1863–1945) is generally recognized as both the inventor and first user of factor analysis, although Pearson was working along similar lines at the same time. In 1904 he presented the results of analysing test scores in this way. He concluded that individual differences in test performance could be accounted for by one general factor, common to all the tests, and a series of specific factors, each peculiar to one task. The general factor he labelled 'g' or general intelligence. This was the origin of the 'two-factor' theory of intelligence, which led to the extremely influential hierarchical model developed by later British workers. Spearman believed he could identify the essential nature of intelligence. This was, in brief, the ability to see relationships. This concept has been embodied in very many subsequent test items.

Sir Cyril Burt and the hierarchical system
Cyril Burt (1883–1971) was the first British educational psychologist (1912) and remained an influential figure to the end of his life. It now seems certain that in later life, from about 1950, he fabricated data on twin studies to support his views on intelligence. Those views, however, cannot therefore be ignored.

One of Burt's major theoretical contributions was the extension of the two-factor notion to a hierarchical model. He argued on both theoretical and empirical grounds for four types of factor: general, group, specific and error factors. As already mentioned, this seemed to be consistent with Sherrington's work on the organization of the nervous system. As Burt put it: 'The measurement of any individual for any one of a set of traits may be regarded as a function of four kinds of components: namely, those characteristic of (1) all the traits, (2) some of the traits, (3) the particular trait in question whenever it is measured, (4) the particular trait in question as measured on this particular occasion' (Burt, 1970).

The first of these Burt identified as intelligence or 'innate general cognitive ability'. At the next level, a number of studies show that the most important distinction is between verbal and non-verbal abilities. Figure 17.3 shows how such a hierarchical model might be conceived.

L. L. Thurstone and primary mental abilities
As we previously noted, the method of factor analysis, whilst providing the means by which we may simplify and interpret complex performances, does not in itself tell us how to do this. It provides a set of interpretations; to choose between them, a new mathematical or psychological model is needed.

Such a principle was introduced by Thurstone (1938) under the name 'simple structure'. This he derived from intuition, reasoning that in a large and representative set of cognitive tests some abilities will be

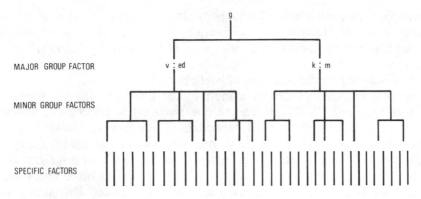

MAJOR GROUP FACTOR

MINOR GROUP FACTORS

SPECIFIC FACTORS

g   = GENERAL INTELLIGENCE
v : ed = VERBAL - EDUCATIONAL ABILITY
k : m   = SPATIAL - MECHANICAL ABILITY

Fig. 17.3 Suggested arrangement of the hierarchical arrangement of intellectual abilities. It should be noted that this is a suggestion. No studies have firmly established that this is a correct model in every detail. (After Vernon.)

relevant to some of the tests and not to others. For example, it would not be expected that verbal ability will influence performance on a test of numerical ability. It is these separate factors which are most meaningful to isolate. However, it was found that a satisfactory simple structure was not always present in the data analysis. This led to a second innovation, the use of correlated factors. The previously mentioned studies used statistically independent factors, which means that there could not be a systematic relationship between general intelligence and, say, spatial ability. Thurstone argued that such relationships are, indeed possible, and based much of his work on this premise.

In a series of studies Thurstone identified seven factors or 'primary mental abilities':

S—Spatial ability
P—Perceptual speed
N—Numerical ability
V—Verbal meaning
M—Memory
W—Verbal fluency
 I or R—Inductive reasoning

With younger children, not all these factors were found, and Thurstone eventually produced three versions, for different age groups, of his test for primary mental abilities.

An interesting outcome of this approach is that since all the scores on these factors are correlated it is possible to compute a 'second-order' analysis of the factors themselves. The resulting super-factor which emerges is clearly comparable with the 'g' of Spearman or Burt.

J. P. Guilford and the structure of intellect

The most extreme version of a multi-factor theory so far developed is that of Guilford (1966). He argued that we must consider three dimensions in analysing intellectual capacities. These are (a) the basic psychological functions involved, e.g., memory, or *operations*; (b) the type of material being processed, e.g., semantic or symbolic, or *products*; and (c) the form that the information takes in the course of being processed, e.g., units or classes, or *contents*. According to Guilford, the number of possible operations is five, of products six, and of contents four. This gives a total of intellectual abilities of $5 \times 6 \times 4 = 120$. This is expressed diagramatically in Figure 17.4.

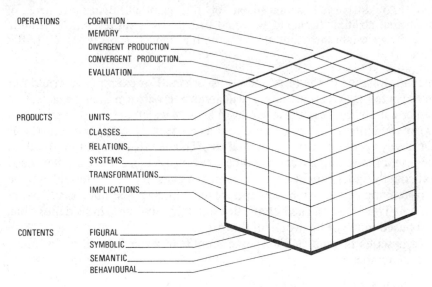

Fig. 17.4   Guilford's scheme of ability factors. (After Guilford.)

This was a theoretical analysis. Guilford has carried out extensive investigation to test the reality of the theory, and see how far it describes real-life behaviour such as solving problems. It appears that there is good evidence for some of the factors or abilities, and less good evidence for others. Guilford and his co-workers seem a little like astronomers searching for new stars which they know ought to be there but which have not yet been established. It also seems that for practical purposes of predicting what a given person will be able to do in certain circumstances, say at school or university, Guilford's complex of abilities is less useful than the simpler models or indeed just one measure of 'general intelligence'.

R. B. Cattell and crystallized and fluid intelligence

Cattell (1963) proposed a theory of intelligence which presupposes that the general factor found in tests is in actual fact a function of two conceptually distinct, but correlated, factors. These he named crystallized and fluid intelligence. Crystallized intelligence applies where what is required are habits of skilled judgement which have become set through learning and experience. Such skills are of less use in new situations, requiring new or adopted responses. Here fluid intelligence is appropriate. Although Cattell suggests ways of separating these two experimentally, it is not clear whether they are in fact two abilities or merely two modes of working.

Cattell has also argued that intellectual factors cannot really be isolated from personality factors. The establishment of measurable traits of personality is more difficult even than for intelligence, but Cattell has shown correlations between some of these, such as motivation, with others such as achievement, which in turn is related to intellectual abilities.

The origins of intelligence

Much of the debate over the origins of intelligence has centred on the issue as to whether it is a product of the environment or, on the other hand, inherited. Practically every possible position has been proposed and attacked, and the issue has at times been utterly confused by misunderstandings, ignorance, and political arguments. Psychologists must be aware of such factors, and of the social and moral effects of their work. But they must strive to distinguish the various issues, while acknowledging the importance of each.

We should distinguish here between two related areas of enquiry: behaviour genetics, which is a name for the investigation of hereditary correlates of behaviour, and genetics, which refers to the structure and workings of the physical mechanisms of inheritance.

While the term 'hereditary' usually implies resemblances between parents and offspring, there are also systematic lacks of resemblances which give information as to how the mechanisms of heredity works. We must distinguish between the phenotype and the genotype: that is, the characteristics which an individual manifests and the genetic characteristics which an individual inherits but may or may not exhibit. The hereditary units that an individual receives from his parents are carried by *chromosomes* which are structures found within every cell of the body. A chromosome is composed of many individual determinants

377

of heredity called *genes*. These are large molecules of deoxyribonucleic acid or DNA. Genes occur in pairs, one of each pair coming from the sperm (male) chromosomes, and the other from the ovum (female) chromosomes. There are 46 chromosomes per body cell and approximately 1000 genes per chromosome: hence, it is extremely unlikely that, by chance, any two human beings would have the same heredity. There are exceptions to this in the case of multiple births, including twins. Twins occur in the human population at a frequency of 12.5 per 1000 births; triplets at 6.4 per 1000. Only twins are sufficiently frequent to yield reliable psychological results. However, only *monozygotic twins* share the same heredity. In this case one fertilized ovum splits into two, each with the same chromosomes and genes. These are the only truly identical twins. In the case of *dizygotic twins*, two separate ova are fertilized at the same time (by two sperms): the resulting twins are no more alike than any pair of siblings (brothers and sisters).

It is best to regard as 'nature' only the genetic constitution of the individual, a particular combination of genes determined at the moment of fertilization. All other influences from that point on should be regarded as 'nurture' or environment. Thus both pre-natal and post-natal conditions are 'environmental'. Now it is known that a given environmental factor can interact differently with different specific genetic material. For example, a rise in temperature affects the number of eye facets in the fruit fly *Drosophila*. But identical changes in temperature have different effects upon flies having different gene constitutions. Further, every individual member of a species has a slightly different environment; even identical twins are born one after the other. And it is a fundamental characteristic of living things, which becomes more important the more complex the organism is, that they interact only with some aspects of the environment. Animals, and above all humans, select from the environment (see Ch. 14).

Thus, apart from having a unique genetic constitution, each member of the species has a unique environment; and each developed individual is the product of the interaction between the two. This interaction effect led D. O. Hebb (1949) to postulate two 'types' of intelligence, which he named Intelligence A and Intelligence B. These correspond to genotype and phenotype: A is an innate potential, the capacity of the brain for development; B is the ability of the developed brain. While neither can be directly observed, Hebb claimed that B is ' . . . a much more direct inference from behaviour than Intelligence A , the innate potential.'

There would probably be general agreement that it is meaningless to regard any psychological characteristic as the result of either heredity or environment alone. However, it is possible to investigate empirically the relative contributions of each set of influences. Anastasi (1958) lists five main methods: selective breeding; normative development studies; structural factors in behavioural development; the effects of prior experience upon behaviour; and studies of family resemblances, of which twin studies are a special case. As far as intelligence is concerned, it is the last method that has received the greatest attention.

Studies of family resemblances
Perhaps the most obvious move is to compare a child's intelligence with that of his parent. A representative result is that of Conrad and Jones (1940) who found that the score of either parent taken alone correlated 0.49 with that of the school-age child. This is approximately the same as the correlation they had obtained between parent and child for physical attributes such as height, and it clearly gives some indication of hereditary influence.

However, under normal conditions the environment provided by the parents presumably influences development. One way to test this is to study children raised by foster parents. There are two questions: (a) does the intelligence of children adopted early in life correlate more highly with that of the natural (biological) parents or that of the foster parents? (b) will the conditions of the foster home have an effect on the level of the children's intelligence? (generally, it is assumed it would raise it, since the most common reason for fostering is the inadequacy of a natural home.)

As may be seen from Table 17.3, Leachy (1935) found that correlation is higher with the biological parents; and later studies support this. However this is far from conclusive for several reasons. Foster parents' attitudes may be different towards children who are not their own, with unknown effects. Then again, foster parents are selected for all sorts of reasons and are not a good experimental control; for example they tend to be a much less varied group than are the natural parents.

Table 17.3 Correlation between child's IQ (Stanford Binet) and parents' IQ.

	Foster	Control
Father's IQ (Otis)	0.19	0.51
Mother's IQ (Otis)	0.24	0.51
Cultural index of home	0.46	0.51

It has also been found that placement in a 'good' home does tend to raise the intelligence scores of the adopted child beyond that predicted from the biological parents. Skeels (1966) reported the results of a long-term study first started by Skeels and Dye in 1939. Studying deprived orphanage children of approximate age nineteen months, they found a mean IQ of 64. These children were adopted between the ages of two and three years and by the age of six years the mean IQ of the group was 96. As adults they lived normal lives and the mean IQ of their children was 105. A control group of children who were not placed for adoption at an early age showed retardation throughout life. Once again, there are difficulties, for example, the measurement of IQ at so young an age as nineteen months is far from reliable.

It was Galton who suggested the study of twins to disentangle the effects of heredity and environment. As he pointed out, the advantage is that at least one side of the equation is under control, since monozygotic (MZ) twins have identical genetic constitutions.

Numerous studies of children's intelligence have shown that ordinary siblings are least alike, dizygotic (DZ) twins more alike but still close to siblings, and MZ twins most alike. Table 17.4 gives sample findings from two such studies.

Table 17.4   Resemblance of IQs of children of the same parents

Pairs of children	Number of pairs	Coefficient of correlation (r)
Ordinary siblings*	384	.53
DZ twins†	482	.63
MZ twins†	687	.87

* Source: McNemar (1942).
† Source: Nichols (1965).

The question is whether this close resemblance between MZ twins is due to their identical inheritance, or to the fact that they also share one environment. One attempt to answer this is to see what happens when MZ twins are, for one reason or another, reared apart. The result of three such studies are given in Table 17.5.

Table 17.5   Correlations between intelligence test scores of MZ twins reared apart

Study	Number of pairs	Coefficient of correlation (r)
Newman, Freeman & Holzinger (1937)	19	.76
Shields (1962)	8	.77
Juel-Neilsen (1965)	12	.68

Another relevant source is the Louisville Twin Study (Wilson, 1977), in which over 400 pairs of twins have been followed longitudinally from birth. The monozygotic pairs, reared together, correlate about 0.8. This contrasts with correlations of about 0.45 for both dizygotic twins and ordinary siblings, again reared together.

Further considerations
Galton raised three important questions regarding the origins of intelligence, and there is some, albeit inconclusive, evidence on each. These are: whether intelligence is inherited at all; if so, by what

380

mechanism does this take place; and what is the relative importance of the genetic and environmental factors.

Evidence for the inheritance of intelligence comes from the numerous findings that the closer the family, that is, the genetic relationship, the higher the degree of similarity on a range of psychological characteristics, and certainly on intelligence. One of the most convincing demonstrations of this was presented by Erlenmeyer-Kimling and Jarvik (1963), who collected the correlation coefficients from fifty-two studies of different degrees of family relationship. The results, summarized in Figure 17.5 show very clearly that correlations rise with increasing closeness of relationship. They also show, of course, that correlations rise with similarity of environment. Even unrelated persons reared together show correlations of up to 0.3.

CATEGORY		·00 10 ·20 ·30 ·40 ·50 ·60 ·70 ·80 ·90	GROUP INCLUDED
UNRELATED PERSONS	REARED APART		4
	REARED TOGETHER		5
FOSTERPARENT-CHILD			3
PARENT-CHILD			12
SIBLINGS	REARED APART		2
	REARED TOGETHER		35
T W I N S	TWO-EGG OPPOSITE SEX		9
	LIKE SEX		11
	ONE-EGG REARED APART		4
	REARED TOGETHER		14

Fig. 17.5 Correlation coefficients for intelligence test scores from 52 studies. Vertical lines represent median scores. Horizontal lines indicate the ranges. (From Erlenmeyer-Kimling and Jarvik.)

The mechanisms by which intelligence, and other characteristics, are genetically transmitted has been the subject of a great deal of modern research, of which the most famous landmark is probably the 'cracking of the genetic code' by Crick and Watson (1962). This research has concentrated on the way genetic information is coded in DNA molecules and converted into proteins via RNA (ribonucleic acid). Detailed discussion of this lies outside the scope of this Chapter.

The issue that has raised most discussion is that of the relative importance of genetic and environmental factors. It is fairly clear that both of these must be involved; and it is also self-evident that, within any population selected at random, there is a wide variation in intellectual capacity. The argument turns on attributing values to sources of variation within populations. It should be noted that it is not possible to say, in the case of any individual, how much of his intelligence (or any other trait) is inherited or otherwise, since it is impossible to partition the

381

variance in a sample of one. Further, even when variance can be partitioned, it is not justifiable to conclude that there are fixed environmental or hereditary components of intelligence: intelligence is not a product like a cake, with constituents of so many ounces of flour and so many of butter.

Thus it is rather misleading to speak of intelligence being X per cent inherited. Such a charge can be levelled against some writers, such as Burt (1966). Using a statistical method of partitioning the sources of variance in a variable, he concluded that intelligence is 80 per cent inherited and 20 per cent environmental. This was based on Burt's own twin data, which are not reliable; but Jensen (1969) reached the same conclusion from other data. The psychological difficulty is that while a potential for development is inherited, it is not known how this interacts with environmental factors to produce behaviour that can be labelled 'intelligent.'

Two sorts of criticism can be made of twin studies. There are, first, technical statistical arguments about the appropriateness of the methods used. These are highly complex, and we shall not enter into them. It is unlikely that they would affect the results very dramatically. There are also, however, some objections to the use of twin studies. Vandenberg (1966) distinguishes four main arguments. First, while we know that for MZ twins that the hereditary factors are equal, there is no way of controlling the genetic variability between groups of twins. One sample of twins may include inherited tendencies towards certain sorts of behaviour which are not, in fact, typical of twins in general. Related points that Vandenberg might have made are that twins themselves are not necessarily typical of the general population; and there is known to be a 'twinning factor', such that certain families tend to produce twins, presumably due to constitutional factors. Second, when MZ and DZ twins are compared, it is assumed that the environment is held constant; but this is not necessarily so. Third, the twin method deals only with variance within families, which is only part of the total variance; no account is taken of variance between families. Lastly, many early studies suffered from errors in identifying identical twins, which is a much more technical matter than might appear. This does not really constitute a problem now, however. On the other hand, evidence has recently been found that even so-called 'identical' twins are not necessarily genetically identical, due to the assorting of genetic material that occurs at the first splitting of the fertilized egg.

These are all important points, but Vandenberg is probably right to conclude that they are unlikely to affect the general results very greatly. On the whole, errors in one direction will be balanced out by those in an opposite direction.

A more general matter is that there seems to be fairly common agreement that, rather than attempting to quantify hereditary and environmental factors, it is more helpful to consider an interaction between different sets of factors, only some of which can yet be identified. In the next part of this Chapter we look at some of these from a slightly different point of view.

Race, culture, and class

Race
In everyday use the word 'race' most often refers to some discriminable group to which the speaker can identify himself as belonging or not belonging. Just what constitutes a separate race of human beings is often not clearly defined. The so-called 'Aryan race' which Hitler's National Socialists sought to preserve was defined by a confused collection of cultural, physical, and supposed historical factors.

The clearest, although still quite complex, way to consider race is biologically. In particular, it seems best to start with the definition that a race is a reproductive community sharing a common gene pool. This definition applies to the human population as a whole: and, thus, different races are sub-groups. All the sub-groups overlap to a greater or lesser extent. For example, Eysenck (1971) reports that estimates suggest an admixture of about 25.30 per cent white genes in present-day negroes in the USA. The overlapping is caused partly by the common origin of groups which have subsequently separated, and partly by interbreeding.

Early attempts to distinguish races depended upon obviously observable characteristics. For example Blumenbach (1775) proposed a classification based on skin colour. This is both invalid and unreliable. Modern methods make use of advances in serological genetics, which enable us to identify specific genes from the chemical reactions of the components of human blood. As the number of blood genes identified increases, so it becomes necessary to increase the number of recognized races. Morphological, that is bodily, characteristics can also be used, and Dobzhansky (1962) has proposed a system involving as many used, and Dobzhansky (1962) has proposed a system involving as many as thirty-four different characteristics. Some studies, e.g., Pollitzer (1958) use both morphological and serological methods in attempting to classify subjects according to race.

Taking the definition of a common gene pool, it is widely accepted (e.g., Garn, 1961) that three types of genetic populations can be distinguished. These can be termed geographical, local, and microgeographical or minor races. The largest unit is a population confined within a broad geographical area, such as Australian, European, Asiatic. Another example is the native population of the Americas, the Amerindians, who share, among other characteristics, a low incidence of the genes for Type B blood. The separate American peoples within the Amerindian group, such as Navahos or Guarani, are examples of 'local' races. Other examples are Basques, Gypsies, Bantu: such groups are often separated from others by physical and/or social barriers. The smallest groups it is generally useful to distinguish are termed by Gottesman (1963) 'significant pockets of variation'. He reports, for example, distinct micro-races, differing by blood-group genes, in Wales.

Thus, it is certainly possible to distinguish between races on purely biological grounds, without considering cultural factors. As has been pointed out, the races so distinguished do overlap considerably; and where the lines are drawn depends upon decisions as to the degree of difference that is important. The questions that arise for psychologists concern the possibility of behavioural differences between the races that are distinguished. There is ample evidence for differences, in, for example, sensory-motor and perceptual abilities; but here we are concerned with intellectual abilities. As it happens, it is this question that has aroused the greatest controversy. The most hotly-debated issue has concerned the Negro population of the United States, and it is on this that the greatest amount of research has been done. This issue illustrates some of the general problems.

Shuey (1966) comprehensively reviewed some hundreds of studies comparing intelligence test scores of white and Negro children. She found that these studies, with very small variance, showed that groups of white children had a mean IQ some fifteen points, or one standard deviation, higher than Negro groups. It has also been generally found that, among Negroes, females tend to score higher than males. Jensen (1969) gives an average of three or four IQ points difference. These findings are shown in Figure 17.6.

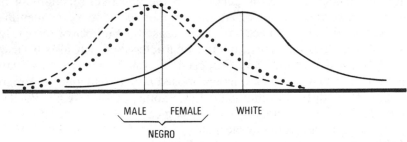

Fig. 17.6 Diagrammatic distribution of intelligence quotients of whites, and Negro males and females. (From Eysenck.)

A great variety of criticisms has been made of these and similar investigations. It has been suggested, for example, that groups of Negroes and whites are not comparable for various reasons. Shuey (1966), however, quotes a study in which two groups were matched on age, education, occupation of parents, geographical areas of childhood home, army rank, number of years in the service, marital status, urban or rural background, personality, and attitudes to test-taking. A difference of nearly one standard deviation still emerged. Again, it is suggested that Negroes are at a disadvantage when the tester is white. But Shuey gives the results of nineteen studies in which Negro children were tested by Negroes. There was no difference as compared with similar investigations using white testers.

In general, it must be accepted that the difference is a consistent one, and not due to accident or error. It is more difficult to say what can be concluded from this. Shuey argued that there must be a strong genetic component to intelligence; and Jensen (1969) and Eysenck (1971) agree. Shuey found, for example, that the differences were greater on abstract test items, which are relatively environment free as compared to verbal items. Further, genetically hybrid groups of subjects score closer to the white average than do the purer Negro groups. On the other hand it appears that southern Negroes are inferior to northern on IQ; and that those who migrate to the North gain in IQ. But it could well be, of course, that these groups are also genetically different. Indeed this is possibly an example of different genetic constitutions interacting differently with different environments.

Jensen (1969) has further argued that Negro and white children should be given different styles of education, fitted to their different modes of intellectual functioning. This is far more contentious, since we do not really know what sorts of education are best suited to different children.

It must also be remembered that the difference is only an average one: even on the standard tests, very many individual Negroes score above the white average.

However, perhaps the crux of the argument is that, as has already been explained, any test of intelligence is only a selection from the extremely wide range of intellectual skills that human beings can display. This sample is, in general, correlated with success in the society in which the test was constructed. But we cannot infer from test scores anything about superiority in general. Nor can we conclude that groups who score below the average of the standardizing population are necessarily less competent generally. This is because competence is defined by the environment, not by tests. As Cole and Bruner (1971) put it: 'The problem is to identify the range of capacities readily manifested in different groups and then to enquire whether the range is adequate to the individual's needs in various cultural settings'.

Although the greatest amount of attention has been paid to the Negro-white issue, there is increasing evidence from other groups. For example, Lesser, Fifer and Clarke (1965) compared six- and seven-year-

385

old children of Chinese, Jewish, Negro, and Puerto Rican communities in New York City, in respect of their verbal reasoning, numerical, and spatial abilities. Distinctively different patterns appeared, which were quite consistent across social classes within the communities. The Jewish group for example, excelled at verbal ability, the Chinese at spatial (the full results are given by Butcher, 1968).

In an important series of studies Vernon (1965) compared West Indian, Canadian, American Indian, Eskimo, and Scottish children. A complex pattern emerges. It is clear that groups from a poor cultural and socio-economic background, with little education and unstable home life, do less well on tests, particularly in practical-spatial and some abstract non-verbal abilities. But perhaps the main lesson is the difficulty of disentangling such test performances from actual attainments, either educational or practical, and sorting out the complicated interaction of causes.

Culture

In the two investigations just mentioned the groups are distinguished by both racial and cultural factors. The latter are even harder to define exactly. Broadly, 'culture' refers to the humanly-created environment in which each individual lives. Culture does not include the physical environment, but it does include the uses to which the environment is put. Similarly, culture does not include genetically determined characteristics, such as skin colour, but it does include the behaviour that may be occasioned by members of a group sharing a particular colour. Cultural groups, even more than racial ones, overlap and intermingle. There are now probably no groups remaining which are not in some measure affected by western culture.

Nevertheless it is still possible to distinguish culturally different groups on the basis of observed differences in basic human practices such as child-rearing, marriage, tool-making, food-getting, religion, and so forth.

There is a good deal of evidence that between such groups there are also more strictly psychological differences. For example Gregory (1966) reports evidence that Zulus are less susceptible to the Muller-Lyer illusion than are Europeans. This is a relatively trivial, but at least measurable, effect, due, Gregory argues, to the 'uncarpentered' environment in which Zulus traditionally live.

The question of intellectual differences is much more complex. Some of the reasons have already been discussed, but there are further problems. It must be first noted that, when any test of intelligence is given to members of a group, what is being measured is a sample of Hebb's Intelligence B. Indeed Vernon (1969) has called this sample 'Intelligence C'. Any cross-cultural comparisons made, are made between Intelligence C samples, which may or may not be valid and reliable.

Further, it must be stressed again that any test of intelligence derives its validity, ultimately, from comparisons with other assessments of behaviour, which are themselves cultural matters. No attempt has, so far, been made to establish tests which would be universally valid. It is true that there are some theories of intelligence, most notably those of Spearman and of Piaget, which claim such validity: but their claims have yet to be tested by investigation. There is some evidence that cross-cultural comparisons can be made using Piaget's stages of cognitive development, but even here it is difficult to be sure just what a particular result means. For example Laurendeau and Pinard (1962) reported a large scale experiment which showed that measures of Piaget's stages could be established in a different population from Piaget's; in this case, children in Montreal. But it is quite a complex and even subjective matter to assess Piagetian stages (see Ch. 20).

Thirdly, the very activity of assessing intellectual functions is one which is strange to many cultural groups. Irvine (1966) points out that the learning task involved in just becoming familiar with and understanding the concept of multiple-choice items is quite formidable for most Africans. He lists six sources of unwanted variance in test scores. Irvine was particularly concerned with African groups, but the problems are more general.

1. The content of the test itself.
2. The form and style of the test.
3. The transfer which takes place between practice items and actual test items, especially when the material is unfamiliar.
4. The particular educational or cultural bias of the test items.
5. The motivational influence of strange (other culture) testers who are likely to be European.
6. Error variance.

It may be pointed out that the only way to equate cultures absolutely would be to make them identical, in which case the possibility of cross-cultural comparisons would cease to exist.

Nevertheless, even given all the difficulties, and the inadequacies of measuring instruments, it is possible to establish some of the factors that definitely do affect the level of test scores in a given population, remembering that it is Vernon's Intelligence C that is in question. Vernon (1965) lists eight such factors.

1. Physiological and nutritional deficit.
2. Perceptual deprivation in pre-school years.
3. Repression of independence and constructive play.

4. Family insecurity and lack of playfulness.
5. Female dominance (this may favour verbal as compared to spatial abilities).
6. Defective education.
7. Linguistic handicaps.
8. Adult roles and adolescent aspirations (in minority cultures, children may be affected by gradual realization of their depressed status, lack of opportunities, etc.).

Although these are all clearly-identified factors, it must still be remembered that they constitute handicaps only in relation to some standard. It is relatively easy to say what is the standard of nutrition required for normal development, but much harder for a psychological variable such as male or female dominance, which in any case varies widely even within a culture. It is very likely that individual children are differently affected by even the 'same' amount of dominance for example.

Despite all these problems, it is possible to explore more and more systematically the modes of thinking characteristic of different cultures. Several of the leaders in this work are or have been based at Harvard University, such as psychologist Jerome Bruner, and anthropologists, such as Michael Cole. Although this work is not strictly on 'intelligence', one example may be given to illustrate the approach.

Cole, Gay, Glick, and Sharp reported a series of studies of the Kpelle people of Liberia in *The Cultural Context of Learning and Thinking* (1971). As well as general observations of cultural practices, they used many experimental techniques to examine such abilities as logical reasoning and conceptual thinking. Probably their major conclusion was that the differences in thought processes between different cultural groups lie, not so much in the processes themselves, as in the situations to which they are applied. The Kpelle subjects, for example, were quite able to reason logically, but were more accustomed to do so in social situations. Abstract problems (such as most intelligence tests include) were new to them.

Cole *et al.* think it significant that the Kpelle equivalent for 'clever' was not applied to such activities as rice farming or car repairing but to skill in social relationships. A farmer might be thought lazy or hard-working, but not 'clever'. Similarly, they found subjects could, for example, clearly explain how children should be raised, but not the principles of good house-building (even though they could, in practical terms, do both).

Class
Like the previous two ways of distinguishing groups (race and culture) social class is not easy to define exactly. Perhaps the simplest criterion is an economic one, since it is a fairly objective fact that some families

have higher incomes than others. This, however, gives us a division which does not exactly match what most people mean by 'social class'. It might be argued, for example, that (say) a grammar school teacher in a country town, a university graduate, is more likely to correspond with what most people mean by 'middle class' than a 'working class' dock worker who may have a higher income. In considering studies of class, therefore, it is desirable to know what criteria are being used: income, occupation, education, style of life, or others.

One of the largest and most famous studies relevant here, however, did not start from a definition of social class. This began in September 1921 when L. M. Terman and his co-workers selected from the state schools in California the 1500 most gifted children aged 3 12: approximately the top 1 per cent on standard intelligence tests. A great deal of other information was also gathered about these children, and the group has been re-examined at intervals over the subsequent years.

About a third of the group came from the homes of professional people, and a half from those in the higher ranks of business. Fewer than 7 per cent came from families of semi-skilled or unskilled workers. A second very conclusive finding was that the more intelligent, in general, excelled in almost every other respect: they were, rather naturally, more advanced in school work; but they were also taller, fitter, better adjusted socially, and more likely to be leaders in group activities. As the group made its way through life, these advantages were, on the whole, maintained. The large majority retained or improved their social status, many becoming distinguished in particular fields.

It will be obvious that this work does not show why high IQ scores are linked to social class; and it is most likely that parents in the middle and upper classes not only transmit through heredity some of their own superior ability, but also provide more intellectually stimulating home environments for their children.

The complex way in which the different variables interact has been illustrated in many other studies. For example Douglas (1964) reports several relevant findings from a sample of 5000 children aged 8–11 years. Social class was determined on the basis of parental employment and parental education. Children from the higher classes tended to be in higher streams at school: not merely higher than average, but higher than would be predicted on the basis of test scores alone. This suggests an attitude or motivation factor; and this is supported by the fact that a change in parental employment was reflected in performance on tests. The importance of the home background is suggested by the fact that, while poor attendance records did not significantly affect the test scores of the upper and middle class children, a record of frequent absences was associated with poor performances in lower-middle and working class children.

Similarly, it is possible to undertake more detailed analyses of the various factors which contribute to social background. Fraser (1959) studied Scottish 12-year-old secondary school pupils. The results are summarized in Table 17.6.

Table 17.6 Correlation of background factors with intelligence and achievement of school children (from Fraser, 1959)

	IQ	Achievement
Parents' education rating	.423	.490
General book reading in home	.208	.329
Newspaper and magazine reading	.381	.398
Income	.350	.444
(Small) family size	.404	.458
Living space	.363	.447
Occupation (not correlated but significant at .001 level)		
Abnormal or broken home environment (not correlated but significant at .01 level)		
Parents' educational and vocational aspirations	.297	.391
Parental encouragement	.604	.660
General family atmosphere	.393	.460
Mother at work	n.s.	n.s.
r_m	.687	.752

It is clear from these results that several indices of socio-economic status are substantially related to measured intelligence, and even more strongly to educational attainment.

An even wider picture results from the extensive surveys reported by Wiseman (1964) and carried out in Manchester, Salford, and Stockport. An entire year-group of 14-year-old children in maintained (state) schools in Manchester was studied in 1951.

Performances on tests of intelligence, reading, and arithmetic were correlated with indices for a number of social variables. Table 17.7 shows the relationships between these variables and the extremes of the performance scores, labelled here 'backwardness' and 'brightness'.

It must be noted that these particular results were obtained from secondary modern school children. The absence of the selected upper stream may account for the higher correlations with backwardness as compared to those with brightness.

In contrast to Fraser's results, correlations are higher for intelligence than for attainment. This may be because the social variables here are more general than Fraser's more specific 'home' factors. Or it might be that these variables are more closely linked to heredity. From a similar study in Salford, however, Warburton concludes that environmental factors play the largest role in determining intelligence test scores; and Wiseman states that an adverse environment affects most seriously children of above-average ability.

390

Table 17.7 Product-moment correlations between attainment and social variables (from Wiseman, 1964)

Variable	Backwardness			Brightness		
	Intell.	Read.	Arith.	Intell.	Read.	Arith.
Mental deficiency	.84	.64	.60	−.55	−.06	−.22
Birth-rate	.69	.37	.53	−.30	.02	−.28
Illegitimate children	.66	.48	.72	−.43	.07	−.15
TB rate	.63	.32	.51	−.16	.16	−.22
Neglected children	.50	.23	.57	−.23	−.25	−.21
J-index	.37	.35	.12	−.25	−.16	−.18
Death rate	.36	.15	−.01	−.08	.14	−.20
Persons per acre	.33	.37	.51	−.19	.14	−.22
Infantile mortality	.25	.16	.14	−.20	−.17	−.09
Infectious diseases	.03	−.21	.08	−.00	−.18	.00
Average correlation	.47	.29	.38	−.24	−.03	−.18

Source: Wiseman (1964).

From the multiplicity of figures produced by these and many other studies, it is perhaps possible to draw some rather general conclusions. Vernon (1969), for example, lists the reasons he feels are responsible for the lower effective intelligence (in terms of test scores) and educational attainment of lower class children.

1. Some genetic differences between the classes.
2. Lower-class children receive poorer pre- and post-natal care.
3. The parents of lower class children do not raise them to be as motivated towards intellectual achievement.

These are of course generalizations, to which there are always many individual exceptions; and they relate, as has been stressed throughout, to measures which are always relative to the culture in which they have been standardized.

FURTHER READING

Kirby, R. and Radford, J. (1976) *Individual Differences*. Methuen.
Tyler, L. E. (1963) *Tests and Measurements*. New York, Prentice-Hall.
Butcher, H. J. (1968) *Human Intelligence: Its Nature and Assessment*. Methuen.
Vernon, P. E. (1979) *Intelligence: Heredity and Environment*. Freeman.

18 Manipulation of information
JOHN RADFORD with Clive Hollin

Thinking

Living organisms are distinguished from inanimate objects by their possession of a number of characteristics. One of these is the ability to reproduce; another, the ability to absorb and incorporate material from the environment. Further characteristics distinguish animals from plants, such as the ability to move from one place to another and the development of sensitivity to stimuli of different kinds, such as heat, light, pressure, and sound. No one of these characteristics constitutes an absolute rule: some plants show such sensitivity, for example, the Venus fly trap. In evolutionary theory, however, a characteristic which is conducive to survival will have a greater chance of being perpetuated. Over many generations, if this condition continues, characteristics will develop further and further, thus bringing about the differentiation of species.

One such evolutionary development which has turned out to be of the greatest importance is the growth of a nervous system. One way of considering the nervous system is as a mechanism for transmitting information within the organism.

Origins of thought
Freud took as a starting point the fact that the human infant comes into existence with certain bodily needs—for air, food, contact, warmth—which can only be satisfied by interaction with the environment. Such satisfaction, which is essential for survival, is not always instantly forthcoming. Freud assumed that human beings are so constructed that they tend to keep their level of excitation as low as possible. Needs such as that for food give rise to excitation, which is reduced

when food is available. Food is particularly relevant, since on the one hand deprivation of air is quickly fatal, on the other, deprivation of warmth is less severe. When food is not immediately available, this results in movements, crying, etc., which end only when food is obtained. Presentation of food is, of course, accompanied by perception of food. The memory of this becomes associated with the excitation. When the need arises again, according to Freud, it re-evokes the memory, and this is equivalent to re-perceiving food. The food 'image' is a powerful one inasmuch as it is invested with energy arising from the need. In a primitive state of development, therefore, the hungry infant hallucinates food. This imaginary food, however, does not satisfy hunger. In order to do so, some of the energy invested in the image has to be inhibited, and directed into seeking a change in the environment. This necessitates the introduction of a test of reality; and this in turn gives rise to a mechanism for controlling movement and expression in order to achieve a purpose. This mental activity is thus 'a roundabout way to wish-fulfilment' and thinking 'is, indeed, nothing but a substitute for the hallucinatory wish', according to Freud in his epoch-making *Interpretation of Dreams* (1900).

This rather strange-seeming account derives partly from Freud's particular background and training (see Burton and Radford, 1978, for a fuller discussion). Piaget, on the other hand, started from a biological training. Thus, while, like Freud, he took as given the reflexes with which the infant is born, he regarded them as examples of elementary 'structures' which develop through the processes of assimilation and accommodation into more complex structures. These structures progressively represent the environment more fully and accurately, and this internal representation becomes progressively less tied to external stimulation, until in the stage of formal operations completely abstract thinking is possible.

Another approach which starts from the reflex is that of several Russian investigators such as A. R. Luria (1902–1977) and E. N. Sokolov. Luria developed Pavlov's concept of language as the second signal system. The first system, shared by both men and animals, is that of reflexes. Language provides another way of controlling behaviour so that it is no longer a matter of automatic responses to changes in the environment. Luria's developmental account stresses the way in which verbal instructions enable a child to carry out progressively more complex sequences of behaviour.

Pavlov's work was a major influence also in the (largely American) behaviourist tradition, since J. B. Watson took the reflex as the basic unit from which all behaviour is built up (see Ch. 2). Later Behaviourists have sought to analyse stimuli and responses rather than reflexes, and have postulated 'internal mediating responses' to account for the connection between the two. More sophisticated writers, such as Howard and Tracy Kendler, regard the stimulus-response analysis more as a convenient way of looking at things than as a necessarily true description. Mediating responses are the best way of looking at the distinction between behaviour which is, or is not, directly controlled by particular stimuli.

J. S. Bruner is a major developmental theorist who began in a Behaviourist tradition but has been strongly influenced by Piaget's ideas and those of Russian workers, among others. His general theory of cognitive development, which is known as 'instrumental conceptualism', emphasizes two aspects in particular. One is that our knowledge of the world is not direct, but is a kind of constructed model, which can be tested against reality only partially and intermittently. This model is developed as a result of use: by a culture and by the individual. Each individual's model of reality is unique, because no two people have identical experiences. Within any one society however (especially if it is relatively traditional and isolated), there will be considerable similarity of experience. These 'models' are partly determined also by the inherited structure of the nervous system, which is, we presume, more alike the more closely related individuals are. An extreme case might be identical twins, brought up together, who do often seem to think alike (as Luria showed in his famous study *Speech and the Development of Mental Processes in the Child*: Luria and Yudovich, 1956).

The second aspect is that Bruner distinguishes three 'modes of representation' or techniques by which such internal models are constructed. These appear successively in the course of individual development, but, unlike Piaget's stages, the earlier mode is not superseded by the later, only added to. The earliest mode is *enactive*: representation of the environment in this mode can be thought of as actions or the stored traces of actions. Bruner instances an infant who grasps and releases an object, then continues the grasping action without the object. It is as if action and object are not distinguished. This is followed by the *ikonic* mode which is characterized by representation in terms of images. This does not necessarily mean the possession of vivid visual imagery, but rather that the environment is thought to be represented internally in a 'concrete' way, 'a match by direct correspondence', as Bruner puts it. This may be clearer by contrast with the third or *symbolic* mode, in which the connection between object and representation is arbitrary. The most powerful example is language: the word 'table' does not look like a table, it merely stands for it; and it stands for any sort of table. Ikonic representation in a sense is more like picture-writing, in which a small, perhaps simplified, drawing of each object is used to represent it.

The different theories which have been briefly summarized (and others, such as Gestalt theory; see Chapter 2) do all seem agreed that

394

what we may call high-level manipulation of information involves some internal representation of the environment in an arbitrary or symbolic way.

Traditionally, textbooks and researchers have tended to concentrate on one or other aspect of information transmission and manipulation, using such familiar headings as sensation, perception, learning, memory, and thinking. All these can be seen as aspects of a process, of input-acquisition-manipulation-retrieval. The third term roughly corresponds to 'thinking'. Similarly, textbooks on thinking generally try to impose some order by the use of a number of sub-headings, such as concept identification, problem solving, creativity, the unconscious, dreams, imagery, and language.

What does thinking consist of?

Perhaps most of these divisions are attempts to analyse the materials of thought. What does thinking consist of? This is a question that puzzled the philosophical progenitors of psychology, at least as far back as Plato and Aristotle. However, picking up the story in the mid-nineteenth century, when psychology emerged as a separate discipline, one of the earliest divisions was into *act* and *content*. Wilhelm Wundt, whose experimental psychology laboratory at Leipzig is regarded as the first (1879), took the view that the task of psychology was to investigate immediate experience (roughly, what we now label sensation and perception), but from the standpoint of the person experiencing. Thinking, as such, was considered to be beyond the scope of psychology. However, other psychologists in the same tradition, led by Oswald Külpe, became unwilling to accept this ban, and started to investigate such thought processes as the making of judgements, using the method developed by Wundt, namely introspection. A skilled observer tried to examine, and report systematically, his experience as he received a certain sensation (e.g., hearing a metronome) or, in Külpe's case, made a judgement (e.g., which of two weights was heavier). Wundt's aim was to analyse experience into units (such as the beats of the metronome) and then show how these linked up to form a whole (e.g., the experience of rhythmical beating). Külpe and his colleagues, who formed what came to be known as the Würzburg school (after the town where they worked), similarly tried to analyse the process of judging into units, which they expected to be mainly perceptions and images. Actually, this turned out to be impossible, and this apparent failure was one reason for the general decision of American psychologists in particular to turn away from the study of experience to that of behaviour.

However, contemporary with Wundt was an alternative view, put forward by the philosopher Franz Brentano, who held that when, for example, we see an object, it is the act of seeing, not the colour and shape of the object, that is the mental phenomenon, and is therefore what ought to be investigated by psychologists. Brentano's ideas influenced Külpe; they influenced several British psychologists such as James Ward and William McDougall, and, in particular, another German, Carl Stumpf, who, in turn, had among his pupils Wolfgang Köhler and Kurt Koffka. These two, with Max Wertheimer, later founded Gestalt psychology (see Ch. 2).

A parallel line of thought to these two is known as Associationism. The best-known proponents are a line of British philosophers: David Hume and David Hartley in the eighteenth century, James Mill (1773–1836), his son John Stuart Mill (1806–1873), and Alexander Bain (1818–1903) in the nineteenth century. The history of Associationism goes back certainly Aristotle but it was perhaps the way in which J. S Mill, in particular, formulated the theory that contributed to so many developments in psychology (see Ch. 2). Mill's Associationism has often been called a 'mental chemistry': he tried to show how the units of which thought seemed to be made up, namely *sensations* and *ideas*, combine together according to certain basic principles. These are the *laws of association*. In Mill's final version there were four principles: similarity, contiguity, frequency, and inseparability. The first two are the fundamental ones, and they can readily be seen in many more recent theories. According to the contiguity principle, if two units (ideas or sensations) occur together on a particular occasion, the presence of one a second time will tend to recall the other. (The frequency principle adds that the juxtaposition must occur several times). Here we have one ancestor of stimulus-response theories. The similarity principle states a different sort of connection between units. What constitutes similarity can be variously defined. Spearman's seeing of relationships is one version. Further, two ideas, connected, may result in a third, new one, and this concept underlies some research on problem solving and creativity.

We should consider one further view of what thought consists of. The notion of a *schema* has been variously used, in particular by F. C. Bartlett and Jean Piaget. Bartlett's use (see Ch. 15) derived from the work of the physiologist Sir Henry Head, who had tackled the problem of how one movement left a trace which was somehow re-excited at the moment of the next movement, and so controlled it. Head, on a number of grounds, showed that such a succession of traces cannot fit what actually happens: there must, instead, be some kind of ever-changing internal representation or postural model of the position of the body. Bartlett extended this idea to deal with cognitive processes, in particular memory. He used the word 'schema' to refer to an active organization of past reactions or past experiences. This idea has similarities with those of Piaget (Ch. 20), the Gestalt psychologists, and J. S. Bruner.

Theoretical orientations

Thought processes have been studied from very many different theoretical points of view, and one reason for the difficulty of integrating all the various results is that different investigators have been asking quite different sorts of questions. The following are the main orientations.

Behaviourist

Behaviourism dominated experimental psychology for about fifty years. In its early, rather dogmatic version, this meant that thinking, as we are considering it, could not be studied at all. J. B. Watson did allow for the study of the supposed very small movements of the mouth and larynx which, he argued, actually were 'thinking'. This was the 'motor theory of thinking', now perhaps only of historical interest.

However, since then, and particularly in the last thirty years, successive attempts have been made to study thinking within a general Behaviourist framework. We have already mentioned the Kendlers. Perhaps the best example is *The Psychology of Thinking* by Bourne, Ekstrand, and Dominowski (1971). They begin by considering two sorts of definition of thinking: one which regards it as an internal process which controls behaviour; and their own, which regards thinking as itself behaviour. The phrase 'he is thinking', they say, describes a person doing something. But in order to specify what he is doing, we must consider four aspects: knowledge, skill, intention and performance. Each of these, they imply, can be observed and measured, and thus thinking can be studied objectively as a complex sort of behaviour.

Psychometric

The attempt to measure abilities, particularly intellectual abilities might seem closely linked to the study of thinking. Historically, however, they have often been carried on quite separately. Spearman believed that his noegenetic principles were the basis of all cognition. Later workers have tried to show just what abilities are involved in problem-solving or in creative thinking. The most complex account is that of J. P. Guilford.

One general conclusion from this work is probably that such accounts do not help us very much to understand or explain thinking. In the case of creative thinking in particular, while a certain minimum level of general 'intelligence' is necessary (Liam Hudson, 1966, suggests an IQ of about 115 for science and 100 for the arts), beyond that the explanation must lie in such factors as personality, motivation, the social setting, etc.

Psychoanalytic

For Freud, thought processes were only one aspect of the total development of the personality. Freud knew little of the academic psychology of his day, but was strongly influenced by evolutionary theory, by his training as a physician and as a scientist in particular in neurophysiology. Freud's concept of the origins of thought has been mentioned. His most notable concept, however, was the distinction between two modes of thinking: the primary and secondary processes. The latter include the (fairly) rational, conscious thought we are normally aware of; the primary processes follow other, non-logical principles and are generally unconscious. Freud by no means invented the idea of unconscious thought; his revolutionary innovation was to see that thought processes which are not conscious must develop first, both in the race and in the individual. Conscious, rational thought comes later in favourable circumstances. Freud believed he was able to unravel some of the unconscious processes, particularly, the basic urges of the child still continue: wishes and thoughts are identical. They show themselves in dreams (and in other ways such as slips of the tongue) in disguised form. Perhaps most psychologists could accept the general concept of unconscious thought, and many also accept that primary processes must be involved, as Freud argued, in other aspects of thinking, such as humour and creative thought.

Gestalt

The Gestalt psychologists reacted against the analytic methods of Wundt; arguing that the mind works with wholes (or 'gestalts') not units: we hear a tune, not a succession of notes. They were primarily interested in perceptual processes, but the principle is readily extended to learning and problem-solving. Problem-solving, they argued, involves seeing a total situation, and then 're-structuring' it so that it is seen in a new way. Once this is done the new way is not forgotten, so problem-solving is also learning.

In Köhler's famous experiments with apes on the island of Teneriffe, restructuring (or 'insight') occurred when Sultan, for example, perceived that two sticks were not just unrelated objects, but could be joined to make a longer stick—a stick the right length to reach a banana. Wertheimer, in later experiments with children, used the same principle: a child who already knew how to find the area of a rectangle, when presented with a trapezoid, solved the problem by restructuring: by cutting off one corner and putting it on the other, to transform the unfamiliar shape into a familiar one. The Gestalt psychologists emphasized the spontaneous nature of such insight, feeling it to be a natural property of the brain. More recent studies of both animals and children (e.g., Jane Goodall, J. S. Bruner) have suggested that a continuous process of learning and experience is, in fact, involved.

398

Piagetian

Piaget's developmental account of cognitive processes is described in Chapter 20. Until fairly recently, his work was not widely known by experimental psychologists, and it still forms a relatively self-contained set of theories and observations, yet to be fully tested by those outside his immediate sphere of influence. This is partly due to the classic Piagetian 'clinical' method of investigation, involving the observation of a subject in a particular situation; altering the situation; further observation; and so on; supplemented by questions and answers. However, rather as with Freud, many of Piaget's concepts have been adopted in some form, either deliberately or not, by other people. Among these are the idea, that thought develops through interaction between the organism and the environment; that there are qualitative changes between processes at different ages; that development involves a sequence of stages; that internal representation of the world is not exact, but rather a kind of model or approximate copy.

Bartlettian

There is no recognized 'School of Bartlett': but there is a line of mainly British psychologists whose ideas partly derive from his. Moreover it can now be seen that Bartlett (1886–1969) was in some ways ahead of his time. Writing in the heyday of Behaviourism, Bartlett (like other eclectic British psychologists such as Cyril Burt) saw no objection to investigating cognitive processes, or to using whatever knowledge was available—experimental, introspective, sociological, etc. Bartlett, in his book *Thinking* (1958) argued that thinking is an advanced form of skilled behaviour. Such behaviour has a number of characteristics which Bartlett considered could be usefully investigated in respect of thinking. He lists, in particular, timing, the momentary pauses that occur between one movement to the next, the 'point of no return' that occurs when one is committed to a movement, and the directional quality of skilled behaviour. Bartlett reported some supporting experiments, but it is perhaps his general influence that is now more obvious, for example, in the work of R. L. Gregory on perception. The Bartlettian approach suggests the control of complex behaviour (not just 'thinking') by internal, adaptable 'models' built up through individual experience in a particular social setting.

Instrumental conceptualism

This is the general name given to the work of J. S. Bruner and colleagues: again, it is not so much a school as a group of related ideas and investigations. The basic concepts have already been mentioned. An important emphasis is on the attempt to isolate variables in the environment that affect cognitive growth, for better or worse—or just

399

differently, for it is stressed that thinking (or 'intelligence') that is well adapted to, and highly successful in, one setting may be less appropriate to another. At the same time, the notion of developing successive modes of representation does imply the superiority of what comes later. Symbolic representation, especially language, is a more powerful and flexible thinking instrument than ikonic or enactive. There has been an increasing interest in comparisons of development between different cultures. Indeed, there has been the related development of a new kind of 'experimental anthropology' led by men such as Michael Cole and John Gay (e.g., *The Cultural Context of Learning and Thinking*, 1971). They push further the idea that the performance of different racial or social groups depends, not so much on differences in thought processes as the requirements of different settings and circumstances.

Computer simulation
Digital computers consist essentially of large numbers of on-off units whose functioning can be compared with that of the neurons making up the brain. (There are also analogue computers on a different principle.) However, this is not the point of computer simulation studies. Rather, the aim is merely to make use of the rapid processing of information that is possible with computers, in order to test out some idea as to how behaviour might work. Such an idea is often called a model. There is some disagreement as to whether, given a model that seems to replicate the behaviour, we have an explanation of that behaviour. It is suggested here that this is not so: we have only a possible explanation. Computer simulations have several potential advantages: they can be a convenient and quick way of testing; they can make a theory more explicit and clear; they may throw up new ideas. The most extensive work on simulating problem-solving is probably that of Alan Newell, J. C. Shaw, and H. A. Simon (1958; 1972). Their programme named the General Problem Solver (applied mainly to logical and mathematical problems), involves the use of symbols for objects, for differences between pairs of objects, and for operators which can change objects. Problem-solving can then be analysed into sequences of simple steps, coupled with a number of general strategies. For details, and assessment, the reader must be referred to other books, such as *The Computer Simulation of Behaviour*, by Michael Apter, 1970.

Phenomenological
The word 'phenomenology' has had various uses in philosophy. Perhaps most generally, it refers to the study of things as they appear to be, rather than of some supposed reality lying behind the appearance. Edmund Husserl (1859–1938) tried to give accurate descriptions of phenomena as they present themselves in consciousness: or rather of the

essences of phenomena, devoid of all the usual presuppositions and pre-judices of the mind. Part of Husserl's doctrine was that consciousness is intentional: the mind is not a passive receiver of objects. This is one of the sources of the ideas of Maurice Merleau-Ponty, whose theory of cognition stresses the way in which what we know of the world is, so to say, created in the act of knowing it. In recognizing an object, we do not note a set of items and put them together: rather the object emerges from the general perceptual field, and only afterwards can we identify the particular stimuli that make it up. This process centres on the body and its movements, since it is through these that we relate to the world; or rather, perhaps, they constitute the relationship. The body is part of the 'I' that knows and perceives, just as we do not say 'my body is hungry' but 'I am hungry'. These complex ideas which are only hinted at here, have perhaps not directly inspired a great deal of experimentation, but have contributed to important changes in attitude in psychology. For example, the work of Liam Hudson; and the general revival of interest in conscious experience.

Language and concepts

Among the processes that become progressively more sophisticated—more finely attuned to reality, we might say—in the course of the development of both species and individual, are those of discrimination and categorizing. These processes involve concepts and language.

Concept identification

A useful working definition of a concept is given by Lyle Bourne (1966):
    'We may say that a concept exists whenever two or more distinguish-able objects or events have been grouped or classified together and set apart from other objects on the basis of some common feature or property characteristic of each.'

This is more or less a Behaviourist sort of definition, and other sorts could be given. It is useful here, however, because most of the experimental work on concept identification has originated in a Behaviourist tradition. This work has been mainly concerned with the ways in which such classifying is done by different groups of subjects under various conditions. The ways in which children come to develop conceptual thinking have been studied rather differently (see Ch. 20).

The Behaviourist approach produced a number of experiments such as that of Hull (1920) which, essentially, required subjects to learn to classify sets of stimuli (Hull used Chinese ideograms, others used words or pictures) which possessed some element in common. Such tasks can be learned quite quickly, even when subjects do not know—and never learn—what the common elements are.

A major set of experiments which involved several new developments was reported by J. S. Bruner, Jacqueline Goodnow, and G. A. Austin in *A Study of Thinking* (1956). Their basic method involved a set of cards (such as is shown in Fig. 18.1) which were displayed to the subject. The

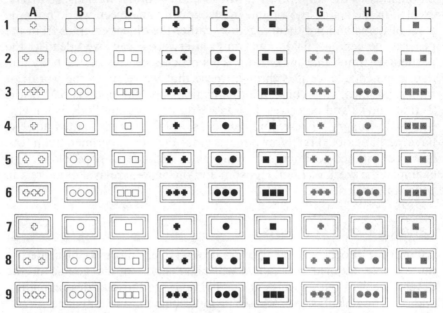

Fig. 18.1 Material used by Bruner, Goodnow and Austin (1956). Plain figures were in green, striped figures in red, solid figures in black. (Reproduced from J. S. Bruner, J. J. Goodnow and G. A. Austin, *A Study of Thinking*, 1956, Wiley, New York.)

experimenter decided in advance on a rule (a concept) such as 'circles' or 'red triangles'. The subject had to work out the rule. In one procedure (reception method) he was told which of a series of cards was an example of the rule; in another (selection method) he himself could choose which cards to be told about. Brumer *et al.* thought that this situation exemplified the way in which concepts are formed in real life. From a lengthy series of experiments they drew several important conclusions, briefly, as follows:

1. Subjects did not choose randomly, but according to what Bruner *et al.* called *strategies*. These were plans or methods for reaching the solution, though it is not really clear whether the subjects followed such plans deliberately. The most basic varieties of strategy were named wholist, or focusing, and partist, or scanning. The distinction was essentially this: in the wholist strategy the subject takes the first positive instance he gets as constituting the concept, and then amends

this as successive instances give further information; in the partist strategy the subject takes one characteristic of the first positive instance and checks this against successive examples until proved right or wrong. If wrong, he has to start again with another characteristic. There were many sub-varieties of these basic approaches. Perhaps the most important point is not the particular nature of the strategies, but the fact that Bruner *et al.*, in employing the notion of strategies at all, had moved so far from the Behaviourist-dominated 'learning' approach.

2. It was possible to show the effects of relevant conditions on the use of strategies (e.g., reception method vs. selection method).

3. Subjects tended to fall back on cues that had been successful in past problems, regardless of whether these were relevant.

4. Negative or indirect information was much harder to use than positive or direct.

5. Conjunctive concepts (e.g., ('black circles') were easier than disjunctive ones (e.g., instances are positive if they are either black or contain circles).

Following this work, other experimenters have explored further variables using similar methods. Rather than trying to summarize all these here, it is better to see if we can distinguish the main theoretical approaches to the experimental study of concept identification. One main distinction may be said to be between stimulus-response, Associationist theories on the one hand, and cognitive or 'hypothesis' theories on the other. Within the general S-R approach, we can further distinguish mediated and non-mediated theories. The early experiments of Hull and others take a non-mediated approach: concept identification is simply a matter of learning the connection between a set of stimuli (having something in common) and one response. A similar view is taken by Skinner, in line with his general principles of operant conditioning (see Ch. 11). A response such as 'thin' is regularly reinforced (that is, understood, approved, etc.) when made in the presence of thin objects, and not otherwise, and so becomes established. The process of generalization enables it to be made to new thin objects.

Most S-R theorists have found it necessary to postulate some process, intervening, or mediating, between the stimulus and the response. Such an approach is taken by Kendler and Kendler (e.g., 1962). They gave subjects two concept problems in succession (see Fig. 18.2). The second problem involved either a *reversal* shift or a *non-reversal* shift. That is, the subject either had to relearn each association: each stimulus that was formerly A is now B; or only half of them: red squares are still A, red triangles are still B. It was found that reversal shifts were easier for children and non-human subjects; non-reversal shifts were easier for

403

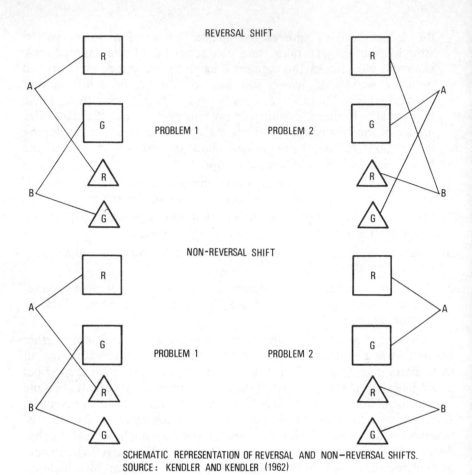

Fig. 18.2 Schematic representation of reversal and non-reversal shifts. (After Kendler and Kendler.)

adults. The Kendlers argued that adults can use a mediating response, probably verbal, which is involved in a non-reversal shift.

In contrast to the S-R approach is one that sees the subject as actively seeking information; forming a hypothesis, whether consciously or not, and so trying to test it. This approach is seen in the work of P. C Wason (see p. 409). Bruner's experiments started from an S-R procedure, but one which did allow the subject to make and test hypotheses.

There is in fact no absolute boundary between experiments on learning, concepts, problems, and reasoning. A useful classification devised by Bourne (1966) helps to show how the various techniques fit together. Experimental tasks, he suggests, can be based on either attributes (e.g., in the case of playing cards, colours, suits, values) or on rules (e.g., all the even numbers). The subjects may have to learn the attribute or the rule; or he may have to use it. This gives the classification shown in Table 18.1.

Table 18.1

Task element		Learning	Use
	Attribute	A. Perceptual learning, concept formation	B. Concept identifications
	Rule	C. Formation of learning sets	D. Rule identification, (some) problem-solving

Examples of the different experiments (described elsewhere) might be:
A. Learning of new concepts by children or adults.
B. The experiments of Hull and of Bruner.
C. Harlow's learning-set experiments.
D. Wason's reasoning tasks.

Language and thought
It is generally accepted that language is the most powerful and flexible means we have for representing and manipulating the environment—for 'thinking'. Language is in itself a subject for psychological investigation, which is discussed in Ch. 19. Here, we are concerned with the particular issue of how language relates to thought. The main views of this can be summarized as:

1. Thought is dependent upon language
2. Thought is language.
3. Language is dependent upon thought.
4. Language and thought have independent roots.

1. Thought is dependent upon language. This view was propounded by, among others, Edward Sapir (1927) and Benjamin Lee Whorf (1957) and is, accordingly, often referred to as the Sapir-Whorf, or Whorfian, hypothesis. Whorf noticed the differences between various American Indian languages and European languages: for example, Hopi Indians used the same word for insect, aeroplane and air-pilot; and Hopi expresses time relationships quite differently. Whorf considered that vocabulary and grammar determine thought. Another rather well-known example is given by Roger Brown (1965) (Fig. 18.3). It is not clear, however, whether a different naming of parts of the colour spectrum means that it is seen, or thought of, differently.

Greenfield, Reich, and Olver (1966), part of the 'instrumental conceptualism' group, asked children of different cultural groups —Mexican, Eskimo, Wolof (Senegal), and white North American

English

purple	blue	green	yellow	orange	red

Shona

cips wuka	citema	cicena	cips wuka

Bassa

hui	ziza

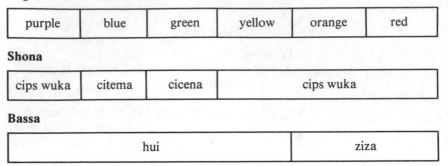

Fig. 18.3   The colour spectrum in three languages. (After Brown.)

—to classify objects, to say in what way objects were alike or different. They distinguished three ways in which language could affect this, through different vocabulary, different lexical structure (e.g., possession of words for classes of things) and different grammatical structure. They concluded, however, that these were outweighed by differences between cultures; in particular by the difference between a 'modern, urban' and a 'traditional, rural' background. This difference is most clearly manifested when children do or do not receive western-type schooling. It seems from this and other studies that the Whorfian hypothesis cannot be supported in any simple form.

2. Thought is language. The extreme form of this view was proposed by J. B. Watson, who held that thought was nothing more than talking to oneself and could, in fact, be reduced to the movements of the larynx, tongue, etc. Although such movements may occur even during silent thought, they do not seem to be essential to it. Smith *et al.* (1947) found that subjects could think clearly even when all the vocal apparatus was completely paralysed by curare. George Humphrey (1951) listed numerous arguments against the 'identity' view: for example, the finding we have already noted, that concept rules can be correctly followed without subjects being able to state them.

3. Language is dependent upon thought. In Piaget's account of the development of cognitive processes, language is one of several mechanisms or tools of thought, of which deferred imitation, symbolic games and mental imagery are other examples. For Piaget, thinking can be said to begin as soon as there is any internal representation of the world. Thus, a child who sees an action and later copies it is already 'thinking'; and Piaget has described the operation of pre-linguistic thought in great detail. In the related theory of Bruner, language is an example—the most obvious and important example—of symbolic

406

representation. Other examples are the use of tools and various forms of skilled behaviour.

4. Language and thought have independent roots. This view was put forward by the Russian psychologist Lev Vygotsky (1896–1934). In his influential book *Language and Thought* (1934) he took issue with some of Piaget's early work. Piaget had argued that early speech, like early thought, was 'egocentric'; as thought processes mature, speech loses its egocentric character and becomes socialized. Language and thought, according Vygotsky, have different origins, as can be seen in both animals and children. Thinking, he seems to argue, originates in the need to re-structure a situation, as in Köhler's experiments; language originates in expressive utterances and in the need to communicate. Vygotsky considered that language for the child had two functions: one, that of monitoring and directing internal thought; the other, that of communicating with other people. It is the inability to separate these two that results in egocentric speech. The latter, however, gradually separates out into inner speech and external speech. These are quite separate modes or 'planes' as Vygotsky calls them, with different syntax. Inner speech appears relatively disconnected and incomplete. It deals in 'sense' rather than 'meaning'. By 'sense' Vygotsky meant the whole complex of psychological events aroused by a word. 'Meaning' is a restricted part of sense; what a word stands for, like a dictionary definition. (An example could be 'cat', which 'means' a furry quadruped; but the sense shifts with the context—I'd like to have a cat; have you put the cat out; what a cat she is.) Language and thought can be considered as two partly overlapping circles: the area of overlap is 'verbal thought'. Both thought and language, however, can exist independently. Much thought has no direct connection with language: Vygotsky's example is the thought involved in tool using. Language without thought occurs, he says, in repeating a poem learned by heart.

To some extent the argument between these four views is a matter of definitions: of what is to count as thought and language respectively.

Problem-solving and creative thought

We can group here various sorts of investigation in which subjects more or less deliberately set out to achieve some end, the route to which is not at first apparent. Like all classifications of psychological investigations, this is only an approximate one.

Problem-solving
E. L. Thorndike (1898) put cats in puzzle boxes, from which they could escape, and so get food, if they accidentally pushed against a pole in the centre of the box. After a number of trials they learned to do it quickly:

the connection between stimulus and response had been 'stamped in' according to the Law of Effect (Ch. 11). Thorndike called it 'learning by trial and error with accidental success'. The Gestalt psychologists considered that such a situation was too artificial to give a true picture of how learning occurred. From his observations of apes (and also of children) in situations more suited to their natural abilities, Köhler argued that they could learn, that is solve problems by 'insight'. This has always been a rather vague concept: it meant to Köhler a kind of mental restructuring of the situation: the evidence that it took place was that it was followed by behaviour that was sudden; novel; and without hesitation. Köhler did not specify how sudden or novel it was to be, and he was criticized for ignoring the repertoire of responses his subjects must already have learned before he tested them. For example, Birch, (1945) found that chimpanzees did much better on 'insight' problems when he allowed them to play freely with suitable objects (sticks) for three days beforehand.

Harry F. Harlow (1949) carried out an extensive series of experiments on what he called 'learning sets'. In his procedure, subjects, usually rhesus monkeys, had to solve a whole series of similar problems (such as choosing the odd one out of three objects to get food hidden beneath it). Over the series, they became better, until they could choose the odd one out of any three objects at once. This, Harlow thought, might exemplify the sort of way in which 'insight' came about.

Max Wertheimer (1945), in his book *Productive Thinking*, reported extensive studies with children. He was careful to stress the role of experience, but insisted that what mattered was what sort of experience. A problem situation, he held, set up 'tensions' in the thinker, and solution, or insight, involved resolving these tensions to produce a stable, harmonious whole.

The influence of Gestalt ideas can be seen in the work of Karl Duncker (1945), who described the way in which the 'general' or essential properties of a solution emerge first: from them comes the precise individual solution. Norman Maier (1930) also showed some Gestalt influence. In some famous experiments, subjects had to use familiar objects in a new way to reach a solution; e.g., to re-classify or 'see' a pair of pliers as a pendulum.

This sort of problem can be seen in a more behaviouristic way, in terms of a number of more or less likely responses that the subject has available. The most thorough-going behaviouristic analysis of thinking is probably that of Berlyne (1965). A problem occurs, he argues, when there is a condition of high drive that cannot be promptly relieved. This is usually due to the existence of a number of learned responses which are in conflict. Such a conflict can be resolved in various ways; for example new information may show that apparently incompatible

408

responses are not really so; or a new response may be introduced, stronger than any of the others.

These different approaches have only been suggested here.

Logic and reasoning

A long philosophical tradition, from Aristotle onwards, regarded logic as the analysis of thought processes. Wertheimer criticized this as inadequate, inasmuch as traditional logic concentrated on form rather than content: an argument can be formally correct, yet in substance without application, or indeed, nonsense. Freud, too, showed that logic could not provide a complete analysis of all thought processes. On the other hand, some writers such as Mary Henle (1962) have defended the role of logic, pointing out that it is often involved in the practical choices of everyday life, and in communicating with others; and that it appears to be a natural way of functioning of the conscious mind. Failure to think logically, she argued, is often due not to lack of ability to do so but to misunderstanding of the task, or the materials involved. This is supported by some of the early experiments on logical reasoning, e.g., on the 'atmosphere effect'. Woodworth and Sells (1935) suggested that the general impression (affirmative or negative) of a logical proposition was a factor in erroneous reasoning. This was by no means conclusively proved, but gave rise to several experiments, since overtaken by the work of Peter Wason.

This work (by Wason himself and others) has now become very extensive, and it raises numerous complex issues. It starts, however, from some apparently very simple experimental situations. In one of the earliest, Wason gave subjects a set of three numbers such as 2, 4, 6, and asked them to discover the rule that made the set a series. They were to do this by suggesting other sets of three numbers and in each case they would be told whether the new set conformed to the rule or not. The rule was, in fact, simply 'ascending numbers'. Many subjects found it difficult or impossible to discover this rule. In another typical situation, subjects were shown four cards, with the following symbols on them:

$$E \quad K \quad 4 \quad 7$$

They were told that each card had a letter on one of its sides and a number on the other. The task was to turn over those cards, and only those cards, which had to be turned over in order to verify the following rule: 'If a card has a vowel on one side, then it has an even number on the other side'. This, too, is very difficult. The correct answer is E and 7 but most subjects chose either E and 4, or only E.

From these and many other experiments the following general findings emerge (Wason and Johnson-Laird, 1972).

It is difficult to understand negative statements, particularly when a

409

negative premise has to be subsequently contradicted in order to draw a valid conclusion. The corollary of this is a strong tendency to try to verify statements rather than disprove them. In the 2, 4, 6 experiment, subjects persisted in giving more examples of what they thought the rule to be, rather than test this hypothesis by asking about an example that contradicted it. Further, when given a hypothesis, or a general statement, and asked to do something to find out whether it was true or false, many subjects acted as if it must be true. Another related tendency was to make use only of information or terms explicitly named, excluding anything else that might exist. In a simple form this is shown by concluding, from the statement, 'All A are B', that 'All B are A'. Wason and Johnson-Laird conclude that such effects are the consequences of one general principle, namely: when two items, or classes, can be matched in a one-to-one fashion, then inferences are readily made, whether they are logically valid or not.

This work has many implications. For example, it may relate to the difficulty of unconvincing people who are prejudiced; it shows how sensitive to disruption is logical thinking; it illustrates Karl Popper's general theory of scientific procedure, and why this is so difficult.

Creative thinking

As with intelligence, there have been seemingly endless arguments as to what is 'really' creative thinking. Many definitions stress originality and/or usefulness or effectiveness. It is clear, though, that these depend largely on context: Robinson Crusoe could be said to be highly creative even though much of what he did had often been done better by other people. There is no sharp line between creative thought and problem solving, reasoning, or other aspects of thinking. Taylor (1958) suggests five levels of creativity, from the simplest or Expressive (free play) to the highest or Emergentive (entirely new principle such as the theory of relativity).

Much energy has likewise been spent on trying to measure creative ability by tests analogous to intelligence tests. This came to the fore with the work of Guilford (1950), whose theory of cognitive abilities (see Ch. 17) included half-a-dozen factors said to underlie creativity. Many of these tests, following Guilford at least in part, have been 'divergent', i.e., requiring a multiplicity of responses in contrast to the one correct answer of the usual 'convergent' intelligence test item. Well-known items include giving as many uses as possible for a common object such as a brick, making up stories to given titles, etc. It has never been possible, however, to establish high levels of validity and reliability for such tests, as has been possible for intelligence tests. In particular, there is little evidence that they can predict really creative work in later life.

Just how such work is achieved is not well understood. In a famous early analysis G. Wallas (1926) distinguished four stages: preparation, incubation, illumination, and verification. There is some evidence for these, but just how illumination emerges from incubation is unclear. Nearly all the various theoretical approaches listed earlier have something to say; for example, Bartlett discussed 'filling in gaps' and the Gestalt psychologists spoke of insight. Perhaps the most influential have been the S-R or associationist, and the psycholoanalytic approaches. Sarnoff Mednick (1962) held that the essential element was the forming of associations into new combinations. This involved the ability to put together 'remote' associates, i.e., ideas not usually associated. The ability can be assessed, he claims, by his Remote Associates test (RAT); and it can be improved by training. The psychoanalytic approach stresses what are thought to be unconscious mechanisms. Kris (1953) argued that creative thinking involves 'regression in the service of the ego', that is, a kind of partial and safe activation of primary process which normally do not reach consciousness. Such an assumption partly underlies the technique of brainstorming (Osborn, 1957), in which a group of people deliberately let their ideas flow freely, even if apparently silly or objectionable. The flow of each, it is held, is stimulated by the others. A more complex method is that of synectics (Gordon 1961), which uses the sort of metaphorical thinking thought to be characteristic of primary processes. Liam Hudson (1968), more influenced by the phenomenological/existential approach, sees the emergence of a self-identity as the important factor. This is partly a matter of balance of forces, including unconscious ones, within the personality, and partly of perception of oneself in a particular context. Hudson found, for example, that boys responded quite differently to a 'creativity' test if they were asked to play the role of someone else—either a creative, divergent thinker or the opposite.

Other investigators, such as Barron (1969) have found creative scientists, at least, to have well-developed, self-directed, rather dominant personalities, while Roe (1952) stressed their high level of motivation. History and anecdote show, however, that creative people have, at different times, had very various personalities. They can emerge even from the most unlikely backgrounds, but it is perhaps plausible to suppose that some cultures produce more than their share of such people, others very few. However, the complexity of possible causes of this is too great to discuss here.

Thinking and experience

Experimental psychology began as the study of conscious experience, and after a period of rejection it is now generally recognized that it is nonsense to try to understand human beings while ignoring one of their

411

most characteristic attributes. One might say two such attributes, inasmuch as consciousness seems very closely linked to language.

Introspection

Thought processes can be studied by all the methods available to psychologists, including observation, experiment, and psychometric tests. From data obtained thus, inferences can be made about the internal processes of thinking. Common sense suggests, however, that these processes can also be observed directly, by introspection. Originally the basic method of psychology, this was rejected by Watson but has more recently been revived. In fact, 'introspection' can refer to several rather different things. The method of Wundt may be called introspection proper: the scientist tried to observe and report on his own mental processes, as objectively as he could, in just the same way as an astronomer observes stars. The difference, of course, is that in the case of the psychologist, no one else can possibly make the same observations. What can be done, though, is to compare the psychologist's observations with those of other people under the same conditions, and with his own behaviour under different conditions. This is, essentially, the strategy that is adopted in all psychological work. As a general principle, it is unscientific to reject any source of information; but it is scientific to realize that every source needs checking against others.

Freud's methods of free association are sometimes called introspective. This is a little misleading, since Freud was more interested in what patients actually said than in whether their reports of their own dreams were really accurate or not. Several experiments (such as Duncker) have had subjects 'think aloud' as they solved problems, or at least offer hypotheses (e.g., Wason). Again, this is not introspection proper. It is rather a matter of observing both verbal and non-verbal behaviour to see, first, if they are consistent with each other. In fact, it often happens that they are not. Subjects frequently get the right answer with either the wrong, or no, reason verbally stated; and sometimes the opposite, i.e., right reasoning but wrong response. Wason is the latest to observe this, but, as we noted, Hull found the same thing: and it is a very common report from highly creative people that they cannot say how good ideas come, except that it is not by conscious reasoning (e.g., Albert Einstein, in Ghiselin, B. *The Creative Process*, 1952).

This is not particularly surprising, since most major theorists since Freud have held that information is processed in more than one way, these ways often going on side by side and sometimes interacting. Ulric Neisser (1967) tried to tie together several such theories by distinguishing multiple and sequential modes of information processing. These concepts were derived from two alternative ways of programming computers for pattern recognition tasks. He suggested that conscious awareness is a sequential process—a 'train of thought'—whereas the unconscious, primary processes are multiple in nature. More accurately, perhaps, thinking, as such, is a multiple process, since the step-by-step course of waking, conscious thought is accompanied by other processes going on simultaneously, of which we may or may not be aware.

Dreams and imagery
While introspection can be readily admitted as one source of information, it can tell us only about some aspects of information processing, and those not completely. The rest must be inferred from what is reported and from behaviour. This was what Freud did. He considered reports of dreams particularly useful because, he believed, they allowed a partial expression of the processes normally not conscious, in disguised forms. Freud described four main disguising mechanisms. *Condensation* refers to the ways in which one idea or image can stand for another with which it has some connection. The connection would be a physical or a conceptual resemblance or a learned association. In *displacement*, emotions normally attached to one object or idea are transferred, in the dream, to another. *Making representable* is the process whereby the underlying material of the dreams (the latent content) is put into dream form, that is into imagery. *Secondary revision* is a further stage in which the dream is made more connected and rational. Bartlett reported a similar process which he termed 'effort after meaning' when subjects in long-term memory experiments tried to make a connected account of partially remembered material. Other experimental work has supported the existence of Freud's mechanisms. For example, Ian Oswald, while subjects slept, played the name of a girl- or boy-friend on a tape recorder then woke them to see what dreams they had been having. In several cases the name seemed to be incorporated in a disguised form: red-haired Jenny as a red-coloured jemmy; Robert as a 'distorted rabbit'.

The experimental work on sleep and dreams which Aserinsky and Kleitman first reported in 1953 has shown, of course, that the vast majority of dreams are not recalled at all; but this has little bearing on Freud's theories.

Together with the new work on dreams there has been a great revival of interest in imagery generally. Imagery can exist in any sensory modality, but visual imagery has been far more extensively studied than any other form. Francis Galton was almost the first to investigate it systematically, largely by means of questionnaires sent to his friends and acquaintances. His most important result was the extremely wide range of variation between individuals, from no imagery, to that which was almost indistinguishable from the real thing. He also turned up several still unexplained oddities, such as number forms and calendar forms: the representation of these abstract concepts by particular visual shapes unique to the individual.

Developmental theorists such as Bruner and Piaget, as we have seen, regard some form of visual representation as a stage in the growth of cognitive processes. Bruner, for example, quotes the work of Clementina Kuhlman (1960). She found that children who scored highly on a test of imagery did well in a task involving the learning of a list of concrete nouns, but less well in learning a concept which necessitated grouping together several perceptually diverse objects. Low imagery scorers showed the reverse. Furthermore, in the first two grades of (American) primary school there was a positive correlation between imagery score and school achievement. After that, it dropped to zero, thus supporting the idea of imagery as an earlier mode of thinking.

Piaget has discussed the function of imagery in great detail (*Mental Imagery in the Child*, 1966). As a mode of thought it has, in his view, two characteristics: it always retains an element of the concrete in that it cannot fully express abstract thought: and it cannot be wholly mobile. This is much like the effect studied by Gordon (1949), among others, as *controllability*: the extent to which one can freely manipulate an image. (Imagine a black car; now make it turn red.) Richardson (1969) regards this as one of two basic dimensions along which imagery can be measured, the other being *vividness*. The role of imagery in thinking cannot be sharply separated from its role in memory, which has been intensively studied and is discussed in Chapter 15.

Obstacles to thought
The full development of effective thinking seems to be a rather rare phenomenon, late to emerge in the evolution of species and in the individual, and easily disrupted by all sorts of factors. Brain damage is perhaps the most obvious case. A. R. Luria (1966) found two major categories of effect of brain lesions:

1. The disruption of spatial and logico-grammatical relationships resulting from lesions in the parieto-temporo-occipital zone.
2. The disruption of the performance of skilled movements, and disturbance of the 'regulatory role of speech' by lesions in the frontal, prefrontal, temporal, and central areas.

These effects are consistent with the idea of two sorts of information processing, the first areas being associated with simultaneous, and the second with sequential processes.

Similarly, various sorts of mental illness without obvious brain damage, are accompanied by deterioration in thought. The schizophrenic group, in particular, seems to manifest loss of ability to think logically and abstractly, disruption of thought by false beliefs (delusions) or false perceptions (hallucinations), and the presence of bizarre and idiosyncratic associations. (It was the disruption of normal associations that led Eugen Bleuler to adopt the word 'schizophrenia' in 1911; it has nothing to do with so-called 'split personality'.) However, there is no general agreement on how consistent these effects are, nor on their causes. There are apparent similarities between some of these symptoms, and some of the effects of 'psychedelic' or 'psychotomimetic' drugs, of which lysergic acid diethylamide is perhaps the most famous. This has led to attempts to increase access to unconscious processes, and thus the flow of creative thought, by the use of such drugs. The evidence, reviewed by Brian Wells (1973) gives little support for such attempts.

Distortions of thought process often occur in conditions of temporary deprivation as in prolonged social isolation, insufficient oxygen, or starvation. Hallucinations and loss of ability to think logically are experienced by at least some subjects in states of sensory deprivation, investigated experimentally in the well-known 'coffin' experiments (Bexton, Heron, and Scott, 1954). Many such conditions have been combined for a more evil purpose in what is called 'brain-washing' or 'thought reform'. There have been many varieties of such attempts to achieve submission or conversion of individuals by forcible means. Perhaps the most basic feature is 'milieu control' (Lifton, 1961), the domination of all communication, and all social interaction. The effects are diverse, but, as far as thinking goes, there does often seem to be a loss of the ability to test what is being propagated against reality, and to consider possible alternatives.

These abilities have often been shown experimentally to be quite vulnerable even under favourable conditions. There is, for example, a long tradition of experiments on 'set', which can be defined as the tendency to respond in one particular way rather than in other possible ways. In the 'water-jar' experiments of Luchins, for example, subjects trained to use one solution to a problem find it harder to use an alternative, better, solution later. Duncker referred to 'functional fixedness' when subjects failed to see a new use for a common object. 'Set' however, is simply a phenomenon, not an explanation. The more sophisticated analyses of Bruner, Goodnow, and Austin, and particularly of Wason, show the difficulties of consistent reasoning more clearly.

FURTHER READING

Apter, M. (1970) *The Computer Simulation of Behaviour.* Hutchinson.
Bolton, N. (1972) *The Psychology of Thinking.* Methuen.
Burton, A., and Radford, J., eds. (1978) *Thinking in Perspective.* Methuen.

Radford, J., and Burton, A. (1974) *Thinking: Its Nature and Development*. Wiley.

Vernon, P. E. (1970) *Creativity*. Penguin.

Wason, P. C., and Johnson-Laird, D. N. (1968) *Thinking and Reasoning*. Penguin.

DEVELOPMENT OF THE INDIVIDUAL

This Section constitutes, so to speak, the other half of 'individual' psychology, balancing Section 3. A notion which goes back at least to Thomas Hobbes (1588–1679) is that a complete account of behaviour must include three levels of phenomena: physiological, individual and social. Psychology, as a distinct discipline, has perhaps spent most time and energy on the middle level, which is peculiarly its own. At the other two levels, specialists are closely allied to other disciplines: physiological psychologists to physiology; social psychologists to sociology and anthropology.

There are not many systematic accounts of behaviour that attempt, still less attain, an explanation consistent at all three levels. Freud, for example, believed he had dealt successfully with the individual and social levels. He had originally embarked on a physiological psychology (in the *Project for a Scientific Psychology*, 1895) but abandoned the attempt and never returned to it. J. B. Watson might be said to have believed in the possibility, since he thought that reflexes and their conditioning (physiological) could be made to explain all behaviour, both individual and social. Perhaps the latest psychologist to offer such an ambitious programme is H. J. Eysenck. How far he is successful you must judge.

19   Developmental psychology
HARRY FISHER

Introduction

Age-related changes in behaviour

Developmental psychology is concerned with age-related changes in human behaviour. Age is simply an index of the passage of time, so that while there is an evident relation between age and behaviour, age, or the passage of time which it indicates, cannot be used as an explanation of the changes. It is rather to various processes going on in time that such an appeal must be made. One way of classifying these is to divide them into two broad groups, those whose influence comes from within the individual and have to do with biological changes, and those whose influence comes from without. While this is a convenient way of dividing the processes for discussion it is a dangerous one in that it carries the suggestion that the processes themselves are separate and independent. This suggestion provides a statement of the nature versus nurture problem which is to be found within psychology in a number of different contexts. More detailed discussion will follow in Chapter 21, but in the context of developmental psychology this two-fold division has taken the following form.

MATURATION VERSUS LEARNING

Biological changes are taking place within the individual throughout his life. Probably the most vigorous and extensive of these occur in childhood and adolescence. They include the physical, anatomical, and biochemical changes associated with the transformation of the neonate into the mature adult, and these processes are included under the general heading of maturation. Maturation, nevertheless, depends upon a benign environment. Physical growth may be retarded by want of nourishment and stunted from inappropriate feeding. In the same way, motor development may be inhibited where infants are not allowed adequate practice. The newborn babe is all but helpless, his first movements being limited to gross and undifferentiated movements of the limbs. Under normal circumstances, he quickly becomes able to make co-ordinated movements and to sit without help, then to crawl, to stand, and within a few months of his first birthday, to walk with rapidly increasing competence. Dennis (1960) described institutionalized children who were unable to walk at over three years of age. Care in the institution was adequate in the sense that the children were fed and kept clean, but shortage of staff meant that as soon as this was finished infants were returned to their cots where they remained until the next meal was due. A prolonged regime of this sort was blamed for the substantial retardation. Indeed, once a routine allowing daily practice and exercise had been brought in, the children soon learned to walk. This study usefully illustrates the interdependence of maturation and learning.

SOCIALIZATION

Learning comes about through the contact the child is constantly making with the world around him. It is a world inhabited by other people who influence his development in a number of different ways. It is also a world of things and natural forces and elements, like gravity, wind, and rain. Thus the child's environment has a social and a physical aspect. Through contact with the people in his life the infant and child is led to approximate to the standards of, and to hold the values of the community to which he belongs. The several processes involved in achieving this end are referred to collectively as socialization. They include direct and explicit instruction in the skills and manners expected, with rewards when the child conforms to, and punishment when he violates, these expectations. But the influence may be less direct, the standards being implicit in the cultural activities in which the child is constantly taking part, or may involve the imitation of a powerful or admired member of the group to which he belongs. The term 'socialization' was originally used to refer to the effects of the social aspect of the environment on the young child. It is clear, however that socialization is a life-long process and some further consideration of this will be found in Chapter 22.

Learning also comes about through the contact the child makes with the physical aspect of the environment. The infant learns to use his maturing powers to control ever wider domains. At first he is able to obtain only those objects which are within his reach; then, by rolling over, he is able to use a larger area, and later still, by crawling and by walking, he is able to expand the borders of his world yet further. For up to two years or so he must make his discoveries largely without the aid of words, relying only upon what his senses tell him, together with an increasing ability to remember. Once he is able to use words the two areas of learning we have distinguished begin to overlap. For words can be used to ask questions about his world: and asking questions involves him with those around him.

Scope

Since changes in behaviour and experience are going on throughout life, it might be supposed that developmental psychology would span the period from birth to old age. In fact, the great majority of studies have been concerned with childhood and adolescence. Over this period developmental changes are both rapid and extensive, and such as to give rise to a wide range of problems, domestic, social, and educational. During the last hundred years the advances in education have both pointed up problems and supplied means of investigation. Further, over this age range, it is relatively easy to elicit information from the individuals concerned, whereas very young children present special methodological problems because of communication difficulties. There has, nevertheless, been a considerable increase in the volume of research involving the young child since the mid-1950s. At the same time, increasing interest has been shown in development in the neonatal period. There has been a similar increase of interest in the behavioural correlates of ageing. At the two extremes of the age-range, biological factors tend to impose some regularity on development which holds across cultures. Examples are the developmental milestones found in the acquisition of motor and language skills in the young and the decline of various skills in the aged. Between these extremes the changes which take place reflect the influence of social and cultural pressures, so that findings generalize less easily across different groups. Indeed, cultural anthropologists have argued that adolescence, for example, both as a phenomenon and as an experience, owes much to its social context, the trials of a 'western' adolescence being greater than those experienced in societies whose way of life involves a more gradual passage toward adult status. Ageing, likewise, will reflect cultural variations; not only are there wide variations in life expectation—so that 'old' age in one culture may relate to the over-sixties and in another to the over-forties, but attitudes to ageing also vary widely. The development of those between the very

421

old and the very young is likely to reflect these complexities, and to exhibit significant regularities related to cultural context.

Aims and methods
Developmental psychologists are motivated by a number of different ambitions which can be broadly divided into two groups. The first group embraces those who pursue their studies in order to understand the processes involved in child development. Such understanding as is gained frequently produces further questions, and these, in their turn, are investigated. It may be that, incidentally, the findings suggest practical applications which eventually find their way into real-life situations. The second group of motives makes the solving of practical problems its goal; for example, the most effective ways of helping those children who are slow to read. Incidentally, this sort of research may turn up questions which are of theoretical rather than practical value. The two differ, then, in emphasis, but the problems which they face and the methods used to solve them have much in common.

The basis of the scientific approach to psychology is observation in some form. It may be carried out in a 'natural' setting, possibly in the home, in a classroom or playground, and the observation intended to sample a range of behaviour; alternatively, the observation may take the form of a carefully controlled experiment where conditions are standardized. These are but two of a wide range of methods to be considered in what follows. Observation is meant to lead to description, that is, to some way of summarizing what has taken place. The observation will, of necessity, be selective but will include details of factors likely to affect the outcome. For instance, in a study of the early phases of speech-development, the primary data will be the recorded utterances of the child, but it may be important to include in the description details of any factors which might have influenced them (the presence of distractions, of parental promptings, and the like) as well as some indications of the general conditions under which the observation took place. Description may sometimes be an end in itself, particularly in the early stages of a study. It may serve to prompt further observation. Usually, however, it is expected that the description of the observation will lead to some sort of explanation. In broad, general terms this means it may be possible to identify principles which serve not only to account for what has been observed, but also suggest ways in which the principles themselves may be verified. In what follows, some of the methods of developmental psychology will be examined and then some of the modes that explanation may take.

Philosophical beginnings

Problems relating to the growth and development of children have confronted mankind from the beginning. For the greater part of history, pronouncements on both theoretical and practical issues have been in the hands of philosophers, and based on casual as distinct from systematic observation. Three contributions of this sort are of interest because they represent approaches which have recent counterparts.

Plato (c. 427–347 BC)

Plato, a Greek philosopher of the fourth century BC, held that differences among individuals was a matter of 'natural gifts'. That is, that on each child nature has bestowed such potentialities as will characterize him throughout life, and that the bounds of development are set by these natural gifts. This is still widely held, though less so now, perhaps, than ever before on account of the difficulty of providing rigorous supporting evidence, as well as the demonstrable influence of environmental factors on development. For Plato this was a premise which lead to recommendations for the running of an ideal society. These included a division of labour, a eugenics policy, and plans for selective education, all based on the notion of a development the principal constraints on which were genetic. Thus people were to be employed in life in that occupation for which they were naturally suited. Government was to be in the hands of the intellectuals, the so-called philosopher rulers. The task of implementing the decisions they made was entrusted to a class of auxiliaries, which included the civil service and forces to maintain law and order. The third class distinguished was that of the producers, which included craftsmen, tradesmen, merchants and farmers. It was held that the members of these classes should be controlled in respect of numbers and quality by controlling their breeding and by subjecting them to such education as would ensure their fullest development within their class. Plato also proposed that movement between classes should take place, according to merit and ability, during the education of the child. The concept of the child implicit here is of one who is in a measure, what he will be. He is a little 'philosopher-king', a little 'auxiliary' or a little 'producer', separated from the adulthood that will follow by the sequence of instruction that his education will bestow. Any ideas of a qualitative change whereby the little producer may become a philosopher-king by dint of hard work are absent. The child is seen as 'the father of the man', as a little adult.

Locke (1632–1704)

John Locke, a seventeenth century British philosopher, shared this view of the child. Like adults, he held, children were to be treated as 'rational creatures'. But Locke's view differed from that of Plato in respect of what was held to be the dominant influence in development. For Plato, this was 'natural gifts'; for Locke, it was the experience provided by the child's environment. Locke saw the mind of the neonate as a *tabula rasa*, a blank slate, upon which the symbols which appeared were those reflecting the experiences of the child. The young child, in particular, is seen as susceptible to the moulding influences of his environment. The implications of this approach for child-rearing are that the environment should be manipulated so as to encourage that which is held to be desirable and to inhibit the undesirable, and that such manipulation be undertaken as early as practicable. This approach has been adopted throughout history, both before Locke and after him. Solomon, the third king of Israel in the tenth century B.C. urged his subjects, 'Train up a child in the way he should go; and when he is old, he will not depart from it' (Prov. 22.6.) The Behaviourist, J. B. Watson, wrote in the same vein:

> 'Give me a dozen healthy infants, well-formed, and my own specified world to bring them up in and I'll guarantee to take any one at random and train him to become any type of specialist I might select—doctor, lawyer, artist, merchant-chief and, yes, even beggarman and thief, regardless of his talents, penchants, tendencies, abilities, vocations, and race of his ancestors.'

Rousseau (1712–1778)

Writing a century later than Locke, the French philosopher Jean-Jacques Rousseau presented a view of the young child different from that of Plato as well as that of Locke. Rousseau saw the child as a 'noble savage'. Like the savage, he derived the knowledge he needed from the world around him. Left to himself Rousseau held that his active involvement with his world would lead him through a natural sequence of developmental stages at each of which his adaptation to it would be appropriate to his needs and capabilities. His nobility, rooted in the concept of his being qualitatively different from the adult he was to become, capable of learning from his own experience and independent of formal educational methods was enhanced by his innate insight into right and wrong. 'The typical interventions of parents and teachers mar and distort the natural succession of the changes of childhood; the child that man raises is almost certain to be inferior to the child that nature raises'. This quotation from Rousseau's work, *Emile*, leads to a view of the task of parents and teachers as providers of the right sort of conditions for the natural course of development to proceed with a minimum of formal education or intervention.

Thus Plato, Locke, and Rousseau present very different models of the young child. While not completely different, they represent different

424

emphases, one underlining genetic factors, one the importance of environmental factors and the third the importance of the interaction between them. These views are important because they represent recurrent themes in psychology. They are all present in some form in current debates.

Observation, experimentation and explanation

These views rest on casual observation. With the advent of a scientific approach to human behaviour it became clear that useful conclusions can be drawn only if observation is systematic. Among the early attempts to incorporate this requirement in studies of development was the keeping of diaries. In the course of time, observation was supplemented by controlled experimentation, where observation produced description and experiment produced explanation.

Diaries of infancy

A move towards a more systematic approach to observation is to be found in diaries kept by those with a practical interest in children. In the eighteenth century, Pestalozzi, the Swiss educationist, published notes (*A Father's Diary*, 1774), based on his extensive and thorough observation of his young son. The nineteenth century saw the publication of a number of such diaries. Darwin, himself the author in 1877 of *A biographical sketch of an infant* (his own son), held that, by careful observation of the infant and child, one could see the descent of man. Diarists, of course, did not set out to record everything, and some useful information about child development has been obtained where observations were concentrated over a limited range of behaviour. In 1877, such a diary was produced by Taine, containing details of the early use of sounds and words as labels. It underlined the way in which, at an early stage in the development of language, one 'label' is used to refer to a range of similar objects.

While these diaries proclaim the enthusiasm and perceptiveness of their authors, they fall short of the standards of scientific accuracy. The observations themselves were frequently irregular, and constrained by the interests and theoretical persuasion of the observer. As this was frequently the parent, the selection and interpretation of items were liable to bias. Even when the observer was scientifically motivated, as Darwin was, it is possible to see in the account items which appear to have been included because they fell into particular theoretical contexts. Certainly, the usefulness of Darwin's diary is limited by a want of objectivity and a tendency to go beyond what was observed in the interest of further speculation. A further limitation of these diary studies is that each refers to only one child, who may, or may not, be typical. It would be unjustified to draw any conclusions about children in general from such evidence. But while these early studies had considerable limitations, they served a useful function in showing up methodological difficulties as well as, in a number of cases, providing a wealth of data against which that from subsequent studies could be compared. Most of the limitations discussed are by no means inherent in the diary approach, and later diarists have increased the objectivity of the data they collected by deciding beforehand what was to be observed, how frequently observations were to be made, and what criteria were to be used in classifying data.

G. Stanley Hall (1844–1924)

The publication of Darwin's *Origin of Species* in 1859 provided further grounds for the detailed study of child development. It was thought that this might throw further light on Darwin's hypothesis of a continuity between the animals and humans. Indeed, a notion was enthusiastically entertained that ontogeny repeats phylogeny, the doctrine of recapitulation. This holds that each individual develops in such a way as to pass through, during the prenatal months, a shortened form of the ascent of man from 'the lowest forms of life' and that, after birth, the 'recapitulation' is continued. It was espoused by many biologists, educationists, and psychologists. One of its fervent proponents was G. Stanley Hall, one of the founders of American psychology. He saw this as the basis for an account of various aspects of human behaviour, for example the undulating movements of the body, like breathing and the beating of the heart, as well as the universal pleasure in repetitive and rhythmic activities. 'It is', Hall wrote, 'as if the waves of the primeval sea whence we came still beat in them.' This was one of a number of theories entertained by psychologists on the basis of plausible hypotheses; while they offered little or no means by which they might be tested, they persisted because of this same plausibility. It was a theory still popular among psychologists and educators of the 1930s but has now long since been abandoned in the absence of satisfactory empirical support. While this occupied much of Hall's energies, he was also concerned with methodological innovations which would reveal something of the contents of children's morals. He used the questionnaire, a method originated by Galton, to obtain a considerable amount of new material about children's anger, their fears, their games, and their ideas about themselves, as well as much other material, which was published in his two-volume work *Adolescence* in 1904.

Methodologically, his work represents a significant step forward from the approaches of the philosophers and the diarists, and it stimulated a wide variety of psychological research centred on children. Hall, who played a distinguished role in the introduction of psychology to the

United States, is also justly held to be the founder of developmental psychology there.

Normative studies and practical applications
In the early decades of the twentieth century, work in child-development might be divided into two broad areas: one concerned with studies which were descriptive and normative; and the other with practical applications. The former sought accuracy of description of norms, using large numbers of children and observational techniques designed to allow careful evaluation of the behaviour studies; while the latter aimed to put the growing body of psychological knowledge into practical ends.

ARNOLD GESELL (1880–1961)

An outstanding example of the systematic observation of children is in the work of Arnold Gesell at Yale University. In *Infancy and Human Growth* (1928) is catalogued, in considerable detail, the results of his observations of the perceptual, motor and social behaviour of infants, indicating norms and the observed range of individual differences. In subsequent works, normative descriptions are made of development throughout childhood. Gesell's studies were limited, however, to American subjects.

Education both drew upon psychology and contributed to it, having long had an interest in turning such psychological information as existed to practical ends. Binet (1859–1911) in France, together with a collaborator, Simon, produced the first intelligence test, the Binet-Simon scale, in 1905. This came in response to the need for detecting defective children at an early stage so that they might be placed in special schools. In England, in 1912, the London County Council Education Authority appointed a psychologist to advise on educational problems. This was Cyril Burt, later to become professor of psychology at University College, London. The study of delinquent and problem children was also expanding. Five child guidance clinics were founded in the late 1920s in the United States, and, in England, 1929 saw the founding of the London Child Guidance Clinic. Such practical problems continued to make demands on psychology, but the emphasis on description, which continued to dominate developmental studies late into the first half of the present century, set it apart from other aspects of psychological inquiry increasingly being undertaken with an intent to supply explanatory acounts, and the 1940s saw a decline in activity in the field of developmental psychology.

Clinical observation
Within ten years a vigorous reversal of this trend was to be seen, which has continued to the present day. The most significant single influence

427

was undoubtedly related to the interest in the theoretical aspects of development which demanded an experimental approach. It would be misleading to suggest that there had been no theoretical side to the work of developmental psychologists before this time. Jean Piaget of Geneva University had begun, in the 1920s, the monumental work in which he aimed to provide both a descriptive and theoretical account of development from birth to maturity. For a number of reasons, one of which was that his work up to that time was not generally available in translation, his work was less appreciated among psychologists than educationists. In the 1950s his work began to take on the stature of a major edifice (now available in translation) in psychology; and while it still fails to sit comfortably in the psychology of the seventies, it continues to provide a major stimulus to current developmental research. A distinctive feature of the Piagetian school was its 'clinical' method of enquiry. This involves both observation and individual interview.

Freud, whose work has had considerable influence on developmental psychology, also used the clinical approach in a rather different sense. He was concerned to trace the influence of early childhood experiences on personality development. His scientific contact with children was very limited. He obtained his information about them from the adults who visted his clinic in search of relief from various forms of what are usually called 'mental illnesses': hysteria, phobias, and the like. He encouraged such patients to talk of their early life as a means of identifying the possible source or sources of their disturbance. Thus, Freud drew on information on children by retrospective means. Others who took Freud's point of view inaugurated some of the clinics already mentioned.

The ecological and ethological approaches
The transition betwen the developmental psychology of the 1940s and that of the 1950s marked a change of emphasis. The earlier represented an approach to science primarily in terms of description, the later an approach which, to observation, added the generation of testable hypotheses and the development of experimental procedures which made it possible to assess the value of the proposed hypothesis. While contemporary developmental psychology reflects this emphasis, it also includes a considerable volume of work based on observation and aimed primarily at description. Not all of those interested in developmental problems are convinced that the experimental approach is optimal. Those who question its value argue that the laboratory experiment constitutes an artificial situation which, all too frequently bears little similarity to 'real life'. In order to observe the effect of one variable on another, all other variables or as many of them as possible, must be held constant. In 'real life', behaviour is influenced by factors which are free to vary and which collectively affect it. The gap between the controlled

428

experiment and 'real life', runs this line of argument, means that generalization from the former to the latter is rarely, if ever, valid. As an extreme example, the behaviour of the laboratory rat may be contrasted with that of a rat living in its natural surroundings. The laboratory rat, bred within the laboratory and fed and tended so that its part in the experimental schedule will be played efficiently, has little of either nature or nurture in common with his wild counterpart, so that what the laboratory rat does in the laboratory can tell us little about the behaviour of the wild rat. Those who hold this sort of view, use the method of observation and concentrate on description.

Two interpretations of this approach have continued to make significant contributions to contemporary developmental psychology. One of these is known as the ethological approach, a description which indicates its link with the approach to animal behaviour, which bears the same name, and which concentrates on the observations of animals in their natural environment. The other has taken the name ecological. Methodologically the two have much in common, using a vast array of technical aids to ensure accuracy of observation and much ingenuity to retain natural circumstances. One of the claims from both approaches is that children, particularly young children, soon learn to disregard the observation even when this cannot be concealed, and that this is a much more effective way of obtaining information than, for example, by clinical interview.

One main difference between the ethological and ecological approaches is the scale of the investigations involved. The principal centre for the latter is Oskaloosa, a small town in the midwest of the USA. Virtually the entire town is involved in the enterprise, and observations of what are known as 'behaviour episodes' may involve the various aspects of the behaviour of children of all ages.

The characteristic feature of the ecological approach is the emphasis on the environment as a determinant of behaviour. Thus, for example, the city-town project was a study of children's behaviour in communities of different size; a small school-large school study was a further attempt to assess the influence of the size of the community on behaviour. Other behaviour settings in which studies have been carried out are drug stores, boy scout examinations, and hikes and camps. For each of these there exists a detailed descriptive account of the typical behaviour pattern and its relation to important aspects of the particular setting. This emphasis thus differentiates it from, as well as links it with, the ethological approach; the difference lies in the aim of the ecologist to demonstrate the nature of the differences in behaviour which occur as a result of the environment. Such differences the ethologist takes as his starting point for an account of the way in which the behaviour represents an adaptation to the surroundings.

429

The study of play-fighting by Blurton Jones in 1972 provides an example of the complexity and thoroughness of the child ethologists' approach. It would be very unusual to find a group of pre-school children sitting still and quiet unless it was story-time. Much more usually they are to be found moving about and making a noise. To casual observation, much of what they do appears to be without pattern, but here and there recurrent themes can be identified. Frequent among these is aggressive behaviour in which voices are raised, arms and feet are raised and battles joined. Careful observation and analysis indicated that some of the behaviour which might be classified as aggressive, was in fact, of a different order, much more like play than fighting. For this, the name 'rough and tumble play' has been used.

The method of the ethologist includes identification of individual components of behaviour in as objective terms as possible. A 'dictionary' of behavioural terms with agreed 'physical' definitions may then be used as a check-list during observations of sequences of behaviour. These may be filmed to provide repeated observation. Thus behaviours described as wrestling, tumbling, rolling over, open-handed (often making no contact) beating of another child, jumping up and down, broad smile, squealing, and chuckling were among the cluster of acts found in rough and tumble play. (It should be noted that the terms are free of motivational intent, e.g., attack, aggression, or moral gloss, that is, spiteful or naughty, in order to obtain as parsimonious and accurate a description as possible). The description includes specification of when each 'act' occurs and the purpose of (statistical) analysis is to identify what acts are frequently associated with which other acts. In this way 'clusters' of acts may be identified and given an accurate and objective description. Blurton Jones, using this kind of analysis on data recordings of acts which occurred within five-minute periods, identified those listed earlier and interpreted them as 'rough and tumble play'. It is suggested that among the acts there are some which serve as an indication of the non-aggressive nature of the activity (the smiling and the jumping up and down), and, further, that it is failure to detect such signals that may result in misinterpretations of the activity by adult supervisors and peers alike. In the former case it may lead to pointless admonition, and in the latter to either an aggressive involvement which is inappropriate, or to avoidance of involvement in the activity altogether.

Longitudinal and cross-sectional methods
Two sorts of approach are used in the study of age-related changes, one involving a single group of subjects who are observed from time to time over a period (usually extending over a period of years), and the other involving several groups of subjects of different age groups. The former is known as the longitudinal method, the latter as the cross-sectional.

For example, if the acquisition of language is to be studied over the years from age one to age five inclusive, this might involve a single group of children observed from their first birthday to their fifth at, say, yearly intervals. Alternatively, five groups of children might be used, one of each age group. The two approaches have their own advantages and limitations. Some of these may be seen by considering the relative demands they make on time and subjects and the extent to which they are capable of producing information about individual differences.

It is seldom of value to set up longitudinal studies for a short period of time. Sometimes they are undertaken for a decade or more. It is characteristic of this method that it is time-consuming, both in terms of the necessarily limited rate at which the data can be collected, but also in respect of the administrative problems involved in keeping track of subjects over a number of years. While a longitudinal study set to cover a five year span of development takes five years at least, a cross-sectional study which uses, say, five different groups, takes little more than the time to collect the data and complete the analysis. This approach is thus relatively expensive in terms of the number of subjects required, but much less time-consuming than the longitudinal approach.

The usefulness of the two approaches is further differentiated, for, since the longitudinal approach uses a single group of subjects, it is capable of providing details about individual differences in development, whereas the cross-sectional approach cannot. Where the interval between successive observations is appropriately small, the longitudinal approach is sensitive to changes which take place quickly. This approach is necessary where the effect of early experience on subsequent behaviour is being examined. The use of retrospective data, which, for example, is obtained from parents who are asked to provide details of childhood matters, is clearly much less reliable. Early behaviour patterns may disappear, details may be forgotten, or exaggerated. In cases of this sort, where, for example, it may be important to assess the effect on later behaviour of hospitalization in early childhood, the longitudinal method provides the most objective way of collecting information. In contexts of this kind, and where individual developmental details are important, the cross-sectional approach has relatively little to offer. Yet it is capable of providing information relatively quickly for an introductory survey. In the study referred to above this approach might be used to assess the extent to which later behavioural problems were associated with early hospitalization, by comparing the incidence of such problems in groups of individuals who had had this experience with groups who had not, over a range of age-groups. A further particular value of the cross-sectional approach is in the provision of age norms.

It is possible to combine the longitudinal and cross-sectional approaches to obtain some of the advantages of both. The combination is sometimes known as the accelerated (or short term) longitudinal approach. Essentially, it consists of two or more longitudinally observed groups overlapping in age. A first group might be examined at say three, four, five and six years of age, and a second at six, seven, eight and nine years. Thus, data covering seven years development can be collected in four years.

Recent developmental research.
The acquisition of language

In what has been said so far, an attempt has been made to trace the origins of developmental psychology, to examine the sorts of methods it uses and the theoretical orientations it embraces. The remainder of this Chapter is devoted to the consideration of the acquisition and development of language.

Since language is such a pervasive and characteristic part of human behaviour, influencing and being influenced by other aspects of development, its acquisition and development bears on much of what is to be considered in the following Chapters. As a topic of much recent interest in developmental psychology, consideration of the progress made may serve to complement the earlier part of this Chapter by indicating something of the relation between recent research and that of the past, the methods employed, and the theoretical positions brought to bear in the attempt to clarify what happens when a child acquires his first language. Most of the work on the psychology of language has appeared since 1960. Psychologists were, of course, interested before this, but in the early 1960s the work of linguist Noam Chomsky began to make itself felt and, for the decade or so which followed, stimulated a large volume of research in psychology. One of the important aspects of this field to which attention was drawn was the phenomenon of the acquisition of language. It had been taken largely that acquisition could adequately be accounted for in terms of imitation, conditioning, reinforcement, and the like. Chomsky disagreed. While such mechanisms may well be implicated, they were by no means capable of giving an adequate account of acquisition by themselves. It was against such a background, that of a challenge to long-held assumptions, that the research began.

Central problems
In the most general terms, the central problems can be put as follows: what exactly does a child acquire when he acquires language, and what factors influence the process of acquisition? The first question requires clarification for 'language' is a label for a range of behaviour of a particular sort and begs the question as to the defining characteristics of this behaviour. It is at this point that agreement is difficult to find. Yet

some sort of definition of language is required if the question is to be given a meaningful answer. Linguists and others have described it in a number of different ways. A common element of such descriptions is the systematic nature of language. To say that language is systematic is one thing; to describe accurately the nature of the system is another. Linguists have distinguished a number of 'systems'. These include phonology, which concerns the sounds of language and the ways in which they may be combined; syntax, which relates to the rules governing the combination of words; and semantics which has to do with the meaning of words and combinations of words. Any such division is artificial and tends to convey the notion of separate entities. While the divisions provide a useful framework for research and discussion, most of the language used in the world goes on without conscious regard to their existence.

The young child must first understand what is going on around him in order to decide about the significance of the words he hears; thus 'meaning' illuminates both phonology and syntax. By the time he is four or five years old a child will have acquired a wide range of basic skills. He can understand and make himself understood in everyday situations. For some part of the first year of life his own production of sounds is only vaguely language-like: crying, cooing, babbling, laughing, and shrieking. Yet these sounds are serving at least some of the functions of language, for they serve as a basis for a wide range of social interactions as well as communicating information about the transient conditions of the infant.

The 'first word' usually occurs around the first birthday, followed, slowly at first by other words, and then at an explosive rate sometime following the second birthday. Utterances, having started with a single word, begin to include combinations of two, then three, words in lawful combination. Thus acquisition seems to begin—at least in performance terms—somewhere round about the age of eighteen months and to have reached a stage of useful communicative competence by about four and a half years—that is, in a period of about three years.

This appears all the more remarkable when it is realized that, at least for most children, this occurs without systematic instruction. They just seem to 'pick it up'. Moreover it is all done in terms of sound. Very few children can read before they enter school at five years, so that language acquisition has taken place without whatever advantage is conferred by a written representation. Development of language goes on, of course, beyond five years of age. Indeed, in the sense in which people go on acquiring new words and learning to use them more accurately, it can be regarded as a continuing process. But development is slower beyond five years, and by nine or ten years of age the child is performing at virtually adult standard.

The answer to the 'how' and 'what' questions of language acquisition will rest to some extent on the assumptions made about the nature of language behaviour. These assumptions will also influence the sort of empirical studies made. Four different approaches will be considered here, together with some empirical work. This will, for the most part, though not exclusively, bear on what it is that the child acquires. A later part of the Chapter will be devoted to a consideration of work done, which bears on how acquisition is influenced by a range of social factors.

B. F. Skinner (b. 1904)

As a learning theorist, Skinner sees no need to differentiate between language and other behaviour. Speech and language are held to be acquired by operant conditioning. The emphasis is upon learning through experience, according to the principles proposed by learning theorists. The innate prerequisites for the acquisition of behavioural responses are few: the capacity to form stimulus-response associations, and to discriminate between and to generalize among stimuli. This capacity is not confined, of course, to humans.

According to this view, the random or imitative sounds uttered by infants become, through the selective reinforcement afforded by parental attention and praise, increasingly like adult sounds. The verbal responses are shaped by the parents, who, as time goes on, tend to withhold rewards until the standard sound is matched by the child's own, or until the word used matches the situation. Thus a parent might say 'what's this' holding up a biscuit, but delay handing it over until the infant has produced the appropriate verbal response (which may, of course, be anything between 'b' and 'biscuit' according to expectation).

The case that Skinner proposes for language acquisition is, thus, a simple extension of his views about behaviour in general. The acquisition of language, or to use Skinnerian terminology, verbal behaviour, comes about according to the same laws of reinforcement by which animal behaviour is shaped.

In this way, Skinner deals with both of the central questions posed. 'What' a child acquires when he acquires language is a set of verbal responses; 'how' he acquires them is by the process of operant conditioning.

The strict Skinnerian view has been criticized on the grounds that the child is seen as being only passively involved in language acquisition. The opponents of this sort of approach point to the way in which children behave creatively with language. That is, not only do children understand sentences which they have never heard before, but they also utter both words and sentences which are novel. Thus, words like 'sheeps', 'goed' and 'oftenly' are unlikely to be products of imitation alone. The thrust of these criticisms is not that the proposals are

434

implausible, but that they fail to fit the facts of language acquisition.

The quantity of empirical evidence bearing directly on the Skinnerian view of acquisition is small; some work assessing the influence of various types of model for imitation will be discussed later (see p. 439).

Noam Chomsky (b. 1928)

Noam Chomsky, in a thorough review of Skinner's book, *Verbal Behaviour* (1957), presented a number of arguments aimed at demonstrating the inadequacy of a learning-theory approach to acquisition. He contended that it is untrue that children learn language only through the meticulous care of adults who shape their verbal repertoire, and that '... a grammar is no more learned than, say, the ability to walk is learned'. Since the late 1950s Chomsky has advocated a view diametrically opposed to that of Skinner. For, while Skinner emphasizes the influence of 'nurture', on acquisition, Chomsky sees 'nature' as playing the dominant role. He holds that the structure of language, that is, the sound system (phonology), the rules for forming words by combining sounds (morphology), and the rules for combining words (syntax), is to a considerable degree, specified biologically. That is, just as it is a part of 'human' nature to walk upright, so it is also natural to speak and understand language. Experience serves not so much to teach, as to activate this innate capacity for language.

An infant, whatever the nationality of his parents, or his country of birth, if placed in a foreign language community where he had contact only with the new language, would acquire that language in much the same way as a native infant. While the Behaviourist sees in this something about the universality of the way in which caretakers shape the language of children, it can also be interpreted as indicating the presence of universal structural elements in language. Chomsky holds that implicit knowledge of these linguistic universals must be part of the innate equipment of each child. The acquisition of language takes place as the development of this endowment. Two sorts of universals are distinguished: 'formal', and 'substantive'. Formal universals are those relating to the overall structural properties of language, whereas substantive universals are linguistic elements found in all languages—for example, certain kinds of sounds are common to all languages, as are such categories as noun and verb.

Chomsky's theory has stimulated an enormous volume of research both on acquisition and adult usage. (It is important to note that Chomsky, a linguist, has conducted no psychological experiments himself. Nevertheless, many psychologists have undertaken work stemming from his proposals.) While some of the work (on linguistic universals, for example) has produced findings consistent with Chomsky's predictions, at least in broad outline, other work has begged the question as to whether the similarities in acquisition across languages are to be accounted for in terms of innate and universal linguistic information, or in terms of common innate cognitive capacities underlying the capacity for language.

Chomsky has, further, argued that the child acquires the grammar of his language, not so much by learning it, as by using the speech he hears to choose among possible grammars stored in what he has termed the child's language acquisition device (LAD). It is held that this is the more remarkable because of the 'meagre and degenerate' sample of speech usually available for this purpose. The speech used in the home is rarely formal, and frequently consists of the abbreviated and half-finished sentences used among intimates. It is questionable, however, as to whether the grammar needs to be obtained from speech only. For the child hears this speech in a social context, and it seems possible that he uses this as a means of deciding what the sounds mean.

Chomsky's work has provided an elaborate and cogent statement of the nativist position. It was not intended to suggest that mechanisms like imitation and reinforcement were inappropriate explanations, but rather to demonstrate that learning-theory approaches by themselves were inadequate. There is a measure of agreement among psychologists here, but research carried out since 1960 has produced only limited support for Chomsky's account.

Eric Lenneberg (1921–1975)

Eric Lenneberg, in his book, *Biological Foundations of Language* (1967), drew on a wide range of studies, anatomical, physiological, neurological, genetic and pathological to support the thesis that biological endowments make language uniquely possible for man. These include some which suggest that verbal behaviour is linked with a considerable number of anatomical and physiological characteristics of the human physique; for example, the lateralization of the speech function in the left cerebral hemisphere of the brain, special co-ordination centres in the brain for speech, and special respiratory tolerance for prolonged speech activities. Lenneberg drew attention to the difference in development potential between the human and chimpanzee brain. The human brain at birth is about 24 per cent of its adult weight while the chimp brain is some 60 per cent. He further held that there was no evidence to suggest that any non-human form had the capacity to acquire even primitive stages of language development. In the late 1960s and early 1970s, a number of chimps were trained in language-like behaviour. To what extent Lenneberg's claim needs to be modified in the light of such studies, if at all, is not clear. It is possible that several chimp studies, now in progress, may provide further light. While animals do not acquire human language, however much they are exposed to it, in humans,

436

acquisition of language goes on in spite of dramatic handicaps for some children. Children of parents who have no spoken language, or who are themselves deaf, for example, acquire language without any great delay. Lenneberg also points to linguistic features common to all languages as consistent with the notion of human language as species specific. He further cites the regularity of the developmental sequence of acquisition: babbling at about six months, the first 'word' at about twelve months, the two-word 'sentence' by about two years and competence in communication which is complete in a basic sense by five years of age.

That this sort of pattern is to be found across widely differing languages and cultures is attested by the work of Slobin and his colleagues. Pathological case histories also indicate that beyond the age of puberty, when language function has been lateralized in the left hemisphere (for the great majority), the capacity for further language acquisition decreases dramatically. This, then, is some of the material brought to bear on the thesis of the uniqueness of language to man. Lenneberg held that human language is a species specific cognitive capacity, a view shared by Noam Chomsky.

In spite of the clear demonstration of the involvement of physical maturation in the acquisition of language, it is impossible to specify in neuro-physiological terms the relationship between them.

Jean Piaget (b. 1896)

Piaget cannot accept either the Behaviourist or the Chomskyan view of language acquisition, and, while his own approach entails the notion of a strong maturational influence, he proposes that language development grows out of the changing cognitive processes of the child, which in turn reflects the changing nature of the interactions between the child and his environment. This view sees the period before the onset of language as one in which the child comes to know his world in such a way as to enable him to make sense of at least some of the vocal sounds that he hears. Interaction with the environment will be largely in terms of caretakers, food, the consequences of an increasing ability to move about, and such like; and it is not surprising that his early words are dominated by those referring to salient aspects of his world. This is a plausible account of the onset of speech, but one which is difficult, in practice, to test. Clearly, infants do understand much about their world before they begin to speak. It may even be that this understanding is an essential ingredient for language. The important question, however, is whether, by itself, the understanding is sufficient to account for language acquisition. Helen Sinclair-de-Zwart (1969), one of the team of Genevan researchers, has provided data which offer some support for the supposition that cognitive changes precede rather than follow language changes.

It will be seen in the next Chapter that this theme is central to Piaget's view of development. What evidence is there to support this point of view? It was noted earlier that the bulk of the work performed by Piagetian psychologists is based on a clinical approach, in which children are required to perform tests and answer questions in situations ingeniously contrived to investigate changing cognitive strategies.

Four- and five-year-old children appear to believe that the amount of a liquid changes with the shape of a container. Thus water from a standard beaker poured into a narrower vessel elicits a response indicating that the amount of liquid is now considered to be greater. Most children of four years of age will respond in this way while most children of six years and more will be able to compensate for the decrease in the width of the container, and maintain that the quantity of liquid is identical (has been conserved) across the two situations. This task, conservation of volume (one of a range of Piagetian conservation tasks), was used to divide the children into three groups; total absence of conservation, intermediate stage, and conservation present.

The children's verbal capacities were explored, using both production tasks (where the children's use of language is examined) and comprehension tasks (their understanding of words used by others). The following linguistic features were examined:

1. Use of comparatives (larger, smaller) as opposed to absolute terminology (big, small).
2. Use of differentiated terms like 'short' and 'thin' as distinct from an overall application of 'little'.
3. The type of sentence used to co-ordinate the two dimensions, e.g., 'This is tall but it's thin'.

The comprehension task 'find a pencil which is longer but thinner' was performed correctly by practically all the children; but, while the three groups did not differ in this task, there were striking differences between the extreme groups on the description tasks. Of those children who 'conserved', the large majority used comparatives; those who did not, used absolute terminology almost exclusively. Those with conservation all used different terms for different dimensions; of those without, three-quarters used a single term, e.g., 'small' for both 'short' and 'thin'. Those with conservation were more skilful in combining descriptions: 'this pencil is longer but thinner, and the other is short but thick'. The group without conservation mostly described only one dimension, or used four separate sentences.

A further series of experiments attempted to teach the group without conservation the verbal skills which distinguished the other group. Having completed this verbal training the children were again assessed to see whether this had made a difference to their ability in the conservation task. In the event, it had not for 90 per cent of the children, whose ability to conserve remained unchanged. It had, indeed, proved difficult to teach the non-conservers some of the verbal skills. It was relatively easy for them to learn to use differentiated terms like 'short' and 'thin', harder for them to use 'plus' and 'minus' ('*plus*' and '*moins*') to produce comparatives, and still more difficult for them to learn combined descriptions. While the verbal training did bring about an awareness of the relation between the height of the liquid and the width of the stem, it did not bring about the ability to 'conserve' for volume.

This provides some support for the Piagetian view of the relation between language and intellectual operations, that language is not a sufficient condition for bringing about intellectual changes; and that, indeed, it is changes in intellectual operations which initiate changes in language.

Some methodological approaches

The four views of language acquisition outlined give rise to somewhat different lines of enquiry. The purpose of this part of the Chapter is to consider a further, small sample of the empirical work in this area with a view to indicating something of the variety of methods employed.

Non-nutritive sucking
It is a matter of common observation that, within a few months, babies respond readily to human speech. Those interested in a view of an innate capacity for language have recently examined children from birth onwards in respect of their response to human speech, taking the view that evidence of early selective responses would provide support for this position. Using a number of different approaches it has been demonstrated that babies respond selectively to those sounds within the range of normal speech frequencies; they respond selectively to patterned sounds as against steady sound stimuli. Babies have been observed to respond in a specific way to adult speech as early as the first day of life, and some recent research has suggested that, even in the early weeks of life, a baby can distinguish between the voice of his own mother and other voices. This was inferred from differences in non-nutritive sucking rates recorded at the sound of the voice of the mother as compared with rates for other voices. The baby sucked on a device designed to measure sucking accurately; this proved to be more vigorous for the voice of the mother than for other voices.

Tape-recorded models for imitation
While Chomsky has demonstrated that the stimulus-response account of language acquisition is inadequate, it is clear that imitation and selective reinforcement are involved, for example, in the establishment of dialect

differences. Critical experiments, that is experiments which serve to differentiate clearly between alternative explanations, are difficult to devise when the alternatives lead to the same sort of predictions. The study to be described, carried out by Ricks in 1972, while not critical in this sense, does throw light on the sort of linguistic material which infants imitate. He played, to children of about one year of age, tapes of three different kinds of word. Each parent involved spoke a list of 'dibby' words, meaningless combinations of sounds—like 'dibby'—which the child was capable of uttering but had not; a list of 'dada' words, which the child had used in babble but which had either no known referent or loose referents; the third list consisted of 'label' words, the child's normal labels for items and events in his environment. Having been exposed to each group of words the child's immediate imitations were recorded. Imitation was low for 'dibby' words, somewhat greater for 'dada' words but greatest of all for 'label' words. Imitation, here, was influenced by things in the environment to which particular sounds had already been assigned, suggesting the importance of meaning as a basis for imitation.

Tape-recorded home studies

Laboratory-based studies have obvious limitations; language acquisition takes place in the home, and it was inevitable that studies should be undertaken in this context. The pioneer work in this field was carried out by Roger Brown and his colleagues from Harvard University. They made an intensive study of the development of the language of three children, known as Adam, Eve, and Sarah. In the early 1960s when the study began, Eve was eighteen months old, Adam and Sarah twenty-seven months old. The minimum schedules involved a two-hour visit every other week for Adam and Eve and half an hour for Sarah. When there were interesting, new things happening, additional recordings were made. This, then, was a longitudinal study covering one year for Eve and five for Adam and Sarah. The principal data gathered were recordings of the spontaneous speech of the subjects in conversation with the mother and occasionally, others. Two investigators made the visits and, while one tended the tape recorder and acted as a playmate for the child, the other made notes of significant features of the content to aid subsequent understanding of the tape transcriptions. The recordings, transcribed into typescript formed an archive for subsequent study.

This approach has its limitations. It is expensive on time and manpower, not to mention the storage space for the transcribed tapes. The data gathered relate to only three, carefully selected, children which clearly limits the extent to which findings may be generalized. To offset this, the vast amount of data provides material for numerous independent studies; indeed, it seems likely that this data will continue to

440

furnish further studies for some time to come. Studies of this data have yielded details of the way in which children of this age use such negatives as 'no' and 'not', and the way in which self-reference changes. At first the child invariably uses his own name, then 'I' and 'me' are used sometimes correctly, sometimes not, and finally they are used in accordance with grammatical function. The succession of stages has been seen as a series of rules, increasing in complexity, used to refer to an entity which does not change—the self. This is one example of increasing grammatical competence, gained, for the most part, in the absence of direct instruction, thus supplying some support for the nativist position.

Other studies have traced similar, apparently rule-governed sequences in respect of the development of phonology, as well as syntax. (While it is convenient to describe language in this way for discussion the division is artificial, the development of each being related to that of the others.)

Such tentative conclusions as can be drawn about the acquisition and development of language, while based on the types of study which have been considered above, must also be seen in the light of the other aspects of the child's development. In particular, there is a question as to how language is related to other aspects of cognitive development. In a review of a variety of evidence from the language acquisition literature, Cromer (1973) distinguished two trends. One of these comes from evidence which supports the notion of acquisition as preceded by appropriate cognitive development. It includes experiments like those of Sinclair-de-Zwart (1969) and Ricks (1972), discussed earlier, and is generally in line with the Piagetian approach. The second trend is one to be found implied in many studies, and is consistent with the development of language independent of other cognitive progress and implicating maturation factors as regulating the acquisition process. This draws heavily upon the sort of evidence adduced by Lenneberg, the stability of the age of onset, and the regularity of the development schedule across cultures. It also draws some support from studies like that on 'self-reference', considered earlier, where the development of the language appeared unrelated to any cognitive change, since the individual to whom 'John', 'I' and 'me' all refer remains, esssentially, unchanged. Further, comparison with attempts to teach language-like behaviour to chimpanzees suggests that, while cognitive development may be a necessary condition for acquisition and development of language, it is questionable whether it is a sufficient condition. Thus, two broad groups of factors are implicated, the one biological and the other cognitive.

Social influences on language acquisition

Much of the discussion so far has related to what the child acquires: sounds, words and rules for creating sentences. Some mention has also been made of how acquisition comes about. The orderly sequence of development suggests the regulating influence of biological factors, and the work of the Genevan school indicates the involvement of other aspects of cognitive development. It is also clear that acquisition and development are influenced by other people, and in this part of the Chapter the evidence from a number of social studies is considered. This relates to the influence of parents, size of family, and social class.

Social class

Hess and Shipman (1965) studied 163 American mothers and their four-year-old children. While their study was concerned with the much wider issue of cultural deprivation, its results have a direct bearing on processes involved in language acquisition. The authors, aligning their position with that of Basil Bernstein (1961), present data to indicate that there are class-related differences in communication, which, they argue, influence the intellectual development of the child. In particular, they draw attention to a 'lack of meaning in the mother-child communication system' for low-status children, and argue that this is a central factor contributing to the child's deprivation. 'The meaning of deprivation', they claim, 'is a deprivation of meaning.'

BERNSTEIN AND CODES

Bernstein distinguished between *restricted* and *elaborated* codes of communication. The former are characterized by brevity and lack of specific information. Statements tend to include a considerable number of cliches but little modification of meaning in terms of subordinate clauses. Elaborated codes, in contrast, are characterized by statements where the content is specific to the situation and the other people involved. They are more precise and permit expression of a more extensive and complex range of thought. According to Bernstein, middle-class people use both codes, but the restricted code dominates the communications of the lower class. It is argued that early experience with these codes affects not only future patterns of the child's communication, but also the complexity of the contact he has with the world around him. (In this form it is a variant of the Whorfian hypothesis discussed in Chapter 18.)

The following example may further clarify the distinctions between the two proposed codes. Where the mother is engaged in a telephone conversation and becomes increasingly aware of intruding noise from her child, a 'restricted code' reaction might simply be a request to 'be quiet' or 'shut up' or similar short explicit commands. The elaborated code reaction would include some sort of reason for the request, 'do be quiet for a moment, I want to talk on the telephone'. In the one case, the child is required to conform to the request, in the other, whether he conforms or not, he has been invited to 'share' in the whole event. Hess and Shipman distinguish between status-orientated families where control is exercised through status appeals ('You do that because I say so'), and person-orientated families. In these, the status appeals are modified by being orientated towards persons ('You do this, John; I believe it to be to your advantage to do so'). This distinction, it will be seen, matches the 'restricted' and 'elaborated' code distinction. Thus it is proposed that 'deprivation of meaning' is built into the family situation of the low-status child, and the growth of cognitive processes is fostered by those family control systems which offer a wide range of alternatives of thought and action via appropriate verbal exchanges.

The data collected by Hess and Shipman bear out the distinctions they draw. The research plan involved interviewing the mothers in their homes, and mother and child in a laboratory-based interaction session in which the mother was taught three simple tasks and then asked to teach them to the child. While this instruction was going on, the mother-child communication was examined. It did reveal marked differences of the sort expected between low- and high-status mothers, the latter providing a more extensive and detailed framework within which the child could learn. The conclusions drawn about the mother-child communication system by Hess and Shipman rest largely on data collected from three specific tasks. To what extent these tasks under laboratory conditions offer insight into 'real-life' interactions must remain an open question. However, a more fundamental question which must be considered is whether the differences between the codes of the low- and high-status children can be seen in terms of relative deficit (or enrichment) or whether they must simply be regarded as different.

LABOV AND 'BLACK ENGLISH'

Labov has drawn attention to the very common evaluative approaches to those who speak dialects different from some accepted standard. In most countries there are dialects which are associated with some form of deficit, however vague, when compared with some standard, for example, 'the Queen's English' or the 'Hochdeutsch' of Germany. It is contended that there is no evidence to support the notion that those speaking a non-standard dialect are deficient in communication skills. Labov (1970) has demonstrated that the social situation is a powerful determinant of verbal behaviour. He has described the dramatic changes which took place when the testing conditions changed. In the first of these, a young black boy was shown a toy and asked by a friendly, white interviewer to tell him everything he could about it. The boy said very little and was silent for much of the time. Had the testing been limited to this situation the experimenter might have been inclined to conclude that this boy was relatively non-verbal. In a second situation a black interviewer was used. Leon, the eight-year-old black boy, answered his questions with single words or indistinct sounds. He, too, appeared to be inarticulate. But when, seated on the floor sharing a bag of potato crisps with his best friend, the same black interviewer introduced topics in the local dialect, Leon emerged as a lively conversationalist. It was quite clear that Leon could not be described as 'non-verbal'. However, if standard testing conditions resemble the first two interviewing situations, it seems very likely that this is the label he would have been given. That the findings of Hess and Shipman accord with what most would regard as clear and expected differences between social classes, is not in doubt. Neither is there doubt that the differences found were reliable within the particular setting of the study. What is challenged by the work of Labov and others is whether the standard tests were valid measures of the normal mother-child interaction.

Family size and deprivation
While doubt exists as to the usefulness of the notion of 'deprivation of meaning' to describe differences in verbal behaviour between social groups it may have some relevance within those groups. Halliday (1975) argues that language is used to regulate the behaviour of others, and that the mastery of this function is one of the essential elements of the developmental process. Not only does the child learn to regulate behaviour, but he uses language to assist in the development of understanding. He is, in Halliday's terms, 'learning to mean'. It thus seems plausible to suppose that opportunities for 'learning to mean' may differ from child to child, and that these may significantly affect language acquisition. The extreme case of feral children (children who by some accident grow up with only animal companions) whose vocalizations consist mainly of animal noises lends some support.

A considerable amount of work has been carried out to investigate home and parental influences on acquisition. The effect of family size on language development, for example, has been studied. Several investigators have noted an impairment of verbal intelligence, i.e., a poor performance on the verbal section of an intelligence test— in children reared in large families—and there is evidence which suggests that it is the environment rather than genetic factors which are involved. It may be the case that, while such children may have adequate social stimulation, its quality is predominantly that afforded by brothers and sisters. This may well be less rich than that of the parents. The distinctly 'adult' form of the language of an only child tends to support the assumption that the acquisition and development process is influenced by the linguistic environment. It has also been argued that, since large families tend to be noisy families where several people may be speaking at once on different topics, the impaired clarity of the language environment makes acquisition more difficult in large families.

Studies which have examined the influence of caretakers and parents suggest the importance of meaningful language interactions in the process of acquisition The Ricks (1972) study cited earlier, indicates the importance of meaning for the child's imitations, for it was the 'label' words which were imitated most. At the babbling stage, babies vocalize more when spoken to each time they do so. Even a tape-recorded voice will produce a significant increase in babbling. In contrast, the mere presence of a (non-speaking) adult has little effect. The greatest effect is obtained in the presence of a person who will 'respond' to the child's babbling. The same sort of thing is to be found in older pre-school children. Extension of play sessions with toys brings about very little development by itself; but when the play session involves an adult who makes a point of engaging the child in conversation, considerable progress is observed. It seems, then, that the quality of the child's linguistic environment plays a significant part in acquisition and that important elements in the environment are how the child is talked to and the meaningfulness of what is said.

Parental models: expansion and imitation
In the course of day-to-day verbal interactions between parents and children, there are a number of repeated patterns which appear as potential influences on acquisition. One of these is the expansion-imitation pattern. For example:

Child: Mummy drink.
Mother: Yes, mummy is having a drink.

Here, the child initiates the sequence, and the mother, using cues provided by the context, expands what the child says. Or the sequence may be initiated by the mother thus:

Mother: Would you like some milk?
Child: Like milk.
Mother: Yes, would you like some milk?

It seem possible that these expansions and imitations could provide part of the mechanism of acquisition. However, at least the first of these two patterns presents some difficulty, for 'mummy drink' could mean for example that the child simply wishes to draw his mother's attention to his own wish for a drink, so that the mother's expansion fails to match the child's meaning.

A different sort of pattern occurs when, instead of expanding what the child says, the mother makes some appropriate comment. Thus:

Child: Girl cry.
Mother: Yes, she's fallen and hurt her knee.

445

Cazden (1965) compared the effects of expansions and comments on the development of language in two-and-a-half-year-old, working-class children. They were divided into three groups, one receiving no special linguistic training, a second group had each statement a child made expanded by an adult, and the third group had their statements commented on rather than expanded. These regimes extended over three months for one hour per day and five days a week. The first group served as a control, and, while the expansion group showed slightly greater improvement, it was the 'commented on' group which showed the most progress. It is also possible that language development is influenced by direct instruction from the parents, particularly from the parental correction of mistakes. Roger Brown and a colleague reported that, from data they collected, parents rarely correct children's grammatical errors, except perhaps for such words as 'eated' and 'goed'. Otherwise corrections relate mainly to 'naughty' words, faulty pronunciation and the truth of the statements made. On some occasions, even when grammatical suggestions are made, the child appears unable to imitate them accurately. An example of this is taken from McNiell (1966):

Child: Nobody don't like me.
Mother: No, say 'nobody likes me'.
Child: Nobody don't like me.

Then, after eight repetitions of this exchange

Mother: No, now listen carefully; say 'nobody likes me'.
Child: Oh, nobody don't likes me.

From this restricted sample of studies aimed at examining some of the factors influencing the acquisition and development of language, some very general conclusions can be drawn. While clear differences exist between social classes as to the style or code of language acquired, there is doubt as to whether it is easy to judge between them in respect of superiority or inferiority. There is also evidence which suggests that children of large families are disadvantaged in respect of language environment, and that the obvious possible mechanisms for 'learning to mean', parental expansion, comment and correction, and imitation by the child, are differentially effective. By themselves, these studies, representative of a range of others, give only a glimpse of the possible ways in which language is acquired. For a more complete account, they need to be supplemented by explanations which draw on maturational notions, like Piaget's concept of 'readiness' to account for the changing use the child is able to make of his environment; that, for example, McNeill's child in the above conversation would, possibly within months

446

of the conversation quoted, find it quite easy to imitate 'Nobody likes me'.

The study of language acquisition is important in its own right. That is, since language forms a significant part of human behaviour it is a proper interest for psychologists. It has been reviewed at this point for two main reasons. First, as a means of underlining the more general issues involved in developmental psychology, considered in the first part of the Chapter, in terms of one of the most recent of its new fields of interest. In spite of its importance, the spread of interest dates only from the early 1960s. Thus, it has been possible to look at some of the problems posed—'what' does a child acquire when he acquires language and 'how' does he acquire it. It has been possible to examine some of the ways in which these problems have been investigated using naturalistic observation and experiment. It has also been possible to use a number of different explanatory approaches to the phenomenon of language acquisition—the Behaviourist, the Piagetian, the biological and the linguistic. This, then, will serve as a backcloth to the sorts of issues to be met in other contexts within developmental psychology.

The second reason for the treatment of language acquisition at this point has to do with its intrinsic importance, not only in developmental psychology, but within human psychology as a whole. For language is both a distinctive and pervasive activity of mankind. It is distinctive because no other species communicates in this way, and because this particular kind of communication has been stored (by printing and other forms of recording) and used in such a way as to allow one generation of men to use and develop the knowledge of previous generations. No other species does this. Each generation of bees, dolphins and chimpanzees must start where their ancestors started—rather than where they left off. Language pervades all parts of man's behaviour. Not only can man talk about his activities and his experiences, he can also translate the absence of these things into words. Like men, animals perceive, remember, reason, experience fear and emotion, and so on. Possession of language means that mankind has an additional dimension at his disposal, by means of which he is able, in some cases, to manipulate the activities and experiences themselves, and also to record them, to reflect on them and to allow others to do so. Further, it provides a means for patterns of social interaction which are distinctly human. Insight into what is involved in language acquisition thus provides an important point of departure for the study of human development.

FURTHER READING
Foss, B. M., ed. (1974) *New Perspectives in Child Development*. Penguin.
McGurk, H. (1975) *Growing and Changing*, ed. P. Herriot. Methuen (Essential Psychology Series).

Mussen, P. H., Conger, J. J., and Kagan, J. (1974) *Child and Personality*. 4th edn. Harper and Row.

Oldfield, R.C., and Marshall, J. C. (1968) *Language*. Penguin.

Turner, J. (1975) *Cognitive Development*, ed. P. Herriot. Methuen (Essential Psychology Series).

20 Three accounts of human development

HARRY FISHER

In many ways, age-related changes in the behaviour of children are similar, in spite of variations in cultural backgrounds. One aim of an account of development must be to supply a theoretical framework which will accommodate these similarities and provide a basis for the prediction of others. One of the accounts to be considered is made in terms of processes held to be involved in all behaviour-change. This is the learning theory account which takes the view that 'development is just learning'. The other two accounts are framed in terms of pervasive aspects of human behaviour, Piaget's being concerned with intellectual, and Freud's with personality development. These three accounts provide an introduction to some of the basic issues involved in contemporary research and to the vocabulary of developmental psychology.

Learning-theory and development

Learning is the process by which more or less permanent changes in behaviour come about, through experience or practice. Behaviour-changes related to temporary states of the organism, like illness, fatigue, drugs, and injury are not in this category; neither are changes which take place due to maturation. As has been seen in the case of language acquisition, it is not always possible to decide which factor, if either, dominates, since it seems likely that both are at work most of the time and that each may influence the other. It is characteristic of maturational processes that there is a regularity about the developmental milestones. The development of mobility in the infant normally progresses from sitting to crawling and thence to kneeling, standing and walking. Many hold that, in this sequence of changes, maturation is dominant.

Learning-theory is the name given to the body of knowledge based primarily on studies in which an external stimulus becomes associated with an overt response, in most cases, by procedures known as conditioning. Three approaches to learning will be considered here. Two use conditioning procedures as the means of establishing new associations, while the third involves changes in behaviour brought about by observation. The general aim of learning-theory is to provide the basis for an explanatory account of as wide a range of behaviour change as possible, animal as well as human, in terms of a small number of principles for establishing new stimulus-response bonds. The validity of these principles has been widely demonstrated in animal experiments. A considerable volume of research in the developmental context has investigated the extent to which these same principles may apply to human behaviour, and much recent research has been concerned with conditioning and learning in early infancy.

Classical conditioning

Not all behaviour is learned. Some, like sneezing, salivating and eye-blinking appears to be elicited automatically by appropriate stimuli. This is known as reflex behaviour. Classical conditioning is the name given to the process whereby an association is formed between a previously neutral stimulus and the reflex behaviour. The best known example, possibly, is that in which Pavlov, the Russian physiologist-turned-psychologist, succeeded in inducing a dog to salivate to a previously neutral stimulus like the ticking of a metronome. Thus the reflex response of salivation, usually reserved for digestive purposes, became conditional on (or conditioned to) the ticking of the metronome. This was brought about by allowing the metronome to tick for a few seconds, stopping it and at the same time presenting the dog with some dry food. After a dozen or so trials the dog salivated at the sound of the metronome, and the *conditioned reflex* had been established. (Further details of Pavlov's experiments are to be found in Ch. 10). It was for this that Pavlov became famous, and he believed that his method provided a means of gaining fundamental insight into the learning process.

The American Behaviourist, J. B. Watson, was of the same mind. He believed that there were three distinguishable emotions, love, anger and fear, each initially evoked by a limited set of stimuli. He argued that these responses were innate, since, for example, loss of body support, or a sudden increase in noise invariably produced distress in young infants. He demonstrated how fear could be learned, by conditioning this response to noise to other, previously neutral, stimuli. In particular, he set out to condition a fear of furry creatures in a nine-month-old infant.

Albert, as the infant was called, had no such fear at the outset of the procedure. In the initial session, as the child reached out to stroke a tame white rat, a loud gong was struck behind him. Naturally the child was startled. By the end of the seventh such weekly session, the child began to exhibit fear and avoidance in the presence of the rat without the sounding of the gong. In particular, this was seen as the way in which irrational fears could be acquired in childhood. In general, it was interpreted as showing that it was possible, in principle, to imagine the establishment of all sorts of stimulus-response bonds in this way. Conditioned reflexes were, thus, seen as providing a sound, explanatory basis for a wide range of behaviour-change. Indeed, there were those who held that all learning could be explained in terms of chains of conditioned reflexes.

It was observed that Albert had also become afraid in the presence of other objects which were white and furry—a rabbit, a dog and a white-bearded man. The fear had generalized. Generalization provided a further explanatory concept for accounting for the extension of the response to similar stimuli. Discrimination was seen as a complementary notion, conditioned responses being elicited only by specific stimuli. The concept of higher-order conditioning—whereby a further neutral stimulus becomes conditioned to a previously conditioned neutral stimulus—was seen as a possible way of accounting for complex human behaviour.

It is possible to see this sort of behaviour-change in infants. They suck innately at a nipple, but not at the sight of a feeding bottle. Yet, after several months of bottle feeding, infants frequently make sucking movements when they see the bottle. A considerable amount of recent research has demonstrated the wide range of the neonate's susceptibility to conditioning. It has, at least in principle, indicated that this means of learning may be extensively involved. It has been suggested that both conscience and language, for example, may be areas in which classical conditioning operates.

Operant conditioning
This mode of learning is associated with the name of B. F. Skinner, the American Behaviourist. Sometimes also called *instrumental conditioning*, it involves the learning of associations between the responses of the organism and events in the environment. It differs from classical conditioning in that it is the response which initiates the process of learning. In the animal experiments in which it has been demonstrated, as soon as the animal makes a response, usually a movement, of the sort required by the experimenter, a 'reward', usually a food pellet, is delivered to it. This is repeated the next time a suitable response is made, so that the animal comes to associate the response with the arrival of the

food pellet. In this way the behaviour of animals has been shaped, and they have been taught a range of behaviours not usually associated with them. Skinner has, for example, conditioned pigeons to play a version of ping-pong by this means. In this case pecking at the ball constitutes the operant (or instrumental) response while the consequent food serves as reinforcement, and the associations learned are between the emitted response and the reinforcement (rather than between a stimulus and a response as in classical conditioning).

Reinforcement
This is needed to maintain as well as to shape new responses, and has been extensively investigated under laboratory conditions. In some experiments, reinforcement has been given every time the required response was made (continuous reinforcement), in others not every time (partial reinforcement). In this last category, a rat may receive reinforcement on, say, every tenth trial (fixed ratio) or every ten seconds (fixed interval). Other schedules of partial reinforcement used are variable ratio and variable interval.

In general, continuous reinforcement produces the quickest learning, while partial reinforcement produces the strongest, that is, the learning which will persist for longest in the absence of the reinforcers. The persistent gambler seems to provide a fair example of this sort of behaviour. His reinforcement (winnings) come only occasionally but, in view of his persistence, sufficiently often to maintain the operant responses of picking the 'winner'.

In common with a host of other psychological concepts reinforcement, while useful, is difficult to define. What is particularly difficult to decide is what makes a reinforcer reinforcing. It is easy to see why a hungry rat is reinforced by a food pellet, but, once the concept is used in the context of human behaviour, the matter becomes more difficult because of the vast range of environmental events—food, sympathy, information, attention, absence of attention, and so on—which function as reinforcers. To avoid this difficulty, an operational definition of reinforcement is given. Thus, any stimulus-event which, following a particular response, increases the probability of the repetition of the response is regarded as a reinforcer. While it is unsatisfactory to be unable to be more specific about the nature of reinforcement, perhaps it is not altogether surprising in the light of the range of complexity of possible learning situations.

Reward and punishment
Prior to Skinner's work on operant conditioning, one of America's early psychologists, E. L. Thorndike, proposed that animals learn responses, the consequences of which they find 'rewarding', and drop those found

'punishing'. That is, it was the effect of making the response which determined whether learning would take place or not. This was Thorndike's Law of Effect, a law which has an immediate intuitive appeal.

It supposes that 'punishment' will have an effect opposite to that of reward (or reinforcement), that is, instead of increasing, it will decrease the probability of repetition. Thorndike's own experiments obliged him to abandon the punishment half of the law. Subsequent animal experiments have confirmed these findings.

Since punishment is practiced both by society and by parents as a means of changing the behaviour of deviants, it is important to try to assess the relevance of the experiments. One possible reaction is to refuse to accept the relevance of laboratory-based experiments in contrived and restricted contexts as valid for wider, real-life situations. If, however, the principles are accepted as valid, it seems that punishment, as a strategy for removing unwanted behaviour, has only limited potential. Further experiments have suggested that unwanted behaviour can be removed more efficiently by experimental extinction. This is a procedure whereby an animal continues to respond but no reinforcement is given. Under such a regime, the frequency of responding gradually weakens until it disappears. In human terms, the suggestion is that raids on the biscuit tin can be more efficiently discouraged by leaving it empty than by smacking or admonishing the raider.

Sufficiently severe punishment will, of course, suppress the undesired response but will not deal with the motivational origins. Indeed, it is argued that such punishment with children may produce undesirable emotional consequences in the wake of the frustrated aim and the fear of future punishment.

Punishment may be effective if the suppression of the undesired response is seen in a context where alternative responses exist which may be rewarded. Thus milder punishments, the criticisms of a trainer or teacher, low essay grades and the like, usually serve these ends. Sporadic punishment of the same offence may only serve as a reinforcer. Some of the persistently undesirable behaviour of children in classrooms has been seen in this light. In the interest of keeping the lesson moving, a teacher may well ignore minor offences for most of the time. The times when he stops to rebuke offenders may produce such a diversion as will reinforce the behaviour. Operant methods have been systematically used in some schools with acute behaviour problems. The basis of the system is the rewarding of desirable behaviour (by praise or the awarding of privileges) and the ignoring of undesirable behaviour as far as possible. When it is not possible, offenders are moved to a 'time out' room. This approach has been used at widely differing levels from English primary schools to down-town ghetto schools in New York. The reports published claim a measure of success.

Language acquisition
Reference has already been made (Ch. 5) to Skinner's account of language acquisition in terms of operant conditioning and of Chomsky's objections to it. It is sufficient here to restate that it was not Chomsky's intention to suggest that operant conditioning was not involved, but rather that such an explanatory device was inadequate to account for all aspects of language acquisition.

Operant conditioning in infancy
As with classical conditioning, recent research has shown that infant behaviour can be modified by operant procedures within the first days of independent life. There are, of course, limits to the variety of response in the neonate's repertoire, but sucking, headturning, and later, vocalization and smiling, for example, have all been brought under the control of operant procedures. Learning by operant conditioning is thus a potentially powerful source of influence on behavioural development from a very early stage.

Classical and operant conditioning—limitations
The learning theorists believed that the central issues involved in giving an account of human behaviour were those which had to do with learning. Classical and operant conditioning were regarded as fundamental principles of behaviour, capable of providing an objective insight into all learning in animals, children, and adults. Subsequent work questioned the validity of assuming so comprehensive a role for conditioning. In particular, the validity of transferring findings from laboratory experiments on animals to real-life situations with humans has been questioned. As has been amply demonstrated, human learning is influenced by language, and to that extent is qualitatively different from animal learning. Furthermore, classical and instrumental conditioning appear to describe acquisition of associations by an organism which is largely passive and virtually at the mercy of the environment. Viewed in this way, accounts based on conditioning appear appropriate only to limited areas of human and animal learning.

Learning by observation
In contrast to the early conditioning experiments, based mainly on animals, learning by observation has been studied using mainly nursery school children. That children learn in this way is no new discovery but it was not until the early 1960s that systematic studies were undertaken. The experimental design involved, first, showing a group of children a real-life episode, or a film, in which a model (usually adult) behaved in a given context in some extraordinary way. The children were later observed individually in a similar context, to assess the extent to which

this behaviour was imitated. It was important that the piece of behaviour filmed should be extraordinary and not a usual part of the child's repertoire, so that the criterion for its imitation could be clear. The behaviour of these children was compared with that of a control group who did not see the film.

A considerable number of experiments have studied the learning of aggressive behaviour. In a typical episode the model would be seen making an attack on an inflatable (Bobo) doll of a size usually a little larger than the watching children. The unusual feature of the attack was that it might involve, say lifting and throwing the doll, or attacking it with a wooden hammer. The findings indicate that, compared with a control group, those children who saw the episode behaved in a much more aggressive way with the doll, much of the aggression following that of the model. This was the same whether the experimental group saw a real episode or a film, or whether the model was child or adult. Using this basic design Bandura and Walters and a number of colleagues have investigated the sorts of factors that influence the likelihood of imitation of observed behaviour.

In a further experiment where the model exhibited aggressive behaviour, one group saw the model rewarded (with sweets and lemonade) for his behaviour; another saw the model 'punished' (in terms of a severe scolding for his brutality), while the control group observed neither the rewarding nor the punishment. Subsequent individual observation showed that the levels of imitation differed among the three groups. The 'model-punished' group showed much less aggression than the other two. Thus, the 'model-punished' group might be seen as sharing the punishment of the model, and the differences between the groups seen in terms of the *vicarious punishment* as against *vicarious reinforcement*. When the children taking part in this study were individually asked to imitate the behaviour of the model and were directly rewarded for doing so, there were no differences. Children from all three groups were equally aggressive. The vicarious punishment was associated, therefore, with the lower performance of aggression in the previous phase of the study. It appeared that the acquisition of the aggressive behaviour was not different from that for children in the other groups.

It is of considerable importance to notice that the aggressive behaviour acquired came about by mere exposure. The children were not instructed to attend to and to try to imitate what they saw: just seeing it was sufficient. Furthermore, Bandura has shown that absence or weakness of performance cannot be construed as absence of acquisition.

What is true for aggressive responses has also been demonstrated for a range of others. Thus, children have been shown to learn to solve problems, and to make moral judgements, among other tasks, by observing others. Learning complex tasks would be extremely difficult if conditioning were the only means. Thus, learning to drive a car, to play golf, or to play a piano can be done more efficiently by the intervention of a teacher who can demonstrate what is required.

Further studies have investigated a range of model-variables involved in the performance of observed behaviour. For example, models whom the subjects perceive as similar to themselves elicit greater imitation than those perceived to be dissimilar: a child is more likely to imitate another than to imitate a cartoon character. Similarly, the perceived warmth, power and attractiveness of the model have been shown to increase performance. However, it has been shown that acquisition is no less likely with models seen as cold or lacking in power or unattractive.

The studies of learning by observation have raised a number of problems as well as providing a wealth of information about the way in which learning may take place outside the laboratory. Of the problems, the notion of imitation is an important one, for it provides no clue as to how the learning takes place, merely an index that it does. Imitation of others is so common that some have seen it as a human instinct. In a study where children were directly rewarded for imitating one aspect of a model's behaviour, it was found that other aspects were also being imitated. Many children imitate their parents in this way, reproducing attitudes of stance and gait, verbal mannerisms and tone of voice, as well as similar opinions. This more general imitation of the characteristics of another has been called identification. It has been seen as an important process in personality development by Freud and others, and this concept will be further considered later. Recent research with infants has suggested that learning by observation is possible within the first three months, and is therefore a potentially powerful means of adaptation.

There is some overlap between the concepts of conditioning and learning by observation. Both, as has been seen, draw on the notion of reinforcement. But they appear to relate to different sorts of tasks. Observational learning relates to the combining of a number of established acts, for example, learning to co-ordinate arms, feet, head and breathing in learning to swim. The shaping of behaviour, on the other hand, appears to be specially suitable for the establishment of behaviour patterns which are, in total, new. There is, thus, a sense in which these two sorts of learning can be seen as complementary.

While two approaches to learning have been considered here, one in terms of conditioning, classical and operant, and the other in terms of observation and imitation, other forms have been described. Gagne, a learning theorist, has proposed a hierarchically organized system of eight different types of learning which he describes as signal learning, stimulus-response learning, chains (of stimulus-response connections), verbal associations, multiple discrimination, concept learning, principle learning, and problem-solving.

Evaluation
As an account of development, the approach in terms of conditioning is general rather than specific. It was the aim of early Behavourist researchers to identify principles underlying the learning process, and to demonstrate their relevance to behaviour-change in general, including, of course, developmental changes. The principles identified stem mainly from animal experiments, but there have been, from the earliest days of the Behaviourist enterprise, experiments demonstrating the effects of conditioning procedures on children, albeit in no great volume and in widely differing contexts. More recently, studies with infants have underlined the potential importance of conditioning from an early age. In many cases, however, experiments have involved highly specific stimuli within strictly controlled environments unlikely to correspond closely to real-life conditions. A cautious conclusion, therefore, is that such experiments demonstrate that conditioning processes may be involved in development. Other experiments, like the conditioning of fear of things white and furry in Watson's subject, Albeit, (see p. 451) demonstrate the principles in action in a more realistic setting. Particular experiments, however, permit only limited generalizations. The generality of the involvement of conditioning in development must, thus, be regarded as inferred, rather than demonstrated.

It seems likely that, whatever the importance of the role of conditioning, other factors are involved. The notion of maturation is not denied by Behaviourists so much as held to be of limited explanatory value. Thus this approach makes no appeal to changing biological factors to account for significant changes in behaviour.

In the case of learning by observation, systematic empirical work, using a range of modelling and imitation techniques on children of different age groups, provides a coherent demonstration of its role in development.

The single feature of child development which poses perhaps the most serious question for the learning-theory approach is that class of responses which may be regarded as 'novel' in the sense that it seems unlikely to have come about as a result of deliberate teaching or the imitation of a model. Child language at certain stages contains examples of such innovations—new words or near-lawful errors like 'gonned' or 'wented' for went, 'Weetabik' as a singular for an apparent plural Weetabix—which suggest a rule-governed behaviour distinguishable from repetition. This same sort of innovation is to be seen also in early locomotor behaviour, where individual children develop highly original means of moving from place to place.

457

Thus, while there seems little doubt that both conditioning and imitation are involved, neither, alone, would appear capable of providing the basis for an adequate account of development.

Piaget's account of development

Intellectual development

Piaget's work as a psychologist dates from 1921. His research, thus, at the time of writing extends over fifty-seven years. The large volume of work he and his associates have produced cannot easily be condensed. It has, however, been dominated by a single theme, the development of intellectual structures. These last two words need some clarification, for Piaget uses them in a singular way. Piaget's account of development is set within a biological framework. For survival, each organism must be able to adapt to its environment. Adaptation includes the possibility of structural changes. By analogy, intellectual development is seen as adaptation involving psychological structural changes. Piaget holds that we inherit a specific mode of doing business with the environment and that it is this which makes intellectual development possible. This mode is seen as remaining constant throughout life (in Piagetian terminology, it is a functional invariant), and changes in structure are due to its operation. Two conceptually distinct processes are seen to be operative in adaptation: assimilation and accommodation. A biological example of these aspects of adaptation can be seen in the case of intake of food by an organism. Assimilation, the process of applying existing structures to new functions, occurs in the processes of ingestion and digestion. The food is incorporated, i.e., assimilated by the organism. Accommodation, a process whereby the organism modifies existing structures to meet the demands of the changed environment, may be seen in the physical changes which may be necessary to incorporate the food as well as the biochemical changes which take place as a result of the intake of food. Intellectual development is seen in analogous terms. The existing cognitive structures operate on the environment in the assimilation of new information, which, in turn, is accommodated by, and produces changes in, existing structures. These two aspects of adaptation will be seen as serving complementary functions. In the same way, Piaget pairs the term organization with adaptation to indicate the progressive nature of intellectual functioning. Each time a child solves some new problem in his interaction with the environment, his intellectual development moves one step nearer to maturity. Confronted by the same problem, a procedure is now available for its solution. The attainment of this new level of adaptation is called equilibration.

Piaget describes the structure of the intellect in terms of schemas and operations. Schema is used to denote the internal representation of a well-defined sequence of physical or mental actions. Neonates are held to possess a number of innate schemas, relating to such actions as sucking, grasping, looking, and crying. As development proceeds, these schemata will be further elaborated, and links formed among them.

The term schema thus covers the most elementary sort of cognitive structure. Operations are more complex structures, usually acquired in middle childhood, and form the basis of the most complex forms of mental functioning. An operation in the sense used by Piaget has been described as 'an internalized action' or 'an action which takes place in imagination'. As with the term schema, Piaget nowhere sets down an exhaustive definition. A distinctive property of an operation is that it is reversible, that is, a child who is able to think 'operationally' is able to imagine not only a particular action, but also that action which will undo the first. Thus, subtraction may be used to reverse addition. A different sort of example of reversibility is to be found in the knowledge that pouring back all the individual glasses of water into the water jug will result in the same quantity of water as was present before the glasses were filled. Operational thinking is essential to intellectual activity; without it Piaget holds that the child is unable to recognize that, in the above example, the quantity of water is invariant, in spite of the transformation which takes place when the glasses are filled from the jug. Piaget holds that it is because the four-year-old is unable to think in terms of inverse operations that he is unable to perform accurately on conservation tasks. That is, he is unable to appreciate that, when the liquid from a tall slim glass is poured into a wider glass, the amount of water is the same. The different liquid levels appear to persuade him against conservation. It is central to Piaget's aim to give an account of the development of intellectual structures from the simplest beginning, the innate schemas, to operational thinking.

Stages of intellectual development

Piaget has identified a series of stages and substages, the order of which he regards as fixed since each presupposes the level of adaptation reached in the previous stage. The stages themselves are thus structurally distinct, and the four main stages are named in accordance with the dominant cognitive structure, as follows: sensori-motor (birth to about two years), pre-operational (two to seven years), concrete operations (seven to eleven years), and formal operations (upwards of eleven years). While most people reach the stage of concrete operations there are some who do not reach the final stage.

The child in the *sensori-motor period* knows his world dominantly in terms of perceptions and actions. When other means of knowing, memory and language, become available, this stage is at an end. The neonate has a few ready-made independent schemas, which gradually become co-ordinated into more complex schemas. Piaget describes how this comes about in terms of six sub-stages, beginning with actions described as reflex exercises, which come about through the gradual organization of action-perception schemas. Early in this stage a small object is something to be grasped, sucked, and looked at. Later it will be shaken, but if it drops it will quickly be forgotten. Most parents have observed babies drop things out of their cots and prams. At first they pay no further concern to the object, but later it becomes a good game to drop it and 'insist' on its return. Thus what seemed earlier to be 'out of sight, out of mind', is no longer so; the child appears to be able to think of an object which is not present. Piaget calls this the concept of object permanence. It suggests the establishment of a capacity to represent actions and objects internally. At about twelve to eighteen months children begin to use words and this provides a further means of representing aspects of the environment. Action-perception schemas are no longer the child's sole means of knowing his world.

While this first period is dominated by interactions involving a present environment, the final stage (formal operations) is characterized by a mode of thinking which can be completely dissociated from the environment. Between them are two stages representing the relative facility with which internal representations are handled. In the first they are handled imperfectly, being tied to a single, egocentric, viewpoint. In the second, released from this restriction, the individual is no longer constrained by his own viewpoint, but is able, by using reversible operations to see other possibilities. When this is the case the stage of concrete operations has been reached.

The pre-operational period can thus be differentiated from the previous stage by an increasing use of internal representation of the environment. The child can remember, imagine, and pretend. It is differentiated from the operational stage by the limitations of egocentricity. At this stage, a child's judgements are dominated by his own unique viewpoint. Such a child is unable, for example, to select from a series of photographs of a model landscape one that represents a viewpoint different from the one he sees it from. Similarly, a boy who asserts that he has a brother will deny that his brother also has a brother. At this stage, the child fails to realize the invariance of matter against perceptual, change. He also fails to conserve for number. If two rows of pennies are placed in one to one correspondence, a child at this stage will agree that each row has the same number. Yet, if in one of the rows of pennies some are placed closer together, he will now judge there to be fewer in this row than the other. He is apparently unable to perform the reverse operation of spreading them out again in his mind's eye.

The period of concrete operation is characterized by the acquisition of reversible operations, demonstrated in terms of success in conservation tasks. This process, however, takes time. In the early part of the period, conservation mistakes are still possible. For example, suppose a child is presented with two balls of clay of the same weight and size. If one of them is subsequently rolled into a sausage shape, the child at the pre-operational stage will say that mass, weight, and volume have all changed. A child in the early concrete operations stage is clear that the mass remains constant, but holds that weight and volume are changed. Later still he appreciates the conservation of both mass and weight—but not volume, until somewhere around eleven years of age. This period concerns concrete operations, because the child needs to be set problems relating to concrete objects rather than abstractions in order to understand logical relationships. For example, the child who is mid-way in the period and competent at seriation tasks, where he is required to arrange in order blocks of different size, may well find difficulty when presented with a similar abstract task (e.g., John is taller than Jack, Jack is smaller than George, who is smallest?).

The period of formal operations is characterized by the ability to solve problems in the absence of the concrete objects and situations to which the problem relates. Thus, a child at this stage is able to manipulate propositions like those above to obtain the correct answer. He is further able to regard the several possibilities of a given problem as hypotheses to be tested, and to locate salient variables, and examine their effects in isolation and in all possible combinations.

An experiment used to investigate formal operational thinking is one described by Piaget and Inhelder on the oscillation of a simple pendulum. The subject is set to determine what governs the time taken to complete one swing of a pendulum, in this case a weight suspended by a string. Possible variables involved are the length of the string, the size of the weight, the length of the swing and the strength of the initial push. It is in fact, the first of these which is the relevant variable. The subject's task is therefore, to isolate its effect from that of the others. The pre-operational child tends to believe that it is the strength of his initial push which matters, but he is incapable of separating the effects of the several factors. The child at this stage of concrete operations can vary each fact or factor systematically and observe the relation between the length of the string and the time of the pendulum's swing, but he too is incapable of isolating the effect of this variable. This isolation is typically, only achieved by the child in the period of formal operations.

Evaluation

An evaluation of Piaget's account of development is difficult because of the immensely detailed body of work on which it must be based. While it has received a general measure of acceptance, there have been a number

461

of recurrent criticisms. One of these involves the notion of distinct and separate stages which permeates Piaget's work. While it is likely that empirical work will raise some data which suggest transitional anomalies between one stage and the next, there are psychologists who hold that characteristics of each stage can coexist in the same individual, for example, counting on fingers to check arithmetical solutions when for some reason these are in doubt. Others have seen characteristics of the formal stage in pre-operational children. For example, something related to the raising of hypotheses is seen as implicit in the child's ability to pretend. As for abstract thinking, this has been seen, at least in embryo, in the recurrent question, 'What would happen, Mummy, if . . .'

Among other questions raised has been whether the emphasis on the activity of the sensori-motor stage is as important as Piaget teaches. (It is these actions which, internalized, lead to operational thinking.) It would follow that children with paralysed limbs but otherwise normally endowed would be seriously disadvantaged in respect of intellectual development. This is, in general, not the case.

The failure of children in the pre-operational phase to cope with conservation tasks has been interpreted by some psychologists in terms of the difficulties the children had with the word-meanings. It is by no means clear that children differentiate between words in the same way as adults do. Much of the work done by Piaget and his colleagues seems to assume that they do. It has been demonstrated that children at this stage can, by indirect methods, be trained to succeed in some conservation tasks. This line of criticism, together with the earlier question concerning the importance of activity, ultimately questions the theoretical validity of the operation, the centre piece of Piaget's account of development. Can the developmental sequence be accounted for in some other way? There is no question that an important qualitative change in thinking takes place. What is not clear is whether the psychological differences are best accounted for in terms of operations.

It has further been noted that Piaget's account of intellectual development pays little attention to the involvement of social and emotional variables.

Criticisms have also been levelled at the use of the clinical method, the restricted population on which findings are based, and, for much of the earlier work, the use of evidence based almost exclusively on Piaget's observation of his own children. Those who work with Piaget today would meet such objections by pointing out that rigorous experimental methods have, for some years now, been employed in addition to the clinical approach, and that this, together with experimentation outside Geneva, has produced substantial support for earlier work, as well as areas of disagreement. This applies, too, in respect of findings drawn from other populations. Psychology is indebted to Piaget for an account of intellectual development which is extensive in its coverage, coherent in that its varied aspects are linked by a relatively simple structural plan, and well-scrutinized in view of the large volume of research it has attracted and continues to attract.

An account of cognitive development which demands neither distinct stages nor a specific link with maturational forces is that described by J. S. Bruner, who sees the infant as an intelligent and active problem-solver from birth, with intellectual abilities basically similar to those of the mature adult. He describes three different ways in which the child represents the world to himself. These are called the enactive, iconic and symbolic modes of representation.

Enactive representation appears first. The child is seen as representing past events through motor responses. An infant will 'shake' a rattle which has just been removed or dropped, as if the movements themselves are expected to produce the accustomed sound.

Next comes iconic representation, when the child is capable of making representations in the form of images or spatial schemes. (These might be described as 'pictures' in the mind's eye. For some people, iconic representation is something of which they are conscious. Others appears to have no such experience.) Symbolic representation develops last. This is the most adaptable form of representation, for actions and images have a fixed relation to that which they represent. A symbol, for example, has only an arbitrary relation with its referent ('*dog*', '*chien*', '*hund*' are symbolic representations of a single class of referents). Symbols are also a more flexible means of representation in that the symbols themselves can be manipulated, ordered, classified, etc., thus facilitating manipulation of the user's world without the constraints of actions or images.

The similarities between this account of cognitive development and Piaget's are clear. An important difference is that the modes of representation are not related in the same way as Piaget's stages, in which any stage presupposes the one which precedes it. Further, while there may be periods when each mode is the one dominantly used, they may coexist.

Bruner argues that what determines the level of intellectual development in a particular area is the extent to which the child has been given appropriate instruction, together with adequate practice or experience, and that any concept, however formal or complex, can be communicated to a child if presented in a way that the child can initially comprehend, and developed in a manner which it can assimilate. He has demonstrated, for example, that children of eight years of age can be taught to appreciate the significance of the algebraic identity,

$$(x + 1)^2 = x^2 + 2x + 1$$

463

using square and rectangular blocks of wood. Another major difference between this account and that of Piaget is that Bruner attempts to describe the part played by influential adults in the instruction of the child, and, in this way to reveal something of the link between culture and cognitive growth. This approach thus carries a well-defined educational component.

Freud's account of development

The development of personality

An important key to the understanding of Freud's account of development is the context in which it was made. Freud was a clinician, interested in patients who were 'mentally ill' and in one way or another maladjusted. His interest in the origins of the abnormalities suggested the prior history of the individual and, in particular, childhood as likely sources. His account of development thus grew out of the details he gained from what his patients told him about themselves and has, therefore, an implicit goal, the attainment of emotional maturity. Freud's central concern is the development of personality and the contingencies which mould it. In particular, Freud saw these as being in large measure related to the way in which the natural urges (in Freudian terminology, instinctual energy) were regulated by the individual and the world around him.

The biological energy model

The notion of biological energy, of inborn instinctive forces, is central to Freud's concept of human personality. It is in this sense that this theory of personality is referred to as 'dynamic'. That human life is regulated by physical energy is incontrovertible. Freud was not concerned with physical but psychological energy. He distinguished three sources or channels for the instinctive drives, one concerned with self-reproduction (sexuality—sometimes called the libido) one with self-preservation (which includes drives like hunger and pain) and one with dominance—aggression. Plausible as this notion of psychological energy is (often compelling in the clinical situation) it has remained untestable. It was further assumed that the amount of energy for a given individual was fixed, and that energy could be invested in or tied to (Freud called this cathexis) thought, action, objects, and people, but that cathexis in respect of one object depleted the total supply of energy.

Personality structure

In broad, structural terms, development starts with the id, viewed as the storehouse for instinctual energy. The neonate is regarded as all *id*, which demands instant cathexis. Frustration cannot be tolerated. As the infant becomes increasingly aware of his environment the second structure, the *ego* develops. This is the executive part of the personality which mediates between the demands of the id and the constraints of reality. The *superego* emerges between about four and six years of age and, continuing the analogy, represents something like a combination of the judiciary and the legislature, adding to the combination constraints in terms of ideals, conscience, and the demands of society. The ego is not always capable of wise mediation among the conflicting demands. The outcome of unresolved conflict is anxiety. Freud saw the ego as continually engaged in the reduction of anxiety by realistic means. Failure is marked by ego-defence mechanisms, symptoms of which are held to be seen in aggression, depression, phobias, rituals, and obsessions. Repression is held to be the most powerful of these defences, as, by it, the ego is seen as removing the source of anxiety from consciousness to the unconscious. It is in repressed sources of anxiety that Freud saw the most significant roots of mental pathology.

Stages of psychosexual development

Dominant among the urges for satisfaction is the libido. Freud described development in terms of the body zones primarily associated with libidinal satisfaction at successive stages. Libidinal satisfaction assumes a more explicit sexual form as the child grows. Its earliest form, in the first year of life, is concerned dominantly with the mouth. Satisfaction, warmth and comfort are gained by sucking, licking and tasting. Freud called this the *oral* stage. In the second year of life it is the anal region which is the most cathected, and the child shows much interest in defecation and urination and the associated activities. This *anal* stage is succeeded at about four years of age by the *phallic* stage, when the source of libidinal pleasure is the genital region. It is during this stage that the Oedipal (Oedipus, in Greek mythology, killed his father and married his mother) conflict is said to confront the child, who at this time, Freud saw as desiring direct sexual relations with the opposite sex parent, but experiencing anxiety in the face of the discovery of his desires by the same-sex parent. The boy is said to fear castration at the hands of his father, and the girl punishment from the mother to add to her believed castration. Resolution of the conflict for both boy and girl is to identify with the like-sexed parent, identification involving not only the showing of affection for, but also the adoption of the ideals of the like-sexed parents. The illicit incestuous desires are repressed and the resolution of the Oedipal conflict is marked by the birth of the superego, based on the identification made, and the societal norms mediated by the parent.

The period which follows is, in contrast, one of relative calm and stability. This, the *latency* period, sees no major personality development, but is a time of considerable social and intellectual development. It continues until the onset of the adolescence. A new stage, *the genital*, marks the beginning of a period of renewed sexual interests and the establishment of a coherent set of sexual attitudes.

Freud saw each of the stages as entailing a unique set of problems to be solved in the interests of the future personality. The prevention of cathexis or its over-indulgence could result in *fixation*. Freud used this term to carry the notion of biological energy so firmly engaged at a less mature level, that it is not available for more mature functioning. Fixation at the oral stage was associated with later gluttony, alcoholism, optimism or pessimism, and at the anal stage with adult obstinancy and meanness. Fixation at the phallic stage is held responsible for the great majority of adult neuroses by psychoanalytically orientated clinicians.

Evaluation

Freud's account of development, like Piaget's, concerns a major dimension of human functioning. For Piaget, the development of the child was seen in intellectual terms, for Freud it is in personality-emotional terms. In contrast with Piaget's developing child, whose intellectual development is built upon his interaction with the world around him, Freud's child is passive and a product of inner forces and outer restrictions.

The overwhelming appeal of his account must rest partly in its plausibility and partly in the potential it offers as an account for a wide range of human activity and experience. Estimates of the originality of the notions he handled have varied, but it is indisputable that his presentation of these notions stimulated a great deal of research inside psychology as well as much interest and speculation outside it.

Much of the experimentation which has gone on has failed to produce any considerable body of support. Three main areas of general criticism may be identified, relating to source of data, methods, and explanations. The source of Freud's data was his patients, who were exclusively adult and abnormal in some way. Freud observed no children directly. This would seem to detract from a developmental account, for it can, at best, be only partial. Further doubt has been expressed as to the validity of making generalizations from an abnormal population.

As with Piaget, the limitations of the clinical method have been raised. With Freud, the case is more extreme since the evidence collected concerns events, some of which were long gone and subject to selection, interpretation and fallible recollections.

While it is not difficult to find evidence consistent with Freud's view of development, it has not been possible to establish it as clearly preferable to others. His approach to scientific discovery was based on observation and induction. Theory emerged as a result of his extensive clinical experience. The nature of the theory put forward puts much of it beyond experimental test, because of the difficulty of drawing falsifiable hypotheses from it; those hypotheses which have been derived (by others) from the theory and tested have produced equivocal findings. Even among psychoanalytically-inclined clinicians there have been significant objections to Freud's theory, as will be seen in the next part of this Chapter.

Freud's work has, notwithstanding these alleged weaknesses, been effective in the founding of a vigorous tradition of interest in child development from the psychoanalytic viewpoint.

Post-Freudian alternatives

Those who have followed Freud can be divided into (a) those who developed the work along strictly Freudian lines, and (b) those who challenged basic assumptions in Freud's theory. Among the former were Anna Freud, daughter of Sigmund, who holds that factors such as parents' attitudes towards their children play as important a part as instinctual factors, and Melanie Klein, who claims that forerunners of the superego are evident during the first two years and that the aggressive drives play a more important part than sexual ones. Both have worked extensively with young children, and have developed methods of analysis suitable for children as young as two years.

Among the latter, Horney, Sullivan and Fromm have challenged most of Freud's assumptions. Though differing among themselves, they agree that:

1. Rather than biological factors, it is the social and cultural ones which are basic to our understanding of human personality.

2. Features of Freudian theory, like the Oedipus complex and the formation of the superego, are cultural rather than universal traits.

3. Interpersonal relationships are important contributors to the development of personality.

4. Personality determines sexual behaviour, rather than being determined by it.

It is characteristic of these post-Freudians that they concern themselves principally with the ego and the social context with which it deals. Erik Erikson has proposed an alternative account of personality development to that of Freud. He lists eight *psychological stages*, each of which is held to be critical for the development of certain fundamental aspects of personality. As Freud emphasized the influence of psychosexual crises, so Erikson emphasizes psychosocial crises. The similarity between the two will be seen in Table 20.1, which summarizes Erikson's proposals.

467

Table 20.1

Psychosocial stages	Personality dimensions
1. Oral-sensory (first year)	Basic trust v mistrust
2. Muscular-anal (2–3)	Autonomy v shame and doubt
3. Locomotor-genital (3–5)	Imitation v guilt
4. Latency (5–12)	Industry v inferiority
5. Puberty and adolescence	Indentity v role confusion
6. Young adulthood	Intimacy v isolation
7. Adulthood	Generativity v stagnation
8. Maturity	Ego integrity v despair

It will be seen that Erikson's analysis of personality development embraces the full life span from birth to maturity.

Comparison: which theory of development?

There are considerable differences among the three accounts outlined. These include differences in generality; the learning theory account differs from the others in that it is a general while they are special theories. It also differs from the two others in respect of attainable goals; for, while Piaget's child is approaching intellectual and Freud's child emotional maturity, it prescribes no such goal or direction for development. Furthermore, both Freud and Piaget draw on biological changes to account for development but the learning theorists do not. A further difference concerns the part played by the child: Piaget's child develops only in terms of his transactions with the world around him, but the other two accord the child a passive role, where development is dominated by either environmental stimulation on the one hand, or the conflict between instinctual forces and the demands of an external reality on the other.

It is perhaps understandable to want to ask which account is right? Or, at least, which is to be preferred? To be in a position to give an answer implies the existence of criteria for being 'right' or 'preferable'. Features of the theories like testability, the range of empirical data accommodated, and the extent to which elaboration is possible, give some guide to the second question but not the first. As has been seen, the different approaches have their own internal strengths and weaknesses and it is probably at this level that evaluations can most easily proceed. For the three accounts are undoubtedly different because of their different viewpoints, and differences of this sort are not necessarily to be seen in terms of contradictions. Each account has something to contribute to an understanding of development; where marked differences occur, these serve to underline the complexity of the task involved in the construction of a single integrated account.

468

FURTHER READING

Baldwin, A. L. (1967) *Theories of Child Development*. Wiley.

Erikson, E. H. (1963) *Childhood and Society*. Norton.

McGurk, H. (1975) *Growing and Changing: A Primer of Developmental Psychology*. Methuen.

Mussen, P. H. (1974) Conger, J. J., and Kagan, J., *Child Development and Personality*. 4th edn. Harper and Row.

21 Nature, nurture, and development
HARRY FISHER

The controversy

Controversy arises when facts are difficult to obtain. They may be difficult to obtain because of the problems inherent in translating conceptual distinctions into real situations capable of furnishing facts. The constraints of reality may make it difficult to decide which questions to ask. The possible outcome that investigations may yield suggestions of important human inequalities may be expected to add further to the controversy. The nature-nurture controversy has all of these ingredients. For, although nature and nurture may be conceived as exclusive of each other, since each organism needs an environment in which to develop, the two are inextricably linked in practice. It has been argued, therefore, that questions like, 'which determines human intellectual capacity, heredity or environment?' presupposing as it does that their influences may be contrasted, are invalid. Answers have nevertheless been supplied, by equally eminent students, some favouring one, some the other. The question of 'how much' each of the two groups of factors contribute to, say, intelligence or some aspect of personality has also been seen as incapable of satisfactory answer in the absence of means of quantification. As will be seen, some tentative efforts have been made in this direction. The question of 'how' specific sets of factors, genetic or environmental, influence development, though posing some of the same problems, offers some hope of solution, and most of the empirical work considered in this Chapter will be of this kind.

The central methodological problem to be solved is that of control of the variables involved, so that, for example, observations might be made of the influence of different environmental conditions, while holding genetic factors constant. Quantification of the variables involved in the way in which it is known in physics is, at present, not known in psychology to any significant extent. Nevertheless, as will be seen, some of the simpler genetic variables admit of accurate description, as do also simple environmental variables, providing useful suggestions for more complex cases.

Naturally, more complete control of variables is possible with animals than with human subjects. While there are obvious limitations to the extent to which generalizations may be made from animal to human studies, the additional control provides results which give rise to useful suggestions.

Among the approaches to be considered in this Chapter are the following:

1. *Genetic methods*, relating known or inferred genetic factors to specific areas of behaviour, including breeding studies in animals and twin studies in humans.
2. *Clinical methods*, drawing on studies of effects of the intra-uterine environment.
3. *Survey methods*, which draw inferences from the distributions of specific facets of behaviour from large samples.
4. *Experimental methods*, designed to assess the influence of the early environment.
5. *Statistical methods* aimed at providing an estimate of the relative contributions of nature and nurture.
6. *Cross cultural studies*, to provide a wider context to the problems of describing development and the influences brought to bear by cultural constraints.

The mode of hereditary transmission
Since the early days of the nature-nurture controversy, it has become increasingly clear that environmental conditions exert a modifying influence on the expression of genetic endowment from conception. Conception takes place when a sperm cell from the father penetrates the wall of an ovum from the mother. This sets in motion the process by which the fertilized ovum divides to make two cells. As this process of cell-division continues, the cells take on special functions as part of the new organism. The sperm cell carries twenty-three minute structures called *chromosomes* which it releases into the ovum where they join twenty-three further chromosomes. The pairs of chromosomes in the original fertilized ovum reproduce themselves, so that each cell that arises as a result of the division carries a duplicate set of the original twenty-three chromosome pairs. It is these chromosomes which are the carriers of the

child's heredity. Each bears somewhere around 20 000 smaller particles, complex chemical chains, called *genes*. A significant clarification of the possible processes involved in cell-division and the mode of hereditary transmission was made by Watson and Crick in 1953. They suggested a possible structure for the gene, a double helix (like a ladder with a vertical twist) of deoxyribonucleic acid (DNA).

The fertilized ovum is known as a zygote. In occasional instances, this divides into two separate entities, each of which develops into a separate individual. The two have identical genetic constitutions and are known as monozygotic or identical twins. Fraternal (dizygotic) twins result when two ova, discharged into the fallopian tubes at the same time, are independently fertilized. In this case the genetic endowment of the twins is no more alike than that of other pairs of siblings.

In some instances, the influence of the genetic endowment is relatively easy to trace, as in the case of certain discrete characteristics, for example, eye colour. Genes function in pairs to influence hereditary characteristics, one from each parent. Individual members of a pair of genes are known as *alleles*, and it is the relationship between alleles which regulates the occurrence of certain discrete characteristics. In some pairs, one allele is dominant, in that its influence will be expressed. The other allele is said to be recessive. Thus the brown-eye gene is dominant while the blue-eye gene is recessive. In other pairs neither allele is dominant. Gregor Mendel, a nineteenth century Austrian monk, demonstrated that different discrete characteristics are distributed with different proportions, reflecting the 'with and without dominance' relationship between alleles. Only a very small number of single gene characteristics are known in man. Most of these are recessive. The disease phenylketonuria provides an example of a genetic defect which can lead to mental retardation. The lack of a gene associated with the production of a critical enzyme leads to our over-production of phenyl-pyruvic acid which attacks the central nervous system. (Knowledge of the specific nature of this metabolic disorder has led to widespread screening of babies. Those found to be at risk are placed on a diet which limits the production of this acid and its consequent effects.) There are few other examples where the influence of the genes is so clear.

While heredity is thus known to act directly on individual biological characteristics, the evidence linking it with psychological traits is much less clear. The inheritance of physical defects or weakness may in some cases lead to psychological withdrawal, but it would be wrong to regard the withdrawal as inherited, for the physical defects might also lead the individual to attempt to compensate for such defects, and appear asser-tive and perhaps over-confident. The distribution of psychological characteristics like intelligence is continuous, rather than in the discrete proportions of the Mendelian laws. Like height and weight, intelligence is normally distributed in the population, and this suggests the interactive involvement of large numbers of genes.

The effect of the prenatal environment

As has been seen, the individual's genetic make-up is determined at conception. The twenty-three chromosome pairs carrying the gene contribution of the parents are to be found in every cell and remain constant throughout life. Between conception and birth, development will go on in the species-specific manner dictated by the genes, but it is clear that this development can be influenced by the prenatal environment in a number of different ways which may radically affect future life and behaviour. Prenatal development can be divided into three phases on the basis of the characteristic changes taking place. They may be labelled as the phases of the zygote, the embryo, and the fetus. The earliest phase, extending about two weeks from conception, is concerned with the passage of the fertilized ovum from the Fallopian tubes to the uterus, where it becomes implanted. During the time before this happens the zygote has developed into several dozen cells. The environment of each of these, and the sole constraint on gene function is the cytoplasm, the living substance surrounding the cell nucleus. This phase comes to an end when tendrils from the outer layer of cells attach the cell mass to the receptive mucous membrane of the uterus. From this point on, the formerly free-floating organism is linked with, and dependent on, the mother. The phase of the embryo which now follows depends on the area of implantation (which becomes the placenta) and the umbilical cord which develops to link the bloodstream of the embryo to that of the mother. The link is not a direct one. Both bloodstreams pass into the placenta, but they are separated by cell walls within the placenta. The nourishment which the embryo receives is utilized in the rapid differentiation of cells to take on the increasingly specialized structures and functions which will serve the organism as sensory cells, blood cells, nerve cells, etc. Rapid differentiation of cells characterizes this phase, which lasts about six weeks; that is, from implantation at two weeks to about eight weeks of age. As differentiation proceeds, so the survival of each cell, and of the entire new organism, depends on the integration of the different functions. It is at this stage that the organism is vulnerable to adverse changes in the prenatal environment. As the important functions are in the process of formation, such changes have potentially more far reaching consequences than if the same changes took place later. Consider, for example, the possible consequences which might ensue from mechanical damage, where physical injury arises as a result of an accident. Such injury is capable of interfering with the establishment of some vital function. At a later date, the more fully developed organism may be in a much better position to withstand the effects of similar

473

damage. It is at this time, for example, that the effects of German measles in the mother is likely to be associated with brain damage in the child. At a later stage in the pregnancy this is less likely.

Although the bloodstreams of the mother and the embryo are separated by semipermeable membranes in the placenta which prevent the passage of blood cells, other substances do penetrate; for example, nutrients of various sorts from the mother's blood to the embryo, and waste products from the embryo to the mother. The maternal bloodstream thus constitutes an important feature of the prenatal environment from the embryonic stage onwards. Contrary to what was believed earlier, it is now clear that the placenta does not form a barrier against the harmful contents of the mother's bloodstream. While minor variations have little or no effect on development, more extreme variation in its constituents, like those associated with the presence of drugs or with malnutrition, can have far-reaching effects. The effects of drugs in the maternal bloodstream has been dramatically demonstrated by the birth of deformed children to mothers who used the sedative drug, thalidomide during pregnancy. Research on the effects of maternal smoking during pregnancy has revealed significant correlations between heavy smoking and babies who were small and underweight. Several studies indicate the potentially serious consequences of malnutrition during pregnancy. This is also associated with deficit in size and weight at birth. More serious is the possibility of the limitation of brain development, the effects of which are irreversible. The most rapid increase in the size and number of brain cells occurs between conception and birth; six months after the child is born there is no further increase in the number of brain cells. Adequate maternal nutrition is thus a vital part of the prenatal environment of the embryo.

This is, of course, true also for the phase of the fetus which occupies the period from the eighth to the fortieth week from conception. The cell differentiation and integration begun in the embryonic stage continues, but the marked characteristic of this phase of development is growth. It is, thus, important that the maternal bloodstream is healthy, well supplied with the proper nutrients, and free of abnormal concentrations of specific constituents. Sustained maternal anxiety may be associated with an abnormally high level of adrenalin in the bloodstream. Since this will pass through the placental barrier it is a potential threat to cell metabolism. Recent studies of children whose mothers suffered sustained anxiety during pregnancy showed them to exhibit significantly more signs of psychological malfunction than those whose mothers had no such stress. It has also been shown that anxiety during pregnancy is significantly related to colic in the newborn. (This is a condition which includes such symptoms as long and continuous periods of crying, distension of the stomach and signs of considerable pain. It is mostly found in neonates under three months). So far, causal connections between anxiety in pregnancy and such subsequent ills have not been established.

Thus, the emotional state of the expectant mother as well as the adequacy of her diet may substantially affect the fetal environment. To this may be added exposure to irradiation, and the general health of the mother-to-be. Exposure to X-rays in large therapeutic doses is associated with a high incidence of mental and physical abnormalities. Since the placental barrier is only partially effective, the fetus may take infection from the mother, and infants may be born infected in this way.

The birth process itself may present prenatal environmental hazards. Strong pressures on the head of the fetus may result in the breaking of blood vessels in the brain. If there is undue delay in the neonate beginning to breathe once it is separated from the maternal oxygen supply, damage may follow. Both of these hazards affect the supply of oxygen to the nerve cells of the brain. In extreme cases, brain cells will die and the infant may suffer serious brain damage or death.

There have been a number of studies on the effects of drugs administered to the mother just prior to delivery. In general, they indicate that the effect of such depressant drugs as pentobarbital is passed to the fetus without any considerable delay. Babies whose mothers had been given the drug were observed to be generally less attentive than babies delivered to mothers who had not. The serious effects of sedation generally seem to be gone by the time the child is a week old. Such studies, however, indicate the dangers to the fetus which may arise from a consistent and heavy use of drugs.

The prenatal environment thus plays a considerable role in the development of the genetic potential of the organism.

The above considerations have been in terms of the hazards the prenatal environment holds. Recent work has suggested ways in which many of these hazards might be minimized, and one major study, concentrating on providing an oxygen-enriched environment for the fetus, has shown promising results in the form of brighter and healthier neonates. While the findings have been challenged on the grounds that those who received treatment were likely to produce such children any way, it indicates the sort of possibilities open for manipulating the intrauterine environment to advantage.

Genes and maturation

Related to the nature-nurture controversy is the contrast drawn between maturation and learning. It was noted earlier that, traditionally, the learning theorists have regarded the concept of maturation as being of limited explanatory value. It is the purpose of this part of the Chapter to examine some of the evidence, the argument for the retention of this concept, and the contention that, without it, it is impossible to give an adequate account of development. This is not a return to a position which regards either learning or maturation as being 'the key' to development—this belongs with the nature-nurture controversy as part of psychology's history—rather, it is to examine appropriate empirical evidence which may throw some light on the interaction between them.

The concept of maturation is of interest to the psychologist only to the extent that it is of value in accounting for empirical evidence. Maturation is not easy to define, and several different proposals have been made. One of these is to distinguish between physiological and behavioural maturation and to argue that the latter reflects the former. In the previous part of this Chapter the influence of the genetic control of physiological maturation in the sequence and patterning of prenatal development was described. Within a given species, the course this takes is highly stable, and resistant to wide variations in environment. There is evidence that genetic factors influence physiological development throughout life. For example, the adolescent growth spurt, while clearly subject to the provision of an adequate diet, is a stable feature of physiological development. So, also, are the characteristic features of puberty, though the timing of these does seem to show some cross-cultural variation. The onset of menstruation has been shown to be much closer for identical than for fraternal twins. Some genetic effects are not evident until much later in life. Huntington's chorea, a degenerative disease of the nervous system, due to a single dominant gene, and thus running in families, usually does not show until the age of thirty-five to forty. A study of twins over the age of sixty suggests that genetic factors play a major role in the maintenance of physical and mental health in old age. To the extent that genetic factors influence physiological maturation throughout life, behavioural maturation may be seen as reflecting the influences of these factors also.

The necessary involvement of environmental factors makes direct evidence for behavioural maturation difficult to obtain. As children grow, for example, adults tend to deal with them in different ways. Expectations relating to toddlers are quite different from those for three and four year olds. The appearance of new behaviours thus begs the question of the extent to which they are influenced by such expectations, or give rise to them, or both. A number of different lines of evidence will be outlined which appear to require the concept of behavioural maturation for an adequate account of development.

The pattern of development
The first relates to the sequential order and patterning of behavioural development and their constancy across widely differing environments. Reference has already been made in earlier Chapters to the patterns of locomotor and language development. Arnold Gesell and his colleagues

476

made a study of the development of children over the first five years of life. Among other indices of development, those relating to motor development in general were found to show a marked correspondence in their sequence and patterning. Other studies indicate the robustness of the sequence of behavioural development to outside influences, that they are resistant alike to factors designed to accelerate or to retard their progress. An early attempt to induce bladder control showed that those twins who were given regular training from an early age were no better than the two co-twin controls whose training was not undertaken until they were well over a year old. The stability of the age of onset of language across widely different cultural backgrounds suggests that this is governed by genetic constraints. Similarly, Lenneberg has pointed to the largely unhindered development of language in those children whose parents are deaf and dumb, and whose language background is thus impoverished. At the motor level, the study by Dennis of Hopi Indian babies appears to make the same point. Traditionally, these babies are strapped to a board for the first three months of life. Other infants of this tribe are cradled and subject to no limitation on their movements. It was found that there was no difference, on average, in the ages at which the two sets of infants learn to walk. This constancy of developmental milestones and their limited vulnerability to environmental variations makes a strong claim for the necessity of the concept of behavioural maturation.

The physiological basis of behavioural maturation
Some studies aim to demonstrate the link between physiological and behavioural maturation. Three different lines of enquiry will be considered in this category. The first seeks to correlate changes in behaviour with changes in physiological structure, the second to compare the behavioural maturation of individuals having known similarities and differences in genetic constitution, and the third to demonstrate the relative constancy of certain measurable behavioural traits. It is clear that certain sorts of behaviour demand specific levels of physiological maturity. Sexual behaviour provides a good example, particularly in lower species whose sexual behaviour is relatively stereotyped. Here, not only is sexual maturity necessary for sexual reproduction, it also determines the form taken by sexual behaviour. In higher species, this line of evidence is by no means so clear. Harlow has demonstrated that social deprivation in infancy can radically restrict the sexual competence of mature monkeys. In human adults, while puberty is a necessary condition of sexual reproduction, social and cultural factors play an important role in the corresponding behavioural maturation. Lenneberg's proposed critical period for language development sees the acquisition of language as related to the maturation of the brain, and the establishment of

maturity in terms of laterality of functioning in the two hemispheres as defining the upper limit of this period.

The second type of study under this heading seeks to compare developmental profiles against known genetic constitutions. Identical (monozygotic) twins have identical genetic inheritances and their development ought, if related to this factor, to be more similar than that of fraternal (dizygotic) twins, who have not. In general both sort of twins will (separately) have similar environmental stimulation, though it has been argued that identical twins receive more similar treatment than fraternals. A recent study of the developmental profiles of groups of infant twins bears out the expectation of significantly greater similarity between the identical twins as compared with the fraternals.

A further possible line of evidence would be the demonstration of the constancy of a measurable trait for an individual under conditions in which relevant environmental factors were known to be variable. Studies of the constancy of measures of intelligence quotient throughout life go only part way towards this. While, for a given individual, investigations indicate a marked stability of IQ, as shown by high correlation among successive tests throughout life, this may reflect, for those surveyed, that such environmental factors as might influence IQ scores have remained stable. The suggestion that the stability is genetically linked awaits further investigation.

The previous part of this Chapter reviewed evidence suggesting ways in which prenatal environment may have an influence on the fetus. This part has, in contrast, reviewed some of the evidence suggesting that the genes impose constraints of their own, and that the pattern of behavioural maturation may reflect their influence throughout life.

Genes and behaviour

The studies to be considered here are selected as examples of work performed to investigate the link between genes and behaviour and to provide further insight into the problem and methods of doing so. The basic requirements of such an enterprise are means of holding environment constant, and of manipulating the genetic constitutions of the subjects whose behaviour is being observed. It is important that such behaviour can be precisely defined, so that objective observations are possible. With human subjects, holding environment constant is patently impossible. The best that can be done is to exercise a limited control by selecting groups having similar environments. Using animal subjects facilitates much more rigorous control. In experiments using humans, the variation in genetic constitution has to be achieved by selecting people whose family relationships are known. This enables inferences to be made about their hereditary similarities. Thus, identical twins, whose

478

genetic constitutions are identical would head the list, with fraternal twins and other siblings, cousins, and step siblings following in order. Again, with animals this factor can be more closely controlled by suitable breeding techniques. Most of the studies to be considered involve human subjects. Although generalization from animal studies to humans has limited validity, it will be seen that the tighter experimental control afforded by animal studies offers some useful insights.

Selective breeding of rats

Long before the recent advances in genetics, both plants and animals were bred for specific qualities. More recently, rats have been bred for behavioural traits which resemble both intelligence and emotionality. The measure of 'intelligence' was the time taken to learn mazes. From a single population, two groups of rats were identified, one of which learned quickly to run new mazes. The other group was slower to learn. By breeding within the members of these two groups for a number of generations, and by selecting at each stage those rats performing at opposite ends of the behavioural range, Tryon produced two strains, the one 'maze bright', the other 'maze dull'. While the breeding was directed to the selection of this single trait, it is clear that the capacity for learning mazes is part of a wider group of traits. For example, the 'maze bright' rats were much more strongly motivated by food and got on with the task, while the 'maze dull' were more susceptible to distraction at choice points and prone to 'spontaneous activity', that is, activity unrelated to the task. It has also been shown that maze dull rats' performance can be dramatically improved by dietary supplements after weaning. No such improvement was found in similarly treated bright rats. A further study showed the two strains to be differentially susceptible to environmental stimulation. Both strains were raised in either an enriched or an impoverished environment. An enriched environment meant that home cages were provided with such 'toys' as wheels, ladders, and the like, and situated in a brightly lit room. Performance was compared with a control group raised under normal laboratory conditions. Dull rats raised in the enriched environment showed considerable improvement, but were not affected by the impoverished conditions. On the other hand, the impoverished condition was associated with a much poorer performance from the bright rats. They showed no improvement in the enriched condition.

Selective breeding has also been used by Broadhurst to produce two strains differing on a trait which resembles emotionality. The tests for this trait, involved the observation of rats' reactions to being placed in a situation intended to induce fear. The rat was taken from its home cage and placed in an open field apparatus, a circular enclosure about one metre across with a vertical rim. Noise was used to add to the contrast

479

between the open field and the quiet home cage. The reaction of the rat was measured in terms of the extent to which the new situation inhibited a normal tendency to move about and explore (latency and extent of ambulation), as well as by the increase in defecation rates. Two strains were bred whose reactions in these terms were clearly distinguishable, one of which was relatively unmoved by the open field situation, (Broadhurst called these 'non-reactive') and the other markedly inhibited by it (the reactive group). In order to infer the link between genetic constitution (genotype) and behaviour it was important that rearing conditions were kept as similar as possible for the two groups. For example, diet, handling, and details of the physical environment were carefully controlled. Cross-fostering was employed to control for rearing differences due to the mothers, that is, litters of reactive offspring were divided equally between reactive and non-reactive mothers in exchange for a similar division of the non-reactive litter.

Such studies as these thus provide strong support for the influence of genotype on these traits. They give some idea of a considerable volume of work directed to this end, involving the investigation of a number of behavioural traits and using a variety of species.

Human studies

With humans, neither genotype nor the environment can be subject to control. Such conclusions as may be drawn must be inferred using family relationships as a guide to genotypic similarity and living conditions as a rough guide to environmental similarity. Francis Galton (1822–1911) observed that outstanding gifts were distributed among a restricted section of the population. The eminent men he studied came from a relatively small group of able families. Galton found this compelling to the point of his enthusiastic advocacy of eugenics ('well-born') as a means of social progress. This was to improve the human stock by encouraging those endowed with desirable characteristics—health and intellectual and artistic ability—to marry with a view to the creation of a population in which such gifts were widespread. The evidence on which Galton was able to draw to support these ideas is described in his book *Hereditary Genius* (1869). This details his studies of the family trees of men of eminence in respect of scholastic, legal, and athletic prowess and his findings that there were strong relations among them. It was clear, for example, that eminent fathers had eminent sons with far greater than chance probability. Galton was persuaded that it was dominantly heredity which accounted for this association. His work is frequently criticized because it seems to neglect the possibly large environmental benefits bestowed upon the sons of eminent fathers. Galton's early work also included pointers to means of investigation which have been developed in subsequent studies. One of these was the notion of the eminent man as the nucleus of a hereditary family, whose gifts diminished as the kinship distance from him increased. Another was the suggestion of the usefulness of twin studies as a means of insight into the relative contributions of heredity and environment to these gifts, a method which is discussed in Chapter 17.

The statistical approach

Two further methods will be considered, both drawing on statistical techniques in a somewhat different manner from those considered above. Both arrive at similar conclusions regarding the genotypic contribution to measured intelligence, putting this roughly at 80 per cent. There are good reasons for supposing that the hereditary influence on intelligence is brought about by the joint effect of a large number of genes. Burt and Howard (1956) proposed a multifactorial theory of inheritance, and, from it, predicted the correlations of measured intelligence for a range of family relationships. Their preliminary study produced correlations which agreed well with their predictions.

Raymond Cattell has proposed a statistical technique which he names the Multiple Abstract Variance Analysis (MAVA). It is claimed that this method is capable of yielding information on the extent of the influence of hereditary and environmental factors with which it is concerned, as well as a means of assessing the extent to which these are correlated. The method is based on four possible sources of variance for any particular personality dimension. These are due to differences of environment within the family (e_w), of environment between families (e_B), and of hereditary differences within and between families (h_w and h_B respectively).

For brothers reared together the total variance (BT) on a given trait is due to the environmental differences within families (due to changing age of parents, number in family, family position, etc.) and hereditary factors within families (due to the transmission of differing selections of parental genes to different children). This is represented as follows:

$$BT = e_w + h_w \tag{1}$$

In a similar manner for brothers raised apart.

$$BA = e_w + h_w + e_B \tag{2}$$

In the case of identical twins raised apart (TA), the equation will be as (2) except for the term h_w which will be zero because of identical genotypes. Thus:

$$TA = e_w + e_B \tag{3}$$

All equations are in terms of variance. It will be seen that by administering tests to appropriate populations—brothers reared together, brothers reared apart and twins reared apart—that each of the variances represented by BT, BA and TA can be given a numerical value. It is then a relatively simple arithmetical task to obtain values for each of the four prime sources of variance by suitably combining pairs of equations (1), (2) and (3).

This approach has critics who maintain that the model is unsound because it treats heredity and environment as independent whereas in real life they are so inter-related as to defy separation. Bright children are usually brought up by bright parents, which may mean that e_w and h_w are not independent but correlated. This suggests a model which will include a large number of intercorrelations. Cattell has anticipated such difficulties and has gone some way to meet the criticisms in terms of a systematic study of the possible intercorrelations. This method of analysis has the further disadvantage of requiring large (of the order of 5000 subjects) and carefully selected samples to obtain reliable estimates of all the components. Nevertheless, there are a number of workers who see it as a powerful approach to the nature-nurture issue. It has already been used to provide information on a number of personality factors as well as intelligence.

Further details may be found in *The Scientific Analysis of Personality*, by R. B. Cattell.

Early experience and development

Animal studies

J. P. Scott, a distinguished student of animal behaviour, interested in the effects of early experience, relates how he was given a newborn female lamb which he raised on the bottle for the first ten days. It was hardly surprising that, when put out to graze at the end of this time with a small flock of sheep, it showed a preference for people (those who had fed it) over sheep. What was more surprising was the extent to which the behaviour of this individual sheep remained atypical. Sheep normally follow the flock. At three years the sheep in question was still following an independent grazing pattern. When, eventually, it had lambs of its own, while they were allowed to feed, the mother made none of the usual attempts to prevent them straying. The experience of the first few days of life had a marked and permanent effect on its behaviour as an adult.

This section will be devoted to a consideration of attempts to trace the links between early experience and subsequent behaviour. Earlier, the effects of the prenatal environment were considered. The studies to be considered here relate to the effect of the early post-natal environment. Some of them relate to animal subjects, and generalizations to human behaviour need to be made with great caution. Nevertheless, this research has provided new perspectives for the study of human behaviour. If firm conclusions are to be drawn about environmental effects, genotype must be controlled in some way. As has been seen earlier, this problem can be more readily approached with animal subjects than with humans. Animals can also be subjected to environmental extremes which would be impracticable with humans. A division may be drawn between the physical and social aspects of the environment. This is, of course, a conceptual division only, and the effects of one aspect to the exclusion of the other are rarely met in practice. In the studies to be considered, the emphasis is on one aspect or the other and, wherever possible, the confounding of the two is limited. Some relate to the effects of the enrichment or the impoverishment of the environment, some to social or to sensory variables, some to animal subjects, and some to children.

Scott performed an experiment to investigate the effect of an impoverished environment on dogs. Scottish terriers were reared from weaning at four weeks in cages which deprived them of normal social and sensory experience. Their diet was normal but administered by an unseen attendant. When released at eight months of age they were found to be markedly different from control animals (reared under normal conditions) in the way they reacted to painful stimulation. The deprived animals, for example, took four times as many trials to learn to avoid an electric shock as the free-environment dogs. These latter also learnt at once to avoid a threatened pin-prick and the heat of a match flame held by the experimenter. The deprived animals returned again and again, moving their noses into the flame, recoiling suddenly only to repeat the movement moments later. It appears that the early deprivation had served to inhibit, for the time being, the normal escape response to painful stimulation.

Some mention has already been made of the differential effects of enriched and impoverished environments on rats of contrasting genotypes. An experiment by M. R. Rosenzweig was set up to investigate anatomical and biochemical correlates in the brain of rats being reared in these environments. Thus, for each rat assigned to the enriched condition—cages with a varying selection of toys and a regime which included daily 'exploratory' sessions—a litter mate was put in the impoverished condition. They were introduced into these as early as possible (about twenty-five days after weaning) when their brain might be most plastic, and kept there for eighty days. The enriched animals were found to have developed brains which were significantly heavier and structurally distinguishable from those of impoverished animals. There was also a difference between the enzyme activity of the brains. The exact implications of the anatomical and biochemical differences are not clear. The overall conclusion, however, that these brains had adapted anatomically and chemically to the two environments, seems important, for it suggests that the early environment is capable of modifying to

483

some extent the effects of genotype. This experiment raises a number of interesting questions to which more recent studies have supplied tentative answers. First, what features of the enrichment are significantly associated with the brain development? In addition to the enrichment features described above, the enriched rats lived in cages of twelve while the impoverished lived alone. This accounts for part of the effect, adding the toys for a further part. The two daily exploratory sessions seem to add relatively little. Is this brain growth possible only in young rats? Further experiments with mature rats suggest not; they showed further brain development as a result of an enriched environment, albeit at a reduced rate. But does this brain development have any practical consequences—greater learning ability, for example? Answers available at the present are equivocal; for some tasks the answer seem to be yes, for others no.

Other experiments in this field indicated the facilitating effect (on subsequent instrumental conditioning) of extra stimulation even when this was no more than the transitory experience of being handled each day in infancy. In an open field situation the stimulated rats behaved much less emotionally than control animals, whose handling was minimal. Physiological investigations indicated that in the stimulated animals there was evidence of earlier maturation of the stress-response pattern in which the animal's biological resources are recruited to meet the needs imposed by the stress. Levine, by whom these experiments were carried out, interpreted the evidence as consistent with the view that stress and handling stimulate the maturation of the central nervous system and thus enhance development. Victor Dennenberg, a distinguished worker in this field, interpreting the results of a wide range of studies into the effects of stimulation in infancy (rats and mice) concludes that such stimulation, when administered between birth and weaning brings about a reduction of emotional reactivity, and that the greater the stimulation in infancy, the less emotional will the adult be. Dennenberg has produced evidence to support the hypothesis that emotional reactivity is inversely related to the amount of infant stimulation.

Harry Harlow of Wisconsin, who has made extensive studies of the behaviour of monkeys, has described how a group of them reared for their first year of life in comparative isolation in the laboratory became adults who were immature, abnormal, and troubled. They lived in wire cages so arranged that they could see, hear, and call to the other infants but could make no contact with them. Their 'troubled' behaviour was apparent in the way that some, holding the head in both hands, would rock to and fro, indifferent both to people and other monkeys. Further abnormalities were to be seen in the way some became enraged without apparent cause, frequently inflicting injuries upon themselves. As five- to seven-year-old adults and sexually mature, their sexual behaviour was marked by a singular ineptitude and immaturity. In the case of females, this sociopathic syndrome includes the absence of anything resembling the normal skills of mothering for those few who produced offspring. Harlow describes them as 'helpless, hopeless, heartless mothers—almost devoid of any maternal feeling'. This condition of the mothers who never knew a real mother suggests that the entire syndrome is related to the manner in which they were raised. Neither monkeys reared in the wild for the first twelve to eighteen months, nor those reared in the laboratory with the opportunity of normal mother-infant and infant-infant contacts developed these abnormalities. Attempts to relieve these met with only limited success. This early social deprivation was associated with radical and apparently irreversible changes in behaviour, resembling those noted in Scott's lamb.

From a survey of some of the literature on the effects of early experience Dennenberg (1969) drew five general principles:

1. Early experience may drastically modify the effect of genotype.
2. It may have long term effects which may also affect progress.
3. It is one major source of individual differences.
4. It may have multiple effects (Harlow's socially deprived monkeys provide a good example).
5. The age when stimulation is administered is important. For rats, it appeared that pre-weaning stimulation has its greatest effect on emotional behaviour, whereas stimulation after weaning had its effect mainly on cognitive functioning.

Dennenberg, with others in this field, expressed the view that these principles have implications for human development. The effect of the experiences of the first two years of life were seen as capable of bringing about consequences as radical for the human infant as for animals, with an analogous division (pre-weaning/post-weaning) for human infants, handling stimulation being most effective up to six months of age, and the enriched-environment type of stimulation from six months onwards.

Child studies

ENVIRONMENTAL STIMULATION

Generalization across species is, however, a hazardous operation at the best of times. Workers investigating the effects of social deprivation on rats found that the maternal behaviour of deprived rats was not fundamentally different from that of the non-deprived. Their failure to replicate Harlow's findings underlines the importance of species-specific differences. Nevertheless, the study of human development has produced evidence which is generally consistent with that from animal studies. Evidence in support of Dennenberg's personal convictions has yet to be

485

produced. This may well have to do with the practical difficulty of carrying out the appropriate research. Extensive experiments on infants is clearly limited by the constraints of normal domestic circumstances. Deliberate deprivation studies are out of the question. One recent attempt to overcome at least some of these difficulties used a control group of infants subjected to a 'normal' regime against an experimental group exposed to extra handling and stimulation. The results go some way towards providing limited support for the view of the importance of early stimulation in human infants. The Dennis study referred to in Chapter 19 seemed to indicate that the absence of varied experience in the institution, of handling, and verbal communication and such things brought about a general retardation of both physical and mental development. It further indicated that, in most of the children, the worst of the effects of the deprivations were not irreversible. This poses the general question as to what extent the effects of early environmental impoverishment are lasting in humans.

SOCIAL STIMULATION

Considerably more research has been carried out into the effects of a child's early social environment. For most children, the key figure is the mother or other caretaker; (in what follows 'mother' applies to all who perform the role). Not only does she regulate the details of the numerous aspects of his physical environment during his considerable period of helplessness, but also becomes the focus of his developing social world. It is hardly surprising that a special bond comes into being between infant and mother. Some aspects of this attachment will be discussed, followed by a consideration of recent findings concerning the consequences of failure to form, or the loss of this bond between mother and infant.

This bond affects both mother and child. In the complex interaction which goes on between them, the behaviour of each is modified by the other. The present context, however, is concerned with its effect on the infant. Psychologists from the major theoretical positions have recognized the psychological importance of this relationship and, according to their individual orientations, have sought to describe and account for it in different ways. As has already been described, Freud's clinical approach involved the interpretation of his patients' problems in terms of their passage through the psychosexual stages. The mother-infant bond was seen as originating at the breast in the oral phase and formed the basis for subsequent social development. Behaviourists have likewise concentrated explanatory accounts on the part played by the feeding activity, seeing it as either 'need-satisfaction', the bond being formed on the basis of the mother's regular involvement in supplying vital nourishment, or, more neutrally, as primary reinforcement. In either case,

486

feeding was seen as providing a primary basis for the bond, investing the mother with a widening range of influence as a secondary reinforcer. Evidence will be considered later which casts doubt on this view. John Bowlby, a British psychoanalyst, sees attachment as an innately determined system of responses designed to serve the adaptive function of keeping the infant within a safe distance of the mother. He sees the mother-child interactions as complex control systems maintaining a degree of proximity related to such factors as the infant's hunger or fatigue, and the degree of familiarity with the environment. Bowlby has concentrated on a list of five attachment responses: sucking, clinging, and following (by looking as well as by movement), by which the infant maintains or seeks proximity with the mother, and smiling and crying, used to recruit the mother's active cooperation in maintaining proximity.

In this area, research has been carried out to throw light on a number of questions. Three will be considered briefly here. All are related to the five attachment responses listed above.

1. Are these responses directed principally to the mother, or are they equally likely to be used on strangers?

2. What are the conditions necessary for their formation?

3. Can empirical evidence be found to support the notion that these responses are a linked, unified system of attachment behaviour.

As to the first it seems clear that crying, smiling and following are behaviours selectively directed to the mother. Taking crying as an example, a demonstration of its selective use was made by observing infant 'separation protest', crying and fussing. Crying is, of course, frequently a response to pain, but infants may also learn to use it to exert control on a caretaker. The basis of the experiment was the observation of the infant when either of the two adults with him, the mother or a stranger, left the room. Infants from three to nineteen months old were used. Some cried irrespective of whether it was the mother or the stranger who left. Only those over twelve months old protested significantly more when the mother left rather than the stranger. Another study put the age of selective protest earlier, at about eight months, but both demonstrated clearly that this response is eventually directed selectively to the mother.

Both the psychoanalytic approach of Freud and the need-satisfaction view hold the feeding activity as the basis of the subsequent positive evaluation of the mother by the child, and thus as a necessary condition for the establishment of attachment. There is evidence available which appears to deny this. Indirect evidence may be drawn from a study by Harlow who provided two artificial 'mothers' for his infant monkeys.

One was covered with cloth to which the infant could cling, but provided no milk. The other was made of wire but fitted with a nipple that provided milk. Reared with both mothers from birth the rhesus monkeys soon showed a marked preference for the cloth mother, visiting the wire surrogate only to feed. More directly, it is clear that much of human infants' social activity takes place, even early in life, when comfortable and well fed, and, so far as can be ascertained, free from urgent biological needs. Other studies have shown that infants make attachments to people who do not perform caretaking activities, and with whom there is no link of need satisfaction. Such studies appear to provide ground for discussing the feeding function as a necessary condition for the formation of attachment.

The answer to the third question must be, as in so many other cases within the scientific enterprise, that empirical evidence falls far short of present speculation. One recent piece of research (Bell, 1970) representative of a number of correlation studies, succeeded in showing a relation between the development of object constancy and attachment responses. Infants younger than seven months rarely seek objects that disappear. When they begin to do so it is suggested that they have some way of representing the object in its absence. The study showed a correlation between the development of this capacity and attachment responses to the mother. Correlational evidence of this sort, while consistent with the notion of a linked system of attachment responses, is at best weak since it does not rule out other possible reasons for the correlation. Evidence for the unitary nature of attachment must wait on further research.

Maternal deprivation

The effects of such early social circumstances as prevent the formation of such attachment and all that goes with it, or which bring about significant disturbances in such a bond have long attracted the attention of psychologists, particularly those engaged in the clinical field. It is hardly surprising, in view of Freud's view of the importance of the mother-child relationship, that psychoanalytically-inclined clinicians should interpret many of the problems of their child patients in terms of the early quality of this relationship. Mother-love in infancy and childhood was held by such clinicians to be as important for mental health as a balanced diet was for physical health. Others were less convinced. Thus the studies in this field have continued to attract wide attention and the debate about the effects of maternal deprivation has continued to reflect diverse views. It is clear that the experiences covered by the term 'maternal deprivation' are varied and complex, but in view of the tendency of the several types of deprivation involved to occur together, it appears to have been generally accepted that the term could be meaningfully employed.

One of the early studies was a report by Bowlby in 1940, then a psychoanalyst working in a child guidance clinic, concerning forty-four juvenile thieves. These were compared with forty-four juveniles who were emotionally disturbed but who had not been accused of theft. The first group was seen to contain more 'affectionless characters', (individuals who were deceitful, evasive, and inaccessible with little capacity for making friends or caring for people) than the other. Further, about half of the first group, as compared with only two in the second had experienced long periods of separation from mother figures during their first five years. Bowlby concluded that maternal deprivation during this period appeared as highest on the list of possible causes of delinquent character development. Other studies have linked maternal deprivation in a similar way with such diverse conditions as mental subnormality, dwarfism and depression. Research findings in these several areas have produced conflicting evidence. This is hardly surprising in view of the inherent methodological difficulties. Consider, for example, the problems in establishing a valid control group. The most desirable group would differ only in respect of the experience of maternal deprivation. Even if this concept was itself well defined, the problem of matching individuals in the two groups on all other variables is a formidable task; and, since different researchers have interpreted 'maternal deprivation' in different ways, this has further added to the inaccuracy. It is clear, for example, that while there is empirical evidence of a link between delinquency and maternal deprivation, the deprivation itself need not be the necessary cause. Rather, some aspect of the deprivation, the absence of appropriate moral guidance, for example, may constitute a more immediate link with the delinquency behaviour.

A reappraisal of the concept of maternal deprivation has recently been made by Professor Michael Rutter of London University, which, accepting the general proposition that 'bad child care' has 'bad effects' points to the need for a more accurate description of both. He has provided a review of the qualities of mothering needed for normal development, together with a consideration of both the short-term and long-term effect of maternal deprivation.

Four qualities considered necessary for adequate mothering are a loving relationship, the development of enduring bonds, a stable but not necessarily unbroken relationship, and a stimulating interaction between mother and child. There are others, like the provision of food, care, protection, and models of behaviour, but these probably play somewhat different psychological roles. The suggestion that the relationship should necessarily be limited to a single person is rejected in the light of evidence regarding successful multiple mothering in Israeli kibbutzim, for example, where responsibilities are shared among several (but not many) 'mothers', thus ensuring a high level of continuity of contact. The notion that the relationship must necessarily take place in the child's own home—'a bad family is better than a good institution'—is also rejected. The concept of maternal deprivation is in need of clarification here: it begs the question of the nature and meaning of deprivation if the mother is 'bad'. Evidence for the rejection of the child's 'own home' requirement is drawn again from the generally satisfactory adjustment of kibbutz children, who, while maintaining contact with parents, live and sleep in the kibbutz. Further, while institutional children show more deviant behaviour than the norm, this is still below the level of deviant behaviour associated with children from the most disturbed homes.

Short-term effects
While there can be no rigid distinction between short-term and long-term effects of maternal deprivation, it is convenient to regard the former as applying to the immediate response to deprivation, extending to the subsequent few months, and the latter to refer to effects experienced after a period of some years.

The most frequent situation in which short-term effects have been studied is when, for one reason or another, a child is admitted to hospital or to a residential nursery. Many, but by no means all, children react immediately by crying and exhibiting other forms of distress. When this ceases the mood changes to one of misery and apathy, to be followed at length by the appearance of adjustment to the situation and loss of interest in the parents. This sequence of protest, despair and detachment has been called the syndrome of distress. In some cases there appears to be an early reaction to maternal deprivation in terms of widespread restriction of developmental progress (the syndrome of developmental retardation). Language and social responsiveness are frequently involved.

While many children experience effects in both categories, there are also many who do not do so. Much depends on the age of the child. Hospital-admissions studies show that under six months there is usually no emotional distress. It appears to be most marked in children of between six months and four years. Other factors which influence the effects of maternal deprivation of the child include the sex and temperament of the child, previous separation experiences and their nature and duration, and the extent to which the mother-child bond is disturbed. (In some cases of hospital admissions, mothers have virtually unrestricted access to their children.)

In an endeavour to identify the psychological mechanims associated with the two syndromes, Rutter concludes that there is strong evidence to suggest that the retardation syndrome is best explained in terms of

490

lack (or privation) rather than loss. In contrast, the distress syndrome is probably best seen as due to loss (deprivation) rather than lack. Thus, retardation is seen as related to the lack of environmental stimulation while the distress reflects the loss of the opportunity for a well established attachment behaviour.

Long-term deprivation

The long-term effects of maternal deprivation pose similar questions. Abnormalities of all sorts—of physical growth, personality, language, and cognition—have been found to be associated with children with early family troubles. But the evidence comes from widely different circumstances and there are many children, deprived of perhaps both mother and father who appear not only to have suffered no such ill effects, but rather to have 'profited' from their experience.

In the case of long-term effects, much seems to depend on the length of the separation, whether it was very short and transient or lasting several weeks, or whether an early separation became permanent. Also, much depends on what happened during the separation. In some cases institutionalization is accompanied by adverse and in others by beneficial effects. Again the age, sex, temperament, and personal experience of the child are significant variables. In view of the wealth and diversity of influencing factors it is hardly surprising that only tentative conclusions can be drawn as to the possible psychological mechanisms involved. Most of the long-term effects can be linked with privation of some kind, for example, dwarfism with a nutritional deficiency, intellectual retardation with different kinds of stimulation deficits (e.g., language and perceptual deficits of some institutional contexts) rather than any type of loss. Delinquency, too, appears to be closely associated with the lack of a stable, harmonious child-parent relationship, and affectionless psychopathy with a failure to develop attachment bonds. The loss of a mother figure appears to play only a subsidiary role in respect of long-term consequences.

Rutter accordingly concludes that the term 'maternal deprivation' gives a misleading description of the origins of the long-term effects considered. Having served to draw attention to the severe consequences sometimes associated with disturbed early social experiences, he concludes that the extremely varied range of experiences with which it has become associated seriously restrict its usefulness. He proposes that the concept be abandoned and that future work should aim at a more precise linking of the various aspects of 'bad' child care with their separate effects together with a consideration of the sources of individual differences.

The interested reader is referred to Rutter's book, *Maternal Deprivation Reassessed* (1972).

Normative studies and the concept of normality

The evidence considered above can leave little doubt about the complexity of the nature-nurture interaction involved in development, or of the potentiality of either to bring about radical changes or to modify the effect of the other. It may well appear that any attempt to describe normal development of the normal individual is doomed to failure. Yet it would seem to be a reasonable demand from a scientific discipline to provide such descriptions. It is proposed here to consider briefly the extent to which developmental psychology is able to do this, and the value and limitations of doing so. Three approaches will be considered, by which attempts have been made to chart the course of normal development.

Gesell's approach

Arnold Gesell, one of several contenders for the title 'father of child psychology', was engaged at Yale University during the 1930s and 1940s on perhaps the most elaborate enterprise of this kind. With colleagues, and using an array of purpose built apparatus including observation domes, film cameras and one-way screens he published general descriptions of development in children from birth to ten years of age. Descriptions were made for each year, with the first year being further subdivided to cover descriptions of the rapid changes. The descriptions are divided into five sections to give details of the behaviour profile, the behaviour day, cultural and creative activities, nursery behaviour, and nursery technique (the two latter for the under-sixes). The behaviour profile provided a survey of the characteristic items of behaviour for a child of a particular age, drawing attention to significant changes in the interval covered, while the behaviour day described what the typical child of a given age would be doing at various times of the day. The other sections are self-explanatory, except perhaps for the last named which aimed to provide practical guidance for parents and other caretakers. At a different level, detailed developmental and diagnostic scales were constructed.

The work represented a laudable scientific enterprise—an ethological characterization of the normal child, based on the belief that what was being observed was a reflection of the effects of maturation. Its value has been limited because of the sampling limitations and the effects of cultural pressures. This latter is perhaps most apparent in the descriptions of the older children: the descriptions which accurately described the children of the 1930s and 1940s probably no longer typify the American children of today, not to mention the children of other cultures. Probably the most useful part of the work was that relating to neonates and infants, whose development more clearly reflects maturation. Some contemporary students of infant behaviour make extensive use of Gesell scales, while attempting to extend this type of characterization of the infant, described as 'just a beginning'.

While description is basic to the scientist's needs, undirected by the aim of hypothesis-testing, it is capable of indiscriminate collection of data, and the accumulation of barren and arbitrary facts.

The second approach to a description of normal development is to be found in the contrasting theoretical orientations described in Chapter 19. While Gesell's data were intended to give a comprehensive view of the typical individual, these focus on particular aspects of development, the Behaviourists with the processes involved in behaviour change, and Piaget, Freud and Erikson with different aspects of individual development.

The clinical approach

The third approach draws on both of the others, for both have been involved in the production of tests designed to give measures of performance of various sorts. This is the clinical approach to normality, based on the administration of standardized tests of physiological indices including electroencephalography (brain waves) and skin resistance, tests of intelligence, personality, memory, and perception, and a range of tests of educational attainment and vocational interests. The usefulness of this approach is that it offers a straightforward comparison of an individual's performance with that of the population upon which the test has been standardized. The individual can be given a position on the distribution of performances derived from this population, and thus seen as an 'average', or 'above average', etc., performer. The accuracy of the placing will depend on the validity and reliability of the test; it will also depend on the breadth of the standardization and the way in which the individual relates to the population for standardization. This list of provisos for the clinical/statistical approach to normal development underlines the relative nature of the evaluations made.

This is true of all three approaches to normal developments. Whatever conclusions are drawn must be seen as limited by the context of the 'standardizing' research population. Thus the 'behaviour day' of an American nine-year-old in the 1940s must not be expected to give too clear a picture of a similar child in the 1980s, nor of a nine-year-old Chinese child. The course of personality development in terms of psychosexual stages might be different between Austrian and Samoan children, and even in respect of such trusted instruments as intelligence tests, it seems possible that they may give a less reliable guide to the intelligence of rural children when the standardizing population is dominantly urban.

What is true of normal development is true also of normality. The concept of normality is bounded by the context in which it is evaluated.

Normality is used in two somewhat different senses. One refers to a standard which is generally accepted, as opposed to another which is not. From a social standpoint, 'normal' means well adjusted to the environment as opposed to ill-adjusted; from a moral standpoint, normal means 'good' rather than 'bad'; from a medical point of view, it means 'well' as opposed to 'ill'. It also has the somewhat finer-grained sense of 'average' or not significantly different from average, but in this case, instead of differing from a single group, the 'normals' are to be constrasted with those both 'above' and 'below' them.

What is generally accepted in respect of individual behaviour changes from one culture to another. Ruth Benedict, one of the pioneers of cultural anthropology describes the Dobu society, until recently cannibalistic. The normal Dobu was by western standards cruel, lawless, resentful, and deceitful and his life was dominated by violence, magic, and fraudulent dealings. A child growing up in this society who failed to develop the manners and the highly suspicious nature of members of this tribe would have been regarded as abnormal. Correspondingly, a child displaying the typical Dobuan attitudes in western society would be regarded as exceptional, at least. What is 'normal' also changes in the same place from one time to another. The child of Victorian England who was 'seen and not heard' and expected by one and all to 'mind his p's and q's' was different in many ways from the child of the 1980s. Thus, while development is influenced by nature and by early experience it is also radically affected by the customs and expectations of the culture in which it takes place. This topic will be taken up more fully in the next Chapter.

FURTHER READING

Booth, T. (1975) *Growing up in Society*. Methuen.
Boulter, L. R., Endler, N. S., and Osser, H. (1976) *Contemporary Issues in Developmental Psychology*. 2nd edn. Rineholt and Winston.
Cattell, R. B. (1965) *The Scientific Assessment of Personality*. Penguin.
Dennenberg, V. H. (1972) *The Development of Behaviour*. Sinauer Associates.
Rutter, M. (1972) *Maternal Deprivation Reassessed*. Penguin.
Sluckin, W. ed. (1972) *Imprinting and Early Learning*. Methuen.

22 Socialization and development
HARRY FISHER

Introduction

Socialization

Within the first year of life the infant begins to take on features of his cultural environment. Among the earliest are the sounds he makes. As time goes on speech, manners, ideals, and motives are all taken up. The longer he remains in the group the more he comes to reflect its 'norms'. These will be different between one sub-culture and another, each producing its own 'normal' personality. The process by which the individual acquires culturally-valued attitudes and behaviour patterns is known as socialization. This term was once used almost exclusively of the learning by young children of the ways of its culture. It has become increasingly clear that, while early experiences are important in shaping subsequent behaviour, the process of socialization does not cease suddenly at some stage beyond adolescence, but continues throughout life. Thus, socialization is intimately linked with the concepts of personality and normality. While personality refers to the 'more or less stable and enduring' characteristics which make each individual unique, socialization is concerned with those which make the individual like others in his society, that is, with those characteristics which are 'normal' for a particular sub-culture.

This description of socialization in general terms is all right as far as it goes. It is much more difficult to provide a definition of adequate socialization. This is because such a statement must, of necessity, include value judgements. In any society, being well socialized implies above-average prowess in the major social areas valued by the culture. In a 'western, industrialized society' this would usually mean having a circle of friends, or being 'good with people', in the sense of being able both to lead where necessary or simply to co-operate with others, having appropriately masculine or feminine ideals and accomplishments, and of doing all of these things at about the right age (precociousness can sometimes hinder socialization by isolating the individual from his peers). It would also mean taking 'full advantage' of educational opportunities. Even within an industrialized society such a list can hardly be regarded as definitive. There are, for example, differences in attitudes towards education. The predominant 'middle class' view of the importance of ambition and achievement is only one view of 'what life is all about'. An alternative is to be found among the lowest social classes in the USA. Here, the pleasures of life which are highly valued have to do with gratification of a much more immediate nature, involving a more spontaneous enjoyment of the environment as well as interpersonal relationships. Educational ambition among the children is much less frequently found. A second reservation concerns those children who are selectively deviant from the norms of society—delinquents, for example, who may be otherwise well adjusted in terms of the above list. There is evidence to suggest that such children are usually successful in making good an 'adequate' socialization, once the deviant allegiance has been broken. While 'adequate socialization' is difficult to define, its accomplishment in practice is a matter of importance to all those actually involved with the developing child. It is brought about in terms of the various methods used by different cultures, and prompted by continuous monitoring of progress, principally by parents at first, but later by an increasing number of those who represent the expectations of the culture. It is in terms of such vigilance that action may be taken to ensure that 'socialization' approaches the 'adequate' ideal. Parents who observe their child's shyness in a social context may take such action as they deem appropriate. This will be based on a range of variables, including the child's age (chronological, physical, and mental), sex, and social class, together with the generally accepted ways of behaving in the culture within which development takes place.

Sociometric measures of socialization

A method which has been found to provide an acceptable guide to the socialization of children of four years and over within school groups asks each of them to name three (sometimes five) best friends. Choices are limited to children of the same sex. In addition they are sometimes asked to name three (or five) least-liked members of the group. The data obtained may be presented in diagrammatic form (sociogram) or tabulated to show for each child the number of times he or she has been chosen (or rejected). This sociometric approach to socialization thus provides a first approximation measure of the interpersonal relations within a group. Using the two measures together, it is possible to detect those children who may have socialization problems, namely, those least liked by a majority of their peers (the rejects), and those never chosen as 'liked' (the isolates). It appears that children chosen by a majority sometimes also have socialization problems, the excessive popularity reflecting special efforts to overcome them, by overgenerosity, for example. 'Adequate' socializaton is usually indicated within this sort of group for a child who is chosen as 'best friend' by at least one or two others.

These measures may be added to by further specifying content by asking such questions as, with whom would you prefer to plan an outing, or, with whom would you choose to do your homework?

Other sociometric approaches to socialization use childrens' ratings of others to give measures along specific dimensions; for example, they might be asked to name those associated with masculine attitudes 'those who are always involved in the rough games'. Such work is usually carried out with due regard to the child's right to opt out if he so wishes, and the views of school authorities who may deem it inadvisable for the child to be involved. While giving a useful guide to the assessment of socialization within specific contexts, such work falls far short of providing insight into the wider aspects of socialization discussed earlier.

Socialization training

Every culture maintains its identity and continues to exist in terms of the pattern of collective life which has grown up among it members. This includes the expectations in regard to developing children as well as the means by which these may be realized. Both what is expected and how it is realized vary between cultures, but there are a number of substantial problems they have in common. These include the feeding and toilet-training of young children, the management of the child's early dependency towards ever increasing autonomy, attention to the fears and anxieties of the growing child, and the direction of aggression into activities approved by the culture. These are some of the problems investigated by developmental psychologists in respect of younger children. Other problems of socialization arise in the context of the transition to adult maturity. Some of these are to be considered later.

As has been seen, the earliest social influences centre around the mother and her caretaking activities. In many cultures this is a continuing source of influence. This single influence is soon added to as the child becomes mobile. Other adult members of the immediate family—peers and adults outside the family—in due course come to provide further indicators of cultural expectations. At the same time, the child's increasing competence means that socialization training can be intensified.

497

Before considering in more detail the ways in which the course of socialization is affected by such factors, it will be useful to consider briefly some of the characteristics of the individual which may impede or facilitate socialization.

Individual differences and socialization

At first sight, the end product of the socialization process would appear to be influenced principally, if not entirely, by one or more of the types of learning discussed in Chapter 10, representing the specific socialization training entailed by cultural expectations. Yet, because maturational factors must, of necessity, regulate the susceptibility of the developing child to certain sorts of socialization training (for example, explanations of 'right' and 'wrong' would not be very effective with the average eighteeen-month-old), the dominance of nurture must certainly be less than total. Some instances of the modifying effects of individual differences on socialization will now be considered which must further reduce this and indicate that socialization is the result of the dynamic interaction of the effects of training with the capacities and disposition of the individual.

Infants show considerable differences in their willingness to be cuddled; some like to cuddle, others tend to resist it. Clinical evidence suggests that girls may, on the whole, be more cuddly than boys. This willingness (or otherwise), genetic or congenital in origin, would seem likely to influence ease of early handling. The cuddly infant may well attract more handling and thus increased contacts with socializing agents. The evidence available at present is limited but consistent with the general proposition.

Another dimension along which infants show considerable individual differences is that of activity level. Again, there is little in the way of empirical evidence, but it would seem reasonable to suppose that a high activity level would, other things being equal, be conducive to more extensive early socialization opportunities than a low activity level.

There is evidence which indicates that a child's socialization is linked with his body build. From four years onward those with 'medium' and 'skinny' builds are better accepted than those with distinctly short and fat builds. This applies to both boys and girls. The 'medium' build is consistently preferred to the other two, and when children are asked to attribute traits to these body types, this build attracts all manner of desirable social graces, leadership, good sports, etc. The skinny build attracts some positive attributes—'likeable', 'gentle' but also some distinctly negative ones like 'withdrawn' and 'neurotic'; while the little fat boy or girl attracts mainly negative descriptions including poor sportsmanship and possible delinquency.

While there is again only limited evidence, it would appear that in

498

view of the complexity of the environment with which the developing child has to deal, measured intelligence must play a major role in the socialization process. Not all socialization training is explicit and direct. When it must be obtained by 'reading between the lines', the child of low intelligence may be at a disadvantage.

The age of sexual maturation has also been shown to influence the course of socialization. Sexual maturation is accompanied by a number of characteristic events. One of these is a marked increase in the rate of growth (the growth spurt). As for each of these events, onset may occur over a wide age range. For the growth spurt, onset may take place as early as ten-and-a-half years of age and as late as sixteen. The corresponding figures for girls are seven-and-a-half and eleven-and-a-half years. A number of studies suggest that in a typical western culture early sexual maturation may confer distinct social advantages in the case of boys. Since such boys are usually both taller and stronger, they are in a good position to exploit these in sporting pursuits, highly valued in western and westernized cultures. Their mature appearance also opens the possibilities of leadership roles as well as inviting adult contacts and thus increasing the available social outlets. Thus, for the early maturing boy the socialization process appears to be facilitated.

These examples give some indication of the complexity of the interaction between nature and nurture in the socialization process, for some of the differences considered not only have an influence upon the course of socialization, but may themselves be modified by it. Intelligence, for example, as has been seen above, may influence the course of socialization. There is ample evidence to show that intelligence is itself subject to environmental forces. A further example may be seen in the attitudes an individual may hold towards himself as a member of a particular culture. Negative attitudes, such as those which might be experienced by individuals within 'oppressed' minority cultures, themselves the product of socialization, may well modify the ends of normal socialization.

The agents of socialization
Children become socialized through constant interaction with others. A host of important people act as agents of the society to direct each child in the way it should go. They include the mother, other members of the family, friends and neighbours, peers, and 'official' socializing agents such as teachers, and law-enforcers. Their relative importance changes with context and the age of the child. In the first year, as has already been seen, the mother or other caretaker plays an important role in socialization. With the increasing mobility and the development of language, the range of 'agents' expands to include those outside the immediate family circle. It is adults whose influence dominates in the first few years. In those cultures which provide schooling, the child nor-

mally comes under the influence of his peers to a greater degree than before in this context, as well as becoming subject to further socialization at the hands of his teachers. From the middle years of childhood onwards the influence of the peer group tends to increase, while that of the home declines. The conflicts which might result from such movements are limited because influential peer friends tend to be chosen so that they reinforce parental views. Parents, families, neighbours, peers, educators and law enforcers carry out their functions as agents of socialization in a direct, face-to-face way. They do so as representatives of the social class and cultures within which they operate; educators and law enforcers, while not necessarily belonging to the same social class as the children they meet, generally work within guidelines consistent with class ideals. All, however, are concerned that the child should be brought up in accordance with cultural expectations. Different social classes exist within the same culture. Culture is defined in terms of the traditions and laws of a people who frequently have ethnic or natural ties. Information about cultural ideals is transmitted by mass media where these exist. Social class is usually defined in occupational and financial terms and, where these variables create special conditions (e.g., the relative isolation of some farming communities), the aims of socialization may be modified. The agents of socialization bring both cultural and social pressures to bear on the developing child.

As the child gets older both those involved in the socialization process and the methods used change. For the very young, methods need to be simple, manipulative, and authoritative. Required behaviour-changes may be brought about by rewards and punishments. Corporal punishment is regarded as of little value in many cultures, but in others is used as a matter of course. Withdrawal of the usual signs of affection is sometimes used to show disapproval. This usually has to wait on the acquisition of some language. As this progresses, the moulding of behaviour into approved patterns can be undertaken by direct instruction and discussion.

Some specific areas of child socialization

Dependence
The long period of helplessness of the human infant means that it relies for survival on the efforts of caretakers. This reliance on others from infancy, throughout childhood and beyond, is one of the most pervasive forms of social behaviour. It changes with age, both in the form it takes, and the people it involves. In the first year of life the dependency is expressed in the attachment behaviour discussed in Chapter 21 which seeks to maintain contact or proximity and concerns principally the mother. In the second year, it is usual to observe the beginnings of what

has been called 'spontaneous progressive detachment'. In the presence of the mother the infant begins to explore the wider aspects of his environment and to move towards increasing autonomy. Later, dependency behaviour tends to take more explicit forms such as seeking attention or help from others, and, as time goes on, involves peers as well as adults. The overdependent child, who seems to exist almost entirely in terms of others, is commonly held to be as ill-adapted as the underdependent child—the 'loner' who lives to a large extent without reference to others. (A distinction is here made between being 'underdependent' and being independent, which will be taken up later). The socialization of dependence behaviour is concerned with avoidance of such extremes.

Dependence has been studied in infants of a year old by observing play and exploratory behaviour in one of four conditions: the presence of the mother alone, the presence of a stranger alone, the presence of both, or of neither. Play and exploratory behaviour were both greater and the incidence of crying less when the mother was present than when she was absent. Even when the mother was there, the presence of the stranger was associated with a tendency for the child to stay nearer the mother.

In a situation where children between one and four years of age were allowed freedom to explore an unfamiliar environment in the mother's presence, the distance separating the child from the mother was seen to increase with age.

A study of dependence behaviour in three- and four-year-old children in a nursery school used a rating scale to assess such things as seeking help or attention from the teacher, and their reliance on other children. Two sorts of dependence behaviour were distinguished, *task-orientated* (sometimes called instrumental dependency, where the teacher's help was sought in order to solve a particular problem), and *person-orientated* (or emotional dependency, involving proximity or affection seeking). These were differently related for younger as compared with older children. For the three-year-olds the two types of dependence behaviour were significantly correlated, while for the four-year-olds they were not. Further, for the younger children, task-orientated dependence was not significantly correlated with rated autonomy, as might be expected, while for the older children there was a significant negative correlation. These results suggest that, by four years of age, the child uses 'self help' or help from others as alternative approaches to problem-solving.

This selection from the available evidence underlines the changing nature of dependence behaviour with age, and the strong link between its occurrence and situations which the child finds anxiety-producing. It seems likely that if dependence behaviour were either always rewarded or never rewarded by the person or persons to whom it was directed, extremes of 'over' and 'under' dependence might be the respective consequences. It is for teachers, parents, and others to judge in which situations their intervention will best serve the quest for autonomy. Studies of both normal and overdependent children have indicated the potential dangers of the inconsistent handling of dependency, and the use of the 'withdrawal of love' technique. Inconsistency may arise, for example, when, possibly for good reasons, a mother may at first brush off a child's move for reassurance and then later relent, satisfying a dependent need which may no longer be salient. Together with 'withdrawal of love' by a usually loving parent, which may be construed by the child as similarly inconsistent, this sort of rearing has been seen as likely to increase the child's anxiety and to open the way to extreme emotional dependency.

Independence and achievement
One way of viewing the independence or autonomy sought as one of the goals of socialization, is that it is simply the absence of dependent behaviour. This, it might be argued, fails to capture what is meant by independence; absence of practically all dependence on others leads to the way of the hermit and the recluse which, while independent, is hardly a social norm. Positively, independence suggests the involvement of such features as self-assertion, initiative, and unaided enterprise in the child's behaviour, accompanied by comparatively rare and selective attempts to draw help from others.

In the normal course of events, children become progressively more independent, probably partly due to the implicit reinforcement arising out of increasing competence in reaching goals unaided, and to explicit reinforcement for independent behaviour.

The link between independence and achievement was made in an early study by Marian Winterbottom in 1953. Achievement behaviour is that which carries the suggestion of an aim to complete a task in a particularly meritorious way with as little outside help as possible. The Winterbottom study was directed towards achievement motivation rather than achievement behaviour. Measures of achievement motivation were obtained for twenty-nine boys aged from eight to ten years. They were shown Thematic Apperception test (TAT) pictures (see Ch. 23) and said what they thought was happening. Their answers were carefully scored to produce a (widely accepted) measure of achievement motivation. (Subsequently evaluation has shown, however, that the measure has only low reliability.) Winterbottom also interviewed the boys' mothers in order to find out how the boys had been brought up with particular attention to demands for independence. She found that the difference between high- and low-achievement boys was related to their independence training. Mothers of high-achievement motivation boys looked for self-reliant behaviour relatively early. Whenever their sons demonstrated their independence, these mothers provided larger and more frequent rewards than the mothers of the low-achievement boys. This evidence, then, consists of a significant correlation between achievement motivation and child-rearing practices. Correlation evidence, however, cannot be used to establish a relation between cause and effect. One possible interpretation is that the son's motivations developed as they did because of the mother's expectations and encouragement. But there are other, equally valid, interpretations. For example, the mother's expectations and the subsequent achievement motivations may both have been produced because of the boys' innately determined competence.

In 1959 Rosen and d'Andrade published a paper entitled *The Psychosocial Origin of Achievement Motivation*, which describes the evidence they gathered to clarify what it is that parents do which fosters achievement motivation. They visited forty families in their homes, twenty of which had a son with high, and twenty a son with low, achievement motivation scores. The experimenters observed each parent as they watched their blindfolded son build a tower from irregularly-shaped blocks. They were allowed to say anything they desired to the boy, but forbidden to touch the blocks. This was one of a series of tasks the boy performed while his parents observed in this way. The data gathered by Rosen and d'Andrade indicated that the parents of high-achievement motivation boys typically set higher standards for their sons and expected better task performance than parents of boys with low-achievement motivation. There were also differences in the behaviour of the two sets of parents as they looked on. In the tower-building task, for example, parents of high scorers, especially the mothers, spent considerable effort on encouragement and were generous in praise of a successful outcome. In contrast, the fathers of low-scoring sons tended to give specific instructions, and to react with annoyance when things went wrong. The authors interpreted their results as indicating the strong influence of parental attitudes, in standard setting, in their own interest and involvement of their son's performance as well as in their provision of both achievement and independence training.

The findings of these two early studies have been supplemented by others in more recent years. One such suggests that the impact of parental attitudes and practices on children's achievement behaviour may depend on a number of factors, including the sex of the child, the sex of the parent, and the type of achievement behaviour. For intellectual achievement, for example, the mother's behaviour is often more predictive for a son than for a daughter. There is also evidence which suggests that girls may employ achievement behaviour as a means of attracting adult approval, while boys work to achieve for its own sake.

A further group of studies has suggested a number of characteristics which distinguish 'high' from 'low' achievers in respect of intellectual pursuits. These include an expectation-related capacity for application: those who expect to do well, in general, work harder than those who do not, indicating a sense of the importance of the part they play in their own success; high-achievers tend to believe that they, rather than other people, are responsible for their success and their ability to work for long term goals.

Aggression
While most of those actively involved in the socialization of children would be prepared to use rearing techniques aimed at the inculcation of independence, ideals of achievement, and the development of sex-appropriate behaviours, few would be inclined to include aggression in such a list. For society at large, aggression is disruptive and something to be constrained. Nevertheless, it is widely regarded as important, at least for boys, that they should be able to 'stand up for themselves' in a fight. The term is also used with positive overtones, for example, in the context of the pursuit of some professional or athletic end with unusual diligence—thus, the 'aggressive' hurdler or managing director. This ambivalence underlies some of the difficulties of arriving at an unambiguous definition. It has been proposed that, from an experimental point of view, what is aggressive should be judged for particular contexts, bearing in mind a variety of antecedent factors. A number of studies have demonstrated the usefulness of the rigour of this social-judgement approach.

A more direct characterization of aggression is that it covers actions intended to produce anxiety or injury in others. It includes physical actions such as kicking, punching, destruction of property, as well as such verbal acts as abuse, derogation, and quarrelling.

The developmental research into aggression may be divided into two parts, one concerned with identifying antecedents of aggression, the other with investigations of means which might be used to inhibit it.

Under the first heading, four general areas can be identified. The first of them, as yet relatively undeveloped, relates to a recently-proposed hypothesis that male aggression is, at least partly, innate. Supporting evidence must, of necessity, be indirect. The proposers cite the early establishment of sex differences in aggression and the greater involvement of males in aggressive behaviour throughout childhood and adolescence. It has, further, been shown that aggressive behaviour is a stable and enduring characteristic throughout development, but more so for boys than for girls. It also appears that it always falls to men to engage in tribal or national warfare. Even among the Arapesh, where both men and women had 'feminine' manners, and the Tchambuli, where sex roles were 'reversed', it is the men who were the warriors. Such considerations, viewed in the light of the earlier discussion of sex differences in behaviour, provide grounds for further investigation.

The second area relates to the frustration-aggression hypothesis, first proposed in 1939, that aggressive behaviour is always linked with antecedent frustration, and that frustration always gives rise to some form of aggression. While support for the link between aggression and frustration has been provided in terms of observations of the greater aggression of a frustrated as against a control group of children involved in projective doll play, the second part of the hypothesis was subsequently modified in the light of a study which demonstrated that, while aggression frequently follows frustration, it does not do so exclusively. Children who were frustrated by being deprived of 'new' toys and obliged to play with a less attractive range, engaged, not in aggressive, but regressive behaviour, that is, less mature behaviour. For example, the children asked to be allowed out of the room, or approached the wire screen which separated them from the new toys, their play being considerably less constructive than before. Other studies have shown that personality differences are important in determining the reaction to frustration.

A third area includes studies which suggest that aggression may be directly inculcated. Antisocial aggression among delinquent boys has been shown to be associated with parental praise for past aggression. An experimental study demonstrated that adult permissiveness towards aggression, where the child is allowed to express aggression freely, may have the same effect as open encouragement. It is also clear that much aggression is learnt in direct interaction with peers.

The fourth area relates to studies of the effects of children's observation of aggressive models. The Bandura study referred to in Chapter 20 shows the influence of such exposure on subsequent aggressive behaviour. A laboratory demonstration of this type naturally begs the question of the extent to which such processes operate in the free environment, and, in particular, the effect of exposure to violent scenes on television. An early study obtained ratings of aggressive behaviour of eight-year-olds by their peers, and these were compared with the violence rating of favourite television programmes as estimated by mothers and fathers. A significant positive relationship between the two was found for boys but not for girls.

The second group of studies concern the inhibition of aggression. Verbal punishment of children for aggressive doll play was found to be effective in bringing about a temporary decrease. There are a number of studies which appear to suggest that physical punishment has little effect in inhibiting child aggression. However, the typically high correlation between high incidence of aggression in children and highly punitive parents poses problems of interpretation. Does the aggression arise because of the exposure to a punitive model? Does the punishment arise simply because the child is already aggressive? Or are both related to some common, predisposing condition arising from combination of natural and environmental factors?

Successful attempts at inhibiting aggression have been reported from down-town ghetto schools in New York and from the nursery school situation. The approach used is to persuade teachers to reward only desirable behaviours and to ignore aggressive and other undesirable acts. While this is a potentially important approach since it avoids some of the consequences of the punishment of aggression, the early reports for the success of the approach need to be interpreted with some caution. It seems possible that at least some part of the success may be attributed to the special conditions which accompany such field studies. The arrival of the behaviour modification team in the ghetto schools meant that pupils had the unusual experience of a stable educational regime. Its effect may well have been compounded with that of the methods of control they employed.

Moral development

The study of moral development involves the identification and description of processes by which children internalize the norms and expectations of social conduct. Psychological studies may be divided into groups corresponding to investigations of cognitive, behavioural, or affective aspects of morality. Probably the most coherent developmental account is to be found in studies of the cognitive aspect, based on the work of Piaget, which investigated the ways in which children of different ages viewed rules and made judgements about hypothetical situations involving moral conflict. The behavioural aspect of morality has provided information as to what children do in a moral conflict, as distinct from what they judge. Investigations have been made, for example, of the child's ability to resist temptation, providing information as to his capacity for implementing internalized rules. The affective dimension of morality in children has been concerned with the emotional reaction associated with transgression, using reactions of guilt to infer the existence of these rules, and as an index of the influence of individual differences. Each aspect will be considered in turn. The question of the effects of child-rearing practices on moral development will also be considered briefly.

Piaget used his own sensitive method of clinical interrogation to gain insight into the development of the child's moral judgements. In one extensive study he questioned children of various ages about the rules governing a popular local game of marbles. In another, he presented them with short, 'moral' stories, which they were asked to evaluate. The stories came in pairs. Typically, one would describe an individual who, through a clumsy, if well intentioned, act occasioned extensive damage, while the other described a similar individual, engaged on some deliberate mischief, which brought about little damage. The child was then asked which of the two was morally worse, and why. Younger children selected the one who did most damage, older children the intentional villain. Piaget used the data he gathered to construct some preliminary description of the developmental sequence of moral judgements. He proposed two clear stages of moral development, an earlier, heteronomous and a later, autonomous, stage, the age of seven to eight years providing an approximate division between them. Heteronomous means 'subject to another's law', autonomous, 'subject to one's own law'. Thus, for the younger children moral sanctions are external and vested in parents and adults. Older children regulate their own conduct, having made the principles largely their own, as a result of socialization, with due regard to the views of others—both peers and adults—but from time to time in defiance of them.

Piaget saw two defects of cognitive functioning in the earlier stage which determined the characteristics of both stages. Because of the first defect, 'moral realism', the child is unable to distinguish 'subjective' from 'objective' phenomena, and tends to view adult rules as fixed and inevitable. The second defect, egocentrism, viewing the rules from his own point of view alone, entails an inability to regard moral rules as relative to persons and situations. The later autonomous stage sees the child disabused of both limitations. Children in the two stages thus differ in their view of rules, their view of right and wrong, and consequently their view of justice. In the earlier stage, rules are regarded as absolute and unchangeable; in the later stage, rules are viewed as means of regulating social intercourse, to be changed if all concerned consent. Right and wrong to the immature child are judged by the letter of the 'absolute' rules. It is only in the autonomous stage that intentionality is used in evaluating right and wrong. Justice, for the younger children, is concerned with the punishment of misdeeds, again according to the letter of the law. Only in autonomous children is the punishment regarded as a means of demonstrating corporate displeasure for antisocial acts. Piaget describes the change from one stage to the next as a change from a 'morality of authority' to a 'morality of co-operation'.

Building on the work of Piaget, Lawrence Kohlberg, using somewhat more complex moral problem stories for his subjects to evaluate, has confirmed the notion of developmental stages in moral development. He has distinguished three levels of moral judgement. The lowest of these is described as 'premoral', the second as 'morality of conventional rule conformity', and the highest level as 'morality of self-accepted moral principles'. Each level is subdivided into two. The final stage, for example, includes judgements consistent with a view of morality in terms

507

of 'contractual obligations and democratic law', and those which indicate 'morality of individual principles of conscience.'. Kohlberg's work has thus added detail to Piaget's scheme.

The second aspect of morality to be considered is concerned with how children behave when placed in a situation that involves them in a choice between alternatives, one of which is seen to be morally wrong. The Character Education Inquiry published in 1932 by Hartshorne and May was an attempt to provide insight into this sort of problem. Twelve thousand children were put into situations where they could cheat, lie, or steal—at home, in the classroom, in athletics, and at party games. They were mistakenly under the impression that their actions were private. The data was used to provide an answer to the question as to whether honesty is a general trait or whether it is situation-specific. Hartshorne and May produced evidence which surprised them. The correlation between bad behaviour in one setting and bad behaviour in another was low, averaging about 0.34. Even when the settings were similar, in school tests, for example, children behaved inconsistently. It was concluded that in the terms of the tests performed, honesty was largely situation-specific rather than a general personality trait. A subsequent re-analysis of the data modified the latter part of this conclusion, by showing that there was a significant, if small, tendency for children who were honest on one test to be so on others. Subsequent studies of different measures of honesty have tended to confirm that they are positively correlated. Thus, whether a person resists the temptation to cheat, lie, or steal is clearly determined by his personality, as well as by the situation. Other methods, including questionnaire, and projective story completion have also been used to gain information about the resistance to temptation in private.

A large body of clinical detail relating to the affective dimension of morality is contained in the writings of Freud. Much recent work in this area has been concerned with the experience of guilt following transgression. In one such study, 112 boys were asked to complete stories describing various forms of misdemeanour: theft, disobedience, and wishing someone dead. The story endings were scored to obtain a measure of the guilt associated with each of those. It was found that the intercorrelations between these measures was low. The individual who experienced guilt to the same degree for all offences was rare. It was concluded that experience of guilt, also, was more specific than general.

Investigations of the affective or emotional aspects of the violation of some moral principle have been carried out by a number of researchers. Psychoanalytic theory predicts that an individual with a strong conscience or superego will be unlikely to violate moral principles because of the discomfort associated with guilt. It has recently been suggested

508

that resistance to temptation and guilt-reactions have different antecedents and are not highly correlated; knowledge of the guilt reactions of an individual should thus be of little value in predicting his resistance to temptation. A recent study has examined the relation between child guilt-responses and three different types of parental discipline. Parental disciplines were classified according to whether they were based on (a) punishment and material deprivation (b) withdrawal of love or (c) a reasoned approach to the consequences of the child's deviant acts. The data gathered showed that the reasoned approach was highly correlated with guilt responses. (These were assessed from a story completion test.) The punishment regime was negatively correlated and the withdrawal of love regime uncorrelated with guilt responses. The reasoned approach was also highly correlated with other measures of indices of moral development such as acceptance of responsibility, consideration for other children, and readiness to confess. Father's and mother's disciplinary practices were separately assessed. It was the mother's practices that provided the substantial part of the overall results, indicating that, in general, she may play the more important role in moral development.

Investigations into the relations among the cognitive, behavioural and emotional aspects of moral development have revealed only low correlations. In some cases no correlations were found and there were no high correlations. This seems to cast doubt on the notion of a single, integrated, moral system. Knowing the difference between right and wrong does not of necessity pre-empt the wrong, nor entail experience of guilt when wrong has been done.

It would appear reasonable to assume that early experience within the family plays an important role in moral development. In general, the direct evidence collected allows very few generalizations to be made apart from the pervasive influence of the mother. Clearest evidence regarding the influence of child-rearing practices comes from a comparison of family conditions between delinquents and matched non-delinquents. The non-delinquent typically comes from a home where the bonds of affection between child and parent are strong, where moral demands on the child are firm and explicit, and where misdemeanours are punished consistently and with some emphasis on reasoning and explanations. Punishment rarely involves physical means. The delinquent, by contrast, usually come from homes where bonds of affection are weak, and where punishment for wrong-doing is based largely on physical or verbal assault, punishment is both inconsistently applied, and is variable in its severity. From studies which use non-delinquents and employ experimental (rather than survey) methods, no such clear relations have, so far, been found between child rearing practices and moral development.

509

Theoretical orientations

Theorizing about socialization is beset by a number of obstacles. These include problems of definition and usage and that of raising criteria for what should count as a comprehensive theory. The term is only loosely defined; usage tends to include both what is happening from the individual's viewpoint in socialization, as well as the techniques and practices used to bring them about. What is to satisfy as a comprehensive theory is difficult because of the large number of variables involved. Thus, it might be argued that a minimum requirement would be for the theory to accommodate developmental and personality data, as well as those relating to social processes. Consider, say, Piaget's structural view of intellectual development. This may appear to be of only restricted relevance in this context. Certainly, its immediate end was not to account for socialization. It will be clear from the account of moral development above, however, that Piaget used general principles from that approach to give an account of the differences between the heteronomous and autonomous moralities. His 'marbles' and 'moral stories' data could scarcely be neglected in a theory of socialization. A further difficulty is general to psychology, in that commonly used concepts refuse to fit a tidy arrangement when subject to scientific investigation. A given phenomenon might invite explanation from a number of different theoretical backgrounds. Guilt reaction after transgression, for example, may be interpreted in learning-theory terms as well as in terms of the superego.

Identification as an explanation

In the discussion of areas of socialization covered earlier, so far as has been possible, theorizing has been restricted. This, in order to consider here, the pervasive notion of identification as a possible explanatory basis of some generality. It is one of the marks of a good theory that it integrates a broad spectrum of data. Identification, as will be seen, takes on a number of very different shades of meaning, as with socialization, confusing process and product. Nevertheless, within this diversity there would appear to be areas of unity which offer useful theoretical starting points.

The processes by which socialization comes about include some which are clear and demonstrable: changes resulting from direct instruction met with understanding; changes associated with social reinforcement of approved behaviours, or contingent on learning by observation. To some degree, each of these has been satisfactorily specified and put to empirical test. Such descriptions, however, say nothing of the motivational basis of the processes, nor do they refer to the people involved and the relations between them. A theoretical account of socialization would appear to require an account of the part played by

510

both, for the socialization of children proceeds in terms of people who supply both models and motivation. Social reinforcement, for example, has been shown to be related to the individuals involved. If, for example, a pupil has little respect for his teacher, words of praise are less likely to be valued than if the relationship were one of respect and admiration. It is in this context that the concept of identification has been useful, in that it links the notion of imitation with that of social reinforcement, supplying thereby some part at least, of the need for a motivational basis for socialization. The requirements for an adequate account of motivation are complex. The concept of identification by no means meets all the requirements but it does offer some ways of obtaining useful insights, particularly so in that it has a wide currency in psychology. The aspects to be considered in what follows will be concerned with

1. Freud's use of the concept of identification.
2. The learning theory 'version' of this concept.
3. The connection of identification with role playing.
4. Identification as generalized imitation.
5. A view of the motivational basis of imitation in terms of 'power'.
6. A comparison of the parts played by the concept of identification and psychosocial development (Erikson) in an account of socialization.

1. Freud distinguished four sorts of identification: narcissistic, goal orientated, object loss, and defensive. He saw identification as concerned with the incorporation by the child of the qualities and ideals of another person. The tendency to identify with people who already have some features in common with the child (provided the child values these features) is called *narcissistic identification*. (Narcissism is Freud's term for self-love.) It is this kind of identification which is seen as responsible for the ties between members of a group based on physical or mental traits, on interests or possessions which the members share, constituting a wide basis for socialization.

Freud saw the source of *goal-orientated identification* as being anxiety and frustration. Typically, one individual who has a problem identifies with another who has successfully solved the same kind of problem. For example, a boy may identify with his father if the father is achieving goals valued by the boy. If the members of the immediate family are not obtaining such goals, the child may look elsewhere, for example, to eminent figures of sport or entertainment.

Object loss identification is seen as an attempt to secure or recover a 'lost' object (the 'object' is usually a person) by making oneself like the lost object. Classical psychoanalysts saw this in the identification of children with parents who had rejected them. Alternatively, to gain parental affection children may attempt to be like someone who represents the ideals and expectations of the parents.

511

Defensive identification, or identification with the aggressor, seeks to avoid punishment by conforming with the demands of a potential enemy. It represents an 'If I am like you, you will not harm me' position. Thus a child may avoid punishment or anxiety by regulating his behaviour in conformity with the requirements of influential others. In the early years these will normally be the parents, but, as time goes on, may include identifications with other authority figures. These four proposed types of identification offer plausible approaches to different aspects of socialization.

2. It is not difficult to see identification in learning theory terms. The hypothetical process of internalization of standards and ideals translates well into behavioural terms. Thus, identification on this basis means behaving in accordance with 'ideals or standards', defined in reward and punishment terms. The learning theory approach of Robert Sears is one of several which elaborates this viewpoint. It is, in essence, a three-stage theory of motivational development. The first stage is characterized by motives based on the 'trial and error' learning in which the child engages in order to solve these problems. The mother plays an important role in this context and mother-child attachment is seen as originating in the transaction from this first phase to a second characterized by direct reward. The mother's role in the satisfaction of primary needs establishes her as an agent of reward. The child's dependence upon her extends to other caretakers, and becomes the basis of a secondary motivational system based on direct rewards and punishments. This second stage is thus related to learning situations which arise within the immediate family. This is further generalized by the inclusion of learning situations outside the family (the third stage). It is the secondary motivational systems which regulate behaviour, as they are potentially more powerful than the primary drives. The child's early attachment means that, as dispensers of direct rewards, the parents exercise control over its behaviour. Later, this control is taken over by the child in accordance with the motivational constraints exercised by the parents. Thus, identification is seen as a motivational system in that the child learns to regulate his own behaviour in terms of the established pattern of rewards and punishments.

3. Social psychology also provides something akin to the notion of socialization as influenced by identification. This comes from role theory, which suggests that a child learns to operate in social situations by acquiring knowledge about the roles involved. The learning comes about by role-playing which is real (in the sense that children actually play at being 'fathers and mothers', or 'teachers' or 'nurses') or fantasy—that is they imagine what they would do if they were mothers

512

or teachers, etc. The role learned may involve not only the behavioural externals, but induced principles and ideals. It involves knowledge of complementary roles (the 'teacher' must also know how the 'pupil' behaves), and is clearly influenced by the intellectual skills and sensitivity of the child. Thus, so far as the content of the behaviours acquired is concerned, identification and role-learning have much in common. The major difference rests on the motivational basis which the concept of identification entails but that of role-playing does not.

4. Role-playing entails imitation, an aspect of behaviour long of interest to psychologists, because it raises the question of its motivational origins: that children imitate the behaviour of both parents and peers is self evident; why they do so is far from clear. Theories which see imitation as an instinct, or the result of classical conditioning have been proposed. These have now given way to an operant analysis, where reinforcement is given for a response similar to that of a model. Matching the response of the model may thus acquire the status of (secondary) reinforcment, and, through generalization, a child may imitate responses of the model not previously reinforced. Imitation (or modelling) is usually used to refer to the copying of specific items of behaviour, and it has been proposed that identification can be regarded as generalized imitation. Here a child will imitate a whole range of behaviours. Some workers use the three terms imitation, modelling, and identification interchangeably, arguing that, since the copied behaviour constitutes the sole evidence, there are no logical grounds for differentiating among them. It is, however, conventional to do so.

5. In 1965, H. M. Wolowitz suggested that the motivational basis of imitation might be characterized, at last in part, by the child's observation in others of various sources of power which may be related to his own goals. A person may be said to have power if he has something that someone else wants or fears, and is known to be willing and able to share it, or, in the case of a feared entity, to be prepared to dispense it. Types of power include physical power, expertise, prestige and nurturance. Physical power for disciplinary purposes is widely used. In spite of disadvantages it has the immediate effect of making the one who uses it appear master of the situation. Even small children, both boys and girls attempt to gain advantage by this means. Expertise also acts as an inducement to imitation. It may include a variety of activities, intellectual, sporting, artistic among others. Boys who 'model themselves on' sportsmen or entertainers by mimicking, not only their professional style, but other attributes of appearance and dress, illustrate well the notion of generalized imitation or identification. As with physical power, the inducement to imitate expertise will vary from one social

situation to another. The influence of physical power tends to decrease with age; that of expertise tends to increase with the child's increasing ability to appreciate it. Expertise and prestige may be related, in that the former may confer the latter, but, in the sense of prestige which relates to status, expertise need not be involved. As an inducement to imitation, prestige has also been seen as status envy; as with expertise, it is more likely to influence older children. By nurturance is meant the property of affording a congenial environment, of providing comfort and generally being able to meet both physical and emotional needs. In respect of nurturance the social-learning literature abounds with studies which contrast the influence of nurturant as against non-nurturant models, showing in general the greater tendency of children to imitate the former. Nurturance has been interpreted, in a variety of ways, from highly specific responses like smiling to more general attitudes including friendship behaviour, attention, approval, acceptance, and the like. The wide range of investigations attest with considerable uniformity to the effectiveness of nurturance as an inducement to imitation.

This brief discussion of the analysis of the 'power' of the model as a motivational basis for imitation behaviour will give an indication of its usefulness as a starting point for an explanatory account of at least some aspects of socialization.

It is the aim of scientific enterprise to provide explanatory accounts of phenomena, and to do so using a minimum of 'basic' ideas to embrace as wide as possible a range of empirical data. Here, the single basic idea of the 'power' possessed by the model is elaborated to include several different types of power to account for a wide range of imitative behaviour. It may be seen that this approach can be applied to all of the aspects of socialization considered earlier—dependency, achievement, motivation, aggression, sex-appropriate behaviour, and moral development. The social-learning literature contains much empirical evidence to suggest its wider applicability. The 'power' approach to imitation thus provides one way of accounting for a large volume of the socialization data.

6. It would seem that in view of the extent of the related theoretical areas, to look for a single, elegant, all-inclusive theory of socialization is to seek the impossible. It may help to throw some light on the nature of the contribution provided by the imitation/power approach if a summary comparison is made with Erikson's theory of psychosocial development. This is a stage theory which seeks to describe the characteristics of each of the eight stages in terms of a bipolar dimension (trust versus mistrust) etc. Thus, while it seeks to describe, the social learning position aims at explanation in terms of motivational processes. As with all stage theories Erikson's emphasizes the discontinuities

between the stages to the possible neglect of transition behaviours. In contrast, the process approach emphasizes the continuity of development in terms of motivation. Erikson's theory stems from a clinical background which included close contact with children. The stages are defined in general terms and await clarification and the demonstration of empirical validity. The social-learning theory approach is an attempt to organize and account for a large body of empirical data. This comparison—which does less than justice to either approach—serves to emphasize the broad differences between them.

Social learning theories rest on the principles of classical and operant conditioning discussed in Chapter 10, but these principles apply only indirectly in socialization. While both modes of conditioning may apply to some early socialization, the advent of language adds considerably to the means available, so that 'pure' conditioning becomes an increasing rarity. The processes which take place are simply analogues of these procedures.

There are, of course, modes of social learning which are not encompassed by the modelling approach, such as the processes of learning by direct social reinforcement, or verbal instruction where the modelling component is absent, or where learning takes place because of a wish to please, where, while the modelling component may be present, the motivational component may be construed in terms of affectional bonds, rather than in terms of problem-solving.

The pervasive notion of identification may thus be seen to present one possible avenue of approach to the complexities of at least some areas of socialization.

Play

In the mid-morning, on five days per week during term-time, children in countless primary schools emerge from their classrooms into the school grounds. Within minutes, the scene becomes one of intense activity and noise, running, shouting, 'cartwheels' being turned, noisy (imaginary) motorcycles ridden recklessly in and out with appropriate sound effects and actions, games of tag, of football . . . this is play-time. At least some of the younger children will have emerged from an educational regime—a descendant of a much older approach to education—named the 'play-way', which includes periods of play. This will involve the use of numerous pieces of apparatus—Wendy houses, mobile toys, scales, paints, counters, plasticine—available for use in accordance with the child's preference. All of these varied activities may be grouped under the single term play. The use of play to facilitate the educational process indicates something of the intense interest in the subject shown by psychologists, psychiatrists, and educators. In what follows, a brief account of some of the main trends of this interest will be given.

Play is a pervasive and characteristic part of the behaviour of the normal healthy child, and it has a developmental sequence. The amount of time spent in play decreases as the child gets older, though there are probably wide cultural and individual differences. It also has a variety of social contexts: it may involve groups of people taking part in some organized game and the groups may be large or small. Indeed, play may be solitary. The great variety of activities, its place in education, and the wealth of social contexts, suggest that play covers a much wider domain than do the several aspects of socialization discussed earlier. Here, a brief summary will be given of a number of different approaches to this area, in a roughly historical sequence. Three periods will be distinguished, the first largely influenced by Darwin's theory of evolution in the nineteenth century and distinguished by inductive theories of play. The second period, occupying approximately the first half of the present century, is marked by the development of major psychological theories, play being viewed in the light of these different orientations. The remaining period covers the third quarter of the century (much of the distinctive work dates from the mid-1960s onward). The nature of this work includes laboratory studies of restricted areas of play and ethological studies.

Three theories of play
Just as children play, so young animals are, likewise, much involved in activities which might well be interpreted as play. In the climate of the Darwinian theory of evolution, it is not surprising that frisking lambs, puppies in mock battle, leaping fish and somersaulting chimpanzees were seen as involved in the same category of behaviour as the 'tagging', 'cartwheeling', children referred to earlier. This may prove to be a valid assumption. Those who theorized about play in the latter half of the nineteenth century assumed that it was; and they were, therefore, concerned with giving an account of play which would apply generally across species. The types of behaviour included in this category were social games, like the rough and tumble play of monkeys, explorations, such as those carried out by a wide range of species to investigate novel aspects of their environment, general bodily activity, involving the expenditure of much energy to apparently little effect, like the galloping of the colt and the prancing of a kitten with a ball of wool, together with activities which seemed to hint at adult behaviours. These categories were neither mutually exclusive nor exhaustive, but it may be seen that they can be applied to both animal and human behaviour. It was widely accepted that the common features of play included the following: it is pleasurable; it appears to be undertaken for no immediate biological or practical end, appearing to be performed 'for its own sake'; it is more

characteristic of the young of the species than the old; the particular forms of play behaviour are largely species specific and the amount of play seems to be greater in 'higher' than in 'lower' animals. It was on the basis of such descriptive findings that nineteenth century theories were put forward. Three of the more famous are the Surplus Energy Theory attributed separately to two philosophers, Friedrich von Schiller (1759–1805) and Herbert Spencer (1820–1903). The central notion was that of energy being continuously collected into a limited capacity store which would eventually overflow and predispose the organism to play. It seems inadequate in that it fails to give an account of the different forms play takes, or why children often play when they are tired. Yet the theory has a certain face validity; over-long deprivation of physical activity is frequently followed shortly by some energy disposing routine—and conversely periods of vigorous physical activity tend to be succeeded by a time of relative inactivity. But while the theory was, at least in principle, testable, it remained untested.

G. Stanley Hall's *recapitulation theory* proposes that individual development (ontogeny) repeats that of the race (phylogeny). It provided parallels for a range of children's play: enjoyment of play in water is linked with the fish phase, tree climbing with the monkey phase and gang behaviour with primitive tribal life. But there were no clear analogues for other play behaviours—the boy with the (imaginary) motorcycle for example. There were also a number of ambiguities; for example, what was the analogue of the primitive tribesman—the boy of ten with his gang-play, or the small child with his 'uncivilized' manner? At this descriptive level, the theory clearly meets with difficulty. Geneticists have rejected the idea of the transmission of acquired characteristics from one generation to the next, and the theory is no longer generally regarded with anything more than antiquarian interest.

Karl Groos in his books *The Play of Animals* (1896) and *The Play of Man* (1901), developed a theory proposed earlier, which has been called the *practice theory* of play. He argued that play was used to practice inborn skills for the purpose of adaptation. It was upon adequate adaptation to the environment that survival depended. Thus the play of the kitten with any small mobile object was seen as practice in mouse catching, and the puppy play-fighting as practice for the sterner fighting of adult life. Play is thus seen as teleological, anticipating the future needs of the animal. Groos collected supportive evidence from a wide variety of sources, but the theory was not subjected to careful testing. Hall was naturally critical, holding as he did that play is reminiscent rather than anticipatory. The theory loses something of its simplicity when seen in the context of the great variety and complexity of child's play: Groos held, nevertheless, that much of this was itself anticipatory of complex adult activities. Likewise, the play of the mature adult is not comfortably accommodated by the theory. The practice theory, nevertheless, in a form which does not draw on the large range of instincts invoked by Groos, still attracts some support.

These three theories, provided some valuable insights into the complexities of play. That none of them has been taken up and developed is probably due to a great variety of reasons. Among these must have been the difficulty of dealing with so large a range of behaviour. While, at the time they were made, theories of such wide scope seemed appropriate, subsequent students of play have become increasingly sensitive to the dangers of over-generalization. In trying to draw conclusions which would fit both animals and humans, for example, it is clear with hindsight, that justice was done to neither.

The turn of the century saw psychology in the process of change from a regime dominated by biological and philosophical constraints to one centred on rigorous experimentation. This new phase of psychology produced its reactions to the study of play. As has been seen, significant influences on psychological thought during this period came from the Behaviourists, from Freud and from Piaget. The Behaviourists excluded the subject of play, as such, from their studies. Freud conceived of play in emotional terms, describing its purpose as cathartic. This term, also applied to play in the writings of Aristotle, was probably originally a medical term meaning to purge or to cleanse; play is thus seen as a means of relieving pent up emotions. Freud's view of play elaborates this notion. Piaget's view of play is linked with his conception of intellectual development. It was during this particular period that the study of animal play and human play were undertaken as separate enterprises, albeit frequently with a view to the provision of mutual insights.

Two considerations alone were sufficient to banish the topic of play, as such, from the Behaviourist programme. First, the term itself is a label for a variety of behaviours which do not lend themselves to collective investigation. Second, play was held to warrant no special explanation. With other behaviours, its acquisition and modification come within the general principles of learning. The psychoanalytic theory of play is a special case of the more general cathartic theory. Freud saw wish-fulfilment as conferring on the child both pleasure and catharsis. Wish-fulfilment may be achieved by the child's indulging in fantasy or day-dreams, in which he may imagine himself as the possessor of all manner of desirable gifts. A further kind of wish-fulfilment described by Freud was that in which the child takes the active role in unpleasant encounters. Thus a child recently subjected to (unpleasant) medicine taking, may indulge in play fantasies involving the repeated administration of medicine to her dolls. The catharsis resulting from this play was thought to produce a sense of mastery.

Piaget on play

Piaget conceived of play in terms of the interplay between assimilation and accommodation. Where the two are in equilibrium there is intellectual adaptation. Where assimilation dominates (that is where the child is dealing with an object or action in such a way as to fit it into established patterns of thinking) play results. Where accommodation dominates, (that is, where information is being used in such a way as to modify existing views) the result is regarded as imitation. This cuts across the common notion of play. For example, it removes the distinction usually made between work and play, behaviours being regarded as more playful (where an attempt is being made to deal with things as they are) or less playful. Piaget distinguished three broad sequential categories of play. Practice play involves the repetition of new motor skills in one new context after another. The child clearly derives pleasure from fitting new objects into such a pattern, regardless of their suitability. Thus, an infant who has learned to pick up an object and convey it safely to his mouth makes the most of opportunities to repeat this action, without regard to the size or edibility of the object. Symbolic play involves the use of one entity to symbolize another. A stone might be used for a mouse, or a wooden block for a battleship. The third category covers games with rules. In each of these can be seen Piaget's emphasis of play as concerned with thought, and objects bent to fit existing concepts, ignoring or playing down some of the logical anomalies incurred.

The eventual decline of play is also seen in terms of the balance between assimilation and accommodation. Before the establishment of these processes there is no play. Up to middle childhood, an ever widening experience promotes a dominance of assimilation. As the child becomes increasingly capable of dealing with things 'as they are' (rather than in terms of his own pre-existing scheme of things), his responses to them become more appropriate.

The third phase, covering the period from the early 1950s and embracing the rapid growth of interest in child development, includes a considerable range of studies of play, widely different in both methodology and behavioural content. Of these, two areas will be considered which will indicate something of the nature of the changes which took place. The ethological approach to child approach to child development, noted in Chapter 5, and representing a more highly articulated approach to observation, has provided a range of further insights into children's play. The immediate aim has been to provide an accurate description of typical play situations within the surroundings in which they occur; studies have been made within the home, the classroom, the playground, and the park, some concentrating on broad bands of activity, like rough-and-tumble play, others on more restricted areas such as smiling. Eight different kinds of smiles, for example, have recently been distinguished by means of detailed descriptions. These indicate certain clear motivational contexts—for example the smile which is called 'play-face' and which is used to communicate the smiler's evaluation of the activities in which he is engaged. It would be misleading to suggest that the application of ethological methods to child play was entirely new, for Gesell, whose work extends into this period made extensive observation of children's play. But, while much of this work related to play situations which could be accommodated within, say, his observation dome, recent work has been conducted in natural settings. This has added detail by making particular studies of child-child interaction and child-adult interaction, for example, from infancy. Earlier studies had suggested that children pass in turn from solitary play to parallel play (in which, although playing in each other's presence, they pay little attention to each other), then to associative play and finally to cooperative play. It had long been suspected that social play begins much earlier than this sequence suggests. Recent work has indicated that once simple motor skills are established the baby clearly enjoys involvement with others in grasping, holding and pulling activities, as well as games of the peep-bo and pat-a-cake type. Again, recent studies of early child-adult interactions have suggested that imitative play may begin within the first month of life.

Play and exploration
In contrast, much insight into play has been gained within much more formal experimental settings. One area widely researched in this way has been that relating to exploratory behaviour among young children. Exploration and play are concepts frequently used synonymously. Young children spend much of their time exploring new aspects of the environment, as well as the new features of their own prowess. The former gives rise, for example, to the examination of novel objects to find out what they do and what makes them work, and the latter to the practice of physical skills of various sorts. Whether these two belong together is at least questionable. It has also been questioned as to whether exploratory behaviour is properly identified with play.

Corinne Hutt, a contemporary researcher who has made a large contribution to this field, attempted to clarify the issue by means of an investigation reported in 1966. Nursery school children (three- to five-year-olds) were, one at a time, introduced into a room containing a novel object and five familiar toys. The novel object was a red metal box—probably somewhat smaller than a ten-inch portable television set—mounted on four brass legs. From its upper surface, a lever ending in a blue wooden ball protruded; this surface also contained four counter dials. Thirty children were asked, one at a time, whether they would like to play for a few minutes, while the questioner (the observer) completed some work in another part of the room. The typical sequence of events began by an examination of the novel object—a 'what does it do?' response, followed by a game involving the object—a 'what can I do with this?' response, this latter sometimes involving some of the familiar toys, which may then have taken over from the novel object as the centre of the child's attention. A number of behavioural indices were used to differentiate the earlier, exploratory, behaviour from the later, play, behaviour. On the basis of the evidence collected, Hutt proposes a distinction between specific exploration and diverse exploration, and suggests that, while play may be similar to the latter, it contrasts with the former. It is further proposed that a possible reason for the traditional confounding of these activities is that, in the young, they are difficult to distinguish. This is partly influenced by the repetitive nature of early exploratory actions, occasioned, perhaps, by restricted memory capacity. The same tendency to repeat is also to some extent present in much early 'play' activity, and it is this which may make it difficult to distinguish the two in practice. Indeed, it seems likely that in a 'real life' situation both may be present in the same activity. The conceptual distinction is clear, however, and there is a similarly compelling distinction to be found in mature behaviour. There is a further possible source of confusion: both specific as well as diversive exploration are facilitated by factors of novelty and complexity. There is laboratory evidence to show that children are more likely, given the alternative, to choose 'new' toys rather than familiar ones, more 'complex' rather than less, within the limits of the child's capacity. The study of exploration behaviour has shown that this preference for novelty and complexity controls infants' visual exploration of patterns as early as two or three months of age. Over a large range of different experimental situations, and responses (including looking, listening, approach, manipulation, and questioning) it is found that an increase in the extent of the 'interest' (novelty or complexity) in a situation is associated with an increase in exploratory activity.

The extensive study of exploratory behaviour has, thus, raised again the matter of the diverse behaviours subsumed under the term play and the necessity for empirical distinctions among them. In this brief summary mention has been made of social play, imitative play, fantasy and make-believe play, as well as 'exploratory' play. Each forms an important aspect of child behaviour and while, as the Hutt study demonstrates, this does not constitute a sufficient condition for an activity to be designated as play, it is possible that it is only in terms of the results of further detailed studies of these and related areas, that the study of child-development may be expected to yield a more systematic description of the complex of behaviours at present called play.

Adolescence

Puberty

During the period of puberty the body of the child is transformed into that of a young adult. The complex of processes involved takes, on average, three to three-and-a-half years for girls, and anywhere from two to four years for boys. The onset of puberty for girls is earlier than it is for boys by about one year. At the close of this phase of development, the body is capable of mature sexual functioning. Under the influence of the pituitary hormones, the sex glands increase their production of sex hormones, and the growth of mature sperm in the male and ova in the female begin. At the same time, related endocrine activity stimulates the growth of bone and muscle and initiates a marked and rapid increase in height (the growth spurt). The complex of changes includes those relating to the size, shape, and proportion of the body, as well as its functioning, among a host of others. These include development of pubic hair, of other secondary hair and the eruption of second molars (the wisdom teeth) for both sexes, the enlargement of the breasts and pelvic breadth, and the onset of menstruation for girls. Boys develop a change of voice, enlargement of genitals, the appearance of beard, and seminal emissions. It seems reasonable to suppose that some of these changes may precipitate problems, physiological, social, and psychological, to which the individual needs to adapt.

Adolescence

It has been the traditional view of adolescence that pubertal changes and the demands they make on the necessity for adaptation bring about this phase which has been labelled 'the terrible teens'.

'Adolescence' derives from a latin verb which means 'to grow' or 'to grow to maturity'. It is used to refer to that period which marks the transition from childhood to maturity, but, while the onset is associated with the several physical changes appearing at puberty, a criterion for its completion is problematical. While some use the mature sexual function as the mark of adulthood, others use an arbitrary age criterion such as that relating to possession of voting rights, or certain legal responsibilities. A behavioural criterion begs the question as to what constitutes mature or adult behaviour. Adolescent behaviour has been described as 'negative'. In more detail it has been seen as including such features as a need for isolation, a disinclination to work, antagonism to family, friends, and society, indulgence in 'martyr' type fantasy, heightened sensitivity, irritability, obstinacy, and frequent revolts. It is unusual to find correspondingly positive descriptions of adolescent behaviour, although they are undoubtedly present. The traditional picture of adolescence is that of a period of 'storm and stress' contrasting sharply with the behaviour and experience both of the child and the adult. In giving an account of the psychology of adolescence, the developmental psychologist is faced with a number of questions. These include the following: to what extent are descriptions of adolescence in the above terms accurate and typical of youth across both social and cultural divisions? To what extent are any psychological changes attributable to physiological changes? What is the importance of cultural context?

Among the chief sources of information in this area are detailed questionnaires concerning the adolescent's view of himself and the society in which he lives. Complementary detail is obtained in the same way from parents, teachers, and others. A recent survey (Rutter, 1976) of this type was carried out in the Isle of Wight, and studied an entire population of 2303 fourteen- and fifteen-year-olds. It found that adolescent turmoil was a fact and not a fiction as had been suggested. The data gathered indicated, however, that the psychiatric importance of the turmoil had been overestimated in the past. Evidence from two primitive cultures, to be considered later, suggests that such turmoil reflects cultural pressures.

The problems of late and early maturing

Considerable differences occur in both the age of onset and the rate of progress of pubertal maturation. In general, early maturers develop more rapidly than late maturers, and this tends to produce, among adolescents of the same chronological age, large differences in maturity. Thus, at fifteen years of age an early maturer might appear as a fully grown adult, while a late-maturing contemporary is still very much a 'child' in appearance. Data from standard personality inventories suggest that there are strong links between physical and psychological maturity. A number of studies show that early maturity for boys is a social asset. They were rated high on such variables as self-assurance and socially appropriate behaviour, where late maturers were rated low. These latter were also rated as low in physical attraction and poise. Thus, late development for a boy—that, is to be still a 'small boy' among young men—is something of a handicap. A study carried out in men in their early thirties, who had previously been studied as adolescents, showed that psychological differences between early and later maturers had persisted to a marked degree. Late maturers were still more dependent than those maturing early.

Early maturity in girls, that is, to be 'grown-up' among mainly immature contemporaries may not confer an advantage, as it appears to do for boys. Among twelve-year-old girls, highly-valued personality traits were attributed to those girls who made up the majority and whose development was prepubertal. One year later, the early-maturing girls scored more, and in the two following years they attained the sort of preference accorded to early-maturing boys. Late-maturing girls have also been shown to have problems of social development which persist beyond the attainment of biological maturity, but less so than in late maturing boys. This is probably related to the fact that physical stature is highly valued for boys in our society but not for girls.

Evidence of the effect of cultural values on the adjustment problems of late maturers comes from a study which compared early and late-developing adolescents of Americans living in America, young Italians living in Italy and adolescents of Italian parents living in the United States. Italians show less preference for stature and more for dependent behaviour from their young people, sometimes well into and beyond adolescence. Little difference was found between early- and late-maturing Italian boys in terms of attitudes to self and behaviour, as compared with those noted for the American boys. Among those with an Italian background in the United States, late-maturing boys exhibited some of the same difficulties as their American peers. For them, it regulated the reaction of the adolescent to his own physical development.

Adolescence and the quest for ego-identity

The development of a sense of identity has been seen as an important task of adolescence. To obtain some answer to the question 'Who am I?' might indeed be seen as a task which continues, to some extent, throughout life, but there are a number of plausible reasons for considering it of particular relevance during adolescence. These are to be found in the rate and extent of the changes which accompany adolescence in an industrialized society. After a period of childhood which is characterized by gradual changes and a consistency of role, the adolescent becomes quickly immersed in a complex of biological, social, and intellectual changes which provide grounds for self-consideration not met before. The evidence considered earlier indicates something of the way in which the changes of puberty draw reactions from society and from the individual concerned. There are numerous related problems to which the adolescent must adapt. To take but two, the problems associated with growth and the general increase in muscle which has been seen as producing the 'clumsy' adolescent; and the now more insistent sexual urges. These latter may give rise to conflict in view of social constraints. Indeed the 'storm and stress' attributed to adolescence by some of the early investigators, was seen as stemming from such conflict. The adolescent also becomes subject to new patterns of social pressure. Following a period where dependence—for physical, social, and emotional sustenance—has been vested in the parents, who also initiated and regulated independent behaviour, the adolescent is confronted with expectations of a more radical sort. These concern his ability to cope with vocational matters and the attendant crises of choice and readjustment. There are additional pressures to conform to peer group expectations, again frequently representing a radical break with the conduct of the preceding period of childhood. Piaget contends that it is as a result of the interaction between biological changes and social pressures that 'adolescent thinking', that is, formal operational thinking, is born. It is this which confers the capacity to think about his own thought, about what is possible as distinct from what now pertains, and about the future. This widening of the conceptual horizons thus suffuses adolescent thinking, providing the possibility of new solutions to old problems, so frequently a theme among adolescent activists, and labelled idealism. Since there are those for whom formal operational thinking is never realized to any considerable extent, this period must also provide in cohesive adolescent school communities the greatest possible contrasts in intellectual functioning, and a correspondingly extreme range of approaches to the quest for identity, a source of further confusion for those involved in it.

It is Erikson who has characterized the extreme possible outcomes of adolescence in terms of 'identity versus role confusion'. His account of the search for identity sees it as a quest to establish a new sense of continuity, the former having been broken by the complex of changes entailed by puberty. The adolescent's task is seen as an attempt to integrate previous identifications, the former 'self' and the present social opportunities and constraints, in order to attain a sense of continuity for himself and for those with whom he has to do. In order to achieve this, adolescents will sometimes temporarily over-identify with popular figures, almost to the point where their own identity is obscured. Where the quest for identity is frustrated, role confusion results, and delinquency and psychopathology may follow. This view of adolescence has found some measure of acceptance, particularly within the United States. As with Freud's views, it is descriptive and based on clinical observations.

It is clear that a sense of identity will be influenced by a number of factors. There are a number of studies which show the importance of child-parent relationships to this end. A warm, interactive relationship between the adolescent and both parents facilitates the establishment of a strong sense of identity. The same-sex parent provides a model for personal and social standards, while the opposite-sex parent provides a source of critical approval of this model. Adolescents with such parents typically have fewer conflicts, and a greater capacity for coping with those which do arise, than those without. They also, typically, have clearly defined and favourable perceptions of themselves. Studies of the family regime have revealed that the 'democratic family' (one in which

525

the child enjoys, as part of a warm relationship with parents, the freedom to disagree with them, involvement in family decisions, and a fair measure of autonomy) produces self-reliant adolescents. The 'authoritarian family', in which the parents institute plans without reference to the adolescent members of the family, and administer (mainly physical) punishment in accordance with rules adopted, again without reference to the children, tends to produce adolescents who, while they are compliant, incline to be deceptive and lacking in self-esteem. The search for ego-identity is thus facilitated by the existence in the home of adequate models of autonomy and co-operation, and an active involvement in the democratic family regime.

Kohlberg's studies of moral development, described earlier, support the general thrust of Piaget's views of the effects of the dawning of formal operational thinking. It further serves to contrast the moral views of childhood with those of adolescence, and to draw attention to the great sensitivity of the adolescent to moral issues. The morality of middle childhood is described as conventional, in that it reflects the expectations of the individual's immediate social context. By contrast, adolescent morality is capable of reaching a level which is characterized by the application of autonomous principles which have a validity apart from such authority contexts.

The sudden engulfment of the adolescent in so wide and radical a set of changes provides possible grounds for the 'negativity' of adolescents described earlier, as well as the storm and stress which has traditionally been associated with adolescence. Common experience suggests that to describe all adolescents as 'negative', and invariably involved in stress during this period of development would be to overgeneralize. An adequate account of adolescence must accommodate the facts that wide differences exist in these respects, and that while some, perhaps many, are 'negative' and 'storm-tossed', others apparently by-pass calmly from a pleasant childhood to agreeable young adulthood, even within the constraints of the social competitiveness which exists in an industrial society. For it seems at least possible to view this sort of pressure as largely responsible for adolescent troubles, since the major transition from formal education to work, occurring, as it does, in close relation to pubertal changes, is beset with social problems.

Adolescence in two primitive cultures
Margaret Mead has provided anthropological evidence that adolescence is not necessarily accompanied by the troubles reported in industrialized society. Her study of the coming of age Samoan girls, and the experiences of young people of the Arapesh of New Guinea, strongly suggest the involvement of cultural pressures as the origin of adolescent stress in industrialized society. For, in both of these 'primitive' societies,

526

where such pressures are largely unknown, the course of adolescence described by Mead is one which much resembles the gradual and continuous development associated with our middle childhood, where dependence and independence coexist, the change from the former towards the latter progressing gradually, without marked discontinuities.

In the case of adolescence among Samoan girls, Mead records that the only differences between adolescent girls and the prepubescent sisters were the obvious bodily changes. There were certainly no differences in respect of revolt against authority, emotional distress or displays of idealism. She also reports negligible differences between late- and early-maturing girls. Comparing these phenomena with those for American adolescent girls she concludes that it is the differences in social environment which offer an explanation. The detailed differences cited may be divided roughly into two groups. The first concerns the characteristic way of life of the Samoan people (in the late 1920s). This was casual in the extreme, the distresses and disagreeable episodes of life being susceptible of speedy solution by mutual agreement. Thus, adolescents, growing up in a society where harrassment was virtually unknown, were themselves subject to no extraordinary pressures. The second relates to the extreme simplicity of Samoan life, in respect of the limited number of choices available for each individual. For while the children of an industrialized society are faced with an array of groups differing in religion, standards of morality, and politics, the Samoan child is confronted by no such range of choices, but lives and grows with social constraints which are simple, minimal, and clear. It is the effect of the wide range of alternatives, and the pressure to choose among them which Mead sees as the discontinuity, making for unrest among the adolescents of 'civilized' societies.

Much the same sort of evidence is cited in the case of both boy and girl adolescents of the Arapesh. The choice of a wife for a boy in childhood means that the two may use both homes for a considerable time before the formal marriage, and in this way one of a number of possible discontinuities at adolescence is dealt with.

This view of adolescent development points plainly to the pressures exerted in a competitive and status-conscious society as a potential source of storm and stress experienced by its adolescents.

Alienation

Adolescence, perhaps more than any other phase of development, tends to throw into sharp relief those individuals who, for one reason or another, fail to fit in with the great majority of their contemporaries. Such individuals have been described as alienated from society; and alienation is the general term under which a wide variety of antipathetic reactions may be subsumed. The three to be considered here relate to

527

activists, drop-outs, and delinquents. Classification into these categories is, of course, in terms of overt and unambiguous behaviour. The data collected are largely of a sociological nature, providing descriptive detail of the nature and context of the alienation. Much of the available data refers to studies performed in the United States; but studies reported from elsewhere suggest similar findings. The interest of the developmental psychologist in alienation is the opportunity it affords for the investigation of related antecedent conditions.

Activism is a broad category, used here to cover a range of adolescent activities in the affairs of society. Protest and attempts to reform are two such activities. Frequently, they are both employed as different aspects of the same movement, but in other cases may be carried out separately where one is thought to be more effective or more practicable than the other. Objectives of such activities have included the banning of atom bombs, campaigning against American involvement in Vietnam, against the building of nuclear power stations and motorways, among a host of others. Protesters typically use all possible means to impede the progress of activities of which they disapprove, while reformers use available means to bring pressure to bear on the legislature to bring about changes. Both concern themselves with what are considered to be the ills of a sick society and the ways in which they are to be treated.

Although the term 'activists' covers a collection of individuals with common aims, they are by no means homogeneous in other respects. Nevertheless, surveys carried out among those involved in such movements have produced evidence of recurrent characteristics. The people involved are mainly students who are, typically, brighter, academically more successful, more imaginative, and more anxious than non-activist peers. They are usually drawn from high status families, where they have enjoyed a warm and affectionate relation with parents, holding similar views on the social issues giving rise to their activism. Indeed, this might well be interpreted principally in terms of identification with parental values.

Social drop-outs also reject the values of society, but, instead of becoming actively involved against it, they elect to live outside it in accordance with their own standards. Sometimes this reaction follows some well-ordered plan; alternatively it may be aimless dissent. Gypsies and hippies, the first having continuous tradition, the second having shown a sudden decline after a sudden blossoming in the late 1960s, are examples of collective social dropping-out. The hippies provided a wealth of opportunity for the study of this kind of reaction to society. While there was no single type of 'hippy', some were philosophically-orientated; others were simply 'adherents' out for a new experience; and yet others, paradoxically, 'part time' hippies. Rejection of the established social order was the common cry, and, in particular, it was the

528

materialistic, competitive, status valuing, conforming aspects, among others, which were repudiated. The alternatives proposed were intended to produce a new social order among its followers, based on concepts like love, gentleness, sharing, and freedom, as well as a new principle, for individual living based on self-realization and 'doing one's own thing'. These ideals were pursued with much dedication by some members of the movement who attempted to influence those outside by their individual commitment. Such ideals proved no easier to achieve under this regime than under other philosophic and religious auspices, and self-realization was frequently sought in terms of hard drugs.

Information collected from the followers of the movement suggest that they are, in general, above average in intelligence and have good academic records. Personality tests indicated a number of features common among them, including deficiencies in cognitive functioning in recalling past events and concentrating on a given task, as well as a general lack of ability in organizing day to day matters, and in relating to others. Perhaps the most outstanding bond between them was the unusually high level of stress and turmoil which they reported. While they came largely from middle class homes, many appeared to have been exposed to extended periods of parental conflict, family and personal illness, frequent changes in homes and medical calamities. From such circumstances, escape was sought for longer or shorter periods of relief, a reaction bearing some likeness to their adoption of the 'hippy' way of life.

Adolescents who break the law are called delinquents or juvenile delinquents. A precise definition of this term for specific purposes usually exists within each community, but, between them, both the maximum age and the range of indictable offences vary. Within most industrialized societies, the activities of delinquents have come to account for a major proportion of serious crime in respect of both crimes of violence and crimes of property. These crimes are committed both by groups (social delinquency) and by individuals. From about the mid-1960s there has been an increase in all sorts of delinquency, with an ever-increasing proportion of the adolescent population involved. Until recently, delinquents were mainly boys. However, the number of girls involved has shown a marked increase, and the gap between the two is decreasing.

There is no common delinquent type. Delinquents come from 'good' homes as well as 'bad', from among rich and poor as do non-delinquents. Sociological and personality surverys have, however, identified some common features. The delinquency rate, for example, is highest in neglected city centre areas and dormitory suburbs. It is lowest in rural areas. This may well reflect the opportunity afforded by the anonymity of the looser social coherence of densely-populated areas. A

529

large proportion of delinquents come from broken homes and very poor homes, but, while the delinquency rate is lowest in middle class areas, it is in these that there has been the most rapid increase in recent times. The single most reliable indicator of juvenile delinquency is the relationship between the young person and the parents. Where this is good, the incidence of delinquency is less. A 'poor' relationship is frequently found in those homes where parental discipline takes either a very casual form or a strict and punitive form, or changes unpredictably from one to the other.

Related to this, it would seem, is the other frequent characteristic of the individual delinquent, a history of misdemeanours. Low intelligence cannot be considered a major factor, for comparisons made between matched groups of delinquents and non-delinquents shows considerable overlap between them, with the average intelligence for the delinquents being only marginally lower. There are, however, marked differences between such groups in terms of personality traits. Delinquents are much more likely to be high on measures of impulsivity, hostility and destructiveness than non-delinquents, and they are much more assertive and defiant of authority. They are also more likely to express poor estimation of themselves, seeing themselves in such terms as undesirable people, lazy, and bad.

While delinquency is a major social problem, sociological and psychological research to the present time permits of only tentative generalizations. It seems clear that young people living under uncongenial and indifferent home conditions within neglected and over-populated areas are especially at risk. Yet, since young people do live under such conditions without necessarily becoming delinquent, this is clearly not the whole story. A general increase in prosperity seems to have been associated with an increase rather than a decrease in delinquency. Confinement in Borstal institutions appears, at least for some, to have served as a preparation for further criminal activities.

There is no lack of suggestions for possible psychological approaches to the problem. Among them are the devising of means for the early identification of children at risk. Timely counselling, it is thought, might save some. Then there is the suggestion that the treatment of the convicted should be guided by the recommendations of suitably qualified psychologists, so that the treatment might fit the individual as well as (perhaps, rather than) the crime.

Life-span development
It is evident that, while adolescence need not be a time of storm and stress, it often is, particularly within an industrialized society. While the biological changes of adolescence need not initiate undue distress, in the regime of a competitive society, they often do, because of pressures

530

implicitly or explicitly brought to bear. As has been seen, the sense of conflict between society and the adolescent is heightened by his mental as well as his physical maturity, which add weight to his idealistic strivings, as they do to his antisocial activities. Where storm and stress occur, the evidence suggests that the roots are to be found in a complex of individual, social, and cultural factors.

Adolescent troubles may thus be seen largely as the result of a crisis arising at a social boundary. Psychological studies of adults have been carried out within this framework. Life, of necessity, involves a number of 'boundary' conditions, shared in some way by most people, the effects of which are to bring about psychological changes over time. In this sense, developmental psychology has been extended throughout the life span, in terms of investigations of what might be termed significant life-crises. Thus, the effects on the individual brought about by such events as marriage, divorce, the birth of a child, the death of a relative, prolonged illness, onset of a serious disability, the menopause, the departure of the last child from home and retirement, have all been studied. In some areas, it has been possible to make recommendations for the alleviation of some of the undesirable effects involved. Adjustment to retirement for example has been shown to be a complex process; while some individuals thrive on a complete break with work, others prefer a more gradual disengagement. A number of large industrial concerns have already adopted gradual disengagement schemes.

Such studies show that, although major life crises may bring about changes, sometimes radical, the changes themselves reflect the persistence of personality traits. They have provided much supporting evidence of the dictum that 'the child is the father of the man'.

FURTHER READING

Brown, R. (1965) *Social Psychology*. Collier Macmillan.
Herron, R. E. (1971) *Child's Play*. New York, Wiley.
Lewin, R., ed. (1975) *Child Alive*. Clarke, Doble and Brendon.
Parke, R. D., ed. (1969) *Readings in Social Development*. Holt Reinhart and Winston.
Reese, H. W., and Lipsitt, L. (1970) *Experimental Child Psychology*. Academic Press.
Rogers, D., ed. (1969) *Issues in Adolescent Psychology*. Appleton-Century-Crofts.

23   Personality

MARIAN PITTS

Introduction

It has been claimed that there are as many definitions of personality as there are personality theorists. Each definition reflects the approach of the theorist who suggests it. A widely-accepted definition of personality is that offered by Gordon Allport. He describes personality as 'the dynamic organization within the individual of those psychophysical systems that determine his characteristic behaviour and thought' (Allport, 1961). Personality theorists study not only particular aspects of a person, they also try to study the whole person. Consequently, the study of personality can overlap with many other areas of psychology such as perception and memory.

There are a number of major controversies in the study of personality and we will examine these first and then consider some of the major schools of personality theory. Finally, we shall consider the ways in which personality can be assessed.

A primary consideration is whether or not one can determine a *general disposition* to behave in one particular way rather than another. The Behaviourist movement in psychology did not accept the idea of a general disposition of behaviour. Behaviour was regarded as a number of stimulus-response sequences and general patterns of responses occurring across situations were not considered. Other psychologists place great emphasis on a general, usually in-born, predisposition to behave in certain ways. These theorists may not take sufficient account of the ways in which a specific situation may influence a person's behaviour and reactions to that situation. A more useful approach to personality probably lies somewhere between these two extreme points of view. A person may, in general, have a tendency to be sociable and outgoing, but his behaviour in any given situation will be determined not only by that predisposition, but also by the way in which he perceives the specific situation.

A second major difference between personality theories is the degree to which they emphasize each person's individuality. Some personality theorists, such as Gordon Allport, place great emphasis on the uniqueness of each individual's personality. The approach is known as an *idiographic* approach. Idiographic theorists try to study an individual for a long period of time and believe that comparisons between people are of limited value only. In contrast, other personality theorists, such as Cattell and Eysenck, try to establish the major dimensions of personality on which people may differ, but which are present to some degree in everyone. This is known as the *nomothetic* approach to personality. Once again, the resolution of this disagreement may be a compromise. We can look for similarities between people and yet also consider the individual's own adjustment and expression of his predispositions. It is worthwhile to bear in mind whilst reading this Chapter that these initial orientations of the personality theorist will lead him to emphasize some concepts at the cost of others.

Finally, some theorists discussed in this Chapter make use of the concept of *traits* as a means of investigating personality. Cattell could be called a trait theorist. Traits may be defined as covariant sets of behavioural acts. They are organizing principles which can be deduced from human behaviour. Examples of traits would be sociability and impulsiveness. These are recurrent, and stable, aspects of an individual's personality. Other theorists place more emphasis on the concept of *type*. A type may be regarded as a group of related traits; it is a more general concept than trait: several traits may correlate with each other and these correlated traits can be subsumed under a type. For example, the traits of shyness, subjectivity, and rigidity are included in Eysenck's dimension of introversion. Some typologists, however (e.g., Kretschmer and Sheldon), have supposed that every individual can be so placed in one of a limited number of categories, or types, having certain specified characteristics.

We shall now examine several personality theories and try to evaluate them. What do we require of a good personality theory? In general, we can expect a good theory of personality to offer an explanation or account of why a person should behave as he does, and, to some degree, we wish to be able to predict how he will behave in future. A good

533

personality theory should describe, explain, and predict a person's behaviour in terms which are meaningful to us.

The first school of personality we shall examine is the psychoanalytic school.

Psychoanalytic theories

Sigmund Freud

Sigmund Freud was born in 1856 and died in London in 1939. For most of his life he lived in Vienna and it was there that he devised what is probably the most influential theory of personality ever produced. Freud studied medicine and became interested in the physiology of the nervous system: on a visit to Paris he was introduced to the use of hypnosis for the treatment of hysteria. Freud used this technique for some time with his patients, but, gradually, he came to the conclusion that it was unnecessary to hypnotize the patient, and he moved on to use the technique of free association. In this method, the patient is asked to relax on a couch and then simply describe what is in his mind, no matter how absurd or irrelevant it might seem. Freud found this method useful in helping him to understand the causes of his patients' problems. This technique formed the basis of all Freud's observations and led him to suggest the theory of personality we shall now consider.

For Freud, all behaviour had a cause: no form of behaviour, however bizarre, arises without a reason and it was the search for these reasons which occupied most of Freud's theorizing. Freud also believed that the reasons for behaviour are not always immediately apparent to an individual. He suggested that unconscious processes exert a powerful influence over a person's behaviour. The free association technique might reveal some of these influences. Freud emphasized the importance of the early years of life. He argued that experiences in these years moulded the psyche and determined the personality which would develop in later life. The technique of free association tapped experiences which were associated with these early years. For a discussion of Freud's theory of the development of personality see Chapter 20.

Freud also analysed the dreams of his patients. He described the interpreting of dreams as the 'royal road to understanding the unconscious'. He argued that we are able to give free expression in our dreams to emotions and ideas which we censor from our waking thoughts. He found many symbols in dreams which he interpreted as sexual in origin. The principle of causality also underlies Freud's interest in the mistakes people make in their everyday lives. Again, he argued that these apparently random events have causes and are the expression of unconscious processes. Thus, even accidental errors of speech were considered by Freud to be worthy of examination and explanation, since they offered insight into the unconscious.

534

Freud describes the personality as made up of three major systems: the id, the ego and the superego. Each system has its own functions and course of development, but in the mature personality the interrelations between them are very strong. The *id* is the driving power behind a personality: it is the psychic energy of a person. The id is a combination of sexual and aggressive needs: by sexual needs Freud meant the seeking of pleasure and the gratification of bodily needs.

The *ego* develops in order to control the energy of the id and its effect on the relation of a person to his world. We need to modify our basic drives towards immediate gratification and it is the ego that enables us to do this. It operates by what Freud called the reality principle: via this the ego manages to curb the impulses of the id in order that immediate gratification can be put off for a more fulfilling, longer-term gratification.

The third element in Freud's theory of personality is the *superego*. This develops as the child learns, through its parents, the values and ideals of society. The child incorporates these values and gradually adopts the moral and ethical code of the parents. The superego is sometimes represented as the conscience: Freud referred to it as the primitive, unconscious conscience. It can be seen that the forces of the superego and the id may be in conflict: the id will seek gratification of wishes, whilst the superego may try to curb these primitive responses if they conflict with societal norms. It is the job of the ego to try to balance these two opposing forces and this implies that, for Freud, man is continually in a state of conflict and that man's behaviour is determined, in part, by how this battle is faring. If the id is dominant anxiety may develop in the person, and he may cope with this in a variety of ways. Perhaps the best known of these ways is by means of *defence mechanisms*. Many defence mechanisms have been suggested and we shall discuss only one or two here. Anna Freud (Freud's daughter) describes some of the major defence mechanisms as *repression, projection* and *regression*. All these mechanisms are said to work at the unconscious level: the person is not aware that he is, for example, repressing something.

Freud emphasized the importance of repression. It is motivated forgetting, but the material is not lost; it is stored in the unconscious and can be regained into consciousness at a later time. Freud argued that if a person becomes anxious about something he may seek to deny its existence: thus, he reduces his anxiety. This can, however, lead to a disruption of his normal behaviour since he is no longer aware of the reasons for his actions. Thus, we may have apparently unreasonable fears which are based on an experience we have repressed or 'forgotten'. While repression is held to be a feature of the ego, it may also develop as a consequence of a strong superego.

With projection, a person copes with anxiety, not by denying its cause, but by unconsciously attributing the feelings to someone else. If he feels hostile to someone, he copes by telling himself that the person is hostile towards him. This can be effective in relieving anxiety and can also give the person an excuse for expressing his true feelings. He can rationalize and legitimize the expression of his hostility. Ultimately, however, this is not a very effective way of reducing anxiety since the person who receives the projection may well resent the hostility expressed and become hostile in his own right.

Freud believed that regression is the process by which an individual reverts to former ways of behaving and of gratifying his needs. For example, a person who feels himself threatened may find himself chewing his nails without being aware of it. Regression is a mechanism sometimes seen in a child who has recently had a new baby brother or sister. The child may have been fairly independent until the birth of the new sibling, but will suddenly become much more clinging and reliant on his parents. Thus, by means of the defence mechanisms described above (and it is suggested that there are others), the ego manages to control the inevitable conflict between the demands of the superego and those of the id.

To summarize these ideas: it is possible to think of Freud's three major components of personality in the following way: the id is the biological basis of personality. It provides the driving force behind a person's behaviour. The ego is the psychological component of personality and it develops measures to cope with the demands of the id and the superego. The superego is the (unconscious) moral component of a personality; it develops from the pressures an individual faces from living in a society. Because the wishes of society are often in conflict with the desires of the individual, the ego is equipped to cope with the reconciliation of these two opposing forces.

Evaluation: Probably no other theory in psychology has created such controversy, not only amongst psychologists, but also in the general population. It is difficult for us to imagine the outrage the theory originally caused. Freud's emphasis on man's sexuality and its origins in childhood was out of keeping with the general views of the time, and ideas that we now find acceptable were thoroughly shocking to Freud's early readers.

It is a demanding task to evaluate a theory of personality which seeks to be so broad and to encompass all human behaviour. If there are so many different processes at work within a person, how can we say at any given time which are directing behaviour? One of the major difficulties is that it is hard to find methods suitable to test Freud's theory. Freud regarded his careful collecting of data from his patients and his emphasis on the principle of causality as the basis of a scientific approach to personality. Nevertheless, it is important to be aware that much of his evidence comes from single case studies and, when the theorist is also the therapist, as was the case with Freud, it is not possible to be confident that bias has been removed.

Critique

Let us consider certain features of Freud's theory and examine the evidence for them.

Freud described repression as 'the cornerstone on which the whole of psychoanalysis rests'. There have been many attempts to demonstrate experimentally that repression will occur after information threatening to the ego has been encountered. An example of this work is an experiment by Zeller (1950). Zeller gave subjects a set of nonsense syllables to learn: he then sorted his subjects into two groups, such that both groups were of equal ability on the syllable learning task. Both groups of subjects were then required to perform a psychomotor task. The control group of subjects was allowed to succeed at this task, but the experimental group was forced to fail. In this way, Zeller argued that ego threat had been introduced into the experimental group. Zeller suggested that the ego threat would be generalized from the psychomotor task to the learned syllables. On a further testing of recall of the syllables the experimental group performed less well than the control group. Zeller argued that the former had repressed the syllables. Both groups then performed a second time on the psychomotor task, but, this time, both groups were allowed to succeed. Hence, for the experimental group the ego threat was lifted, and, as Freud would predict, on a subsequent test of the learning of the nonsense syllables both groups performed equally well. This experiment and others like it were thought to provide strong support for Freud's explanation of repression.

Holmes has criticized these experiments. He suggests that it is not repression that causes the experimental group to perform poorly after failure in the psychomotor task. Rather, Holmes claims, response competition, or interference, is the basis of these results. Subjects who have performed poorly on the psychomotor task are likely to be concerned and will reflect on their performance. This will cause interference in their ability to recall the syllables. In order to test this suggestion, Holmes and Schallow (1969), designed a similar experiment to that of Zeller. Three groups of subjects learned a list of high frequency nouns. Each group was then shown a series of Rorschach ink-blots (this test is discussed in greater detail on p. 556). The groups were given the nouns from the learning task and were asked to choose which were appropriate to describe the ink-blots. Group 1 (the ego threat group) was told that its choices of nouns indicated some degree of pathology. Group 2 (the control group) was told it was simply helping to test a scoring system and the experimenter was not interested in their individual responses. Group 3 (the interference group) was told that the ink-blots test investigated perception and it was shown random film sequences between presentation of the ink-blots to cause interference. All these groups were then retested on their recall of the high frequency nouns. They were then debriefed (that is, the true purpose of the experiment was explained to them) and they were tested again for their recall of the nouns. Figure 23.1 shows the results for these three groups. It is clear

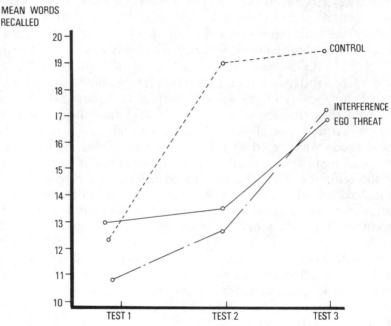

Fig. 23.1 Mean number of words recalled on: Test 1, before experimental manipulation; Test 2, after experimental manipulation; Test 3, after debriefing. (Holmes, 1974.)

that there is little difference between the interference Group and the ego-threat Group. Both differ from the control Group. Holmes and Schallow argue that interference can account for the results of both Groups 1 and 3. Furthermore, if ego threat were operating in Group 1 then one would expect it to be reflected in the repression of those words which had been associated with the 'pathological' responses to the ink-blots. The patterns of recall for the nouns did not differ for this group from the pattern for the interference group. Thus it would appear that the concept of interference is sufficient to explain all the results that have been taken to provide evidence to Freud's theory of repression. This does not of itself, of course, refute the theory, which in any case is concerned with emotional development in childhood, not with laboratory situations.

Eysenck has also criticized the experimental work which is cited to support Freud. He discusses an experiment by Daston (1956) which examines the relation between paranoia and homosexuality. Freud suggests that paranoids have repressed homosexual tendencies. Daston found that paranoids recognized words relating to homosexuality which were presented tachistoscopically more readily than did normal subjects. This experiment has been cited as evidence to support Freud, but Eysenck argues that, if the homosexual tendencies of paranoids are repressed, then perceptual defence should operate and these words should be recognized less easily by paranoids than by normal people.

This study, and many others, are reviewed by Kline, who argues that there is a wealth of evidence from both experimental and cross-cultural studies which supports Freud. Eysenck has reviewed the same evidence and cannot find any specific support for Freud's theory. He describes the theory as follows: 'what's new in these theories is not true, and what's true is not new'. This debate is likely to continue, so let us look elsewhere to evaluate Freud further.

A good way to evaluate Freud's theory is to look at its applications. Much of Freud's theory developed from his observations of his patients in Vienna. The techniques he used, such as that of free association, have formed the basis of many of the therapies used today; the relationship between therapist and client is still central to all forms of psychotherapy. Many of us make use of concepts emphasized by Freud (for example, the concept of unconscious motivation), and his influence has spread beyond psychology to literature and anthropology.

The neo-Freudians

During his lifetime Freud attracted followers to his way of thought. Many of them came to reject certain aspects of his theory and developed theories of their own. All of them, however, show a clear debt to Freud in their writings. Two of his most famous followers are Carl Jung and Alfred Adler.

CARL JUNG (1875–1961)

Carl Jung was, for a time, looked upon by Freud as his successor. Jung, however, found himself increasingly in disagreement with Freud and broke away from the psychoanalytic group. The major disagreement between the two men was about the nature of the libido, or driving force of the id. Freud said it was primarily sexual, or pleasure-seeking. Jung regarded it as a more general life-force.

Jung went on to develop his own approach to personality. This is often known as analytic psychology. Jung's theory differs from that of Freud in a number of important respects. The first we have already mentioned: Jung thought of psychic energy in more general terms than Freud. He also characterized the structure of personality in a different way from Freud. Personality is considered by Jung to be composed of a number of interacting systems; the ego, the personal unconscious, and the collective unconscious.

The *ego* is the conscious mind and is regarded as the central core of the personality. The *personal unconscious* is similar to the unconscious dimension of Freudian theory. It is the total of the individual's experience, much of which has been repressed or forgotten. It is the third dimension of Jung's structure that differs most markedly from Freud's account of the structure of personality. Jung postulates a *collective unconscious*. This holds ancestral and racial memories; it is the psychic residue of man's development. Within the collective unconscious are *archetypes*. These are the result of experiences which have been constantly repeated over the centuries and have become embedded in the human mind. Evidence for the existence of archetypes can be found in myths and folk-lore. Some examples of archetypes would be God, the wise old man, death, and rebirth. Jung uses the evidence of these recurrent themes in the mythologies of a number of different cultures to argue for the existence of archetypes. He claims that they are also recurrent in free association and in the phantasies of psychotics. The validity of this can be questioned. Many of man's experiences are common to all cultures and so it should not surprise us to find these common experiences reflected in our dreams and our literature. We do not need to postulate a collective unconscious in order to account for them. Carl Jung is also known for his use of the terms introversion and extraversion. These concepts will be discussed in the part of this Chapter on H. J. Eysenck.

Jung also popularized the technique of word association. In this technique, a person is presented with a word and asked to respond with the first word he thinks of. For example, the experimenter might say 'black', and the subject would probably respond, 'white'. Jung suggested that hesitations before responding, or bizarre associations, might be indicators of complexes within the individual. This assertion is very difficult to test, but it seems, intuitively, to have a certain validity.

We have discussed the difficulty of evaluating Freud's theory; how much more is this the case with Jung! Very few workers have elected to investigate the validity of his suggestions about the structure of personality. He is widely admired and regarded by some as a great thinker but his influence on main-stream psychology has been slight. Nevertheless, we can find in Jung's writings a more optimistic view of man and his future than is found in Freud, and this is certainly a characteristic of later approaches to personality, such as those of Maslow and Rogers.

540

ALFRED ADLER (1870–1937)

Adler broke off his association with Freud in 1911. He, like Jung, disagreed with Freud's description of the libido and its sexual nature. He argued that man is motivated primarily by social drives. He further postulated that we should examine psychological maladjustment in terms of man's relation to society. Adler introduced a concept which has passed into our general vocabulary: the 'inferiority complex'. Adler believed that man is born with a striving for superiority and perfection that causes him to move constantly towards new goals. With the achievement of any goal, man sets himself a higher one. Feelings of inferiority arise from a sense of imperfection in the tasks attempted. The course a man will take to achieve his goals is an individual one; hence, each man has his own unique life-style. Adler's theory of personality places a greater emphasis on the social factors which affect personality; he places less emphasis on the unconscious processes that are central to the theories of Freud and Jung.

Evaluation: Because Adler stresses the individuality of any person's struggle against inferiority, it is extremely difficult to arrive at any clear predictions of behaviour from his theory. Possibly the only certain prediction is that every individual will be different. That does not take us very far!

However, Adler has made some predictions about the effects of birth-order on the patterns of behaviour which will typify each child in a family. The first-born child is secure and happy until he has to cope with the change that comes with the birth of a second child. Until then, he is the centre of attention, and anxiety could arise if the child no longer feels himself to be the chief recipient of his parents' love. This child may have problems in later life; Adler predicts he could become delinquent or neurotic. The second child will be ambitious. He will constantly strive to outdo his elder sibling; he will be orientated towards the world and will strive for recognition there rather than within the family where he shares attention with his elder sibling. The youngest child will be the 'baby' of the family. In later life he will be a sociable person but will not strive for success in the way the second child might. He may also have difficulties in adjusting to the world beyond the family.

The evidence that has been collected in support of these suggestions is rather slight. Goodenough and Leahy (1972) asked teachers to rate children on a number of traits such as aggression, introversion, submission, etc. For the fourteen traits they used, they found that the average percentage of unfavourable ratings that the children received were as follows: for oldest children 22.5 per cent of the ratings were unfavourable, for middle children 20.6 per cent, and for youngest children 16.5 per cent. These differences are very small: the difference between the oldest and the youngest child is only 6 per cent, and it is difficult to establish the basis for deciding that a trait was unfavourable.

Another study by Fenton and Stuart reported no relationship between birth order and emotionality. Thurstone (1938), in a separate study confirmed these negative findings. It is also clear that other factors besides birth-order could be very important in determining personality; the sex of the child could be as important as its place in the family; the age-gap between the children could also be influential. Hence, the evidence for Adler's view is very slight and it would be unwise to place too great credence on his views.

We have reviewed three of the major theories of the psychoanalytic school of personality. All three are imaginative and thought-provoking, but only Freud's has played a major part in the experimental investigation of personality. The theories we shall examine next are type theories, based on observations of body size and shape.

Constitutional theories

Since the time of the ancient Greeks, there have been those who believed that a person's personality can be deduced from their physique; we tend to think that fat people are jolly and that muscular men are aggressive. Advertisements urge us to change our physique; if we develop our bodies the change will be reflected in the way people respond to us. What truth is there in the belief that there is a relation between personality and physique?

Ernst Kretschmer (1918–1964)

Kretschmer was one of the first psychologists to examine scientifically the relationship between physique and personality. As is often the case in this area of psychology, he based his observations on patients in clinical institutions. He compared those patients who had been diagnosed as schizophrenic with those diagnosed as manic depressives. He found major differences between them in terms of their average body size. Schizophrenics, typically, were tall and rather thin; he called this type *asthenic* (weak). Manic depressives were, in general, short and plump (so much for our notion that these people are always jolly!). He called this body type *pyknic* (thick). Kretschmer also examined people not in clinical institutions and described their average body size as *athletic*.

These are interesting findings, but there is doubt about their validity. Schizophrenia typically develops in late adolescence, thus Kretschmer's sample of schizophrenics was mainly of young people. Manic depression, on the other hand, is often a disease of middle age. It might be argued that Kretschmer was classifying the body changes that occur through a life-time: middle aged people are generally stouter than young

542

ones. This would have biased his results and produced evidence which tells us very little about personality.

William Sheldon (b. 1901)

Sheldon's work began where Kretschmer's ended. His concern was to try to map the relationships that might exist between physique and temperament. Sheldon believed that biological factors were extremely important as determinants of human behaviour. He sought to identify these factors to provide a firm basis on which to build a study of human behaviour. He hypothesized a biological structure (the morphogenotype) which underlies physical characteristics. He suggested that this morphogenotype influenced, not only the observable physical characteristics of a person, but also, indirectly, that person's personality.

His studies began in this way: Sheldon took photographs of 4 000 college men and sorted them into types of physique. He identified three major dimensions of physique which he called endomorphy, meso-morphy and ectomorphy. The type of physique which he called *endomorph* was round and soft (rather like Kretschmer's pyknic type). *Mesomorphs* were muscular and broad-shouldered (athletic in Kretschmer's typology), and *ectomorphs* were narrow-shouldered and skinny (asthenic). These are descriptions of body types at the extremes of the dimensions. A person can be described in terms of how much he resembles each of these three types of physique. Using a seven-point scale, one might score him: two for endormorphological characteristics, six for mesomorphical characteristics and one for ectomorphological characteristics (2, 6, 1). These ratings result in a description of a person's physique. Sheldon calls this the person's *somatotype*.

Having characterized and classified a person's physique, Sheldon turned to temperament and attempted a similarly ambitious task. He scoured the literature on personality and drew up a list of the trait names that he found there: there were 650 in all. He reduced this list to fifty by considering the overlap between them. Sheldon and his fellow workers then selected a group of thirty-three men and carefully observed them for a period of a year. They rated each of the men on each of the fifty traits. By the use of factor analysis Sheldon reduced these fifty factors to three major clusters. He called them viscerotonia, somatotonia and cerebrotonia.

A person who scores highly on those traits describing *viscerotonia* is a lover of comfort, someone who needs approval for his actions and who can relax easily. Sheldon describes him as 'bold as a rabbit'. A person who would be classified as extreme in *somatotonia* is noisy and aggressive, always on the move, Sheldon says he is 'fearless as a mastiff'. The third type, the extreme *cerebrotonic* is tense and hesitant, rather a social isolate and not fond of action. Sheldon says that in the face of a problem he 'closes up like a clam and seeks a hole to crawl into'.

After this analysis, Sheldon was able to consider the relationship between his typology of physique and that of temperament. In 1942 Sheldon reported the results of a five-year study he had made of 200 men. He rated them for temperament as a result of interviews and observations and he typed their body build according to the dimensions described above. He then looked at the degree of association between his two sets of figures: those for physique and those for temperament. He found a highly encouraging set of relationships. Endomorphy correlated highly with viscerotonia, mesomorphy with somatotonia, and ecto-morphy with cerebrotonia. These correlations were all of the order of +.80: a degree of correlation which is rarely found in psychology.

Evaluation: The extent of Sheldon's work is impressive, but in this lies one of its major flaws. Sheldon himself scored his subjects both for physique and temperament. He firmly believed there was a strong relationship between the two and had clear ideas of what this relationship might be. Indeed, he thought he was measuring the same factor at two different levels: that physique was directly related to temperament. This in itself must make his findings rather suspect. Rosenthal and others have shown how an experimenter can unwittingly bias his findings in the directon he expects. We are not suggesting that Sheldon deliberately rated his subjects in ways which would confirm his theory, but, in psychology, we place greater credence on work carried out by independent observers who do not have clear preconceptions of what the findings might show.

Sheldon maintains that to require total ignorance on the part of the investigator would make it impossible to obtain meaningful results and there is much to be said for this point of view. Furthermore, even if independent judges rated the subjects for temperament we would not remove completely the problems of bias. As we mentioned earlier, most of us have stereotypes of the fat, jolly person and, because of these stereotypes, it is difficult to guarantee that a rater will not be influenced by them.

Bearing in mind these criticisms of Sheldon's work, there are some experiments which lend support to his theory. In a major study of delin-quents, Sheldon and Glueck showed that delinquent boys differ from non-delinquent boys in body-type. The delinquents tended to be mesomorphic rather than endomorphic or ectomorphic. This is not an unlikely finding. It is probable that a good muscular physique is likely to suit the life-style of a delinquent. An individual who has a certain physique may be rewarded for certain behaviours and punished for others. The mesomorph may be successful if he is aggressive and dominant, whereas the ectomorph may often fail to gain success through aggression and so learns other techniques of gaining his own way. The relationship that Sheldon found is therefore a plausible one, but one cannot argue that the differences in physique are directly the cause of differences in personality—except in the general way just indicated, where social expectations and differential success and failure rates may mediate the relationship.

Sheldon's typology is not a strong theory: he is concerned to type people on the basis of careful observation, and the predictions that can be derived are not numerous. Nevertheless, it is important to recognize that his contribution to the study of personality is great. He set standards of observation and insight which are clear guidelines for current research.

Factor analytic theories

Raymond Cattell (b. 1905)

Let us now turn to two psychologists who have also tried to use statistical analysis to aid the development of a personality theory. The first of these is Cattell. Cattell sees the aim of personality research as enabling us to predict what a person will do in a given situation. His investigations of personality make use of the factor analytic technique described in Chapter 17. Cattell began by looking at the names used to describe traits or characteristics of personality. He used a list of 18 000 trait names and reduced this enormous number to 160 by looking at the clustering he found by factor analysis: he reduced this number again to about sixteen factors which he considered to be the major ones which underlie personality. These factors he called *source traits*. He claims that these source traits manifest themselves in clusters of *surface traits*. These are relatively unstable, and Cattell maintains that many psychologists have been misled by observation of these surface traits; he claims that only by factor analysis can we uncover the source traits which are stable and which form the basis of our personality. Figure 23.2 shows a list of these major source traits. Cattell prefers not to label them with names because he thinks this is misleading; he simply gives each a letter.

Further factor analysis of these source traits has revealed *second order* factors; that is, some traits are themselves correlated and can be subsumed under a more general second order category. The two most important second order traits are those called exvia-invia and anxiety. Cattell considers that these, whilst interesting, are not as useful for prediction of behaviour as the source traits and it is at the level of source traits that he claims useful predictions of behavioural responses can be made. Cattell emphasizes that personality traits are only some of several

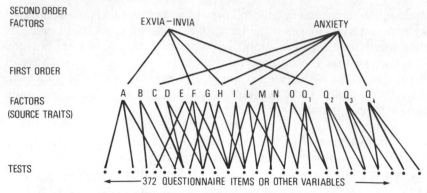

Fig. 23.2   Diagram to illustrate Cattell's level of factors.

factors which can influence behaviour. A person's state of mind, at any given time, can also affect behaviour. For example, I may, in general, be a sociable person, but on a particular evening I may choose not to go out with friends.

Hans Jurgen Eysenck (b. 1916)

Hans Jurgen Eysenck published his first account of his model of personality in 1947. Since then, he has expanded and modified his theory several times. The basis of his theory, however, remains the same. Eysenck claims that personality can be represented on two dimensions which are uncorrelated with each other. He isolated these dimensions, labelled extraversion and neuroticism, by factor analysis. In 1952 he isolated a third dimension which he calls psychoticism.

Eysenck places his work in a historical context by pointing out the similarities between the dimensions he has found and those described by Galen and others through the centuries. Galen described four main types of personality: choleric, melancholic, sanguine and phlegmatic; and these four types have recurred at regular intervals in personality descriptions. Kretschmer, for example, made use of a typology very similar to that described above. Eysenck's attempt to type personality was not, therefore, new but it has a number of novel features. He has tried to make his theory of personality scientific: he has used psychometrics and experimental techniques and has generated hypotheses which can be tested. The theory is new in attempting to establish dimensions on which individuals can be measured, rather than intuitively inferring a number of groups, into one of which every individual is supposed to fall.

Eysenck has also tried to make his theory a total one in that he has worked to give it validity at different levels of analysis. At the lowest level of analysis, there are specific responses or acts of behaviour; on a higher level, there are habitual responses, i.e., acts which recur under similar conditions. On a yet higher level are found traits. These are theoretical constructs which are based on correlations that have been observed at the level of habitual responses: these traits are characteristics such as rigidity and persistence. Finally, Eysenck claims there is the level of the type: this is a second order factor; for example, extraversion. In this way, knowledge of the type of a person should enable us to predict not only the general characteristics of that person, but also how they may respond in specific situations.

The foundation of Eysenck's theory of personality is a reliance on the biological basis of his dimensions. A person's location on the extraversion-introversion scale is held to be a function of the balance between the excitatory and the inhibitory processes within the cortex; whilst the degree of neuroticism he possesses is presumed to be a function of the relative liability or excitability of the nervous system. This part of Eysenck's theory is a development of basic ideas about the relationship between physiology and behaviour postulated by Pavlov, and another Russian worker, Teplov.

Pavlov noticed that certain of his dogs were more difficult to condition than others and he suggested this was because they were more cortically inhibited. He also noticed that certain patients called hysterics were also difficult to condition and extinguished conditioned responses quickly. Hysterics tend to be neurotic extraverts, whilst dystemics tend to be neurotic introverts. Eysenck verified these observations. Thus, on the neurological level certain predictions can be made and experimentally tested. Some of these predictions will be, for example, that:

1. Extraverts condition less easily than introverts (demonstrated by Franks).

2. Extraverts would show greater figural after-effects (demonstrated by Eysenck).

3. Introverts would be more difficult to sedate (shown by Shagass).

4. Drivers prone to accidents would be high on extraversion and neuroticism (shown by Shaw and Sichel).

Evidence from these sorts of experimental studies has been used by Eysenck to argue that his theory of cortical inhibition has been supported. But the link he claims between the neurological and behavioural levels is not at all clear. Other workers, for example Claridge, have suggested that the findings could be explained more simply in terms of basic differences between people in their levels of arousal.

The level of traits of behaviour is most simply measured by a questionnaire devised by Eysenck. This questionnaire will be discussed

547

in the part of this Chapter on personality assessment. Eysenck claims that his theory is useful, not only at the biological and individual levels, but also at the social level. He suggests that beliefs and attitudes can be linked to his two major dimensions. He further suggests a dimension which he calls 'tough-mindedness' (someone who is practical and materialistic). This is a projection onto the field of attitudes of the characteristics of the extrovert. 'Tender-mindedness' (someone who is thoughtful and idealistic) is a projection of the characteristics of an introvert. This dimension of tough/tender-mindedness has been isolated, again by factor analysis, and is considered to be orthogonal to the dimension of radicalism/conservatism. According to Eysenck, someone who is a communist in his beliefs is likely to be tough-minded and radical: a person who is fascist is likely to be tough-minded and conservative; whilst a person who is pacifist may be tender-minded and radical. Persons who have strong religious and moral beliefs tend to fall in the quadrant of tender-minded and conservative.

Evaluation: Eysenck has extended his theory into a number of areas. He has, for example, attempted to explain criminality in terms of inadequate socialization as a result of poor conditioning. Thus, according to Eysenck's theory, criminals should be high on the extraversion and neuroticism dimensions. In fact, it has been suggested that there are two sorts of criminal: the introverted sort who condition quickly to their undesirable environments, and the extraverted sort who do not condition at all and so do not learn to obey the rules of society. The evidence for these assertions is confused. Some workers have found support for Eysenck's suggestions, but many have not.

Even the basic prediction that extraverts condition less easily than introverts has been shown to be far more complex than was originally thought. Conditioning seems to be determined, at least partially, by the intensity of the unconditioned stimulus and the sort of reinforcement schedule employed. In particular, Gray and others have argued that highly extraverted and highly neurotic individuals should be difficult to condition by a passive avoidance schedule (Gray calls this fear-conditioning), and that this is the basis of the differences found in conditioning, rather than more general differences in conditioning by all types of schedule.

There are other problems with Eysenck's theory. He has been accused of concentrating too much on extraversion and has not expanded, to any degree, the supposed biological basis of neuroticism; he has used the terms excitation and inhibition of cortical activity very loosely. Recently, these concepts have been linked with the concept of a strong or a weak nervous system (briefly, the ease with which the person can be aroused). Evidence seems to confirm that introverts have a weak nervous system and extraverts have a strong one as measured by the electroence-phalogram (EEG).

A further problem for Eysenck is that the unitary nature of extraversion has been questioned. It is known that questions concerning extraversion on the Eysenck Personality Inventory (EPI) tap two factors—sociability and impulsivity. Eysenck claims that the dimension of extraversion is nevertheless unitary, but Carrigan suggests that the two factors should be considered independently. She proposes that the sociability factor may result in a well-adjusted type of person, whilst the impulsivity factor may result in a maladjusted type.

Problems of factor analysis

Factor-analytic approaches to personality are a welcome alternative to the abstract theorizing which has characterized many of the approaches we have described in the Chapter so far. Use of this technique makes it more likely that we can derive experimental hypotheses about the theory, and, by putting these to the test, we can evaluate the theory and consider possible modifications.

There are, however, many problems associated with the technique. A worker in this field has to decide whether to employ orthogonal or oblique systems of factor analysis. Analysis by orthogonal methods requires that the factors extracted are uncorrelated, or at right angles to each other. Oblique analysis allows factors which are partially correlated with each other to emerge. Cattell uses the latter method and derives several major traits. Eysenck prefers the former and, hence, arrives at his two major factors. The orthogonal method has the benefit of economy on its side; but this method can produce factors which are too gross to enable us to make many specific predictions, although Eysenck's theory has probably given rise to more testable hypotheses than any other. The oblique method can give rise to a further set of correlations between the factors that emerge. Cattell reports second order factors which, to some extent, represent the relationships between his original first order factors.

Methods of factors analysis can be used to test observations made by people working in the clinical setting. If the two, very diverse, methods—clinical judgement and factor analysis—agree about the major dimensions of personality, then we can be a little more confident about them. But, as was mentioned earlier, Cattell claims there is an important difference between source traits and surface traits, and it seems likely that there might be disagreement about which of these two kinds of traits the clinician is examining.

Another major difficulty with the use of factor analysis is the contention that one only gets out what has been put into it. This means that an analyst has to have a theoretical basis to determine the measures he chooses to consider. This is perfectly in order as long as he is aware of this: factor analysis is merely a tool for use in personality research; it cannot produce a new theory of personality 'out of the blue'.

Finally, there is the problem of labelling and identifying the factors which emerge. Cattell was unwilling to do this; certainly, once we have called Factor A, say, neuroticism, we have reified it and given it a reality which does not make it readily apparent that, far from being a single, unified characteristic, it is a bundle of factors which cluster together.

Nevertheless, bearing these observations in mind, it does not seem unreasonable to welcome an approach to personality theory which attempts to cut through the large subjective element at present contained in many major theories. Certainly, factor-analytic theories such as Eysenck's have encouraged more empirical research than almost any other type of theory—and this can only be to the general good of the area.

Self theories and self-actualization

Gordon Allport (1897–1967)

Gordon Allport has often argued against the main trends in personality theory. Whilst most of the theorists have been looking for common characteristics between individuals and attempting to classify these into broad bands, Allport has maintained the idiographic viewpoint that each individual is unique and unlike any other. His approach relies heavily on case study as the basis for investigating and reporting personality findings.

It is often useful for an area of investigation to have its critics: personality theorists are fortunate to have had one of the good sense of Allport. Allport emphasized the self and the essential unity of the individual's personality. His approach may be useful in describing an individual's known behaviour, but it is of little use as a predictor of future behaviour in a variety of situations. One can make few generalizations, even about one individual, which will hold in all future cases. We need to be able to generalize in order to explain, and it could be argued that without this faculty, personality has no place in a science of pyschology.

Carl Rogers (b. 1902)

Carl Rogers shares Allport's views about the importance of studying the individual. Rogers is primarily a therapist and, from his work with his clients, he has developed an orientation to personality which concentrates on the self. As we have seen from the descriptions of the psychoanalytic school, it is not unusual for personality theorists to begin their investigations from a clinical setting.

Carl Rogers and his followers have a view of man which differs in many ways from the other major theorists we have considered. Rogers sees man as a rational and a whole being who has the greatest knowledge about himself, his feelings, and his reactions. Thus, Rogers differs from the psychoanalytic theorists who stress the degree to which a man's personality is unconscious and hidden from himself. Rogers stresses self-knowledge as the basis of personality.

Unlike the factor-analytic theorists, Rogers emphasizes the uniqueness of the individual: his consideration is not 'in what ways are these people the same?' but 'what makes each of them different?' The major concept of Rogerian theory is the self. The self is the core of the individual. Some of the major properties of the self are that it develops from interactions with the world, that it aims for consistency, and that it can change as a result of interactions. Rogers also claims that there is a basic need for positive regard which can overshadow all other needs; there develops out of this a need for self-regard. Rogers suggests that an individual may have problems, such as neurotic disorders, if there arises a discrepancy between his experiences of others responding to him, and his self-concept. For example, he may think of himself as a generous person, but he may find others responding to him as though he were mean. He will have to modify his self-concept or cope with what may be a distortion in his perception of others' responses to him.

Evaluation: Many psychologists have welcomed Rogers' attempts to consider the totality of the individual and his positive regard for his clients in therapy. Certainly it is a useful antidote to the general view that one can treat aspects of an individual without concern for him as a person in his own right.

However, as a theory of personality, the Rogerian approach has certain drawbacks. It may well be a naive approach that uses as its basis the self-report. Can we be sure that a person knows himself as clearly as Rogers would claim? Rogers does not explain fully how the personality develops and it is again difficult to make specific predictions from his theory. Rogerian theory has had its major impact in psychotherapy, and here its influence is very largely to the good. The client-centred therapeutic approach moves away from the ideas of the therapist as expert and places the emphasis on the client. Rogers has made extensive use of tape-recordings of his therapy sessions, and this has allowed others to check claims made by the therapist of success in changing the viewpoint of the client. We cannot evaluate the logic of Freud's deductions from his therapeutic sessions; we can at least make some beginning with Rogers.

Self-actualization

The term 'self-actualization' has been variously used and it is not always clear that different writers have meant the same thing by it. One source of the concept is Jung's theory of 'individuation'—approximately, the realization of oneself as a person. Another source is a theory of motivation proposed by Henry Murray, which supposes that human needs are arranged in a hierarchical system. Some, such as those for food and shelter, are more basic, and must be satisfied before those that are higher can receive attention. A. H. Maslow developed these ideas and argued that the highest need is for 'self-actualization', which involves the development of an individual's potential for those characteristics which make us most human: love and affection, aesthetic experiences, altruism. He considered that this implied a new alternative to the two main traditional approaches to psychology, behaviourism and psycho-analysis.

This has given rise to a very large number of related theories and programmes designed to increase self-awareness and self-development. At the present time any objective assessment of the value and efficacy of these is lacking.

Personality assessment

So far in this Chapter we have looked at several different approaches to personality. As you will have learned from the other Chapters in this book, psychologists endeavour not only to describe behaviour, but also to measure it. We want to know not just that John is aggressive, but by how much he is more aggressive than his fellows. We come now to the variety of attempts that have been made to measure personality. There are two assumptions behind these attempts: that a person's personality, once formed, can be constant across situations and time; but also, paradoxically, that it can change as a result of experience. There are at least three major ways in which we can measure personality: by questioning the person himself about his feelings and behaviour, by making inferences as a result of his responses to material we give him, and by directing, observing, and measuring his behaviour.

Self report

INTERVIEWS

We conduct interviews for many different reasons but the purpose of most of them is we are trying to understand and assess a person. Interviews form the basis of many types of therapy; by listening to and questioning a person the therapist hopes to gain insight into his motivations and personality. Freud and Rogers both began with the patients' verbal report and made their inferences from it. This is largely a subjective method: it can pinpoint areas of a person's psyche which it might be fruitful to explore. However, there is a danger that the interviewer may read into a person's report what he expects to find there.

Attempts have been made to make the interview less subjective and more open to public scrutiny and evaluation. Rogers tape records many of his therapy sessions, so that the basis of his conclusion can be examined by others. Another frequently used method is a content analysis of the verbal report. The core of this method is that one constructs categories and counts the amount of verbal behaviour which falls into each. One might look, for example, for the expression of defence mechanisms or of conflict in a person's report. Changes in the structure of the content analysis over a number of sessions can be used to check against a therapist's reports on the progress of the individual. The therapist may report that the person is feeling less hostile as the therapy sessions progress; the expression of hostility, as measured by the content analysis, should also decrease. If this is the case then there would seem to be some basis for the therapist's claim.

Even a relatively structured interview is subject to bias. The person may report his feelings in a way that he thinks the therapist will approve. There is also no guarantee that a reduction in the expression of hostility within the interview is an indication of a general reduction of hostility in the person as he moves from situation to situation.

A major way in which psychologists have tried to measure personality is by the use of paper and pencil tests. These have the advantage that, whilst relying still on the person's report, they are quicker to administer than an interview and they are less open to accusation of bias. It is possible to administer the same test to a person at different times and check whether the responses are similar on all occasions. To re-run an interview is more difficult.

QUESTIONNAIRES

The most widely used of all questionnaires is the Minnesota Multiphasic Personality Inventory (abbreviated to MMPI). This test was devised in 1942 to discriminate between different types of patients in a psychiatric unit; it is now widely used in a variety of settings. The test has 550 questions, to which a person is asked to respond 'true', 'false', or 'cannot say'. These questions fall into nine clinical scales which are shown in Table 23.1.

A problem with these scales is that they are based on traditional diagnostic categories which have, to some extent, been abandoned in recent years. The scales are not independent of each other in the way one would require for orthogonal factor analysis, and this may also be a problem. Nevertheless, the devising of the MMPI, was a step forward in the objective testing of personality.

Other widely used paper and pencil tests of personality are those devised by Cattell and Eysenck. Cattell's 16PF Questionnaire is a direct test of his sixteen factors (source traits) of personality that have been

Table 23.1 Clinical scales of the MMPI.

Psychiatric disorder	Manifestation
1. Hypochondriasis (Hs)	Concerned about physical functions
2. Depression (D)	Depressed, dejected
3. Hysteria (Hy)	Unrealistic, insecure
4. Psychopathic deviate (Pd)	Irresponsible, egocentric
5. Maculinity-femininity (Mf)	Degree of gender identification
6. Paranoia (Pa)	Aggressive, sensitive to criticism
7. Psychasthenia (Pt)	Insecure, apprehensive
8. Schizophrenia (Sc)	Withdrawn, oversensitive
9. Hypomania (Hm)	Confident, lacking persistence

described above. The Eysenck Personality Inventory (EPI) is an attempt to measure the two major factors which he claims underlie personality—neuroticism and extraversion. This is a comparatively short questionnaire. People are asked to respond 'Yes' or 'No' to questions such as 'Do you like to go to parties?' 'Are you impulsive?' From responses to the questionnaire the person can be scored for how neurotic he is, and how extravert. Eysenck has paid particular attention to the reliability and validity of his questionnaire and it is widely used, especially in experimental settings.

A major problem with personality questionnaires is that subjects may try to 'fake good'; that is, they may try to fill in the questionnaire in such a way as to give the most favourable impression of themselves. Some questionnaires, such as the EPI, try to overcome this problem by introducing into the questionnaire certain questions which will show this response bias if it is operating; but this works only to a limited extent.

In spite of these drawbacks, the questionnaire method of assessing personality seems to be one of the most successful and appropriate. It is increasingly used and is often supported by other techniques in order to gain as accurate a picture as possible of an individual's personality.

OTHER TYPES OF SELF-REPORT

A rather less limiting test of personality than the questionnaire has been developed by Stephenson. It is called the Q-sort technique. A person is presented with a large number of statements of the sort 'I am an anxious person'. He is asked to sort these into a number of piles according to how well he thinks each statement reflects his self-concept. The examiner can then build up a picture of the individual. Alternatively, the person may be asked to sort the statements in such a way that they reflect how he would like to be. Thus, the examiner can compare how a person sees himself with his ideal-self. This technique makes use of Rogers' approach to personality which sees the self as a central construct. A therapist could see from this technique whether therapy was leading to a closer relationship between a person's self-concept and his ideal-self.

You will remember that the EPI had a sub-scale incorporated into it to counteract the possibility of a person 'faking good'. The Q-sort has no such scale; the examiner is forced to assume that the responder is not influenced in his sorting by what he thinks is desirable. The examiner also has to place complete reliance on what the person knows of himself.

Another test which faces similar problems to those encountered by Stephenson's Q-sort is Kelly's Role Construct Repertory Grid. This test has been constructed from Kelly's Personal Construct Theory. Kelly sees man as being in many ways like a scientist. He develops constructs which enable him to predict and interact with his world. The Repertory Grid test is designed to elicit these constructs. A person is given a list of a number of roles, for example, teacher, employer, friend. He is asked to list people who fulfill these roles. The names of these people are then presented in threes to the person who is asked to indicate how two of the three are similar and the third one different. For example, he may say that two of them are generous whilst the third is mean. Gradually, a matrix can be built up by this process and examination of this matrix may indicate which dimensions are important to that person.

This technique is designed to inquire into the way a person sees the world. The test is useful as a preliminary investigation of personality, but it has only very limited predictive power and suffers from one of the problems we have mentioned before, that of interpretation; it offers very few clues as to why a person sees the world as he does.

Projective techniques
Side by side with the attempts just described to standardize and objectify the assessment of personality there is another approach. Some psychologists see a questionnaire as too limiting: they do not seek to impose their own organization of personality on others. They have tended to use much less restrictive methods of assessment.

WORD ASSOCIATION TESTS

These tests have a long history in psychology. The psychologist presents a subject with a word and asks him to respond with the first word he thinks of. It is hoped that an analysis of the sorts of responses given to this task will lend insight into the primary concerns and desires of the person being tested.

AMBIGUOUS STIMULI TESTS

There are other, more refined tests which share the rationale just described. In these tests, the emphasis is on finding stimuli that are ambiguous and that have few clues of how the subject is expected to respond. It is hoped that in this ambiguous setting the subject will reveal his concerns. The most famous test of this type is the Rorschach Ink-blots test. This was devised in 1921 by a Swiss psychiatrist, Hermann Rorschach. He chose ten ink-blots from a larger number which he generated. The person is asked to tell the examiner what he sees in each ink-blot. When he has responded in this way to all ten ink-blots the examiner then questions the subject about his interpretations to try to elucidate what determined his responses. Originally the ink-blots test was used as an aid to diagnosis in psychotherapy. The usual responses to the ink-blots were established and unusual responses were examined for clues to the person's state of mind. The Rorschach test assumes that much of the person's response is determined by unconscious processes; that he will project his feelings into the ink-blot. Therefore it is supposed that this technique will give valuable insights which would not be found by direct interviewing or by a standard paper and pencil test.

Another frequently used projective test is the Thematic Apperception test (TAT) which was developed by Morgan and Murray in 1930. This test comprises thirty pictures which are highly ambiguous the subject is asked to tell a story around each picture. Again, there is no correct or incorrect answer to this test and so the subjects have very few clues to guide the stories that they make up. The examiner can record the time taken to begin to tell the story, he can also look for themes which recur within the stories. Major themes that are frequently studied by this test are, for example, to what degree the stories told indicate a motivation for achievement, a desire for affiliation, or a fear of failure.

The TAT, like the Rorschach test, suffers from problems of validity and accuracy of interpretation. The examiner may have expectations about the sort of themes which could be contained in the stories and this may bias his interpretations. Many studies have shown that training examiners to recognize indicators of themes has not led to great agreement between them in interpreting the stories.

It is clear, then, that the advantages of projective techniques—their flexibility and the provision for freedom of expression—lead directly to several major disadvantages. The tests are difficult to score, and the scores themselves need careful interpretation. Precisely what does the frequent appearance of a theme in the stories tell us about a person's personality? Projective techniques can be useful, then, but their drawbacks have led many workers to search for other methods of personality assessment.

Direct observation

If we wish to know how a person behaves why do we not simply observe him? Occasionally we do; but the observation can never be total: personal privacy does not permit that. Instead, we can sample some part of a person's behaviour. During a period of time we can count how much of a particular sort of behaviour is occurring, for example, how many times a child behaves aggressively in a playground. This can be very useful: the psychologist could use conditioning schedules to try to reduce the amount of aggression the child displays; direct observation scores could indicate how successful the schedule has been. However, this does not really explain the behaviour that is measured. The psychologist is still at the stage of observation and description. We can, however, use how a person behaves in a specific situation as an indicator of his personality and this is discussed below.

Behaviour tests

There are numerous laboratory situations which are used to distinguish between different types of personality. Some of them will be discussed here to give a flavour of the sort of work that is done.

THE ROD AND FRAME TEST

Subjects in a laboratory are asked to adjust a rod which is in a tilted frame. The apparatus is in a darkened room and so subjects have no clues to what is the true horizontal or vertical. This test is designed to measure field dependency. This concept was suggested by Witkin in the 1940s. Field dependency is the degree to which a person is influenced by the situation which surrounds him. In the laboratory it could be clues about the perceptual field, in the social setting it might be the attitudes of the people he is interacting with. Thus performance on the rod and frame test may give valuable insight into a person's more general behaviour patterns.

THE EMBEDDED FIGURES TEST

This task is also designed to measure field dependency. A person is shown a figure and then asked to find it in a larger and more complicated design. Again, it is possible to tell from his performance on this task whether he is greatly or only slightly influenced by his surroundings.

These tests are very useful: they are objective, and it is possible to check their reliability by retesting the subjects and the findings suggest that these characteristics of field dependency endure for a long time in a person's life.

THE LEMON DROP TEST

Eysenck and his followers have used a large number of experimental tests to discriminate between extraverts and introverts. Some of these have already been mentioned in the discussion of his theory. A test not previously discussed is the lemon drop test. Introverts have a greater state of cortical arousal than extraverts; they react more strongly to sensory stimulation. If a standard number of drops of lemon juice are placed on a subject's tongue he will tend to salivate much more if he is an introvert than if he is an extravert.

FIGURAL AFTER-EFFECTS

It can also be predicted from Eysenck's theory of personality that highly extraverted people will develop figural after-effects more rapidly and more strongly than will introverts. This has been found to be the case, and so the test will successfully discriminate between the two personality types.

We have seen here that experimental tests can successfully be used to measure personality. These sorts of investigations enable psychologists to record results in an objective and unambiguous manner, and the conclusions drawn from the tests can be re-examined to determine their generality. It seems probable that future work in the area of personality research will make greater use of these techniques.

24 Abnormal psychological states

PHILIP EVANS

Who's who?

You are at a social gathering of some sort and somebody approaches you with the usual question: 'And what do you do?' You reply (if you are, as yet, inexperienced in matters of convenient untruths): 'Well, actually, I'm a psychologist.' Immediately you will be assumed an expert in all things concerned with bizarre behaviour, funny experiences, and, of course, nervous breakdowns. In short you are taken to be an expert in *abnormal psychology*. The reason why this specialization within psychology should become synonymous with psychology as a whole on the part of a majority of the lay public is not hard to glean. For a start, there are many superficially similar words in existence: psychologist, psychiatrist, psychoanalyst, psychotherapist, and so on. Little wonder that this creates some confusion.

It would be true to say that the last three persons mentioned are always in some way concerned with the 'abnormal'; so are *certain* psychologists: those who have made it their academic interest for teaching and research; and more narrowly those *clinical* psychologists, who have taken a specific post-graduate training to enable them to work professionally in the applied field, dealing with the mentally ill—a concept which we shall have to explore the meaning of a little later. First the reader should carefully examine the definitions below, which will clarify the 'job specifications' of those confusing people whose professional titles share the same five initial letters.

Psychiatrist: A qualified medical practitioner who has subsequently undergone training in what is termed 'psychological medicine'. In this country the usual professional qualification will be the DPM—Diploma in Psychological Medicine. The psychiatrist may undertake a diagnostic and therapeutic role, or he may refer patients to a clinical psychologist or psychotherapist. In any event, he usually fulfils the global role of being finally medically responsible for the patient.

Clinical psychologist: A qualified psychologist who has subsequently specialized and undergone professional training in the discipline of clinical psychology which involves the diagnosis and psychological treatment of mentally ill patients. His therapeutic role does not include the prescribing of physical treatments, unlike the psychiatrist. As psychological treatments have become more diverse and, arguably, more powerful, so the therapeutic role of the clinical psychologist has grown. It is usual to find the clinical psychologist 'eclectic' in his approach to therapy, with perhaps a bias recently towards the use of behavioural therapy. This is in contrast to the psychoanalyst.

Psychoanalyst: Strictly speaking, a therapist who more or less rigidly follows the method of psychological treatment devised by Sigmund Freud during the first thirty or so years of this century. The term is sometimes expanded to include practitioners of allied methods of therapy: analytic psychologists—followers of Carl Jung; individual psychologists—followers of Alfred Adler; and a host of post-Freudian and neo-Freudian schools of therapists. Most but not all psychoanalysts are also medically trained and are also psychiatrists. Because of the time-intensive nature of this kind of treatment—and, some would say, because of its limited applicability and efficacy—in Britain it tends to be practised privately on the middle classes of London and the home counties.

Psychotherapist: An umbrella term to describe anyone who undertakes the psychological treatment of patients. The only exclusion has been a group of belligerent 'behavioural' therapists, who have wanted to contrast their methods totally with the rest of psychotherapy. The present author has little sympathy for such zealots and sees nothing odd about being a behaviourally-orientated psychotherapist.

Who's ill?

We have now dealt sufficiently with the overlapping array of authority figures—the professionals. In search of their diverse talents come the so-called mentally ill. What are we to make of such a label?

Throughout history, and across societies, there have always been people who have been singled out by the rest of the community as odd, because of their behaviour. The term 'abnormal psychology' therefore, in its strictest sense, presents us with no problems. If a piece of behaviour is odd or abnormal in the statistical sense it can be justifiably studied under the rubric of abnormal psychology whether the behaviour in question be an incoherent and apparently meaningless flow of verbiage from a hitherto normally-speaking adult or a coherent and meaningful flow of musical compositions from a four-year-old child prodigy.

Abnormal, in essence, should be a neutral adjective in terms of its application. It is equally clear that the adjectival phrase 'mentally ill' is not. Quite clearly there is something 'wrong' with the mentally ill. The trouble is that the term 'illness', borrowed from the field of medicine to describe physical suffering and physical damage, or something capable of finally producing suffering or damage, loses a lot of its exactitude when prefixed by 'mental'. Treating physical and mental illness in this kind of parallel fashion would not be so bad if the resulting confusions did not often raise serious moral questions. Let us examine some of these.

A physically ill person is usually in a position to admit he is suffering and in need of treatment. Moreover, the doctor can usually point to something which can be identified as a cause. (This can be an over-simplification but we cannot explore every avenue of argument.) People who are often, and perhaps conveniently, labelled mentally ill by a society do not always subscribe to the view that they are suffering from an illness; still less would they agree that they are in need of treatment; still less can any doctor point to a simple cause. The big moral issues are easily highlighted by careful choice of example. In the Soviet Union perfectly sane (by Western criteria) dissidents are labelled mentally ill and delivered into the hands of Soviet psychiatrists. Closer to home, it has, until quite recently, been common practice to commit homosexual men and women for treatment as mentally ill, subject them to such procedures as receiving electric shocks while viewing photographs of lovers (aversion therapy), or asking them to imagine their lovers covered with vomit (covert sensitization). This was done despite the lack of any evidence to show any abnormality other than a different, but by no means rare, sexual orientation. The truly abnormal willingness of some homosexuals to undergo such procedures is, of course, amply explained by his living at odds with a society which can countenance such modern-day tortures.

The examples I have used are, of course, the easy ones, much used by other writers (see Szasz, 1970) who are antipathetic to the term mental illness. Perhaps we can agree that practices in the Soviet Union are a travesty of psychiatry. Perhaps we can point to the recent decision in the United States to remove homosexuality from its official list of psychiatric conditions.

Is the remaining area of psychiatric attention meaningfully covered by the term mental illness? Let us take a very common and less controversial mental illness: depression. However much one is concerned with definitions and exact use of terms and their moral implications, it is sobering occasionally to conjure up pictures of real people. Anyone who has worked in psychiatric establishments will have seen the real suffering, anguish, and despair of the truly depressed patient. Moreover, he will have felt it his primary duty to help this patient, and the question whether the patient is really ill will not readily enter his head in the performance of that perceived duty. However, it is possible to ask oneself afterwards what aid it has been to have called that condition an illness. Moreover, one can also perhaps see the dangers in labelling psychological mood-states in terms of illness. People who may be sad, very sad, for good reason become, with the wave of a verbal wand, victims of depression. People who are justifiably anxious in their day-to-day lives become sufferers from neurosis. And the trouble with such conceptual transformations is that they can be positively harmful in directing attention away from genuine causes of suffering requiring social and, perhaps, ultimately, political attention towards a vague and ghostly inner cause, which may be a mere convenient fiction. This really is the source of disagreement between those who advocate a so-called medical model (many psychiatrists, for obvious reasons) and those who do not (an increasing number of clinical psychologists whose training has emphasized the importance of social learning in the development of normal and abnormal behaviour). However, it is important to turn the above argument round and admit the possibility that in certain cases it may be equally frustrating to divert attention away from possible causes of a physical nature. To make an extreme point, one would not appreciate a misdiagnosis where a psychological confusional state, caused in reality by the consumption of toxic substances, has been interpreted in the light of a disturbed childhood. Equally, it is a plausible hypothesis to see certain forms of very severe and irrational depression as being caused by a biological predisposition to toxicate one's own brain periodically.

What, then, do we conclude from this argument? The term 'illness' cannot be said to be either rightly or wrongly applied in this area in any general sense. Undoubtedly, as our knowledge progresses certain 'conditions' or 'disorders' will be able unambiguously to be called illnesses; equally, others will not. The term 'mental illness' is, therefore, not a particularly helpful all-round term. Do we, then, for the present, do away with all the well-known labels of pyschiatry—schizophrenia, neurosis—along with their less well-known subdivisions and types? I think not. It is wrong to confuse the question of illness labels with the question of classification. Classification can, and should, be a neutral term, just as it is for the psychologist interested in classifying 'normal' personality types, response strategies, or whatever. Every science must go beyond the individual case in order to find some order before further work can be done. One could draw a parallel with botany and the pioneering work of Linnaeus, whose contribution was primarily a classificatory one. If we forget about illness as such, and simply ask ourselves how we can understand and help people with manifest, psychological problems, it is surely helpful if we can discover some order in

562

such problems. One does not have to be committed to any form of medical model in order to appreciate that words like 'symptom' and 'syndrome', traditionally medical words, can have a sort of classificatory value even when we are not sure about the 'illness status' of the condition we are describing.

The classification of 'disorders'

Organic syndromes and the psychoses

Let us then look at a traditional type of classification in the field of psychiatric disorders. We could begin, closest to the field of medicine in general, with those disorders which, despite their observed pathology in terms of intellectual and emotional functioning, are clearly related to physical factors: mental retardation, and organic brain syndromes. The latter can encompass a wide variety of conditions: bizarre behaviour resulting from specific traumatic injuries to parts of the brain, damage to the brain as a result of acute or chronic poisoning (e.g., alcoholic), and last, but not least, chronic deterioration of mental functioning as a result of arteriosclerosis affecting the brain of the aged which accounts for many of the so-called *senile dementias*. In addition, there is a host of rarer specific syndromes leading to mental and physical deterioration, e.g., Huntington's chorea which is genetically transmitted. Some of these disorders are qualified by the adjective *psychotic*, which is a kind of shorthand way of saying that the disorder is characterized by very severe impairment of mental functioning, impairment of language, perception, and memory processes, as well as emotional dysfunction.

Non-organic psychoses

Not all psychotic behaviour can be so readily attributed to physical factors, and this brings us to our next category of psychiatric disorder: psychoses not directly attributable to physical causes. By far the biggest subcategory here is *schizophrenia*. The schizophrenic is the layman's traditional idea of a madman, the lunatic: he is the patient who thinks he is God, or Christ, Napoleon, or a computer, and he can weave a more or less coherent *modus vivendi* around such a *delusion*—he has, in other words, a delusional system. We shall look at schizophrenia in a little more detail after our survey of psychiatric disorders in general and we shall find that not all schizophrenics have such a florid delusional system. At present it suffices to point out that the schizophrenic does not suffer from a split personality, as is so often assumed—a disintegrated personality is nearer the mark.

The other major psychosis within this category is variously known as manic-depressive psychosis or psychotic affective disorder. As those names suggest, the disorder is characterized by very severe mood swings, which periodically affect the patient for no apparent reason. The clearest cases involve a cycle from abnormally elevated mood (*mania*) proceeding down through normality to a deep depression, where the patient lies in bed, for perhaps weeks at a time, completely unresponsive to other people or to his own needs. However, not all cases are so simple, and the cycle may, for example, miss out mania entirely and consist simply of periodic bouts of severe and inexplicable depression.

It will have struck the reader that, although at present these disorders are not clearly related to organic causes and are, hence, not categorized as such, they nevertheless do not seem readily explicable in terms of learning or psychological experiences—they seem too bizarre and unrelated to life events. For this reason, many are of the opinion that the eventual causes (and remedies) will come from traditional medical and biologically-slanted research. The psychologist's present role in therapy has more to do with management than cure (though in the case of schizophrenia there is a vocal minority opinion, represented in the writings of R. D. Laing, that schizophrenia can be seen as a psychological adjustment to an existence felt to be truly terrifying and self-destroying. This view is still most easily assimilated by the reader through the pages of Laing's early book *The Divided Self*).

Neurotic disorders
The psychologist's major theoretical contribution comes in our understanding of the next category of disorders known as the neuroses. Unlike psychotic patients, neurotic ones are not grossly out of touch with reality. By and large, they live their lives much as everyone else but with an awful, handicapping sense of anxiety which sometimes becomes too much, so that the patient is forced temporarily to opt out and seek help—the only meaning that can really be given to the confusing term, nervous breakdown. Some neurotics have more specific symptoms, unlike the general anxiety neurotic just described. For example, phobic patients are even more like normal people, except that they have some object or situation which, when encountered, fills them with absolute terror. They may be so incapacitated by having to avoid the source of their phobia that they are forced to seek treatment. Yet another, and rarer, form of neurosis involves the patient in a compulsion to engage in senseless rituals, such as washing one's hands a hundred times a day, counting every advertisement hoarding on the way to work and so on. Such behaviour may strike the reader as so odd as to justify the term psychotic. However, unlike the psychotic type of patient, the obsessional neurotic has complete insight into his behaviour—he is the first to admit that it is crazy. Since anxiety enters the picture in some way in all neuroses, and since the conditioning of anxiety responses is something the trained psychologist can claim to know something about, it is not

surprising, as I have just said, that psychology has increased our understanding of the nature and treatment of these disorders.

There is, however, one particular neurotic disorder, where it is sometimes claimed that anxiety (or at least conscious anxiety) does not enter the picture. These are so-called *conversion hysterics*, much treated in the early years by Freud. The patient develops a physical symptom such as a paralysed arm (or even blindness!) and yet, there is no physical damage to account for the symptom and, indeed, before Freud's time, these patients were officially classified as malingerers. Freud's own view was that the symptom had symbolic meaning and could be traced back to some forgotten source of trauma. Anxiety becomes too intense to be felt consciously and is repressed, eventually finding indirect expression in some meaningful physical symptom. Other than complaints about his symptom, the patient seems totally carefree, showing what the text-books refer to as *la belle indifférence*. It is, however, questionable whether more than a few patients really exhibit such happy indifference. A modern psychological theory of conversion symptoms would probably simply point to the possibility of their being learnt because of some reinforcement value (after all, many internal responses, felt previously to be involuntary, are now known to be susceptible to shaping by reinforcement—see Chapter 11). However Freud writes very eloquently in general and still deserves to be read. The reader could do no better than consult Freud's original writings—perhaps the intriguing case of Fräulein Anna O.—if he wishes to consider the possibility that a symptom may be learnt because it has meaning for the individual at an unconscious level.

Usually categorized alongside the neuroses is depression. Sometimes one speaks of *reactive* depression to contrast this with the psychotic depressions already mentioned. Reactive implies that the depression can be linked to life events, even though, it may since have developed its own momentum leaving the patient depressed in the absence of good reason. Depression which does not seem to relate to any circumstances, such as psychotic depression is referred to as endogenous, suggesting an inner cause.

Psychosomatic disorders
Related to anxiety and stress, but usually categorized separately are the psychomatic or psychophysiological disorders. Unlike hysterical conversion symptoms, these disorders are real physical disorders with manifest pathology: an ulcer, a skin rash, an attack of asthma are all physical and sometimes very dangerous symptoms. The term psychosomatic merely emphasizes that psychological factors, such as exposure to chronic stress, are heavily implicated in the onset of such symptoms. Of course, since most illnesses can be said to be multi-determined (being in

the presence of a flu virus is not sufficient to catch flu) it has become fashionable to talk of nearly all illnesses having a psychosomatic component. It is therefore best to think of a continuum of psychosomatic illnesses from things like asthma and ulcers (heavy psychosomatic loading) through heart attacks and certain cancers (medium loading) to broken legs from climbing accidents (virtually nil loading?).

When someone makes a move, of which we don't approve . . .

To end our survey of types of disorder we move on to a rather dust-bin type of class, sometimes not very aptly called personality disorders or character disorders. This is also the area where ethical considerations, which we noted earlier, occur. Soviet dissidents and homosexuals would have to belong here; so would any person who is an embarrassment to his society rather than himself—Jews in Nazi Germany were taken to be hopeless cases of flawed characters and there were professors of psychiatry who argued the case in favour of the Third Reich. That said, there are undoubted examples of the need to have some sort of category for a psychopathic murderer (the subdivision psychopathy: a deeply anti-social personality, incapable of feeling guilt, shows no evidence of learning pro-social behaviour through exposure to society's normal sanctions, and, on these criteria, can be usually differentiated from the ordinary criminal) or for someone who actively seeks sexual intercourse with six-year-old girls (paedophile), or someone who is quietly killing himself with injections of heroin or slugs of whisky or meths (addict).

We need no longer, I think, dwell on the difficulties of making hard and fast rules about who to commit to care under the auspices of this label: marijuana users but not tobacco users; the cocaine sniffer but not the obese, unless, of course, the obese smoker wants to break his habits. The psychologist has, probably sensibly, devoted more of his time to studying obesity and smoking behaviour than to studying what society officially disapproves of in terms of illegal, but perhaps less harmful, substances than tobacco or food in large quantities.

If this were an abnormal psychology text, it would be time now to begin Chapters in detail on all the separate disorders which have been outlined. In these more limited pages, that is not possible. Therefore, the best approach is perhaps to consider just one or two topics in further detail, giving the reader some introduction to the methods that psychologists and allied workers use in both the investigation and treatment of various symptoms. The reader who wishes to go beyond a simple introduction can consult one of the many text-books given over exclusively to abnormal psychology. I should particularly recommend *Abnormal Psychology—an Experimental-Clinical Approach* by Davison and Neale.

More about Schizophrenia and something about research

Schizophrenia is a good topic with which to begin; and it is so for several reasons. First, it is by far the most common severe mental disorder affecting adults. The majority of the in-patients of a psychiatric hospital are likely to be diagnosed as schizophrenic. Hence research into finding the aetiology (essentially, the main causative factors) of schizophrenia and, it is hoped, a remedy is a formidable enterprise. Secondly, the problems that arise in attempting to do research are legion and also highlight methodological difficulties which can be generalized to other areas within the field of abnormal psychology.

Problems are first encountered when we try to give a strict definition of schizophrenia. Let us take a fairly typical attempt at a definition given by the psychiatrist Stafford-Clark (1964):

Schizophrenia is a generic name for a group of disorders characterized by a progressive disintegration of emotional stability, judgement, contact with, and appreciation of reality, which produce considerable secondary impairment of personal relationships and intellectual functions.

Now, in the case of a florid schizophrenia we may be presented with a picture of someone very clearly 'out of contact with reality', and so on, since he is suffering, perhaps, from delusions of the kind we have already mentioned earlier in the Chapter, and perhaps also, he may appear to be hearing and answering to non-existent voices (auditory hallucinations). But what if the patient shows no such florid symptoms but just seems to have withdrawn into a world of his own, showing no interest in anything outside himself? He may show a few eccentric mannerisms, but that is all. How do we diagnose this case? The answer is unfortunately that some psychiatrists would say that this was still a case of schizophrenia, whilst others would not. The symptom of withdrawal in the presence of a few eccentricities is far more likely to be diagnosed schizophrenia in the United States than it is in Britain.

This unreliability of diagnosis has, of course, disastrous implications for carrying out thorough research. Let us illustrate this by the following example. Suppose a researcher is interested in showing that schizophrenia has a substantial genetic component and that heredity is largely responsible for the transmission of the 'disease'. A powerful technique of investigation is to look at identical and non-identical twins and establish concordance rates for them. If, for example, you had ten pairs of identical twins where one twin was always schizophrenic, you would go on to investigate the status of the other twin, and you may find that in seven out of ten cases the other twin was also schizophrenic, thus giving a 70 per cent concordance rate. Now, suppose you have done this for a sample of identical and non-identical twins and you now have two figures for concordance. If the figure for identical twins is substantially higher than that for non-identical twins which we will also assume is, in turn, higher than for ordinary siblings, then we have presumptive evidence of a genetic factor; and if the absolute figure is itself high then we have evidence of a substantial genetic factor. Needless to say, such research has been carried out by many researchers in many countries. One of the earlier North American studies obtained monozygotic (identical twin) concordance rates of between 69 and 86 per cent—very high compared with dizygotic (non-identical twin) rates of only 10 to 15 per cent. This, of course, appears to be presumptive evidence for a strong and significant genetic factor in schizophrenia. However, more recent Scandinavian research (admittedly on smaller samples) puts concordance rates for both kinds of twins below 6 per cent! A recent English study by Gottesman and Shields (1972) comes somewhere in between, confirming the American work in terms of a big difference between identical and non-identical twin studies, but putting the concordance rate for monozygotic pairs somewhat lower than the American study at around 40 per cent. There can be no question that inadequately agreed criteria for diagnosis is the single most important factor accounting for such discrepancies.

Quite recently, Rosenhan (1973) created a storm in psychological and psychiatric circles by publishing an article in *Science* magazine entitled 'On being sane in an insane place'. The import of the article was, quite simply, to shock people into considering the vagaries of diagnosis in schizophrenia. He sent members of his research team into psychiatric hospitals and instructed them to fabricate just one symptom: that they heard voices. Any other questions about their current psychological state or their family history or whatever were to be answered honestly. After being diagnosed as schizophrenic and admitted to hospital the pseudo-patients had instructions to drop the faked symptom and behave totally normally. Rosenhan describes how this was all to no avail and that even quite normal activity on the part of the pseudo-patient (taking notes about what was happening) was reported by the nursing staff as evidence of abnormality. Only certain fellow-inmates gave evidence of having certain suspicions. Rosenhan's study has since been exposed to some criticism, but it had its intended effect of raising severe doubts about the use of schizophrenia as a diagnostic label.

Despite diagnostic difficulties, research carries on, as indeed it should; and most researchers try to make sure that at least the sample of schizophrenics they use is reasonably homogeneous, i.e., similar in type to one another so that any conclusions reached may, hopefully, be generalized to similar types in the population. But further difficulties can then arise. Let us take another line of research to serve as an example in this respect.

There has been much speculation that schizophrenia and its attendant psychological symptoms are primarily the result of the faulty operation of certain brain chemicals, with perhaps the propensity for such faulty operation being genetically programmed. Thus, a search has been under way for many years to isolate offending substances and a long list of candidates have gone in and out of fashion; adrenalin, and related compounds, taraxein, and currently, dopamine. Many years ago now, some researchers thought they had solved the enigma of schizophrenia by discovering a simple, but apparently inexplicable, deficiency in iodine compounds; it remained inexplicable and fascinating just as long as it took to discover further that the hospital salt was bought cheaply and lacked the usual iodine nutrients. Control for diet in such studies now goes without saying. However, the difficulty of determining whether any finding is truly causative rather than a result of anything to do with background and life-style, including diet, can be a formidable difficulty.

Psychologists have tried to tell us more about the schizophrenic by studying his cognitive behaviour. Has the schizophrenic got some sort of specific memory deficit? Does he have difficulty storing, coding, or retrieving information? Does he have difficulty filtering irrelevant input from relevant, and, if he does, is this because he is perhaps chronically under-aroused or over-aroused? Models are constructed, and the psychologist goes about testing the models by giving batteries of cognitive tasks to do. Now, although much useful work has been done in this area, interpretation is often difficult because schizophrenics are usually receiving very powerful medication in the form of drugs known as the major tranquillizers, notably chlorpromazine, and the effects of these drugs is confounded with the schizophrenia under investigation. Attempts to get round this difficulty present other problems: for example, the simple solution of taking patients off their drugs a week or so before the research, as well as raising ethical questions if the drug seems to be controlling the schizophrenia fairly well, may be useless if the schizophrenic is thereby made incapable of concentrating on the relevant task.

So is there any reasonable methodology which is problem-free? The answer is certainly no, but that is, arguably, what research is all about, and, in all the above areas of research, good work has been done and is being done, simply because the researcher is aware of the type of problems we have outlined. Perhaps we should end this discussion of schizophrenia by outlining what might seem to be a common sense research project. You may say that, since we have no complete evidence that the causes of schizophrenia are biologically based, and because the very existence of some identical twins who are discordant shows that any genetic factor must have to interact with the environment to determine schizophrenia, we should therefore look very carefully at the past histories and present environments of all the schizophrenics we can lay our hands on. Why not simply gather all the information we can, and perhaps we may come up with the vital missing ingredient?

The answer is that this has been done by many people across many years. A lot of the resulting work has also run into the last of the methodological problems that I want to mention. Such work has for the most part been retrospective: such information as has been got has been acquired after the person in question has been diagnosed schizophrenic. Now, the trouble with retrospective information is that it is notoriously unreliable, especially if it is 'family history' sort of information got from relatives and friends of the patient, who are quite understandably influenced in their response by the current situation of the patient. Not only that; the researcher himself may want to discover certain patterns in the backgound of the schizophrenic and thus unconsciously bias his research. It would be much better all round if the information could be acquired and documented before the person became schizophrenic, but the problem here is one of numbers: how many people do you have to collect masses of information from over many years before you get enough records of people who later become schizophrenic? This kind of longitudinal research—following up your subjects over a period of time—is extremely expensive and time-consuming. However, Scandinavian researchers, led by Mednick, are at present engaged in just such an enterprise but have got round the problem of prohibitive numbers by adopting a so-called 'high-risk group' methodology. Mednick and his colleagues have chosen to study limited samples of children over many years and have included the key sample of children with schizophrenic mothers, who are deemed, therefore, to be high-risk for schizophrenia. Already, the high-risk group has divided itself into those showing signs of disturbance and those not, and Mednick *et al.* have reported that birth complications are strongly implicated in differentiating the two sub-groups. It is certainly a long-term project which promises future pay-offs.

We have deliberately approached this outline of schizophrenia with the aim, not of giving a potted portrait of schizophrenics, but of showing what kinds of questions have been raised by those interested in finding out more about its nature and origin; in particular, we have tried to show the pervasive difficulties that the genuine researcher will always encounter. For the reader to appreciate those difficulties is of very general value.

More about neurosis and something about behavioural therapy

If psychologists have been able to offer little in the way of a cure for schizophrenia as yet, they have managed to make therapeutic inroads with respect to certain neurotic disorders. Before the 1960s the psychological therapies given to neurotic patients tended all to be based, sometimes strictly, sometimes not so strictly, on the psychoanalytic method developed by Sigmund Freud. Unfortunately there was (and still is) no hard evidence to show that the method achieved more than chance success rates: neurotic patients do improve with time, even in the absence of formal therapy. What appears to be the case is that such therapy does help certain individuals but might actually make others worse by encouraging the patient to talk forever about himself, his past, his complexes, anxieties, guilt-feelings, and dreams, and never get round to doing anything about changing himself. With its emphasis on neurosis being caused by an interplay of blind unconscious forces, the Freudian model does not naturally give the patient a feeling of responsibility or control. Hence, the improved and what may be termed 'recovery-retarded' patients cancel each other out, leaving, as I have said, a chance level of performance for the therapy as a whole.

In 1958, a psychiatrist called Joseph Wolpe published a book entitled *Psychotherapy by Reciprocal Inhibition*, which can be seen as the beginning of the Behaviourist movement in the field of therapy. Wolpe had previously been using psychoanalytic-type methods and had become disenchanted by them and, searching for something new, started reading articles and books from the field of academic psychology, in particular the field of learning theory (see Chapter 10). It occurred to Wolpe that, since everyone, including Freudians, tended to agree that people become neurotic as a result of experience, that was tantamount to saying that neurotic behaviour is learned; and, if it is learned, it should be governed by the same laws of learning which were being espoused by learning theorists in their psychological laboratories; moreover, psychologists had also studied 'unlearning' or extinction processes, and surely they should, if applied to neurotic behaviour, approach the status of therapy.

Now, the learning theorists had traditionally dealt in stimuli and responses, and Wolpe's first job was to try to conceptualize neurotic behaviour in similar terms. The easiest neurotic disorders to begin with were phobias, where it is possible to see the feared object or situation as a stimulus and the fear as a response. The principle of reciprocal inhibition in the learning theory of Clark Hull states that if two incompatible responses to a stimulus are put in competition, the stronger will come to dominate and gradually extinguish the weaker by the process of inhibition. Earlier in the century, Watson and Rayner had reported the famous case of 'Little Albert' who was made phobic of furry objects by pairing the presentation of a white rat with a loud noise; Albert's phobia was then extinguished by feeding him chocolate in closer and closer proximity to the rat. The pleasant response of eating chocolate could be seen as vying with the fear and since this response competition took place at first some distance from the phobic object the pleasant responses won the battle. The next battle, taking place a metre or so nearer the rat, was made easier and so on till the phobia was completely extinguished.

Now, Wolpe realized two things: firstly, he could not readily feed chocolate to his adult patients and, secondly, not all objects of phobic response can be positioned so many metres away from a patient in a consulting room. In terms of learning theory, he had to find alternative, reciprocally inhibiting, responses and, in certain cases, alternative stimulus substitutes. He solved the first problem by suggesting three responses which could be said to be antagonistic to anxiety: assertiveness, sexual interest, and self-governed relaxation. With respect to ordinary phobias, as opposed to social and sexual anxieties, it is the third type of response which has become important: patients can be given training in progressive muscular relaxation or, alternatively, a sort of self-induced, semi-hypnotic state, which would limit the capacity to feel afraid. Wolpe solved his second problem by suggesting that the mere imagination of the phobic object should conjure up enough anxiety to enter into the deconditioning process and that such deconditioning would generalize to the real-life situation. Thus, by imagining oneself closer and closer to one's source of fear but always remaining relaxed and never moving ahead too fast, Wolpe envisaged the successful extinction of a phobia. He was right. This method of *systematic desensitization* has had tremendous success in the eradication of many phobias, particularly relatively clear-cut and simple phobias, and it is still one of the most widely-practised behavioural therapy techniques. That said, it is still a matter of much debate as to why the technique works, and Wolpe's original rationale in terms of reciprocal inhibition is not the only one nor the most plausible.

This is instanced by the more recent success of another behavioural technique which is so much the opposite of desensitization at first appearance that it would seem to contradict the rationale of the earlier treatment. It is called 'flooding'—the patient is literally flooded with as much anxiety as possible in the presence or imagined presence of his phobic object. Under the supervision of the therapist he is encouraged to tolerate as much anxiety as he can until the anxiety is forced to dissipate itself by the very passage of time. The fear that such a procedure may make the patient worse is very much contradicted by experience and, indeed, sometimes the phobia is cleared up in remarkably fewer sessions than required by desensitization. The fact that both methods of treatment have creditable track records suggests an at least partly shared rationale: both treatments deliberately confront patients with the source of their fears and both treatments, at different paces, could be said to be teaching a certain tolerance of anxiety which may effectively prevent the patient from allowing fear to feed on fear to the point of panic-responding. In a simple fashion, both treatments refuse to reward the patient for escaping from the source of his fears; equally simply, learning theory states that a systematically unrewarded response will be supplanted in an organism's repertoire of behaviour.

Although not all neurotics have phobias, it is still true that phobic features are present in a number of cases of general anxiety neurosis, and, thus, the treatments described have some place in therapy. Moreover, it is possible for the therapist to identify inner sources of anxiety—thoughts and preoccupations—which he may wish to desensitize. In this way these treatments can be seen as general techniques for anxiety relief.

The behaviourally-orientated therapist adopts, in the case of neurotic patients in general, an attitude which can best be described as 'problem-solving'. He tries to see the patient as being under the control (in a learning theory sense) of his present environment, rather than being the victim of his past lingering on in the form of inner and unconscious determinants of his present behaviour. The difference is one of emphasis. In stressing the present situation, the therapist can try to discover real contingencies between the way the patient feels and acts and the shifting background of his immediate environment, including the way other people behave towards the patient himself. By focusing on particular sources of anxiety, the therapist may be in a position to encourage the patient to experiment with new and alternative responses which, in turn, will shape a new environment which will, in its turn, shape the patient's existing modes of feeling and acting. The same sort of strategy is often used to treat depressed patients, who may be seen as having lost control over sources of 'reinforcement' in environment as a result of a severe upheaval, such as a loss of a loved one. The traditional emphasis on past history, beloved of psychoanalysis, is not totally ignored by the eclectic Behaviourist; he is, however, usually, and correctly, quick to point out that current factors maintaining abnormal behaviour are possibly more important than past factors precipitating such behaviour.

Finally, with respect to neurosis and depression, it needs to be said that psychological treatment is still very time-consuming, especially in view of the numbers of possible patients seeking it. It is therefore not surprising that chemotherapy (use of drugs) has come to play an important role in bringing symptom-relief, just as is the case in schizophrenia. Minor tranquillizers such as the benzodiazepines (Valium and Librium) are prescribed in millions, to combat anxiety. In the case of depression, drugs of the tricyclic group are often extremely valuable even when psychological therapy is offered, since really depressed patients can start off so low that they are effectively beyond other means of help.

FURTHER READING

Abnormal psychology and applied clinical psychology is one of the largest branches of psychology as a whole. The interested reader should, therefore, if he wants to know more about the subject, first consult one of the introductory text books in the field—the Davison and Neale text has already been mentioned—and these texts can, in turn, guide the reader towards books on specific topics. In addition, there are many journals specializing in this area. Some are quite geared to the practising of clinical psychology as a profession; others, such as the *Journal of Abnormal Psychology*, publish a more wide-ranging selection of papers.

PSYCHOLOGY AS A SOCIAL SCIENCE

It is sometimes said—indeed it is sometimes the subject of an examination question—that all psychology is social psychology. This is really one of those rather frustrating 'it all depends on what you mean' remarks. It is true that (as far as we can guess) very little normal development would take place if a child were reared in complete isolation. (The nearest examples are the 'feral' children: but there is never any certainty that they were normal to start with.) On the other hand, it is not true that you cannot study any important aspects of behaviour without taking all the social factors into account simultaneously. All the preceding Sections demonstrate that.

Conversely, there are many aspects of behaviour which are more or less defined by their social context. It is meaningless to speak of racial prejudice without the existence of at least two races, or of group dynamics without a group. Just as with physiological psychology, there is a fairly distinct group of social psychologists who have developed particular techniques for dealing with these sorts of behaviour. And there is, once again, the question of deciding on an appropriate level of explanation.

25 The foundations of social behaviour
JUDY GAHAGAN

Introduction

Human behaviour and experience always occurs within some kind of social context. A hermit, isolated in the wilderness and fending for himself, nevertheless brings with him knowledge, ideas, feelings, and attitudes from the social environment he has left behind. They colour his experience of his solitary state.

The social context affects not only the ways in which we perceive form and colour, form judgements about actions and people, and develop theories about the world past and present, it also affects the ways in which we relate to other people. This implies that psychological processes in different cultures and at different periods of history may take varied forms. Our task as psychologists is to unravel those psychological processes which are a product of social context from those which are invariant. Social psychology is specifically concerned with the ways in which social contexts do influence psychological processes. It is additionally concerned with how people interact with one another and influence the behaviour of one another. In this Chapter we shall focus on some common ways in which social environments determine behaviour and experience, and affect patterns of interaction. Before we do this, however, it is useful to consider some very general characteristics of social life among humans, social life amongst other species, and the parallels which can be observed.

Compared with any non-human species, human behaviour shows astonishing variations. For example, in response to threat or attack, humans have the capacity to attack physically with a large range of weapons and techniques, to attack verbally using strategies ranging from sarcasm to direct insult, to stay silent and impassive, or to turn the other cheek. Which response occurs depends on the actor's interpretation of the reason for the attack, the circumstances surrounding it, the cultural rules of the group to which the actor belongs, his status within the group, his age, sex, personality, and so forth. The most intelligent of the higher primates will display many fewer ways of reacting to threat or attack. This potential variability characterizes human responses, not just to attack or threat, but to many common situations. This large repertoire of behaviour potentially available to humans means that it is complex to understand and furthermore potentially very unpredictable. If any one of a range of fifty possible reactions to a situation were equally probable then co-ordinating our behaviour to others would be impossible and social life would be chaotic. In fact, social life runs relatively smoothly, and people show a degree of predictability which makes it possible for us to anticipate their actions and to behave in accordance with this anticipation. Two men meet at the entrance to their offices, exchange glances, smiles, perfunctory remarks about the weather, and, after a very slight moment of confusion, one will hold the door, the other pass through, and they will part amicably. All this occurs with no problem or even much thought on the part of either actor. Yet, such a co-ordinated sequence involves complex processes of prediction feedback and adjustment. Many processes and mechanisms of social behaviour appear to have evolved to reduce the uncertainty and unpredictability which could follow from man's complex intellectual processes and large repertoire of responses. Some of these processes will become apparent in the ensuing discussion. Let us start, however, by comparing social life amongst other species with the social life of human beings.

Social behaviour in non-human species

As we saw in Chapter 9, social life in animals is functionally related to their survival. The major dimensions of social behaviour are concerned with mating, care of the young, territoriality and dominance, protection from predators, and, in some species such as termites, co-operative behaviour, serving all these functions.

Sexual and reproductive behaviour constitutes a large sector of social behaviour in many species. However, there is great variety across species in the form these take. Sexual behaviour, for example, varies in the elaborateness of the courtship rituals involved and the permanence of the behaviour ensuing from sexual contact. Gibbons, for example, form permanently mated pairs, whereas sexual behaviour amongst many herd animals consists of a single contact. Similarly, with social behaviour arising out of parent-offspring relationships, complexity and extent of care and contact varies. Elephants, for example, show both prolonged care and fierce protection of the young. At the other end of the scale cuckoos lay eggs and then abandon them. In many species the male plays no parental role at all. Offspring care involves more than protection and sustenance, it involves training and preparation for independence. Amongst birds, cats and dogs, to mention a few, complex behaviour associated with training the young is an important component of parental care.

Another major sector of social behaviour is concerned with ritualistic displays of dominance and with fighting. This sector of social behaviour fulfills a number of purposes. Much of the fighting and competition within the species is territorial in nature, that is, it is limited to each individual establishing and controlling a territory for himself. Territorial behaviour ensures dispersal of the species and, therefore, adequate food supplies. Territoriality is also a component of reproductive fighting. In song birds, for example, failure to establish a territory entails a failure to mate and therefore to reproduce. Where territoriality is not a component of mating behaviour, competitive fighting between males for females is, nevertheless, widespread and tends to lead to the strongest and fittest member of the species obtaining priority in mating and reproduction. Aggressive competition is often not restricted to the mating season. Some species establish a dominance hierarchy (or pecking order) which is maintained all the time. This order ensures that priority for food and access to females is allocated to the more dominant member. Because fighting in animals infrequently results in injury to an individual, being limited to ritualistic displays of dominance and submission or appeasement gesture by the defeated, it does not endanger the survival of the species as a whole.

Co-operative behaviour amongst other species is most marked in termites and bees. Here, a complex division of labour exists, in which some ants are workers foraging, carrying food, and building the nest, others are soldier ants who protect the group from predators, and others are solely concerned with reproduction. Although co-operative behaviour of this sort appears closely analogous to human social behaviour the mechanisms responsible for it are very different.

The behaviours briefly described here constitute the major areas of social behaviour in other species. There are two further areas of interest: play, and grooming behaviour. The young of many species and the adults of some engage in play both solitary and social. In no species is play as complete and as socially-orientated as in man. Grooming refers to the mutual cleaning behaviour which can be observed in cats, monkeys, and other animals. This behaviour has no obvious parallels in human social behaviour, although there have been suggestions (Argyle, 1969) that it might be akin to the 'small talk' or phatic communication which humans indulge in in certain kinds of encounter. The significance and functions of these two types of behaviour are obscure and their

579

parallels in man difficult to draw. For this reason they will not be discussed further at this point. Let us turn now to those patterns of social behaviour which show a clearer biological continuity from animals to man.

Some parallels between animal and human social behaviour

When we consider those patterns of behaviour which are found universally across different human societies and cultures, we realize that these are the patterns serving clear biological functions and which have clear parallels with behaviour patterns found in other species. A great deal of our behaviour is quite obviously about sex and reproduction, parents and children, dominance and aggression, co-operation and play. It is equally true, too, though, that much social behaviour in humans is not obviously related to biological processes. However, for the moment let us stay with the obvious patterns and see in what ways they provide a basis for social relationships, Although biologically-based social behaviour is universal, the forms which it takes vary from culture to culture. For example, sexual behaviour is regulated in some way in most societies, not by biological factors, but by beliefs and rules particular to a society. This is so, too, with respect to patterns of child-bearing, as with dominance and status and co-operation. Let us look in more detail at these basic patterns, beginning with patterns of behaviour arising out of the regulation of sexual conduct.

Social structure

The regulation of sexual behaviour and marriage

Societies vary in the ways in which sexual behaviour is regulated. In the first place there is enormous variation in the degree to which it is regulated. In some societies, sexual behaviour is restricted to marriage relationships; in other societies, marriage is only one of several settings for sexuality. Almost all societies, however, whether restrictive or permissive, recognize some form of marriage as a legitimate context for sexual behaviour—usually the most important one.

Forms of marriage vary. In western society, we are accustomed to monogamous marriage, although this varies from one culture to another in how far it is lifelong, divorce not being recognized, or serial in which an individual, over the years, may divorce and marry several times. However, in many parts of the world, the wealthier men of the community may take several wives concurrently. In other parts of the world, women may take several husbands concurrently. These two forms are called polygamy and polyandry respectively. Marriage varies, too, in the degree of choice couples exercise with respect to their marriage partner.

In many societies the marriage of a couple forms an important link and basis for economic exchange and co-operation, and the social group into which an individual can marry is closely specified. Marriage, then, does more than regulate sexual behaviour, it legitimates offspring, provides a principle for the inheritance of property and forges economic and co-operative links between different groups. It forms the basic unit of the family. For, even in polygamous societies, a man, his several wives, and their children often constitute several distinct nuclear families. And in societies where biological paternity is less important than social paternity, a woman's husband will have his own distinct role with respect to her children, even though they are not his. Marriage provides for legitimate sexual contact between a man and a woman. However, it is a contract which binds a couple in many other respects. Marriage normally carries with it rights and obligations on the part of the couple to each other—in our society, a wife has a right to economic support and a man to domestic support. In other societies a wife may be obliged to work on her husband's land, and he may be obliged to share his property with her. Similarly, beliefs about the relationship and the behaviour proper to it vary widely. In our society, we stress equality and intimacy, but in many, distance and inequality between the couple is considered a desirable characteristic. This is reflected in the arrangements for and sentiments surrounding the selection of marriage partners. In our society, we think of strong emotional and physical attraction between a couple as a legitimate, even essential basis for marriage. We may have further views about compatibility of personality and interests as important bases for a marriage relationship. Yet, both views are fairly unusual across the world's cultures. Often, people will have no choice at all about their marriage partners, the arrangement being left to negotiations between the families and kinship groups concerned. The important criteria for mate selection in such societies are to do with economic links between the families involved; and, although personal qualities are relevant, they are qualities to do with health, industry, and stability, rather than uniquely personal ones. By and large, it is assumed that the necessary attractions and sentiments will result from marriage itself. Romantic love is an experience produced by the economic and social conditions and the religious philosophies that have been prevalent in modern societies for some time. Even in our society, where mate selection is presumed to be a function of attraction, in fact, many hidden social factors influence choice of partners. For example, homogamy is a rule of mate selection rather than an exception. Homogamy refers to the mating of people of similar social characteristics, such as social class, religious affiliation, age, ethnic group, and even occupational specialization. Of course, in densely populated communities even choosing a partner from the same class, age, religion, and ethnic group still leaves a pretty wide choice and therefore opportunity for personal attraction to operate in bringing people together.

The character of married relationships also depends on the economic and social status accorded to the sexes. In many societies, women have inferior status to men and this is also reflected in the kinds of sentiments which the partners are supposed ideally to hold for one another. The superior economic position of men in our society is supported by a popular view that men are assertive and women compliant and this stereotype has often shaped people's behaviour in marriage and their feelings about it. However, in many societies wives and husbands may have similar, and similarly important, economic roles, and stereotypes about gender differences in personality are not firmly held. To summarize at this point, we can see that sexual behaviour is regulated in various ways and that its regulation provides the basis for a variety of patterns of interaction. Even though sexual acts may be universally identical, beliefs and sentiments attached to them vary widely.

Parent-child relationships

As with animals, a large sector of social behaviour is that which occurs between parents and offspring. Beliefs about child-rearing and even about the notion of childhood itself vary widely across cultures and periods of history. In our own society at the present time, where life-expectancy is high, childhood is a prolonged phase of life compared with some cultures where the physically viable child was, and still is, treated as an adult. However, we must remember that attitudes towards and beliefs about pregnancy, childbirth, and the neo-natal phase vary considerably, so that a child's very earliest experiences are affected by the culture into which he has been born. It is neither possible nor necessary to document these variations here, but worth perhaps noting some of the more significant ones. In many parts of the world where pregnancy and childbirth have minimal medical attention, a woman continues her normal activities up to and immediately after the birth. In fairly recent history here a woman would be secluded and her movement curtailed for a prolonged period before and after the birth. Births in modern society are often attended only by medical personnel. In many parts of the world a woman would be surrounded by a group of relatives. A baby here is usually put in his own bed and often his own room for long periods of time, starting at birth. In many parts of the world the baby is held continuously by his mother or, more often, by a variety of women who will probably feed him as well. This means that the infant, from birth, is involved in adult community life from the start, whereas here he is secluded from it. Childhood, in our society, constitutes a specific and prolonged life-phase. Children remain dependent on their parents financially, legally and emotionally well beyond puberty. In our society, children wear different clothes to adults, have special artifacts, such as toys, created for them and are largely absolved from the obligations of adult life. We have theories about children's needs and capacities at various ages, and they are educated in accordance with these theories in institutions secluded from the main adult community. Again, when considered historically and cross-culturally, this view of childhood is quite rare. In many parts of the world, children participate in adult activities as soon as they are physically viable even if certain kinds of roles are withheld until puberty. In most societies, infants are treated indulgently—probably more so than in our own society. However, frequently, children are not awarded any special care or consideration and are expected to fend for themselves. Again, this contrasts with our own society, where children, ideally, if not in reality, are awarded a very special kind of concern.

In the next Chapter on socialization we shall look into different kinds of child-rearing practice in various cultures. At this stage, we simply need to understand that conceptions of childhood profoundly affect the way in which parents and children behave to one another and the kinds of sentiments which characterize the relationship. Thus, a parent may expect to influence and control his child's behaviour as well as physically caring for him—or he may exert no authority over his child at all but simply maintain the bond through affection. Similarly, a child may expect to respect and even fear his parents and to anticipate caring for them in old age, even though they still have authority over him. The exclusive and secluded ties of the small family child to his two parents, especially his mother, are characteristic of our society but fairly rare across time and space. In most societies, women have economic functions to fulfil which are not affected by childbearing. The care of infants and children is shared by an extended group of relatives of different generations. It is highly likely that the emotional intensity of parent-child relationships in our society are not characteristic of cultures where the child is brought up in a wide network of adults.

Kinship

In discussing two basic types of social relationships, those generated by the regulation of sexual behaviour through marriage, and those generated by reproduction, we have isolated the two elements which provide the basis for systems of kinship. These systems are, in many societies, responsible for a large section of social relationships and behaviour.

All human societies recognize links between people brought about by blood relations and by marriage. These ties link together groups of people through gift exchange, rights to assistance, and obligations to aid.

They are also cemented by rules governing the proper conduct and sentiments between members of different kinship relations.

In our society, kinship is less of a major principle for organizing social relations than it is in many societies. This is partly indexed by the number of kinship terms existing in the lexicons of different languages. For example, we have the single words 'aunt' and 'uncle' referring to four distinct types of relationship: mother's brother/sister; father's brother/sister; mother's brother's/sister's spouse; father's brother's/sister's spouse. In societies where there are important differences between these relations, the language will index that difference by having four distinct terms for 'aunt' and 'uncle'. In some societies, individuals are able to trace their complicated relationships with several hundred people.

The status and importance of different categories of relatives are a function of principles of lineage. In a matrilineal society, the family name is passed through the mother and the female line, as are property, goods, and money. In a patrilineal society, it is passed through the male members. In our society, names are passed patrilineally, but property may go through either males or females. Principles of lineage are often accompanied by characteristic patterns of residence. In many matrilineal societies, a man on marrying goes to live in his wife's village or in her mother's house. In a patrilineal society, a woman will live with her husband and his male relatives in their village or house. These principles often carry with them constraints on marriage partners, for example, cross-cousin marriage is often a favoured arrangement in matrilineal societies.

Relationships of kinship have implications for behaviour in a number of ways. For example, in most societies and even in our own society, where kinship is relatively unimportant, kin have priority in gift-exhange and in hospitality. In our society, we are more likely to give presents to relatives than non-kin on ritual occasions like Christmas and birthdays. Similarly, people expect to spend some time at Christmas with immediate relatives and to offer and receive hospitality from them. This is so even in our society, where we may not get on with our relatives and be quite prepared to admit to antipathies. In many societies such gift exchanges would be more important, more frequent, and closely specified for different categories of relatives. Of course, in simpler societies, economic co-operation between relatives is absolutely necessary and has an entirely different status to the rather vague, loose obligations we know here.

Within a kinship system we can see rights and obligations which constrain peoples' behaviour towards one another and their feelings about one another. We can also see different patterns of authority and influence. Some kinship positions carry greater prestige and power than others. In a matrilineal society, both the maternal grandmother and her eldest son will have considerable influence and authority over other members. In a patrilineal system, the oldest male may enjoy that position. In a polygamous family, the husband's first wife and perhaps his favourite will enjoy prestige and power not accorded to his other wives. Age and principles of lineage determine patterns of authority; and in simpler societies this authority is very real, since the economic resources will be controlled by the highest-status member. In our society, very little authority resides within the kinship system once children have established themselves in work. In general, influence and status decline rather than increase with age, again a feature specific to our society.

Marriage, parenthood, and kinship are the fundamental biological principles which underlie large sections of social behaviour in man and the first two are closely paralleled in animal societies. There are further principles which are important in humans: age, gender, and occupational specialization. The first two vary across societies in importance; the second is particularly important in modern societies.

Age

We mentioned earlier the rule of homogamy in mate selection, one aspect of which is that people tend to marry within a few years of their own age group, women tending to be slighty younger. Age, however, is an important determinant of social relations other than marriage. In our society, because of the prolonged and specialized education from pre-school to college, which young people receive, most of our social contact is with people of the same age. Even in adulthood, the retired tend to be segregated from the rest of the community; and patterns of housing in Britain and America particularly lead to young marrieds living in close proximity to other couples of the same age, and similarly for older groups. Age-grading, a technical term for this principle, is particularly marked at adolescence in our society. The adolescent consumes products especially designed for him, occupies leisure spaces reserved for his age group, and in general constitutes a segregated, clearly identifiable culture. His closest friends will be other adolescents. In many societies, adolescence is not a recognizable phase, since at puberty, after initiation the child becomes a fully-functioning adult. The indeterminate phase we call adolescence, where, for some functions the individual has a child status and for other functions adult status is not widespread.

The importance of age as a principle organizing social relationships is not confined to our own society. Though it is true that in many parts of the world people of different generations participate in the affairs of the community and interact with one another to a greater extent than here, there are examples of simple societies where age-grading is important. In some African societies, males born within a number of years of each other are recognized as being in an age grade. In particular, they will go through an initiation ceremony together. The nature of the relationship is quite clearly specified. Members of the same age-grade are friends and are absolutely obliged to offer each other hospitality, gifts, help, and even to share their wives with each other. They are brought up together, live in the same huts, go on hunting and warring parties together, and so forth.

The importance of age in our own society stems from prolonged socialization and education process and also from the organization of work which, in different jobs, follows distinct phases and usually culminates in rather early retirement.

Gender

In all societies, men and women are marked off from one another in some way—by dress and artifacts, by attitudes and work, and by rules about personal conduct.

Dress and artifacts are the most obvious ways in which men and women differ in most places. Dress and cosmetics probably originate in sexual display, which is an intrinsic part of sexuality. We are accustomed to thinking of sexual display as a peculiarly female characteristic. That is, it is women who adorn and paint themselves and wear a wide variety of clothes and hair styles. Considered historically and cross-culturally, however, this is not an exclusively female characteristic. In, for example, eighteenth century England men and women preoccupied themselves equally with personal adornment and grooming. In the Marquesan Islands, it is the men who are expected to be beautiful and desirable and groom and dress themselves accordingly. Human societies offer the whole range of differentiation in this respect. The norms governing dress and appearance in men and women are not lightly held. In many societies, an individual who appears in garb reserved for the opposite sex not only arouses consternation and ridicule but often sanctions against him too. It should be easy to see how customs relating to such apparently superficial areas of behaviour such as dress, might permeate experience of sexual relationships and feelings about sexual identity.

The question of job specialization by gender is closely linked with the legal and political status that women have in a society. For the most part, the wider the range of activities which are equally available to men and women the more similar is their political and legal status. Our ideas of kinds of work women are able to do is extended during periods of change and crisis, like war time, and by the example provided by societies where explicit attempts are made to minimize the gender factor, as, for example, in some communist countries. There, we see women as builders and train drivers and aeroplane pilots. Increasingly, in non-communist European countries we see men as nurses, nursery teachers and child-minders in the family home. Currently, in our own society, however, it is still the case that technology, heavy industry and hard manual work is done by men, with women predominantly in teaching, nursing, social work, and in subordinate roles in commercial settings. The main points here are twofold.

Firstly, the range of activities taken up by men and women is considerably influenced by their social and political environment, and this varies across time and place. Secondly, the division of activities is partly maintained by theories about the basic disposition of men and women and, thus, becomes self-perpetuating. Thus, the theoretical notion that women are emotional and intuitive and their interest focused on interpersonal matters, may be based on real physiological differences between the majority of men and the majority of women. Whether they are so based or not, this belief will lead to girls being brought up and educated in a manner appropriate to the belief.

Occupational specialization
In many simple societies, most jobs can be and are done by most people, although men and women may carry out different functions. In a society whose economy is based on fishing, hunting and some agriculture, with carving, building, and pottery any adult male will acquire the relevant skills for all these jobs, as will the women, for those jobs customarily allocated to them.

In technologically advanced societies, the volume of knowledge and techniques required for many jobs is such that people have to specialize in order to master them. Furthermore, mass production of goods is so organized that the individuals comprising the labour force have to spend most of their time engaged in a single activity, as, for example, on a production line and, even though the work itself requires little skill, it demands both time and complex schedules to co-ordinate the efforts of the different sections of labour.

In many simple societies, no particular division is made between 'work' and leisure. People simply continue with the particular tasks which provide subsistence until they are done, and work is not necessarily continuous, or regular. Many activities, like fishing, carving, and pottery are engaged in for their own sake anyway and in our society would be regarded as 'play' rather than work.

Occupation, however, is an important source of social relationships, particularly in our society, and particularly for men. Shared burdens, hazards, and interest in occupational settings create the conditions for strong ties of friendship. Shared interests and knowledge provide the basis for attachment amongst members of professions. Professional associations and conferences, although having the instrumental function

587

of disseminating knowledge among members of that profession, also have components which are obviously to do with sociability and the formation of friendship ties. Although rights and obligations to members of the same profession or job are not explicitly laid down, semi-formal systems often emerge purely for extending help and support to members and their dependants who are in need. Furthermore, 'leisure' activities, too, may be provided within the work context. Many firms and factories have sports and social clubs and even clubs for activities like music and drama.

Of course, the ties and interdependence generated by shared occupations have political functions, and the trade union is the most formal system for organizing the activities and safeguarding the interest of its members. It is sufficient at this point simply to illustrate the importance of work as a context for the formation of relationships and attitudes.

Locality and community

In both animal and human societies, geographical proximity can produce networks of social relations and a basis for organizing interests and activities. Except perhaps in the case of the dormitory suburbs of industrial countries, people living in a common locale acknowledge ties which are absent between them and people of a different locale. These ties are often a shared obligation to offer help and friendship but they may also bring about norms of conduct, for example, in 'expensive' neighbourhoods where children 'don't play in the street' or the village where gardens are 'beautifully maintained'.

In simpler societies than ours, ties of kinship and ties of locality may completely overlap since the extended families of a kin group often live close to one another. In industrial and urban societies this is rarely so, although it is more common in working class communities. Often, there is an overlap between occupational specialization and locality. For example, in mining villages, the vast majority of men work at similar jobs in the same pit.

The term 'stranger', in many societies, means an individual who is not a kinsman and comes from different locality. Differentiation between 'strangers' and 'familiars' is an important dimension of social behaviour in many societies. Strangers bring about varied reactions across the world. These range from customs of extreme and lavish hospitality offered automatically to any stranger to customs permitting automatic murder of any stranger. These are very rare in our own society, although we can document instances where a stranger in extreme need has been ignored by passers by, and we can similarly document the overwhelming response to strangers caught in a disaster. We shall consider this topic a bit more closely later in the Chapter.

Ties of locality or community generate shared rules of conduct as well as providing a basis for co-operation and shared, social activities. These rules of conduct range from religious beliefs and political affiliation to customs of entertainment and dress. Such rules and social ties are more strongly maintained in isolated communities where there is little movement in or out of them. Such isolation anywhere is nowadays fairly rare and we have to travel away from industrial societies to find pure examples of local communities unaffected by influences from outside.

One important feature of geographical proximity is the emergence of particular manners of speech which we call dialect. Dialects are most distinguished by their deviant pronunciation rules but often they include different vocabularies and rules of grammar (as for example the absence of the article in Lancashire dialects). Special forms of language can be shared by very small groups of people indeed. One may be able to distinguish several dialects in the different quarters of a large town. Although speakers of different dialects of a language can usually understand each other, the dialect has the important function of marking off individuals as members of a particular community—thus, it can mark off one community from another and express communal solidarity to the outsider.

Communities may evolve rules of conduct and shared beliefs and customs. Perhaps more importantly, communities can function to maintain conformity to rules and beliefs derived from the larger society. For example, rules about drinking and about sexual conduct may originate in state legislation and religious institutions. But it is the neighbours' eyes and tongues which bring about conformity to them since neither Church nor State can provide continuous surveillance of everyone's behaviour. It is this process which leads many people to believe that the erosion of kinship and locality ties has produced more anti-social and criminal behaviour than was formerly prevalent. How far this is true it is hard to establish, but mobility means that conduct has to be regulated by some process other than by the opinions of the immediate social group.

Status and dominance

One important component of social behaviour in other species, which was discussed earlier, was the establishment of dominance or status hierarchies. During the discussion of social structure in human societies, status was touched on as a component of kinship relations and of relations between the sexes. Let us focus on status more precisely. Human societies share, to varying extents, the idea of differential worth amongst their members. This differential worth may be indicated as expressions of esteem or by the allocation of rights and duties. Typically, high-status members of a society enjoy privileges and incur responsibilities which are different from those of lower-status members. The prime minister, for example, has a right to two fine houses, first class travel by train and air, and a chauffeur driven car, as well as the obligation to be involved in political affairs during most of his waking hours. Societies vary in the degree to which status is an important dimension, and the degree to which it is rigidly assigned. Caste systems, such as those known in India until very recently, are examples of status as an important dimension of social life and one which is rigidly assigned. People born into a particular caste, whose boundaries derive from religious beliefs, are assigned a particular range of occupations which determine their wealth or poverty and, thus, their living conditions. They also determine with whom, and on what basis, they may have social relationships. Marriage, for example, may be rigidly restricted to partners of the same caste. In contrast, some European democratic societies such as Denmark and some primitive societies, found, for example, in the Amazon regions, show markedly fewer signs of status hierarchies.

We normally make a distinction between status which is achieved and status which is ascribed. The latter is well exemplified by caste systems, where, from birth, one's status is established and cannot be altered. It is also exemplified by societies where age or sex provide a basis for status. With sex, as with caste, one's status is unalterable and many societies award higher status to men than to women. With age, higher status may be tied to a particular phase in life—in some societies it is later life; in our society, if at all, it is to younger people. The point is that, once the appropriate age has been reached, the status is awarded and is automatically enjoyed. Achieved status on the other hand is brought about by the individual's own activities. In our society, for example, it is usually through work and profession; in societies like that of communist China, it is through political activity and commitment. The important point about achieved status is that, theoretically, it is open to almost everyone to achieve it and also that achieved status can be lost again.

With both achieved and ascribed status, societies vary in the qualities or activities of the individual which are necessary. In some societies, physical strength, among both men and women, is a characteristic which receives esteem and possibly recognition. In our society, academic intelligence and physical beauty are widely admired. In fact, our society recognizes an interesting mixture of achieved and ascribed status. For example, physical beauty, particularly in women, may provide the holder with high status; intelligence may produce the same effect. Both are, arguably, examples of characteristics which cannot be achieved and are therefore bases for ascribed status. On the other hand, qualities like initiative, bravery, hard work, can also carry status, though these qualities are brought about by the individual's behaviour.

Status invites esteem from other people and it usually carries differing patterns of rights and obligations. For example, train drivers and social workers may enjoy esteem from many people in society but, typically, they do not enjoy the same allocation of money and its attendant pleasures as rock stars or footballers. Again, prime ministers and brain surgeons get high salaries and enjoy a comfortable standard of living but, compared with rock stars and footballers, their obligations are of a different order. Looking at society from a distant vantage point, one can obtain a fairly clear picture of status arrangement from examining the differential allocations of money, property, possessions, and space. This vantage point does not, however, allow us to see very clearly the esteem that higher status members enjoy, and in a complex society like our own a myriad different viewpoints will produce very different attitudes towards social status.

In modern societies, this structure is embodied in the idea of social class. Social class rests variously in accumulated or inherited wealth or on occupation. Occupations differ in different countries in terms of the status they carry although in most countries professions involving long training and specialized skills carry more status than others. Social class is measured objectively by reference to some scale which classifies occupations according to skills involved, prior education, and earning power. Although it can be measured objectively this does not mean that all people are necessarily very aware of their class membership. Nowadays, although we attempt to minimize the importance of social class in people's lives, nevertheless, class, based on occupation, has a persuasive influence on life-styles, that is patterns of leisure and consumption, housing, sociability, attitudes toward child-rearing, and political views. Patterns of consumption of goods and life style in modern life expose social class or status in a particularly significant way through status symbols. Status symbols are personal possessions or even activities (like going to film premieres or to the opera) which accrue to a status group and therefore, indeed, to an individual as a member of that group. Frequently, of course, people try to get hold of status symbols which index the group they aspire to join. The importance of the symbolic aspects of status are clearly seen in advertising where products are presented as being the symbols of a higher prestige group than the majority of people actually belong to. It is clear, too, that many people, beyond a certain level of affluence, are concerned more with the symbolic nature of material things than with their actual convenience, usefulness, beauty, or value, although their function may be seen as valuable and important by many people.

The whole question is a complex one and it is not necessary to examine it in more detail here. Two points, however, should be stressed. One is that status arrangements can contribute to a division of labour and a more or less agreed allocation of resources. The second point, arising out of the first, is that, where a status order is established, these things do not need to be continually disputed. The advantage is there can be a certain continuity and therefore predictability in social life. Finally, it is important to remember that dominance and submission in social life are very pervasive, whether we are talking about competition between business managers, academics, football teams, or people involved in casual and informal discussions. Many people are concerned to control their own outcomes and to control other people's behaviour, and this process, contributing to status, can be identified in everyday behaviour. Thus, the status dimension in society affects people's behaviour, opinions, and their evaluations of themselves.

Among other species, the existence of status hierarchies appears to have a direct biological function, that of giving priority in food and mating to the strongest members. The establishment of such hierarchies is brought about by the male of the species. The idea that status structures allow dominant members of a society to exercise power and weaker members to remain subordinate and to accept influence is a pervasive underlying theme in some political ideologies. Yet it is clearly counteracted both by other beliefs and by values which have gained ground over many hundreds of years. If we look at human societies, it is difficult to tell how status arrangements contribute to optimal functioning and, thus, to survival. As we have seen, many people enjoying high status do not necessarily perform very useful functions.

Two further aspects of status should be mentioned: status congruence, and distributive justice. Status congruence refers to the arrangement whereby symbols of status are comparable across the various areas of an individual's activities. For example, a managing director probably has wall-to-wall carpeting in his office, a large desk, and his own cloakroom. Not only that, he probably has a special parking place allocated to him, and perhaps someone parks his car for him. Furthermore, he is expected to wear expensive suits and to carry quality props around with him in the form of a good, leather brief-case, silver cigarette-case, and so forth. Groups go to a good deal of trouble to maintain status congruence, so that the entire array of status symbols accruing to a high-status person are all superior to the array of status symbols held by a lower-status individual.

Distributive justice refers to an arrangement where a person's resources or characteristics are seen to be commensurate with his rewards. For example, at work, a person may acquire status through seniority or age, through recognized qualifications, through acknowledged skills, or some form of relevant experience. It is then expected that his outcomes in the form of pay and working conditions should excel those of someone lacking those resources and therefore of lower status. The notion of distributive justice is a pervasive phenomenon: for example, it can be seen quite clearly in the maintenance by trade unions of 'differentials' in pay structure, and is clearly the single most potent force in producing satisfaction or dissatisfaction with wages, and living standards.

Roles, norms, and stereotypes

Roles

We have looked at some of the most general patterns of social behaviour which emerge from a study of social structure. It is now possible to approach the study of individual social behaviour a little more closely. Social structure refers to the most general principles of social organization. The link between these general principals and the individual is through the social role.

Social roles are slots in a social system and those slots are occupied by individuals. The most widely-recognized roles are those which derive directly from social structure: there are kinship roles, like daughter, father, grandmother; there are gender roles, age roles, and occupational roles. The important point about a social role is that it exists independently of the person occupying it. Take, for example, a football team. The game itself defines the roles that members of the team play. There must be a goal-keeper and similarly a centre forward and a full-back and the other positions if the game is to be properly played. Individuals occupying these parts may play them with different styles and different degrees of success. Nevertheless, much of their behaviour, while engaged in the game, is constrained by the nature of the role requirements. Let us look at the nature of roles systematically.

A social role involves a recognized position or slot and, additionally, a set of expectations about the behaviour of someone occupying it. We can further distinguish between expectations of the role-occupant and his actual role-performance.

Role-positions do not exist in isolation from one another; they interlock and constitute social systems. We cannot conceive of the role of mother without a child, of a teacher without a pupil, of a salesman without customers. From the point of view of the occupants, other roles in a given system are counter-positions and their occupants role-partners. Where one position is countered by many others which are similar, then that position is a focal position. For example, a salesman occupies a focal position for his many customers. It is possible to see many social groups in precisely this way, for example, a family, an office, or a school.

The expectations associated with a role vary along a number of different dimensions. Firstly, they differ in the degree to which there is a general consensus of expectations, covering all aspects of the role. For example, almost everyone will agree that the role of mother implies caring for a child physically when he is unable to look after himself. Most people would similarly agree that a mother should feel and show affection for her child. However, there might be considerably less consensus about whether she should teach him to read, or whether she should spend most of her time playing with him. Even general consensus about caring for the child physically may not imply consensus about the definition of physical care, and mothers may have very different criteria in this respect. It is possible for different role-partners in a system to disagree with one another on many aspects of role-expectation and, further, to disagree with the role-occupant. Nevertheless, for most role expectations there is a hard core of commonly held expectations and an outer layer of controversial ones.

Secondly, role-expectations vary in their permeation. Some roles pervade all areas of the occupant's behaviour, other roles only affect the occupant's behaviour at particular times in particular places. For example, a nun is required to be a particular kind of person, devout, charitable, humble, and chaste all the time. In contrast, a bus conductor as long as he collects the fares, records the transactions, does not overload the bus, and ensures that passengers do not fall off it, can think about whatever he likes. Furthermore, once he is off the bus, and away from the bus station, role-expectations need make no demand on him at all.

Thirdly, some role-expectations may be backed up by sanctions. For example, a mother can be sent to prison for neglecting her child physically but not for failing to teach him to read or for failing to play with him. Many aspects of role-expectations are not backed up, however, by sanctions and it is of considerable interest to ask why people conform to their roles as much as they do. Role-expectations may be formally laid down or explicitly codified. For example, many professional roles involve the signing of a contract before the occupant takes up his position. This contract will specify fairly precisely what the role expectations are. The marriage ceremony, for example, has this feature.

In some cases, professional roles, for example, medical ones, are covered by a code of conduct. These codes do not specify particular expectations about behaviour but lay down certain guiding principles for covering a variety of contingencies. Very often, ceremonies and rituals evolve to establish that the individual has entered a particular role which is publicly impressed on him, and he is asked to make a public commitment to the expectation accruing to the role. A good example of this is the confirmation ceremony or indeed, again, the marriage ceremony.

Role-expectations, then, carry with them norms of behaviour. The word 'norm' has a number of closely-related meanings. It can have a statistical meaning, namely, 'what the majority of people do in this role'.

594

It can mean 'value', namely 'what would be ideal for people to do in this role'. It can mean an explicit rule: 'what all people must do in this role'. The norm involved in role expectations can carry all three meanings. Furthermore, a norm can acquire a kind of superhuman quality so that it appears more as a natural law than as a social contract; as one sociologist has put it, 'the necessary becomes the right'. Gender roles clarify this process well. Women, for example, are expected to be concerned about how they look to a far greater degree than men are. For a women to be excessively unconcerned and for a man to be excessively concerned appears to many people to be unnatural, deviant behaviour. During an earlier discussion, it was pointed out that such a norm is located in particular societies at particular times: it is not a biologically-programmed aspect of gender.

A person, then, in the position of bank manager, will (a) usually be punctual and efficient, or (b) ideally punctual, neat, and efficient or (c) if not punctual, neat, and efficient he will be sacked. These customs, ideals, and rules will affect an individual strongly while he occupies his role-position, because they will be expressed in many obvious and in many subtle ways by the behaviour of his role-partners.

It should not be too difficult at this point to think of the ways in which social roles have profound influence on one's behaviour, and to see that knowledge of someone's role and the expectations associated with it is highly predictive of many areas of his behaviour.

Stereotypes

Stereotypes are shared theories about the personality characteristics of role occupants, and, as such, they can enter into role expectations. However, they generalize some way beyond the role itself. Stereotypes are about characteristics which endure. For example, a stereotype of the bank manager may be that he is honest, punctual, diligent, shrewd, unimaginative, and conventional and these qualities are his whether he is in the bank or at home on holiday or in any other role. Of course stereotypes may be based on some element of truth in the sense that people with particular qualities choose, for example, occupational roles which express them. Nevertheless, they are probably often inaccurate and people may go to some lengths to dissociate their real selves from their role stereotypes. How often, for example does one read of an actor or rock star trying to persuade the general public that he is a modest, unassuming person who most enjoys quiet private family life? Stereotypes become attached to the most general roles in the social structure, like age, sex, and kinship. Young people are radical, rebellious adventurers; old people are conservative, complacent, and timid. Women are emotional, intuitive, narcissistic; men are unemotional, logical, and aggressive. Mothers are kind, long suffering, and self-sacrificing, and so forth. When someone enters a social role for the first time, in some sense he enters a ready-made personality which may fit him well or badly. His experience of and satisfaction with his social slot will vary according to that fit. However, as with role-expectations, some roles involve stronger stereotypes than others do. For example, it is dubious that there are strong stereotypes associated with occupational roles such as printer, or house-decorator, or taxi-driver, whereas artists, social workers, and property speculators, etc., probably elicit much stronger ones.

Multiple-position-occupancy and role conflict

It must be obvious by now that people usually occupy more than one role and some people occupy a great many. A woman, in addition to being a woman, may be simultaneously wife, mother, teacher, and Samaritan. A man may, similarly, be husband, father, solicitor, secretary of a local political organization, and a minor tennis champion. The possibilities of occupying many roles are clearly greater in large, complex societies than in small, simple ones. One role can entail others. for example, being a father usually entails being a husband and always entails being a man. But many roles have no such entailment and then they must be segregated, spatially and temporally, if they are not to collide and cause role conflict.

Social systems are usually structured in such a way that an individual will not encounter expectations deriving from one role when he is engaged in another, or at least not expectations which entail conflicting behaviours. Work is normally segregated in time and space from family life and from leisure activities. Even within the work situation, spaces are so arranged that only consistent role-performance is called for. For example, the formal role-behaviour of a managing director towards his junior subordinates is easily managed within the office but is sustained with more difficulty in the canteen. For this reason, he may use a special entrance and lift and a dining room shared only by other directors.

Nevertheless, it is possible for roles to collide and for the individual to feel conflict. A teacher with her own child in her class is such an example. A corporal promoted to sergeant with his former rank-mates is another example. In both cases, the roles involved entail conflicting expectations. The mother as teacher exercises harsh discipline in the classroom but is more permissive and indulgent with her own child at home. If he misbehaves in the classroom, she has to decide whether to behave as a parent or teacher. Similarly the sergeant has evolved informal equal relationships with his friends which by army protocol are now ruled out by his new rank.

Role-conflict arising out of multiple-position-occupancy is often partly resolved by priority being allocated to particular roles. For example, many organizations make explicit rules about when a familial role may take precedence over an occupational one, so the serious illness or death of a close relative, or moving house will be occasions when a man may abandon, temporarily, his occupational role, its expectation, and obligations, for his familial one. Some large firms may further attempt to reduce such conflict by providing company housing close to work, leisure facilities for whole families, and, indeed, may go so far as interviewing employee's wives when they are taken on in order to both assess her degree of commitment to her husband's occupational role and possibly to her suitability as a partner to it. Even so, many aspects of working life cut across expectations associated with family roles, for example, shift work, frequent travel, and general job mobility.

Other sources of role-strain

Role-strain can arise from other sources than the conflicting expectations arising out of multiple-position-occupancy. Earlier, we saw how role expectations vary in the degree of consensus supporting them, and later, how personal qualities associated with a role may not be matched by the occupant's personality. Let us look at role-strain arising out of lack of consensus. Firstly, there may be lack of consensus between the occupant of a role, on the one hand, and all his role-partners on the other hand. For example, a girl who is used to interacting quite freely with boys, taking the initiative in meeting them, paying for herself, and having definite opinions about how their encounters should be spent, may find, on going to live in another country, that not one of her potential boy role-partners shares her expectations at all. Both she and they will experience puzzlement, embarrassment, and possibly anger; that is, they will all suffer role-strain. Secondly, the expectations of one's role-partners in a social system, may conflict with each other. For example, a headmaster might suppose that he is expected to be concerned with academic work in school. The parents of the children in that school share this expectation. The governors expect him to be largely concerned with administering school finances, and resources. Some teachers think he should largely be concerned with discipline and control, and still others think he should be concerned with public relations and building up the image of the school in the eyes of the local community. Given that each set of role-partners has different expectations, which will lead them to demand of him priority for their own goal, he, too, will feel the strain of their conflicting demands.

Thirdly, consensus about role-expectations may be low because they are vague; that is, no one is very sure what the expectations of that role-occupant actually are. This can happen when a new job is created to cope with a number of vaguely related problems, for example, 'information officer' in a firm where it is, in fact, a new role. The occupant has to create the expectations of it for himself out of the vague formulations inferred from the behaviour of his role-partners and from his own perception of the function of the role in the system. Fourthly, a role may demand certain qualities of the occupant that he simply does not possess. By and large, we expect people to choose roles where the expectations are congruent with their aptitudes and personalities, but they are not always successful in doing so. A retiring and compliant individual may find himself in a situation, as father of teenage children, as leader in a work team where he must exercise direction and authority. In such a case, the actor will again feel role-strain.

Role theory, of which only a brief outline has been provided here, provides a formal analysis of the way in which large sectors of our everyday behaviour and experience are constrained by our positions in a social system. It is an analysis which is sociological rather than psychological since it is concerned rather with the dynamics and demands of a system, rather than the cognitive and affective processes of the individual. Yet it reinforces the view that the latter cannot be understood without reference to the context in which they are occurring. Furthermore, it has been an over-simplistic analysis because it has ignored the fact that individuals respond to expectations of their roles differently and that these responses are generated by factors within the individual. A mother interprets her role in ways which are congruent with her own personality and experience. If she generally feels a lot of hostility, she may pay more attention to the disciplinary aspects of the role than to other aspects. A bank manager who enjoys having a lot of attention from others may spend a lot of time joking with his colleagues, flirting with the secretaries, and being very charming and informal to his clients. Thus, the individual brings idiosyncratic components to his role-performances. Similarly, his manner of resolving problems of role-strain reflects processes arising out of his personality. For example, with multiple-role-occupancy he may rigidly segment the demands of his different roles so that he is unaware of their conflicting demands. Thus, the army chaplain can preach peace and participate in war. He may try to respond fully to all the demands and have a breakdown. He may quite happily ignore some of them and be unconcerned with his relationship with his various role-partners. Nevertheless, a person's personality expresses itself within the constraints of the social system of which he is part.

Social structure, roles, and mass society

Roles, as they have been examined here, stem directly from social structure as it was expounded earlier in the Chapter. Neither analysis does adequate justice to the context of the modern industrial society in which we operate. Both simply provide some principles and framework for examining the potential effect of societal contexts on behaviour and experience. However, in conclusion, let us consider some of the ways in which modern society provides a context for behaviour, transcending our analysis of social structure and social roles. Categories of social structures and the roles which derive from them carry norms and expectations which permeate the conduct and experience of the individuals of that society. No one, except those who are insane or in some altered state of consciousness, can remain quite impervious to the expectations and values of those around him. The reason that social life is a relatively ordered affair is because, sharing so many implicit norms, we can anticipate the behaviour of others and adapt our own behaviour accordingly, participating in, as Irving Goffman the sociologist has put it, 'an infinite regression of mutual consideration'. Yet, the illustration of social roles based on fixed and enduring categories of sex, kinship, and occupation grossly under-represents the complexity and refinements of roles enacted in modern society. Take, for example, the role of 'mother'. Knowing that someone is a mother in our society provides us with only the most general outline of how she is likely to behave and the kind of attitudes she may have. Within such a gross category, we can identify many sub-categories or stereotypes which will be recognized by people within a section of society. A 'mother' can be a tree-climbing, kite-flying fun-mother; she can be a long-suffering, devoted mother; she can be a jolly, indulgent, anything-goes mother; she can be an intellectual, I-just-want-to-get-child-rearing-over mother. Any stereotype that she occupies will have social recognition and she will express this stereotype or identity by clothes and personal style, by verbally expressed attitudes and many other insignia. These will enable those around her to recognize her identity and provide her with the cues to enact this identity. Thus, within the gross social roles generated by the social structure can be found stereotypes which generate identities. By enacting identities and by role-partners responding appropriately to them, social life can run as smoothly as a good production of a Shakespeare comedy (or tragedy). If we behaved towards a 'long-suffering devoted' mother as if she were a 'fun mother', our encounters with her would suffer from a sense of strain. When social interaction is strained or breaks down because participants fail to recognize, or are unable to respond to another's projected identity, the phenomenon we call 'embarrassment' results.

The wit whose joke is old and stale cannot support his momentary claim to his identity of the 'wit'. The 'expert' who suddenly shows ignorance of some fundamental aspect of his field cannot support his claim to his identity of 'expert'. The lady who behaves as if she were an irresistible 'femme fatale', while totally failing to get any response from those present, fails to support her identity. In these examples, both the individuals concerned and those present will experience embarrassment—a sense of discomfort and a momentary inability to continue the encounter. Why is embarrassment contagious in this way? One possibility is that when an actor fails to support his claim to an identity he also invalidates the identities of those present. If, for example, a performer on stage breaks down or, forgets his lines, he makes us all uncomfortable because our identities as audience are also thus undermined. The phenomenon of embarrassment clearly points to (a) the need to elaborate on conceptions of role to include the identities and stereotypes which we project to the outside world, and (b) the realization that a great deal of social interaction is dependent on the mutual recognitions of identities and stereotypes. In spite of its actual importance for understanding social interaction, embarrassment has received very little systematic treatment from social psychologists. Work by Goffman, Gross and Stone (1900) has shown how the breakdown of an encounter, which embarrassment signals, can uncover the implicit underlying rules of that encounter and the dimensions of the participants' identities. Yet we are variously vulnerable to embarrassment, just as we are variously likely to project false or unsupportable identities. The individual psychological factors responsible for this variability remain to be examined.

Different social groups within society have different norms and expectations of behaviour. For example, the role of 'good husband' in a working class community entails different behaviour to that in a middle-class community. In the latter, for instance, far more emphasis will be put on intimacy, shared interests and companionship. Thus, the modern society in which most of us spend our lives consists of a myriad of miniature societies which may differ as much, in many respects, as an American Indian might from an East Anglian farmer. Members of these miniature societies however, unlike the simple societies on which much of our previous discussion has been based, do not all remain in them. People are geographically and intellectually mobile; that is, during a lifetime we may move to different parts of the country, through different institutions, and live in different communities. Even if we do not, through the mass media we are exposed to the customs and conduct of other groups, even if we do not encounter them directly. What are the consequences of this mobility? One major consequence is that the norms of behaviour and definitions of roles which have been acquired in one context may become irrelevant and possibly disapproved of in another context. For example, in one setting, friendly overtures to neighbours is regarded as extremely important and desirable; an another context, they may be regarded as intrusive and irritating. In one community, a lot of emphasis may be placed on one's children appearing immaculate and beautifully dressed; in another, children may uniformly wear old jeans and look fairly scruffy. People moving from one context to another have to adjust their behaviour and expectations accordingly or suffer a sense of social strain. Pure exposure to such different forms of conduct through secondary sources like the media, although less compelling, will nevertheless give us room for some doubt about our dearly-held values. Of course, mobility is not restricted to modern society. Nomadic communities can be found in many parts of the underdeveloped world. The difference is, however, that such communities move as communities. They may move geographically but they carry their social structure, norms and customs, with them. In our society, people move as individuals or nuclear families into strange environments. As individuals, then, they must frequently renegotiate their relationships with others. It is, then, difficult to sustain a view that any codes of conduct and values are right or absolute: they are relative in the sense that they are tied to a particular context at a particular time. Furthermore, earlier in the discussion, it was pointed out that it is one's immediate group which controls conformity to norms and values. We adhere to standards of conduct partly because we are concerned about the opinions of those around us. Yet, mobility may prevent us from establishing sufficient integration into a community for its collective views to have much power to constrain our behaviour. Thus, more constraints have to be generated from within the individual. Not only, then, do his values and norms have to be generated individually, conformity to them has to be sustained individually. It is not surprising that modern sociologists have become preoccupied with problems of deviance (that, is, behaviour which runs counter to the 'official' values of society at large), with problems of anomy and alienation (that is, a state of normlessness in which an individual feels quite uncommitted to a consistent set of role-definitions and moral values). Although these ideas cannot be pursued further here, it must be remembered that they have great relevance for our understanding of mental illness and other forms of social pathology. The mobility and resultant complexity of modern society demands great adaptability. The capacity to react to novel expectations and definitions is a component of healthy survival, and man's cognitive flexibility is specifically geared to realize that necessary adaptability.

26 Social interaction

JUDY GAHAGAN

In Chapter 25 social psychology was presented as the study of two major aspects of human behaviour and experience. The first aspect, considered at some length in that Chapter, is concerned with the effects of social context on cognitive, affective, and behavioural processes. The second aspect is concerned with social interaction, that is, the way we perceive other people, feel about them, the ways in which we may influence one another, and, finally communication. In this Chapter, we shall examine each of these components of social interaction in turn. Let us look first at the processes involved in perceiving other people.

Person perception

In the study of person perception, we are concerned with a number of overlapping processes. We study, for example, the ways in which people perceive one another as physical objects and form impressions of their physical appearances, actions, and the social categories to which they can be assigned. These processes are clearly salient when we consider how people identify and recognize strangers or assign people to role-categories, such as chinese waiter, policeman, drunk, or whatever, on the basis of their physical appearance. We also study the ways in which people perceive one another as psychological entities. People guess at the feelings, intentions, attitudes, and underlying disposition of others and make judgement about their characters. The perception of other people as psychological entities will be the focus of discussion in this section of the Chapter.

The study of person perception is the study of man as psychologist.

Human beings try to make sense of one anothers' behaviour, and they try to predict one anothers' behaviour. In so doing, they are engaging in the same activities with the same objectives as the professional psychologist. The two are trying to make sense of behaviour, decide its causes, and predict future action. The differences between everyman as psychologist and the professional psychologist are twofold. The professional psychologist attempts to follow systematically scientific and logical principles in the inferences that he makes from what he observes, and these principles have to be made explicit to other psychologists. The lay psychologist, on the other hand, may be quite unaware of the reasoning he is following when making inference about others and, indeed, his reasoning may change from one situation to the next. Similarly, he may be unaware of the actual data, or aspects of another's behaviour, which he is using as a basis for judgement, and, therefore, is unlikely to make these bases explicit. However, we must recognize that there may be great individual differences in the extent to which lay psychologists do reason like professional psychologists. The professional psychologist studying the reasoning of man as lay psychologist is not concerned with the validity of that reasoning, only the reasoning itself. For example, we study how people make judgements about personality on the basis of limited information, such as physical appearance or dress. We are not concerned very much with whether such judgements are correct or valid, but with the conditions under which people make such judgements and the steps they follow in their reasoning.

There are certain respects in which the processes involved in perceiving people are similar to those involved in perceiving objects. For example, there is a degree of stability about perception, such that we recognize others as the same, even though we encounter them in different roles and different circumstances. Similarly, we attend only to those aspects of people which are relevant for our purposes at hand, just as we do in perceiving non-human entities. There is one crucial way, however, in which the perception of others differs from the perception of anything else and that lies in the fact that we recognize others as human beings and as sharing our own characteristics. Therefore, to varying degrees, our perception of others is coloured by our belief that they are or may be like us. Person perception, then, is liable to a greater degree of subjectivity than is the perception of other entities. The professional psychologist, of course, attempts to minimize his subjectivity where the ordinary person may not. Assumed similarity and the projection of our own feelings and beliefs onto others and the effect of this process on judgement is a central component in person perception and is studied in its own right by social psychologists.

Person perception is essentially predictive. We make judgements about people's immediate intentions and feelings and construct theories

603

about the general character which underlies these in order to guide our behaviour with them. Having made judgements about intentions and dispositions, we often then only attend to behaviour which confirms this judgement, and we act towards them in ways which are congruent with this judgement. This can be seen most clearly in stereotyping, where, having decided that someone is a comedian or a social worker our expectations blind us to bits of behaviour incongruent with our beliefs about comedians and social workers. It should, then, be clear by now that the perception of others is as much a product of the perceivers' own mind, as of the real characteristics of the perceived. Let us look now in more detail at some aspects of person perception.

The attribution process

Most of our data about other people is derived from their overt behaviour and the settings in which this behaviour occurs. Occasionally, we hear about someone from other people's reports or other secondary information and perhaps make judgements on this basis. The latter is less common in everyday life although very standard in psychological experiments on person perception. The basic data, then, for making inferences about others are their actions. However, actions in themselves cannot provide us with much information about another unless we can decide what caused the action. For example, if we see someone stumble and fall over, we might infer that he is absent-minded and clumsy; if, however, we find that he tripped on a well-camouflaged rock in the grass then his action is not informative about his psychological characteristics. The process of determining the causes of actions is called the attribution process by social psychologists.

The degree to which we can use behaviour as a basis for making judgements about a person's psychological traits depends on where we locate the cause. We can locate the causes of actions either to factors within the person or to factors outside him in the physical and social environment. If we locate the cause of an action to some factor within the person, we have further to discriminate between his ability to carry out the action and his motivation for doing so; or, as the social psychologist, Fritz Heider put it, to discriminate between power and trying. For example, if a boy of fifteen is making a muddle out of a simple problem, we may infer that his motivation is low and he is not trying very hard. If a boy of seven is making a similar muddle out of the problem, we may infer that though motivation is high and he is trying very hard: the problem is simply beyond his present capabilities.

The point is that inferring lack of ability, as opposed to inferring lack of motivation, leads to very different inferences about the person's other qualities, partly because ability is seen as a stable trait, motivation as a fluctuating one.

Let us return to the first point, that, initially, we must judge whether the cause of an action lies within or outside the person. Causes outside the person may be physical forces or social psychological forces. Since we have already provided an illustration of the first kind of force, a physical force, let us have a look at the second social force. Our problem is to decide whether an action reflects some individual, enduring feature of the person's character or attitudes and is caused by these traits or by something outside.

First, where an action is strongly normative, that is, it is behaviour which is expected by most people in that situation we may be less inclined to attribute it to character or attitudes. For example, if we observe someone weeping or looking very subdued at a funeral we are less confident in inferring a melancholy disposition than if we saw him behaving in this way at a garden party. That is, we imagine his behaviour is determined by the setting, and the rules governing behaviour in that setting. We ask ourselves the question, how likely is it that most people would behave in this way in this setting? If we think that the behaviour is unusual, then it is a more potent basis for inference than if it is conventional. The attribution theorists E. Jones and K. Davis have summarized this discussion by arguing that the less normative behaviour is, the more informative about character and attitudes it is. They use the term correspondence to describe the extent to which we can link behaviour with psychological states. Perhaps, at this point, we should think briefly about what contributes to norms or expectations about behaviour.

We have already come across the term 'norm' in Chapter 25. It refers to a set of beliefs or expectations about the 'proper' or 'normal' or 'best' behaviour in a particular setting or by people in particular roles. Whatever a person's character or inclinations, some of his behaviour will be determined by his knowledge of the norms and expectations held by others in various settings. Some norms are rules about behaviour in a particular setting (in the example above, behaviour which can be reasonably expected at a funeral, or at an interview for a job). Other norms may be rules about behaviour of particular role-categories such as mother, priest, old man, or whatever. Some expectations may be generated simply for one occasion. For example, if someone is telling a joke a strong expectation held by those present is that the co-participants will both listen to the joke and make a stab at laughing at it.

Jones and Davis suggest that an actor's knowledge of shared rules and expectations about behaviour are regarded by the lay psychologist as sufficient cause of his behaviour. Note that we cannot ever really 'know' whether behaviour is caused by an enduring psychological trait or by social pressures in the form of implicit norms, only that many people in the attribution process balance up the two possibilities when ascertaining the causes of behaviour and when utilizing that behaviour as a basis for further inference. Consider the following experiment: subjects were played a tape-recording of what was apparently an interview between a personnel officer and an applicant for a job. All subjects knew what character qualities were required for the job and they were all led to believe that the applicants knew this too. Half the subjects heard the applicant describing himself along the lines required for the job; the other half heard him describing himself rather differently to the job requirements. The subjects were asked what they thought the applicant was really like and how confident they were in their judgement. Subjects showed a clear tendency to assign with confidence the trait attributed to the applicant to himself where these were incongruent with the job requirements. The inference, presumably, was that in the congruent condition the demands of the situation were in themselves sufficient to explain the applicant's behaviour and little could be determined about the person's real personality.

Kelly's analysis

A somewhat different way of analysing the attribution process is provided by A. Kelly. He argues that we take into account three factors when assigning causes to a piece of behaviour. The three factors are *distinctiveness*, *consensus*, and *consistency*. What do these terms mean? Let us imagine a man showing extreme anger at his wife. Distinctiveness is high where extreme anger is shown only to his wife and not to other people, it is low if the man shows a lot of anger to a lot of people. Now, which level of distinctiveness tells us most about the man? In the first case, since his anger is reserved exclusively for his wife, we may assume that his behaviour is a product of her and of their joint situation. In the second case, his anger appears in many contexts and, since he is the only common factor, we are likely to think his anger has something strongly to do with factors associated only with him, for example, his personality. Therefore Kelly would argue that where the factor of distinctiveness is low then we assign causes of behaviour more confidently to something within the person.

What about consensus? This factor is concerned with the degree to which many people behave in the same way in that situation. Thus, it relates to Jones and Davis' idea of social pressures in the form of norms and expectations. In Kelly's analysis and in the example that we have just examined, consensus would be high if everyone showed anger at the man's wife. We might assume that, since many people respond in a similar way then the cause of behaviour lies more in the wife as a stimulus than in the actor. Therefore, where consensus is high we are able to attribute less of the cause to the man's behaviour than to the stimulus. Useful information about the actor's character is only provided where consensus is low.

Finally then, let us have a look at consistency as a factor in causal attribution. If a piece of behaviour occurs on a single occasion and is never repeated, then we are more likely to assume it is a product of that situation. If it occurs repeatedly across a range of situations of a roughly similar type, then we consider that some of the cause is located within the person or, at least, there is an interaction between the person and the situation. Therefore high consistency will contribute to attribution of cause within the person. This point is an important one, since it suggests the obvious point that a minimal degree of information about an action may have to be made available before people make causal judgements at all. In Kelly's model these three conditions of low consensus, low distinctiveness, and high consistency should co-occur for attribution of cause within the person to be made.

Experimental demonstrations of the attribution process at work have largely consisted of presenting subjects with an account of an actor's behaviour, information about the context, and the behaviour of others in that situation; they then ask the subject either to attribute traits to the actor or to locate the cause of his action. Under these conditions, subjects behave largely along the lines presented in the above analysis. However, many questions about the attribution process remain unanswered. For example, the three conditions specified by Kelly as the conditions necessary for making causal judgements can assume a variety of values. Experimental work has shown that within-the-subject attributions are made where high consistency, low distinctiveness, and low consensus obtain. What happens if one of these values is changed? We have little clear evidence. Secondly, individuals will vary, particularly if some of them have training in psychology, in the confidence with which they will make causal attributions. After all, there are many erroneous assumptions in the attribution processes outlined above. For example, a person behaving in a conventional way may still be doing so because this behaviour reflects his inner traits and attitudes, not because he is succumbing to social pressures. Indeed, he may be quite unaware of such pressures and the norms surrounding them. This possibility is a logical one and, insofar as the lay psychologist follows logical principles in his processes of judgement, it should occur to him too. A similar point can be made with respect to the factor of consistency and distinctiveness. The 'sophisticated' lay psychologist might argue that precisely the single action (low consistency) and the behaviour related to one particular stimulus (high distinctiveness) may be highly revealing about someone's 'inner nature' and contribute strongly to an understanding of his character. Whether or not the individual subject does consider these possibilities in making causal

607

inference depends on his own private theory of human motivation.

Although the attribution process is likely to vary with the intelligence and sophistication of the observer, even the quasi-logical process so far described can be illogically distorted by further factors. For example, there is some evidence that people will be more inclined to make within-actor causal attributions if the outcome of his behaviour is severe (Chaikin and Darley, 1973). For example, if someone spills ink over a large, valuable book we may hold him more responsible than if an identical action resulted in ink being spilled over an old newspaper. Logically speaking, of course, the outcome of an action can be quite unrelated to the causes of it and therefore the seriousness or otherwise of that outcome should not affect our judgements of where the responsibility for it lies. Nevertheless, even in institutionalized settings; for example, within the judicial process, severity of outcomes is properly considered when assigning responsibility to the accused.

Not only may the severity of an outcome affect our causal attributions, but the personal relevance of that outcome will do so too (Jones). Thus, for example, I may assign more reponsibility to an actor spilling ink over a large, valuable book than if he spilled it over an old newspaper; I will assign even more responsibility if he spills it over my large, valuable book than if he spills it over someone else's. Once again, however, we must allow that people will vary in the extent to which their judgements will be thus influenced. For example, we might well expect children's causal attribution to be more distorted by outcome factors than adult causal attributions would be. Furthermore, we might expect the purposes for which we are making a causal attribution to affect the degree of distortion through outcome values. For example, if an actor faced a court case as a result of such a process, we might be particularly cautious in linking outcome values with intention or responsibility. As yet, unfortunately, there has been no investigation of any of these points.

Finally, attribution processes have been found to vary quite systematically for actors and for observers. An actor is likely to locate the causes of his own behaviour rather differently to how he will do so as an observer of someone else's behaviour, even though action and setting are identical. An actor is more likely to attribute the causes of his behaviour to factors external to himself, the observer is more likely to attribute the causes of behaviour to factors within the actor. The work of Jones and Nisbett in this connection has shown that, even where action and context are identical, these differing perspectives of action and observers will lead to different causal attributions. There are some fairly obvious reasons for these differing perspectives. Firstly, the attention of the actor is likely to be focused outwards towards situational factors and he is therefore likely to place more weight on these cues. An observer considering the behaviour of an actor is likely to focus on the actor and therefore attach more weight to what appears to be internal factors. The actor also has information about himself which the observer does not have. For example, he has experience of the great variability of his own behaviour. The observer seems to infer that a given piece of behaviour of an actor reflects a stable tendency. This is probably due to the considerable need we all have to set up stable expectations about others to provide guidelines for our behaviour with them. Again, individual differences influence the degree to which we attribute the causes of our actions and our outcomes to internal or to external factors. These differences have been examined by Rotter and Phares and, indeed, they have developed a questionnaire which measures people's tendency to feel internally or externally controlled themselves and to attribute internal or external causation to others.

Implicit personality theory
Assigning causes to the behaviour of others is one of the many steps in forming impressions of others. Let us now look at the process at a further stage. Having decided that an action or series of actions results from some attribute of the actor, what further inferences do we make? A rather large area of psychological research suggests that we do, indeed, make inferences which extend beyond the information given by a person's behaviour. This research is concerned with what social psychologists call 'implicit personality theory'. The term means, as was suggested earlier, that all of us, whether professional psychologists or not, have 'theories' about how personality is structured, or in other words, which traits tend to co-occur within individuals. If, for example, you are told simply that an individual is 'punctual' then you may infer that he is conscientious and tidy, probably cautious and inhibited, and possibly unimaginative. We could probably set a similar psychological process in motion by describing someone as 'vivacious'.

STEREOTYPING
'Implicit personality theory' has been demonstrated through a number of experimental techniques, and it has been shown to manifest itself in a number of different ways. Perhaps one of the most compelling manifestations of 'implicit personality theory' emerges in the phenomenon of stereotyping. The example given in the previous paragraph was illustrative of how a single item of information about another character will generate inferences about other aspects of his character. With stereotyping, the information is limited to either some external aspect of a person, such as his appearance or to the fact that he belongs to some ethnic or occupational category. This information in itself will generate judgement of what an individual belonging to such categories or having such an appearance is like. Take, for example,

physical attractiveness. It has been found in a variety of studies that subjects attribute a number of favourable characteristics to individuals who are physically attractive. For example, subjects presented with people who are good looking rate them more highly on intelligence, poise, emotional adjustment, kindness, and a number of other desirable characteristics than they do people who are physically unattractive (Dion Berscheid and Walster, 1972); that is, where the only information available is the person's level of physical attractiveness observers will infer the presence of certain 'psychological' traits. Stereotyping emerges in a similar way with respect to ethnic group membership. A number of researchers have provided subjects with a list of ethnic groups, for example, American, Jew, or Negro (84 in all), and a list of words describing personality, for example, intelligent, superstitious, or pleasure-loving (100 in all). They asked these subjects to indicate the five characteristics most closely associated with an ethnic group.

Three studies conducted at considerable intervals from one another over the last fifty years have shown the pattern summarized in Table 26.1 (p. 152, Harvey and Smith).

Table 26.1   Stereotyping by three generations of Princeton men

1933		1951		1967	
American					
Industrious	48	Materialistic	37	Materialistic	67
Intelligent	47	Intelligent	32	Ambitious	42
Materialistic	33	Industrious	30	Pleasure loving	28
Ambitious	33	Pleasure loving	27	Industrious	23
Progressive	27	Ambitious	21	Intelligent	20
Favourableness	(.99)		(.86)		(.49)
Jew					
Shrewd	79	Shrewd	47	Ambitious	48
Mercenary	49	Intelligent	37	Materialistic	46
Industrious	48	Industrious	29	Intelligent	33
Grasping	34	Ambitious	28	Industrious	33
Intelligent	29	Mercenary	28	Shrewd	30
Favourableness	(.24)		(.45)		(.66)
Negro					
Superstitious	84	Superstitious	41	Musical	47
Lazy	75	Musical	33	Happy-go-lucky	27
Happy-go-lucky	38	Lazy	31	Pleasure loving	26
Ignorant	38	Ignorant	24	Lazy	26
Musical	26	Pleasure loving	19	Ostentatious	25
Favourableness	(−.70)		(−.37)		(.07)

Stereotypes exist for many classifications of people. We may stereotype others not only on the basis of their level of physical attractiveness but on the types of features they have. We may stereotype others because of their age-grouping, their occupations, or even their Christian names. Stereotyping is basically an overgeneralization. It involves first the assignment of an individual to a social or physical category, that is the judgement that he is Chinese or that he is attractive or whatever. Secondly, it involves the belief that certain traits characterize people in that category. Thirdly it involves the inference that the individual, as a member of that category must possess the associated traits.

Psychological studies of stereotyping may, of course, exaggerate people's tendency to engage in the process. For one thing, they present their subjects with no information other than an individual's appearance or his ethnic group membership. In real life, or course, we are usually exposed to more information about a person than this and his behaviour may soon differ from that of the stereotype. On the other hand, the belief in such a stereotype may cause us to attend only to those features of his behaviour which are congruent with it.

Stereotyping illustrates dramatically the process of 'implicit personality theory', which is central in forming impressions of others. One of its most interesting features is that, although we may hold individual stereotypes, there is ample evidence that the beliefs associated with them are very widely shared by members of a common culture.

The origins of stereotypes and their effects on behaviour and attitudes towards the group involved is a question of some complexity, such that we cannot pursue it further here.

Other research on 'implicit personality theory' using various techniques (Bruner, Schapiro and Tagiuri; Asch; Wishner) has shown clearly that we share common beliefs about how traits co-vary. In one study, for example (Bruner, Schapiro and Tagiuri), subjects were given a trait, for example, intelligence, and asked to indicate whether people who are intelligent

$$\left.\begin{array}{l} \text{very often are} \\ \text{tend to be} \\ \text{may or may not be} \\ \text{tend not to be} \end{array}\right\} \text{ aggressive, awkward, active, etc.}$$

(A list of fifty-nine associated traits was presented to the subject.) Subjects were asked to complete a task using two or three given traits in combination. One of the main findings of this study was that subjects concurred in a majority of cases in the inferences they made from the given trait. For example, given the trait intelligence, a majority of subjects stated that a person possessing this trait would very often be imaginative, active, and independent.

611

In the various studies of 'implicit personality theory', as with stereotyping, the most striking feature of the results is the degree of consensus between subjects about how traits co-vary, even though the individuals may hold 'personal implicit personality theories'. More recently, there have been studies of the 'individual implicit personality theory'. One example is the study by Rosenberg and Jones (1972) of the use of personality description of women in the novels of Theodore Dreiser, where the writer shows clear configurations of associated traits in his fictional characters.

Critique
What contributions do these pieces of research make to our understanding of the processes of impression-formation as a whole? They show, firstly, that people are able to go beyond the fragmentary information given about another and to infer other qualities. However, it is not clear to what extent people actually do this and do make global judgement of personality outside the psychological laboratory. We need to know more precisely under what conditions people will be drawn to use information in this way and make inferential judgements. Then, in many studies of impression-formation, subjects are provided with lists of trait words with which to describe someone. We do not know whether these provided traits are the ones they habitually use outside the laboratory. It was suggested above that people have individual theories of how personality is structured; that is, how given traits co-vary. The work of one psychologist, George Kelly, indicates that people have their own particular construct systems, through which they perceive others; and the constructs which people choose vary markedly, as does the manner in which they relate to one another. For example, dominance, intelligence, and aggressiveness may be, to me, the most salient dimension for describing people. For you, warmth, friendliness and honesty may be salient. Furthermore, the opposite of friendly for you may be unsociable; for me it may be cold or reserved. This suggests that the researchers in many experiments were simply eliciting people's common definitions of word meanings and of the closeness and overlap of word meanings. Thus, people assume shared meanings of such terms as sincere, sociable or whatever when they have very little else to go on except words. When they are describing real people with whom they have some experience then they may well express themselves in more idiosyncratic, less conventional ways.

Finally, of course, many studies of impression-formation present a picture of the process as static. That is, having used some information about someone and inferred the presence of other qualities, this judgement then holds. But people may modify their impressions. Indeed, the extent to which they do so is a subject of considerable interest in its own right.

We have looked at some processes which appear central in person perception. There are other questions which cannot be examined here. Two of these are:

1. How does one's attitude towards oneself affect the way in which one perceives another?
2. How does the situation in which we are engaged with another affect our perception of him? For example, certain dimensions of people may be salient in, say, the work setting, and others in academic settings. These have been explored in social psychological research.

One of the most enduring questions about person perception, which is at the same time very difficult to investigate is the question of accuracy. Earlier in the discussion, it was suggested that social psychologists have been more concered with the processes of person perception than they have with the accuracy of person perception. The question here is, to what extent do people make accurate judgements about others; or, more precisely, what kinds of people make accurate judges of others? The question can be examined at a number of levels. We can look to see how far people can detect others' emotional states from such cues as facial expression, body movement, and so forth. Insofar as we can obtain an objective measure of the emotions another is feeling, it is reasonably easy to see whether people guess them accurately or not. In general, people can discriminate grossly different emotional states such as fear against calm or happiness against anger. They can do so using many non-verbal cues as well, of course, as verbal behaviour. They are not much good at discriminating closely-linked emotions like jealousy as against anger, unless the person is providing a full verbal description of their feelings. There is also some evidence that we are quite adept at detecting the extent to which people like each other (Tagiuri, 1958).

At the more complex level of assessing enduring personality traits, the question becomes more difficult. The difficulty relates partly to the problem of finding an objective measure of what someone is really like. If we could be sure that personality was, indeed, entirely stable and accurately measurable, then it would be a matter of comparing a sound measure against a subject's judgement. In practice, what is involved is that we ask one target person to fill in a self-report inventory purporting to measure his personality (assuming he is a truthful and accurate judge of himself); we then ask a subject to predict the former's responses on that measure. The degree of discrepancy then becomes the measure of accuracy of our subject's perception. The problem here is that there are a number of ways of obtaining small discrepancies which are not the result of accurate perception on the part of the subject.

First, it is possible to predict the typical response on many instruments for a whole class of people, e.g., female college students or old men. That is, both subject and target person may share a common stereotype. In this case the subject is not showing accuracy on the unique traits of the individual. Then, it has been shown that many subjects assume others are like themselves. They will predict the other's responses in terms of what their own would be. If the target person is, indeed, similar then the small discrepancy arises out of the assumed similarity, not out of accurate perception. Furthermore target people may have a bias towards presenting themselves in a favourable light and subjects may share this bias in describing others. Yet, again, the small discrepancy could arise out of a shared bias rather than from accurate perception. Now, many studies have not taken account of these problems. Therefore, their results, showing accuracy of different subjects and presenting typical profiles of the accurate subject, cannot be accepted with much confidence. It is likely that subjects, particularly those who have experience or who have received specific training, may become skilled in detecting the presence of specific qualities in others. Studies of successful interviewers throw some light on this.

Perhaps it is not surprising to find that man, as psychologist, construes the intentions, motivations, and personalities of others in ways which reveal much about his own cognitive processes, but which may be fairly inaccurate when it comes to reality. After all, the knowledge of the professional psychologist is still largely incomplete where motivation and personality are concerned. Nevertheless, understanding the perceptions that people do have of others, whether valid or not, gives us some insight into their behaviour with others.

Attraction

We have considered, in the previous part of the Chapter, some of the processes involved in knowing others. Let us turn now to the affective dimension of interpersonal relations, in particular let us focus on attraction between people. The question that we all ask, social psychologists included, is why we are attracted to some people and not to others.

It may be the case that people are attracted to one another for myriads of different reasons which defy any attempt at description or analysis. The social psychologist, however, works on the assumption that there are certain underlying laws of attraction, complex though they may be, which will account for its varying manifestations. How have they attempted to uncover such patterns?

Sociometry
One of the earliest approaches to the topic involved identifying the 'popular' or 'attractive' people in various groups and seeing whether they showed characteristics which differentiated them from the unpopular.

The argument here would be that there are certain characteristics of people which we all find attractive, and we like people to the degree that they possess such characteristics.

Using a technique known as sociometry the researcher would ask members of a group (it might be a college fraternity; it might be workers on a factory floor) to indicate which other member of the group they preferred to associate with, work with, spend leisure time with, and liked. The resulting patterns of choices were then represented on a sociogram. (There are, of course, many ways of doing this; we may also ask who people do not like; we may ask them to rank the whole group on the liking dimensions; we may ask them to make one nomination, several or as many as they wish.) Figure 26.1 illustrates part of a hypothetical sociogram; the circles represent group member and the arrows the choices that they made. In this case, we can see quite clearly that 2 and 4 are highly chosen and next in order came 6 and 3. 7 makes no choice and receives none, and 1 and 5 are not chosen. We can also see where choices are neutral or one-sided.

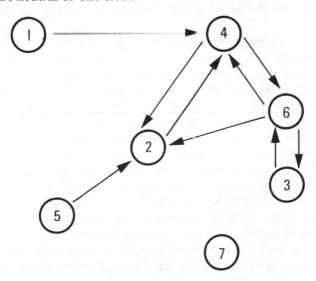

Fig. 26.1 A hypothetical sociogram.

This hypothetical sociogram is not unusual in the sense that, here, choice or 'popularity' is unevenly distributed, and some people are popularity 'stars' and others are 'isolates'.

The second part of the procedure involves the rating of the group members on personality traits, either by each other or by people outside the group who are acquainted with them. Summary of many of the research findings using such procedures suggests some unsurprising conclusions. The over-chosen tend to be more intelligent, attractive, well-adjusted, sociable, and competent at skills relevant to the group in which they are participating.

The examination of attraction between people through the technique of sociometry and of its interpretation presents some problems. Firstly, choices are based on people's 'ideal choices', or verbal sociometric behaviour. Clearly, everyone cannot spend his time with the most socially desirable individuals and it is unlikely that he does not like less popular individuals at all. In a class of students, for example, one or two people may indeed be very popular but nevertheless most of the other members will pair off into little groups and dyads and will presumably 'like' each other. This suggests that there must be further determinants of attraction between people other than the factors producing popularity in a group as a whole. This notion leads us to a different approach to the problem of understanding interpersonal attraction.

The second part of the procedure in this type of research involves the rating of the members of the group on traits of personality, these ratings being obtained either from group members about each other or from people who know the member of the group but who are not members of it.

A summary of many findings from research using these procedures reveals some rather expected conclusions. Over-chosen, popular individuals are described as markedly more intelligent, attractive, healthy, well off, well-adjusted, sociable, kind, and competent at skills which are important for the group as a whole than are isolates. What does this research tell us? It tells us that, if asked, people will express liking and a desire to associate with individuals who have characteristics which most people consider highly desirable. However, it does not tell us who actually associates with whom. Given that the kinds of choice obtained in this way converge on very few people clearly only a few individuals will actually be friendly with or associate with the over-chosen. The rest will find companionship with other people and, if attraction or liking have anything to do with actual behaviour, that is, spending time and sharing activities with others, then that liking or attraction must be of a different order to that expressed in sociometric choices.

Perhaps, there may be other reasons which draw us to those with whom we mainly associate and for whom, presumably, we have positive sentiments. Of course, it may be that friendship and association is very much a compromise process. That is, though we would all like in our friends the qualities which characterize popular people, we have to settle for fewer of the qualities or smaller amounts of the qualities in our actual friendships—the degree to which we like or are attracted to people we associate with may not have much to do with the association itself. However, let us keep in mind the other possibility that other factors, rather than socially desirable characteristics determine our attachment to others.

Social reinforcement

Continuing the discussion of attraction rather than association or friendship, we have been told that certain characteristics lead to attraction or popularity. We have also seen, however, that these are unlikely to be the only factors which make others attractive to us. What then are other factors or processes which social psychologists have identified?

One such process is of reinforcement. Reward, or reinforcement, is a central concept in the psychology of motivation (see Ch. 11). It is therefore not surprising that some social psychologists should have explored the possibility that we are attracted simply to those who provide us with rewards. Although this idea is not only quite plausible and, in a very general sense, true, it is not, as it stands, very predictive. That is, it does not tell us precisely who will be attractive to whom.

Firstly, different things are rewarding to different people. For example, one person may find help given by another a most potent form of reward. Another person may find expression of esteem and approval from another a most potent form of reward. A third may simply find an attractive physical appearance some kind of reward.

Secondly, what a person finds rewarding on any occasion will depend on his needs; not only generalized and enduring needs, but also needs on particular occasions. For example, when a person's confidence is somewhat low he may value the reward of another person's esteem and approval and therefore be attracted to that person. On another occasion, having more regard for himself, he might find rewarding the other characteristics, such as his physical appearance. Therefore, it is very difficult to predict in advance which rewards will be potent for particular people on particular occasions.

Thirdly, the rewarding value of a person's behaviour or of his perceived characteristics depends on our evaluation of other factors to do with him. For example, the approval or esteem of someone who continually approves of and admires practically everyone he ever meets is surely less effective as a reward than that emanating from someone who is highly selective in his admiration and approval of people. Similarly, a person may provide us with admiration and approval in the context of a situation in which he is asking us for a loan or some other favour. The value of his approval is surely altered in such a context, simply because we attribute the causes of his approving behaviour differently. Nevertheless, casual observation and introspection and a wealth of experimental demonstration show that with no other information available other than that a stranger approves of us, helps us in an experimental task, shares some of his own reward with us, and so forth, we will express greater liking for people whose behaviour, by common consensus, is rewarding, than for people whose behaviour is not rewarding (Clore and Bryne, 1974; Lott and Lott, 1974).

Reinforcement theorists further argue that even receiving rewards in the mere presence of another person will generalize attraction to him. For example, a number of studies have shown that strangers, brought together for the purposes of some experimental game-like task, showed greater liking for each other where they were rewarded after participation in the game, than where they were unsuccessful. This was the case, even though the allocation of reward was determined by the tossing of a coin and the subjects knew this (Rabbie and Horowitz, 1969). This, of course, can be considered to be an example of secondary reinforcement, where a previously neutral stimulus acquires reinforcing properties through association with a reinforcer. Anyway, this suggests that, if we receive some form of reward as reinforcement, we shall express liking for a person who happens to be around at the time. Let us remember again, however, that this holds where no other information about the person is available and indeed where the expression of liking for the stranger has no implications of interaction with him at all. The exact process, whereby reward, either directly or secondarily associated with someone, should lead to expressed liking for that person, is a complex one and cannot occupy our discussion at this point. One aspect of the process, the emotional arousal associated with reward and the degree to which arousal might become associated in the mind of the subject with someone present, will be taken up a bit later when we discuss sexual attraction and romantic love.

Let us try to summarize our knowledge of the attraction process so far. First, sociometric studies suggest that certain qualities of people are highly regarded and many people seem to concur on what these qualities are. People who are perceived as having such qualities are also recipients of verbally-expressed choices which imply liking. These qualities include physical attractiveness, competence, and general stability. Secondly, we find that being rewarded in some way by another person leads to our expressing liking for him. Thirdly, we find that being rewarded in some way simply in the presence of another person will lead to our expressing liking for him. However, we must still remember that (a) there are great individual differences in what kinds of stimuli are found rewarding; (b) whether a person's behaviour is rewarding or not depends on other characteristics of the person and on characteristics of the situation in which the behaviour occurs; (c) reward, or reinforcement, has been found to affect liking when virtually no other information about the person is available; (d) therefore, the way in which reward interacts with a person's perception of another's qualities may well affect the reinforcement-liking relationship.

Let us recall at this point, that we are talking about interpersonal attraction as measured by a subject's reported liking for another (often a stranger). So far, we have not considered interpersonal attraction as measured by the incidence or by the strength of an actual relationship.

The processes involved in evolving and maintaining a relationship may be similar to those involved in generating initial attraction between strangers and similar to those involved in producing popularity in a group. However, we cannot make an assumption about this and the whole question will be examined later in the Chapter.

Similarity and attraction

Let us now have a look at a different strand of research on interpersonal attraction, that is, research on similarity and attraction. Here, we are looking at principles which relate the qualities of two individuals to each other. There are two types of methods involved in examining the relationship betwen similarity and attraction. One involves looking at the attitudes, values, and tastes of pairs who are already engaged in some kind of relationship, and comparing the similarity of actual pairs with randomly compared, unrelated couples. Another involves the following experimental format: a subject fills in a questionnaire on his views on a variety of topics. Some time later he is shown the responses or profiles apparently provided by other individuals. These profiles show either that the stranger is very similar to him in attitudes and tastes or is very different. He is then asked to indicate how much he feels attracted to this stranger. A typical finding is that the subject is strongly attracted to the similar stranger but not to the dissimilar stranger. More precisely, the amount of attraction to the other person has been found to be directly related to the proportion of similar to dissimilar attitudes the other is alleged to hold (Byrne, 1969).

Research on the similarity-attraction relationship has not been confined to paradigms in which the stimulus is a hypothetical person with a set of similar or dissimilar attitudes, and the measurement of attraction, hypothetical liking (i.e., a measure of liking derived from responses to questions like 'How much do you think you would like the person who filled in this questionnaire?). A number of researchers have examined the similarity in attitudes of people who had, in fact, formed a relationship. For example, some early studies have shown that spouses have similar views on a variety of issues (Newcombe and Svehla, 1937) as do friendship pairs (Winslow, 1937).

In one study (Newcombe, 1961), intending students (male) of a university were offered free board and lodging in return for participating in a research project which was concerned with the acquaintance process. They were initially strangers, and the research took place during the few months preceding their university enrolment. Newcombe again found similarity to be a predictor of friendship-choices. He also found that similarity increased with acquaintance. We might suppose that this method of investigation, which uses real-life relationships as a criterion for attraction might be more powerful evidence for the similarity-attraction relationship than the attraction-to-strangers paradigm discussed above. However, the difficulty lies in interpreting where the causal element lies. It may be that couples or friends *become* similar in attitudes as a result of their relationship, rather than the relationship developing as a result of similar attitudes. Newcombe's findings did suggest that the relationship, in itself, produced increasing similarity. However, he also showed that a degree of similarity predicted friendship between previously unacquainted people.

The results from all the studies using both types of methodology, taken together, do suggest that similarity of attitudes plays some part in interpersonal attraction. Why should similarity in attitudes generate attraction? A number of views have been put forward. Byrne (1961), for example, has argued that when people have similar attitudes to one another they provide each other with rewards. This is because agreement from someone else 'validates' one's own point of view. However, it is a complex matter to find support for Byrne's theory. For one thing, people tend to assume that other people, similar to them, will like them (McWhirter and Jecker, 1967), and we are more attracted to those who we think like us (Aronson and Worchel, 1960). Therefore, it may be that attraction to similar others (particularly to strangers as in Bryne's research) is generated not by their attitudes, but by the expectation that they will like us. Newcombe argued on a slightly different basis. He propounded the view that to like person x and to be strongly in favour of attitude y when x is strongly against it, is cognitively 'uncomfortable'. We find it simpler to live in a world where the people we like like the things we like. In fact, Newcombe argued that much of the acquaintance process was occupied with the 'strain toward symmetry'. (The process, of course, involves the converse of this: symmetry or balance obtains if people we dislike like things that we dislike.) There is some evidence (including Newcombe's own data) which suggests that acquaintance or attraction produces a cognitive restructuring which brings attitudes into line between friends and couples. However, a more extensive discussion of research on Newcombe's and other 'balance' theories is available in Chapter 27.

A rather different interpretation of some of the similarity-attraction data derives from sociological studies of marriages and friendships. Many sociologists have examined patterns of both marriage and friendship. Both cases are characterized by homogamy, that is, the tendency to select partners who are similar in age (Bowerman, 1956), in social class (Warren, 1966), and of the same race (Schmitt, 1971), and religion

(Bumpass, 1970). This is particularly marked with respect to marriage partners, on which most relevant research has been based. Obviously, social background or demographic factors play an important role in patterning relationships of friendship and marriage. Society is structured in such a way that the field of eligibles, in which mate and friend selection occurs, is highly restricted in terms of age and social background. That is, most people we meet in situations relevant for either type of relationship to occur, are similar in age and in social background. Thus, we do not 'choose' others, nor are we 'attracted to' others drawn from the total population but only others from a highly restricted sample similar to us in these factors. Now, when we consider that attitudes towards political and religious issues are highly dependent on such variables as race, class, and religious group (that is, people who come from similar backgrounds hold rather similar political and ideological views), then the relationship between attraction and similarity appears in a different light; that is, studies showing that couples and friends are similar in attitudes and values are probably only further illustrating the fact that their partners are drawn from similar backgrounds to each other. This could imply that they were not attracted to one another because of their similarity, only that they were choosing from a restricted field anyway. This interpretation would further suggest that they were attracted for reasons beyond their similarity, since they would presumably have already been 'exposed to' many similar others and failed to evolve a relationship with them. However, although this interpretation is quite plausible when we consider the similarity of attitudes observed between couples and friends, it requires considerably more elaboration if we consider the similarity-attraction relationship for strangers.

It may well be that subjects in Byrne's research simply classify an unknown person apparently sharing their views as someone within their 'field of eligibles' and therefore automatically more 'attractive' than someone who is not. As the research stands we cannot decide whether this is a valid possibility or not.

Common sense, however, would suggest that, when it comes to actual choices of partners, similarity may operate as a fairly low-level filtering mechanism. That is, many of those we meet (and we must remember that the research cited above is largely based on restricted samples of young, middle-class undergraduates and graduates) do already share our general views on major issues and further criteria must be brought into play to make us more attracted to some of these 'similar people' than to others of them.

These explanations of the similarity-attraction relationship are not, of course, incompatible with one another. The last one, however, involves a suprapersonal, a sociological level of analysis, since it suggests that

621

forces beyond the individual restrict his choices of friends or mates. The first two explanations, similarity as rewarding and similarity as 'cognitively comfortable', may be simply alternative ways of describing the same process. Research which would clearly distinguish between these two explanations has yet to be carried out.

Similarity of attitudes is, of course, only one kind of similarity. What about similarity of personality? The bulk of research examining this relationship is concerned with ongoing relationships rather than initial attraction. For example, Izard (1960) examined the relationship between attraction and similarity of personality amongst fresher (first-year undergraduate) girl students. Initial strangers were asked to complete personality tests and six months later asked to name the girls they liked best in the class and those that they liked least. Izard found substantial similarity of personality between the choosers and favoured chosen but not unfavoured chosen.

A number of subsequent studies have not substantiated Izard's findings; others have left the picture quite unclear. Since different researchers use different measures of personality, different measures of attraction, subjects of different ages and in different settings, there are many possible reasons why the results show such variability. One study (Cattell and Nesselroade, 1967) examined the similarity of personality profiles of married couples who reported themselves to be either happily or unhappily married. They found clear evidence that similarity was associated with stable or happy relationships but not with unhappy ones. However, again we have to query the extent to which the factors which influence initial attraction play an important role in sustaining a relationship; that is, whether 'attraction' is to be regarded as an initial and ephemeral psychological phenomenon or whether it is to be considered a factor of importance in determining the course of a relationship. Research reported by Levinger (1972) already suggests that different factors assume differing amounts of importance in the later phases as compared with the earlier phases of a relationship—for example, similarity in attitudes appears more important at earlier stages than it does when the relationship has advanced to greater intimacy.

What further factors, then, might influence the attractiveness of another person in a relationship, beyond similarity of attitudes and similarity of personality? One further strand of research has been concerned with the complementarity of needs between partners in a relationship. The idea here is that we would get on best with others who 'complement' us in some way; for example, a domineering person might find greatest satisfaction with a submissive retiring partner.

An initial study (Winch, Ktsanes and Ktsanes, 1954) measured the need patterns of twenty-five married couples (they had all been married for less than two years) and found evidence for complementarity. Some

622

similar studies did not find this pattern; others, particularly those that examined only those needs which the partner felt were relevant to the marriage-relationship, supported Winch's data (Levinger, 1972). It is hard to reconcile studies which suggest that need complementarity (i.e., dissimilarity of personality) is a factor both in attraction and in sustaining a relationship, with those studies which suggest that similarity of personality is likewise an important factor.

As was suggested above, differing measures, criteria of attraction, and subject samples could account for the confusing picture presented by the research data. However, we must bear in mind certain critical points.

Firstly, actual relationships may be partly generated by circumstantial non-psychological factors which are as important as attraction. Secondly, some of the variability reported may be due to individual variation amongst subjects, that is, depending on their major personality needs, some people may be attracted by similarity, others by complementarity. Perhaps the major fault of psychological research, so far, has been its efforts to paint an over-simplistic picture of the forces involved in attraction. Certainly individual differences have been largely ignored. Let us briefly summarize again at this point.

We find similarity of attitudes being apparently allied to attraction, both in studies involving hypothetical strangers as well as in studies of actual relationships. The main question generated by these findings is whether or not the similarity-attraction relationship is simply one manifestation of demographic selection processes which present people with a restricted field of eligibles from which to form relationships and which determine their expectations about who will be 'attractive'. If this is the case, further factors must operate in the selection, from nevertheless fairly large fields of eligibles, to produce particular pairs of friends or spouses. One such further factor may be similarity of personality, another may be complementarity of personality needs. Which of these factors is most important may well be a function of further individual differences, as yet unexamined. Let us now turn to some of the questions raised earlier in the discussion.

Social exchange theory

It was suggested earlier in this discussion that 'liking' or 'attraction', particularly that generated in the setting of the research laboratory might be independent of the formation or maintenance of a relationship. For example, we might as often reason along the lines 'I must like x or find x attractive since I seem to spend a lot of time with him' as 'I spend a lot of time with x because I like him'. We can consider the problem in more depth if we focus now on the formation and maintenance of relationships rather than focusing on expressions of liking or attraction.

The first thing to remember about relationships in everyday life is that they are produced by both parties. Most of the research considered so far has simply concentrated on choices expressed by one individual. However much we may be attracted to someone, they have also to be attracted for a relationship to form. When we 'choose' others as friends or partners these choices are fairly unlikely to be ideal choices but compromises which represent the best available in the prevailing circumstances—this is true for both partners in the transaction.

This point emphasizes again that research based on sociometric techniques may tell us little about the choice or relationship process. It also casts further light on research suggesting that we like/choose others who reward us: another may reward us but they have, in turn, to be rewarded if a relationship is to evolve; furthermore, our evaluation of the rewards provided by another will depend on our evaluation of rewards potentially available from others in the field. This evaluation will affect whether a relationship ensues or not. One approach to attraction and interaction which takes account of these points is that embodied in social exchange theory. The authors of two versions of the theory, G. Homans, a sociologist, and J. Thibaut and H. Kelly, who are social psychologists, independently suggested a model of social interaction which accounts for 'choice', mutuality, and for the potential separation of 'attraction' or liking from the relationship formation.

The theory
In social exchange theory, relationships, or the interactions which constitute relationships, can be seen as exchanges of behaviour: A talks, B listens; A frowns, B smiles. Behaviour is, thus, viewed as a kind of commodity and the social world a kind of market in which this commodity can be exchanged; and interactions or relationships can be seen as transactions. The behaviours thus exchanged assume values for the participants in the sense that they are variously rewarding for them. (Social exchange theory, as you may have guessed, is a form of reinforcement theory.) Now, a central assumption in this theory is that people's major motive is to maximize their outcomes or rewards. This means that we will seek out people who we believe can produce the most rewarding behaviour. Since they are doing the same, we may not get the most rewarding people but those who will be at once rewarding and satisfied with what we have to offer. Thus will one strike a bargain.

Social exchange theory is an advancement on reinforcement theory in that it incorporates the idea that we like others who reward us in some way, but we will only evolve a relationship with those whom we can also reward. In its treatment of reward or reinforcement, it provides a further elaboration. Firstly, it is argued that any kind of event is only rewarding when assessed against some kind of scale or standard. This scale is constructed out of our past experience, and of our perceptions of what people similar to us obtain. For example, a new car is more rewarding if it is the first one we have ever had than if it is simply one in a succession. Furthermore, if most of the people we compare ourselves with are always having new cars, we will find our own less rewarding than if it is a pretty unusual event. Therefore, in short, to decide how rewarding one person's behaviour is to another, it is necessary to know about their scale of comparison—in the terms of social exchange theory, their *comparison level*.

Also, in assessing the reward value of another person's company we consider what rewards may be available from others—in exchange theory terms, a *comparison level for alternatives*. A further way in which exchange theory amplifies reinforcement theory is that it stresses that not only do we aim to obtain rewards, but we also aim to reduce costs. Interaction with others may involve us in behaviour which is 'costly'. An obvious example might be the cost associated with the efforts of shouting at a deaf person, or undertaking a long, awkward journey to visit someone. Our outcomes from an interaction with someone will, then, be made up of rewards minus costs, just as theirs will be. We both have to emerge with a profit for the interaction to continue. Furthermore, costs are made up, not only in terms of effort, embarrassment, boredom, or whatever else might be associated with interacting with someone, they are also made up in terms of the rewards foregone from others we might have interacted with. Just as the cost of a new car is not just its price but also the rewards of the holiday abroad we have now had to forego, so the cost of investing time and attention with person B is the rewards foregone from not interacting with person A. Again then, no event is rewarding in itself, it is rewarding, firstly, when assessed against a comparison level, secondly, when assessed against the costs associated with obtaining it, and, thirdly, when assessed against the rewards potentially available from another source (comparison level for alternatives), these rewards contributing towards the cost. Two people then engage with another when these computations reveal that their mutual outcomes are the best prevailing in the circumstances. We should also discriminate between at least two phases of the relationship. In the 'estimation phase' individuals are computing the potential rewards and costs. If they perceive profitable outcomes, they will embark on further interaction, in which they will begin to sample actual outcomes. This suggests the obvious point that relationships are dynamic not static. At any point, estimated rewards and costs may be revealed, on sampling, to be very different. Furthermore, in a social context of changing people, comparison levels for alternatives will also fluctuate. Thus, on this analysis, relationships are potentially unstable.

Before commenting on this approach and affiliation let us look at the 'outcome matrix', the main technique by which Thibaut and Kelly have illustrated their theory. Figures 26.2 and 26.3 represent one tiny component of a relationship between members of a pair. They form on two bits of behaviour which are components of this relationship. The hypothetical value for the two people, A and B, are represented in the top and bottom diagonals of each cell. In Figure 26.2, both A and B get equally high reward (+5) when they talk politics, but all other combinations of behaviour produce poor or even costly (minus figure) outcomes for one or other of them.

The hypothetical reward values in this illustration are aimed at with reference to the general comparison level. If, as in Figure 26.2, both parties stay with talking politics, their profits are high. If someone else came along who could produce talk which either person valued at say +6 or +7, then the relationship or interaction might be terminated. In this example, we see that at least one bit of A and B's repertoire of behaviour is rewarding to both of them. We can imagine a much larger matrix, in which many more bits and combinations of bits of behaviour could be represented and values assigned. The more cells like the bottom right hand one then the more likely that the pair would form a relationship. In Figure 26.3, we see a very different state of affairs. Here, either can engage only in behaviour rewarding to him at the expense of the other. Unless they have other bits of behaviour which can be combined to produce favourable outcomes for both, this relationship appears quite incompatible.

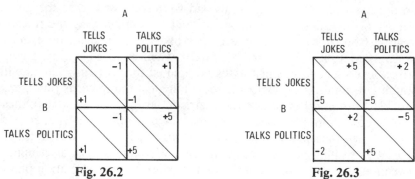

Fig. 26.2   Fig. 26.3

Before looking more critically at this analysis, let us summarize its contributions to our understanding of interpersonal attraction. The analysis focuses on behaviour directly rather than on perception of personality attributes, attitudes, and values in others. It expands other conceptions of the reward-attraction equation by taking into account costs and comparisons. It takes as central the fact that people are making decisions and choices when they affiliate with others, and it takes as central that both parties must compromise in their 'interpersonal bargains'. It suggests, indirectly, that 'liking' or 'felt attraction' is a secondary process to the primary one of behaviour exchange and reward. It allows that relationships and interactions may not be stable and the outcome matrices representing them may change in their moment to moment values. Finally, the motive to maximize outcomes, regardless of other factors, is central to exchange theory.

Evaluation

However plausible this analysis may be, there are severe drawbacks to this theory as a theory. First, along with other reinforcement theories in psychology, there are major difficulties about saying exactly what a reinforcement is. In the case of exchange theory, we cannot define rewards or costs, nor can we quantify them for any particular individual. In effect, this appears to make social exchange theory quite circular. If people form a relationship, we can argue, it is because their behaviour produces the most profitable outcomes in the prevailing circumstances. We cannot, however, predict who will interact with whom. As we saw from the illustrative matrix, costs and rewards are somehow seen as equated along a common scale. Thus, the costs of someone's deafness can be quantified against the pleasures of their hospitality. In real economics this can be done. Money relates the costs of a bag of peanuts to the cost of a new record player (although economists have to consider values not expressible in money terms too). Secondly, a central assumption is that people always make choices in relationships solely on the basis of personal satisfaction. Although this may hold plausibly in some societies and in some sections of a society, it does not hold plausibly everywhere. As we saw in Chapter 25, in many societies relationships are controlled by social norms and role structures which are not created by the individual at all, though he may well never question them. In many societies, friendship and marriage is based on kinship, or on class, or on community, or on age, or even on occupation. The point was raised earlier in the discussion that suitability of marriage partners appears to be at least partly constrained by supra-individual factors. Thus, the relevance of social exchange theory may have to be limited to certain kinds of social context.

Nevertheless, because a theory appears to be limited in its application and weak in its predictive power, this does not imply that it is invalid. The task of the researcher is to uncover its range of applicability and strengthen the definition of its central terms, in this case those relating to rewards and costs.

If we reconsider some of the research discussed earlier, we can see that much of it can be subsumed within the framework of social exchange theory. Sociometric research shows rather clearly the kinds of characteristics that most people value highly. These characteristics entail behaviour which many people find rewarding. So, although some rewards are particular to individuals and difficult to assess, many are widely shared and suggest a basis for uncovering the rewards inherent in many relationships. Research on similarity and complementarity again suggests some definitions of reward for many people: that is, that agreement on issues is rewarding, or for some behaviour to be enacted which you find hard is rewarding. Thus, research is supportive of social exchange theory, although it is supportive of many other theories, too. Research directly designed to test theory has largely been restricted to testing some aspect of it. For example, in a series of experimental studies, Aronson showed that the reward value of approval by another person depends on the level of approval shown in their previous behaviour. Someone who is initially uncomplimentary and later complimentary is found more attractive than someone who remains at a consistent level or who is initially complimentary and later changes. This provides some support for the idea that a reward like approval depends on context for its value, that is on a comparison level.

Other researchers have examined the proposition that relationships represent a compromise. That is, although we may all seek for partners with highly rewarding attributes, we will end up with someone who more or less 'matches' our own (someone who fits our purse). Thus, Murstein predicted that, given physical attractiveness is perceived as a rewarding characteristic, nevertheless, couples (opposite sex) will largely end up with others somewhat similar in level of attractiveness to them. Taking as subjects couples with an established relationship, he had them independently rated on attractiveness. He then compared the correlations of ratings between randomly-paired subjects with those of actual pairs. He found a clear tendency for real couples to be more similar in their received ratings than for pseudo-couples. Many other studies (Backman and Secord, 1958; Berscheid and Walster, 1967) have provided similar support for this aspect of exchange theory.

Nevertheless, taking the theory *in toto*, it has not been really tested and in its present form it may be untestable *in toto*.

Love

We have strayed somewhat from the concept of 'attraction' as understood in everyday life—that is, as a kind of magnetic psychological force. This conception is often concerned with romantic or sexual attraction. Our discussion so far has focused on the rather mundane process of 'liking'—which may, in fact, really mean many things such as 'approving of', 'anticipating rewards from', and so forth—and it has also focused on interaction. What about love? We shall not add to the pile of definitions of love which have accumulated over the centuries, but simply point to the few features common to many of them. Romantic

628

love involves physiological arousal, is impervious to reasoning about the loved object's real qualities, is short-lived and frequently one-sided. Until recently, academic social psychologists ignored this phenomenon. Recent work on emotional states has, however, begun to provide a possible interpretation of 'romantic love'. This interpretation runs as follows. Firstly, an individual may become physiologically aroused for a variety of reasons. He may have been angered, frightened, elated or surprised, or, of course, sexually aroused. Frequently, he has located the cause of this arousal to its proper source. Sometimes however, he is not aware of the source of his emotional state. Under these conditions, the presence of someone who is eligible and reasonably desirable and a situation in which 'romantic attraction' would be reasonable can lead to the individual labelling his arousal as 'love'. Thus, this argument suggests that romantic love is really the accidental labelling of physiological arousal under conditions where 'falling in love' is acceptable and even encouraged.

A number of studies have supported (if rather weakly) this idea. For example, in one study (Brehm, Gatz, Geothals, De Crommon, and Ward, 1970), fear was aroused in male subjects by leading them to expect (erroneously) very severe electric shocks. As part of the experiment, they were introduced to an attractive female assistant and asked to estimate their liking for the girl. Compared with a control group, liking was significantly higher amongst the aroused group than amongst those not aroused. The research, of course, did not claim that subjects 'fell in love' with the girl and, in that sense, contributes rather weakly to this theory of romantic love. Nevertheless, it demonstrates how expressions of liking can be manipulated by conditions which have nothing to do with the stimulus person. This further supports the argument that feelings of liking may be independent of the formation of relationships. It is worth noting in this context that, in our society, 'falling in love' has, until perhaps recently, been considered a reasonable basis for marriage (so long as it occurs between 'eligible' partners: falling in love with a ninety-year-old, a small child, or a Carthusian monk is usually considered abnormal and undesirable). However, in many societies 'romantic love' is either said not to exist except as a rare phenomenon or is in no way considered to be relevant to marriage. Some research shows that the 'romantic love' component of marriage is salient only where men and women have a fair degree of economic independence from one another, where marriages are not arranged by the families involved, and where the range of eligibles is very broad. Here, we have considered only some of the social-psychological approaches to attraction. Major contributions have been made by psychologists in other fields, notably in ethology, and, of course, by proponents of Freudian psychoanalytic theory. This work, and its relation to the approaches described, fall far beyond the scope of this text. A thorough study of the psychology of attraction would demand their inclusion.

Social influence

We come now to a further dimension of social interaction: that of social influence. We have examined some processes involved in the perception of others and processes of attraction towards others. In what ways and for what reasons are people able to influence one another's behaviour and beliefs? In Chapter 27, the discussion focuses on ways in which people's opinions can be modified and generally manipulated through communication and persuasion. Here, we are concerned with the ways in which people modify their behaviour when others are present, even without direct pressure to do so. Some of the earliest experiments in social psychology demonstrated that, apparently, the mere presence of other people facilitated an individual's performance of a simple task. If others were there he worked more quickly and more accurately and completed more in total than if he was alone. This came to be known as the social facilitation effect. It was demonstrated in a number of studies, both where the subject was observed by others as he worked at a simple task, and also where he worked together with others engaged on the same task. However, a number of researchers, in particular Zajonc (1960), observed that the effect only held with tasks which were very simple or were already overlearned by the subject. With new or complex tasks, the presence of other people in either capacity often produced a decrement in performance. Zajonc suggested that the presence of others heightens physiological arousal. This arousal enhances what he called 'dominant responses' (in effect, very well learned ones). In the case of novel or complex tasks, most of the subjects' responses, initially, are incorrect; therefore, when arousal from the presence of others facilitates the emission of responses they are incorrect, hence the performance decrement. Many arguments surrounded the social facilitation phenomenon, particularly those relating to whether 'mere presence' of others affects arousal. For the moment, the phenomenon simply serves to illustrate how quite simple behaviour changes can be caused by the presence of other people.

Let us turn now to some other demonstrations of social influence which can be more clearly interpreted. In a classic series of experiments, Sherif (1935) demonstrated how a person's judgement on a simple task could be influenced by the judgement of others. Using the auto-kinetic effect, he obtained estimates of the extent of the movement from subjects making their judgement alone. (The auto-kinetic effect is obtained when a stationary spot of light is projected onto a dark screen in an otherwise dark room, and, to the subject, it appears to move about. The cause of this effect has to do with the physiology of vision.) All individuals decreased the variability of their responses over time. However, there was marked variation across subjects in the mean estimates they gave. He then tested subjects in groups of five or six on the same task. Within a few trials, he found that the judgement of subjects tested together became closer and closer—there emerged for each group what Sherif called 'a group norm'. The subjects did not communicate with one another in any way since they were only required to call out the judgements in turn. No one attempted to bias their judgements at all. We are left with a clear demonstration of social influence, and the question as to the reasons for its existence. Before we consider that question, let us consider a different paradigm demonstrating social influence.

Conformity
In another series of classic experiments, Asch (1956) had subjects making simple judgements of length of lines in a group which was unknown to the subjects, composed of stooges instructed to give unanimously wrong answers on certain trials. Now, when the subjects made their judgement alone they were always correct, the task being a quite unambiguous and very simple one. However, under group conditions when the majority gave a unanimous wrong judgement, about one third of Asch's subjects gave the same wrong judgement. Note here that, unlike in Sherif's experiment, there was an unambiguously correct answer which subjects, when alone, never failed to produce. Asch (and subsequently other researchers) introduced various conditions into their basic paradigm in an effort to understand the factors controlling these manifestations of social influence, which he called experimental studies of conformity. For example, varying the difficulty or the ambiguity of the task affected the number of conforming responses obtained. Where the ambiguity or complexity of the task is increased and subjects become presumably less certain about their own judgements, they are more swayed by the opinions of others.

Another manipulation involves varying the apparent credibility of the other members of the 'group' and of the subject. This is achieved by giving the subject a pre-experimental test on some task closely related to the experimental one and then providing him with a false feedback about his performance on it, either that he has done well or badly (irrespective of his actual performance) relative to the others. Again, a subject who thinks others are better at the task than he is, is more likely to conform and, similarly, if he thinks they are worse, he is more likely to stay with his own judgement. Variations in the size of the unanimous majority only produce variations in conformity up to around four; increases beyond that making little further difference. However, stooges instructed to 'defect' from the majority at some point during the experiment and to

631

'support' the subject in his correct answers have a dramatic effect in reducing conformity. Using slightly different experimental techniques, other researchers have found that whether the response is made privately or face-to-face with others in the group also affects conformity, 'public' conditions producing more conformity. These, and related findings have suggested that we accept the influence of others in an attempt to assess reality, to validate our opinions, to arrive at correct answers. In Asch's and similar experiments, presumably the subject is reasonably concerned to give the right answers. In arriving at it, we may imagine that a number of sources of information play some role in his judgement. Firstly, he has information from his own senses about the task itself. In Asch's original experiment, the subject was simply asked which of three lines was the same length as a standard line, and it was sufficiently obvious that, alone, he always got the correct answers. However, supposing the task were really ambiguous or difficult, or maybe, as in Sherif's experiments, there were no 'right' answers. Under these conditions, one would expect subjects to be influenced by other kinds of cues while arriving at a judgement, for example, the cues deriving from other people's behaviour. In the face of a very ambiguous reality, other people's definitions of it seem very credible. When we see a new work of art, a new fashion or hear a new piece of music, the knowledge that other people, particularly highly credible people like critics, have assessed it as good, exciting, or important can easily make us feel that way about it too, and, indeed, make us actually see aspects of the stimulus which we had not previously considered. So it is with subjects in an experiment on conformity. Where the stimulus is ambiguous or complex, subjects are more likely to be swayed by majority opinion; where it is clear they are less likely to be influenced.

Of course, some subjects are susceptible to influence, even with an unambiguous task, and some subjects are immune to it with an ambiguous one. Individual differences account for certain components of social influence. A subject's evaluation of his own ideas versus other people's behaviour as a source of influence on his judgements depends on his assessment of his and their credibility, or competence. We have seen that when a subject is led to believe that he is not very good at the task, relative to others present, he is, indeed, more likely to be swayed by their opinions. Similarly, if their credibility is increased (enjoying the status that the critic has in the everyday world), then, again, the power of their behaviour with respect to the stimulus is increased. Not surprisingly we find that individual differences in self-esteem (that is, the degree to which one has a generally good opinion of one's abilities and other characteristics) relate to susceptibility to social influence when variables like task difficulty and the experimental conditions are held constant. People with a generally low level of self-esteem have, in some studies,

632

been found to be more susceptible to social influence. Thus, in summary, we see that one root of the general tendency to be influenced by others is man's need to evaluate correctly the world in which he lives and to compare his opinions and judgements with those of other people.

This, however, is not the whole story. We found that some studies showed that responding publicly in a conformity experiment produced more conformity than responding privately did. This suggests that people in these experiments might be conforming because they were worried about the impression they might be making on those present. It is possible, of course, that in the public conditions, the majority sounds a more convincing informational source than when one simply reads or hears of their responses. Nevertheless, common observation and other research data suggest that we conform for affective as well as cognitive reasons: we also conform in order to be accepted and liked by other people. We find some evidence (Festinger, Schachter and Back, 1964) that groups, that is real-life groups, which are cohesive and tightly-knit (that is, the members are strongly attracted to the group and to each other) show a greater uniformity of opinions on issues which affect them than groups which are less cohesive. Clearly, if disapproval of non-conformity by the majority of members is anticipated by individuals, then the more is risked in the more cohesive groups than in the less cohesive ones.

Dyadic influence
Social influence does not only occur in the small-group setting any more than it only occurs through the persuasive messages of mass communications. People exert power and influence over one another in dyadic relationships too. We can use the opinions and behaviour of a friend or partner to form opinions, make judgements, and attempt to validate those already formed. We can also be influenced by another in a dyadic relationship by our desire for approval acceptance or some related affective need. Before we leave the topic of social influence, let us return to the outcome matrix used to illustrate a social exchange theory of interaction; for the theory is not simply concerned with attraction in a relationship, it is concerned with further features of it. Thibaut and Kelly (1959) have suggested an analysis of power and influence between people which follows their analysis of interaction being controlled by outcomes. They argue that, in any kind of relationship, power and influence can be exerted to the extent that one party has resources (attributes or behaviour) which the other values highly and which are not currently obtainable elsewhere to a greater extent than his partner has resources which he similarly values and are unobtainable elsewhere. Power is contributed to by resources and dependencies. Once one member of a relationship is dependent on behaviour which only his

633

partner can enact, then the latter can make that behaviour contingent on services he requires from the former. As the Chinese say, 'one picture is worth a thousand words', so let us look at Figure 26.4 to see this point illustrated.

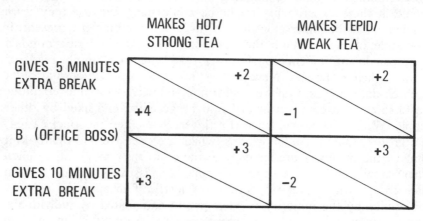

Fig. 26.4

In Figure 26.4 we have represented some possible combinations of responses available to a hypothetical tea-lady and her hypothetical boss. Again, her outcomes are represented above the diagonal of each cell, and his below. She can either make hot, strong tea, which he likes very much, or tepid, weak tea which he dislikes. He, in turn, can let her have either five or ten minutes extra break. Now, we can see that she cares less about the break time than he does about the tea (the difference between his maximum outcome +4 and his minimum outcome −2; as against her maximum of +3 and minimum of +2). She then has potential power over him in the sense that she can make decent tea contingent on the extra break time or anything else she likes to ask for. (This can happen without much being said on either side.) This, of course, only represents one segment of their relationship (or total behavioural repertoire). The boss, at this point in it, can curb the tea lady's power (a) by caring less about the kind of tea he drinks, (b) by finding something that the tea lady cares more about than the extra minutes break, (c) by having available another potential tea lady. This latter point reminds us that, as in the comparison level for alternatives, power in a group or dyad is limited by the other partner's potential for obtaining the valued resources elsewhere in some other relationship. This analysis, then, suggests conformity, and compliance not motivated by cognitive factors is made possible by the motive to maximize one's outcomes. Unfortunately, in much of the data we have on power influence and conformity it is difficult to separate out these components. Social exchange theory, in effect, suggests that conforming or complying with someone in order to be 'accepted' is simply behaviour which is reinforcement-determined.

Communication

Intrinsic to all forms of social interaction is the process of communication. Animals communicate through signalling systems which often carry complex, fixed, and specific messages. These signals regulate their social behaviour and have evolved to carry no other meaning. Humans have two partially overlapping systems. One of these is, of course, language; the other is bodily communication—usually called non-verbal communication. It consists of body and facial movements as well as the use of space, artifacts, and also paralanguage, the non-linguistic aspects of speech. Language and non-verbal communication are usually used in conjuction with each other. Watching a film with the sound switched off heightens our awareness of the amount of non-verbal communication which normally accompanies speech. Language, in its written form is an autonomous self-contained communication system, and, indeed, non-verbal communication can be markedly restricted, as with telephone conversations or formal lectures without language being impaired as a communication system. Non-verbal communication, except in very unusual instances such as American sign language for the deaf, or ritualized gesture in dance and mime, cannot stand alone as a communication system in humans. Language is used for communicating about events and abstractions of many sorts. Non-verbal communication carries information about the immediate social situation, the feelings of the actor, his attitudes towards others present, and the impression of himself, or identity, which he wants conveyed; it can also modify the meaning of what is being verbally expressed. Most basically, it functions to regulate the mechanics of social interaction, that is, for example, the initiation and termination of encounters and the sharing of the conversational floor. Although this suggests that the two systems show wholly separated functions this is not quite the case. Firstly, this is because, as we have already suggested, verbal and non-verbal communication supplement each other. A remark made with a smile can have a very different meaning to one made with a frown or a cold look, or a lugubrious tone of voice. Secondly, it is because our choice of words and style of speech can also carry information about our feelings toward the listener. Indeed, a whole class of verbal communication, called phatic communication is largely concerned with enhancing social relationships as with cocktail party talk, or remarks about the weather, or end of term speeches in school. We will consider this aspect of language very briefly later in the discussion. At this point, let us have a look at some of the research on non-verbal communication, its characteristics and functions.

Difficulties in studying non-verbal communication
There are considerable difficulties in studying non-verbal communication, firstly because we do not really know how much body-movement and voice and speech qualities are communication and not random. By and large, we consider behaviour to be communicative where the message is understood in the same way by both sender and receiver; that is, the sender intends the message, the receiver responds to it, the message carrying some common code of meaning. However, with non-verbal communication people respond to signals without being aware of having done so (for example, the glance which accompanies the termination of the speakers utterance and provides the cue for the listener to take over, is crucial in meshing conversation, but neither party is usually aware of the glance). Many body signals, although potentially informative about the sender, are not under his control. For example, blushing or rapid blinking are informative about the actor's state of arousal, but they are not intended to be so by him, and he cannot control them.

The second major problem encountered in studying non-verbal communication is that we know little about its structure, if, indeed, it has one. We know, for example, that all human languages are structured in such a way that sound units combine into meaning units, meaning units into words, words into clauses, clauses to sentences, sentences to paragraphs and so on. We know, too, something about the combination of syntax rules which underlies this hierarchy. We also know that all speakers and listeners have an innate understanding of the units and their syntax. Non-verbal communication consists of many modalities, but in none of these modalities are we yet able to identify the units. What constitutes a single gesture—the movement of hand and figures, or the slight shift in body orientation and the arm movement that accompanies it? Given that we could identify the primary component, how does it relate to the stream of body movement and paralanguage in which it appears?

Notwithstanding these ambiguities about non-verbal communication, research has unearthed some interesting findings about its role in social interaction.

The management of social encounter
Looking, or eye-catching, and smiling are specifically social signals. Meeting the gaze of someone whom we know makes it almost obligatory to interact with him at least briefly. (Conversely, avoiding the gaze is a method for avoiding social interaction, as attempting to engage a reluctant shop assistant or waiter will demonstrate.) The ethologist, Eibl-Eibesfeldt, has collected data which suggest that the gaze with raised

eyebrows and slight smile (or as he calls it, the eyebrow flash) is common in many cultures as a signal for interaction with someone out of earshot. Similarly, encounters (other than extremely negative ones) end with smiles from both participants and slight head movements. Some greeting signals, of course, are highly ritualized and often reserved for specific types of encounters between particular people, for example, shaking hands in our culture, or bowing amongst the Japanese.

At the start of an encounter people orientate themselves spatially to their partners, both so that they can attend to feedback from the other's eyes and facial expression, as well as being able to hear what is being said, and also to provide the other with feedback as to one's attention to, comprehension of, and interest in what he is saying. During the encounter, apportionment of talking time is managed through patterns of looking. Film recordings have shown that looking, on the part of the speaker, relates to the content of his speech. When one participant starts to talk, he looks briefly at the listener and, while he is talking, will send him intermittent, very brief glances. When he has finished, he then gives him a much longer look which provides the signal for the other to take the floor. If the content of his speech becomes complex, and this will also be indexed by a higher rate of pausing and longer pauses, he will withdraw eye-contact. This is partly so that the listener will not interrupt during pauses but may also reduce the amount of information from the others behaviour to him so that he can concentrate on planning his utterances. The listener, in contrast, looks more often at the speaker and with prolonged glances. These glances and his facial expression provide evidence of his attention, understanding, and attitude to what is being said (Kendon, 1967).

Film recordings have also shown that the body movements of two people talking very often mirror one another, and two people engaged in conversation often take up congruent postures (for example, both lean forward or both cross their legs). In fact, some research in psychiatric settings has suggested that body position congruence reflects the ease of relationship between the participants (Scheflen, 1964; Kendon, 1970). A speaker also changes the position of his body and his head as he changes the subject or theme of his discourse. This provides additional signals to the listener to help him follow the content of the speech. Furthermore, some people (in some cultures more than others) also illustrate the content of their speech by ikonic hand gestures (that is gestures which mime or picture what is being said).

Terminating an encounter (unless some external event intervenes to bring it to a close) is brought about by a variety of non-verbal as well as verbal signals. (Some people appear to find terminating encounters extraordinarily difficult.) First, between friends and casual encounters between people of equal status it is very common for one person or both

637

to say 'I must get along and do x now', and extremely rare to hear them say that they want to do x, and even rarer to hear them say that they want to terminate the interaction. The reason behind this, as behind the smiles which are exchanged at the close of an encounter are probably, as Irving Goffman has suggested, to make the withdrawal appear absolutely mutual and also to minimize the potential threat to the affability of the relationship which separation might entail. Another piece of evidence supporting his suggestion is that both greetings and farewells are more prolonged and elaborate the greater the preceding or anticipated separation and the greater the distance to be put between the parties. (An interesting project might be to measure the time and elaboration of greetings and farewells at transcontinental airport lounges as opposed to suburban train stations or bus garages.) As with greetings, some farewells may be ritually signalled by waves, handshakes, or standing stiffly to attention; and, again, these vary cross-culturally and at different periods in history in the same culture.

Signalling interpersonal attitudes

Aside from signals concerned with managing the mechanics of interaction, other kinds of information are transmitted, such as, information about the speakers' attitudes to each other, about their definitions of the situation and the nature of the encounter, about their feelings, and the identities they may be projecting. People will show, by their posture and their spatial orientation, their closeness to, and equality with, each other. It has been shown in a number of studies that in a formal situation, people of unequal status maintain a greater physical distance from one another, as, indeed, they will if they do not like each other. Looking and mutual gazing also signal the degree of intimacy of the participants—that is, people look more at those they like and those they approve of. Eye-signals are complex in this respect. Looking, particularly mutual looking between opposite sexed partners, is a signal of intimacy and mutual involvement, as well as liking among those not particularly involved. However, staring is threatening to most people and is interpreted as a signal of hostility and/or dominance. Gaze-aversion signals indicate both submission and self-concealment or even deception. In this case, the direction of gaze is only one of the other signals such as facial expression and, of course, the nature of the interaction—and the interpretation of gaze will depend partly on these other cues.

The definition of the situation

If an encounter is going to run off smoothly the participants have to agree on what it is to be about; whether, for example, it is to be consultative, casual, sexual, serious, funny, or whatever. Many encounters take place in circumstances where the definition is imposed by shared norms.

638

We know in advance, for example, that requesting a book from the librarian at the public library is likely to be casual and consultative, that an encounter at a party may be sexual, that a drink in a pub may be funny. The settings in which such encounters take place already provide cues as to the definitions of the situations which will occur in them. It is difficult to hold a party in an office usually occupied by the Social Security Department, and almost equally difficult to discuss one's career plans with one's tutor in a ballroom. However, in modern society, many of our encounters are not thus structured in advance and we have to improvise definitions of the situation with our co-actors. We do this partly by the use of clothes, artifacts and props (such as brief cases, shopping bags, etc.); we do it by the style of speech that we adopt; and we do it by means of general demeanour in the form of gestures and postures. During an encounter which had previously been casual-consultative, one participant may attempt to redefine it as sexual. This may be done by increasing physical proximity, by increased touching, by increased looking, and changes in tone of voice. If the other participant does not accept this redefinition it can be signalled by body movements which reduce proximity and congruity, gaze diversion, 'stiffer' postures, and so forth. All this can be achieved without any verbal 'discussion' at all.

Information about emotional states

So far, we have discussed those aspects of non-verbal behaviour over which actors can achieve some degree of control and, through this control, the course of an encounter. Emotional states or 'real feelings' are revealed by many cues which the actor cannot control, like blushing, or which he may attempt to conceal, like facial expression.

Research has revealed that facial expressions, body movement, and tone of voice can all give clues to the observer about emotional states. Some facial expressions appear to be innately linked with emotional states, such as anger, disgust, or happiness, and are very similar across cultures where other aspects of non-verbal communication are remarkably dissimilar. If we take the facial expression associated with the few 'basic' emotions, observers are quite accurate at interpreting them (Woodworth, 1938; Ekman, 1967). However, many facial expressions are not very interpretable, particularly those which reflect similar emotional states like surprise and awe. The meanings of facial expressions in any case derives both from the sequence in which they occur (Cline, 1956) and from the context in which they occur (Frijda, 1969). Perhaps most importantly, some people have some control over their facial musculature and they may hide emotional expression. (In some cultures, such as among the Japanese, concealment of unpleasant emotion in particular is absolutely obligatory.) It has been found that emotional

639

states are more easily detectable the more 'leakage' cues are provided by body movement and voice qualities (Duncan, 1969; Ekman and Frieson, 1969). It is important for actors to detect signs of emotional arousal in others during interaction since, for one thing, they provide warning lights of impending embarrassment. Embarrassment, as we noted in Chapter 25 is disruptive for all parties in an encounter.

Projecting impressions of self

In order to make social encounters run smoothly, we have to agreee upon a definition of the situation. Part of this definition is the roles which the participants are to play. We saw in Chapter 25 that a projected role which is discredited (as, for example, with the unfunny wit, or incompetent performer) leads to a hiatus in interaction which we call embarrassment. A situation where someone's conduct is being investigated calls for an investigator and an accused. A situation where someone is to get advice about his personal problems requires a client and a counsellor. Although, often, definitions and roles are established in advance, and much of the substance of the interaction is carried by language, nevertheless, we use appearance in the form of clothing, furniture and other props to sustain them. Where they are not classified in advance, the communcation carried by these artifacts plays an important part in making the interaction comfortably predictable. It is difficult to sustain a seduction scene dressed in a pin-striped suit and bowler hat or in industrial overalls, and similarly, it is difficult to sustain an admonitory conversation with someone dressed in tennis shorts. Clothes and posture tell those present what kind of role we are planning to take up and they may adjust themselves accordingly. This is possible because people share stereotypes based on appearance, for example, that jeans and T-shirts imply informality and tolerance, and heavy make-up and exotic dress, sexual availability.

Non-verbal communication has a degree of ambiguity about it. This ambiguity is, however, important. So much of social life is improvised. We may attempt redefinition of situation; we may attempt to set up a role relationship with someone. In both cases, this can be achieved non-verbally. However, failure to achieve it non-verbally because of the other's non-acceptance can leave the relationship unimpaired, since non-verbal statements can be ignored or misunderstood in a way that verbal signals cannot be. This allows for considerable flexibility in our relations with others.

One important aspect of non-verbal communication is that it varies cross-culturally. It varies in the sense that although components of it, like eye-contact, proximity, touching, and so forth, express the same dimensions, they do it in different ways. For example, proximity signals intimacy and equality across many cultures. However the degree of physical proximity expected overall varies. Amongst Arabs, all situations demand greater physical proximity, frontal orientation, and eye-contact than in northern Europe. As we have seen, facial expressions signify emotional states amongst different races. However, the overall degree of facial expressiveness is controlled by norms of conduct, so that it is distinctly inhibited in Japan and amongst some American Indians and distinctly uninhibited amongst Italians and Arabs. This means, of course, that managing encounters with members of other cultures can be distinctly tricky and lead to serious misunderstandings. Of course, books of etiquette are often designed to clarify the ritual components of non-verbal communication, yet that which manages most interactions can only be learned through experience.

Language and sociolinguistics

Let us now consider very briefly the social functions of language. It was suggested earlier that some verbal interactions are phatic, that is, concerned with the maintenance of social relationships. Our choice of language in a bilingual community, our choice of standard or dialect in a mono-lingual one, our choice of style, literary or vernacular, all depend on the setting, the relationships between participants, and the topic of conversation. Phatic communication, such as speeches by visiting heads of state or party chat carries little information in itself: it is simply a celebration of existing relationships. The main difference between language and non-verbal communication, aside from the former's capacity to carry information displaced in time and space, is the ambiguity of non-verbal communication. Also, with the management of encounters and relationships carried by the non-verbal channels, language is freed from overloading on its main function. The effective use of both types of communication can be regarded as a skill which can be acquired, and a skill which is important for a successful social life.

In summary, then, we have looked at four components of social interaction: perception, attraction, influence, and communication. The research discussed has focused on these components separately. However, in the flow of complex behaviour and cognition typical of social interaction, these processes are not really separable. For example, whether we like someone or not depends on how we perceive his actions, assign causes to them, and the inferences we make from them. Our perceptions, in turn, depend on what an actor communicates about himself and how he communicates with us. For example, a person's facial expressions and gestures modify the meanings we attach to his words and actions. The experimental techniques described demand an artificial control and separation of variables which normally interact. The development of new research techniques may, at some time, make it possible to examine the components of social behaviour as they interact in 'real-life' settings.

27   Attitudes

DENIS GAHAGAN

Introduction

It could well be argued that the study of social psychology has largely been the study of social influence. This is particularly evident when we consider the vast amount of attitude research reported in the psychological literature during the past few decades. This is not really very surprising. Social psychology has developed mainly in North America and has always had a distinctly utilitarian bias. Underlying theory and research in American psychology is a belief that, once the principles and processes of human action have been uncovered, then this knowledge can be put to practical use in reducing social discord and improving the quality of human existence. We find this belief most clearly expressed in the Behaviourist's allegiance to the methods of natural science and the stated aim of ultimately achieving complete prediction and control.

Some psychologists may well deny the reality of this utilitarian ideology and argue that they are pursuing psychological knowledge for its own sake. Nevertheless, most psychological research is funded directly or indirectly by government agencies or by large foundations whose wealth comes from national and multi-national corporations, and such funding is premised on the expectation that the research will eventually lead to some practical application. However, the application of psychological knowledge can be for good or for evil, and which it is will depend largely on the values and attitudes of not only the persons applying it but also of whoever is judging it. What may seem a vital and valuable application to one person may strike another as an abomination. The use of psychological techniques in the interrogation of guerrillas will be judged as good or evil depending on whether they are seen as 'terrorists' or as 'freedom fighters'. The application of psychological methods in advertising will doubtless be applauded or deplored, depending on whether one sees advertising as a means of deceiving and manipulating people or as a healthy way of encouraging consumption and thus promoting economic growth. If there is disagreement as to both means and ends in the quest for human happiness, then the development and application of a social science technology is no more a guarantee of social harmony and well-being than is the development and application of nuclear physics.

Thus, in considering what social psychologists have discovered about attitudes, it behoves us to keep in mind that the vast body of research reflects a desire to be able to change people's attitudes and, by implication, their behaviour. Advertisers wish to sell more products, politicians to sway more voters, and health authorities to change health practices.

The nature of attitudes

Why do we use the term 'attitude'? It is useful on two counts: firstly, when trying to explain someone's past or present behaviour towards some person or object, and, secondly, when predicting how he will behave in the future towards this same person or object. If we observe that an individual goes out of his way to avoid homosexuals, frequently makes disparaging remarks about them, and visibly bristles when one enters the room, then we attribute to that individual a negative attitude towards homosexuality. Thus, an attitude is an attribution. We do not see it in the same way in which we see a cat or a razor blade. All that we observe is that a person behaves *consistently* towards a category of persons or objects across a large number of situations. It is this consistency which leads us to make the attribution. _an example!_

643

An attitude is, therefore, a psychological construct. It is an invention of the observer in his attempt to make sense of someone's behaviour. It is for this reason that psychologists differ in their definitions of an attitude. On the one hand, there are those who hold what is called 'a *latent process conception*'. What this means is that they postulate the operation of some hidden or hypothetical variable, functioning within the behaving individual, which shapes, acts upon, or 'mediates' the observable behaviour. Thus, they attribute a genuine, but unobservable, existence to our inner attitudes. A good example of a definition reflecting this conception is that given by Gordon Allport: 'An attitude is a mental and neural state of readiness, organized through experience, exerting a directive or dynamic influence upon the individual's response to all objects and situations with which it is related.'

On the other hand, psychologists who dislike postulating hidden intervening variables have adopted 'a *probability conception*' of attitudes. They question the internal reality of attitudes and argue that, as we know them, attitudes consist solely of the external constructs which we develop on the basis of our observations of consistencies among an individual's behaviour. For these psychologists, then, an attitude is no more than a convenient shorthand description of a set of empirical relationships and not a genuine psychological entity. Which conception a psychologist adopts will be largely a matter of personal preference. In this Chapter, we shall adopt the latent process conception, since this approach has tended to dominate both theory and research.

Three components of attitudes

In analysing attitudes, a distinction is usually made between three components: cognitive, affective and behavioural. To illustrate this three-fold classification, we will consider the issue of vivisection:

The cognitive component consists of the beliefs which a person holds with respect to the attitude object. Thus, an individual may believe that most advances in medical knowledge could not have been achieved without the use of animal experiments; that the saving of human lives is more important than any suffering caused to animals; and that the laws regulating animal experiments ensure that efforts are made to minimize suffering and that animals are used only when there is no alternative method of investigation. These beliefs relating to vivisection make up the cognitive component of one individual's positive attitude towards the issue.

The affective component consists of the feelings which an individual has towards the issue. They may vary in kind from one person to another. For example, one person may feel anger at the notion of vivisection, whereas another person may feel horror, and yet another person only mild regret. Whatever the case, the feelings will vary in direction and

644

intensity; that is, they will be either positive or negative and will differ in strength. The affective component of many attitudes is often the most deep-rooted of the three and, hence, the most resistant to change.

The behavioural component consists of the tendency or disposition to react to an attitude object in certain ways. Thus, if a person has a negative attitude towards the issue of vivisection, he is likely to speak out against it, whenever the occasion arises; he will withhold a donation to a medical research project if he believes it will involved animal experiments; and he may write letters to newspapers condemning such practice. These actions would demonstrate the behavioural component of a person's attitude towards vivisection.

This analysis of the structure of attitudes raises a number of questions: How are the components of an attitude related to one another? How is it that two people may hold the same set of beliefs about an attitude object but feel very differently? If one of the components changes, will this lead to changes in the other components? If one of the components is a tendency or disposition to react to the attitude object, will this reaction occur invariably? In trying to provide answers to these and related questions, psychologists have generated a large body of theory and research, some of which we shall have cause to refer to in this Chapter.

Consistency of beliefs, feelings, and actions

Let us suppose we hear someone expressing his beliefs about the Irish. We might hear him make the following assertions:

> The Irish are mentally inferior.
> The Irish are intolerant bigots.
> The Irish drink too much.
> The Irish are violent.

Now, it would be very surprising if we then heard the speaker say:

> I like the Irish.

This would probably strike us as rather bizarre and we should wonder whether he was being deliberately ironic or perhaps was not quite right in his head. This is because the cognitive, affective, and behavioural components will normally be congruent. If you have negative feelings about an attitude object, then, in general, your beliefs about that object will support these feelings. Furthermore, we can expect that your actions will be largely in keeping with your feelings and beliefs. There will be an overall consistency between the three components. Firmly-entrenched beliefs are usually accompanied by strong feelings, and strong feelings are usually supported by firmly-held beliefs.

Most attempts at changing people's attitudes implicitly acknowledge this principle of consistency. In attempting to persuade someone, we usually communicate new information to him. If he accepts this information, it means that his beliefs will have changed. The expectation is that his feelings will follow suit. This approach is often successful, provided the individual has no strong feelings about the issue in the first place. For example, if I have no strong feelings about any particular make of car, then my attitude towards different makes is likely to be influenced by various sources of information such as knowledgeable friends, advertisements, and reports by motoring correspondents in the media.

On the other hand, if I already have strong feelings on an issue, then I am likely to resist any new information which contradicts my beliefs. I may do this by ignoring it or distorting it in some way as to make it consistent with these beliefs. The orator, the demagogue, and the propagandist are, of course, well aware of this resistance and try simultaneously to manipulate people's feelings in order to change their attitudes. It may well be that the reason for the failure of so many attempts to reduce racial prejudice is because the approach has been through education. Dissemination of information which contradicts false beliefs about ethnic minorities will have little impact if people already have very strong feelings.

In order to demonstrate that a change in the affective component of an attitude would produce a consistent change in the cognitive component, Rosenberg (1960) conducted the following experiment. Students who had negative attitudes towards racially integrated housing acted as subjects. In the experimental group, they were hypnotized in individual sessions and given the following instructions: 'When you awake, you will be very much in favour of the idea of Negroes moving into white neighbourhoods. The mere idea of this will give you a happy, exhilarated feeling. Although you will not remember this suggestion having been made, it will strongly influence your feelings after you have awakened'. When the subjects awoke, they were unable to remember the hypnotic suggestion having been made, and their attitudes towards integrated housing were measured again. It was found that they had not only undergone a change in feeling towards integrated housing, but, more importantly, they had changed their beliefs also. In order to be consistent with their hypnotically-induced feelings, they now believed that integrated housing would neither lower property values in the neighbourhood nor harm race relations. The effects lasted a week, until in a second hypnotic session Rosenberg reversed the feeling change and carefully debriefed the subjects. Subjects in the two control groups, who either rested or engaged in role-playing 'someone who feels one thing and believes another', showed relatively little change in their beliefs or feelings about integrated housing.

We do not know, of course, from this study whether the changes in belief would have persisted for a long time, nor whether the subjects would have behaved differently with respect to integrated housing. Nor, indeed, can we be certain that subjects who are susceptible to hypnotic suggestion are typical in their need to re-establish consistency. Nevertheless, Rosenberg has provided a dramatic illustration of how change in one attitude component will produce change in another.

Consistency between attitudes

So far, we have considered how each attitude has an internal consistency. However, we can often go beyond a single attitude and see how this principle applies to whole clusters of attitudes. We will illustrate this with a hypothetical case of someone who feels very strongly about the introduction of artificial, synthetic elements in food. No doubt, he will support his feelings with a set of beliefs about the harmfulness and non-nutritional value of such foods and will probably examine the labelling on tins and packages when buying his groceries. However, he is also likely to feel strongly about factory farming and the use of chemical fertilizers. We can probably go beyond the food area and predict with some confidence that he will value traditional craftsmanship against mass-produced articles, would prefer to live in the country, perhaps shuns the mass media, and entertains himself doing pottery or singing madrigals. We might even predict, though with less confidence, that he would go to a homeopathic doctor. What we have here, then, is a man with a coherent set of attitudes which reflect an underlying theme or value system which is based on a love of the 'natural' and a dislike of 'progress'. The more strongly we know him to feel about any one of the objects or issues which we have described, the more confidently can we predict his position on any of the others. Such a set of attitudes constitutes a syndrome.

From this example, we can see that we do not hold an attitude in isolation from other attitudes. Rather, it exists in a matrix of relationships with other attitudes and reflects one or more important values that we hold. Values can be viewed as those ultimately desirable goals or end-states about which we have very strong feelings. Examples might be 'happiness', 'a healthy body', 'fame', 'security' or 'a loving family'. It is towards the attainment of our values that we strive and by our values that we judge the actions both of ourselves and of others. Rosenberg (1956) has shown that the strength and nature of the feelings we have towards any attitude object is correlated with our beliefs about that object's instrumentality in attaining or blocking the values which we hold. This means that the more instrumental I believe something to be in leading to the attainment of one or more of my values, the more favour-

647

able will be my feelings about it. It is for this reason that there is affective-cognitive consistency in any attitude.

For each individual, then, there will be a number of attitudinal arenas in each of which a number of attitudes are related to each other in a consistent manner as a reflection of one or more values. We can see now why two individuals may share the same attitudinal belief but differ in their feelings. For example, they both might believe that the Baader-Meinhof group are determined to destroy the existing political structure of West Germany, but feel the exact opposite to each other. This could well be because they differ in the importance they attach to a number of values, such as freedom, national security, and non-violence.

Attitudes and behaviour

If one of the components of an attitude is the tendency to react to the object in certain ways, will the reaction always occur? Or, to rephrase the question, do people behave in a manner which is consistent with their attitudes? In the very early years of attitude research, many researchers, rather naively, assumed that they did. Any failure to predict behaviour from a knowledge of attitudes would be attributed to inadequacy of the attitude-measuring instrument. However, in 1934 LaPiere published the results of an investigation which strongly challenged this assumption. During a period of two years, he travelled extensively through the United States in the company of a middle-aged Chinese couple. They stayed in numerous hotels and ate at many restaurants. Of the 251 establishments visited, only one refused them service. Six months after each visit, LaPiere then wrote to the proprietor to enquire whether the establishment had any policy about accepting custom from orientals. Approximately 93 per cent of the hotel proprietors and 92 per cent of the restaurant owners indicated in their responses to the questionnaire that they would refuse to serve Chinese people. This indicated a marked inconsistency between their actions and their verbalized attitudes.

However, since LaPiere and his Chinese friends had visited the hotels and restaurants *before* sending the questionnaire, it was just possible that the Chinese couple might have caused the prejudiced attitude in some way through their visit. So, LaPiere sent the same questionnaire to a random sample of one hundred similar establishments, which they had not visited, and obtained a similar negative response. Here we have, then, an instance of a clear discrepancy between an attitude (as measured by a questionnaire) and actual behaviour. In fact, since LaPiere's classic study, many researchers have confirmed this attitude-behaviour inconsistency.

Why are we unable to predict other people's behaviour from a knowledge of their attitude? Why is there this discrepancy? There are several good reasons. In the first place, many attitudes are relevant to a

648

single action and, in some circumstances, may be in activated opposition to one another. For example, I may find myself defending the right of a National Front supporter to address a meeting, not because I have a favourable attitude towards the aims and policies of the National Front—they may actually be an anathema to me—but because I have a stronger attitude towards the issue of free speech in a democratic society. Secondly, many of our attitudes are stereotyped, so that, when confronted with an instance of the attitude object, it may bear little relation to the stereotype. Unless the feeling component is very strong, the action tendency is likely to be fairly weak in such an instance. Thus, in LaPiere's study, the proprietors may have shared a negative stereotype of the Chinese as sinister, cruel, and violent—a stereotype popular in comics, detective stories and 'B' feature movies of the period. However, when confronted by a respectable middle-aged Chinese couple in the company of an equally respectable-looking American, the negative stereotype was simply not evoked. Finally, and perhaps most importantly, a person's behaviour is determined, not only by his attitude, but also by his evaluation of the immediate situation and of the likely outcome of his behaviour. A person will take into account the norms operative in the situation and the consequences likely to result from his behaviour. A racist may hesitate to give vent to his prejudice if there are strong laws forbidding such behaviour. Cyrano de Bergerac was un-willing to declare his passion for Roxane, because he feared she would scorn him on account of his grotesque nose. A guest at a dinner party may publicly praise the cook and privately deplore her cooking.

So, we cannot rely solely on our knowledge of a person's attitudes to predict his behaviour. Knowledge about the situation is equally important. Nevertheless, in our day-to-day interactions we do manage fairly well to predict how other people are likely to react. This is because we also take the situation into account. It is only when, as psychologists, we try to measure people's attitudes in a manner divorced from situa-tions, that we usually come unstuck in our predictions. Even when attempting to predict how people will vote in an election, where we might expect the effect of the immediate situation to be minimal and the effect of their attitudes to be paramount, psychologists still have very variable success.

The measurement of attitudes

Given that we do not have the time to observe people's behaviour across a wide variety of situations in order to infer their attitudes, how do we set about measuring them? What we do in most cases is actually to ask them what their attitudes are. We might choose to do this in a perfectly straightforward manner with a direct question during an open-ended interview. However, since accurate measurement is an essential element of scientific research and since, in many cases, we want to go beyond a simple pro-con dichotomy and be able to make fine discriminations between different individuals or groups, psychologists have developed a number of systematic techniques for this purpose.

Attitude scale techniques, largely employing questionnaires, have been in existence for nearly fifty years, but the earliest ones, developed by Thurstone in 1929 and by Likert in 1932, are still widely used today, albeit in modified form. They illustrate quite well the problems intrinsic to measuring attitudes—problems of sampling and of establishing reliability and validity. If we return to our notion of an attitude object, then how do we set about measuring, that is, quantifying, for example, an individual's attitudes towards synthetically produced foods? Firstly, we must look for questionnaire items which are relevant to the attitude and, secondly, we must produce a scale of items, so that people with different attitudes towards such foods appear at different points on it. Accepting these two criteria, we will examine the different ways in which Thurstone and Likert set about constructing attitude scales.

The Thurstone method

A person is presented with a set of statements and asked to tick those with which he is in agreement. For example, a selection of such items relating to synthetically produced foods might be:

10.5 *Synthetically produced foods make a wide range of nourishment available to even the poorest sections of the population.*

9.2 *Synthetically produced foods are made under the most hygienic conditions.*

8.0 *Synthetically produced foods are nourishing but rather tasteless.*

7.5 *Synthetically produced foods are unappetizing.*

4.3 *Synthetically produced foods are lacking in vitamins.*

2.2 *Synthetically produced foods contain chemicals whose effects on the body we do not really understand.*

1.0 *Synthetically produced foods are dangerous and probably carcinogenic.*

The numbers beside each item refer to the scale value of the item and an individual's score is the mean of the scale values of the items he ticks. Normally, of course, the scale values are not shown on the questionnaire, and the items are randomized in terms of favourableness to the attitude object. The scale has eleven points, such that an individual can obtain a score anywhere between one and eleven. Thus, if he does have an attitude towards synthetic foods, he will tick only *some* of the items and it is the mean value of these items which gives us his attitude score. One assumption is that an item of value ten is twice as favourable as an item valued at five, that is, that we are using an equal interval scale. However, in order to understand how Thurstone came to make this assumption, which has not gone unchallenged, we have to see how the numbers or values are arrived at.

The procedure for constructing such a scale begins with the researcher collecting a large number of evaluatively-tinged statements about the attitude object. Each statement is put on a card and then a large number of judges—probably between fifty and one hundred—sort these statements into eleven piles ranging from most favourable through neutral to least favourable. Statements which are assigned to widely different piles by different judges are discarded as ambiguous. Then the scale value of the remaining items is calculated as the median position of each item among the eleven piles. Finally, the researcher selects between twenty and forty of these items to constitute the questionnaire, ensuring that they cover the full range of the eleven-point scale and that the median score of each item is approximately equidistant from that of its closest neighbour.

Of course, the judges' ratings do not necessarily have to be along a favourable-unfavourable dimension. It will depend on the particular attitude you are interested in measuring. For example, if you are interested in sexism, you may have judges rate several hundred statements for degree of sexual discrimination.

There are two major difficulties involved in the use of Thurstone-type scales. Firstly, a subject is asked to tick those items in the questionnaire with which he agrees and, by implication, those items closest to his position and having roughly the same scale value. However, there is nothing to stop him ticking any item he agrees with, so that two subjects could well end up with the same attitude score obtained from very different patterns of responding. Secondly, the values attributed to the statement items as a result of sorting by judges may well be affected by the judges used. Thurstone did not think this would be the case and argued that all judges would sort objectively, uninfluenced by their own attitudes towards the issue. However, Hovland and Sherif (1952) looked at the sortings of statements about negroes and found that Negro and pro-Negro white judges shifted neutral and moderately favourable statements towards the unfavourable end of the scale, while anti-Negro judges shifted neutral and moderately unfavourable statements towards the favourable end of the eleven piles. So, what Thurstone had hoped would be a technique for constructing an objective equal-interval scale, can only safely be regarded as an ordinal scale.

The Likert method
A person is presented with a number of statements which are clearly favourable or unfavourable towards the attitude object and is asked to

rate his agreement with each one on a five-point scale. For example, a sample of such items relating to immigration might be:

There are too many coloured immigrants in this country.

Strongly agree	Moderately agree	Undecided	Moderately disagree	Strongly disagree
(5)	(4)	(3)	(2)	(1)

Anti-immigration arguments are a thinly-veiled cover for racist beliefs.

Strongly agree	Moderately agree	Undecided	Moderately disagree	Strongly disagree
(1)	(2)	(3)	(4)	(5)

Immigrants should be given assisted passage back to their country of origin.

Strongly disagree	Moderately disagree	Undecided	Moderately agree	Strongly agree
(1)	(2)	(3)	(4)	(5)

There should be no restriction on the entry to this country of the relations of settled immigrants.

Strongly disagree	Moderately disagree	Undecided	Moderately agree	Strongly agree
(5)	(4)	(3)	(2)	(1)

The numbers in brackets are the score values of each response and would not normally appear on the questionnaire. An individual's total attitude score is the sum of the scores for all the items in the questionnaire. In order to expose any response bias of always checking on one side of the scale or of always acquiescing with a statement irrespective of its content, there are usually an equal number of favourable and unfavourable items, and the direction of the five-point agree-disagree scales is systematically varied. Since each item can contribute a varied amount from one to five to the total score, there is no basis for saying that a total score of 43 is half as hostile to immigration as a score of 86. All we have is an ordinal scale on which we can rank individuals.

To construct a Likert scale, the researcher selects a large number of favourable and unfavourable items and gives them to a trial group of representative subjects, who have to check each item on the five-point agree-disagree scale. Computing the total score for each subject, the researcher then carries out an item analysis. To do this, he ranks all the subjects in terms of their total scores and then selects the top and bottom 25 per cent. He then examines each item to see which ones best discriminate between these two groups of subjects. Those items which do not discriminate are discarded. Those remaining constitute the final questionnaire.

This Likert procedure is often used by researchers who wish to construct an attitude questionnaire quickly. It is a good deal less time-consuming than the Thurstone method, and measures of the same attitude, made with the two methods, correlate highly. However, as with the Thurstone method, the Likert method is liable to difficulty in interpreting the meaning of a total score, since many different patterns of responding can yield the same total. Nevertheless, it does give a more sensitive measure of each individual's response to any particular item than the Thurstone method and, therefore, its reliability can be more accurately assessed using the test-retest technique. Recently, however, another easily-used measuring device has grown increasingly popular: the semantic differential.

The semantic differential

A person is presented with a bi-polar scale on which he has to mark the point which he thinks represents his attitude. Thus, he might be asked to rate his feelings about immigration on the scale below:

Favourable :——:——:——:——:——:——:——:——: *Unfavourable*
(+3) (+2) (+1) (0) (−1) (−2) (−3)

The choice of bi-polar construct will depend on the nature of the attitude being measured, but will usually be evaluative, that is, it will primarily indicate a person's feelings about the object. Thus, alternatives which might be used are *like-dislike*, *support-reject* or *pleasant-unpleasant*. The researcher can choose how many points to use on his scale. We have given as an example a seven-point scale, but the range can be anywhere between five and about sixteen. The values may or may not appear underneath each scale point, largely depending on the researcher's personal preference.

All that the subject has to do, then, is to put a mark on the scale point which indicates his attitude. Most subjects readily respond to this request and have little difficulty in representing their attitudes in spatial terms. Even quite young children, who would be unable to cope with a Thurstone or Likert questionnaire, can be given the semantic differential. Since the test-retest reliability tends to be high, this technique does provide a useful method for measuring attitude change following an influence attempt.

However, as with most measuring instruments employed by psychologists, the semantic differential is not without its problems. For example, there is no control for any position response bias. If a subject will always respond by marking at the extreme ends of a scale irrespective of his attitude, this will not be revealed to the researcher unless a large number of measures are taken for a range of issues. Secondly, it is not easy to interpret the meaning of a response which falls in the centre of the scale; for example, if a subject scores zero on the seven-point scale above. If a scale indicates both the direction—whether positive or negative—and the strength of a person's attitude, then what does a score of zero indicate? There are three possibilities. On the one hand, it could indicate *indifference*. Thus, for example, if I were asked to indicate my attitude towards veteran tricycle runs from London to Brighton, I would mark the centre of the scale, since I am completely indifferent to this activity. Alternatively, it could indicate *ignorance*. If asked my attitude about some issue of which I am totally ignorant, then the only sensible response I can make on the scale is to mark the mid-point. But, the most likely reason for a score of zero is *ambivalence*. Our attitudes to many objects and issues are frequently quite complex. For example, let us take the case of a person's attitude to oil fires. Probably included in his attitude will be a whole set of beliefs relating to such factors as initial purchase cost, efficiency of heating, actual running cost, no quarterly bills, smell and dirt, possible effect of fumes on health, danger of fire where there are young children, and so forth. Attached to each of these beliefs will be an evaluative reaction, for example, that low running cost is desirable and that fumes and dirt are unpleasant. Thus, most people probably have very mixed attitudes to oil fires and, in order to be able to indicate their attitude on a single scale, they will have to weigh up all these pros and cons. The outcome may well be that the rating is made at the mid-point of the scale and reflects the ambivalence which people feel.

The techniques we have considered so far are all self-report techniques. That is, they rely on the individual actually reporting in some way or other on what his attitude is. They are all liable, therefore, to what is called the *social desirability bias*. This simply means that, since subjects are aware of or at least guess at the implications of their responses, they may well distort their responses in such a way as to convey what they believe will be a favourable impression of themselves to the investigator. Thus, what the investigator gets is not an accurate measure of a person's real attitude towards an issue but rather a measure of what the subject thinks the investigator will approve. This could well happen when the issues involved are controversial or sensitive; for example, when trying to measure attitudes to immigration, sexual equality, the mentally or physically handicapped, and so forth. However much the investigator tries to disguise the purpose of the enquiry or to reassure the subjects that there are no right or wrong answers, he would be naive to assume automatically that social desirability did not contaminate the responses.

Indirect methods
Despite many of the drawbacks which we have mentioned, standardized scales of attitude measurement are useful. We can estimate their reliability fairly accurately, and they are certainly invaluable when measuring attitude change. Nevertheless, they must be treated with caution and, where possible, the information they yield should be supported by other evidence. For this reason, indirect methods have

654

been explored. Of particular interest are those situations where an individual expects to have to commit himself to an attitude. Thus, in a study by DeFleur and Westie (1958) subjects were first asked to fill in a questionnaire indicating their attitudes towards Negroes. Later, they were provided with a specific action opportunity, when the experimenter asked them if they were willing to be photographed with a Negro of the opposite sex in order to provide him with photographic slides for use in his research. Some subjects indicated willingness, but others categorically refused. Those who agreed were then presented with a *photograph release agreement* containing a graded series of uses to which the photograph could be put, ranging from a laboratory experiment of the kind which the subjects had previously experienced to a nationwide publicity campaign advocating racial integration. They had to sign their names on this document to each 'use' which they would permit. DeFleur and Westie were able then to determine (a) the degree of correspondence between anti-Negro attitudes as indicated by responses to the questionnaire and (b) commitment to these attitudes as indicated by the range of uses which subjects were willing to allow. They reported that, although the correspondence was high, it was by no means one-to-one. For example, a few subjects who appeared unprejudiced on the questionnaire nevertheless refused to have their photograph taken with a Negro. This and similar findings from other studies highlight the dangers of over-reliance on self-report measures of attitudes.

An alternative indirect approach has been to present subjects with partially structured material and to infer their attitudes from the responses given. For example, subjects may be asked to describe what is happening in an ambiguous picture on the assumption that they will project their underlying feelings onto the material. However, there are difficulties here of interpretation. For instance, if, when asked to describe a scene containing whites and Negroes, an individual assigns the Negroes to menial positions, we cannot be certain that this reflects anti-Negro prejudice. He may simply be reflecting the more likely social arrangement as he knows or has experienced it. Also the test-retest reliability of such techniques is low, and any comparison between the responses of different individuals is difficult. Their main advantage is that subjects are often unaware of the dimension on which they are being assessed and so are likely to give 'genuine' responses. Therefore, used in conjunction with other methods, this approach can provide limited supportive information.

Yet another approach which attempts to eliminate the effects of the social desirability bias and to achieve an accurate estimate of the attitudes of individuals is the recording of physiological responses or reactions to actual members of the attitude object group, to pictorial representations of situations involving such members, or even to the

655

words or labels by which we identify them. For example, Westie and DeFleur (1959) recorded galvanic skin response (GSR), vascular constriction of the finger, amplitude and duration of heartbeat, and duration of heart cycle, while subjects were viewing pictures of whites and Negroes. The assumption underlying such studies is that the intensity of arousal recorded is directly related to the strength of the individual's feelings about the attitude object. However, even if we accept this assumption—and there are many physiological psychologists who would not—we still do not know whether it is positive or negative. All we really have is a measure of arousal. Considerable excitement was generated briefly in the 1960s when Hess and his colleagues reported findings indicating that subjects' pupils dilated in the presence of pleasant stimuli and constricted in the presence of unpleasant stimuli. Here, at last, it seemed psychologists had a measure of both the direction and strength of a response to an attitude object which would not be under the conscious control of subjects. However, subsequent research, using more refined photographic techniques and analysis, has cast serious doubt on this dilation-constriction relation to attitudes and suggests that such differential responses indicate only intensity and not direction of feeling.

Because each of the different approaches to attitude measurement has its advantages and its limitations, many psychologists advocate the use of more than one approach in any study. As with most research in psychology, unfortunately, practice often falls a long way short of precept and researchers often choose to rely solely on a single technique —usually a single, self-report measure. The choice of a measuring instrument is all too frequently dictated by considerations extrinsic to the nature of the enquiry: considerations of expediency determined by the availability of time and resources. This is particularly serious when the outcome of the enquiry is envisaged as having practical application. Social planners, government agencies, market researchers and other agents of social change who blithely ignore the complexities of measurement and evaluation do so at their peril.

Theories of attitude change

Theories of attitude change are primarily an attempt to answer the question: under what conditions will a person change his attitudes? During the 1950s and early 1960s, there was a burgeoning of theories of attitude change in the psychological literature. Insko, in a book published in 1969, reviewed no less than fourteen major theories. Lest the reader feel daunted at the prospect of considering such a multiplicity of approaches, we shall begin by examining a conceptual framework, which will allow us to compare and contrast social psychological theories. We will then

656

select for scrutiny three types of theory of attitude-change by way of illustration. The selection will be determined partly by the conceptual framework and partly by the impact which the theories have had in the psychological literature.

A conceptual framework
According to Richard Stevens (1976) social psychological theories can be seen as differing in a number of important ways:

BASIC ASSUMPTIONS

Theories differ in their assumptions about the nature of man, the significance of factors which influence his behaviour and experience, and the appropriate methods of enquiry. Thus, for example, a behaviourist approach to socialization assumes that the infant is virtually a *tabula rasa* to be moulded by the patterns of stimuli which impinge upon him— a totally deterministic and very largely passive view of man. On the other hand, personal construct theorists and symbolic interactionists regard man as a reflexive being who constructs social reality, exercising choice and making decisions in the light of his constructions. This distinction between man as determined and man as self-determining in turn leads to assumptions—often not made explicit—as to the importance or otherwise of biological factors in human development. Furthermore, theories are premised on assumptions as to what methods of enquiry should be employed. Thus, the behaviourist subscribes to the methods of natural science, whereas theorists holding a reflexive view of man adopt a more phenomenological approach and stipulate that we must take into account how a person perceives and experiences the world.

CONCEPTS

Theories differ in the nature and range of concepts used. Some theorists coin new words (e.g., reactive inhibition, reaction formation, reactance), but more often they use words 'selected as approximations from everyday language and given a meaning of their own in the context of the theory' (e.g., arousal, projection, dissonance, identification). Some concepts are given highly precise definitions (e.g., releaser), while others are used variably and their meaning is determined by the context in which they are used (e.g., displacement). This certainly creates difficulties for the student of psychology, not only when he tries to compare one theory with another, but also when he tries to understand the different meanings of the same word when used in different theories.

KINDS OF EXPLANATION

There are also differences in the kinds of explanation which theories propose. For example, the stimulus-response, cause-effect analysis of infant learning by a behaviourist is totally at variance with the structuralist approach of Piaget and his colleagues. Similarly, mother-child interaction will receive very different kinds of attention and explanation from ethologists, social learning theorists and psycho-analysts. Also, as we have already noted earlier with regard to attitudes, some psychologists prefer a latent process conceptualization, whereas others are very chary of postulating hypothetical constructs or mediating variables.

FOCUS AND RANGE OF CONVENIENCE

There are vast differences in the range of phenomena to which theories apply and which they are capable of accounting for. Some consist of little more than a single hypothesis applied to one aspect of social behaviour; for example, Michael Argyle's 'equilibrium' theory of eye contact and physical proximity. Other, middle-range theories are applicable to a much wider range of phenomena; good examples of which are exchange theory, discussed in Chapter 26, and dissonance theory, which we shall be considering later. Finally, there are grand theories which claim to be able to account for the entire repertoire of human behaviour. Both psychoanalysis and learning theory are at this end of the continuum.

'INSIDE' OR 'OUTSIDE' PERSPECTIVE

This refers to whether theories take account of the personal experience of individuals or take the viewpoint of an outside observer. The 'inside' perspective is usually referred to as the phenomenological viewpoint.

LEVEL OF ANALYSIS

Just as theories differ in the kinds of explanation they provide of the same phenomena, so they differ in the level or unit of analysis adopted. We will touch on this issue in Chapter 28, when considering the nature of social influence. Thus, analysis can be at the level of social forces, group dynamics or individual processes. And, even when focusing on the individual, we can adopt more molecular levels of analysis and reduce behaviour to the interaction of physiological operations. Levels of analysis are not reducible, and an explanation of behaviour at one level cannot be translated normally to another without loss.

FORMALITY OF EXPOSITION

Theories vary considerably in the rigour or formality with which they set out their propositions. Some attempt to define their concepts clearly and systematically and to state their principles formally. Hull's drive reduction theory of learning is a good case in point. Other theories have a much looser structure and develop more haphazardly in the context of discussion of experimental or clinical findings or of general issues. In general, the more molecular the theory, the more formal the exposition. This is because they are better able to operationalize their concepts than are molar theories.

METHODOLOGICAL BASE

Theories emerge from different sources and social contexts. For example, whereas social learning theory developed in the context of rigorous hypothesis-testing by academic psychologists in experimental laboratories, psychoanalytic theory developed in the context of the observation and treatment of patients in a clinical setting. Thus, the techniques and methods associated with the emergence of different theories tend to reflect the objectives of the theorist. The aim of the social learning theorist is to provide reliable knowledge and, hence, he will concentrate on the evaluation of his theory through the rigorous testing of hypotheses. On the other hand, the psychoanalytic theorist has as his primary aim the alleviation of his patients' distress, so he is likely to be concerned with the development of techniques which will give him access to the patient's unconscious.

EMPHASIS ON TESTABILITY OR DIFFERENTIATION

Theories differ in the emphasis they place on testability. A theory dealing with simple behavioural events that can be given clear operational definitions will focus on experimental testability. But a theory which goes beyond simple behavioural events and is concerned with complex factors such as experience, ideas, meaning or language will tend to focus on the subtlety and complexity of relations. This may well involve a network of hypothetical constructs, inextricably linked to one another, and which preclude rigorous testability, but which the theorist will regard as essential, if the complexity of human behaviour and experience is to be understood.

EMPHASIS ON DESCRIPTION OR EXPLANATION

The final dimension on which theories can be regarded as differing is in the degree to which they are explanatory. At one end of the scale we have theories which offer little more than a classification or taxonomy of some area of human behaviour. At the other, there are theories whose primary objective is to offer a comprehensive explanation of this same behaviour. McDougall's 'instinct theory' is an example of the former, while Skinner's 'reinforcement theory' is an example of the latter. Within the domain of theories of attitude change, as we shall shortly see, functional theories have tended to be descriptive, whilst consistency theories are more explanatory.

659

We have, then, ten features of psychological theories in which they can be thought to differ. However, this is simply one possible conceptual framework and there may be alternatives, since this is no more than a theory about theories. The categories are not mutually exclusive, and the reader may feel there is overlap in some cases; for example, in discriminating between a theory's methodological base and its emphasis on testability or differentiation. Nevertheless, we believe it will prove useful in helping the reader to evaluate different theories of attitude change.

We have chosen to examine three types of theory of attitude change by way of illustration. These are, firstly, functional theories; secondly, consistency theories; and finally, attribution theories.

Functional theories

The key feature of functional theories has been to stress that we cannot understand, let alone predict, attitude change, unless we know the needs or motivations that an attitude serves for an individual. The emphasis of such theories, therefore, has been on describing the different functions which attitudes perform. One such theory is that of Daniel Katz (1960), in which he suggests that there are four major functions:

UNDERSTANDING

Many attitudes help us to understand the world and to make sense of events around us. They provide us with consistency and clarity in our attempts to explain and interpret events. For this reason, it has also been called the *knowledge function*. It does not imply that attitudes provide a factually truthful picture of the world, but simply one that is meaningful to the individual. For example, whereas for one person, Russian involvement in Africa may be understood with reference to an attitude that 'all large nations have imperialist ambitions', another person may relate it to a belief that 'communism is an inevitable process'. In both cases, the beliefs or attitudes provide a context for the appraisal of new information, assisting in its interpretation and incorporation into the individual's belief systems.

NEED SATISFACTION

We develop favourable attitudes towards those objects which maximize the rewards that we get and unfavourable attitudes towards those which lead to punishment. Once formed, such attitudes tend to be stable as long as they are useful in helping us to satisfy our needs and to reach our goals. Katz has also called this the *utilitarian or adjustive function* to reflect this idea of attitudes being useful in helping us to achieve our goals and to adjust to life situations. Thus for example, my attitudes towards the police may be favourable or unfavourable, depending on whether they have recovered property stolen from my house or whether they have apprehended me in the act of burgling someone else's.

EGO DEFENCE

This is where a person's attitudes function to bolster his self-esteem and to protect him from unpleasant truths about himself or about the harsh realities in the external world. We all use defence mechanisms to some extent, but they are used much more by those who are insecure, or feel inferior, or who have internal conflicts. Deep hostility towards individuals or groups may well reflect the operation of such mechanisms. Thus, prejudiced attitudes towards Negroes can be one way in which some people bolster their egos.

VALUE EXPRESSION

This fourth, and final function of attitudes has three main aspects to it. Firstly, it gives positive expression to an individual's central values. Thus, for example, sending a donation to the National Council for Civil Liberties or canvassing for the National Front Party would give expression to, and be a reflection of, different values. Secondly, it facilitates the definition of an individual's self-concept; for example, a West Indian teenager may adopt Rastafarian hair style, clothing, and mannerisms in order to define himself as a member of a West Indian peer group and to establish his status in that group. Thirdly, it helps an individual to relate to a group. Thus, when joining a group, we often internalize the values of the group and their expression helps us to relate to other members.

Since Katz is concerned to emphasize the motivational basis of attitudes, he has specified conditions which will lead to the arousal of an attitude and the conditions which will bring about change:

ATTITUDE AROUSAL

Since we hold literally thousands of attitudes, only a few of them at any one time will be the focus of our conscious attention or directly influence our behaviour. Katz maintains that it requires the onset of some environmental cue or of some internal need to arouse any particular attitude into an active state. The anti-Semite is not continuously seething with anger towards Jews. His attitude will only become active, when he encounters Jews or references to Jews or is, for some reason, minded to think about them.

ATTITUDE CHANGE

Katz maintains that an attitude will undergo change only when it ceases, for whatever reason, to fulfill the function it serves. Therefore, it will take different forces and pressures to change attitudes that serve different functions. For example, the factors which may facilitate change in an 'understanding-oriented' attitude will probably be quite different to those which will have any impact on an ego-defensive attitude. Thus, communication of new information about an attitude object, which contradicts the previous beliefs of a person, may be successful in the former case but hopeless in the latter. This may be why, as we have remarked earlier, racial prejudice is extremely resistant to change through information and argument.

Functional theories have been neither widely accepted nor frequently studied by researchers. There are several good reasons for this neglect. Firstly, functional theorists are by no means agreed either on the number or kinds of functions involved in attitude formation and maintenance. Katz, as we have seen, suggests that there are four major functions. On the other hand, Smith, Bruner, and White (1956) postulated only three functions. These were (1) social adjustment; (2) externalization; and (3) object appraisal. In addition, they argued that the expression of attitudes was not a need in the individual, but simply a reflection of his individual style of operating. Yet again, Robert Lane (1969), in attempting to understand the attitudes of young Americans, came to the conclusion that the categories used by these earlier theorists were too blunt and ignored important differences. In his theory, he proposed that attitudes, in the political arena alone, might serve any one or more of ten needs. These are (1) instrumental guide to reality; (2) cognitive needs; (3) consistency and balance needs; (4) social needs and values; (5) moral needs and values; (6) esteem needs and values; (7) personality integration and identity information; (8) aggression needs; (9) autonomy and freedom; and (10) self-actualization. Thus, the theories differ in terms of both the nature and range of concepts used. It is not a question of determining which theory is the correct one, but rather of realizing that they represent varying degrees of differentiation within a largely descriptive framework.

A second reason for the neglect by researchers—which follows directly from the first—is that the theories are difficult to assess. Although their theoretical stance seems very plausible, it is not clear how the functions can be *operationally* defined. We need to know which function is being served by a particular attitude if we are to make predictions that can be tested. Unless we can measure and predict, we cannot easily verify the theory. Thirdly, since an attitude may serve more than one function, it increases the difficulty involved in identifying the functions, which, again, is a necessary step if a theory is to be tested.

Consistency theories

We have already discussed how consistency obtains not only between the belief, feeling, and behavioural components of an attitude, but also within clusters of attitudes. It is not surprising, therefore, to find that this notion of consistency has featured as a key principle in a number of theories of attitude change. And, indeed, during the past twenty years or so, consistency theories have received more attention and have generated more research than any other group of theories. Functional theories, as we have seen, are essentially concerned to delineate the nature and relationship of various motivations which underlie the formation, maintenance, and shift of attitudes—of which the need for consistency is but one possible motive. Consistency theories, on the other hand, focus specifically on the need for consistency and explore its implications for attitude change. Therefore, whereas functional theories are largely motivational in their orientation, consistency theories, insofar as they emphasize the importance of people's beliefs and ideas, are clearly cognitive.

Underlying all consistency theories, then, is this notion of a basic motivation in humans to be consistent, although they vary in their choice of label to describe this desired state (e.g., balance, congruity, symmetry, consonance). The original idea of consistency theory is usually credited to Fritz Heider (1946), who published a short paper, in which he discussed the organization of attitudes and introduced the notion of cognitive balance. However, the most important theory in terms of its influence on research and on subsequent theoretical discussion has been cognitive dissonance theory, first proposed by Leon Festinger in 1957. It is this theory which we will now examine.

DISSONANCE THEORY

The theory maintains that human beings will strive to maintain consistency or consonance among any cognitions that they perceive to be related to each other in any way. Festinger defined cognitions as 'the things a person knows about himself, about his behaviour, and about his surroundings'. The relation between two cognitions can be consonant, dissonant, or irrelevant. Dissonance will arise when an individual is aware that the opposite of one cognition would follow from the other. For example, the cognition 'I am a heavy smoker' is consonant with the cognition 'I enjoy smoking', is dissonant with the cognition 'Smoking causes lung cancer', and is irrelevant to the cognition 'I forgot to send flowers on Mother's Day'. The quality of the relation between cognitions is determined by the individual's expectations, so that dissonance can be the result of logical inconsistency, of the individual's expectations based on past experience concerning what things go together, or of expectations based on cultural norms and values.

663

The basic propositions of the theory can be summarized as follows:

1. Inconsistencies between cognitions generate in the individual a feeling of dissonance.
2. The individual experiences dissonance as unpleasant, and is, therefore motivated to reduce it or to avoid it.
3. The amount of dissonance experienced is a joint function of the importance of the cognitions for the individual and the proportion of relevant cognitions which are dissonant. For example, smoking is obviously more important for the heavy smoker than for the light smoker and the more illnesses an individual knows to be associated with smoking, the greater the dissonance.
4. The greater the dissonance, the stronger the motivation to reduce it.

Festinger suggests that there are several ways in which an individual will try to reduce dissonance: (a) He may change a cognition about his behaviour, for instance, by giving up smoking or changing to low tar brands; (b) he may change a cognition about the environment, for instance, by deciding that evidence linking smoking with lung cancer is weak or that filter tips largely eliminate carcinogenic substances; (c) he may add new cognitions to bolster one or other of the dissonant cognitions, for instance, 'I know of plenty of doctors who still smoke' or 'I'm just as likely to die in a crash while driving to work as I am from lung cancer'.

What we have here, then, is a theory which claims to explain why and how people's attitudes change. It does so by postulating a hypothetical construct which has drive-like properties. The theory specifies, not only conditions giving rise to the arousal of this drive, but also the means by which it may be reduced. Insofar as the theory proposes that dissonance is aroused through an individual's awareness of inconsistency between his cognitions, it is clearly a cognitive theory. However, many of the cognitions are about the individual's behaviour; and, therefore, it also establishes a firm link between attitudes and behaviour by emphasizing that attitude change *results from* an individual's behaviour rather than causing it.

There are many situations to which the concept of dissonance can be applied, including many outside the domain of attitude research. However, we will confine ourselves here to just two areas of attitude research: firstly, dissonance following upon a decision; and secondly, dissonance created by counter-attitudinal behaviour. Taking each separately, we will briefly outline what the theory predicts and, by way of illustration, describe an experiment designed to test the prediction.

POST-DECISIONAL DISSONANCE

The theory posits that dissonance is aroused by making a decision between two or more alternative objects or courses of action. The resulting dissonance is proportional to (a) *the importance of the decision*, for instance, choosing between two eligible marriage partners is more important than choosing between two brands of detergent—notwithstanding current TV advertisements—and will create more dissonance; (b) *the attractiveness of the unchosen alternative*, for instance, the more difficult the choice, because of the considerable merits of both potential partners, the greater the dissonance; and (c) *the degree to which the alternatives are different in kind*, for instance, there will be greater dissonance following a decision to buy a car rather than to have a holiday on the Continent than there will be after deciding which of two cars to buy.

Two of the ways in which post-decisional dissonance can be reduced are (a) by decreasing the attractiveness of the unchosen alternative, and (b) by increasing the attractiveness of the chosen alternative. There have been a number of studies testing predictions derived from this notion of post-decisional dissonance and, generally, the data have been supportive. For example, in one study by Jack Brehm (1956), of which we will only describe part here, subjects were given to believe that they were assisting in contract work on consumer research for a group of manufacturers. As one of their tasks, they had to rate for desirability on an eight-point scale eight different articles, such as an automatic coffee-maker, a sandwich toaster, a desk lamp, etc. By desirability was meant the attractiveness, quality, and usefulness of the article to the subject. They were then told that, by way of payment for participating in the research, they would receive one of the eight articles which they had previously rated. Subjects in the experimental (dissonance) condition were allowed to *choose* one of two of the articles from the eight. Furthermore, Brehm so arranged the pairings of the articles that some subjects were given a choice between an article previously rated high and one previously rated low in desirability (low-dissonance condition) and other subjects had to choose between two equally desirable articles (high-dissonance condition). Subjects in the control (no dissonance) condition were simply *given* one of the eight articles which they had rated as highly desirable.

Later, all the subjects were asked to rate the eight articles again. The prediction was that there would be systematic changes in the ratings of the chosen and unchosen items in the experimental conditions as compared with the rating of the item given to subjects in the control condition, and that the changes would be greater for the high-dissonance group than for the low-dissonance group. Overall, the results supported the predictions and showed that (a) there was more change on the key items in the dissonance conditions than in the control condition; (b) there was more change in the high than in the low dissonance condition; and (c) changes in the dissonance conditions were reflected by both

665

increases in the rating of the chosen item and decreases in the ratings of the unchosen item.

Though there have been contrary reports, the experimental findings in the area of post-decisional dissonance have largely supported the theory. For example, Knox and Inkster (1968), in an inventive field-study conducted at a race meeting showed that the confidence of punters in their chosen horse increased markedly immediately after they had placed their bet. However, in order to tighten the theory, Brehm and Cohen (1962) argued that two conditions are necessary for dissonance arousal to occur:

a. Commitment. If an individual does not feel committed to or bound by his decision, there is no reason for him to experience dissonance. Hence, a publicly announced decision is more likely to arouse dissonance than a privately considered one. Research evidence supports this argument.

b. Volition or choice. If an individual feels that he had little or no choice in acting as he did, then the amount of dissonance aroused is likely to be minimal. This is why the term 'forced compliance' has been replaced by the term 'counter-attitudinal behaviour' to describe the second type of situation giving rise to dissonance and subsequent attitude change, which we will now consider.

COUNTER-ATTITUDINAL BEHAVIOUR

Dissonance theory postulates that, if we act in a manner that is at variance with our attitudes, then we will experience dissonance. In particular, when there is pressure on us to act in a counter-attitudinal manner, dissonance will be aroused if we comply. The pressure can be in the form of threat of punishment or promise of reward. Given the aversive quality of dissonance, we will try to reduce it, and Festinger argued that it is easier to reduce it when the pressure is great than when it is small. This is because we can attribute the compliant behaviour to the force of the pressure. However, when the pressure is slight, we cannot reduce the dissonance by reference to the pressure. Thus, an alternative means of reducing it may be to change our attitude to make it more consistent with our action.

Now, without foreknowledge of dissonance theory, this prediction is, in many cases, counter-intuitive. For example, we might well expect that, in a case of corruption, the greater the financial inducement (bribe) to break the law or bend the rules, the more likely is a person to justify his actions to himself by modifying his attitude towards the laws or rules. We would regard this as a clear case of rationalization after the event.

Largely because of its counter-intuitive nature, this has proved one of the most challenging predictions of dissonance theory and has generated a host of studies aimed at testing it. As an illustration, we will describe the classic experiment by Festinger and Carlsmith (1959). Male subjects spent an hour working at tasks designed to be boring. At the end of the hour they were told that the experiment was over. Those in the experimental (dissonance) condition were then asked for their help in the further running of the experiment. It was explained that a student helper usually brought in the next subject and told him how enjoyable the task was. However, the student helper had failed to show up and the experimenter would like the subject to act as helper in this capacity. As payment for helping, the experimenter offered some subjects one dollar (low-reward condition) and other subjects twenty dollars (high-reward condition). Having introduced the next subject (a female stooge) to the experiment in accordance with the experimenter's instructions, subjects were later interviewed by a member of the college administration (another stooge) in another part of the building. In the context of general questions about participation in psychological experiments, the subjects were asked to rate how enjoyable they thought the task was and whether or not they were suspicious of the experiment. Subjects who were suspicious or who had refused to comply with the request to act as helper were eliminated from the study. Subjects in the control (no dissonance) condition simply performed the boring task for an hour and later rated the task for enjoyability in the interview; they were not asked to act as helpers. So, here we have then a situation in which subjects have (a) lied or not lied to fellow students about a boring task; and (b) if they have lied, they have been paid different amounts of money for doing so. Comparing the subsequent ratings of task enjoyment, it was found that the low-reward subjects gave significantly higher ratings than the high-reward subjects, who did not differ from the control subjects. Thus, it would seem that high reward for the discrepant behaviour either created less dissonance or enabled subjects to reduce dissonance more easily than low reward, since high-reward subjects felt less need to regard the obviously boring task as enjoyable—as reflected in their subsequent attitudes towards the task.

There have been many replications and extensions of this experimental paradigm, though not always yielding evidence supportive of dissonance theory. Indeed, some experiments using counter-attitudinal essay-writing to produce attitude-behaviour discrepancies have found that the greater the reward or incentive offered, the greater the attitude change—a finding in direct contradiction to dissonance theory. The research findings in this area are still confusing and very complex, but there has been some recent convergence of findings as to the necessary and limiting conditions under which dissonance effects will occur following counter-attitudinal behaviour. These effects will occur provided that the individual engages in the behaviour under conditions of (a) low incentive or reward, (b) high perceived choice on his part to comply or not, with (c) expected unpleasant consequences of his behaviour for someone else, and (d) an awareness of personal responsibility by the actor for the consequences.

EVALUATION OF DISSONANCE THEORY

Although we have only presented the skeleton of the theory and have confined ourselves to a brief consideration of only two areas of application, there are a number of general points worth making in attempting to evaluate its usefulness:

1. If one of the hallmarks of a good theory is its power to stimulate discussion and research, then, clearly, dissonance theory is a front-runner, for it has proved exciting and influential enough to inspire research by hundreds of supporters and opponents.
2. Compared with other consistency theories, dissonance theory is both richer in differentiation and yet more accessible to experimental testing.
3. It is broader in its application or range of convenience than other consistency theories, especially in its application to choice behaviour in conflict situations; and yet, as compared with functional theories of attitude change, its emphasis is nevertheless on explanation rather than description.
4. As with all consistency theories, dissonance theory adopts a latent process conceptualization of attitudes and specifically postulates the operation of an intervening variable to account for attitude change. Indeed, recent research by Zanna and Cooper (1974) offers strong support for the existence of dissonance as an arousal state having aversive motivational properties. Furthermore, apart from the concept of 'dissonance' itself, the theory uses concepts which are in common use, clear in their meaning and easy to operationalize.
5. It is rare for psychologists to experience the delight of confounding common sense, yet, on this score, dissonance theory has produced some intriguing 'non-obvious' predictions which experimental testing has largely borne out.
6. In the process of trying to test dissonance theory, researchers have been inspired to devise many ingenious experiments and to attain a degree of creativity and experimental sophistication rarely found elsewhere in social psychology.

Nevertheless, dissonance theory has not been wanting in its critics, although many of the criticisms apply more to the experiments designed to test the theory than to the theory itself. For example, one major criticism has been the dubious methodological practice of non-random elimination of subjects. In the Brehm (1956) study, which we described earlier, some of the subjects in the experimental (low dissonance) condition, when offered a choice between a highly desirable and a less desirable article, chose the latter. Consequently, they were discarded from the analysis. Now, there may have been very good reasons for this unexpected behaviour. For example, it may have been the case that these subjects already possessed the more attractive article and, therefore chose the less attractive one. Nevertheless, this is speculation, and any discarding of subjects from an experimental condition is worrying.

A more serious criticism is that, because the theory allows for several alternative ways of reducing dissonance, it is often difficult to make clear-cut predictions for any given situation. In an experiment, this can be taken care of by blocking off alternatives and leaving only one avenue of attitude change. But, when we try to apply the theory outside the laboratory, we do not know whether an individual will try (a) to avoid dissonance arousal in the first place by adopting strategies, such as compartmentalization, or switching off, or (b) to reduce the dissonance by either changing his cognitions about his behaviour, changing his cognitions about the environment, or adding new cognitions to either of the dissonant pair. Whatever the case, any explanation in terms of dissonance theory tends to be *post hoc*.

One final criticism is that dissonance experiments are frequently open to alternative interpretations, although it is fair to say that no one alternative theory has been able to explain all the results of the many areas of experimental investigation, nor have they had the degree of parsimony or range of applicability of dissonance theory. The current status of dissonance theory, then, is that of a theory which has withstood the onslaught of many hundreds of experiments designed to test it, but which, in the process, has diminished in scope from its original form, where all kinds of inconsistency were considered to be motivating. As we have noticed with regard to counter-attitudinal behaviour, numerous criteria must be met before dissonance can be considered as occurring. In improving its precision, researchers have reduced its range of convenience.

Attribution theories
During the past few years, attribution theory has begun to replace dissonance theory as the most popular theoretical model in social psychology. Just as with consistency theory, Heider was the seminal influence on attribution theory when he first discussed the major concepts in a short paper published in 1944. However, whereas dissonance theory arose in connection with the study of attitude change and was extended gradually by researchers to many other areas of behaviour, attribution theory arose primarily in connection with person perception, and has only recently been applied to attitude change.

The major contribution of attribution theory to attitude change has been made by Daryl Bem (1967) in his 'self-perception' theory of attitude change. He starts from a behaviourist position in that, although he uses cognitive terms such as beliefs, attitudes, and self-awareness, he tries to define them objectively. He proposes that the way in which an individual comes to know about his own internal states, such as emotions and attitudes, is the same way he learns to attribute feelings and attitudes to other people—that is, through observation. As children, we learn about the external world through discrimination training by the socializing community of adults and older children. Thus, through verbal labelling, we learn to distinguish between spoons and forks, for instance, and also between fear and anger in other people. By extension, we also learn through self-observation to label our own inner feelings and likings. Moreover, since the internal cures we experience are often weak or ambiguous, in order to determine what it is we are experiencing, we have to refer to our overt behaviour and to the situation in which it occurs. Thus, if I am asked whether I like brown bread, I will refer, not to some private internal state, but rather to my awareness that I am always eating it. If I am always eating it, then I must like it. Bem's major theoretical premise is that we attribute feelings and attitudes to ourselves through self-perception, and the cues we use are largely the same publicly-observable responses which we utilize when attributing feelings and attitudes to other people.

In explaining attitude change, then, Bem argues that there is no need to postulate the operation of hidden intervening variables such as 'dissonance'. Attitude change is no more than a reflection of the fact that an individual has up-dated his information as to what his attitude is by referring to how he has behaved and whether or not there was any extrinsic reason for his behaviour in the form of rewards or punishments. If he observes no external reason for his behaviour, he will attribute to himself an attitude which is consistent with the behaviour. Applying this argument to dissonance experiments such as the one by Festinger and Carlsmith (1959), Bem maintains that the reason subjects in the one dollar and twenty dollar conditions later reported different degrees of liking for the boring task was that they reached different conclusions about the causes of their own behaviour. Those in the twenty dollar condition reasoned as follows: 'I told the next subject that I liked the task I'd performed, but since twenty dollars is enough money to induce me to lie, I really don't like it'. On the other hand, those in the one dollar condition reason: 'I told the next subject that I liked the task I'd performed, and since one dollar is not enough to induce me to lie, I must really like it'. In short, subjects offered a small reward for engaging in attitude-discrepant behaviour report greater liking for the boring task later, because they can perceive no other reason for having described it as enjoyable to the next subject.

A number of experiments have been conducted to determine whether a dissonance or an attribution explanation is more accurate. However, so far, the results have been rather inconclusive, with some studies offering support for dissonance and others supporting self-perception. Insofar as there are a number of studies which indicate that cognitive inconsistency is arousing (Kiesler and Pallak, 1976), self-perception theory cannot account for all attitude change, since the theory maintains that an individual, faced with inconsistency, attempts to infer his attitudes from the information available in a totally 'cool' and dispassionate manner. Dissonance theory, in contrast, does suggest that inconsistency will result in the arousal of an aversive motivational state, and there is evidence supporting this. However, since there is little doubt that we do often infer our attitudes from our behaviour, this is probably more likely to occur in situations where our feelings are not very clear or intense. In a recent paper, Fazio, Zanna and Cooper (1977) have, in fact, argued that the two theories are not competing, but rather complementary, formulations of attitude change. They maintain that both theories have their own specialized domain. Self-perception theory most accurately characterizes attitude-change phenomena when the attitude is congruent with behaviour, and dissonance theory is more applicable in explaining attitude change following attitude-discrepant behaviour. It has, thus, become a question, not of which theory has won, but rather of determining which is most appropriate in specific situations.

Factors in persuasive communication

We began this Chapter by pointing out that the interest of psychologists in attitude research largely reflects a general desire to be able to change people's attitudes and, by implication, their behaviour. In this part of the Chapter, we shall consider whether psychologists have discovered anything which can be of use to salesmen, advertisers, politicians, propagandists or any other agents intent on changing people's attitudes. What factors must be sensibly taken into account when planning an influence attempt?

A conceptual framework

Firstly, we must decide how we are going to talk about the influence process. What is needed is a conceptual framework, within which we can organize those factors which psychologists believe to be important. One such approach, suggested by McGuire (1969), looks upon any influence attempt as a communication-persuasion relationship. There is a *communication*, whereby someone says or does something to someone else; and, there is a *persuasion* or resultant change in attitude. The communication can be regarded as the independent variable and embraces a set of factors which can be varied or manipulated in an influence situation. The persuasion can be regarded as the dependent variable and includes several different, measurable responses which occur in reaction to the communication. We can distinguish four major classes of independent variables and five dependent variables. This is illustrated in Figure 27.1:

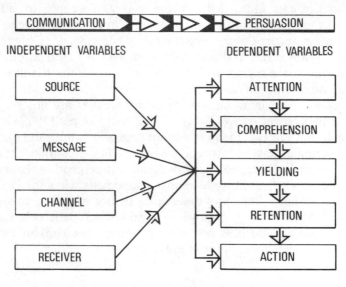

Fig. 27.1

Let us consider what is meant by each of these in turn.

INDEPENDENT VARIABLES

Source variables are the perceived characteristics of the source of the message, such as its expertness, trustworthiness, personal investment in the influence attempt, status, and similarity to the receiver. For example, what effect will the status or prestige of the persuading agent have on the outcome of the influence attempt? A great deal of current advertising is based on the belief that more products will be sold if they are promoted by stars from screen or sport.

Message variables include both the content and structure of the communication, such as the use of emotional appeals, whether or not counter-arguments are presented, what order they occur in, and whether or not they are refuted explicitly or only by implication. For example, does the counsel for defence in a trial have an advantage over the counsel for the prosecution by summing up last?

Channel variables include the various kinds of media which can be used to transmit the message, such as the printed word, radio, television, and face-to-face interpersonal communication.

Receiver variables are the characteristics of the people at whom the message is aimed, their personalities, abilities, interests, and degree of involvement in the communication process. For example, are some people more easily influenced than others?

DEPENDENT VARIABLES

In the process of persuasion there are at least five clear steps which must occur in sequence, each one involving a greater degree of persuasive effect. We need to ask ourselves whether the receiver has (a) *attended* to the message, (b) *understood* it, (c) *yielded* to it, (d) *retained* it, and (e) *acted* in accordance with its recommendations. A message might be perfectly effective at one of the early stages but ineffective at the later stages. Most experiments on attitude change have focused on the third stage—yielding, or acceptance of the message—and have ignored both the earlier and the later stages. Many erroneous conclusions have probably been made through the failure of researchers to measure all the stages. There will be little value in a study which shows that a particular independent variable has an effect on yielding if the researcher neglects to see whether the receivers remember the suggestions contained in the message for more than a very short time.

The independent variables are likely to interact with one another in many ways. Thus, for example, we might expect more intelligent people to be more easily persuaded by reasoned argument, but less intelligent people to be more easily swayed by emotional appeals. The different independent variables will also help to determine which stage in the persuasion process a person reaches. Thus, low intelligence may decrease comprehension, whereas high intelligence or level of knowledge about the message content could decrease the yielding. Any conclusions that are drawn from attitude-change experiments in which one independent variable is systematically varied to bring about a measurable change in one or more of the dependent variables must be treated, therefore, with great caution. The conceptual framework we have outlined is important because it makes distinctions which are all too often forgotten when researchers make generalizations about the effectiveness of persuasive communications.

With these distinctions and cautions in mind, we can now go on to examine some of the research which has been carried out in this area. Many hundreds of experiments have been conducted to determine the effects of the many different variables involved in a persuasive communication attempt. The approach has been, essentially, a pragmatic one and was initiated by Carl Hovland and his colleagues at Yale University. It has been pragmatic insofar as it has examined the effect of different experimental variables without generating an overall theory which posits some dynamic process operating in the receiver. Although the results of such experiments can be, and often have been, interpreted by other researchers in terms of dynamic processes such as dissonance, the Yale Studies were largely confined to seeking answers to pragmatic questions of the form: what effect will X have on Y?

Characteristics of the communicator

The perceived characteristics of the communicator or source of the message will determine his credibility in the eyes of the receiver and will strongly affect the persuasiveness of the communication. Judgements about a communicator's credibility have been shown to be influenced by many different factors of which perhaps the three most important are:

EXPERTISE

If we believe a person to be an expert, we are more likely to be influenced by his suggestions—even when his expertise lies in a different area to the one under focus. It would seem that the effect of experitise can generalize from one area to another; hence the use of well-known television and sporting personalities to advertise products.

INTENTIONS OR MOTIVES

If we believe that someone has no vested interest in persuading us, we are more likely to be influenced by him. This has been demonstrated in a number of experiments which used one of two paradigms. In one paradigm, different groups of subjects are exposed to different communicators, who might be perceived as having different degrees of involvement in the issue; for example, a judge and a known criminal advocating heavier penalties for criminal offences. In the second paradigm experiment, different groups of subjects are led to believe that the communicator is either aware or unaware that they are overhearing his message.

ATTRACTIVENESS

The more a communicator is liked, the more influence he will have. Now, since we tend to like others who are similar to ourselves in certain ways or who are physically attractive, the attractiveness of a communicator can have a strong effect on the persuasiveness of the communication; hence, the tendency in recent years for political candidates to be selected as much for their good looks as for their abilities or integrity and for them to make a point of presenting themselves to voters as 'no different to the man in the street'.

One interesting phenomenon which received a great deal of attention in social psychology textbooks in connection with communicator credibility until quite recently was something known as the *sleeper effect*. This referred to an early observation by Hovland, Lumsdaine and Sheffield (1949) that the influence of low-credibility communicators, while initially weak, increases over time. It is as though the receivers 'slept on' the message. This phenomenon was explained as being due to the fact that with the passage of time the source of a message becomes dissociated from its content. An individual comes to forget the context in which he received the message but retains its content, with the result that *what* has been communicated comes to exert a more powerful influence than *who* has communicated it.

However, a critical review of the sleeper effect literature by Thomas Cook and a series of seven replications by Gillig and Greenwald (1974) of a sleeper effect experiment have cast serious doubt on the existence of the phenomenon. The evidence at the moment suggests that with the passage of time there occurs (a) a decrease in the influence of a high-credibility communicator, but (b) no actual increase in the influence of a low-credibility communicator. Although there is evidence showing that the source does become dissociated from the content (which may help to explain the decrease over time in the influence of the high-credibility communicator), this dissociation does not affect the impact of the low-credibility communicator. In the light of their findings. Gillig and Greenwald suggest that it may well be time to lay the sleeper effect itself to rest!

Fear appeals
One of the ways in which messages can differ is in the amount of fear they arouse in receivers. An example of persuasive communications having strong fear appeal are posters showing the disfigured faces of car drivers who were not wearing their safety belts when they crashed. The assumption behind the use of such unpleasant posters is that the fear they arouse in the viewer will make him more susceptible to the suggestion that he always wear his safety belt when driving. The assumption that a strong fear appeal will be more effective than a weak or neutral appeal has not gone unchallenged. Surprisingly, when Janis and Feshbach (1953) undertook the first experimental study of the effects of different degrees of fear on attitude change, they found that a strong fear appeal was less effective than a medium fear appeal, which in turn had less impact than a minimal fear appeal. This finding continued to be reported in social psychology textbooks for nearly fifteen years at the expense of an increasing body of contradictory evidence. In a review of the relevant literature Higbee (1969) reported that in general the evidence suggested that strong fear messages tend to induce greater attitude change than weak ones, and that this was especially so when concrete recommendations are provided to enable individuals to avoid the fearful outcomes portrayed.

675

There are at least two possible explanations for the greater efficacy of strong fear appeals in bringing about attitude change. First, high fear arousal is more unpleasant than low fear arousal. If, by changing his attitude, an individual can reduce the fear, then the relief which accompanies fear reduction should reinforce the attitude change. The stronger the fear, the greater the relief from its reduction and, hence, the greater the reinforcement. Secondly, an individual may simply reason to himself that anything which frightens him so badly must be convincing and, hence, he changes his attitude accordingly. Whichever explanation is correct—and they are not incompatible—there seems little doubt that frightening someone may well be an effective technique of persuasion.

Persuasibility
So far, in considering the effects of different factors on an influence attempt, we have discussed (a) communicator credibility, as an example of a source factor, and (b) fear, as an example of a message factor. To conclude this part of the Chapter, we shall take a brief look at persuasibility or susceptibility to persuasion as an example of a receiver factor.

The question which psychologists have asked is whether some people are more easily influenced than others. An examination of the research literature reveals very inconsistent findings. However, McGuire (1968), in a review of this literature, concluded that persuasibility on one issue does seem to be positively related to persuasibility on other issues, but that this has been disguised through a neglect of attention to the complex interaction it has with the dependent variables. He argues that personality factors will affect the acceptance of a persuasive message in at least two ways. They will differentially affect (a) comprehension, and (b) yielding. For example, as we pointed out earlier, we might expect the relationship of intelligence to persuasion to be fairly complex: intelligence will probably be positively related to comprehension but negatively related to yielding. Similarly, we might expect self-esteem to be positively related to comprehension since low self-confidence may interfere with an individual's reception of the message; but it will be negatively related to yielding because he will have less confidence in his own viewpoint. Support for this hypothesis comes from a study by Zellner (1970). He found that, compared to a group of subjects high in self-esteem, subjects who were low in self-esteem showed more yielding to a simple message but less yielding to a complex one.

Prejudice

It seems appropriate to end this Chapter on attitudes by saying something about prejudice and discrimination. Much of the early attitude research was motivated by a desire to understand the nature of prejudice, with a view, hopefully, to devising procedures for its reduction. As we have already seen, the development of techniques of attitude measurement and the debate about the relationship between attitudes and behaviour arose largely in the context of studying racial prejudice.

The nature of prejudice

How shall we define this special category of attitudes which we choose to call prejudiced? It is important to appreciate from the outset that any use of the term involves value judgements. What may seem to me to be a prejudiced attitude in another person is unlikely to appear so to him. We are quick to assign the label to others but rarely are we prepared to acknowledge its application to ourselves. It is not surprising, therefore, that psychologists are by no means agreed in their definitions and uses of the term. However, they do all seem to stress that prejudice involves a departure from one or more of three ideal norms: (a) a norm of rationality; (b) a norm of justice, and (c) a norm of human-heartedness or tolerance. Gordon Allport (1954) in his classic book on the subject defined prejudice as:

> 'an antipathy based on a faulty and inflexible generalization directed towards a group as a whole or towards an individual because he is a member of that group. It may be felt or expressed.'

We can see that, in this definition, the emphasis is on prejudice as a departure from rationality. Prejudice can be viewed, then, as a strong tendency to prejudge others on the basis of their racial, ethnic, religious, political or even sexual attributes and to act towards them in a discriminatory or hostile manner.

As with any attitude, prejudice has three components: cognitive, affective, and behavioural. In the case of the *cognitive* component, the beliefs and perceptions often form stereotypes, that is, clusters of preconceived notions regarding various groups. There is a tendency, not only to over-generalize about individuals solely on the basis of their group membership, but also to be unwilling to revise one's opinions in the light of new disconfirming information. As we have suggested earlier in this Chapter, this unwillingness is due to the fact that in many instances the *affective* component is extremely powerful. The emotional feelings of hostility are often very intense, because they serve an ego-defensive function. New information is resisted, because it threatens the support system by which an individual maintains a sense of his own worth.

The *behavioural* component of prejudice refers to the tendency to act in a discriminatory fashion towards some person or group. It can range from mild antilocution to participation in total genocide. Antilocution refers to all forms of verbal denigration, one of the most frequently observed of which is the recounting of racial jokes. The current spate of 'Irish' jokes acts to reinforce and perpetuate a negative stereotype of the Irish as unbelievably thick, bigoted, and drunken.

The persistence of stereotypes of minority groups has been well documented. Katz and Braly (1933) presented Princeton undergraduates with a list of eighty-four character traits and asked them to indicate which were most characteristic of several racial and ethnic groups, e.g., Negroes, Chinese, Jews, etc. They found strong agreement on the perceived characteristics of these groups. Since this pioneering study, two replications have been carried out at eighteen-year intervals with new generations of Princeton students. Although Gilbert (1951) found a weakening of stereotypes, reflected in a reluctance on the part of some of the students to conform with the task instructions, Karlins, Coffman and Walters (1969) found evidence for the continued existence of stereotypes in the late 1960s. Although the content of many of the stereotypes had undergone change, the level of agreement between subjects was as great for many of the stereotypes as it had been in the 1933 study.

The origins of prejudice

What causes people to hold prejudiced attitudes? This is a question which has long been of interest to social scientists, and many theories have been proposed which operate at different levels of explanation. Some stress the origins of prejudice, whilst others lay greater emphasis on factors which contribute to its perseverance. Allport argues that many of the explanations put forward are not mutually exclusive and that it is a mistake to assume that prejudice has one cause. Rather, we must regard it as being multiply caused. Each explanation will reflect the orientation of the discipline in which the theorist works. For example, a Marxist historian will tend to hold an *exploitation* theory of prejudice. According to such a theory, prejudice is propagated by an exploiting class for the purposes of stigmatizing some groups as inferior, so that continued exploitation of these groups and of their resources can be justified. Thus, prejudice is explained as a form of rationalized self-interest of the upper classes. On the other hand, sociologists will tend to stress various *socio-cultural determinants* such as density of populations, community separateness, ignorance and barriers to communication, ease of vertical mobility, and rapid change in the social structure, as well as realistic rivalries and conflict arising out of competition for employment, of which the importation of cheap foreign labour, especially to break a strike, has been a frequent example in the past.

Social psychologists tend to stress the *interaction of personal and social factors.* They emphasize the importance of social norms and the resultant pressure to conformity. Thus, in a society where prejudice and

678

discrimination are a social norm, any violation of this norm by an individual will lead to negative sanctions being applied by other members of his in-group. Therefore, it is largely the perceived costs of conformity and non-conformity which are seen as the major factor determining the maintenance of prejudice in a society. One implication of this approach is that most individuals in a society which has a norm of prejudice will be prejudiced. However, their attitudes will be likely to change if either the norms themselves change or if the individual removes to another society which does not have a norm of prejudice.

Yet other psychologists have stressed factors within the individual. There have been two main approaches: scapegoat theory and character theory. *The scapegoat theory* of prejudice holds that hostile attitudes towards persons or groups arises out of an individual's life experience. It does not assume any specific personality traits but rather sees prejudice as a reaction to a specific situation. Briefly, if an individual is frustrated in some way, this leads to aggression. However, where the source of the frustration cannot be attacked—either because it is distant or because it is too powerful—then the individual will displace the aggression onto targets which cannot easily retaliate. There have been a number of experimental studies testing this frustration-aggression explanation of prejudice and, by and large, the results have supported the hypotheses.

The second approach is in the nature of a *personality or character theory* of prejudice. Prejudice is viewed as stemming from specific traits or personality characteristics which predispose an individual to react with hostility towards ethnic, racial, religious, political and other minority groups. This view originated in the classic study of the authoritarian personality by Adorno and his colleagues at Berkeley in the 1950s. Individuals with an authoritarian personality were thought to have been brought up by harsh, punitive parents who created in them a pattern of submissive obedience and punitive rejection of out-groups. They would tend to view the world in black-and-white categories, so that either someone is a member of their group and they are for him, or he is a member of some rejected out-group and therefore they are against him. Although a number of methodological criticisms were levelled at the original study of the 'authoritarian personality', subsequent investigations have largely confirmed the relationship between the personality syndrome described by the original researchers and prejudice.

From this brief review of the kinds of theory put forward to explain prejudice, we can see that historians and sociologists have been concerned primarily to determine how prejudice has arisen and is maintained *in a society*, whereas psychologists have focused on factors which help to explain prejudice *in the individual*.

The reduction of prejudice

Where a prejudiced attitude is maintained because of its ego-defensive function, it is unlikely that education or the application of persuasive arguments buttressed by 'hard facts' will have any impact on an individual. The most likely outcome is that he will become even more resistant to attempts to change his views, since the information is so threatening.

There have been a number of studies investigating the effects of enforced contact, for example, of racially integrated units in the Armed Forces, of integrated housing projects and of integration in certain occupations such as coal-mining. The general finding is that increased interaction tends to decrease prejudice and discrimination *in situ*, but this does not generalize to situations outside the one which is enforced. Thus, Negro and white soldiers, miners, and department store employees work harmoniously together but spend their leisure hours separately. It is not surprising, therefore, that the current emphasis is on legislation to remove existing inequalities, for example, desegregated schools and busing from one school district to another, and to prevent discriminatory behaviour, for example, the Race Relations Act. Changing people's attitudes is altogether a much tougher problem.

FURTHER READING

Reich, B., and Adcock, C. (1976) *Values, Attitudes and Behaviour Change*. Methuen.

Warren, N., and Jahoda, M. (1973) *Attitudes: Selected Readings*. 2nd edn. Penguin.

Zimbardo, P. G., Ebbesen, E. B., and Maslach, C. (1977) *Influencing Attitudes and Changing Behaviour: An introduction to method, theory and applications of social control and personal power*. 2nd edn. *Addison-Wesley*.

28   Social influence and socialization
DENIS GAHAGAN

Introduction

Much of social psychology is concerned with attempts to describe systematically and explain how we are influenced by others. Indeed, social psychology could well be described as the study of social influence. Though we may, at different times, speak of the influence of culture, society, institutions, groups, or individuals, nevertheless, these influences operate primarily in the context of our interactions with other individuals. It is largely as a result of our continuously changing encounters with our relations, friends, neighbours, and teachers that we come to be and to see ourselves as we are. We are also influenced, though less directly, of course, by others through the written word and other media.

Each of us is a socio-historical creation shaped in large part by the forces operating at the time in the society into which we happen to have been born. Thus, while I may regard myself as uniquely different from everyone else—for each of us has his own biography—I am nonetheless clearly more like my fellow-countrymen and contemporaries than I am like my ancestors of five hundred years ago or the members of a tribe of aborigines living in the Australian outback. It is partly, however, a matter of degree. How differently or how similarly others see me, will depend on the particular perspective adopted. What may seem to me to be a distinctive feature of my personality, may be quite unremarkable to a psychologist interested in personality types. And what may be central for this psychologist may not be salient for a social psychologist or of any relevance to a sociologist or a historian.

In much the same way, when we talk about social influence, we can take any one of a number of perspectives. Which one we adopt will depend on what question we are asking. Let us suppose, for example, that we are interested in the effect of different patterns of child rearing on later adult behaviour and personality. Essentially, what we are asking is how it is that individuals acquire different values, attitudes, and beliefs and develop different personalities. In trying to answer this question, we may choose to talk in terms of cultural or sub-cultural influences. This simply means that, while implicitly acknowledging that child-rearing refers to the ways in which a number of individuals directly impinge upon an infant from the day he is born and control the environment in which he grows up, there are nevertheless sufficient similarities within particular societies or within sections of a society for us to speak of cultural or societal influences. In the same way, if, we are concerned to investigate how being in a group affects an individual's behaviour, we may well speak of group influences, whilst accepting that this is a convenient way of referring to the fact that the individual is reacting in a particular way to a number of discrete persons.

In this Chapter we shall be considering the nature of social influence in its many forms. This will involve us in an examination of the thinking and research not only of those who call themselves social psychologists, but of sociologists and anthropologists as well. We will begin by taking a broad view and consider a number of factors which it is believed are major influences on an infant from the moment of birth. This area of study is traditionally called 'socialization'. You will have already encountered this term in Chapter 22 when considering different theories of child development. In this Chapter, however, we shall not be concerned with the actual mechanisms of the socialization process, for example, identification, reinforcement, imitation, internalization, and so forth, which are thought to underlie the development of personality and the acquisition of values. Rather, we shall focus on the fact that societies differ considerably in their socialization practices, as do also sections within a society. What the consequences of such differences may be for later adult personality and behaviour will be our major concern.

Socialization

Socialization is the process by whch the values and requirements of a society, an institution or a group are mediated to the individual. We are not born with a set of values, attitudes, knowledge, or beliefs. Nor does it seem to be the case that we are born with anything more than a most general constitutional predisposition towards particular personality traits.

An example: sex and gender
Even the possession of distinctive anatomical features which determine whether we are classified as male or female is no guarantee that we shall develop psychologically as masculine or feminine. There may be a world of difference between the sex and the gender of an individual. We can

illustrate this with two examples. Firstly, there are instances reported in the psychological literature of children whose parents strongly desired a child of the opposite sex to the one which happened to be born. As a consequence, the child is treated from birth exactly as if it were of the opposite sex. The effect of this can be, effectively, to create an individual who, though anatomically of one sex, is psychologically of the opposite. Thus, a boy may be a boy insofar as he has a penis and testes but he may be a girl in every other respect. Indeed, he may feel so strongly that he is a girl that he will spend his life passing as female and even, in some instances, seek an operation to effect an anatomical change, so bringing his body into line with his view of himself.

The second example comes from a famous study, by the anthropologist, Margaret Mead, of three tribes living in New Guinea. This study makes us realize just how parochial are our beliefs about what is masculine and what is feminine. In western societies, men are more aggressive and independent than women; they are also more outgoing and extraverted, as well as being more confident in their ability to control and manipulate the external environment. Women are more introverted, nurturant and emotionally labile; they are also more sensitive and perceptive in their interpersonal relationships, as well as being more dependent on these relationships. What Margaret Mead observed was that, not only did the three New Guinea tribes differ markedly from this western stereotype of sex-tied personality differences, but that they differed considerably among themselves. Among the Arapesh, there seemed little evidence for the temperamental differences between the sexes which we call 'masculine' and 'feminine'. The ideal adult in this tribe was gentle, passive, and nurturant, so that, to all intents and purposes, both males and females behaved in a manner which, in western society, we call 'feminine'. Among the Mundugumor there was also little by which Margaret Mead could distinguish temperamentally between the sexes, but here the difference was reversed. Both males and females behaved in an assertive, independent, and aggressive manner which we have traditionally associated with masculinity. Finally, in the third tribe, the Tchambuli, the pattern was different again, with males behaving in what we would call a feminine manner and females behaving in a masculine manner.

From these two examples of gender differences being unrelated to biological sex characteristics in the ways to which we are accustomed in western society, we can see that the possession of a masculine or a feminine temperament is by no means biologically determined. It will depend rather on the set of expectations for behaviour held by those among whom an individual grows up. Indeed, as we shall see later in this Chapter, it is likely that our own stereotypes of what is masculine and what is feminine are undergoing change in western society.

An individual's behaviour, personality, and values are all shaped by the demands of those with whom he comes into contact. And, as we saw in the introduction to this Chapter, we can speak of these demands as being made by society or culture or by particular institutions or groups. A child is initially shaped by the demands of his immediate family—his parents, brothers and sisters, and other kinsfolk with whom he comes into contact. In our society, a child is later shaped by his school and his peer group, later still, by his work and by marriage, and finally by his retirement. Entry into any new institution or group will modify an individual in some way. Whatever new role an individual adopts—be it student, parent, divorcee, professional, or pensioner—he will be affected by it. Thus, the use of the term 'socialization' is not restricted to the period from infancy to the end of adolescence but covers the entire life cycle and refers to processes which are continuously at work. It will be obvious, then, that the study of socialization is concerned with questions of very wide scope and occupies a position intermediate between sociology and psychology.

The questions psychologists ask
Given that the subject area of socialization is so very broad, it may be helpful to divide it into several areas of enquiry based on the kinds of questions which psychologists ask.

First, psychologists are interested in discovering exactly what values are transmitted and what demands are made by different groups and institutions. This question is particularly relevant when we consider whether or not a social deviant is a failure of socialization or a product of it. For example, can we consider juvenile delinquency as being due to socialization? Or, is it more useful to regard it as due to failure of socialization? Let us take the case of a delinquent child who comes from a social milieu where many of the adults and most of his older peers are engaged in crime. It seems nonsense to regard his delinquency as due to a failure of socialization, since most of those with whom he is in constant contact have socialized him into delinquent values. These values are only deviant from the point of view of other sections of society.

Secondly, psychologists are interested in discovering *why* particular values and demands are made. This question is of particular interest when we come to consider the different attitudes to child-rearing of people in different societies or in different sections of a society. Why do they differ? We shall be looking at this question in some detail later in the Chapter, both with respect to political and economic systems, as well as with respect to the social class factor within western society.

Thirdly, psychologists are concerned to explain *how* these demands and values are mediated. What are the processes and mechanisms involved in socialization? Some of those put forward by psychologists to explain socialization in childhood have already been discussed in Chapter 22, for example, reinforcement, punishment, imitation, internalization and so forth. However, there are others which have traditionally been used by psychologists to explain changes in adulthood. We have already considered some of these social influence processes in earlier chapters when we discussed such topics as conformity and attitude change.

Finally, psychologists have been interested in examining what effects socialization procedures have. This leads to two kinds of question: (a) Are they successful? (b) Are they intended? As we have already mentioned, the notion of success and failure raises questions about the nature and causes of social deviancy and delinquency. Failure of socialization can only be said to have occurred, if values have been presented, modelling and reinforcement opportunities have been optimal and yet, despite this, an individual deviates from the norms and values of his group. In fact, it is probably the case that most of those who are labelled as deviant are marching out of step simply because they are marching to a different tune. They have adopted the values of a different group—called by social psychologists a *reference group*—which is different to the group they belong to. Thus, failure and success of socialization is relative and very much a matter of degree. At one end of the continuum we have individuals for whom their membership group is also their reference group. In the middle are those individuals who refer to groups outside their immediate membership group. And at the other end there may be individuals who neither belong to a group nor seem to have a reference group. An example of this last type might be the affectionless psychopath described by Bowlby.

Turning now to the second aspect of the effects of socialization, psychologists are concerned not only with the intended effects of a socializing agent but also with the incidental, unintended effects. For example, in the early half of this century middle-class parents were concerned with early habit-formation in childhood. They stressed, for example, early toilet training in infancy and training babies to sleep in rooms by themselves. Though their concern was with the convenience of the family, doubtless they also believed it to be for the good of the infant. However, if these practices can lead (as Freud and other psychoanalytically oriented theorists believe) to obsessive-compulsive disorders in adulthood in the first example and to anxiety neurosis in the second, then these effects are clearly incidental and unintended. For those psychologists who are interested in the unintended effects of socialization practices, the focus of attention is on particular personality syndromes. Many believe, for instance, that the mildly obsessional personality of some individuals is an unintended effect of severe toilet training in early childhood. The syndrome of the 'authoritarian personality' is also thought to be a direct, if unintended, product of a particular set of child-rearing experiences.

Each of these questions concerned with the content, variations, mechanisms, and effects of socialization has technical problems associated with trying to provide answers. Indeed, there is very little research in the area of socialization which is free of severe methodological weaknesses. There are many theories, but few substantive facts. We shall consider these limitations as we come to them.

The emphasis on early socialization
Although an individual is being socialized at all points in his life cycle, nevertheless, most theory and research until quite recently has concentrated on socialization in early childhood to the almost complete neglect of socialization during adulthood. Exceptions to this have been of a rather dramatic or sensational kind, for example, studies of political indoctrination through coercive techniques of P.O.W.s in Korea during the early 1950s and of priests and Chinese intellectuals following the creation of the Communist Republic of China at around the same time. Another notable exception is the study by the sociologist Erving Goffman of mental patients and other classes of individuals living in total institutions. It is only in the last few years, however, that psychologists have begun to turn their attention to the less dramatic changes which occur during adulthood. For example, psychologists have begun to study certain critical points in the life of adults when change often seems to be accompanied by stress. The term 'mid-life' crisis is used to refer to a period of stress undergone by many adults in our society as they move into middle age, their children leave home, and there is little further progress to be made in their occupational career. Another crisis point now being studied by psychologists and sociologists is the moment of retirement.

Why has there been this emphasis, until quite recently, on early childhood? There seem to be two good reasons. Firstly, the study of early socialization should be highly predictive. A view held by many psychologists—whether Freudian or behaviourist in orientation—is that early childhood experience is a critical determinant of later personality. It is seen, therefore, as a critical determinant of an adult's later response to socialization. Secondly, the aims and content of early childhood socialization are similar across many different societies and cultures. Parents everywhere want their children to feed themselves, to be toilet-trained, to become independent and to inhibit certain aggressive and sexual impulses. But, what emphases are put on each of these particular aspects of behaviour and the ways in which these parental aims are realized vary from one culture to another. This means, then, that since the aims of early socialization are constant, we can examine

686

the effects of different procedures cross-culturally, cross-nationally, and even sub-culturally. Thus, we are provided with what amounts to a natural, albeit crude, field experiment. Much of the socialization literature is, in fact, concerned with just such comparisons. However, as children grow older, the aims and values of the socializing agents become more diverse and it becomes meaningless to examine the effects and methods of different social systems and relate them to personality.

Assumptions underlying the study of socialization
The term 'socialization' in itself presupposes a number of assumptions about the determinants of human behaviour. For one thing, it presupposes an environmentalist position. This, in the case of many theorists, is taken to extreme lengths; for example, that membership of a particular social class brings about distinct types of personality as a result of different child-rearing practices. One assumption, therefore, is that genetically-determined factors such as constitutionally-based personality and intelligence play little part in developing patterns of behaviour, attitudes, and values. The arguments and research of personality theorists like Eysenck, which are discussed in Chapter 24, are unlikely to get much of a hearing in the socialization literature.

A second assumption underlying much of the socialization research seems to be that people, and children in particular, are passive objects in the socialization process. They contribute very little to it themselves. This is a view which is in keeping with any deterministic theory of personality, such as that of Freud. On the other hand, it is at complete variance with theories, such as that of Maslow, which view man as a self-actualizing being who consciously strives to develop his potential and to carve out his own destiny.

A third assumption underlying much of the research into the processes and mechanisms by which socialization is achieved is that the processes and mechanisms are identical at all phases. Thus, theorists who stress reinforcement apply it equally to the infant and the school child, whilst those who stress imitation see it as the sole mechanism regardless of the age of the subject. Yet, our knowledge of the development of cognitive processes in children at the very least suggests that learning strategies undergo distinct changes at different ages.

Comparative studies of socialization

Let us now look at the different kinds of evidence for a relationship between social structure, socialization practices and resultant personality differences. We will consider evidence from three sources. First, there is evidence from cross-cultural studies conducted mainly by anthropologists. Secondly, there is evidence from cross-national studies

687

and, in particular, from a recent comprehensive study of socialization in Russia and the United States by the psychologist Urie Bronfenbrenner (1971). Finally, there is evidence from a host of studies of sub-cultural differences in patterns of child-rearing, where the focus has been primarily on social class.

Cross-cultural studies of socialization

A view held by many anthropologists working in this area is that environmental factors largely determine the maintenance systems of a society. By 'maintenance systems' is meant the economic, political, and social organizations surrounding the nourishment, sheltering, and protection of a society's members. These systems determine the child-rearing practices which, in turn, are responsible for personality development.

These views have been formalized in a conceptual model by Harrington and Whiting (1972) of which the following is a simplified version:

Extra-societal causal events
e.g., environmental/ecological factors such as climate, terrain, etc.

Maintenance systems
e.g., subsistence patterns, economy, residence patterns, household structure, social, and political systems and groups

Child-rearing practices
e.g., time and severity of training, methods, initiation rites, etc.

Child personality
i.e., personality variables and cognitive processes

Child behaviour and cultural products
e.g., beliefs about gods; games; attitudes to theft, etc.

The model has been developed on the basis of anthropological studies of primitive, i.e., non-technological, societies throughout the world. The method used to test it is correlational and consists simply of taking a number of factors and seeing to what degree the presence of one factor in a large number of societies is associated with the presence of each of the other factors. Although the implication is that there is a causal relationship between these factors (as we have indicated by using arrows in the model), nevertheless, the evidence cited in support of it is only correlational. We can illustrate this with the following example given by the anthropologist, Whiting.

Significant correlations have been found between hot, rainy, tropical climates and the presence of kwashiorkor, which is a disease caused by protein deficiency in infancy. Low protein-availability and the risk of kwashiorkor are correlated with an extended postpartum sex taboo. This taboo allows the mother time to nurse the infant through the critical stage before becoming pregnant again. We also find that societies where there is a lengthy postpartum sex taboo tend to be those in which a polygynous form of marriage is practised, thus providing alternative sexual outlets for the male. Polygynous societies in turn are associated with mother-child households and with child-training almost exclusively by women. And, since this is likely to result in cross-sex identity for the male child, we find that these tend to be the societies which have initiation rites for males—presumably to resolve the conflict and properly inculcate male identity.

A study by Barry, Child, and Bacon (1959) shows how the basic economic organization of societies affects their child-rearing practices. They examined anthropological records for a large number of societies and then rated these societies for the relative stress which they placed on various aspects of socialization. In addition, they classified them according to their subsistence levels by placing them into categories determined by the extent of food accumulation—with animal husbandry representing the highest level, and hunting and fishing the lowest level. They found that societies with high accumulation of food put strong pressure on children to be responsible and obedient, whereas societies with low accumulation of food emphasized achievement, self-reliance, independence and assertiveness. The argument here, then, is that the nature of the economy selectively produces child-rearing practices which provide training in behaviour which is necessary for that economy. If the resources of a society reside in cattle or crops, then clearly it is important for the survival of that society that its members are brought up to accept the shared responsibilites involved in looking after cattle or in sowing and harvesting crops. On the other hand, in hunter-gatherer and fishing societies, where there is little opportunity for co-operative activities, it makes more sense to train children to be independent and assertive, since for much of the time as adults they will have to rely on their own initiative to survive.

In another study, the same authors also found that differentiation of children by sex was greatest in societies either where superior physical strength and motor skill were important for maintaining the economy or where a large family with a high degree of co-operation was required. Thus, in both kinds of society, boys were trained to be self-reliant, assertive and independent, whereas girls were trained to be nurturant, responsible, and obedient. We may consider our own society here and the kind of characteristics which it inculcates into boys and girls. It is no accident that the current, and often very heated, debate about the role of women in our society has tended to focus increasingly on the differences in socialization to which boys and girls are exposed. We shall return to this point when we consider the evidence for sub-cultural differences in patterns of child-rearing.

There are, of course, considerable difficulties involved in the collection and interpretation of cross-cultural data. In the first place, the anthropologist is not able to manipulate the variables he is interested in. The data lends itself only to correlational analysis, yet, frequently, the conclusions drawn are causal. Since it is always possible to postulate other causes for an observed association between any two factors—and this is particularly the case with cross-cultural studies—such conclusions need to be treated with extreme caution. Secondly, even the observed association between any two factors is by no means invariable. For example, there are societies whose economies require physical strength and motor skill but in which there is very little sex differentiation of personality and role. This is the case with pygmy tribes in the Congo. Thirdly, the idea of a modal personality, that is, of a personality type which is distinctive of a particular society, is a very dubious one. It is inevitably based on the subjective impressions of an anthropologist, and its status is at about the same level as that of any popular stereotype in our own society; for example, that Italians are musical or Scotsmen mean. Such stereotypes ignore wide individual differences within a society and, in the case of cross-cultural investigations, are usually based on an extremely limited sampling of the members of a society. Finally, although it is possible to demonstrate a strong association between a social structural factor, such as size of household, and a socialization factor, such as the degree of indulgence shown towards infants, it is another matter altogether to say that this relationship has a bearing on child personality. It is something which has to be demonstrated and this can only be done by showing in turn that different degrees of indulgence are associated with different personality types; and, even if this were possible, we would still be left with a chain of associations and not with a series of causes and effects.

When compared with personality research conducted by psychologists in our own society (for which objective tests are developed, adequate sampling techniques employed, and reliability coefficients established), we can see that cross-cultural research has severe limitations and that a healthy scepticism needs to be maintained. However, it seems only fair to point out one enormous benefit to be derived from cross-cultural research, and that is that it provides a vital antidote to the parochialism of most psychological research. The aim of many behavioural scientists is to discover general laws governing human behaviour. By confining their attentions to western society, and in particular to annual intakes of first-year undergraduate psychology students, they run the risk of making very broad generalizations which

690

have scant validity beyond the university campus. The dangers of blinkered thinking are nowhere more apparent than in the area of child-rearing, for controversies over such issues as the importance of the mother-child relationship tend to be debated with a good deal more emotion than is usually realized. Thus, cross-cultural evidence for the great diversity of ways in which infants from different societies are treated by adults provided an important corrective to the early claims made by psychologists about the damaging effects of maternal deprivation. As you will have seen in Chapter 21, cross-cultural research has been largely responsible for switching attention from the biological ties linking mother and infant to the stability of the infant's social environment.

Cross-national studies of socialization

We saw above how it is fairly easy to illustrate the differences in aims and demands of child-rearing systems among primitive societies. It probably comes as no surprise to learn that parents in nomadic societies stress different virtues to those stressed by parents in settled, pastoral societies. Nor do we doubt that the striking differences we observe between ourselves and non-technological societies are largely effected through socialization rather than being due to biological factors. But, what about differences between technological societies? Do political and economic differences between technological societies such as Russia and the United States or Great Britain produce differences in personality and behaviour through the medium of socialization? It is to this question that we now turn our attention.

In North America and the United Kingdom over the past twenty-five years or so, we seem to have become increasingly child-centred. This is reflected in best-selling books on child-rearing by authors such as Dr Benjamin Spock as well as in the educational philosophy of teacher training courses. In the first place, there is a stress on *individuality*. Each child is to be viewed as a unique person who must not be prematurely moulded and whose gifts and talents must be carefully nurtured and developed. (Whether parents and teachers actually do this is another matter, but certainly the current ideology demands it.) Secondly, there is a stress on *creativity*. Childhood is supposed to be fun. It should be creative, and every child an explorer. In the same vein, there is an emphasis on the child as a *potential intellectual*, and an enormous toy industry is geared to meeting and creating parental demands for toys which will develop their children's intellectual and creative capacities. Finally, and perhaps most importantly, considerable emphasis is placed on the fact that children have *feelings and emotions* which must be communicated and taken account of. Thus, we must prepare children for such events as illness and hospitalization, for starting school, for the birth of a brother or sister.

691

This type of empathy or orientation towards children is relatively recent. There have been times when children were viewed as inconveniently small adults who could be expected to learn Greek and Latin and read religious sermons. At other times they have been seen as the exemplars of Original Sin, from whom evil had to be removed by all possible means. But, besides making historical comparisons, we can also contrast our attitudes to children and the little that we demand of them with those pertaining in Russia, where we might expect a rather different ideology to operate. In his book, *Two Worlds of Childhood: U.S.A. and U.S.S.R.*, Urie Bronfenbrenner reports the findings of just such a comparative study. Following a series of lengthy visits to the Soviet Union, he was able to offer a description of both the ideology and practice of child socialization as he found it.

In Russian homes there is a marked indulgence of infants particularly with regard to physical contact. Infants and young children spend a lot of time sitting on adult laps. There is also an involvement of all age groups in concern for young children. Even adolescent boys show an interest in and affection for children, which in western society would probably be regarded as strange, if not actually unhealthy. For example, Bronfenbrenner reports an occasion when, out walking in a Russian city with his wife and two children, he saw a gang of youths approaching. The younger of his two children had run on ahead of his parents and Bronfenbrenner felt slightly apprehensive as the youths reached the toddler. Suddenly, one of them gently lifted him up, hugged and kissed him, then passed him to the next and so on until each of the youths had hugged him amidst much smiling and laughter. Then, as the parents caught up with them, they handed him back and passed on their way.

Because of the high employment of women, many infants go to a creche each day, and most later go to nursery school. From the start, they are encouraged to be self-reliant in such matters as feeding and dressing themselves and keeping themselves clean and tidy. Language-development is heavily stressed and a high teacher-child ratio allows for a great deal of individual language training. Children are continuously encouraged to be co-operative. No fighting is allowed, nor are they allowed to be possessive about toys.

Children start school at age seven, and the first day of the school year is a national holiday, thus allowing parents, relatives, and friends of the family to accompany the child to school with bouquets of flowers for the teacher. School is concerned, not only with the acquisition of skills and knowledge, which is put forward both as a duty and as a privilege, but also with moral training. Teachers encourage obedience and respect for all adults. There is continual emphasis on collective responsibility for everyone in the community, and all aspects of community life are made visible to the children.

692

Teachers are not allowed to use physical punishment. To achieve compliance, love-oriented techniques of guilt and shame are employed. Collective responsibility is reinforced by children's courts which also employ techniques of guilt and shame to enforce conformity. There is no opportunity for discontinuity between home and school. Parents actively engage in their children's education, to such an extent that, in the case of an intractable child, a headmaster might well summon from work both parents to discuss ways of improving the situation.

Competition at school is encouraged at all levels but according to the dialectical principle of conflict at one level being resolved by synthesis at the next. Thus, each child competes to be best in his row of desks; each row competes to be best in the class, each class to be best in the school; each school to be the best in the district and so on. Responsibility for excellence of each individual resides in whatever group is under focus. For example, if a child is having difficulty with maths, then others in his row or class who are good at maths will help him at home with extra homework.

Manuals of advice for teachers, parents, and children are completely consistent in emphasis and content. Bronfenbrenner quotes a passage from one such manual for children:

> '*At home.* Upon rising, greet one's parents, thank them after the meal or for any help received; before leaving, check to make sure you have everything necessary; upon return from school put everything in its place; take care of your own things (sew on buttons, iron, shine shoes, keep desk in order); in accordance with ability, help with house-cleaning, dusting, setting table and chairs in place, serving, clearing, washing dishes, growing and caring for decorative flowers, taking care of younger children—playing games with them and taking them for walks; do homework; follow the rule: "Job done—take a rest, then start another job".'

Let us summarize this necessarily brief survey of Bronfenbrenner's observations of child socialization in the Soviet Union.

1. There is absolute agreement and consistency among all socializing agencies about moral values which matter.
2. To inculcate these moral values, love-oriented techniques of guilt and shame are employed.
3. There is concern by every age level with every other age level in society.
4. From the start, young children are made aware of the community and of the wider society to which they belong.
5. There is a playing down of the individual *qua* individual; the focus is on him as a member of society and on the collective needs and values.

693

If we now contrast this picture of socialization in Russia with what is the case in the United States (and to a slightly lesser extent in Great Britain), we find striking differences. In the first place, there is very clear age-grading in American society. Children spend very little time with adults outside school hours. In general, the ethos or orientation of the peer group is in opposition to that of adults. Nor is there explicit moral training. There is also a strong emphasis on the individual child. His feelings are regarded as important and his creative capacity encouraged. Rebellion and questioning are viewed as part of healthy development. Finally, there are often considerable inconsistencies between the different socializing agencies in the demands that they make—for example, in the discontinuity between home and school. These inconsistencies are probably related to the inconsistencies inherent in a system which is both capitalist and avowedly Christian, a system of contradictions in which individual competitiveness and concern for others make uneasy bedfellows. It seems clear, then, that the two very different types of orientation towards child-rearing which we find in Russia and in North America arise out of two different ideological, economic, and social systems: the one stressing communal responsibility, social roles and networks, and the submergence of the individual; the other stressing individuality, opportunism, and change.

However, one question that still remains is whether the picture which Bronfenbrenner paints of socialization in the Soviet Union represents reality. His observations, based on visits to schools, discussions with education officials and examination of official publications such as the manuals for parents, teachers, and children, might well have led to erroneous conclusions about what actually occurs. For example, how representative of Russian homes and schools were those which he was allowed to visit? Are the precepts and practices advocated in the manuals actually put into practice? We know all too well that widespread dissemination of moral tracts and endorsement of their contents by the authorities in Victorian England was no guarantee of how people would or actually did behave. It is always possible, then, that the aims and procedures which Bronfenbrenner reported are just ideologies with little or no basis in actual behaviour.

Bronfenbrenner was perfectly aware of this possibility, and what makes his study so important is that he took steps to remedy the situation. He conducted a series of experiments on large samples of school-children in Russia, the U.S.A. and several European countries, including Great Britain. In general, the results of these experiments suggested that the ideology of child socialization in the Soviet Union is effective. He found that American and English children are much more willing to engage in anti-social behaviour than Russian children. Furthermore, Russian children were least willing to engage in immoral behaviour if their peers would know about it, whereas American children were more willing if their peers would know. Across all the experiments, he found that Russian children were very reluctant to engage in anti-social acts, whereas English and American children were extremely willing to do so.

Sub-cultural studies of socialization

If we now turn to evidence for intra-societal differences in child-rearing, we find that there are a large number of studies in the psychological literature which suggest that one's economic relationship to the community produces distinctive styles and emphases in child socialization. And, in turn, it is claimed that these differences are reflected in the resultant child personality. Most studies have used social class as the index of one's relation to society. This is almost invariably based on the father's occupation and income. Whilst the majority of studies have been conducted in the United States, their findings do not differ greatly from those reported in the few studies conducted in Great Britain.

Early studies investigating social class differences in child-rearing were largely influenced by Freudian theory of psychosexual development in their choice of variables to examine. Thus, they looked for differences in weaning, toilet-training, and the control of sexual and aggressive impulses. They largely consisted of detailed observations (based on interviews and questionnaires) of child-rearing procedures and the relation of these to personality characteristics which were inferred, observed non-systematically, or, very occasionally, assessed.

Several interesting findings emerged from these studies. In the first place, although there was considerable evidence for social class differences, the pattern was a changing one. Up to World War II, there was a trend towards greater permissiveness, particularly in infant feeding and toilet-training, among working class mothers, but this was reversed after the war. On the other hand, middle-class mothers have become increasingly permissive since the war. Compared with their working-class counterparts, middle-class mothers have been consistently more permissive towards their children's expressed needs and wishes; they are less likely to use physical punishment; and they are generally more acceptant and equalitarian. On the other hand, it also seems that the gap between the social classes is narrowing, with working-class parents beginning to adopt both the values and techniques of the middle-class.

However, despite the widespread belief in the relationship between parental attitudes towards these 'Freudian' variables and later childhood personality and behaviour, there is no evidence to support it. Any relationship between, for example, age and severity of weaning or toilet-training and particular behavioural manifestations in later childhood has yet to be demonstrated. There are several good reasons for this state of

695

affairs. Firstly, most of these studies were retrospective and, therefore, liable to all the flaws inherent in a technique which relies solely on memory. Secondly, since the data are based on mothers' reports in an interview, there may well have been distortion through the bias of social desirability. Interviews and questionnaires may successfully tap parental attitudes to child-rearing but tell us nothing about how parents actually behave. If a mother knows that the current ideology favours permissiveness, then she may well respond in an interview in such a manner as to present herself as conforming to the ideology, though her actual behaviour, which is not open to scrutiny by the researcher, may be quite the reverse. Furthermore, if, as was the case with many of these studies, the assessment of the child's personality is also based on the mother's reports, then we can easily appreciate that there may well be a reluctance to blemish. For a mother to admit to faults in her children may well seem to her to be an admission of failure on her part as a mother. Finally, it ought to be pointed out that the effects which Freud would have predicted as following from particular weaning and toilet-training procedures would not show up with the kinds of measures used in most of these studies; for example, the effect upon later sexual behaviour or the development of an authoritarian personality.

In the last fifteen years or so, there has been some improvement in the situation, in that a number of investigators have switched to longitudinal, prospective studies. Thus, by studying a large sample of children from birth through to adolescence, some of the flaws inherent in the early studies can be avoided. However, the methods used still tend to be based on interviews and questionnaires, so that we still do not know whether we are getting a true picture of how parents actually behave towards children in the home. This is very serious, because, at the same time, there has been a shift of emphasis from the study of rather specific variables such as weaning and toilet-training to the study of more general variables such as control and punishment strategies, parental warmth, and styles of interaction. We would expect such variables to be especially prone to social desirability bias.

A consistent finding to emerge from both American and British studies of social class differences in child socialization is that middle-class parents differ from working-class parents in the control strategies they use. Physical punishment and threats of physical punishment are the major strategies used by working-class parents. The middle-classes tend to be more ideational, that is, they tend to use love-orientated techniques, which, by appealing to empathy and to the child's internal self, are more likely to lead to the formation of strong internal controls based on feelings of guilt. Furthermore, working-class parents tend to respond to children's transgressions in terms of the consequences of the act, whereas middle-class parents respond in terms of the child's intent.

696

Do these differences have any noticeable effect on children's behaviour? There are, of course, many factors which differentiate middle from working-class children. But, how far can we legitimately attribute them directly to differences in child-rearing? Social classes differ, not only in their socialization procedures, but also in their total life styles. It may well be that, for example, poverty is a much more important determinant of observed differences between middle and working-class children than any of the mediating variables investigated by social scientists. This is not to deny the importance of differences in socialization procedures, but rather to point out that the relationship between social system variables, socialization practices, and resultant personality and behaviour is a complex one.

Furthermore, by ignoring the wider social context, we are in danger of accepting uncritically the value judgements which all too often underlie research into social class differences. There is an implicit assumption that the middle-classes are in some sense morally superior to the working-classes and that the world would be a better place if only the working-classes would emulate their middle-class counterparts. It ignores the question why such differences exist in the first place. And when it leads to remedial programmes and intervention projects for those who have come to be classified as 'culturally disadvantaged', it may simply divert attention away from the need to improve the economic status and physical environment of those who are at the bottom of the social class hierarchy.

To take an example, many studies have reported that middle-class children can accept symbolic rewards or delayed rewards as readily as actual rewards, but that working-class children prefer actual rewards and are not prepared to tolerate delay of gratification. The implication here is that delay of gratification is virtuous and ought to be encouraged. However, if we ask why such a difference exists and what function it fulfills, then we may start to doubt the superiority of the middle-class ethos. For example, we might speculate that tolerance of delay of gratification is related to the traditional patterns of employment in our society. Compared with their middle-class counterparts, working-class families are economically insecure. Working-class fathers do not have something called a 'career'; they have a job. They do not earn a monthly salary; they are paid a weekly wage. They do not get fixed annual increments; there is a rate for the job and the same amount is earned at age twenty-five as at age sixty. They do not have security of tenure but may be employed for the day or for as long as the job lasts. A civil servant is not given his cards with his wage packet on a Friday night. Working-class men do not usually receive a pension from their employers equivalent to half their earnings; they draw an old age pension from the State which is proportionately far less. Whilst the Trade Unions have been

697

largely instrumental in mitigating some of the harsher realities of working-class life, nevertheless delay of gratification as a value makes little sense to those members of society for whom there is no likelihood of long-term rewards. Making sacrifices with very limited resources for an uncertain future has little to recommend it. Delay of gratification is a middle-class virtue, because it pays dividends for members of the middle-classes. In a stable economy, saving money makes money, but in a period of inflation money saved in a bank account depreciates faster than the interest accrued. Hence, at the present moment, this particular form of delay of gratification is unlikely to be held up as a virtue. Immediate consumption is the wiser policy and we see the most affluent section of society acting in the most pragmatic fashion by purchasing antiques and paintings as a hedge against inflation.

We have given considerable attention to the notion of delay of gratification, firstly, in order to demonstrate how implicit assumptions underlie much of the research into social class differences in socialization; and, secondly, to stress the importance of viewing this research from a broader perspective. By locating socialization research in a broader social context, we can see that sub-cultural differences in patterns of child-rearing are neither arbitrary nor fixed. Rather, they are a direct reflection of the political and economic structure of society at a given time. Of course, there may well be a time-lag between changes in social structural variables and changes in socialization procedures. Habits and attitudes change more slowly than economies. Nevertheless, as we have already pointed out, research has shown significant changes in patterns of child-rearing over the past three decades with the gap between the social classes narrowing—a reflection possibly of the post-war rise in standard of living for all strata of society.

Significant changes have also been reported in the area of sex-role differentiation. In both the U.S.A. and the U.K. greater sex-role differentiation is found among working-class than among middle-class families. For example, Bronfenbrenner reported in 1961 that the roles of both parents in middle-class families were changing. The father was becoming less authoritarian and more affectionate, and the mother was becoming more important as the adult in the family who disciplines. On the basis of evidence from his own study of 400 American adolescents and their families, Bronfenbrenner argued that the changing roles of middle-class parents would significantly affect the personality development of American middle-class boys. If the mother was now the disciplinarian instead of the father and, if she used love-orientated techniques of control rather than physical punishment, then the effect would be to discourage the development of initiative, independence and self-sufficiency, while at the same time establishing strong internal controls. He wrote: 'Males exposed to love-orientated socialization techniques

698

might be expected to differ from their counterparts of twenty-five years ago in being somewhat more conforming and anxious, less enterprising and self-sufficient, and, in general, possessing more of the virtues and liabilities commonly associated with feminine character structure'. In the case of the lower middle and working class, we still find the traditional pattern of parental preferences, whereby most parents tend to be more affectionate toward the child of the opposite sex. Since these families have a power-orientated structure, the father disciplines the boy through physical punishment and threats of physical punishment and leaves the disciplining of the girl to the mother. Since she uses love-orientated techniques, the outcome of the personality development of boys and girls will be along traditional lines.

Although the effects of a new pattern of parental control for personality development described by Bronfenbrenner are speculative, there is little doubt that there has been a change in patterns of parental control among the middle classes. Similar findings have been reported by the Newsons in their longitudinal study of child socialization in Nottingham and by Bernstein in his study of families in Outer London areas.

There do seem, then, to be clear social class differences in parental role specialization. Whether these have important consequences for sex-role differentiation, as suggested by Bronfenbrenner, has yet to be demonstrated. Furthermore, whether these social class differences will gradually disappear or whether new patterns will emerge, only time and further research will tell.

Socialization after childhood

We have already noted that the major focus of socialization research by psychologists has been on child development, that is, on child-rearing differences and their effects on personality and behaviour. One of the assumptions underlying much of this research is that personality, once it has been formed during childhood, remains stable and undergoes little change during adult life. Here, we shall now consider how far this assumption is justified. If personality development is largely determined by the early social environment, will later changes in the social environment bring about changes in personality? To what extent do we change our beliefs, attitudes, values, and motives as we progress through life? How far can such changes be attributed to social influence? Do we continue to be influenced by the different roles we occupy and the various institutions we pass through? Compared with the study of childhood socialization, there is little information in the psychological literature which will help us to answer these questions; we shall have to rely very much on description and sociological analysis in order to arrive at any conclusions.

Sources of evidence

However, let us look first at what evidence is available. It is derived from roughly four different sources. Firstly, there is evidence based on individual case histories obtained in clinical practice. Usually, the patient's personality is measured and continuity with the past is assumed or inferred, largely depending on whatever theory the clinician is working with. Evidence of this sort is very dubious indeed, since it is based on the recollections of the patient, on the testimony of his family and friends and on the speculations of the clinician. It can hardly be regarded as objective or reliable. A second and more reliable source of evidence comes from empirical studies of continuity of personality. These have usually focused on the durability of early childhood learning, such as the durability of political attitudes, and, in many cases, are based on retestings with the same personality measure. However, the findings are inconsistent and vary from study to study and from sample to sample. Although, overall, the evidence points to some continuity of personality over time, nevertheless, in most studies, there is still a considerable amount of variance which is not accounted for. In other words, the later variance is not predictable from the earlier measurements of personality. This suggests that there is both continuity and change of personality in adult life, a conclusion which is perhaps not so surprising.

A third source of evidence comes from studies of adult socialization, where entry into a given role in adult life is accompanied by measurable changes in personality characteristics, as for example, following entry into an occupational role. In one study which looked at the effect of marriage on personality, it was found that, when compared with a control group of unmarried persons, there was significant change in scores on certain scales of the California Personality Inventory, such as dominance and self-acceptance, for married persons. Unfortunately, such well-controlled studies are rather rare.

A final and more recent source of evidence comes from studies of the effects on personality and behaviour of participation in various kinds of 'relationship' groups. These are groups whose aim is to facilitate personal development and to enhance interpersonal skills. Since the notion of personal development implies changes in personality, such groups are a useful source of information. To date, however, there is little reliable evidence for long-term changes in personality as a consequence of participation in this type of group. One reason for this is that many of the studies have severe methodological flaws. For example, very often, the measures of personality are based on participant self-reports and observer ratings, both of which can produce biased results. Unless expectancy on the part of the participant and knowledge on the part of the observer are controlled in some way, we can set little store by the findings. Another possible reason is that many groups are short-lived, lasting perhaps only for a weekend. Whatever their short-term outcome, it is unlikely that they will have long-term effects on personality, which more permanent, on-going groups, lasting several months or more, might achieve. However, this is a new and exciting area of research which may well yield interesting and reliable information in the future.

Given the current paucity of information in the psychological literature relating to adult socialization in general and to continuity of personality in particular, it will be useful to consider what we might expect. Firstly, however, we must distinguish socialization from other forms of change such as maturation. Secord and Backman (1974) have suggested two criteria for isolating socialization. These are (a) that any changes in attitudes, personality and behaviour must be attributable to learning; and (b) that such changes should be seen to have their origins in interactions with other persons. Whilst these two criteria are clearly important in theory, nevertheless, in practice it is usually very difficult to apply them with any degree of confidence, except in extreme cases of change directly attributable to physical factors such as physical illness and bodily degeneration with increasing age.

However, it is clear that the socialization experienced during childhood cannot prepare an individual for all the roles which he will be expected to fill during his adult life. People move through a sequence of different positions in society in accord with the different stages of the life cycle. Insofar as our beliefs, attitudes, values and motives are affected by the occupation of a role, we probably experience continuous, albeit gradual and often subtle, changes in the view which we have of ourselves as well as the view which others have of us.

The origins of self
Let us take each of these perspectives separately. Self, or personal identity, refers to the set of characteristics which you are aware that you possess, and which is composed of a central core and a number of sub-identities. Personality, on the other hand, refers to the set of characteristics which others believe you have and which are inferred from consistent patterns in your behaviour. Self is you experienced by yourself, whereas personality is you experienced by other people. Self is how you sum up all that you are; personality is how others sum you up. We will examine the notion of self first and then consider personality.

The most widely held view as to the origins of self is that you become aware of yourself in the process of interaction with others. As a young child, you gradually become aware of yourself as an object to others, that others are reacting to you. You feel loved or unloved, you are told you are good or naughty, clever or stupid, pretty or plain, and so on. As a result of these reactions to you, your self-image arises. The image you develop of yourself is simply the reflection of how others see you. You

701

adopt the attitudes, reactions and evaluations of others towards you as your own attitude, reaction, and evaluation of yourself. The phrase 'the looking-glass self' has been used to describe this process by which each of us comes to know or perceive ourselves through our realization of how others see us. Just as we look at our reflection in a mirror to see what we look like, so we see who we are by seeing the reflection of ourselves in other people's reactions to us.

Whatever the biological determinants of your personality and behaviour may be, your notion of your self comes only as a result of your perception of other people's reactions to your behaviour. These biological determinants will be reflected back to you, but, increasingly as you grow up, so will social determinants. You will occupy an increasing number of social roles to which expectations as to how you should behave are attached. As you fulfill these role-expectations—more or less successfully—as student, friend, lover, or player, so will you come to evaluate yourself as others do. Your role partners will not see you solely as a biologically unique individual but as someone occupying a social role who fulfills the expectations in varying degrees. They will evaluate you accordingly and these evaluations will become part of your evaluation of yourself. This is not a process you can escape from or grow out of. You will inevitably evaluate yourself by referring to other's evaluations of you and will use others to compare yourself with. Your self is not your own possession. As Goffman once put it, your self is on loan from society. If society's evaluation of you changes, then your evaluation of yourself will surely change.

We can illustrate this process of social patterning of self by quoting from a brilliant analysis by Cavan of the effect on a man's self-image of switching from the role of an employed person to that of someone in retirement:

> At the point of retirement, we may make a generalized picture of the male. He has a well-ingrained self-image as competent, successful at some level of work, usefully productive, self-supporting, and able to provide for his family. This image has been built up over years of time by the favourable reactions of his family, friends, co-workers, and those segments of society whose opinion he values. He has, moreover, found a kind of work—a social role—that permits him to express his self-image satisfactorily, and he is firmly incorporated into a physical environment and a group of co-workers which make it possible for him to carry out his role.
>
> Using the concepts employed above, let us consider what happens at the point of compulsory retirement. First, the means of carrying out the social role disappear: the man is a lawyer without a case, a book-keeper without books, a machinist without tools. Second, he is excluded from his group of former co-workers; as an isolated person

he may be completely unable to function in his former role. Third, as a retired person, he begins to find a different evaluation of himself in the minds of others from the evaluation he had as an employed person. He no longer sees respect in the eyes of former subordinates, praise in the faces of former superiors, and approval in the manner of former co-workers. The looking-glass composed of his former important groups throws back a changed image: he is done for, an old-timer, old-fashioned, on the shelf.

Although not all re-evaluations of self are as devastating and dramatic as this, nevertheless there do seem to be moments when we take stock of ourselves, realizing that we are no longer the same as we were. This often happens when we have been away from home for a long time and return or meet old friends after an absence of several years. It is then that we are struck by the fact that we have changed in some way, despite the feeling of personal continuity in our own biography. We feel the same person, yet realize at the same time that we have changed. Although this stock-taking is a subjective experience, it is nonetheless an outcome of socialization, since it occurs in a social context. It is a change in self-evaluation which is explicitly or implicitly refracted back to the individual by the reactions of others.

Personality change
If we now consider whether or not we would expect personality to remain stable during adult life, we find that much the same kind of argument applies. The evidence which we briefly reviewed earlier suggested that there is both continuity and change. In the light of our analysis of the inter-relationship between self and social role, this is perhaps not so surprising. Personality is the summary of an individual by others, a summary based on their observation of consistency and regularity in his actions. But the important questions to ask are: Who is doing the observing? What are the social contexts in which these observations take place? Many social psychologists would argue that personality is expressed in and partly determined by the social roles occupied. We are all familiar with biographies which portray an individual as harsh and tyrannical in his occupational role and as meek and gentle as spouse or parent. Several Nazi concentration camp commandants in World War II are a good case in point, manifesting abominable cruelty and sadism in the one context and warmth and kindness in another.

There seem, then, to be at least two reasons why we are rarely aware of changes in other people's personalities. Firstly, we do not usually encounter the same individual in widely different social contexts or roles. When we do, we are most likely to be influenced by the context or role behaviour which we have most frequently encountered. Secondly, any changes which do occur within a particular role are likely to be gradual and go unnoticed for the most part. It is only when we meet people again after a long absence that we are likely to become aware of changes.

This conception of personality as context-bound has serious implications for the validity of 'objective' personality assessment as currently conducted by many psychologists. Personality tests are usually of the self-report kind and involve asking an individual about his actions and feelings in general. They largely ignore the social context in which such actions occur. If the purpose of personality assessment is to be able to predict future behaviour, then, by ignoring social context, psychologists must expect a considerable amount of error.

We can illustrate this point with an example taken from the recent controversial Stanford Prison experiment reported by Zimbardo and his colleagues (1972). In this investigation male college students volunteered to take part in a psychological study of prison life. The major purpose of the study was to determine whether the behaviour shown by prisoners and guards in real prisons stems, to a large degree, from the situation in which they find themselves, rather than from special (personality) characteristics they bring with them to this setting. The question being asked was whether in this study middle-class, highly-educated subjects would come to act very much like real guards and prisoners when placed in an environment which simulated actual prison conditions as closely as possible. Subjects were interviewed and given a battery of personality tests to ascertain that they were all normal, well-adjusted individuals. Before the experiment, they were randomly assigned to the roles of prisoners and guards. The experiment proper began several days later, when the 'prisoners' were arrested without warning by the city police, taken downtown, fingerprinted, photographed and 'booked'. They were then driven blindfolded to a prison at whose whereabouts they could only guess, but which, in fact, had been specially constructed in the basement of Stanford University Psychology Department. Once there, they were stripped of all clothing and forced to dress in uncomfortable, loose-fitting smocks and a tight nylon cap. Their personal possessions were removed and they were given a number to use in place of their names. They were then locked in empty cells containing only the bare necessities of life and from thenceforth were subject to a daily prison regime imposed by their guards.

The guards wore identical khaki-coloured uniforms and silver-reflector sunglasses, which made eye contact with them impossible. They also carried badges of authority appropriate to their role—billyclubs, whistles, and handcuffs. They worked a shift system returning to their own homes when off duty. The investigators observed and recorded the ensuing events unobtrusively through spy holes and one-way mirrors.

The results of the experiment were dramatic and alarming. Although it was planned to continue for a fortnight, it had to be stopped after only six days. The reason for this change was that, even during this short period of time, major—and quite disturbing—changes developed in the behaviour of both the prisoners and the guards. Initially, the prisoners resisted the guards and even tried to overpower them. This attempt was ruthlessly suppressed by the guards and from then on the prisoners became increasingly passive and depressed. Several began to show signs of serious psychological disturbance and one had to be released from prison after only thirty-six hours when he began to demonstrate uncontrollable fits of crying and screaming. Two others were released shortly after when they also showed symptoms of severe emotional disorder.

As the prisoners became increasingly disorganized and depressed, the guards became increasingly brutal and sadistic. They harassed the prisoners constantly, forced them to curse and denounce and denigrate each other, assigned them senseless and tedious tasks, and enforced a variety of physically painful punishments for misdemeanours or non-compliance. Indeed, they tended to dehumanize the prisoners and came to perceive them as somehow less than human.

The conclusion which the investigators reached on the basis of these unexpected and very dramatic results was that prisons may well create the brutal behaviour of guards and the passive, despondent behaviour of prisoners. There was no indication either in the transcripts of the initial interviews nor in the personality profiles derived from the 'objective' testing that the subjects would enact their roles in such an unnerving fashion. Furthermore, although both the prisoners and the guards evinced considerable differences in behaviour among themselves—some prisoners 'cracking', while one remained defiant; some guards behaving sadistically, while others stuck more to the 'rules'—none of these differences in reaction to the situation could have been predicted from their scores on the personality tests.

It would seem, then, that social conditions are paramount in determining how individuals behave and whatever contribution individual differences in temperament or personality may make, psychologists committed to an ideology of objective, psychometric assessment of personality may be barking up the wrong tree.

Socialization and institutions

We will conclude this discussion of adult socialization by examining the manner in which institutions function as socializing agencies. Although early socialization for most people takes place in the context of the family, as soon as we go to school we are subject to a new set of social influences. In fact, much of our lives is spent in institutions or large-scale organizations and, in many cases, a major aim of the institution is to change us. Thus, schools, colleges, offices, factories, mental hospitals, prisons, and the Armed Forces are all institutions which we may at some time pass through. In some cases, there will be little or no incompatibility between the aims of the institution and the values of the individual. Thus, for example, how the individual has been socialized in the past is unlikely to interfere with the acquisition of short-hand and typing skills in a secretarial college or the assembling of a car in a factory. However, in other cases, there may well be a clash between the values and behaviour expected in an institution and those to which the individual has been accustomed. Where this is the case, we find that similar techniques are employed by the institution to mould the individual to its requirements. The process is essentially one of power and control over the individual, and, invariably, the institutions are what Goffman has called total institutions, that is, they are operative and in control over the inmates twenty-four hours of the day. Thus, boarding schools, prisons, mental hospitals, military institutions, indoctrination camps, convents, and monastries are all total institutions. They are characterized by having an overall rational plan supposedly designed to fulfill the aims of the institution and which involves each inmate in a daily programme of tightly-scheduled activities carried out in the same place and under the same authority and usually in the company of a group of other inmates who are all treated alike and required to do the same thing.

From the perspective of society, a child at birth is a blank slate and parental strategies are designed to inculcate gradually a pattern of attitudes, values, and motives. However, in adult socialization, and especially where there is a discrepancy between institutional and individual values, then old patterns have to be erased and new ones impressed. Consequently, we can distinguish analytically two phases in the socialization process in institutions—desocialization and resocialization—though in reality they are taking place concurrently. To achieve the aims of a total institution, desocialization strategies are a necessary complement to any resocialization programme, and each of these phases can be seen to have certain features in common across very different kinds of institution.

We can distinguish three major features of any desocialization programme, all of which are aimed at weakening an individual's ties with other social contexts. Firstly, entry to a total institution effectively cuts an individual off from contact with wider society. For example, recruits to the Armed Forces are not allowed 'out of camp' for several weeks, during which time the identity of 'serviceman' will be expected to have taken strong hold. Secondly, all the symbolic trappings and cues to his previous social roles are removed. For example, he is usually required to have his hair cut very short, his personal belongings are reduced to a minimum, he is given a standard issue of clothing and personal living space is restricted to a small, impersonal sleeping area. Thirdly, continual assaults are made on the individual's self-concept. In the Forces, this is known as 'hazing' and it involves verbal and physical assaults, vilification, and humiliation. This emphasizes the low status of the recruit and denigrates his previous social position. In this manner the individual's self-image is eroded and the new position within the institution for which he is being socialized becomes more attractive.

Turning now to the resocialization phase, we can see that, by completely monopolizing the time of the novice, the institution effectively prevents him from engaging in any other activities which might be incongruent with the socialization programme. By totally separating him from his previous social environment, it makes him dependent on the other novices and encourages the forging of ties in a group within the institution. This is effected also by making rewards contingent on individual compliance within the group of novices. Since in total institutions the individual has no power and no control over the rewards and punishments, he is, in this respect, in much the same position as a young child in a family. Compliance makes life more pleasant.

We have considered the case of total institutions in society, because they highlight in dramatic form the fact that socialization continues after childhood. Just as most army recruits, novices in religious orders and first year 'fags' in boarding schools come to adopt the attitudes, values, and motives of their respective institutions, so, in less dramatic form, do we all undergo changes which enable us to fulfill the many roles which society assigns to us.

FURTHER READING

Booth, T. (1975) *Growing Up in Society*. Methuen.
Danziger, K. (1971) *Socialization*. Penguin.
Oakley, A. (1972) *Sex, Gender and Society*. Maurice Temple Smith.

Bibliography

Abernethy, E. (1940) 'The effect of changed environmental conditions upon the results of college examinations'. *Journal of Psychology*, 10, 293–301.

Adorno, T. W., Frenkel-Brunswick, E., Levinson, D. J., and Sanford, R. N. (1950) *The Authoritarian Personality*. New York, Harper and Row.

Allport, G. (1954) *The Nature of Prejudice*. Reading, Mass., Addison-Wesley.

Allport, G. W. (1961) *Pattern and Growth in Personality*. New York, Holt, Reinhart and Winston.

American Psychological Association (1954) 'Technical recommendations for tests'. *Psychological Bulletin*, 51, pt 2.

Anand, B. K., and Brobeck, J. R. (1951) 'Hypothalamic control of food intake in rats and cats'. *Yale Journal of Biology and Medicine*, 24, 123–140.

Anastasi, A. (1958) *Differential Psychology*. New York, Macmillan.

Annett, M. (1975) 'Hand preference and the laterality of cerebral speech'. *Cortex*. 11, 305–28.

Apter, M. (1970) *The Computer Simulation of Behaviour*. London, Hutchinson.

Argyle, M. (1969) *Social Interaction*. London, Methuen.

Aronson, E., and Worchel, P. (1960) 'Similarity versus liking as a determinant of interpersonal attractiveness'. *Psychonomic Science*, 5, 157–8.

Asch, S. E. (1946) 'Forming impressions of personality'. *Journal of Abnormal and Social Psychology*, 41, 258–90.

Asch, S. (1956) 'Studies in independence and submission to group pressures. A minority of one against a unanimous majority'. *Psychological Monographs*, 70 (9) (Whole No. 416).

Aserinsky, E., and Kleitman, N. (1953) 'Regularly occurring periods of eye motility and concomitant phenomena during sleep'. *Science*, 118 273–4.

Atkinson, R., and Shiffrin, R. (1968) 'Human Memory: a proposed system and its control processes'. In K. Spence and J. Spence, eds., *The Psychology of Learning and Motivation: Advances in research and theory*, Vol. 2. New York, Academic Press.

Ax, A. F. (1953) 'The physiological differentiation of fear and anger in humans'. *Psychosomatic Medicine*, 15, 433–42.

Baddeley, A., and Scott, D. (1971) 'Short term forgetting in the absence of inhibition'. *Quarterly Journal of Experimental Psychology*, 23, 275–283.

Bahrick, H. P., Noble, M., and Fitts, P. M. (1954) 'Extra-task performance as a measure of learning a primary task'. *Journal of Experimental Psychology*, 48, 298–302.

Backman, C. W., and Secord, P. F. (1966) 'The Compromise Process and the Affect Structure of Groups'. In *Problems in Social Psychology: Selected Readings*, C. W. Backman and P. F. Secord, eds., New York, McGraw-Hill.

Barron, F. (1969) *Creative Person and Creative Process*. New York, Holt, Reinhart and Winston.

Barry, H. A., Bacon, M. K., and Child, I. (1957) 'A cross-cultural study of some sex differences in socialization. *Journal of Abnormal and Social Psychology*, 55, 327–32.

Barry, H. A., Child, I. L., and Bacon, M. K. (1959) 'Relation of child training to subsistence economy'. *American Anthropologist*, 61, 51–63.

Bartlett, F. C. (1932) *Remembering: A Study in Experimental and Social Psychology*. Cambridge University Press.

Bartlett, F. C. (1958) *Thinking: An Experimental and Social Study*. London, Allen and Unwin.

Bell, S. M. (1970) 'Development of the concept of object as a result of infant mother attachment'. *Child Development*, 41, 291–311.

Bem, D. J. (1967) 'Self-perception: an alternative interpretation of cognitive dissonance phenomena'. *Psychological Review*, 74, 183–200.

Berlyne, D. E. (1965) *Structure and Direction in Thinking*. New York, Wiley.

Bernstein, B. (1961) 'Social class and linguistic development: a theory of social learning'. In A. H. Halsey, *et al*, eds., *Education, Economy and Society*. New York, Free Press.

Berscheid, E., and Walster, E. (1978) *Interpersonal Attraction*, 2nd edn. Reading, Mass., Addison-Wesley.

Bexton, W. H., Heron, W., and Scott, T. H. (1954) 'Effects of increased variation in the sensory environment'. *Canadian Journal of Psychology*, 8, 70–6.

Birch, H. G. (1945) 'The relation of previous experience to insightful problem solving'. *Journal of Comparative Psychology*, 38, 367–83.

Blakemore, C., and Cooper, J. F. (1970) 'Development of the brain depends on the visual environment'. *Nature*, 228, 477–8.

Blakemore, C., and Mitchell, D. E. (1973) 'Environmental modification of the visual cortex and the neural basis of learning and memory'. *Nature*, 241, 467–8.

Blanchard, R. J., Fukunaga, K. K., and Blanchard, C. B. (1976) 'Environmental control of defensive reactions to a cat'. *Bulletin of the Psychonomic Society*, 8, 179–81.

710

Blurton Jones, N. G., ed. (1972) *Ethological Studies of Child Behaviour*. Cambridge University Press.

Bourne, L. E. (1966) *Human Conceptual Behaviour*. Boston, Allyn and Bacon.

Bourne, L. E., Ekstrand, B. R., and Dominowski, R. L. (1971) *The Psychology of Thinking*. Englewood Cliffs, N.J., Prentice-Hall.

Bowerman, C. E. (1956) 'Age relationships at marriage, by marital status and age at marriage'. *Marriage and Family Living*, 18, 231–3.

Bransford, J., and Johnson, M. (1973) 'Considerations of some problems of comprehension'. In W. Chase, ed., *Visual Information Processing*. N.Y., Academic Press.

Brehm, J. W. (1956) 'Post-decision changes in the desirability of alternatives'. *Journal of Abnormal and Social Psychology*, 52, 384–9.

Brehm, J. W., and Cohen, A. R., eds. (1962) *Explorations in cognitive dissonance*. New York, Wiley.

Brehm, J. W., Gatz, M., Geothals, G., McCrommon, J., and Ward, L. (1970) 'Psychological and interpersonal attraction'. Mimeo available from author.

Broadbent, D. E. (1958) *Perception and Communication*. Pergamon.

Bronfenbrenner, U. (1961) 'The changing American child: a speculative analysis'. *Journal of Social Issues*, 17, 6–18.

Bronfenbrenner, U. (1971) *Two worlds of childhood—U.S. and U.S.S.R.* London, Allen and Unwin.

Brown, R. (1965) *Social Psychology*. New York, Free Press.

Bruner, J. S., and Goodman, C. C. (1947) 'Value and need as organising factors in perception'. *Journal of Abnormal and Social Psychology*, 42, 33–44.

Bruner, J. S., Goodnow, J. J., and Austin, G. A. (1956) *A Study of Thinking*. New York, Wiley.

Bruner, J. S., and Minturn, A. L. (1955) 'Perceptual identification and perceptual organization'. *Journal of General Psychology*, 53, 21–8.

Bruner, J. S., Olver, R. R., and Greenfield, P. M. (1966) *Studies in Cognitive Growth*. New York, Wiley.

Bruner, J. S., Shapiro, D., and Tagiuri, R. (1958) 'The meaning of traits in isolation and combination'. In R. Tagiuri and L. Petrullo, eds. *Person Perception and Interpersonal Behaviour*. Stanford, California, Stanford University Press.

Bugelski, B. R. (1938) 'Extinction with and without sub-goal reinforcement'. *Journal of Comparative Psychology*, 26, 121–33.

Bugelski, B. R., and Alampay, D. A. (1961) 'The role of frequency in developing perceptual sets'. *Canadian Journal of Psychology*, 15, 205–11.

Bumpass, L. (1970) 'The trend of interfaith marriage in the United States'. *Social Biology*, 3, 253–9.

Burks, B. S. (1928) *The Relative Influence of Nature and Nurture upon Mental Development.* 27th Yearbook of National Society for the Study of Education Part 1.

Burt, C. (1940) *The Factors of the Mind.* University of London Press.

Burt, C. (1955) 'The evidence for the concept of intelligence'. *British Journal of Educational Psychology*, 25, 158–77.

Burt, C. (1966) 'The genetic determination of differences in intelligence'. *British Journal of Psychology*, 57, 137–53.

Burt, C., and Howard, M. (1956) 'The multifactorial theory of inheritance and its application to intelligence'. *British Journal of Statistical Psychology*, 9, 95–131.

Burton, A., Radford, J. (1978) *Thinking in Perspective.* London, Methuen.

Butcher, H. J. (1968) *Human Intelligence: Its nature and assessment.* London, Methuen.

Byrne, D., and Nelson, D. (1965) 'Attraction as a linear function of preparation of positive reinforcements'. *Journal of Personality and Social Psychology*, 1, 659–63.

Byrne, D. (1969) 'Attitudes and Attraction'. In L. Berkowitz, ed., *Advances in Experimental Social Psychology*, vol. 4. New York and London, Academic Press.

Cannon, W. B. (1927) 'The James-Lange theory of emotions: a critical examination and an alternative'. *American Journal of Psychology*, 39, 106–24.

Cannon, W. B., and Washburn, A. L. (1912) 'An explanation of hunger'. *American Journal of Psychology*, 29, 441–54.

Carlson, N. R. (1977) *Physiology of Behaviour.* Allyn and Bacon.

Carrigan, P. M. (1960) 'Extraversion-Introversion as a dimension of personality: a reappraisal'. *Psychological Bulletin*, 57, 329–60.

Cattell, R. B. (1963) 'Theory of fluid and crystallized intelligence: a critical experiment'. *Journal of Educational Psychology*, 54, 1–22.

Cattell, R. B. (1965) *The scientific analysis of personality.* Penguin.

Cattell, R. B., and Nesselroade, J. R. (1967) 'Likeness and completeness—theories examined by the 16-personality factor measure on stably and unstably married couples'. *Journal of Personality and Social Psychology*, 351–61.

Cavan, R. S. (1957) 'Self and role in adjustment during old age'. In Rose, A. M (1962): *Human Behaviour and the Social Processes: an interactionist approach.* London, Routledge and Kegan Paul.

Cazden, C. (1965) 'Environmental assistance to the child's acquisition of grammar'. Unpublished doctoral dissertation, Harvard University.

Chaikin, A. L., and Darley, J. M. (1973) 'Victim or perpetrator? Defensive attribution of responsibility and the need for order and justice'. *Journal of Personality and Social Psychology*, 25, 268–75.

Cherry, C. (1953) 'Some experiments on the reception of speech with one and with two ears'. *Journal of the Acoustical Society of America*, 25, 975–9.

Claridge, G. (1967) *Personality and Arousal*. Oxford, Pergamon.

Cleland, B. G., and Levick, W. R. (1974) 'Properties of rarely encountered types of ganglion cells in the cat's retina and an overall classification'. *Journal of Physiology*, 240, 457.

Cline, M. G. (1956) 'The influence of social context on the perception of faces'. *Journal of Personality*, 25, 142–58.

Cohen, B. (1966) 'Some-or-none characteristics of coding behaviour'. *Journal of Verbal Learning and Verbal Behaviour*, 5, 182–7.

Cole, M., and Bruner, J. S. (1971) 'Cultural differences and inferences about psychological processes'. *American Psychologist*, 26, 867–76.

Cole, M., Gay, J., Glick, J. A., and Sharp, D. W. (1971) *The Cultural Context of Learning and Thinking: An exploration in experimental anthropology*. London, Methuen.

Collins, A., and Quillian, M. R. (1969) 'Retrieval time from semantic memory'. *Journal of Verbal Learning and Verbal Behaviour*, 8, 240–7.

Collins, A., and Quillian, M. R. (1972) 'Experiments on semantic memory and language comprehension'. In L. Gregg, ed., *Cognition in Learning and Memory*. New York, Wiley.

Conrad, R. (1964) 'Acoustic confusion in immediate memory'. *British Journal of Psychology*, 55, 75–84.

Corsi, P. *Verbal memory impairment after unilateral hippocampal excisions*. Paper read at 40th annual meeting of Eastern Psychological Association, Philadelphia.

Corteen, R. S., and Wood, B. (1972) 'Autonomic responses to shock-associated words in an unattended channel'. *Journal of Experimental Psychology*, 94, 308–13.

Craik, F. I. M., and Lockhart, R. (1972) 'Levels of processing: a framework for memory research.' *Journal of Verbal Learning and Verbal Behaviour*, 11, 671–84.

Craik, F. I. M., and Watkins, M. (1973) 'The role of rehearsal in short-term memory'. *Journal of Verbal Learning and Verbal Behaviour*, 12, 599–607.

Cronbach, L. J. (1960) *Essentials of Psychological Testing*. New York, Harper and Row.

Crow, T. J. (1973) 'Catecholamine-containing neurones and electrical self-stimulation: a theoretical interpretation and some psychiatric implications'. *Psychological Medicine*, 3, 66–73.

Daston, P. G. (1956) 'Perception of homosexual words in paranoid schizophrenia'. *Perceptual Motor Skills*, 45–55.

Dawkins, R. (1976) *The Selfish Gene*. Oxford University Press.

DeFleur, M. L., and Westie, F. R. (1958) 'Verbal attitudes and overt acts: an experiment on the salience of attitudes'. *American Sociological Review*, 23, 667–73.

Denenberg, V. (1969) 'Animal studies of early experience: some principles which have implications for human development'. In J. Hill, ed., *Minnesota Symposium on Child Psychology*, Vol. 3. University of Minnesota Press.

Dennis, W. (1960) 'Causes of retardation among institutional children'. Iran. *Journal of Genetical Psychology*, 96, 47–59.

Deutsch, J. A., and Deutsch, D. (1963) 'Attention: some theoretical considerations'. *Psychological Review*, 70, 80–90.

Devenberg, V. H. (1972) *The Development of Behaviour*. Sinauer Associates.

Dion, K. K., Berscheid, E., and Walster, E. (1972) 'What is beautiful is good'. *Journal of Personality and Social Psychology*, 24, 285–90.

Ditchburn, R. W., and Ginsborg, B. L. (1952) 'Vision with a stabilized retinal image'. *Nature*, 170, 36–7.

Dobzhansky, T. (1962) *Mankind Evolving: The evolution of the human species*. Newhaven, Conn., Yale University Press.

Douglas, J. W. B. (1964) 'Parental encouragement'. *Home and the School*, 52–9.

Duncan, C. (1949) 'The retroactive effect of electro-shock on learning'. *Journal of Comparative Physiology*, 42, 32–44.

Duncan, S. (1969) 'Non-verbal communication'. *Psychological Bulletin*, 72, 118–37.

Duncker, K. (1945) 'On problem solving'. *Psychological Monographs*, 58, No. 5 (whole No. 1270).

Eibl-Eibesfeldt, I. (1974) *Similarities and Differences Between Cultures in Expressive Movements in Nonverbal Communication*. Readings with commentary, Shirley Weitz, ed., Oxford University Press.

Ekman, P., and Friesen, W. (1969) 'Non-verbal leaking and clues to deception'. *Psychiatry*, 32, 88–106.

Ekman, P., Sorenson, E., and Friesen, W. (1969) 'Pan-cultural elements in the facial displays of emotion'. *Science*, 164, 86–8.

Erlenmayer-Kimling, L., and Jarvik, L. F. (1963) 'Genetics and intelligence: a review'. *Science*, 142, 1477–9.

Ewart, P. H. (1930) 'A study of the effect of inverted retinal stimulation upon spatially co-ordinated behaviour'. *Genetic Psychology Monographs*, 7, 177–366.

Eysenck, H. J. (1952) *The Scientific Study of Personality*. Routledge and Kegan Paul.

Eysenck, H. J. (1955) 'Cortical inhibition, figural after-effects and theory of personality'. *Journal of Abnormal and Social Psychology*, 51, 94–106.

Eysenck, H. J. (1971) *Race, Intelligence and Education*. London, Temple Smith/New Society.

Eysenck, H. J. (1971) *Readings in Extraversion-Introversion*, Vol. 3. London, Staples Press.

Eysenck, H. J. (1972) 'The experimental study of Freudian concepts'. *Bulletin, British Psychological Society*, 25, 261–7.

Eysenck, H. J., and Eysenck, S. B. G. (1969) *The structure and measurement of personality*. London, Routledge and Kegan Paul.

Eysenck, M. (1975) 'I remember you, you're ...'. *New Behaviour*, 2, 222–3.

Fantz, R. L. (1961) 'The origin of form perception'. *Scientific American*, 204 (5), 66 72.

Fazio, R. H., Zanna, M. P., and Cooper, J. (1977) 'Dissonance and self-perception: an integrative view of each theory's proper domain of application'. *Journal of Experimental Social Psychology*, 13, 464–79.

Fechner, G. T. (1860) *Elemente der Psychophysik*. Leip., Breitkopf, Härtel.

Fenton, N. (1928) 'The only child'. *Journal of Gen. Psychol.*, 35, 546–56.

Ferster, C. B., and Skinner, B. F. (1957) *Schedules of Reinforcement*. New York, Appleton-Century-Crofts.

Festinger, L. (1957) *A Theory of Cognitive Dissonance*. Evanston, Illinois, Row, Peterson.

Festinger, L., and Carlsmith, J. M. (1959) 'Cognitive consequences of forced compliance'. *Journal of Abnormal and Social Psychology*, 58, 203–10.

Festinger, L., Schachter, S., and Back, K. (1964) 'Operation of group standards'. In D. Cartwright and A. Zander, eds., *Group Dynamics, Research and Theory*, 2nd edn. 1968. London, Tavistock.

Fisher, A. E., and Coury, J. N. (1962) 'Cholinergic tracing of a central neural circuit underlying the thirst drive'. *Science*, 138, 691–3.

Flynn, J. P., Vanegas, H., Foote, W., and Edward, S. (1970) 'Neural mechanisms involved in a cat's attack on a rat'. In R. E. Whalen, R. F. Thompson, M. Verziano, and N. M. Weinberger, eds., *The Neural Control of Behaviour*. New York, Academic Press.

Frankenhauser, M. (1975) in *Emotions: their parameters and measurement*. Levi, L., ed. New York, Raven Press.

Franks, C. M. (1956) 'Conditioning and personality. A study of normal and neurotic subjects'. *Journal of Abnormal and Social Psychology*, 52, 143.

Fraser, E. D. (1959) *Home environment and the School*. University of London Press.

Freeman, F. S. (1962) *Theory and Practice of Psychological Testing*. New York, Holt.

Freud, S. (1900) *The Interpretation of Dreams*. London, Allen and Unwin, (1938).

Frijda, N. H. (1969) 'Recognition of emotion'. In L. Berkowitz, ed., *Advances in Experimental Social Psychology*. Vol. 4. New York, Academic Press.

Funkenstein, D. J. (1966) 'The psychology of fear and anger'. In S. Coopersmith, ed., *Frontiers of Psychological Research*. Readings from Scientific American. San Francisco, Freeman.

Galton, F. (1868) *Hereditary Genius*. London, Macmillan (repr. Fontana, 1962).

Galton, F. (1893) *Inquiries into Human Faculty and its Development*. London, Macmillan.

Garn, S. M. (1961) *Human Races*. Springfield, Ill., Thomas.

Gesell, A. (1941) *The First Five Years of Life*. New York, Harper and Row.

Ghiselin, B. (1952) *The Creative Process*. Berkeley, California, University of California Press.

Gibson, E. J., and Walk, R. D. (1961) 'A comparative and analytical study of visual depth perception'. *Psychological Monographs*, 75 (15), 2–34.

Gibson, J. J. (1933) 'Adaptation, after-effect and contrast in the perception of curved lines'. *Journal of Experimental Psychology*, 16, 1–31.

Gilbert, G. M. (1951) 'Stereotype persistence and change among college students'. *Journal of Abnormal and Social Psychology*, 46, 245–54.

Gillig, P. M., and Greenwald, A. G. (1974) 'Is it time to lay the sleeper effect to rest?' *Journal of Personality and Social Psychology*, 29, 132–9.

Glaze, J. A., 'The association value of nonsense syllables'. *Journal Genetic Psychology*, 35, 255–69.

Glueck, S., Glueck, E. (1956) *Physique and Delinquency*. New York, Harper.

Goffman, E. (1963) *Behaviour in Public Places: Notes on the social organization of gatherings*. New York, The Free Press.

Goffman, E. (1968) *Asylums: essays on the social attitudes of mental patients and other inmates*. Harmondsworth, Penguin.

Goffman, E. (1971) *The Presentation of Self in Everyday Life*. Penguin.

Goffman, E. (1972) *Interaction Ritual: Essays on face-to-face behaviour*. Oxford, Pergamon.

Goodall, J. (1971) *In the Shadow of Man*. London, Collins.

Goodenough, F. L., and Leahy, A. M. (1927) 'The effect of certain family relationships upon the development of personality'. *Journal of Genet. Psychol.*, 34, 45–71.

Gordon, R. (1949) 'An investigation into some of the factors that favour the formation of stereotyped images'. *British Journal of Psychology*, 38, 156–67.

Gordon, W. J. J. (1961) *Synectics: The development of creative capacity.* New York, Harper and Row.

Gottesman, I. I. (1963) 'Heritability of personality: a demonstration'. *Psychological Monographs*, 77, (9), 21.

Gottesman, I., and Shields, J. (1972) *Schizophrenia and Genetics.* New York, Academic Press.

Gray, J. (1971) *The Psychology of Fear and Stress.* London, Weidenfeld and Nicolson.

Greenfield, P. M., Reich, L. C., and Olver, R. R. (1966) 'On culture and equivalence'. In S. Bruner, R. R. Olver and P. M. Greenfield, *Studies in Cognitive Growth.* New York, Wiley.

Gregor, A. J., and McPherson, D. A. (1965) 'A study of susceptibility to geometric illusions among cultural outgroups of Australian aborigines'. *Psychologicia Africana*, 11, 1–13.

Gregory, R. L. (1966) *Eye and Brain.* London, Weidenfeld and Nicolson.

Groos, K. (1898) 'The play of animals'. In J. Bruner, *et al*, eds., *Play—Its Role in Development and Evolution.* Penguin Education.

Groos, K. (1901) 'The play of man'. In J. Bruner, *et al*, eds., *Play—Its Role in Development and Evolution.* Penguin Education.

Gross, E., and Stone, G. P. (1964) 'Embarrassment and the analysis of role requirements'. *American Journal of Sociology*, 70, 1–15.

Guilford, J. P. (1950) 'Creativity'. *American Psychologist*, 5, 444–54.

Guilford, J. P. (1967) *The Nature of Human Intelligence.* New York, McGraw-Hill.

Haider, M., Spong, P., and Linsley, D. B. (1964) 'Attention, vigilance and cortical evoked potentials in humans'. *Science*, 145, 180–2.

Halliday, M. A. K. (1975) *Learning to Mean: Explorations in the development of languages.* London, Edward Arnold.

Harlow, H. F. (1949) 'The formation of learning sets'. *Psychological Review*, 56, 51–65.

Harlow, H., Dodsworth, R. O., and Arling, G. L. (1966) 'Maternal behaviour of rhesus monkeys deprived of mothering and peer relations in infancy'. *Proceedings of the American Philosophical Society*, 110, 58–66.

Harlow, N. F., Harlow, M. K., and Meyer, D. R. (1950) 'Learning motivated by a manipulation drive'. *Journal of Experimental Psychology*, 40, 228–34.

Harrington, C., and Whiting, J. W. M. (1972) 'Socialization process and personality'. In F. K. L. Hsu, ed., (1972) *Psychological Anthropology*, 2nd edn. Cambridge, Mass., Schenkman.

Hebb, D. (1949) *The Organization of Behaviour.* New York, Wiley.

Hebb, D., and Foord, E. (1945) 'Errors of visual recognition and the nature of the trace'. *Journal of Experimental Psychology*, 35, 335–48.

717

Heider, F. (1944) 'Social perception and phenomenal causality'. *Psychological Review,* 51, 358–74.

Heider, F. (1946) 'Attitudes and cognitive organizations'. *Journal of Psychology,* 21, 107–12.

Held, R., and Hein, A. (1963) 'Movement-produced stimulation in the development of visually guided behaviour'. *Journal of Comparative and Physiological Psychology,* 56, 607–13.

Henle, M. (1962) 'On the relation between logic and thinking'. *Psychological Review,* 69, 366–78.

Hess, E. H. (1965) 'Attitude and pupil size'. *Scientific American,* 212 (4), 46–54.

Hess, R. D., and Shipman, V. C. (1965) 'Early experience and socialization of cognitive modes in children'. *Child Development,* 34(4), 869–86.

Hess, W. R. (1957) *The functional organization of the diencephalon.* New York, Grune and Stratton.

Hetherington, A. N., and Ranson, S. W. (1942) 'The spontaneous activity and food intake of rats with hypothalamic lesions'. *American Journal of Physiology,* 136, 609–17.

Higbee, K. L. (1969) 'Fifteen years of fear arousal: research on threat appeals: 1953–1968'. *Psychological Bulletin,* 72, 426–44.

Hirsch, H. V. B., and Spinelli, D. N. (1971) 'Visual experience modifies distribution of horizontally and vertically oriented receptive fields in cats'. *Science,* 168, 869–71.

Hohmann, G. W. (1966) 'Some effects of spinal cord lesions on experienced emotional feelings'. *Psychophysiology,* 3, 143–56.

Holmes, D. S. (1974) 'Investigations of repression: differential recall of material experimentally or naturally associated with ego threat'. *Psychological Bulletin,* 81, 632–53.

Holmes, D., and Schallow, J. R. (1969) 'Reduced recall after ego threat: repression or response competition?' *Journal of Personality and Social Psychology,* 13, 145–52.

Homans, G. C. (1961) *Social Behaviour: Its elementary forms.* New York, Harcourt Brace.

Hovland, C. I., Lumsdaine, A. A., and Sheffield, F. D. (1949) *Experiments on Mass Communication.* Princeton, N.J., Princeton University Press.

Hovland, C. I., and Sherif, M. (1952) 'Judgmental phenomena and scales of attitude measurement: item displacement in Thurstone scales'. *Journal of Abnormal and Social Psychology,* 47, 822–32.

Howes, D. H., and Solomon, R. L. (1950) 'A note on McGinnies' emotionality and perceptual defense'. *Psychological Review,* 57, 229–34.

Hubel, D. H., and Wiesel, T. N. (1959) 'Receptive fields of single neurones in the cat's striate cortex'. *Journal of Psychology*, 148, 574–91.

Hudson, L. (1966) *Contrary Imaginations*. London, Methuen.

Hudson, L. (1968) *Frames of mind: Ability, perception, and self-perception in the arts and sciences*. London, Methuen.

Hull, C. L. (1920) 'Quantitative aspects of the evolution of concepts'. *Psychological Monographs*, 28, No. 1 (Whole No. 123).

Humphrey, G. (1951) *Thinking: an introduction to its experimental psychology*. London, Methuen.

Hunt, J. McV. (1963) 'Motivational interest in information processing and action'. In O. J. Harvey, *Motivation and Social Interaction*. Ronald Press.

Hutt, C. (1966) 'Exploration and play in children'. *Symposia of the Zoological Society of London*, 18, 61–81.

Insko, C. I. (1969) *Theories of attitude change*. New York, Appleton-Century-Crofts.

Irvine (1966) 'Towards a rationale for testing attainments and abilities in Africa'. *British Journal of Educational Psychology*, 36, 24–32.

Izard, C. E. (1960) 'Personality, similarity and friendship'. *Journal of Abnormal and Social Psychology*, 61, 45–51.

Jahoda, G. (1966) 'Geometric illusions and environment: a study in Ghana'. *British Journal of Psychology*, 57, 193–9.

James, W. (1890) *The Principles of Psychology*. Vol. 2. New York, Holt.

Janis, I. L., and Feshbach, S. (1953) 'Effects of fear-arousing communications'. *Journal of Abnormal and Social Psychology*, 48, 78–92.

Jenkins, J. (1974) 'Can we have a meaningful memory?' In R. Solso, ed., *Theories in Cognitive Psychology: the Loyola Symposium*. New York, Wiley.

Jensen, A. R. (1969) 'How much can we boost IQ and scholastic achievement?' *Harvard Educational Review*, 39, 1–123.

Jones, E. E., and Davis, K. E. (1965) 'From acts to dispositions: the attribution process in person perception'. In L. Berkowitz, ed., *Advances in Experimental Social Psychology*, Vol. 2. New York, Academic Press.

Jones, E. E., Davis, K. E., and Gergen, K. J. (1961) 'Role playing variations and their informational value for person perception'. *Journal of Abnormal and Social Psychology*, 63, 302–10.

Jones, E. E., and Nisbett, R. E. (1972) 'The actor and the observer: divergent perspectives of the causes of behaviour'. In E. E. Jones, D. E. Kanouse, H. Kelley, R. E. Nisbett, S. Valins, and B. Weiner, eds., *Attribution: perceiving the causes of behaviour*. Morristown, N.J., Genevore Learning Group.

Jones, J. M. (1977) *Prejudice and Racism*. Reading, Mass., Addison-

Wesley, reprinted by permission in J. H. Harvey, W. P. Smith *Social Psychology: an attributional approach* (p. 152). Saint Louis, The C. V. Mosby Company.

Jorgansen, C., and Kintsch, W. (1973) 'The role of imagery in the evaluation of sentences'. *Cognitive Psychology*, 4, 110–16.

Jouvet, M. (1967) 'The states of sleep'. *Scientific American*, 216, 62–72.

Kahneman, D. (1973) *Attention and effort*. Englewood Cliffs, N.J., Prentice-Hall.

Karlins, M., Coffman, T. L., and Walters, G. (1969) 'On the fading of social stereotypes: studies in three generations of college students'. *Journal of Personality and Social Psychology*, 13, 1–16.

Katz, D. (1960) 'The functional approach to the study of attitudes'. *Public Opinion Quarterly*, 24, 163–204.

Katz, D., and Braly, K. (1933) 'Racial stereotypes of one hundred college students'. *Journal of Abnormal and Social Psychology*, 28, 280–90.

Kay, H. (1955) 'Learning and retaining verbal material'. *British Journal of Pyschology*, 44, 81–100.

Keehn, J. D. (1969) In R. M. Gilbert, and N. S. Sutherland, eds., *Animal Discrimination Learning*. New York, Academic Press.

Keesey, R. E., and Powley, T. L. (1975) 'Hypothalamic regulation of body weight'. *American Scientist*, 63, 558–65.

Kelly, G. A. (1955) *The Psychology of Personal Constructs*. New York, Norton.

Kelley, H. H. (1967) 'Attribution theory in social psychology'. In D. Levine, ed., *Nebraska Symposium on Motivation*. Lincoln, University of Nebraska Press.

Kendler, H. H., and Kendler, J. S. (1962) 'Vertical and horizontal processes in problem solving'. *Psychological Review*, 72, 229–32.

Kendon, A. (1970) 'Some relationships between body motion and speech: an analysis of an example'. In A. Siegman, and B. Pope, eds. *Studies in Dyadic Communication*, New York, Pergamon.

Keppel, G., and Underwood, B. (1962) 'Proactive inhibition in short-term retention of single items'. *Journal of Verbal Learning and Verbal Behaviour*, 1, 153–61.

Kiesler, C. A., and Pallak, M. S. (1976) 'Arousal properties of dissonance manipulations'. *Psychological Bulletin*, 83, 1014–25.

Kintsch, W. (1970) *Learning, Memory and Conceptual Process*. New York, Wiley.

Kline, P. (1972) *Fact and Fantasy in Freudian Theory*. London, Methuen.

Kluver, H., and Bucy, P. C. (1937) 'Psychic blindness' and other symptoms following bilateral temporal lobectomy in rhesus monkeys'. *American Journal of Physiology*, 119, 352–3.

Knox, R. E., and Inkster, J. A. (1968) 'Postdecision dissonance at post time'. *Journal of Personality and Social Psychology*, 8, 319–23.

Koch, H. L. (1923) 'A neglected phase of the part/whole problem'. *Journal of Experimental Psychology*, 6, 366–76.

Kohler, I. (1964) 'The formation and transformation of the visual world'. *Psychological Issues*, 3, 28–46 and 116–33.

Kohler, W. (1925) *The Mentality of Apes*. New York, Harcourt Brace.

Konishi, M. (1965) 'The role of auditory feedback in the control of vocalization in the white-crowned sparrow'. *Zeitschrift der Tierpsychologie*, 22, 770–83.

Kretschmer, E. (1925) *Physique and Character*. New York, Harcourt.

Kris, E. (1953) *Psychoanalytic Interpretations in Art*. New York, International University Press.

Krueger, W. C. F. (1929) 'The effect of overlearning on retention'. *Journal of Experimental Psychology*, 12, 71–8.

Kuhlman, C. (1960) 'Visual imagery in children'. Unpublished doctoral dissertation, Harvard University. In J. S. Bruner *et al* (1966) *Studies in Cognitive Growth*. New York, Wiley.

Kuffler, S. W. (1953) 'Discharge patterns and functional organization of mammalian retina'. *Journal of Neurophysiology*, 16, 37–68.

Labov, W. (1970) 'The logic of nonstandard English'. In F. Williams, ed., *Language and Poverty*. Chicago, Markham.

Lack, D. (1966) *Population studies of birds*. London, Oxford University Press.

Lane, R. E. (1969) *Political Thinking and Consciousness*. Chicago, Markham.

LaPiere, R. T. (1934) 'Attitudes *v*. actions'. *Social Forces*, 13, 230–7.

Lashley, K. S. (1951) 'The problem of serial order in behaviour'. In L. A. Jeffress, ed., *Cerebral Mechanisms in Behaviour*: The Hiscon Symposium. New York, Wiley.

Laurendeau, M., and Pinard, A. (1962). *Causal Thinking in the Child*. International Universities Press.

Lazarus, R. S., and McCleary, R. A. (1951) 'Autonomic discrimination without awareness: a study of subception'. *Psychological Review*, 58, 113–22.

Leachy, A. M. (1935) 'Nature-nurture and intelligence'. *Genetic Psychology Monographs*, 17, 236–308.

Leeper, R. (1935) 'A study of a neglected portion of the field of learning—the development of sensory organization'. *Journal of Genetic Psychology*, 46, 41–75.

Lesser, G. S. *et al* (1965) 'Mental abilities of children from different social-class and cultural groups'. *Monographs of the Society for Research in Child Development*, 30 (serial No. 103), 1–93.

Lettvin, J. Y., Maturana, H. R., McCulloch, W. S., and Pitts, W. H.

(1959) 'What the frog's eye tells the frog's brain'. *Proceedings of the Institute of Radio Engineers*, 47, 1940–51.

Leumger, G., and Snoek, J. (1972) *Attraction in Relationship: A new look at interpersonal attraction*. New York, General Learning Press.

Levick, W. R. (1967) 'Receptive fields and trigger features of ganglion cells in the visual streak of the rabbit's retina'. *Journal of Physiology*, 188, 285–307.

Levine, S. A. (1962) 'The psychophysiological effects of infant stimulation'. In E. L. Bliss, ed., *Roots of Behaviour*. New York, Harper.

Levinger, G. (1974) 'A three-level approach to attraction: toward an understanding of pair relationships'. In P. L. Huston, ed., *Foundations of Interpersonal Attraction*. Academic Press.

Lifton, R. J. (1961) *Thought Reform and the Psychology of Totalism*. London, Gollancz.

Likert, R. (1932) 'A technique for the measurement of attitudes'. *Archives of Psychology*, 22, 1–55.

Loewi, O., and Navratil, E. (1926) 'Über humorale Überträgbarkeit der Herzenervenwirkung X. Über das Schicksal des Vagusstoffes'. *Pflügers Archiv der gesamten Physiologie*, 214, 678–88.

Lorenz, K. (1950) 'The comparative method in studying innate behaviour patterns'. *Symp. Soc. Exp. Biol.*, 4, 221–68.

Lott, A. J., and Lott, B. E. (1974) 'The power of liking: consequences of interpersonal attitudes derived from a liberalized view of secondary reinforcement'. In L. Berkowitz, ed., *Advances in Experimental Social Psychology*, Vol. 6. New York, Academic Press.

Lotze, H. (1852) *Outlines of Psychology*, tr. G. T. Ladd. Boston, Ginn.

Luh, C. W. (1922) 'The conditions of retention'. *Psychological Monographs*, 142.

Luria, A. R. (1966) *Human Brain and Psychological Processes*. New York, Harper and Row.

Luria, A. R., and Yudovich, E. (1956) *Speech and the Development of Mental Processes in the Child*. London, Staples Press (1971).

Mackworth, N. H. (1950) 'Researches on the measurement of human performance'. *Medical Research Council Special Report*, No. 268. London, H.M.S.O.

MacLean, P. D. (1949) 'Psychosomatic disease and the "visceral brain"'. *Psychosomatic Medicine*, 11, 338–53.

Maier, N. R. F. (1930) 'Reasoning in humans'. *Journal of Comparative Psychology*, 10, 115–43; 12, 181–94.

Maier, S. F., and Sclijman, M. (1969) 'Pavlovian fear conditioning and learned helplessness'. In B. A. Campbell, and R. M. Church, eds., *Punishment*. New York, Appleton-Century-Croft.

Mandler, G. (1972) 'Organization and recognition'. In E. Tulving and

W. Donaldson, eds., *Organization of Memory*. New York, Academic Press.

Manning, A. (1973) *An Introduction to Animal Behaviour*. Arnold.

Maranon, G. (1924) 'Contribution a l'etude de l'action emotive de l'adrenaline'. *Revue Française d'Endocrenologie*, 2, 301–25.

Marler, P., and Tamura, M. (1964) 'Culturally transmitted patterns of vocal behaviour in sparrows'. *Science N.Y.*, 146, 1483–6.

Masserman, J. H. (1941) 'Is the hypothalamus a center of emotion?'. *Psychosomatic Medicine*, 3, 3–35.

Mayes, A. (1973) 'Remember, remember'. *New Society*, 1 March 1973.

McGuire, W. J. (1968) 'Personality and susceptibility to social influence'. In Borgatta, E. F., and Lambert, W. W., eds., *Handbook of Personality Theory and Research*. Chicago, Rand McNally.

McGuire, W. J. (1969) 'The nature of attitudes and attitude change'. In Lindzey, G., and Aronson, E., eds., *Handbook of Social Psychology*, 2nd edn., Vol. 3. Reading, Mass., Addison-Wesley.

McKay, D. (1973) 'Aspects of the theory of comprehension, memory and attention'. *Quarterly Journal of Experimental Psychology*, 25, 22–40.

McNemar, Q. (1942) *The Revision of the Stanford-Binet Scale*. Houghton Mifflin.

McNiell, D. (1966) 'Developmental psycholinguistics'. In F. Smith, and G. Miller, eds., *The Genesis of Language*. Cambridge Mass., M.I.T. Press.

McWhirter, R. M., and Jecker, J. D. (1967) 'Attitude similarity and inferred attraction'. *Psychonomic Science*, 7, 225–6.

Mednick, S. A. (1962) 'The associative basis of the creative process'. *Psychological Review*, 69, 220–32.

Mednick, S. A., and Schulsinger, F. (1968) 'Some premorbid characteristics related to breakdown in children with schizophrenic mothers'. In D. Rosenthal, and S. Kety, eds., *The Transmission of Schizophrenia*. Elsmsford, New York, Pergamon.

Meehl, P. E. (1950) 'On the circularity of the law of effect'. *Psychological Bulletin*, 47, 52–75.

Miles, T. R. (1957) 'Contributions to intelligence testing and the theory of intelligence: I. on defining intelligence'. *British Journal of Educational Psychology*, 27, 153–65.

Miller, G. (1956) 'The magical number seven, plus or minus two: some limits of our capacity for processing information'. *Psychological Review*, 63, 81–97.

Miller, G. A., Galanter, E., and Pribram, K. H. (1960) *Plans and the Structure of Behaviour*. New York, Holt, Reinhart and Winston.

Miller, N. E. (1941) 'The frustration-aggression hypothesis'. *Psychological Review*, 48, 337–42.

Moniz, E. (1936) *Lentatives operatoires dans le traitement de certaines psychoses*. Paris, Masson.

Moray, N. (1969) *Attention*. London, Hutchinson.

Moray, N. (1969) *Listening and Attention*. Penguin.

Morgan, C. D., and Murray, H. A. (1935) 'A method for inventing fantasies'. *Archives of Neurological Psychiatry*, 34, 289–306.

Morris, D. (1959) 'The comparative ethnology of grassfinches and mannakins'. *Proceedings of the Zoological Society of London*, 131, 389–439.

Moyer, K. E. (1968) 'Kinds of aggression and their physiological basis'. *Communications in Behavioural Biology*, 2, 65–87.

Mundy-Castle, A. C. (1966) 'Pictorial depth perception in Ghanaian children'. *International Journal of Psychology*, 1,290–300.

Mundy-Castle, A. C., Nelson, G. K. (1962) 'A neuropsychological study of the Knysna forest workers'. *Psychologia Africana*, 9, 240–72.

Neisser, U. (1967) *Cognitive Psychology*. New York, Appleton-Century-Crofts.

Newcombe, T. (1961) *The Acquaintance Process*. New York, Holt.

Newcombe, T., and Svehla, G. (1937) 'Intra-family relationships in attitudes'. *Sociometry*, 1, 180–205.

Newell, A., and Simon, H. A. (1972) *Human Problem Solving*. Englewood Cliffs, N.J., Prentice-Hall.

Newell, A., Shaw, J. C., and Simon, H. A. (1958) 'Elements of a theory of human problem solving'. *Psychological Review*, 65, 151–66.

Newman, H. H., Freeman, F. N., and Holzinger, K. J. (1937) *Twins: A study of heredity and environment*. University of Chicago Press.

Nicholls, R. C. (1965) 'The inheritance of general and specific ability'. *National Merit Scholarship Corp. Res. Rep.*, 1:1–9.

Olds, J. (1956) 'Pleasure centers in the brain'. *Scientific American*, 195, 105–16.

Olds, J., and Milner, P. (1954) 'Positive reinforcement produced by electrical stimulation of septal area and other regions of rat brain'. *Journal of Comparative Physiological Psychology*, 47, 419–27.

Ornstein, R. (1974) 'The brain's other half'. *New Scientist*, 6 June, 606–8.

Osborn, A. F. (1957) *Applied Imaginations*. New York, Scribner's.

Oswald, I. (1966) *Sleep*. Penguin.

Paivio, A. (1971) *Imagery and Verbal Processes*. New York, Holt, Reinhart and Winston.

Papez, J. W. (1937) 'A proposed mechanism of emotion.' *Archives of Neurology and Psychiatry*, 725, 743.

Peterson, J., and Peterson, J. K. (1938) 'Does practice with inverting lenses make vision normal?' *Psychological Monographs*, 50, 12–37.

Pettigrew, J. D., and Freeman, R. D. (1973) 'Visual experience without lines: effect on developing cortical neurons'. *Science*, 182, 599–600.

Pettigrew, T. F., Allport, G. W., and Barnett, E. O. (1958) 'Binocular resolution and perception of race in South Africa'. *British Journal of Psychology*, 49, 265–78.

Phares, E. J. (1976) *Locus of Control in Personality*. New York, General Learning Press.

Piaget, J. (1966) *Mental Imagery in the Child*. Paris, Presses Universitaires de France.

Pollio, H., and Foote, R. (1971) 'Memory as a reconstructive process'. *British Journal of Psychology*, 62, 53–8.

Pollio, H., Richards, S., and Lucas, R. (1969) 'Temporal properties of category recall'. *Journal of Verbal Learning and Verbal Behaviour*, 8, 529–36.

Pollitzer, A. (1958) 'The Negroes of Charleston, S.C.: A study of haemoglobin types, serology and morphology'. *American Journal of Physical Anthropology*, 16, 241–63.

Postman, L. (1972) 'A pragmatic view of organization theory'. In E. Tulving and W. Donaldson, eds. *Organization of Memory*. New York, Academic Press.

Postman, L., Bruner, J. S., and McGinnies, E. (1948) 'Personal values as selective factors in perception'. *Journal of Abnormal and Social Psychology*, 43, 142–54.

Poulton, E. C. (1953) 'Two channel listening'. *Journal of Experimental Psychology*, 46, 91–6.

Powley, T. L., and Opsahl, C. A. (1974) 'Ventromedial hypothalamic obesity abolished by subdiaphragmatic vagotomy'. *American Journal of Physiology*, 226, 25–33.

Premack, D. (1962) 'Reversibility of the reinforcement relation'. *Science*, 136, 255–7.

Rabbie, J. M., and Horowitz, M. (1969) 'Arousal of ingroup-outgroup bias by a chance minor loss'. *Journal of Personality and Social Psychology*, 13, 269–77.

Raber, H. (1948) 'Analyse des Belzverhaltens eines domestizierten Truthahns'. (Meleagries). *Behaviour*, 1, 237–66.

Rachlin, H. (1976) *Introduction to modern behaviour*. Freeman.

Radford, J., and Burton, A. (1974) *Thinking: Its nature and development*. London, Wiley.

Radford, J., and Kirby, R. (1976) *Individual Differences*. London, Methuen.

Restle, F. (1974) 'Critique of pure memory'. In R. Solso, ed., *Theories in Cognitive Psychology: the Loyola Symposium*. New York, Wiley.

Richardson, A. (1969) *Mental Imagery*. London, Routledge and Kegan Paul.

Richter, C. P., Holt, L. E. Jr., and Barelare, B. Jr. (1938) 'Nutritional requirements for normal growth and reproduction in rats studied by the self-selection method'. *American Journal of Physiology*, 122, 734, 744.

Ricks, D. M. (1972) 'The beginnings of vocal communication in infants and autistic children'. Unpublished doctoral thesis, University of London.

Rivers, W. H. R. (1901) 'Vision'. In A. C. Haddon, ed., *Reports of the Cambridge Anthropological Expedition to the Torres Straits*, Vol. 2 (1) Cambridge University Press and *British Journal of Psychology*, I, 321. (1905).

Roe, A. (1952) *The Making of a Scientist*. New York, Dodd Mead.

Rogers, C. (1951) *Client-centred Therapy, its Current Practices, Implications and Theory*. Boston, Houston.

Rosen, B. C., and d'Andrade, R. (1959) 'The psychosocial origins of achievement motivation'. *Sociometry*, 22, 185–218.

Rosenberg, M. J. (1956) 'Cognitive structure and attitudinal affect'. *Journal of Abnormal and Social Psychology*, 53, 367–72.

Rosenberg, M. J. (1960) 'Cognitive reorganization in response to the hypnotic reversal of attitudinal affect'. *Journal of Personality*, 28, 39–63.

Rosenberg, S., and Jones, R. A. (1972) 'A method for investigating and representing a person's implicit theory of personality: Theodor Dreiser's view of people'. *Journal of Personality and Social Psychology*.

Rosenberg, S., and Sedlak, A. (1972) 'Structural representations of implicit personality theory'. In L. Berkowitz, ed., *Advances in Experimental Social Psychology*, Vol. 6. New York, Academic Press.

Rosenhan, D. L. (1973) 'On being sane in an insane place'. *Science*, 179, 250–8.

Rosenthal, R. (1976) *Experimenter Effects in Behavioural Research*. Irvington, Century Psychology Series.

Rosenzweig, M. R. (1965) 'Environmental complexity, cerebral change, and behaviour'. *American Psychologist*, 21, 321–32.

Rotter, J. B. (1966) 'Generalized expectancies for internal versus external control of reinforcement'. *Psychological Monographs*, 80, 1. (Whole No. 709).

Rutter, M. (1972) *Maternal Deprivation Reassessed*. Penguin.

Ryle, G. (1949) *The Concept of Mind*. London, Hutchinson.

Sapir, E. (1927) *Language*. New York, Harcourt Brace.

Schachter, S., and Singer, J. E. (1962) 'Cognitive, social and physiological determinants of emotional states'. *Psychological Review*, 69, 379–99.

Scheflen, A. E. (1964) 'The significance of posture in communication systems'. *Psychiatry*, 27, 316–31.

Schwarz, M. (1978) *Physiological Psychology*. Englewood Cliffs, N.J., Prentice-Hall.

Schmitt, R. C. (1971) 'Recent trends in Hawaiian inter-racial marriage rates by occupation'. *Journal of Marriage and the Family*, 33, 373–4.

Scott, J. P. (1962) 'Critical periods in behavioural development'. *Science*, 138, 949–58.

Scoville, W. B., and Milner, B. (1957) 'Loss of recent memory after bilateral hippocampal lesions'. *Journal of Neurology, Neurosurgery and Psychiatry*, 20, 11–21.

Secord, P. F., and Backman, C. W. (1974) *Social psychology*, 2nd edn. London, McGraw-Hill Kogakusha.

Segal, E. (1969) 'Hierarchical structure in free recall'. *Journal of Experimental Psychology*, 80, 59–63.

Segall, M. H., Campbell, D. T., and Herskovits, M. J. (1963) 'Cultural differences in the perception of geometrical illusions'. *Science*, 139, 769–71.

Segall, M. H., Campbell, D. T., and Herskovits, M. J. (1963) *The influence of culture on visual perception*. New York, Bobbs-Merrill.

Seligman, M. (1972) *Biological Boundaries of Learning*. New York, Appleton-Century-Croft.

Shagass, C., and Kerenyi, A. B. (1958) 'Neurophysiological studies of personality'. *Journal of Nervous and Mental Disease*, 126, 141–7.

Shaw, L., and Sichel, N. S. (1970) *Accident Proneness*. Oxford, Pergamon.

Sheffield, F. D., Wulff, J. T., and Baker, R. (1951) 'Reward value of copulation without sex drive reduction'. *Journal of Comparative and Physiological Psychology*, 44, 3–8.

Sheldon, W. (1942) *The Varieties of Temperament: A psychology of constitutional differences*. New York, Harper.

Sherif, M. (1935) 'A study of some social factors in perception'. *Arch. Psychol.* 187.

Shields, J. (1962) *Monozygotic Twins Brought Up Together and Brought Up Apart*. Oxford University Press.

Shuey, A. M. (1966) *The Testing of Negro Intelligence*. New York, Social Science Press.

Shulman, H. (1970) 'Encoding and retention of semantic and phonetic information in short term memory'. *Journal of Verbal Learning and Verbal Behaviour*, 9, 499–508.

Sinclair-de-Zwart, H. (1969) 'Developmental psycholinguistics'. In D. Elkind, and J. H. Flavell, eds., *Studies in Cognitive Development*. Oxford University Press.

Skeels, H. M. (1966) 'Adult status of children with contrasting early life experiences'. *Monographs of the Society for Research in Child Development*, 31, 3 (serial No. 105).

Smith, M. B., Bruner, J. S., and White, R. W. (1956) *Opinions and Personality*. New York, Wiley.

Smith, S. M., Brown, H. O., Toman, J. E. P., and Goodman, L. S. (1947) 'The lack of cerebral effects of d-tubocurarine'. *Anesthesiology*, 8, 1–14.

Snyder, F. W., and Pronko, N. H. (1952) *Vision with Spatial Inversion*. Wichita, Kansas, University of Wichita Press.

Spearman, C. (1927) *The Nature of Intelligence and the Principles of Cognition*. London, Macmillan.

Sperry, R. W. (1966) 'The great cerebral commissure'. In S. Coopersmith, ed., *Frontiers of Psychological Research*, Readings from Scientific American. San Francisco, Freeman.

Stein, L., and Wise, C. D. (1971) 'Possible aetiology of schizophrenia: progressive damage to the noradrenergic reward system by 6-hydroxydopamine'. *Science*, 171, 1032–6.

Stephenson, W. (1953) *The Study of Behaviour*. Illinois, University of Chicago Press.

Stevens, R. (1976) *Understanding Social Behaviour and Experience*. D305, Block 1, Social Psychology. Milton Keynes, The Open University.

Stratton, G. M. (1896) 'Some preliminary experiments on vision'. *Psychological Review*, 3, 611–17.

Stratton, G. M. (1897) 'Vision without inversion of the retinal image'. *Psychological Review*, 4, 341–60 and 463–81.

Stroh, C. M. (1971) *Vigilance—The Problem of Sustained Attention*. Oxford, Pergamon.

Stuart, J. (1926) 'On the alleged psychopathology of the only child'. *Journal of Abnormal and Social Psychology*, 20, 441.

Szasz, T. S. (1970) *The Manufacture of Madness*. New York, Harper and Row.

Tagiuri, R. (1958) 'Social preference and its perception'. In R. Tagiuri and L. Petrullo, eds., *Person Perception and Interpersonal Behaviour*. Stanford, California, Stanford University Press.

Taylor, I. A. (1959) 'The nature of the creative process'. In P. Smith, ed., *Creativity*. New York, Hastings.

Terman, L. (1925–1957) *Genetic Studies of Genius*. Vol. 1: 1925, Vol. 2: 1926, Vol. 3: 1930, Vol. 4: 1957. Stanford, California, Stanford University Press.

Thibaut, J. W., and Kelley, H. H. (1959) *The Social Psychology of Groups*. New York, Wiley.

Thomson, T. I. (1963) 'Visual reinforcement in Siamese fighting fish'. *Science*, N.Y., 141, 55–7.

Thorndike, E. L. (1898) 'Animal intelligence: an experimental study of the associative processes in animals'. *Psychological Review Monograph Supplements*, 2, No. 8.

Thurstone, L. L. (1938) 'Primary mental abilities'. *Psychometric Monographs*, No. 1.

Thurstone, L. L., and Chave, E. J. (1929) *The Measurement of Attitude*. Chicago, University of Chicago Press.

Thurstone, L. L., and Thurstone, T. G. (1930) 'A neurotic inventory'. *Journal of Social Psychology*, I, 3–30.

Tinbergen, N. (1952) 'Derived activities'. *Quarterly Review of Biology*, 27, 1–32.

Tolman, E. C. (1932) *Purposive Behaviour in Animals and Man*. New York, Appleton-Century-Crofts.

Treisman, A. (1960) 'Contextual cues in selective listening'. *Quarterly Journal of Experimental Psychology*, 12, 242–8.

Treisman, A. (1964) 'Verbal cues, language and meaning in attention'. *American Journal of Psychology*, 77, 206–14.

Tulving, E. (1966) 'Subjective organization and effects of repetition in multi-trial free recall learning'. *Journal of Verbal Learning and Verbal Behaviour*, 5, 193–7.

Tulving, E. (1968) 'Theoretical issues in free recall'. In T. Dixon and D. Horton, eds., *Verbal Behaviour and General Behaviour Theory*. Englewood Cliffs, N.J., Prentice-Hall.

Tulving, E., and Thomson, D. (1973) 'Encoding specificity and retrieval processes in episodic memory'. *Psychological Review*, 80, 352–73.

Vandenberg, S. G. (1966) 'Contributions of twin research to psychology'. *Psychological Bulletin*, 66, 327–52.

Vernon, P. E. (1960) 'Development of current ideas about intelligence tests'. *Modern Concepts of Intelligence*, Association of Educational Psychologists.

Vernon, P. E. (1965) 'Ability factors and environmental influences'. *American Psychologist*, 20, 723–33.

Vernon, P. E. (1965) 'Environmental handicaps and intellectual development'. *British Journal of Educational Psychology*, 35, 117–36.

Vernon, P. E. (1969) *Intelligence and Cultural Environment*. London, Methuen.

Von Wright, J. M., Anderson, K., and Stenman, U. (1975) 'Generalization of conditional GSRs in dichotic listening'. In P. Rabbit, and S. Dornic, eds., *Attention and Performance* (Vol. 5). Oxford and Stockholm, Academic Press.

Vygotsky, L. S. (1934) *Thought and language*. Cambridge, Mass. (1962). M.I.T. Press.

Wallas, G. (1926) *The Art of Thought*. New York, Harcourt.

Warburton, D. M. (1975) *Brain Behaviour and Drugs*. London, Wiley.

Warren, B. L. (1966) 'A multiple variable approach to the assortative mating phenomenon'. *Eugenics Quarterly*, 13, 285–90.

Wason, P. C., and Johnson-Laird, P. N. (1972) *The Psychology of Reasoning: Structure and content*. London, Batsford.

Waugh, N., and Norman, D. (1965) 'Primary memory'. *Psychological Review*, 72, 89–104.

Wells, B. (1973) *Psychedelic Drugs*. Penguin.

Wertheimer, M. (1945) *Productive Thinking*. New York, Harper and Row.

Westie, F. R., and DeFleur, M. L. (1959) 'Autonomic responses and their relationship to race attitudes'. *Journal of Abnormal and Social Psychology*, 58, 340–7.

Whorf, B. L. (1957) *Language, Thought and Reality*. Cambridge, Mass., M.I.T. Press.

Wilkinson, R. T., Morlock, H. C., and Williams, H. L. (1966) 'Evoked cortical response during vigilance'. *Psychonomic Science*, 4, 221–2.

Wilson, R. S. (1977) 'Twins and siblings: Concordance for school-age mental development'. *Child Development*, 48, 211–16.

Winch, R. F., Ktsanes, T., and Ktsanes, U. (1954) 'The theory of complementary needs in mate selection: an analysis and descriptive study'. *American Sociological Review*, 19, 241–9.

Winslow, C. N. (1937) 'A study of the extent of agreement between friends' opinions and their ability to estimate the opinions of each other'. *Journal of Social Psychology*, 8, 433–42.

Wiseman, S. (1964) *Education and Environment*. Manchester, Manchester University Press.

Wishner, J. (1960) 'Reanalysis of impressions of personality'. *Psychological Review*, 67, 96–112.

Witkin, H. A. (1949) 'The nature and importance of individual differences in perception'. *Journal of Personality*, 18, 145–70.

Wolowitz, H. M. (1965) 'Attraction and aversion to power'. *Journal of Abnormal Psychology*, 70, 360–70. c.f. Reese, H. W., and Lipsitt, L. R. (1970) *Experimental Child Psychology*. Academic Press, ch. 17.

Woodworth, R. (1938) *Experimental Psychology*. New York, Holt, Reinhart and Winston.

Woodworth, R. S., and Sells, S. B. (1935) 'An atmosphere effect in formal syllogistic reasoning'. *Journal of Experimental Psychology*, 18, 451–60.

Worthington, A. G. (1969) 'Paired comparison scaling of brightness judgements: a method for the measurement of perceptual defence'. *British Journal of Psychology*, 60(3), 363–8.

Wulf, F. (1922) 'Über die Veränderung von Verstellunge (Gedächtnis und Gestalt)'. *Psychologisch Forschung*, 1, 333–73.

Wynne-Edwards, V. C. (1962) *Animal Dispersion in Relation to Social Behaviour*. Edinburgh, Oliver and Boyd.

Zajonc, R. B. (1960) *Social Psychology: An experimental approach*. Belmont, California, Wadsworth.

Zanna, M. P., and Cooper, J. (1974) 'Dissonance and the pill: an attribution approach to studying the arousal properties of dissonance'. *Journal of Personality and Social Psychology*, 29, 703–9.

Zeller, A. (1950) 'An experimental analogue of repression: the effect of individual failure and success on memory measured by relearning'. *Journal of Experimental Psychology*, 40, 411–22.

Zellner, M. (1970) 'Self-esteem, reception and influenceability'. *Journal of Personality and Social Psychology*, 15, 87–93.

Zimbardo, P. G. (1972) 'Pathology of imprisonment'. *Society*, April, 1972.

APPENDIX

SIGNIFICANCE TABLES

Table A.1 One-tailed probabilities (p) for values of the standard normal deviate (z). (Abridged from Table 1 of *The Biometrika Tables for Statisticians*, Vol. I, edited by Pearson, E. S. and Hartley, H. O., with permission of E. S. Pearson and the trustees of Biometrika.)

z	p	z	p	z	p
0.00	.5000	0.35	.3632	0.70	.2420
0.01	.4960	0.36	.3594	0.71	.2389
0.02	.4920	0.37	.3557	0.72	.2358
0.03	.4880	0.38	.3520	0.73	.2327
0.04	.4840	0.39	.3483	0.74	.2296
0.05	.4801	0.40	.3446	0.75	.2266
0.06	.4761	0.41	.3409	0.76	.2236
0.07	.4721	0.42	.3372	0.77	.2206
0.08	.4681	0.43	.3336	0.78	.2177
0.09	.4641	0.44	.3300	0.79	.2148
0.10	.4602	0.45	.3264	0.80	.2119
0.11	.4562	0.46	.3228	0.81	.2090
0.12	.4522	0.47	.3192	0.82	.2061
0.13	.4483	0.48	.3156	0.83	.2033
0.14	.4443	0.49	.3121	0.84	.2005
0.15	.4404	0.50	.3085	0.85	.1977
0.16	.4364	0.51	.3050	0.86	.1949
0.17	.4325	0.52	.3015	0.87	.1922
0.18	.4286	0.53	.2981	0.88	.1894
0.19	.4247	0.54	.2946	0.89	.1867
0.20	.4207	0.55	.2912	0.90	.1841
0.21	.4168	0.56	.2877	0.91	.1814
0.22	.4129	0.57	.2843	0.92	.1788
0.23	.4090	0.58	.2810	0.93	.1762
0.24	.4052	0.59	.2776	0.94	.1736
0.25	.4013	0.60	.2743	0.95	.1711
0.26	.3974	0.61	.2709	0.96	.1685
0.27	.3936	0.62	.2676	0.97	.1660
0.28	.3897	0.63	.2643	0.98	.1635
0.29	.3859	0.64	.2611	0.99	.1611
0.30	.3821	0.65	.2578	1.00	.1587
0.31	.3783	0.66	.2546	1.01	.1562
0.32	.3745	0.67	.2514	1.02	.1539
0.33	.3707	0.68	.2483	1.03	.1515
0.34	.3669	0.69	.2451	1.04	.1492

733

Table A.1 *cont'd.*

z	p	z	p	z	p
1.05	.1469	1.50	.0668	1.95	.0256
1.06	.1446	1.51	.0655	1.96	.0250
1.07	.1423	1.52	.0643	1.97	.0244
1.08	.1401	1.53	.0630	1.98	.0239
1.09	.1379	1.54	.0618	1.99	.0233
1.10	.1357	1.55	.0606	2.00	.0228
1.11	.1335	1.56	.0594	2.01	.0222
1.12	.1314	1.57	.0582	2.02	.0217
1.13	.1292	1.58	.0571	2.03	.0212
1.14	.1271	1.59	.0559	2.04	.0207
1.15	.1251	1.60	.0548	2.05	.0202
1.16	.1230	1.61	.0537	2.06	.0197
1.17	.1210	1.62	.0526	2.07	.0192
1.18	.1190	1.63	.0516	2.08	.0188
1.19	.1170	1.64	.0505	2.09	.0183
1.20	.1151	1.65	.0495	2.10	.0179
1.21	.1131	1.66	.0485	2.11	.0174
1.22	.1112	1.67	.0475	2.12	.0170
1.23	.1093	1.68	.0465	2.13	.0166
1.24	.1075	1.69	.0455	2.14	.0162
1.25	.1056	1.70	.0446	2.15	.0158
1.26	.1038	1.71	.0436	2.16	.0154
1.27	.1020	1.72	.0427	2.17	.0150
1.28	.1003	1.73	.0418	2.18	.0146
1.29	.0985	1.74	.0409	2.19	.0143
1.30	.0968	1.75	.0401	2.20	.0139
1.31	.0951	1.76	.0392	2.21	.0136
1.32	.0934	1.77	.0384	2.22	.0132
1.33	.0918	1.78	.0375	2.23	.0129
1.34	.0901	1.79	.0367	2.24	.0125
1.35	.0885	1.80	.0359	2.25	.0122
1.36	.0869	1.81	.0351	2.26	.0119
1.37	.0853	1.82	.0344	2.27	.0116
1.38	.0838	1.83	.0336	2.28	.0113
1.39	.0823	1.84	.0329	2.29	.0110
1.40	.0808	1.85	.0322	2.30	.0107
1.41	.0793	1.86	.0314	2.31	.0104
1.42	.0778	1.87	.0307	2.32	.0102
1.43	.0764	1.88	.0301	2.33	.0099
1.44	.0749	1.89	.0294	2.34	.0096
1.45	.0735	1.90	.0287	2.35	.0094
1.46	.0721	1.91	.0281	2.36	.0091
1.47	.0708	1.92	.0274	2.37	.0089
1.48	.0694	1.93	.0268	2.38	.0087
1.49	.0681	1.94	.0262	2.39	.0084

Table A.1 *cont'd.*

z	p	z	p	z	p
2.40	.0082	2.70	.0035	3.00	.0013
2.41	.0080	2.71	.0034	3.01	.0013
2.42	.0078	2.72	.0033	3.02	.0013
2.43	.0075	2.73	.0032	3.03	.0012
2.44	.0073	2.74	.0031	3.04	.0012
2.45	.0071	2.75	.0030	3.05	.0011
2.46	.0069	2.76	.0029	3.06	.0011
2.47	.0068	2.77	.0028	3.07	.0011
2.48	.0066	2.78	.0027	3.08	.0010
2.49	.0064	2.79	.0026	3.09	.0010
2.50	.0062	2.80	.0026	3.10	.0010
2.51	.0060	2.81	.0025	3.11	.0009
2.52	.0059	2.82	.0024	3.12	.0009
2.53	.0057	2.83	.0023	3.13	.0009
2.54	.0055	2.84	.0023	3.14	.0008
2.55	.0054	2.85	.0022	3.15	.0008
2.56	.0052	2.86	.0021	3.16	.0008
2.57	.0051	2.87	.0021	3.17	.0008
2.58	.0049	2.88	.0020	3.18	.0007
2.59	.0048	2.89	.0019	3.19	.0007
2.60	.0047	2.90	.0019	3.20	.0007
2.61	.0045	2.91	.0018	3.21	.0007
2.62	.0044	2.92	.0018	3.22	.0006
2.63	.0043	2.93	.0017	3.23	.0006
2.64	.0041	2.94	.0016	3.24	.0006
2.65	.0040	2.95	.0016	3.30	.0005
2.66	.0039	2.96	.0015	3.40	.0003
2.67	.0038	2.97	.0015	3.50	.0002
2.68	.0037	2.98	.0014	3.60	.0002
2.69	.0036	2.99	.0014	3.70	.0001

Table A.2 Critical values of chi square. Values of X^2 that equal or exceed the tabled value are significant at, or beyond, the level indicated. (Abridged from Table IV of Fisher, R. A. and Yates, F.: *Statistical Tables for Biological, Agricultural and Medical Research*. Longman 1963. Previously published by Oliver and Boyd Ltd, Edinburgh. By permission of the authors and publishers.)

Degrees of freedom	Level of significance	
	.05	.01
1	3.84	6.64
2	5.99	9.21
3	7.82	11.34
4	9.49	13.28
5	11.07	15.09
6	12.59	16.81
7	14.07	18.48
8	15.51	20.09
9	16.92	21.67
10	18.31	23.21
11	19.68	24.72
12	21.03	26.22
13	22.36	27.69
14	23.68	29.14
15	25.00	30.58
16	26.30	32.00
17	27.59	33.41
18	28.87	34.80
19	30.14	36.19
20	31.41	37.57
21	32.67	38.93
22	33.92	40.29
23	35.17	41.64
24	36.42	42.98
25	37.65	44.31
26	38.88	45.64
27	40.11	46.96
28	41.34	48.28
29	42.56	49.59
30	43.77	50.89

Table A.3 Critical values of t that equal or exceed the tabled value are significant at, or beyond, the level indicated. (Taken from Table III of Fisher, R. A. and Yates, F.: *Statistical Tables for Biological, Agricultural and Medical Research.* Longman 1963. Previously published by Oliver and Boyd Ltd., Edinburgh. By permission of the authors and publishers.)

Degrees of freedom	Level of significance for a one-tailed test			
	.05	.025	.01	.005
	Level of significance for a two-tailed test			
	.10	.05	.02	.01
1	6.314	12.706	31.821	63.657
2	2.920	4.303	6.965	9.925
3	2.353	3.182	4.541	5.841
4	2.132	2.776	3.747	4.604
5	2.015	2.571	3.365	4.032
6	1.943	2.447	3.143	3.707
7	1.895	2.365	2.998	3.499
8	1.860	2.306	2.896	3.355
9	1.833	2.262	2.821	3.250
10	1.812	2.228	2.764	3.169
11	1.796	2.201	2.718	3.106
12	1.782	2.179	2.681	3.055
13	1.771	2.160	2.650	3.012
14	1.761	2.145	2.624	2.977
15	1.753	2.131	2.602	2.947
16	1.746	2.120	2.583	2.921
17	1.740	2.110	2.567	2.898
18	1.734	2.101	2.552	2.878
19	1.729	2.093	2.539	2.861
20	1.725	2.086	2.528	2.845
21	1.721	2.080	2.518	2.831
22	1.717	2.074	2.508	2.819
23	1.714	2.069	2.500	2.807
24	1.711	2.064	2.492	2.797
25	1.708	2.060	2.485	2.787
26	1.706	2.056	2.479	2.779
27	1.703	2.052	2.473	2.771
28	1.701	2.048	2.467	2.763
29	1.699	2.045	2.462	2.756
30	1.697	2.042	2.457	2.750
40	1.684	2.021	2.423	2.704
60	1.671	2.000	2.390	2.660
120	1.658	1.980	2.358	2.617
∞	1.645	1.960	2.326	2.576

Table A.4 Critical values of F at the 5% level of significance. Values of F that equal or exceed the tabled value are significant at or beyond the 5% level. (Abridged from Table 18 of *The Biometrika Tables for Statisticians*, Vol. I, edited by Pearson, E. S. and Hartley, H. O. with the permission of E. S. Pearson and the trustees of Biometrika.)

Degrees of freedom for the numerator

df (denom.)	1	2	3	4	5	6	7	8	9	10	12	15	20	24	30	40	60	120	∞
1	161.4	199.5	215.7	224.6	230.2	234.0	236.8	238.9	240.5	241.9	243.9	245.9	248.0	249.1	250.1	251.1	252.2	253.3	254.3
2	18.51	19.00	19.16	19.25	19.30	19.33	19.35	19.37	19.38	19.40	19.41	19.43	19.45	19.45	19.46	19.47	19.48	19.49	19.50
3	10.13	9.55	9.28	9.12	9.01	8.94	8.89	8.85	8.81	8.79	8.74	8.70	8.66	8.64	8.62	8.59	8.57	8.55	8.53
4	7.71	6.94	6.59	6.39	6.26	6.16	6.09	6.04	6.00	5.96	5.91	5.86	5.80	5.77	5.75	5.72	5.69	5.66	5.63
5	6.61	5.79	5.41	5.19	5.05	4.95	4.88	4.82	4.77	4.74	4.68	4.62	4.56	4.53	4.50	4.46	4.43	4.40	4.36
6	5.99	5.14	4.76	4.53	4.39	4.28	4.21	4.15	4.10	4.06	4.00	3.94	3.87	3.84	3.81	3.77	3.74	3.70	3.67
7	5.59	4.74	4.35	4.12	3.97	3.87	3.79	3.73	3.68	3.64	3.57	3.51	3.44	3.41	3.38	3.34	3.30	3.27	3.23
8	5.32	4.46	4.07	3.84	3.69	3.58	3.50	3.44	3.39	3.35	3.28	3.22	3.15	3.12	3.08	3.04	3.01	2.97	2.93
9	5.12	4.26	3.86	3.63	3.48	3.37	3.29	3.23	3.18	3.14	3.07	3.01	2.94	2.90	2.86	2.83	2.79	2.75	2.71
10	4.96	4.10	3.71	3.48	3.33	3.22	3.14	3.07	3.02	2.98	2.91	2.85	2.77	2.74	2.70	2.66	2.62	2.58	2.54
11	4.84	3.98	3.59	3.36	3.20	3.09	3.01	2.95	2.90	2.85	2.79	2.72	2.65	2.61	2.57	2.53	2.49	2.45	2.40
12	4.75	3.89	3.49	3.26	3.11	3.00	2.91	2.85	2.80	2.75	2.69	2.62	2.54	2.51	2.47	2.43	2.38	2.34	2.30
13	4.67	3.81	3.41	3.18	3.03	2.92	2.83	2.77	2.71	2.67	2.60	2.53	2.46	2.42	2.38	2.34	2.30	2.25	2.21
14	4.60	3.74	3.34	3.11	2.96	2.85	2.76	2.70	2.65	2.60	2.53	2.46	2.39	2.35	2.31	2.27	2.22	2.18	2.13
15	4.54	3.68	3.29	3.06	2.90	2.79	2.71	2.64	2.59	2.54	2.48	2.40	2.33	2.29	2.25	2.20	2.16	2.11	2.07
16	4.49	3.63	3.24	3.01	2.85	2.74	2.66	2.59	2.54	2.49	2.42	2.35	2.28	2.24	2.19	2.15	2.11	2.06	2.01
17	4.45	3.59	3.20	2.96	2.81	2.70	2.61	2.55	2.49	2.45	2.38	2.31	2.23	2.19	2.15	2.10	2.06	2.01	1.96
18	4.41	3.55	3.16	2.93	2.77	2.66	2.58	2.51	2.46	2.41	2.34	2.27	2.19	2.15	2.11	2.06	2.02	1.97	1.92
19	4.38	3.52	3.13	2.90	2.74	2.63	2.54	2.48	2.42	2.38	2.31	2.23	2.16	2.11	2.07	2.03	1.98	1.93	1.88
20	4.35	3.49	3.10	2.87	2.71	2.60	2.51	2.45	2.39	2.35	2.28	2.20	2.12	2.08	2.04	1.99	1.95	1.90	1.84
21	4.32	3.47	3.07	2.84	2.68	2.57	2.49	2.42	2.37	2.32	2.25	2.18	2.10	2.05	2.01	1.96	1.92	1.87	1.81
22	4.30	3.44	3.05	2.82	2.66	2.55	2.46	2.40	2.34	2.30	2.23	2.15	2.07	2.03	1.98	1.94	1.89	1.84	1.78
23	4.28	3.42	3.03	2.80	2.64	2.53	2.44	2.37	2.32	2.27	2.20	2.13	2.05	2.01	1.96	1.91	1.86	1.81	1.76
24	4.26	3.40	3.01	2.78	2.62	2.51	2.42	2.36	2.30	2.25	2.18	2.11	2.03	1.98	1.94	1.89	1.84	1.79	1.73
25	4.24	3.39	2.99	2.76	2.60	2.49	2.40	2.34	2.28	2.24	2.16	2.09	2.01	1.96	1.92	1.87	1.82	1.77	1.71
26	4.23	3.37	2.98	2.74	2.59	2.47	2.39	2.32	2.27	2.22	2.15	2.07	1.99	1.95	1.90	1.85	1.80	1.75	1.69
27	4.21	3.35	2.96	2.73	2.57	2.46	2.37	2.31	2.25	2.20	2.13	2.06	1.97	1.93	1.88	1.84	1.79	1.73	1.67
28	4.20	3.34	2.95	2.71	2.56	2.45	2.36	2.29	2.24	2.19	2.12	2.04	1.96	1.91	1.87	1.82	1.77	1.71	1.65
29	4.18	3.33	2.93	2.70	2.55	2.43	2.35	2.28	2.22	2.18	2.10	2.03	1.94	1.90	1.85	1.81	1.75	1.70	1.64
30	4.17	3.32	2.92	2.69	2.53	2.42	2.33	2.27	2.21	2.16	2.09	2.01	1.93	1.89	1.84	1.79	1.74	1.68	1.62
40	4.08	3.23	2.84	2.61	2.45	2.34	2.25	2.18	2.12	2.08	2.00	1.92	1.84	1.79	1.74	1.69	1.64	1.58	1.51
60	4.00	3.15	2.76	2.53	2.37	2.25	2.17	2.10	2.04	1.99	1.92	1.84	1.75	1.70	1.65	1.59	1.53	1.47	1.39
120	3.92	3.07	2.68	2.45	2.29	2.17	2.09	2.02	1.96	1.91	1.83	1.75	1.66	1.61	1.55	1.50	1.43	1.35	1.25
∞	3.84	3.00	2.60	2.37	2.21	2.10	2.01	1.94	1.88	1.83	1.75	1.67	1.57	1.52	1.46	1.39	1.32	1.22	1.00

Degrees of freedom for the denominator

Table A.5 Critical values of F at the 1% level of significance. Values of F that equal or exceed the tabled value are significant at or beyond the 1% level. (Abridged from Table 18 of *The Biometrika Tables for Statisticians*, Vol. I, edited by Pearson, E. S. and Hartley, H. O. with the permission of E. S. Pearson and the trustees of Biometrika.)

Degrees of freedom for the numerator

Denominator df	1	2	3	4	5	6	7	8	9	10	12	15	20	24	30	40	60	120	∞
1	4052	4999.5	5403	5625	5764	5859	5928	5982	6022	6056	6106	6157	6209	6235	6261	6287	6313	6339	6366
2	98.50	99.00	99.17	99.25	99.30	99.33	99.36	99.37	99.39	99.40	99.42	99.43	99.45	99.46	99.47	99.47	99.48	99.49	99.50
3	34.12	30.82	29.46	28.71	28.24	27.91	27.67	27.49	27.35	27.23	27.05	26.87	26.69	26.60	26.50	26.41	26.32	26.22	26.13
4	21.20	18.00	16.69	15.98	15.52	15.21	14.98	14.80	14.66	14.55	14.37	14.20	14.02	13.93	13.84	13.75	13.65	13.56	13.46
5	16.26	13.27	12.06	11.39	10.97	10.67	10.46	10.29	10.16	10.05	9.89	9.72	9.55	9.47	9.38	9.29	9.20	9.11	9.02
6	13.75	10.92	9.78	9.15	8.75	8.47	8.26	8.10	7.98	7.87	7.72	7.56	7.40	7.31	7.23	7.14	7.06	6.97	6.88
7	12.25	9.55	8.45	7.85	7.46	7.19	6.99	6.84	6.72	6.62	6.47	6.31	6.16	6.07	5.99	5.91	5.82	5.74	5.65
8	11.26	8.65	7.59	7.01	6.63	6.37	6.18	6.03	5.91	5.81	5.67	5.52	5.36	5.28	5.20	5.12	5.03	4.95	4.86
9	10.56	8.02	6.99	6.42	6.06	5.80	5.61	5.47	5.35	5.26	5.11	4.96	4.81	4.73	4.65	4.57	4.48	4.40	4.31
10	10.04	7.56	6.55	5.99	5.64	5.39	5.20	5.06	4.94	4.85	4.71	4.56	4.41	4.33	4.25	4.17	4.08	4.00	3.91
11	9.65	7.21	6.22	5.67	5.32	5.07	4.89	4.74	4.63	4.54	4.40	4.25	4.10	4.02	3.94	3.86	3.78	3.69	3.60
12	9.33	6.93	5.95	5.41	5.06	4.82	4.64	4.50	4.39	4.30	4.16	4.01	3.86	3.78	3.70	3.62	3.54	3.45	3.36
13	9.07	6.70	5.74	5.21	4.86	4.62	4.44	4.30	4.19	4.10	3.96	3.82	3.66	3.59	3.51	3.43	3.34	3.25	3.17
14	8.86	6.51	5.56	5.04	4.69	4.46	4.28	4.14	4.03	3.94	3.80	3.66	3.51	3.43	3.35	3.27	3.18	3.09	3.00
15	8.68	6.36	5.42	4.89	4.56	4.32	4.14	4.00	3.89	3.80	3.67	3.52	3.37	3.29	3.21	3.13	3.05	2.96	2.87
16	8.53	6.23	5.29	4.77	4.44	4.20	4.03	3.89	3.78	3.69	3.55	3.41	3.26	3.18	3.10	3.02	2.93	2.84	2.75
17	8.40	6.11	5.18	4.67	4.34	4.10	3.93	3.79	3.68	3.59	3.46	3.31	3.16	3.08	3.00	2.92	2.83	2.75	2.65
18	8.29	6.01	5.09	4.58	4.25	4.01	3.84	3.71	3.60	3.51	3.37	3.23	3.08	3.00	2.92	2.84	2.75	2.66	2.57
19	8.18	5.93	5.01	4.50	4.17	3.94	3.77	3.63	3.52	3.43	3.30	3.15	3.00	2.92	2.84	2.76	2.67	2.58	2.49
20	8.10	5.85	4.94	4.43	4.10	3.87	3.70	3.56	3.46	3.37	3.23	3.09	2.94	2.86	2.78	2.69	2.61	2.52	2.42
21	8.02	5.78	4.87	4.37	4.04	3.81	3.64	3.51	3.40	3.31	3.17	3.03	2.88	2.80	2.72	2.64	2.55	2.46	2.36
22	7.95	5.72	4.82	4.31	3.99	3.76	3.59	3.45	3.35	3.26	3.12	2.98	2.83	2.75	2.67	2.58	2.50	2.40	2.31
23	7.88	5.66	4.76	4.26	3.94	3.71	3.54	3.41	3.30	3.21	3.07	2.93	2.78	2.70	2.62	2.54	2.45	2.35	2.26
24	7.82	5.61	4.72	4.22	3.90	3.67	3.50	3.36	3.26	3.17	3.03	2.89	2.74	2.66	2.58	2.49	2.40	2.31	2.21
25	7.77	5.57	4.68	4.18	3.85	3.63	3.46	3.32	3.22	3.13	2.99	2.85	2.70	2.62	2.54	2.45	2.36	2.27	2.17
26	7.72	5.53	4.64	4.14	3.82	3.59	3.42	3.29	3.18	3.09	2.96	2.81	2.66	2.58	2.50	2.42	2.33	2.23	2.13
27	7.68	5.49	4.60	4.11	3.78	3.56	3.39	3.26	3.15	3.06	2.93	2.78	2.63	2.55	2.47	2.38	2.29	2.20	2.10
28	7.64	5.45	4.57	4.07	3.75	3.53	3.36	3.23	3.12	3.03	2.90	2.75	2.60	2.52	2.44	2.35	2.26	2.17	2.06
29	7.60	5.42	4.54	4.04	3.73	3.50	3.33	3.20	3.09	3.00	2.87	2.73	2.57	2.49	2.41	2.33	2.23	2.14	2.03
30	7.56	5.39	4.51	4.02	3.70	3.47	3.30	3.17	3.07	2.98	2.84	2.70	2.55	2.47	2.39	2.30	2.21	2.11	2.01
40	7.31	5.18	4.31	3.83	3.51	3.29	3.12	2.99	2.89	2.80	2.66	2.52	2.37	2.29	2.20	2.11	2.02	1.92	1.80
60	7.08	4.98	4.13	3.65	3.34	3.12	2.95	2.82	2.72	2.63	2.50	2.35	2.20	2.12	2.03	1.94	1.84	1.73	1.60
120	6.85	4.79	3.95	3.48	3.17	2.96	2.79	2.66	2.56	2.47	2.34	2.19	2.03	1.95	1.86	1.76	1.66	1.53	1.38
∞	6.63	4.61	3.78	3.32	3.02	2.80	2.64	2.51	2.41	2.32	2.18	2.04	1.88	1.79	1.70	1.59	1.47	1.32	1.00

Degrees of freedom for the denominator

739

Table A.6 One-tailed probabilities associated with particular values of x in the Sign test.

n \ x	0	1	2	3	4	5	6	7	8	9	10	11	12	13	14	15
4	063	313	688	938												
5	031	188	500	812	969											
6	016	109	344	656	891	984										
7	008	062	227	500	773	938	992									
8	004	035	145	363	637	855	965	996								
9	002	020	090	254	500	746	910	980	998							
10	001	011	055	172	377	623	828	945	989	999						
11		006	033	113	274	500	726	887	967	994						
12		003	019	073	194	387	613	806	927	981	997					
13		002	011	046	133	291	500	709	867	954	989	998				
14		001	006	029	090	212	395	605	788	910	971	994	999			
15			004	018	059	151	304	500	696	849	941	982	996			
16			002	011	038	105	227	402	598	773	895	962	989	998		
17			001	006	025	072	166	315	500	685	834	928	975	994	999	
18			001	004	015	048	119	240	407	593	760	881	952	985	996	999
19				002	010	032	084	180	324	500	676	820	916	968	990	998
20				001	006	021	058	132	252	412	588	748	868	942	979	994
21				001	004	013	039	095	192	332	500	668	808	905	961	987
22					002	008	026	067	143	262	416	584	738	857	933	974
23					001	005	017	047	105	202	339	500	661	798	895	953
24					001	003	011	032	076	154	271	419	581	729	846	924
25						002	007	022	054	115	212	345	500	655	788	885

Table A.7 Critical values of T or T^1, whichever is the smaller, in the Wilcoxon Rank-Sum test. Values of T or T^1 that are equal to or less than the tabled value are significant at, or beyond, the level indicated. (Taken from Table L of Tate, M. W. and Clelland, R. C., *Non-Parametric and Shortcut Statistics*. Interstate Printers and Publishers Inc., Danville, Illinois, 1957. With permission of the authors and publishers.)

Number of scores in the larger sample (n_2)	One-tailed	Two-tailed	1	2	3	4	5	6	7	8	9	10	11	12	13	14	15	16	17	18	19	20
3	.10	.20	3	7																		
	.05	.10		6																		
	.025	.05																				
	.005	.01			(4)																	
4	.10	.20	3	7	13																	
	.05	.10		6	11																	
	.025	.05			10																	
	.005	.01				(5)																
5	.10	.20	4	8	14	20																
	.05	.10	3	7	12	19																
	.025	.05		6	11	17																
	.005	.01				15	(6)															
6	.10	.20	4	9	15	22	30															
	.05	.10	3	8	13	20	28															
	.025	.05		7	12	18	26															
	.005	.01			10	16	23	(7)														
7	.10	.20	4	10	16	23	32	41														
	.05	.10	3	8	14	21	29	39														
	.025	.05		7	13	20	27	36														
	.005	.01			10	16	24	32	(8)													
8	.10	.20	5	11	17	25	34	44	55													
	.05	.10	4	9	15	23	31	41	51													
	.025	.05	3	8	14	21	29	38	49													
	.005	.01			11	17	25	34	43	(9)												
9	.10	.20	1	5	11	19	27	36	46	58	70											
	.05	.10		4	9	16	24	33	43	54	66											
	.025	.05		3	8	14	22	31	40	51	62											
	.005	.01		6	11	18	26	35	45	56	(10)											
10	.10	.20	1	6	12	20	28	38	49	60	73	87										
	.05	.10		4	10	17	26	35	45	56	69	82										
	.025	.05		3	9	15	23	32	42	53	65	78										
	.005	.01		6	12	19	27	37	47	58	71	(11)										
11	.10	.20	1	6	13	21	30	40	51	63	76	91	106									
	.05	.10		4	11	18	27	37	47	59	72	86	100									
	.025	.05		3	9	16	24	34	44	55	68	81	96									
	.005	.01		6	12	20	28	38	49	61	73	87	(12)									
12	.10	.20	1	7	14	22	32	42	54	66	80	94	110	127								
	.05	.10		5	11	19	28	38	49	62	75	89	104	120								
	.025	.05		4	10	17	26	35	46	58	71	84	99	115								
	.005	.01			7	13	21	30	40	51	63	76	90	105								

Table A.7 *cont'd.*

n₂	One-tailed	Two-tailed	1	2	3	4	5	6	7	8	9	10	11	12	13	14	15	16	17	18	19	20
13	.10	.20	1	7	15	23	33	44	56	69	83	98	114	131	149							
	.05	.10		5	12	20	30	40	52	64	78	92	108	125	142							
	.025	.05		4	10	18	27	37	48	60	73	88	103	119	136							
	.005	.01			7	14	22	31	41	53	65	79	93	109	125	(14)						
14	.10	.20	1	7	16	25	35	46	59	72	86	102	118	136	154	174						
	.05	.10		5	13	21	31	42	54	67	81	96	112	129	147	166						
	.025	.05		4	11	19	28	38	50	62	76	91	106	123	141	160						
	.005	.01			7	14	22	32	43	54	67	81	96	112	129	147	(15)					
15	.10	.20	1	8	16	26	37	48	61	75	90	106	123	141	159	179	200					
	.05	.10		6	13	22	33	44	56	69	84	99	116	133	152	171	192					
	.025	.05		4	11	20	29	40	52	65	79	94	110	127	145	164	184					
	.005	.01			8	15	23	33	44	56	69	84	99	115	133	151	171	(16)				
16	.10	.20	1	8	17	27	38	50	64	78	93	109	127	145	165	185	206	229				
	.05	.10		6	14	24	34	46	58	72	87	103	120	138	156	176	197	219				
	.025	.05		4	12	21	30	42	54	67	82	97	113	131	150	169	190	211				
	.005	.01			8	15	24	34	46	58	72	86	102	119	136	155	175	196	(17)			
17	.10	.20	1	9	18	28	40	52	66	81	97	113	131	150	170	190	212	235	259			
	.05	.10		6	15	25	35	47	61	75	90	106	123	142	161	182	203	225	249			
	.025	.05		5	12	21	32	43	56	70	84	100	117	135	154	174	195	217	240			
	.005	.01			8	16	25	36	47	60	74	89	105	122	140	159	180	201	223	(18)		
18	.10	.20	1	9	19	30	42	55	69	84	100	117	135	155	175	196	218	242	266	291		
	.05	.10		7	15	26	37	49	63	77	93	110	127	146	166	187	208	231	255	280		
	.025	.05		5	13	22	33	45	58	72	87	103	121	139	158	179	200	222	246	270		
	.005	.01			8	16	26	37	49	62	76	92	108	125	144	163	184	206	228	252	(19)	
19	.10	.20	2	10	20	31	43	57	71	87	103	121	139	159	180	202	224	248	273	299	325	
	.05	.10	1	7	16	27	38	51	65	80	96	113	131	150	171	192	214	237	262	287	313	
	.025	.05		5	13	23	34	46	60	74	90	107	124	143	163	182	205	228	252	277	303	
	.005	.01		3	9	17	27	38	50	64	78	94	111	129	147	168	189	210	234	258	283	(20)
20	.10	.20	2	10	21	32	45	59	74	90	107	125	144	164	185	207	230	255	280	306	333	361
	.05	.10	1	7	17	28	40	53	67	83	99	117	135	155	175	197	220	243	268	294	320	348
	.025	.05		5	14	24	35	48	62	77	93	110	128	147	167	188	210	234	258	283	309	337
	.005	.01		3	9	18	28	39	52	66	81	97	114	132	151	172	193	215	239	263	289	315

Level of significance — One-tailed / Two-tailed. Number of scores in the smaller sample (n₁). Number of scores in the larger sample (n₂).

Table A.8 Critical values of T for the Wilcoxon Signed-Rank test. Values of T that are equal to or less than the tabled value are significant at, or beyond, the level indicated. (Taken from Table 1 of McCormack, R. L. 'Extended tables of the Wilcoxon matched pair signed rank statistic.' *Journal of the American Statistical Association*, 1965, Vol. 60, pp. 864–871. With permission of the publishers.)

	Level of significance for a two-tailed test			
	.10	.05	.02	.01
	Level of significance for a one-tailed test			
n	.05	.025	.01	.005
5	0			
6	2	0		
7	3	2	0	
8	5	3	1	0
9	8	5	3	1
10	10	8	5	3
11	13	10	7	5
12	17	13	9	7
13	21	17	12	9
14	25	21	15	12
15	30	25	19	15
16	35	29	23	19
17	41	34	27	23
18	47	40	32	27
19	53	46	37	32
20	60	52	43	37
21	67	58	49	42
22	75	65	55	48
23	83	73	62	54
24	91	81	69	61
25	100	89	76	68

Table A.9 Critical values of r_s. Values of r_s that equal or exceed the tabled value are significant at, or beyond, the level indicated. (Taken from Zar, J. H.: 'Significance Testing of the Spearman Rank Correlation Coefficient.' *Journal of the American Statistical Association*, 1972, Vol. 67, pp. 578–580. With permission of the author and publisher.)

	Level of significance for a two-tailed test			
	.10	.05	.02	.01
	Level of significance for a one-tailed test			
	.05	.025	.01	.005
n = 4	1.000			
5	.900	1.000	1.000	
6	.829	.886	.943	1.000
7	.714	.786	.893	.929
8	.643	.738	.833	.881
9	.600	.700	.783	.833
10	.564	.648	.745	.794
11	.536	.618	.709	.755
12	.503	.587	.671	.727
13	.484	.560	.648	.703
14	.464	.538	.622	.675
15	.443	.521	.604	.654
16	.429	.503	.582	.635
17	.414	.485	.566	.615
18	.401	.472	.550	.600
19	.391	.460	.535	.584
20	.380	.447	.520	.570
21	.370	.435	.508	.556
22	.361	.425	.496	.544
23	.353	.415	.486	.532
24	.344	.406	.476	.521
25	.337	.398	.466	.511
26	.331	.390	.457	.501
27	.324	.382	.448	.491
28	.317	.375	.440	.483
29	.312	.368	.433	.475
30	.306	.362	.425	.467

For n > 30, the significance of r_s can be tested by using the formula:

$$t = r_s \sqrt{\frac{n-2}{1-r_s^2}} \qquad df = n-2$$

—and referring to Table A.3.

Table A.10 Critical values of Pearson's r. Values of r that equal or exceed the tabled value are significant at, or beyond, the level indicated. (Adapted from Table 13 of *The Biometrika Tables for Statisticians*, Vol. 1, edited by E. S. Pearson, and H. O. Hartley, with the permission of E. S. Pearson and the trustees of Biometrika.)

	Level of significance for a one-tailed test		Level of significance for a two-tailed test	
	.05	.01	.05	.01
Degree of freedom				
1	.988	.999	.997	.999
2	.900	.980	.950	.990
3	.805	.934	.878	.959
4	.729	.882	.811	.917
5	.669	.833	.754	.874
6	.622	.789	.707	.834
7	.582	.750	.666	.798
8	.549	.716	.632	.765
9	.521	.685	.602	.735
10	.497	.658	.576	.708
11	.476	.634	.553	.684
12	.458	.612	.532	.661
13	.441	.592	.514	.641
14	.426	.574	.497	.623
15	.412	.558	.482	.606
16	.400	.542	.468	.590
17	.389	.528	.456	.575
18	.378	.516	.444	.561
19	.369	.503	.433	.549
20	.360	.492	.423	.537
21	.352	.482	.413	.526
22	.344	.472	.404	.515
23	.337	.462	.396	.505
24	.330	.453	.388	.496
25	.323	.445	.381	.487
26	.317	.437	.374	.479
27	.311	.430	.367	.471
28	.306	.423	.361	.463
29	.301	.416	.355	.456
30	.296	.409	.349	.449
35	.275	.381	.325	.418
40	.257	.358	.304	.393
45	.243	.338	.288	.372
50	.231	.322	.273	.354
60	.211	.295	.250	.325
70	.195	.274	.232	.303
80	.183	.256	.217	.283
90	.173	.242	.205	.267
100	.164	.230	.195	.254

Table A.11 Critical values of W. Values of W that equal or exceed the tabled value are significant at, or beyond, the level indicated. (Taken from Tate, M. W. and Clelland, R. C. *Non-Parametric and Shortcut Statistics*, Interstate Inc., Illinois, 1957. Values to the left of the line are from Kendall, M. G. *Rank Correlation Methods*, Griffin, 1948. With permission of the authors and publishers.)

n	Level of significance	k							
		3	4	5	6	7	8	9	10
3	.05	1.00	.82	.71	.65	.62	.60	.58	.56
	.01		.96	.84	.77	.73	.70	.67	.65
4	.05	.81	.65	.54	.51	.48	.46	.45	.44
	.01	1.00	.80	.67	.62	.59	.56	.54	.52
5	.05	.64	.52	.44	.41	.39	.38	.36	.35
	.01	.84	.66	.56	.52	.49	.46	.44	.43
6	.05	.58	.42	.37	.35	.33	.32	.31	.30
	.01	.75	.56	.49	.45	.42	.40	.38	.37
7	.05	.51	.36	.32	.30	.29	.27	.26	.26
	.01	.63	.48	.43	.39	.36	.34	.33	.32
8	.05	.39	.32	.29	.27	.25	.24	.23	.23
	.01	.56	.43	.38	.35	.32	.31	.29	.28
9	.05	.35	.28	.26	.24	.23	.22	.21	.20
	.01	.48	.38	.34	.31	.29	.27	.26	.25
10	.05	.31	.25	.23	.21	.20	.20	.19	.18
	.01	.48	.35	.31	.28	.26	.25	.24	.23
12	.05	.25	.21	.19	.18	.17	.16	.16	.15
	.01	.36	.30	.26	.24	.22	.21	.20	.19
14	.05	.21	.18	.17	.16	.15	.14	.14	.13
	.01	.31	.26	.23	.21	.19	.18	.17	.17
16	.05	.19	.16	.15	.14	.13	.12	.12	.12
	.01	.28	.23	.20	.18	.17	.16	.15	.15
18	.05	.17	.14	.13	.12	.11	.11	.11	.10
	.01	.25	.20	.18	.16	.15	.14	.14	.13
20	.05	.15	.13	.12	.11	.10	.10	.10	.09
	.01	.22	.18	.16	.15	.14	.13	.12	.11
25	.05	.12	.10	.09	.09	.08	.08	.08	.07
	.01	.18	.15	.13	.12	.11	.10	.10	.09
30	.05	.10	.09	.08	.07	.07	.07	.07	.06
	.01	.15	.12	.11	.10	.09	.09	.08	.08

Table A.12 Critical values of H in the Kruskal-Wallis test. Values of H that equal or exceed the tabled value are significant at, or beyond, the level indicated. (Abridged from Kruskal, W. H. and Wallis, W. A. 'Use of ranks in one-criterion variance analysis.' *Journal of the American Statistical Association*, 1952, Vol. 47, pp. 584–621. With permission of the publishers.)

	Sample sizes		Level of significance	
n_1	n_2	n_3	.05	.01
3	2	2	4.71	
3	3	1	5.14	
3	3	2	5.36	6.25
3	3	3	5.60	6.49
4	2	1		
4	2	2	5.33	
4	3	1	5.21	
4	3	2	5.44	6.30
4	3	3	5.73	6.75
4	4	1	4.97	6.67
4	4	2	5.45	6.87
4	4	3	5.60	7.14
4	4	4	5.69	7.54
5	2	1	5.00	
5	2	2	5.16	6.53
5	3	1	4.96	
5	3	2	5.25	6.82
5	3	3	5.44	6.98
5	4	1	4.99	6.84
5	4	2	5.27	7.12
5	4	3	5.63	7.40
5	4	4	5.62	7.74
5	5	1	5.13	6.84
5	5	2	5.25	7.27
5	5	3	5.63	7.54
5	5	4	5.64	7.79
5	5	5	5.66	7.98

Table A.13 Critical values of P in Jonckheere's Trend test. Values of P that equal or exceed the tabled value are significant at, or beyond, the level indicated. (Taken from Jonckheere, A. R., 'A distribution-free k-sample test against ordered alternatives'. *Biometrika*, Vol. 41, pp. 133–145. With permission of the author and publisher.)

		Number of samples (k)							
		3		4		5		6	
Level of significance:		.05	.01	.05	.01	.05	.01	.05	.01
Number per sample (n)	2	10	—	14	20	20	26	26	34
	3	17	23	26	34	34	48	44	62
	4	24	32	38	50	51	72	67	94
	5	33	45	51	71	71	99	93	130
	6	42	59	66	92	92	129	121	170
	7	53	74	82	115	115	162	151	213
	8	64	90	100	140	140	197	184	260
	9	76	106	118	167	166	234	219	309
	10	88	124	138	195	194	274	256	361

Table A.14 Critical values of L in Page's Trend test. Values of L that equal or exceed the tabled value are significant at, or beyond, the level indicated. (Taken from Page, E. B. 'Ordered hypotheses for multiple treatments: a significance test for linear rank.' *Journal of the American Statistical Association*, 1963, Vol. 58, pp. 216–230. With permission of the publishers.)

	Number of samples (k)							
	3		4		5		6	
Level of significance:	.05	.01	.05	.01	.05	.01	.05	.01
Number per sample (n) 2	28	—	58	60	103	106	166	173
3	41	42	84	87	150	155	244	252
4	54	55	111	114	197	204	321	331
5	66	68	137	141	244	251	397	409
6	79	81	163	167	291	299	474	486
7	91	93	189	193	338	346	550	563
8	104	106	214	220	384	393	625	640
9	116	119	240	246	431	441	701	717
10	128	131	266	272	477	487	777	793

For values of k and n beyond those tabled above, the significance of L can be tested by using the formula:

$$z = \frac{12L - 3nk(k+1)^2}{\sqrt{nk^2(k^2-1)(k+1)}}$$

Index

753

Cultures 640

D'Andrade, R. 503
Dark-rearing 282–4
Darwin, C. 4, 8–10, 43, 192, 193,
    425, 426
Daston, P. G. 539
Dawkins, R. 213
Decision-map 88
Decision process 250, 251
Defence mechanisms 535
DeFleur and Westie 655
Degrees of freedom 92–4, 736, 738,
    739
Delay of gratification 698
Delinquency 21, 489, 491, 498,
    528–30, 684
Delusions 563
Dennenberg, V. 484
Dependence 500–502
Dependent variables 52, 53, 61, 673
Depression 561–2, 564, 565, 573
Depth
    binocular cues to 261–2
    monocular cues to 262–5
Depth perception 261–3, 280–82
Derived activities 212
Descartes 4
Desensitization 572
Desocialization 706
Deutsch, A. and D. 311
Development 44, 45, 449–64
    and early experience 482–6
    and learning theory 449–58
    and socialization 495–531
    animal studies 482–5
    child studies 485–8
    comparison of theories 468
    environmental stimulation 485–6
    Freud's account of 464–8
    intellectual 458–61
    life-span 530–31
    normative studies and the concept
    of normality 492–4
    pattern of 476–7
    personality 464, 468
    Piaget's account of 458–64
    post-Freudian alternatives 467

prenatal 473
psychosocial 468, 514
social stimulation effects 486–8
Developmental psychology 32, 43–5,
    419–68
    aims and methods 422
    beginnings of 423–5
    central problems 432
    clinical observation 427
    ecological and ethological
    approaches 428–30
    longitudinal and cross-sectional
    methods 430–32
    normative studies and practical
    applications 427
    observation experimentation and
    explanation 425–32
    recent research 432–9
    scope of 421
Dewey, J. 12–13
Dialects 589
Difference tests 87–8
Discrete variable 76
Discrimination 676
Discriminative stimuli 234
Dispersion measure 65–9
Displacement 210, 413
Dissonance 663–9
Distinctiveness 606
Distributive justice 592
DNA 378, 381, 472
Dobu society 494
Domain of convenience 48
Dominance 206–7, 589–93
Dopamine 178–81
Dreams 27, 413
Dress 586
Drive-reduction hypothesis 237–9
Drive theories 34, 226
Drug effects 137, 178, 179, 181, 414,
    569
Drug therapy 178, 181, 573
Duncan, C. 344
Duncker, K. 408
Dyad influence 633–5
Dynamic psychology 27

Ear 147–8

754

755

761

Developmental psychology
different approaches to study of
32–50
dynamic 27
experimental 138
Gestalt 16–21, 24, 257–60, 398
historical background 1
individual 26
method in 47–9
physiological 32, 36–7, 135–90,
417
recent 32–3
schools of 5, 31
social 32, 37–9
Psychometry 29–30, 368
Psychopharmacology 178–81
Psychophysiology 183–4
Psychoses 563
Psychosexual development 27, 465
Psychosomatic disorders 565–6
Psychosurgery 189–90
Psychotherapist, definition 560
Psychotic affective disorder 563
Puberty 522
Punishment 241–2, 452–3, 455, 509,
512, 693, 707
'Puzzle box' 15
Pyknics 542

Q-sort technique 554–5
Questionnaires 553
Quilliam, R. 361–3

Race 300, 383–6
Random error 55
Random number tables 55
Range 66
Rats, selective breeding of 479
Razran, G. 222–3
Reaction energy 210
Recapitulation theory 517
Receiver Operating Characteristic
Curve 253
Receiver variables 673
Receptive fields 151–3
Rectangular distribution 101
Red deer 207
Reflexes 23, 138, 141, 195, 218, 219,
417, 450

Regression 535, 536
Rehearsal 354–5
Reinforcement 180, 226–7, 230,
233–46, 452, 455, 573, 617
and learning 229
hedonistic theories 240–41
nature of 237–41
partial 233, 235
response theories 239–40
schedules of 233
social 511, 515, 617–9
Rejection region 85
Related measures 56–8, 61
Related t-test 115–7
Relative brightness 265
Relative size 263
Reliability 368
Reliability coefficient 120
Religious issues 621
Repression 350, 465, 535
Resocialization 706
Restle, F. 356
Reticular formation 144
Retinal images 254–6
Reward 180, 226, 452–3, 707
Rivalry 208
RNA 381
Rod and frame test 557
Rods and cones 149–50
Rogers, C. 550–53
Role-categories 605
Role-conflict 596–7
Role Construct Repertory Grid 555
Role-expectations 594, 597
Role-partners 597
Role-performance 593
Role-planning 640
Role-playing 513
Role-positions 593
Role-relationships 640
Role-strain 597
Role theory 598
Roles 593–601
social 593, 598
Rorschach Ink-blots test 537–8, 556
Rosen, B. C. 503
Rosenberg, S. 646, 647
Rosenhan, D. L. 568

762

763